Frommer's®
Cancún & the Yucatán
19th Edition

by Shane Christensen &
Christine Delsol
with Maribeth Mellin

WILEY

John Wiley & Sons, Inc.

Published by:
John Wiley & Sons, Inc.
111 River St.
Hoboken, NJ 07030-5774

ISBN 978-1-118-28758-3 (paper); ISBN 978-1-118-33139-2 (ebk); ISBN 978-1-118-33366-2 (ebk);
ISBN 978-1-118-33480-5 (ebk)

Editors: Emil J. Ross
Production Editor: Heather Wilcox
Cartographer: Guy Ruggiero
Photo Editor: Alden Gewirtz
Cover Photo Editor: Richard Fox
Design by Vertigo Design
Layout, Graphics and Prepress by Wiley Indianapolis Composition Services

Front cover photo: The ruins at Tulum ©Chris Cheadle/All Canada Photos/Getty Images
Back cover photos: Back cover photos: (left) Olmec head statue, Parque La Venta, Villahermosa,
Tabasco ©Luckie Photography; (middle) Sea turtle at the Centro Ecológico Akumal ©Hamid Rad,
Courtesy Centro Ecológico Akumal; (right) Local food in Merida ©Jose Granados

For information on our other products and services or to obtain technical support, please contact
our Customer Care Department within the U.S. at 877/762-2974, outside the U.S. at 317/572-3993
or fax 317/572-4002.

Wiley also publishes its books in a variety of electronic formats. Some content that appears in print
may not be available in electronic formats.

Manufactured in China

5 4 3 2 1

CONTENTS

8 TABASCO & CHIAPAS 304

9 PLANNING YOUR TRIP TO THE YUCATÁN, TABASCO & CHIAPAS 345

10 SPANISH & MAYAN TERMS & PHRASES 370

LIST OF MAPS

ABOUT THE AUTHORS

A former resident of Mexico City, **Shane Christensen** has written extensively for Frommer's throughout Mexico and is the author of *Frommer's Dubai* and *Frommer's Grand Canyon.* He goes back to Mexico at every chance he gets. Author of *Pauline Frommer's Cancún & the Yucatán,* **Christine Delsol** has been traveling to Mexico at every opportunity for 30 years. She has spent most of her career in newspapers and is the recipient of an Associated Press award and two Lowell Thomas awards. **Maribeth Mellin** first drove the two-lane road from Cancún to Chetumal when tires hanging on sticks marked sandy roads to secluded campgrounds. She's kept track of the changes ever since. She's the author of *Traveler's Mexico Companion,* which won the country's prestigious Pluma de Plata award.

HOW TO CONTACT US

In researching this book, we discovered many wonderful places—hotels, restaurants, shops, and more. We're sure you'll find others. Please tell us about them, so we can share the information with your fellow travelers in upcoming editions. If you were disappointed with a recommendation, we'd love to know that, too. Please write to:

Frommer's Cancún & the Yucatán, 19th Edition
John Wiley & Sons, Inc. • 111 River St. • Hoboken, NJ 07030-5774
frommersfeedback@wiley.com

ADVISORY & DISCLAIMER

Travel information can change quickly and unexpectedly, and we strongly advise you to confirm important details locally before traveling, including information on visas, health and safety, traffic and transport, accommodations, shopping, and eating out. We also encourage you to stay alert while traveling and to remain aware of your surroundings. Avoid civil disturbances, and keep a close eye on cameras, purses, wallets, and other valuables.

While we have endeavored to ensure that the information contained within this guide is accurate and up-to-date at the time of publication, we make no representations or warranties with respect to the accuracy or completeness of the contents of this work and specifically disclaim all warranties, including without limitation warranties of fitness for a particular purpose. We accept no responsibility or liability for any inaccuracy or errors or omissions, or for any inconvenience, loss, damage, costs, or expenses of any nature whatsoever incurred or suffered by anyone as a result of any advice or information contained in this guide.

The inclusion of a company, organization, or website in this guide as a service provider and/or potential source of further information does not mean that we endorse them or the information they provide. Be aware that information provided through some websites may be unreliable and can change without notice. Neither the publisher nor author shall be liable for any damages arising herefrom.

FROMMER'S STAR RATINGS, ICONS & ABBREVIATIONS

Every hotel, restaurant, and attraction listing in this guide has been ranked for quality, value, service, amenities, and special features using a **star-rating system.** In country, state, and regional guides, we also rate towns and regions to help you narrow down your choices and budget your time accordingly. Hotels and restaurants are rated on a scale of zero (recommended) to three stars (exceptional). Attractions, shopping, nightlife, towns, and regions are rated according to the following scale: zero stars (recommended), one star (highly recommended), two stars (very highly recommended), and three stars (must-see).

In addition to the star-rating system, we also use **seven feature icons** that point you to the great deals, in-the-know advice, and unique experiences that separate travelers from tourists. Throughout the book, look for:

🎁 **special finds**—those places only insiders know about

💬 **fun facts**—details that make travelers more informed and their trips more fun

☺ **kids**—best bets for kids and advice for the whole family

📷 **special moments**—those experiences that memories are made of

✋ **overrated**—places or experiences not worth your time or money

📎 **insider tips**—great ways to save time and money

🏷 **great values**—where to get the best deals

The following abbreviations are used for credit cards:

AE	American Express	**DISC**	Discover	**V**	Visa
DC	Diners Club	**MC**	MasterCard		

TRAVEL RESOURCES AT FROMMERS.COM

Frommer's travel resources don't end with this guide. Frommer's website, **www. frommers.com**, has travel information on more than 4,000 destinations. We update features regularly, giving you access to the most current trip-planning information and the best airfare, lodging, and car-rental bargains. You can also listen to podcasts, connect with other Frommers.com members through our active-reader forums, share your travel photos, read blogs from guidebook editors and fellow travelers, and much more.

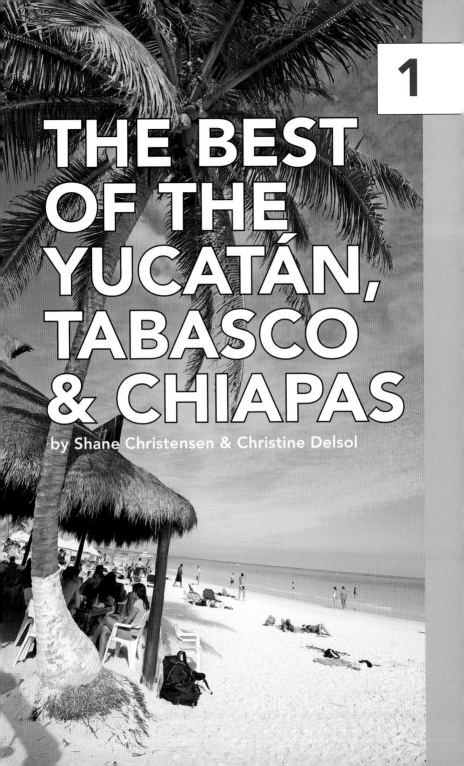

THE BEST OF THE YUCATÁN, TABASCO & CHIAPAS

by Shane Christensen & Christine Delsol

The Yucatán Peninsula welcomes more visitors than any other part of Mexico. Its tremendous variety—from breathtaking beaches, endless water sports, and jungle excursions to visits to Maya ruins, unforgettable walks through indigenous villages, and exhilarating eco-adventures—attracts every kind of traveler. We've logged thousands of miles crisscrossing the peninsula, and these are our personal favorites.

THE most UNFORGETTABLE TRAVEL EXPERIENCES

- **Swimming in the Caribbean:** Slipping into the brilliant turquoise sea from the white sandy beach, it's entirely possible you'll feel you've entered paradise. There's no sensation quite like floating in the warm, welcoming waters of the Caribbean on a clear sunny day. For a more adventurous time in the ocean, you can also swim with dolphins in Cancún, Cozumel, and Isla Mujeres.
- **Catching Island Fever:** Cozumel and Isla Mujeres are two idyllic Caribbean islands far removed from the glitz and revelry of Cancún. Although only 15 minutes away by ferry, sleepy Isla Mujeres feels worlds removed, and Cozumel seems just as far from Playa del Carmen, even though it's less than 45 minutes by boat.

PREVIOUS PAGE: **Tulum Beach.** ABOVE: **The Tulum ruins, overlooking the Caribbean Sea.**

- **Peering Under the Surface:** The Mexican Caribbean boasts magnificent snorkeling and scuba diving, particularly in Cozumel, which is home to one of the planet's most spectacular coral reef marine communities.
- **Exploring Maya Ruins:** Whether Chichén Itzá, Uxmal, Tulum, Palenque, or any of the other ancient Maya ruins dotting this region, the Yucatán Peninsula offers unparalleled chances to view the archaeological legacy of this great Mesoamerican civilization.
- **Experiencing Village Life:** The Yucatán is among the most culturally rich areas of Mexico, the heart of Maya civilization well before the Spanish conquest. Take your time walking village streets, visiting the markets, sampling Yucatecan food, and experiencing a part of the enduring indigenous cultures.
- **Seeing Another World in Chiapas:** The cultural capital of Chiapas, San Cristóbal de las Casas is one of the world's unique cities, where indigenous traditions, Spanish colonial influences, Mexican society, and international tourism all intersect.

THE best REGIONAL EXPERIENCES

- **Exploring the Inland Yucatán Peninsula:** Travelers who venture only to the Yucatán's resorts and cities miss the rock-walled inland villages, where women wear brightly embroidered dresses and life proceeds almost as if the modern world (with the exception of highways) didn't exist. The adventure of seeing secluded cenotes, unrestored haciendas, and newly uncovered ruins, deep in jungle settings, is not to be missed. See chapter 7.

- **Catching Street & Park Entertainment in Mérida:** Few cities have so vibrant a street scene as Mérida. Every night of the week you can catch music and dance performances in plazas about town. Then, on Sunday, Mérida really gets going— streets are closed off, food stalls spring up everywhere, and you can enjoy a book fair, a flea market, comedy acts, band concerts, and dance groups. At night, the main plaza is the place to be, with people dancing to mambos and rumbas in the street in front of the city hall. See chapter 7.

Mérida by night.

- **Exploring San Cristóbal de Las Casas:** The city of San Cristóbal is a living museum, with 16th-century colonial architecture and pre-Hispanic native influences. The highland Maya live in surrounding villages and arrive daily in town wearing

The Yucatán Peninsula

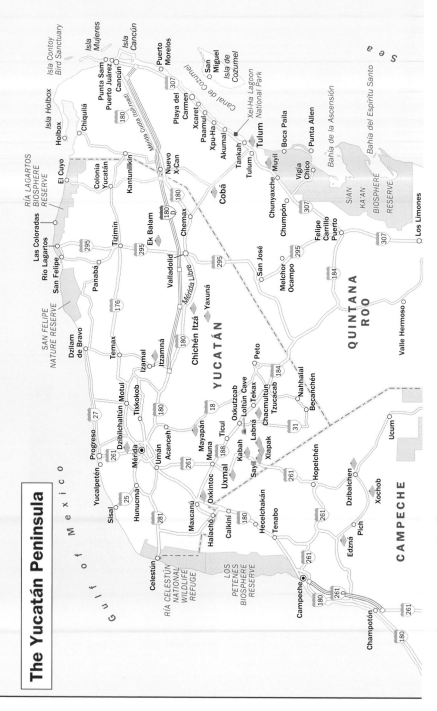

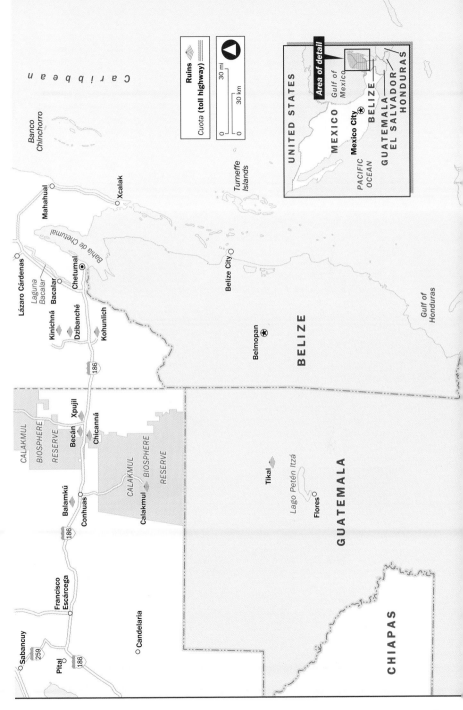

colorful handmade clothing. A visit to the villages is a window into another world, giving visitors a glimpse of traditional Indian dress, religious customs, churches, and ceremonies. See chapter 8.

o **Visiting a Hacienda:** They were built by the wealthy, but you don't have to be rich to stay in a restored hacienda hotel. The fabulous haciendas now owned or managed by the Starwood chain are the best known and most expensive, while places such as Hacienda Yaxcopoil, Hacienda San Pedro Nohpat, and Hacienda San José Cholul, all near Mérida, are not only affordable but far more evocative of life on a hacienda during their heyday. See chapter 7.

THE best FOOD & DRINK EXPERIENCES

o **Feasting in Cancún's Hotel Zone:** This famous (some would say infamous) resort town is home to some of the top restaurants in all of Mexico. Expect internationally trained chefs in the Hotel Zone's acclaimed independent restaurants, where menus tend to focus on fresh Caribbean seafood and Black Angus steaks using Mexican and Mediterranean ingredients. The top-rated restaurants lie in The Ritz-Carlton, JW Marriott, Le Meridien, and Fiesta Americana Grand Coral Beach resorts, and are less often found in all-inclusive hotels. See p. 93.

TOP: **Fresh seafood is abundant.** BOTTOM: *Panucho* **(tortillas filled with beans and topped with chicken, lettuce, and pickled red onion) is a local staple.**

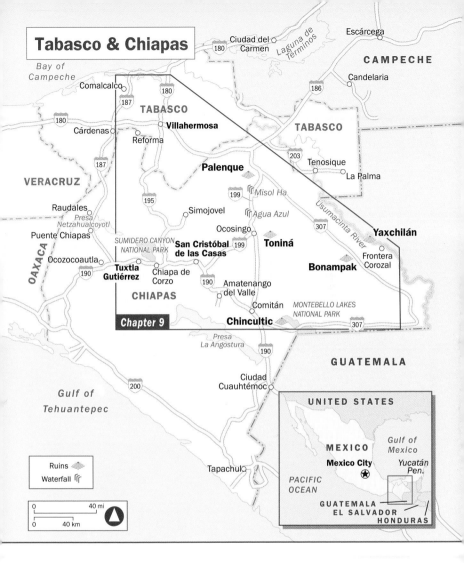

Tabasco & Chiapas

Bay of
Campeche

CAMPECHE

Escárcega

Ciudad del
Carmen

Laguna de
Términos

180

Candelaria

Comalcalco

187

180

TABASCO

180

Cárdenas

Villahermosa

Reforma

TABASCO

186

VERACRUZ

Palenque

203

Tenosique

La Palma

199

Misol Ha

195

Raudales

Simojovel

Agua Azul

Presa
Netzahualcoyotl

Puente Chiapas

Ocosingo

307

Yaxchilán

SUMIDERO CANYON
NATIONAL PARK

San Cristóbal
de las Casas

199

Toniná

Ocozocoautla

190

Tuxtla
Gutiérrez

Chiapa de
Corzo

190

Bonampak

Frontera
Corozal

Usumacinta River

Amatenango
del Valle

CHIAPAS

Chapter 9

Comitán

Chincultic

MONTEBELLO LAKES
NATIONAL PARK

307

Presa
La Angostura

190

GUATEMALA

Ciudad
Cuauhtémoc

200

Gulf of
Tehuantepec

Ruins

Waterfall

0   40 mi

0   40 km

Tapachula

UNITED STATES

MEXICO

MEXICO CITY

PACIFIC
OCEAN

Gulf of
Mexico

Yucatán
Pen.

GUATEMALA
EL SALVADOR
HONDURAS

- **Eating Like a Local:** Downtown Cancún is dotted with tasty, inexpensive eateries, whether you're looking for a spicy sidewalk taco or a sit-down Mexican meal. Steep yourself in traditional Yucatecan culture at **Labná,** which showcases Maya cuisine and music. The Labná Special samples four of the region's best dishes, including baked suckling pig with guacamole. See p. 98.

- **Sampling Yucatecan Cuisine Across the Region:** A trip to the Yucatán allows for a culinary tour of some of Mexico's finest foods. Don't miss specialties such as *pollo* or *cochinita pibil* (chicken or pork in savory achiote sauce), the uniquely Campechan *pan de cazón,* great seafood dishes, the many styles of tamal found throughout Chiapas and the Yucatán, and Caribbean-influenced staples such as fried bananas, black beans, and yucca root. For a glossary of popular regional dishes, see chapter 10.

o **Cracking Open a Fresh Caribbean Lobster on the Islands:** You'll find lobster on the menus of even the most simple seafood establishments in Isla Mujeres and Cozumel, and the great thing is it's completely fresh and not too expensive. If you want an ideally seasoned, succulent lobster dinner in Cozumel, **Cabaña del Pescador** is the place. If you want anything else, you're out of luck—lobster dinner, expertly prepared, is all it serves. See p. 144.

o **Learning to Cook Like a Local:** You won't miss Yucatecan cuisine so much after you get home if you make it part of your repertoire. Cooking schools take all forms: The Ritz-Carlton Cancún's instruction in a gleaming new culinary center; *mercado* shopping, tours and cooking lessons at Los Dos in Merida; and the Little Mexican Cooking School's savory blend of lecture, demonstration, and hands-on practice is spiced liberally with humor in Puerto Morelos. See p. 60.

THE best LOCAL EXPERIENCES

o **Chilling Like a Local on Isla Mujeres:** If uninterrupted relaxation is what you're after, Isla Mujeres offers a quintessential laid-back vacation. Bike—or take a golf cart—around the island to explore rocky coves and sandy beaches, or focus your tanning efforts on the wide beachfront of Playa Norte. Here you'll find calm waters perfect for swimming and snorkeling, as well as beachfront *palapa* restaurants beckoning you to linger over fresh red snapper. If island fever starts to take over, you're only a ferry ride away from the action in Cancún.

o **Sipping an Ice-Cold Cerveza:** The hot weather calls for a frosty beer, whether served on a beach chair or in a traditional cantina. Mexicans love to drink their Corona, Dos Equis, Negro Modelo, Bohemia, or any other number of

Relaxing on the beach in Isla Mujeres.

Mexican brands straight from the bottle and often with a slice of lemon. It should be accompanied by some crispy tortilla chips and hot salsa.

o **Perusing the Local Flea Markets:** Most Mexican towns in this book have flea markets that meet weekly, if not daily. These are the places to buy handicrafts, textiles, and inexpensive jewelry. They're far less expensive, and often more interesting, than shopping malls, and if you look carefully you'll find plenty of hand-made items. Respectful bargaining is expected.

o **Walking the Walk with Campechanos:** After exploring the confection of impeccably preserved centuries-old mansions, domed churches, and stone fortifications in Campeche's Centro Historico, breach the city walls for a walk along the *malecón*. Campechanos congregate on the broad, palm-lined sea walk to visit and cool off, and you'll likely never see a better sunset than the celestial conflagration that stops joggers, strollers, and squealing children in their tracks every evening.

THE best FAMILY EXPERIENCES

o **Kicking Back on the Beach:** In Cancún just above the Hotel Zone, the northern beaches facing Isla Mujeres are protected by the Bahia de Mujeres, making for calm waters that are perfect for swimming. At most of the beaches along this stretch, you can rent a sailboard and take lessons, ride a parasail, or partake in a variety of watersports. There's a small but beautiful portion of public beach on **Playa Caracol,** popular with families because of its shallow sandy bottom. See p. 88.

o **Going Underwater at Cancún's Coolest Aquarium:** The **Interactive Aquarium** at the family-friendly La Isla shopping center in Cancún offers 13 fish tanks (27,800 gallons of water); a contact area for kids to feed a turtle, touch a sea ray, or hold a sea star; dolphin swims and shows; and the chance to feed a shark while immersed in the water in an acrylic cage. Guides inside the main tank use underwater microphones to point out the sea life and answer questions. See p. 92.

o **Getting Wet at a Natural Waterpark:** Xel-Ha, near Tulum, is a beautiful lagoon where you can swim, float, snorkel, or take a zip line surrounded by lush jungle. The clear, protected waters make it a natural aquarium with several species of colorful fish. Swimming with dolphins, Snuba (a combination of snorkeling and diving), or walking under water with a "Sea Trek" are also offered here. See p. 184.

o **Relaxing in the Center of Town:** Head for the central plaza of just about any town in the evening as families gather to end their day with gossip, snacks, maybe a little music, and a chance for children to run out their excess energy. Especially on weekends, it may take on a carnival atmosphere, filling with food carts, balloon vendors, and street performers—or even puppet shows or trampolines.

THE best BEACH EXPERIENCES

o **Drinking in the Sun at Cancún:** Whether or not you believe Cancún is an unrelenting spring break party in which Americans compete with Mexicans for the city's real identity—and I'd say the truth lies in the timing of your

Catching some rays at one of the many luxury resorts in Cancún.

visit—you're likely to agree this man-made resort has some of the most spectacular beaches in the country. The powdery white sand is complemented by warm Caribbean waters that look like a Technicolor dream, so clear that you can see through to the coral reefs below. The northern beaches facing Isla Mujeres just above the Hotel Zone are protected by a bay and ideal for swimming.

o **Zoning Out in Isla Mujeres:** If uninterrupted relaxation is what you're after, Isla Mujeres is your island. Within a few minutes' walk of the main town, you can plant your toes on one of the world's most stunning swimming beaches at Playa Norte. Try to come for more than just a daytrip from Cancún to experience the island's easygoing beach culture. Most accommodations here are small, inexpensive inns, with a few luxury boutique hotels tempting you for at least a night.

o **Soaking in the Waters at Cozumel:** It may not offer lots of big, sandy beaches, but Cozumel promises something the mainland doesn't: the calm, flat waters of the sheltered western shore. It could be mistaken for a giant swimming pool, only this pool has lots of brilliantly colored fish, so take your snorkeling mask even if you don't plan to do any diving, which is among the best in the world.

o **Taking in the Scene at Playa del Carmen:** Stylish and hip, Playa del Carmen has a beautiful beach and an eclectic assortment of small hotels, inns, and cabañas. The social scene focuses on the beach by day and the pedestrian-only Quinta Avenida (Fifth Avenue) by night, with its assortment of restaurants, clubs, sidewalk cafes, and shops offering all the entertainment you could want. You're also close to the coast's major attractions, including nature parks, ruins, and cenotes (sinkholes or natural wells). Fast-growing Playa is becoming homogenized (think Dairy Queen and Starbucks). Enjoy it while it's still a manageable size. See chapter 6.

- **Relaxing in the Shade of Tulum's Ruins:** Fronting some of the best beaches on the entire coast, Tulum's small hotels offer guests a little slice of paradise far from the crowds and megaresorts. The bustling town lies inland; at the coast, activities and partying compete with swinging in a hammock and doing absolutely nothing. If you can pull yourself away from the beach, there are ruins to marvel at and a vast nature preserve to explore. See chapter 6.

- **Going Back in Time on the Southern Caribbean:** For a glimpse of the Caribbean coast as it was before Cancún brought the world rushing in, head for the Costa Maya, beginning at the southern border of the Sian Ka'an reserve and stretching to the Belize border. The wide, white sands seem to go on forever, and beyond the two main towns, it might be forever before you encounter another soul. With some local guidance, you can work your way into a part of Sian Ka'an that tourists rarely see.

THE best HISTORIC EXPERIENCES

- **Standing Over the Ocean at Tulum:** Tulum isn't the most important ancient Maya city, either historically or architecturally, but its seaside setting is uniquely beautiful. The stark contrast of its crumbling stone walls against the clear turquoise ocean just beyond is an extraordinary sight. See chapter 6.

- **Wandering the City of Calakmul:** Of the many elegantly built Maya cities of the Río Bec area, in the lower Yucatán, Calakmul is the broadest in scope and design. It's also one of the hardest to reach—about 48km (30 miles) from the Guatemalan border and surrounded by the jungle of the Calakmul Biological Reserve. Calakmul is a walled city with the tallest pyramid in the Yucatán—a city that continuing research might prove to be the largest in the Maya world, more than equal to Guatemala's Tikal. Go now, while it remains infrequently visited. See chapter 6.

The Palenque ruins.

- **Examining the Carvings at Uxmal:** No matter how many times we see Uxmal, the splendor of its stone carvings remains awe-inspiring. A stone rattlesnake undulates across the facade of the Nunnery complex, and 103 masks of Chaac—the rain god—project from the Governor's Palace. See chapter 7.

- **Visiting the Center of Mayan Life at Chichén Itzá:** Stand beside the giant serpent head at the foot of El Castillo and marvel at the architects and astronomers who positioned the building so precisely that shadow and sunlight form a serpent's body slithering from peak to the earth at each equinox (Mar 21 and Sept 21). See chapter 7.

- **Marveling at the Pyramid of Ek Balam:** In recent years, this is the site where some of Mexico's most astounding archaeological discoveries have been made. Ek Balam's main pyramid is taller than Chichén Itzá's, and it holds a sacred doorway bordered with elaborate stucco figures of priests and kings and rich iconography. See chapter 7.

- **Raiding the Tombs of Palenque:** The ancient builders of these structures carved histories in stone that scholars have only recently deciphered. Imagine the magnificent ceremony in A.D. 683 when King Pacal was buried deep inside his pyramid—his tomb unspoiled until its discovery in 1952. See chapter 8.

- **Avoiding the Crowds in Edzná:** This huge but barely excavated city about 50km (31 miles) outside of Campeche gets fewer visitors in a year than Chichén Itzá does in a day. Its natural beauty; marvelous network of canals, reservoirs, and aqueducts; and ornate architecture—resembling Palenque or Tikal more than anything in the Yucatán—are yours to absorb in utter peace. See p. 279.

THE best OUTDOOR EXPERIENCES

- **Scuba Diving in Cozumel & Along the Yucatán's Caribbean Coast:** The coral reefs off the island, Mexico's premier diving destination, are among the top five dive spots in the world. The Yucatán's coastal reef, part of the planet's second-largest reef system and a national marine park, affords excellent diving all along the coast. Diving from Isla Mujeres is quite spectacular. Especially beautiful is the Chinchorro Reef, lying 32km (20 miles) offshore from Mahahual or Xcalak. See chapters 5 and 6.

- **Fly-Fishing off the Punta Allen & Mahahual Peninsulas:** Serious anglers will enjoy the challenge of

Scuba diving in Cozumel.

Great white herons in Isla Contoy.

fly-fishing the saltwater flats and lagoons on the protected sides of these peninsulas. See chapter 6.

o **Cenote Diving on the Yucatán Mainland:** Dive into the clear depths of the Yucatán's cenotes for a whole new world of underwater exploration. The Maya considered the cenotes sacred—and their vivid colors do indeed seem otherworldly. Most are between Playa del Carmen and Tulum, and dive shops in these areas regularly run trips for experienced divers. For recommended dive shops, see "Cozumel" in chapter 5, and "Playa del Carmen" and "South of Playa del Carmen" in chapter 6.

o **Swimming with Giants on Isla Holbox:** A shark the size of a whale might sound like a science-fiction nightmare, but whale sharks—three times the size of the biggest great white shark—are peaceful, plankton-eating creatures, and swimming with them is a unique and awe-inspiring experience. Isla Holbox, Quintana Roo's northernmost island, is whale shark central, hosting the polka-dotted behemoths from May to September. See p. 303.

o **Birding:** The Yucatán Peninsula, Tabasco, and Chiapas are ornithological paradises. Two very special places are Isla Contoy, with more than 70 species of birds as well as a host of marine and animal life (p. 125), and the Huitepec Cloud Forest, with its flocks of migratory species (p. 332). North America's largest flamingo breeding and nesting grounds lie at opposite ends of Yucatán state's Gulf Coast, in Celestún (p. 255) and Ría Lagartos (p. 301).

o **Trekking to Bonampak & Yaxchilán:** Bonampak and Yaxchilán—two remote, jungle-surrounded Maya sites along the Usumacinta River—are accessible by car and motorboat. Colorful murals of battle and victory at Bonampak have

Exploring the ruins of Yaxchilán.

managed to survive the elements after hundreds of years, and remain some of the best examples of Maya painting on the peninsula. The experience could well be the highlight of any trip. See "Road Trips from San Cristóbal" in chapter 8.

THE best SHOPPING EXPERIENCES

- **Shopping Duty-Free in Cancún's Hotel Zone:** Isla Cancún's luxury malls are filled with international designer fashions and duty-free shopping. "La Isla" is the most enticing shopping center here, an outdoor oasis adjacent to the Nichupté Lagoon featuring high street fashions, quality restaurants, Venetian-style canals, and a spectacular aquarium. This is also a great place for families. See chapter 4.

- **Hunting for Bargains in Downtown:** The best flea markets are located downtown, where polite bargaining is welcome. Authentic handicrafts, inexpensive jewelry, and colorful textiles and clothes fill the local shops and markets of Cancún City. Mercado 28 is generally considered a reliable market for good deals. See p. 100.

- **Searching for Splurges in Playa del Carmen:** Shops and boutiques along busy Quinta Avenida (Fifth Avenue) display amber jewelry, Guatemalan embroidered blouses, Brazilian bikinis, and collectible folk art from throughout Mexico. Hold on to your pesos till you've thoroughly explored the shops from calles 2 to 30. Treasures are hidden among the endless array of tacky souvenirs. See chapter 6.

Campeche has a market outside the colorful Old Town.

○ **Mingling with Locals in the Markets:** San Cristóbal de las Casas and Mérida have some of Mexico's finest market areas filled with local vendors and shoppers wearing traditional embroidered clothing. You'll find hammocks, Panama hats, and *guayaberas* (men's shirts) in Mérida, and woven shawls and *huipiles* (blouses with elaborate colorful patterns) at the Plaza de Santo Domingo in San Cristóbal. See chapter 8.

THE best NIGHTLIFE EXPERIENCES

○ **Going Wild in Cancún:** After baking yourself all day in the sun, your bronzed body deserves to be flaunted. Head to Party Row, where longstanding Cancún favorites **Carlos 'n' Charlie's, Hard Rock,** and **Señor Frog's** offer potent drinks, hot music, and wild (if sometimes sloppy) dance floors. **Dady'O,** as well as its four offspring bars, all lie within a block of each other pulsating with music and tequila-inspired revelers. See chapter 4.

○ **Dancing Like You've Never Danced Before:** Forum by the Sea entertainment center in Cancún has it all: a dazzling array of clubs, sports bars, fast food, and fine dining, with shops open late as well. It's also the home of what remains Cancún's hottest club, **CoCo Bongo,** which regularly packs in up to 3,000 partyers. **The City** is the other mega day-and-night dance club, offering a day club with beach and pool activities and food and bar service, as well as the sizzling multi-level nightclub with nine bars. See p. 102.

- **Having a More Sophisticated Night Out on Quinta Avenida (Playa del Carmen):** Stroll along lively, pedestrian-only Fifth Avenue to find the bar that's right for you. With live-music venues, tequila bars, sports bars, and cafes, you're sure to find something to fit your mood. The intersection with Calle 12 is becoming the de facto club central. See p. 172.

- **Being Out & About on Mérida's Grand Boulevard:** In addition to the nightly free, city-sponsored cultural performances, Mérida has a varied collection of night spots along majestic Paseo de Montejo. Choose from live rock, salsa dancing, and Latin music at clubs clustered around Calle 60, cool hotel lounges, and stellar restaurants that become dance clubs at night. See p. 246.

Playa del Carmen's bustling Quinta Avenida.

- **Clubbing It in San Cristóbal de las Casas:** This city, small though it may be, has a live-music scene that can't be beat for fun and atmosphere. The bars and clubs are all within walking distance of each other, and they're a real bargain. See chapter 8.

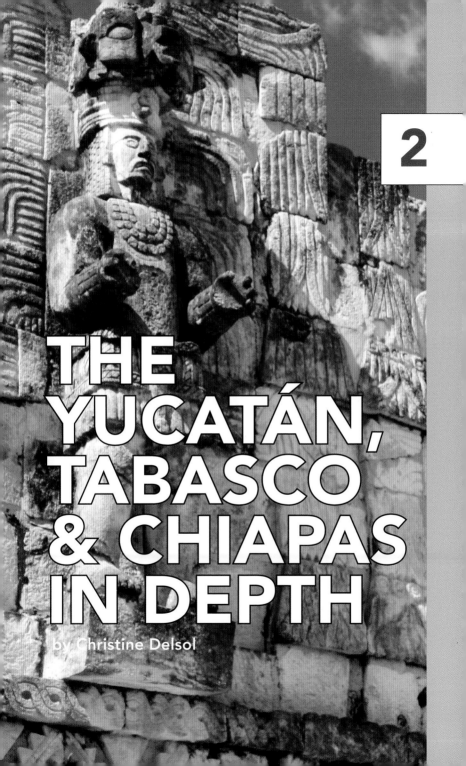

THE YUCATÁN, TABASCO & CHIAPAS IN DEPTH

by Christine Delsol

n the space of a single generation, the Yucatán has been transformed from a forgotten backwater visited primarily by archaeologists, sports fishermen, and scuba divers into a major international destination and economic powerhouse. Cancún's creation and growth have wrought changes as far away as Chiapas and Tabasco, whose significant Maya populations share a history with the Yucatán despite their distance and different personalities and landscapes.

The change is most visible on the coast, where fishing villages and coconut plantations have given way to modern developments, marching in lock step south to Tulum, inching toward the recently minted Costa Maya, and extending to the Belize border. For the young Maya of the interior villages, growth has brought new work opportunities and their first close contact with the modern world—specifically the modern world in vacation mode. The shift from village society to vacation paradise is the very definition of culture shock, which the implacable Maya meet with equanimity.

Less dramatically, tourism also made its way inland to the splendid Yucatán capital of Mérida and the major ruins—Chichén Itzá, Uxmal, and Palenque—and eventually to the barely uncovered ancient cities and time-warp villages of the deep interior. Every year seems to bring new archaeological discoveries.

Curiously, all the excavation and renovation has left small-town life little changed. Coastal natives not swept up in the tourism boom were relocated inland, where they continue their ancestors' ways. Families of workers in the tourist palaces remain in the tropical forest, living in round thatch houses with no electricity, indoor plumbing, or paved roads, gathering plants for food and medicine, cooling off in hidden cenotes, and appealing to the gods for successful crops. To explore an older world where the Mayan tongue's distinctive intonations fill the air and centuries-old traditions endure, you have only to drive inland from the Caribbean coast, venture to Campeche on the Gulf shore, or head south into Chiapas.

The turquoise waters and tropical climate may beckon first, but what will ultimately draw you back, again and again, is the unique character of this land and its people.

THE YUCATÁN, TABASCO & CHIAPAS TODAY

In the five states that make up the Yucatán and southeastern Mexico, great wealth lives alongside abject poverty. Paradoxically, the indexes of both wealth and poverty in this region surpass the national average. A tremendous amount of money flows into the area—from tourism in Yucatán and Quintana Roo, and the oil industry in Campeche, Tabasco, and Chiapas. Yet most residents reap little from this prosperity. These five states have a total population of almost 10 million—10% of Mexico's population—but account for only about 6% of the country's economic activity.

PREVIOUS PAGE: **Mayan sculptures.**

In some cases, development has increased demand for local products and services. For example, fishermen and *palaperos*, the native people who create the thatched roofs (*palapas*) crowning so many restaurants and hotels, are in high demand whenever a hurricane brushes the coast. At the same time, development has destroyed the livelihood of other locals. Coastal coconut growers were wiped out when Cancún developers brought turf from Florida to build a golf course, unwittingly introducing a disease that killed the coconut palms; destruction of mangroves, crucial to the coastal food chain, has diminished fishermen's catches. A similar give-and-take is at play within the oil economies of Tabasco and Chiapas.

> **In the Beginning**
>
> *The animals showed them the road. And then grinding the yellow corn and the white corn, Xmucané made nine drinks . . . and with it they created the muscles and the strength of man . . . After that they began to talk about the creation and the making of our first mother and father; of yellow corn and of white corn they made their flesh; of corn meal dough they made the arms and the legs of man.*
> —From the *Popul Vuh*, the Maya "bible"

While residents' incomes have not improved, tourism and oil money has brought indirect benefits. Lacking a coherent policy to combat social ills, the government still has paved most of the peninsula's roads and fitted out remote villages with electricity. Purified water is widely available. And with the increasing emphasis on ecotourism, some remote villages have formed partnerships with tour companies that allow them to profit from tourism while controlling the number and type of visitors.

Today's Maya Culture & People

The Yucatán peninsula, Tabasco, and Chiapas often feel like a country apart from Mexico. Their *jarana* music, sweetened by clarinets, and a cuisine redolent with capers, achiote, and saffron, exude Caribbean sensuality. And the region's

Old meets new as people surf the Internet in a centuries-old plaza.

A Maya family in Yokdzonot, a small town near Chichén Itzá.

dignified, gentle people display little of the machismo or the relentless huckstering that tries visitors' patience in northern and central Mexico.

The sense of "otherness" grows partly from geographical isolation but even more from the Maya's fierce, centuries-long resistance to being absorbed into the Spanish spoils; some Maya refuse to recognize Mexican sovereignty even today. All of which makes their warm, generous natures as much a wonder as their famous pyramid at Chichén Itzá.

In the Yucatán, especially, your simplest transaction with a local easily evolves into spirited conversation. In the peninsula's interior, where some Maya Indians are uneasy speaking Spanish, you are more likely to encounter initial reticence. Usually, it's quickly overcome with smiles and inventive gestures.

You don't need to leave Cancún to meet the Maya; thousands travel from the interior to jobs at hotels and restaurants. More than 350,000 Maya living in the peninsula's three states speak Yucatec, the local Mayan language. Most, especially men, also speak Spanish, and workers in Cancún usually know at least basic English.

The estimated one million Tabascan and Chiapan Maya, who speak four Mayan languages with dozens of dialects, are more reserved. Highland Maya around San Cristóbal de las Casas tend to remain aloof from outside cultures, preferring to live in mountain hamlets and meeting only for ceremonies and market days. In their chilly cloud-forest homeland they, too, live much as their ancestors did, but with beliefs distinct from their peninsular relatives.

Though they held fast to their language through the Spanish conquest, the Maya lost much of their living memory of pre-Hispanic life; what they retained is cloaked in myth and worked into elements of Catholicism. That process of syncretism, as anthropologists call it, continues today in the many Maya communities that have native churches.

The question of their ancestors' rightful place among the world's ancient civilizations might be as much a mystery to today's Maya people as it is to scholars. But nearly every year, archaeological discoveries of the art and architecture of the ancients add to the growing picture of a complex urban culture that thrived where only sparsely populated jungle exists today.

The Well-Lived Life

Despite economic inequities, Mexican society remains tremendously resilient and cohesive. Mexicans place paramount value on family and friends, social gatherings, and living in the present; worrying about the future takes a back seat. Mexicans always have time to meet with friends for a cup of coffee or attend a family get-together. The many spirited public celebrations Mexico is known for are simply another manifestation of this attitude.

You won't find more amiable people anywhere on Earth, and you can invite the full force of their natural gregariousness by being mindful of some social norms. Here's a start:

SLOW DOWN The stereotype of *"mañana* time" is mostly true. Life obeys slower rhythms, and "on time" is a flexible concept. Arriving 30 minutes to 2 hours late to a party in someone's home is acceptable—in fact, coming at the specified hour would be rude, for your hosts almost certainly will not be ready. Here's the "mostly" part: Dinner invitations are less flexible; arrive within 30 minutes of the appointed hour. And be on time for business appointments, public performances, weddings, and funerals.

MEET & GREET Don't curtail the hellos and goodbyes; social values take precedence over time efficiency. A Mexican must at least say *"¡Buenos días!"* even to strangers. An individual will greet each member of a group separately, no matter how long it takes. Handshakes, *abrazos* (embraces), and, among women, kisses abound. Stick to handshakes until your host initiates a more intimate greeting. But don't back away from an embrace—that would amount to a rejection of friendship.

HAVE A LITTLE RESPECT Mexicans are lavish with titles of respect, so dispense *señor, señora,* and *señorita* (Mr., Mrs., Miss) freely. Teachers, lawyers, architects, and other professionals have earned the right to a title: *licenciado* for lawyers (and some other professions requiring a college degree), *maestro* or *maestra* for elementary school teachers, *profesor* or *profesora* for secondary or college teachers, and so forth. Mexicans have two surnames, father's first and mother's second. Both appear on business cards (the mother's name might be abbreviated to an initial), but when addressing people, use just the first (paternal) surname.

DON'T GET HUFFY Mexicans are genuinely interested in foreigners. If they stare, it's friendly curiosity. They like to practice their English, and might ask

Mayan Terms & Phrases

Hundreds of thousands of Maya living on the Yucatán Peninsula today speak at least some of their mother tongue. Most speak Yucatec Maya (commonly called simply "Maya"), one of more than 30 Mayan languages used today that can be traced back about 4,000 years to a single language believed to have originated in northwestern Guatemala. You will see numerous spelling variations around the peninsula. ***Note:*** The term "Mayan" is reserved for Mayan languages. The noun or the adjective for the people is "Maya." For a glossary of Mayan phrases, see "Spanish & Mayan Terms & Phrases," p. 370.

about family, friends, money, and other intimate matters. If you are over 30 and have no children, they may express deep concern. Don't take it personally.

SHOW SOME CULTURE   Mexicans tend to divide the world into the well-raised and cultured (*bien educado*) and the poorly raised (*mal educado*). Don't be shy about trying out your rudimentary Spanish; even the most elementary attempt is appreciated because it shows your interest in the culture. To be categorized as a foreigner is no big deal. What's important in Mexico is to be categorized as a cultured foreigner and not one of the barbarians.

LOOKING BACK: YUCATÁN, TABASCO & CHIAPAS HISTORY

Pre-Hispanic Civilizations

The earliest "Mexicans" might have been Stone Age hunter-gatherers from the north, descendants of a race that crossed the Bering Strait and reached North America around 12,000 B.C. A more recent theory points to an earlier crossing of peoples from Asia to the New World. What we do know is that Mexico was populated by 10,000 B.C. Sometime between 5200 and 1500 B.C., these early people began practicing agriculture and domesticating animals.

THE OLMEC & MAYA: THE PRE-CLASSIC PERIOD (1500 B.C.–A.D. 300)

Agriculture eventually supported large communities, with enough surplus to free some people from agricultural work. A civilization emerged that we call the

A colossal Olmec head in Villahermosa.

IT'S ALL IN THE game

The ancient Maya played a ball game of such importance that ball courts (pictured below) appear in virtually every Maya city (Bonampak is a rare exception). They were laid out in a capital I shape with sloping walls in the center. Similar ball courts have been found as far south as Nicaragua and as far north as Arizona.

Though we know little about this sacred game, ancient depictions, early accounts by the Spanish, and the Popol Vuh (the Maya "bible") show that the solid rubber ball was heavy and could inflict injury. Wearing thick padding and protective gear, players formed teams of 2 to 10 members, the object being to propel the ball through a stone ring or other goal using mainly the hips.

We also know the game was part sport and part religious ritual based on the Maya's cosmological beliefs. It sometimes involved sacrifice, though we're not sure whether the winners, the losers, or perhaps prisoners of war were sacrificed. In the Popol Vuh, the hero twins, Hunahpu and Xbalanque, challenge the lords of the underworld to a ball game, played in part with the head of one brother. Eventually the twins win and are allowed to return to the world of the living. Playing the ball game, then, might have been one way to cheat the underworld.

Olmec—an enigmatic people who settled the Tabasco and Veracruz coasts. Anthropologists regard them as Mesoamerica's mother culture because they established a pattern for later civilizations from northern Mexico to Central America. The Olmec developed basic calendar, writing, and numbering systems, established principles of urban layout and architecture, and originated the cult of the jaguar and the sacredness of jade. They probably also bequeathed the sacred ball game common to all Mesoamerican culture.

A defining feature of the Olmec culture was its colossal carved stone heads, several of which reside today in the Parque–Museo La Venta in Villahermosa, Tabasco. Their significance remains a mystery, but they were immense projects, sculpted from basalt mined miles more than 80km (50 miles) inland and transported to the coast, probably by river rafts. Their rounded, baby-faced look, marked by a peculiar, high-arched lip—a "jaguar mouth"—is an identifying mark of Olmec sculpture.

The **Maya** civilization began developing in the pre-Classic period, around 500 b.c. Understanding of this period is sketchy, but Olmec influences show up everywhere. The Maya perfected the Olmec calendar and developed both their ornate system of hieroglyphic writing and their early architecture. The people of **Teotihuacán,** north of present-day Mexico City, and the **Zapotec** of Monte Albán, in the valley of Oaxaca, also emerged around this time.

TEOTIHUACÁN, MONTE ALBÁN & PALENQUE: THE CLASSIC PERIOD (A.D. 300–900)

The rise and fall of these three city-states are bookends to the Classic Period, the height of pre-Columbian Mesoamerican art and culture. Achievements include the pyramids and palaces of Teotihuacán; the ceremonial center of Monte Albán; and the stelae and temples of Palenque, Bonampak, and Calakmul. The Maya also made significant scientific discoveries, including the concept of zero in mathematics and a complex calendar with which priests predicted eclipses and the movements of the stars.

Teotihuacán (100 B.C.–A.D. 700—near present-day Mexico City), a well-organized city built on a grid, is thought to have had 100,000 or more inhabitants at its zenith, led by an industrious, literate, and cosmopolitan ruling class. The city exerted tremendous influence as far away as Guatemala and the Yucatán. Its feathered serpent god, Quetzalcóatl, joined the pantheon of many succeeding cultures, including the Toltec, who brought the cult to the Yucatán. Teotihuacán's refined aesthetics, evident in its beautiful, highly stylized sculpture and ceramics, show up in Maya and Zapotec objects. Around the 7th century, the city was abandoned. Who these people were and where they went remains a mystery.

TOLTEC & AZTEC INVASIONS: THE POST-CLASSIC PERIOD (A.D. 900–1521)

Warfare became more pervasive during this period, and these later civilizations were less sophisticated than those of the Classic period. The **Toltec** of central Mexico established their capital at Tula in the 10th century. Originally one of the barbarous hordes that periodically migrated from the north, they were influenced

Elaborate stonework from a Maya construction.

by remnants of Teotihuacán culture at some point and adopted the feathered-serpent god Quetzalcóatl. The Toltec maintained a large military class, and Tula spread its influence across Mesoamerica. But their might was played out by the 13th century, probably because of civil war and battles with invaders from the north.

The Maya of the Yucatán, especially the **Xiu** and **Itzáes,** might have departed from the norm with their broad trading networks and multiple influences from the outside world. They built beautiful cities in and around the Yucatán's Puuc hills, south of Mérida, their architecture characterized by elaborate exterior stonework above door frames and extending to the roofline. Impressive examples include the Codz Poop at Kabah and the palaces at Uxmal, Sayil, and Labná. Chichén Itzá, also ruled by Itzáes, was associated with the Puuc cities but shows strong Toltec influence in its architectural style and its cult of Quetzalcóatl, renamed Kukulkán.

The exact nature of the Toltec influence on the Maya is a subject of debate. An intriguing myth in central Mexico tells of Quetzalcóatl quarreling with the god Tezcatlipoca and being tricked into leaving Tula. Quetzalcóatl heads east toward the morning star, vowing someday to return. In the language of myth, this could be a metaphor for a civil war between two factions in Tula, each led by the priesthood of a different god. Could the losing faction have migrated to the Yucatán and later ruled Chichén Itzá? Perhaps. What we do know is that this myth of Quetzalcóatl's eventual return became, in the hands of the Spanish, a devastating weapon of conquest.

Cortez, Moctezuma & the Spanish Conquest

In 1517, the first Spaniards arrived in Mexico and skirmished with the Maya off the coast of Campeche. A shipwreck left several Spaniards stranded as prisoners of the Maya. Another Spanish expedition, under **Hernán Cortez,** landed on Cozumel in February 1519. The coastal Maya were happy to tell Cortez about the gold and riches of the Aztec empire in central Mexico. Disobeying his superior, the governor of Cuba, Cortez promptly sailed with his army to the mainland and embarked on one of history's most bizarre culture clashes.

He landed in Tabasco, established a settlement in Veracruz, and worked his way up the Gulf Coast during the height of the Aztec empire's wealth and power. **Moctezuma II** ruled the central and southern highlands and extracted tribute from lowland peoples; his greatest temples were plated with gold and encrusted with the blood of sacrificial captives. A fool, a mystic, and something of a coward, Moctezuma dithered in Tenochtitlán while Cortez blustered and negotiated his way into the highlands. The terrified Moctezuma was convinced that Cortez was the returning Quetzalcóatl. By the time Cortez arrived in the Aztec capital, he had accumulated 6,000 indigenous allies who resented paying tribute to the Aztec. In November 1519, he took Moctezuma hostage in an effort to leverage control of the empire.

In the middle of Cortez's maneuverings, another Spanish expedition arrived with orders to end Cortez's unauthorized mission. Cortez hastened to the coast, routed the rival force, and persuaded the vanquished to join him on his return to Tenochtitlán. The capital had erupted in his absence, and the Aztec chased his garrison out of the city. Moctezuma was killed during the attack—whether by his own men or the Spaniards is not clear. For a year and a half, Cortez laid siege to Tenochtitlán, aided by rival Indians and a devastating smallpox epidemic. When the Aztec capital fell in 1521, all of central Mexico lay at the conquerors' feet, vastly expanding the Spanish empire. The king hastened to legitimize the victorious Cortez and ordered the forced conversion to Christianity of the new colony, to be called New Spain. By 1540, New Spain included possessions from Vancouver to Panama. In the 2 centuries that followed, Franciscan and Augustinian friars converted millions of Indians to Christianity, and Spanish lords built huge feudal estates with Indian farmers serving as serfs.

The Rise of Mexico City & Spanish Colonialism

Cortez set about building a new city upon the ruins of the Aztec capital, collecting the tributes that the Indians once paid to Moctezuma. Many paid in labor, which became the model for building the new colony.

Over the 3 centuries of the colonial period, Spain became the richest country in Europe from New World gold and silver chiseled out by Indian labor. The Spanish elite built lavish homes filled with ornate furniture and draped themselves in imported velvets, satins, and jewels. Under the new class system, those born in Spain considered themselves superior to the *criollos,* or Spaniards born in Mexico. People of other races and the *castas* (Spanish-Indian, Spanish-African, or Indian-African mixes) formed society's bottom rungs. Wealthy colonists lived extravagantly despite the Crown's insatiable demand for taxes and contributions.

Criollo resentment of Spanish rule following the 1767 expulsion of the largely *criollo* Jesuit clergy simmered for years. In 1808, **Napoleon** invaded Spain, deposed Charles IV, and crowned his brother **Joseph Bonaparte.** To many in Mexico, allegiance to France was unthinkable. The next logical step was revolt.

Hidalgo, Juárez & Mexico's Independence

In 1810, **Father Miguel Hidalgo** set off the rebellion in the town of Dolores, Guanajuato, with his *grito,* the fabled cry for independence. With **Ignacio Allende** and a citizen army, Hidalgo marched toward Mexico City. Although he ultimately failed and was executed, Hidalgo is honored as "the Father of Mexican Independence." Another priest, José María Morelos, kept the revolt alive with several successful campaigns before he, too, was captured and executed in 1815.

When the Spanish king who replaced Joseph Bonaparte decided to institute social reforms in the colonies, Mexico's conservative powers concluded they didn't need Spain after all. Royalist **Agustín de Iturbide** defected in 1821 and conspired with the rebels to declare independence from Spain, with himself as emperor. However, internal dissension soon deposed Iturbide, and Mexico was instead proclaimed a republic.

The young, politically unstable republic ran through 36 presidents in 22 years, in the midst of which it lost half its territory in the disastrous **Mexican-American War (1846-48).** The central figure, **Antonio López de Santa Anna,** assumed the presidency no fewer than 11 times and just might hold the record for frequency of exile. He was ousted for good in 1855 and finished his days in Venezuela.

Amid continuing political turmoil after ragtag Mexican troops defeated the well-equipped French force in a battle near Puebla in 1862 (now celebrated as Cinco de Mayo), conservatives resolved to bring in a Habsburg to regain control. With French backing, **Archduke Maximilian** of Austria became emperor in

1864. After 3 years of civil war, the French finally abandoned Maximilian, leaving him to be captured and executed in 1867. His adversary and successor as president was **Benito Juárez,** a Zapotec Indian lawyer and one of Mexico's greatest heroes. Juárez did his best to unify and strengthen his country before dying of a heart attack in 1872, and his plans and visions bore fruit for decades.

Yucatecan Independence & the Caste War

In 1845, in the midst of political turmoil, the Yucatán's landed oligarchy declared independence from Mexico. They armed the populace—including Indians who had slaved all their lives on the haciendas—to defend the territory from inva-

A mural depicting the subjugation of the people of the Yucatán.

sion. The Indians, resentful of their serfdom, realized it didn't much matter whether their oppressors lived in Mexico City or Mérida, and raised their arms against the landowners in what became the War of the Castes. The slaughter would continue, off and on, for 60 years.

The peasants soon controlled most of the countryside, capturing several towns and the city of Valladolid. Mérida, too, was on the verge of surrender just as planting season arrived. Rather than press their advantage and take the capital, the Maya inexplicably laid down their weapons to return to their cornfields. Yucatecan troops quickly regrouped, swore fealty to Mexico and called for a government army. Eventually the Maya rebels were driven back into what is now Quintana Roo, where they were largely left on their own, virtually a nation within a nation, until a Mexican army with modern weaponry finally penetrated the region at the turn of the 20th century.

Díaz, Zapata, Pancho Villa & the Mexican Revolution

A few years after Juárez's death, one of his generals, **Porfirio Díaz,** seized power in a coup. He ruled Mexico from 1877 to 1911, a period now called the "Porfiriato," maintaining power through repression and by courting favor with powerful nations. With foreign investment came the concentration of great wealth in few hands, and discontent deepened.

In 1910, **Francisco Madero** led an armed rebellion that became the Mexican revolution ("La Revolución" in Mexico; the revolution against Spain is the

OF henequén & HACIENDAS

Commercial production of *henequén*, the thorny agave that yields the rope fiber we know as sisal, began in 1830. Demand reached fever pitch during World War I; with a virtual monopoly on the *oro verde* ("green gold"), Yucatán blossomed from one of Mexico's poorest states to one of its richest. In addition to their baronial homes along Mérida's Paseo de Montejo, landowners built plantations to meet their every comfort when they traveled to the countryside. Their haciendas were small, self-contained cities supporting hundreds of workers, and each had its own school, infirmary, store, church, cemetery, and even a jail.

Invention of synthetic fibers during World War II devastated the *henequén* industry; abandoned haciendas became grand derelicts until a new generation of wealthy Mexicans began turning them into hotels in the early 1990s.

"Guerra de Independencia"). Díaz was exiled and is buried in Paris. Madero became president, but **Victoriano Huerta,** in collusion with U.S. ambassador Henry Lane Wilson, betrayed and executed him in 1913. Those who had answered Madero's call rose up again—the great peasant hero **Emiliano Zapata** in the south, and the seemingly invincible **Pancho Villa** in the central north, flanked by **Alvaro Obregón** and **Venustiano Carranza.** They eventually routed Huerta and began hashing out a new constitution.

For the next few years, Carranza, Obregón, and Villa fought among themselves; Zapata did not seek national power, though he fought tenaciously for land for the peasants. Carranza, who was president at the time, betrayed and assassinated Zapata. Obregón finally consolidated power and probably had Carranza assassinated. He, in turn, was assassinated when he tried to break one of the tenets of the revolution—no re-election. Not until **Lázaro Cárdenas** was elected in 1934 did the revolution appear to have a chance. He implemented massive land redistribution, nationalized the oil industry, instituted many reforms, and gave shape to the ruling political party, which evolved into today's Partido Revolucionario Institucional, or **PRI.** Cárdenas is practically canonized by most Mexicans.

Modern Mexico

The presidents who followed were noted more for graft than leadership, and the party's reform principles were abandoned. In 1968, the government quashed a democratic student demonstration in Mexico City, killing hundreds of people. Though the PRI maintained its grip on power, it lost its image as a progressive party.

Economic progress, particularly in the form of large development projects, became the PRI's sole basis for legitimacy. In 1974 the government decided to build a new coastal megaresort. To determine the ideal location, data crunchers loaded all the variables into a computer. Out popped Cancún, and Mexico's economy changed forever.

The government weathered several bouts of social unrest caused by periodic devaluations of the peso. But in 1985, the devastating Mexico City earthquake brought down many new, supposedly earthquake-proof buildings, exposing the widespread corruption that had fostered the shoddy construction, and triggering criticism of the government's relief efforts.

Meanwhile, opposition parties were gaining strength. The two largest were the **PRD** (Partido de la Revolución Democrática) on the left and the **PAN** (Partido Acción Nacional) on the right. To ensure its candidate, Carlos Salinas de Gortari, would win the 1988 presidential election over the PRD's Cuauhtémoc Cárdenas (formerly of the PRI and son of former President Lázaro Cárdenas), the government simply unplugged election computers and declared a system failure.

Under pressure at home and abroad, the government moved to demonstrate a new commitment to democracy and even began to concede electoral defeats for state governorships and legislative seats. Power struggles between reformist factions and hardliners within the party led to several political assassinations, most notably of the PRI's next candidate, Luis Colosio, in 1994.

After the crippling economic crisis the same year, Gortari's successor, Ernesto Zedillo, spent his 6 years in office trying to stabilize the economy and bring transparency to government. In 2000 he shepherded the first true elections in 70 years of one-party rule. The winner was PAN candidate **Vicente Fox,** a

A TALE OF TWO hurricanes

By 1988, when Hurricane Gilbert swept through, Cancún had more than 200,000 residents, with more than 12,000 hotel rooms and another 11,000 on the drawing boards. The storm's destruction barely slowed the explosive growth; existing resorts were promptly remodeled and reopened, followed by dozens of new ones. But the decision to slash hotel rates to lure tourists back, combined with the national drinking age of 18, had the unintended effect of making Cancún the spring-break capital of North America. Images of binge-drinking college hordes replaced idyllic scenes of couples and families playing tag with turquoise waves.

Ironically, an even more devastating hurricane turned this image around. On Oct. 18, 2005, Hurricane Wilma parked on top of the region, battering it with 240kmph (150 mph) winds. Bridges linking the island Hotel Zone with the mainland city collapsed, electricity and water were out for 10 days, and the world's most celebrated beaches were scoured down to rock. It was the most destructive natural disaster in Mexican history, surpassing even the 1985 Mexico City earthquake.

The government, insurance companies, and major resort hotel chains mobilized a massive recovery effort. Restoration of more than 11km (6¾ miles) of white-powder beach with sand pumped 35km (22 miles) from the ocean bottom (a solution that proved to be temporary and was reprised in 2009 and 2010 to make the repairs more permanent) grabbed the headlines, but a more important transformation was in the works. Within 3 months, 18,000 of the 22,000 hotel rooms were ready for guests. Crews built new roads, installed better street lamps, planted thousands of palms, and installed modern sculptures. In rebuilding, often from the ground up, resorts took pains to distance themselves from the spring-break crowd, going bigger, better, and more luxurious than ever—with price hikes to match.

A sticky HABIT

Cigar smoking and gum chewing are two pleasures we have the Maya to thank for. Gum, the more innocuous of the two, comes from the sap of a species of *zapote* tree that grows in the Yucatán and Guatemala. Chewing releases its natural sugars and a mild, agreeable taste. The chewing-gum habit spread from the Maya to other cultures and eventually to the non-Indian population. In the second half of the 19th century, a Mexican (said to have been Gen. Santa Anna) introduced gum to the American Thomas Adams, who realized that it could be sweetened further and given other flavors. He marketed chewing gum in the U.S. with great success. Chemists have since figured out how to synthesize the gum, but the sap is still collected in parts of the Yucatán and Guatemala for making natural chewing gum. *Chicle* is the Spanish word originally from the Nahuatl (Aztec) *tzictli*, and those who live in the forest and collect the sap are called *chicleros*. Because the tree takes so long to produce more sap, there is no way to cultivate it commercially, so it is still collected in the wild.

former businessman who ran on a platform of economic liberalization and anti-corruption. Many Mexicans voted for him to see if the PRI would relinquish power more than for any other reason. It did, but Fox didn't prove to be the master politician that the situation required. His efforts to build a coalition with segments of the PRI failed, and he accomplished little during his last 3 years in office.

The whisker-close and bitterly disputed presidential election of 2006 tested Mexico's nascent pluralism. The elections tribunal's ruling, denying the PRD's request for a recount and declaring PAN's **Felipe Calderón** the winner, was profoundly unpopular. Losing candidate **Andrés Manuel López Obrador** did not take defeat gracefully and provoked a constitutional crisis that only time managed to heal. President Calderón, recognizing the PRD campaign's resonance with the poor, announced programs to boost employment, alleviate poverty, and stabilize the skyrocketing price of tortillas.

His biggest challenge, however, has proved to be the alarming escalation of drug-related violence—a conflagration attributed to his crackdown on traffickers who ferry contraband through Mexico on its way to the United States. The violence, directed at journalists and government officials as well as rival drug cartels, is concentrated in six states along the U.S.-Mexico border and parts of northern and central Mexico.

As 2011 began, Calderón could claim a certain success in his war on the cartels: He succeeded in capturing or killing several high-profile drug lords in 2010, and dismantled several cartel networks in the process. Such victories, however, further upset the balance of power as the organizations attempt to preserve their territory and grab turf from their weakened rivals. The result was the bloodiest year in Mexico's history—more than 11,000 deaths, up from 6,000 in 2009. The gory turf wars have boiled up in formerly quiet states such as Nuevo Leon, Morelos, Mexico, Colima, and Jalisco.

Opposition to Calderón's strategy has steadily mounted, and 2011 brought new tactics. He deployed more highly trained and better-paid (therefore less susceptible to corruption) federal police to Ciudad Juárez and other key areas. Perhaps more significantly, the legislature approved harsher prison sentences for terrorist acts while acknowledging that the cartel violence could be classified as terrorism. Simply characterizing the violence as terrorism raises two interesting possibilities. First, it has the potential to spike the level of outrage among the general population, for whom tolerating cartel activity has become a given; second, it raises the possibility of increased U.S. involvement in the conflict. Calderón is walking a fine line; he doesn't want the U.S. to storm the border in the name of counterterrorism, nor can he be sure whether he, rather than the cartels, will bear the brunt of public outrage.

With the July 2012 presidential election approaching, Calderón is boxed in. Since the July 2009 legislative elections ended the majority rule of his PAN party, the rival PRI has gained new strength. He has to reduce the body count, and he's running out of both time and resources. He basically has two choices: Accept U.S. intervention, which carries its own political perils, or give the cartels room to return to a clear division of territory and self-policing. As of this writing, Calderón had not tipped his hand as to which path, if either, he might take to preserve his party's political future.

Southern Mexico—particularly Yucatán and Campeche—remains blessedly removed from the fray, likely because it is undisputed territory. With some of the lowest casualty counts in the country, the region is a safer place to travel than some parts of the United States or Canada. Yet blaring headlines about the drug wars, combined with a tenacious worldwide tourism slump and wariness left over from the 2009 flu scare, have kept travelers away in droves. Mexico's tourism industry, especially around Cancún, showed strong signs of recovery in the winter of 2010 and 2011, and posted record numbers in early 2012. Fortunately for visitors, travel costs still have increased negligibly and in some cases not at all.

ART & ARCHITECTURE

Mexico's art, architecture, politics, and religion were inextricable for more than 3,000 years. The Maya were perhaps the most gifted artists in the Americas, producing fantastically lifelike stone sculptures, soaring temples clad in colors we can only guess at today, and delicately painted pottery. The Spanish conquest in A.D. 1521 influenced the style and subject of Mexican art, yet failed to stamp out its roots.

Pre-Hispanic Forms

Nowhere is the interplay of religion and art more striking than in Mexico's renowned pyramids, which were temples crowning a truncated platform. Maya structures also served as navigation aids, administrative and ceremonial centers, tombs, astronomical observatories, and artistic canvases.

Circular buildings such as Chichén Itzá's El Caracol and Palenque's observatory tower aided Maya priests' astral calculations, used primarily for astrological divination but stunningly accurate by modern astronomical standards. Chichén Itzá's El Castillo itself is a massive calendar, with four staircases of 91 steps, equaling the 365 days of the solar year when the central platform step is added. The stairways also divide the nine terraces of each face of the pyramid into 18 segments, representing the Maya calendar's 18 months; the 52 panels on the terraces symbolize the 52-year cycle, when the solar and religious calendars

Chichén Itzá's El Castillo.

converge. Architects aligned the temple precisely to produce the equinox phenomenon of the stairway's shadow snaking down a corner of the pyramid to join a giant serpent's head at the bottom.

Though ancient architecture shows a variety of influences, building one pyramid on top of another was a widespread practice. Chichén Itzá's strong Toltec influence, with its angular, stepped profiles, emphasizes war and human sacrifice; Uxmal's refined and more purely Maya geometry, including the beautifully sloped and rounded Temple of the Magician, incorporates the varied elevations of the Puuc hills.

The unjustly overlooked Edzná in Campeche state displays roof combs and corbeled arches resembling those of Palenque and giant stone masks similar to Guatemala's Petén style. The alternating vertical and sloping panels of Toltec and Aztec architecture surfaces also in Dzibanché, a partially excavated site that opened in the early 1990s near Laguna de Bacalar in southern Quintana Roo.

The true arch was unknown in Mesoamerica, but the Maya devised the corbeled arch (or Maya arch) by stacking each successive stone to cantilever beyond the one below, until the two sides met at the top in an inverted V.

The Olmec, who reigned over the Gulf coastal plains, are considered Mesoamerica's parent culture. Little survives of their pyramids, which were built of clay. We still have their enormous sculptural legacy, from small, intricately carved pieces of jade to the 40-ton carved basalt rock heads still found at La Venta, Tabasco (some of which are displayed in the Parque–Museo La Venta in Villahermosa).

More intact later cities, built of stone, give us a better glimpse of ancient Maya art, but their exuberant color is all but lost. The stones originally were covered with a layer of painted stucco that gleamed red, blue, and yellow through the jungle foliage. Most of the fantastic murals that adorned their buildings are also lost to time, though surprisingly well-preserved fragments have been found at Bonampak and Ek Balam. Vestiges also remain at Mayapán and Cobá.

Artisans also crafted marvelous stone murals and mosaics from thousands of pieces of fitted stone, adorning facades with geometric designs or figures of warriors or snakes. Uxmal, in fact, evidently had not a single mural; all its artistry is in the intricate stonework.

Murals and stone carvings were more religious or historical than ornamental in purpose. Deciphering the hieroglyphs—rich, elegant symbols etched in stone or painted on pottery—allows scholars to identify rulers and untangle dynastic history. Michael Coe's *Breaking the Maya Code* traces centuries-long efforts to decode Maya script and outlines

A corbeled arch in Uxmal.

recent breakthroughs that make it possible to decipher 90% of the glyphs. "Cracking the Maya Code," a *Nova* program based on Coe's book, is available for viewing on www.pbs.org or on DVD.

Good hieroglyphic examples appear in Palenque's site museum. Several stelae, the large, free-standing stone slabs where the Maya etched their history, are in place at Cobá. Calakmul is known for its many stelae, and good examples are displayed in Mexico City's Museum of Anthropology and the archaeology museum in Villahermosa.

Columns of Ek Balam.

Spanish Influence

The Spaniards brought new forms of architecture to Mexico; in many cases they razed Maya cities and reused the limestone to build their Catholic churches, public buildings, and palaces. In the Yucatán, churches at Izamal, Tecoh, Santa Elena, and Muna rest atop former pyramids. Indian artisans recruited to build the new structures frequently implanted traditional symbolism, such as a plaster angel swaddled in feathers, reminiscent of the god Quetzalcóatl; they determined how many florets to carve around church doorways based on the ancient cosmos's 13 steps of heaven and nine levels of the underworld.

Detailed stonework from Uxmal.

Spanish priests and architects altered their teaching and building methods in order to convert native populations. Church adornment became more explicit to combat the language barrier; frescoes of Biblical tales were splashed across church walls, and Christian symbols in stone supplanted pre-Hispanic figures.

Remnants of 16th-century missions, convents, monasteries, and parish churches dot almost every Yucatecan village. Examples worth visiting include the Mission of San Bernardino de Sisal in Valladolid; the cathedral of Mérida; the vast atrium and church at Izamal; and the *retablos* (altarpieces), altars, and crucifixes in churches along the Convent Route, between the Puuc Hills and Mérida.

Porfirio Díaz's 34-year rule (1877–1911) brought a new infusion of European sensibility. Díaz commissioned imposing European-style public buildings and provided European scholarships to artists who returned to paint Mexican subjects using techniques from abroad. Mérida is a veritable museum of opulent, European-style buildings constructed during the Díaz years; the most striking are the Palacio Cantón, now housing the Regional Anthropology Museum, and the Teatro Peón Contreras.

The Advent of Mexican Muralism

The Mexican revolution that rent the country from 1910 to 1920 gave rise to a new social and cultural era. In 1923, as one way to reach the illiterate masses, Diego Rivera and other budding artists were invited to paint Mexican history on the walls of the Ministry of Education building and the National Preparatory School in Mexico City. Thus was born Mexico's tradition of public murals.

The courtyard and History Room of the Governor's Palace in Mérida display 31 works of Castro Pacheco, the Yucatán's most prominent muralist. Though he painted on large panels rather than directly on the walls, he aligned with other great muralists in his affinity for strong colors and the belief that art is meant for public enjoyment, not just private collectors. Pacheco's murals are a chilling depiction of the bloody subjugation of the Yucatán, including the Popol Vuh legend, a jaguar with fierce warriors in headdresses, a Maya *henequén* worker's hands, and portraits of such heroes as Felipe Carrillo Puerto, the martyred Yucatecan governor who instituted agrarian and other reforms.

RELIGION, MYTH & FOLKLORE

Nearly 90% of Mexicans subscribe to Roman Catholicism, but Mexican Catholicism is laced with pre-Hispanic spiritual tradition. You need only to visit the *curandero* section of a market (where you can buy such talismans as copal, an incense agreeable to the gods; rustic beeswax candles, a traditional offering; and native species of tobacco used to ward off evil) or watch pre-Hispanic dances performed at a village festival to sense the supernatural beliefs running parallel with Christian ones.

Spanish Catholicism was disseminated by pragmatic Jesuit missionaries who grafted Christian tradition onto indigenous ritual to make it palatable to their flock. Nearly 500 years after the conquest, a large minority of Mexicans—faithful Catholics every one—adhere to this hybrid religion, nowhere more so than in Chiapas and the Yucatán.

The *padres'* cause enjoyed a huge boost when a dark-skinned image of the Virgin Mary appeared to an Aztec potter near Mexico City in 1531. The Virgin of Guadalupe, fluent in the local language and acquainted with indigenous gods, provided a crucial link between Catholic and native spiritual traditions. She remains Mexico's most beloved religious figure, smiling from countless shrines, saloons, and kitchen walls. Millions of pilgrims walk and crawl to her Mexico City shrine on her December 12 feast day.

The equally pragmatic native people chose the path of least resistance, dressing their ancestral beliefs in Catholic garb. They gave their familiar gods the names of Christian saints and celebrated their old festivals on the nearest saint's day. Thus we find the Catholic feasts of All Saints' Day and All Souls' Day superimposed on

Santa Elena Church was built atop a former pyramid.

2012: prophecy OR CHICKEN LITTLE?

Within the past 10 years, the year 2012—specifically, December 21, 2012—has morphed into a modern doomsday in popular consciousness. History and time have wiped out much of the ancient Maya's writings and scripture, making it near impossible for scholars to determine what the ancient Maya thought about the approaching date. One thing is certain: The predictions of cataclysmic solar storms, magnetic pole reversal, earthquakes, supervolcanoes, a galactic collision, alien invasion, or even the end of the world aren't coming from today's Maya.

Between the scarcity of actual references to the end of the Mesoamerican Long Count Calendar in the few surviving Maya sources, the obliqueness of those references, and the largely self-serving interpretations of contemporary pseudo-scientists and New Age soothsayers, it's rather like a global game of phone tag. December 2012—the date is unspecified—coincides with the end of one 5,125-year cycle of the calendar, used by the classic Maya (A.D. 250–900) but not by contemporary Maya people. Modern interpretations have settled on December 21 primarily because it coincides with the equinox, though the importance of the equinox to the Maya is a matter of debate among serious scholars.

What significance the Maya attached to the end of the Long Calendar cycle is uncertain. They believed an earlier long cycle ended before their time—significantly, with no mass destruction—which suggests they expected another cycle to follow. Some inscriptions refer to future events or commemorations to come after completion of the current cycle, so we can safely rule out the end of the world as a Maya prediction.

Rather than fearing this date, those Maya today who recognize it at all regard December 2012 as a new dawn: a time for reflection on mankind's failings and an evolution, perhaps a change in consciousness or even a new social order. In some interpretations, the change of time might bring a reawakening of the ancient Maya world, with an appearance of ascending gods to lift the people back up. However much they might have stretched the evidence to make the date jibe with Western astrology and motley spiritual notions, New Agers who deem 2012 the beginning of a new era come closer in spirit to what the evidence suggests. Nowhere does the Western concept of apocalypse appear in surviving Maya inscriptions.

Remodeling that old Cold War–era underground bunker is, to put it mildly, an overreaction—but there's no harm in aspiring to harmony with the universe, and no better place in the world to contemplate the ancient Maya's complex cosmology than in the heart of their ancient land.

the ancient Day of the Dead celebration, and the cult of the "Black Christ"—an amalgam of Jesus Christ and the cave-dwelling Maya god Ik'al—entrenched in the Yucatán, Chiapas, and Tabasco. In one of the most dramatic examples of this spiritual hybridization, the Tzotzil Maya of San Juan Chamula in highland Chiapas carpet their church with pine needles, kneeling among candles and Coke bottles to pray in an archaic dialect under the painted eyes of helpful saints. They bring offerings of flower petals, eggs, feathers, or live chickens prescribed by local *curanderos* (medicine men) in an effort to dispel the demons of disease.

Common themes in the Catholic and Maya belief systems also made the Jesuits' task easier. The Catholics had the Bible, the Maya had the Popol Vuh. Both had long oral and written traditions (although Bishop Diego de Landa burned the Maya codices of Maní in the infamous *auto-da-fè* of 1562). Ceremonial processions with elaborate robes and incense were common to both religions, as were baptism by water and the symbol of the cross.

But the differences intrigue us most. The Maya's multitude of deities, 166 by most counts, is just the beginning. The Popol Vuh's creation myth, similar to Genesis in making man on the last day and striking down imperfect creations with an apocalyptic flood, departs from the Genesis plot in striking ways, not the least of which is fashioning man from corn after failed tries with mud and wood. Maya mythology is a collection of convoluted tales, full of images placing nature on a level equal to man, that attempt to make sense of the universe, geography, and seasons.

The tall, straight ceiba tree was revered as a symbol of the cosmos. Its leaves and branches represented the 13 levels of heaven, the tree trunk the world of humans, and its roots the nine-level underworld—not hell but a cold, damp, dark place called Xibalba.

THE maya PANTHEON

Every ancient culture had its gods and goddesses, and their characteristics or purposes, if not their names, often crossed cultures. Chaac, the hook-nosed rain god of the Maya, was Tlaloc, the squat Aztec rain god; Quetzalcóatl, the plumed-serpent Toltec man/god, became the Maya's Kukulkán. Sorting out the ancient deities and beliefs can become a life's work, but here are some of the most important gods of the Maya world.

Itzamná Often called the Supreme Deity; creator of mankind and inventor of corn, cacao, writing, and reading; patron of the arts and sciences.

Chaac God of rain, striking the clouds with a lightning ax; sometimes depicted as four separate gods based on the four cardinal directions.

Kinich Ahau Sun god, sometimes regarded as another manifestation of Itzamná; appeared in the shape of a firebird.

Kukulkán Mortal who took on godly virtues, sometimes symbolized as Venus, the morning star.

Ixchel Wife of Kinich Ahau; multitasking goddess of the moon, fertility and childbirth, water, medicine, and weaving.

Bacab Generic name for four brothers who guarded the four points of the compass; closely associated with the four Chaacs.

Yumil Kaxob God of maize, or corn, shown with a crown or headdress of corn and distinguished by his youth.

Balam One of numerous jaguar spirits; symbol of power and protector of fields and crops.

Ixtab Goddess of suicide; suicide was an honorable way to die, and Ixtab received those souls into heaven.

Foremost among the Maya pantheon were those who influenced the growth of corn. The Maya worked hard to please their gods through prayer, offerings, and sacrifices, which could be anything from a priest giving his own blood to human sacrifice. They were obsessed with time, maintaining both a 260-day religious calendar and a 365-day solar calendar that guided crop planting and other practicalities. In fact, religion, art, and science were so entwined that the Maya might not even have perceived them as separate pursuits. So from a kernel of corn grew some of civilization's earliest and greatest accomplishments.

THE YUCATÁN, TABASCO & CHIAPAS IN POP CULTURE

Books

HISTORY & CULTURE For an overview of pre-Hispanic cultures, pick up **Michael D. Coe**'s *Mexico: From the Olmecs to the Aztecs,* or **Nigel Davies**'s *Ancient Kingdoms of Mexico.* Coe's *The Maya* is probably the best general account of the Maya. For a survey of Mexico's history through modern times, *A Short History of Mexico* by **J. Patrick McHenry** is thorough yet concise.

John L. Stephens's two-volume *Incidents of Travel in the Yucatán* is not only one of the great books of archaeological discovery but a travel classic. Before his expeditions, beginning in 1841, the world knew little about the region and nothing about the Maya. Stephens's account of 44 Maya sites is still the most authoritative.

Ronald Wright's *Stolen Continents,* published in 1992 for the 500th anniversary of Christopher Columbus's voyage, recounts the story of the European conquest from the point of view of indigenous Americans—Aztec, Maya, Inca, Cherokee, and Iroquois—who had been largely left out of the history every child was taught until then.

Graham Greene's *The Lawless Roads,* covering the brutal religious oppression of the late 1930s, is a dyspeptic travelogue of Chiapas and Tabasco. This compelling look at what was then a remote region—flawed though it is by the author's distaste for Mexico—also was the basis for his masterpiece *The Power and the Glory.*

For contemporary culture, start with **Octavio Paz**'s classic, *The Labyrinth of Solitude,* still controversial because of some of Paz's cultural generalizations. *Our Word Is Our Weapon,* a collection of articulate, often poetic writings by Zapatista leader **Subcomandante Marcos,** provides insight into Chiapas' armed revolt in the 1990s.

The marimba, a traditional instrument of Chiapas and Veracruz.

Lesley Byrd Simpson's *Many Mexicos* is a comprehensive cultural history; *Distant Neighbor* by **Alan Riding** is a classic of cultural insight.

ART & ARCHITECTURE *Art and Time in Mexico: From the Conquest to the Revolution,* by **Elizabeth Wilder Weismann,** covers religious, public, and private architecture. *Maya Art and Architecture* by **Mary Ellen Miller** showcases the best of Maya artistic expression.

NATURE *A Naturalist's Mexico* by **Roland H. Wauer** is getting hard to find, but *A Hiker's Guide to Mexico's Natural History* by **Jim Conrad** is a good alternative. *Peterson Field Guides: Mexican Birds* by **Roger Tory Peterson** and **Edward L. Chalif** is predictably excellent. **Les Beletsky**'s enlightened *Southern Mexico* is a richly illustrated, engagingly written field guide and ecotourism manual.

LITERATURE **Jorge Ibargüengoitia,** one of Mexico's most famous modern writers, died in 1983 but remains popular in Mexico and is available in translation. His novels *Estas Ruinas Que Ves (These Ruins You See)* and *The Dead Girls* (a fictional account of a famous 1970s crime) display deft characterization and a sardonic view of Mexican life.

Juan Rulfo, one of Mexico's most esteemed authors, wrote only three slim books before his death in 1986. His second, *Pedro Páramo,* is Mexico's equivalent of Shakespearean tragedy and has never been out of print since its publication in 1955. The short novel of a son's search for his abusive, tyrannical father is told in competing first- and third-person narration and had a major influence on the magical realism movement. It has been translated twice into English and been made into film several times; Gael García Bernal and Diego Luna are working on a new adaptation.

The earlier novels of **Carlos Fuentes,** Mexico's preeminent living writer, are easier to read than more recent works; try *The Death of Artemio Cruz.* **Angeles Mastretta**'s delightful *Arráncame la Vida (Tear Up My Life)* is a well-written novel about a young woman's life in postrevolutionary Puebla. **Laura Esquivel**'s *Like Water for Chocolate* (and the subsequent movie) covers roughly the same period through a lens of magical realism and helped to popularize Mexican food abroad.

Hasta No Verte Jesús Mío by **Elena Poniatowska** and anything by Pulitzer-winner **Luis Alberto Urrea** offer hard looks at third-world realities.

Guillermo Arriaga, screenwriter for *Amores Perros,* is a brilliant novelist, too. *El Bufalo de la Noche,* about a young man reeling from his best friend's suicide, is available in English. *Retorno 201,* a collection of stories set on the Mexico City street where Arriaga grew up, was published in 2005.

Film
GOLDEN AGE & CLASSICS

During Mexico's "Golden Age of Cinema" in the 1940s, studios stopped trying to mimic Hollywood and started producing unabashedly Mexican black-and-white films whose stars are still cultural icons in Mexico. **Mario Moreno,** aka Cantinflas, was a comedic genius who personalized the *el pelado* archetype—a poor, picaresque, slightly naughty character trading on his wits alone and getting nowhere. Mexican beauty **Dolores del Río** played the steamy Latin babe in

Views from the Outside: Films Starring Mexico

Elia Kazan's 1952 classic, **Viva Zapata!,** written by John Steinbeck, stars Marlon Brando as revolutionary Emiliano Zapata. Orson Welles's 1958 film-noir **Touch of Evil** (preposterously billing Charlton Heston as a Mexican narcotics agent) looks at drugs and corruption in Tijuana—still compelling, even though it feels sanitized compared with today's screaming headlines. The adaptation of Carlos Fuentes's novel **The Old Gringo** (1989), a love triangle set during the Mexican Revolution, was filmed with Gregory Peck, Jane Fonda, and a young Jimmy Smits in numerous locations in five Mexican states. HBO's 2003 flick, **And Starring Pancho Villa as Himself** with Antonio Banderas, is the true story of how revolutionaries allowed Hollywood to film Pancho Villa in battle. **Man on Fire** (2004), with Denzel Washington as a bodyguard hired to protect a little girl, is full of great Mexico City scenes, though the plot is depressing and all too

real. Dylan Verrechia's **Tijuana Makes Me Happy** (2005), focusing on Tijuana's humanity rather than its perceived sins, has won awards in Latin America and at U.S. film festivals. Stephen Soderbergh's Academy Award–winning **Traffic** (2000), with Benicio del Toro, has powerful scenes focusing on Tijuana's drug war, while the documentary **Tijuana Remix** (2002) unveils the city's unique and idiosyncratic culture.

Mel Gibson's controversial **Apocalypto** (2006) cast indigenous Maya to depict the Maya empire's waning days; the rainforests of Veracruz state stand in for the lush jungles that must have covered the Yucatán centuries ago. Mexico, most notably an uglified Campeche, stood in for 1950s Cuba in Steven Soderbergh's **Che** (2008), a two-part epic focusing first on the Cuban revolution and then on his attempt to bring revolution to Bolivia that won the Cannes best actor award for Benicio del Toro.

Hollywood. **Pedro Infante,** the singing cowboy, embodied the ideal of Mexican manhood.

Luis Buñuel's dark *Los Olvidados* (1950) was the Spanish surrealist's third Mexican film, exploring the life of young hoodlums in Mexico City's slums.

THE NEW CINEMA

After a long fallow period, a new generation of filmmakers emerged in the 1990s. The first big *El Nuevo Cine Mexicano* (The New Cinema) hit outside of Mexico was *Like Water for Chocolate* (1992), directed by **Alfonso Arau,** then author Laura Esquivel's husband. He continues to make films, mainly in Mexico. *Sexo, Pudor y Lágrimas* (1999), by director **Antonio Serrano,** is an unflinching look at the battle of the sexes in Mexico City.

After **Alfonso Cuarón**'s debut film, the mordant social satire *Sólo con tu Pareja* (1991), scored critical and commercial success in Mexico, he garnered international acclaim with his ironic *Y Tu Mamá También* (2001), which touches on class hypocrisy while following a pair of teenage boys on an impromptu road trip with a sexy older woman. Cuarón has since directed *Harry Potter and the Prisoner of Azkaban* (2004), the science-fiction thriller *Children of Men* (2006), and other international productions.

In *Amores Perros* (2000), **Alejandro González Iñárritu** (director of *21 Grams*) presents a keen glimpse of contemporary Mexican society through three stories about different ways of life in Mexico City that converge at the scene of a horrific car accident. His Academy Award–nominated *Babel* (2006), another tour de force, features a Mexican border scene that is realistic, exhilarating, and frightening all at once. His *Biutiful* brought a best actor award for star Javier Bardem at the 2010 Cannes Film Festival.

Guillermo del Toro's debut, the dark, atmospheric *Cronos* (1993), won critical acclaim in Mexico. Moving into the international arena, he has directed similarly moody films such as *Hellboy* (2004) and Oscar winner *Pan's Labyrinth* (2006).

Julie Taymor's *Frida* (2002), with Mexican actress Salma Hayek producing and starring, is an enchanting biopic about Frida Kahlo's life and work, from her devastating accident to relationships with Diego Rivera and Leon Trotsky. The exquisite cinematography captures the magic realism evinced in Kahlo's work.

Director **Robert Rodriguez**'s breakout film, *El Mariachi* (1992), is set in a small central Mexican town. Made on a shoestring budget, the somewhat cheesy action flick is at least highly entertaining. His *Once Upon a Time in Mexico* (2003) isn't as great, but it's fun to see scenes of San Miguel Allende. Ditto for San Luis Potosí in *The Mexican* (2001) with Brad Pitt and Julia Roberts. With *Machete*, his over-the-top 2011 action/gore/humor flick, his aim is clear: to make a Mexican Jean-Claude Van Damme out of star Danny Trejo.

Music
MARIMBA & SON

Marimba music flourishes in much of southern and central Mexico but is considered traditional only in Chiapas and the port city of Veracruz, whose bands travel to play in such places as Oaxaca and Mexico City. You can hear *marimba* any night for free in Tuxtla Gutiérrez's Parque de la Marimba.

Dancing in Tuxtla Gutiérrez's Parque de la Marimba.

Son, a native art form from many parts of Mexico, employs a variety of stringed instruments. Ritchie Valens's "La Bamba" popularized one of the most famous forms, *son jarocho,* in the '50s. Often fast-paced, with lots of strumming and fancy string picking, it originated in southern Veracruz. *Jarana,* the Yucatán's principal dance music, is a form of *son jarocho* that adds woodwinds and a sensuous Caribbean beat. The dance was born as part of the haciendas' annual *Vaquerías,* or country fiestas, and are still performed every week in Mérida's central plaza and many smaller parks.

DANZÓN & BOLERO

These musical forms came from Cuba in the late 19th century and gained great popularity, especially in Veracruz and Mexico City. *Danzón* is orchestra music that combines Latin flavor with a stateliness uncommon in later Latin music.

The Yucatán had strong ties to Cuba, and its *son yucateca* probably influenced bolero and the related *trova,* or classical guitar trios. This soft, romantic, and often slightly melancholy music is a linchpin of Yucatecan tradition, and singers sometimes use Mayan lyrics. Mérida's free nightly cultural events include *trova yucateca,* and the city stages an annual *trova* festival.

MARIACHI & RANCHERA

Mariachis, with their big sombreros, waist-length jackets, and tight pants, embody Mexican spirit. The music originated from Jalisco state's *son,* arranged for guitars, violins, string bass, and trumpets. Now heard across Mexico and much of the American Southwest, it is at its traditional best in Jalisco and its capital, Guadalajara. Mariachi is also common in the Yucatán, especially in cantinas and during national celebrations. Yucatecan *trova* music even has mariachi adaptations.

Trova, a classical guitar trio.

The national pride, individualism, and sentimentality expressed in mariachi's kin, *ranchera,* earns it favored status as drinking music. Many Mexicans know the songs of famous composer **José Alfredo Jiménez** by heart.

ROCK EN ESPAÑOL

Mexican rock forged its identity in the 1980s and exploded during the 1990s with bands such as **Los Jaguares** and **Molotov,** out of Mexico City, and **Maná,** based in Guadalajara. Named for the 1920s cafe in the capital's Centro Histórico, **Café Tacuba** has been at it since 1989. Their music is influenced by indigenous Mexican music as much as folk, punk, bolero, and hip-hop. The fast-rising **Yucatán a Go Go**—hailing, despite the name, from central Mexico—fuses a bouncy pop beat to lyrics firmly rooted in cultural tradition. Latin alternative music, which was born as an alternative to slickly produced Latin pop exemplified by

A *Vaquería,* **or country fiesta.**

Ricky Martin or **Paulina Rubio,** has become a genre in itself. Practitioners such as **Panda, División Minúscula,** and **Zoé** have achieved not-so-alternative success.

EATING & DRINKING

The tacos and burritos familiar north of the border are mere appetizers on Mexico's vast and varied menu. Some staples grace plates throughout the country, but long distances and two formidable mountain ranges gave rise to distinct regional cuisines that evolved independently. It is not only possible but also one of life's great pleasures to eat your way through Mexico without downing a single taco or burrito.

When the Spanish arrived, they found Mexico's natives cooking with corn, beans, chiles, tomatoes, and squash, combined with turkey and other wild game. Local women promptly incorporated beef, pork, lamb, nuts, fruits, cheese, spices, and sugar cane (by way of the Caribbean) contributed by the conquistadors. To the dismay of the Spaniards—and the delight of travelers today—the result was not a simulation of European cuisine but new versions of native dishes.

Mexican cooking remains simple at its core; most of the picante flavor is added afterward with the chile and salsa found on every table. Regional variations range from the basic but nutritious dishes of the north and seafood specialties of the coastal

> **Local Wisdom**
>
> "The chile runs in our veins."
> —Laura Esquivel, author of *Like Water for Chocolate* (1989) in introduction to *La Cocina del Chile* (2003)

Tequila and lime.

regions to the complex variety of Mexico City and the central states and the earthy, piquant creations of the Maya in the south.

The Staples

TORTILLAS The tortilla is Mexico's bread, and sometimes its fork and spoon, used to scoop up food. Corn is cooked in water and lime, ground into grainy *masa* dough, patted and pressed into thin cakes, and cooked on a *comal* (hot griddle). Even restaurants that serve bread always have tortillas available. The flour tortilla was developed in northern Mexico and is less common in the south.

ENCHILADAS The most famous of numerous Mexican dishes based on the tortilla was originally called *tortilla enchilada,* meaning a tortilla dipped in a chile sauce; variations include *entomatada* (dipped in tomato sauce) and *enfrijolada* (in a bean sauce). The basic enchilada, still sold in food stands, is a tortilla dipped first in hot oil and then chile (usually ancho) sauce, folded or rolled on a plate, and sprinkled with chopped onions and *queso cotija* (crumbly white cheese). It's often served with fried potatoes and carrots. Restaurants serve more elaborate enchiladas filled with cheese, chicken, pork, or seafood. In Southern Mexico, enchiladas are often bathed in a rich *mole* sauce.

TACOS Anything folded or rolled into a tortilla—sometimes two, either soft or fried—is a taco. Flautas and quesadillas (except in Mexico City, where they are a different animal) are species of tacos. This is the quintessential Mexican fast food, sold in *taquerías* everywhere.

FRIJOLES Most Mexican households eat beans daily. Pinto beans are predominant in northern Mexico, but black beans are the Yucatán's legumes of choice. Mexicans add only a little onion and garlic and a pinch of herbs, as beans are meant to be a counterpoint to spicy foods. They also may appear at the end of a meal with a spoonful of sour cream. Fried leftover beans often appear as *frijoles refritos,* a side dish commonly called "refried beans." In fact, they are fried just once; the prefix *re* means "well" (as in "thoroughly"), so a better translation might be "well-fried beans."

TAMALES The ultimate take-out meal, tamales (singular: *tamal*) developed in pre-Hispanic Mexico and became more elaborate after the Spanish introduced pork and other ingredients. To make a tamal, you mix corn *masa* with lard, beat the batter, add a filling, wrap it, and cook it. Every region has its own specialty. The most popular *rellenos* (fillings) are pork and cheese, but they might be anything from fish to iguana, augmented by pumpkin, pineapple, rice, or peanuts, and tucked into a blanket of yellow, black, or purple *masa*. Tamales are usually steamed but may be baked or grilled; the jackets

A DEBT OF gratitude

Lost among the laurels heaped upon the ancient Maya for their contributions to science, mathematics, architecture, astronomy, and writing is the wide array of foods they introduced. It's no exaggeration to say the Maya changed the world's eating habits in the 1500s. Just try to imagine life without:

Avocado From its origins in southern Mexico, where it was used as an aphrodisiac, the avocado spread to the Rio Grande and central Peru before the Europeans learned about it.

Black Beans Archaeological digs indicate the black bean originated in southern Mexico and Central America more than 7,000 years ago. Still the favorite in and around the Yucatán, it has spread widely throughout Latin America, the Caribbean, and the U.S.

Chiles Chiles have been cultivated in the Americas for more than 6,000 years. Blame Christopher Columbus for calling them "peppers," but credit him for their worldwide reach. Southern Mexico's *Capsicum annuum* species, with its many cultivars, is crucial to nearly every fiery cuisine in the world.

Chocolate The Maya's "food of the gods," made from the toasted, fermented seeds of the cacao tree, is arguably the New World's greatest gift to civilization. Though Cortez learned of chocolate from the Aztec, the Maya ate it many centuries earlier and used cacao beans as currency.

Corn The creation myth in the Popol Vuh, the Maya "bible," attributes humankind's very existence to this domesticated strain of wild grass, easily the most important food in the Americas. Thousands of years after corn became a dietary staple, the Maya started cultivating it around 2,500 B.C. and abandoned their nomadic ways to settle in villages surrounded by cornfields.

Papaya The large, woody, fast-growing herb—commonly referred to as a tree—was used to treat stomach ailments. After spreading from southern Mexico, it now grows in every tropical country.

Tomatoes Even the Italians had to make do without tomato sauce before discovery of the New World. Precursors originated in Peru, but the tomato as we know it came from the Yucatán, where the Maya cultivated it long before the conquest.

Vanilla The elixir from a special species of orchid originally flavored Maya chocolate drinks. Southern Mexico's jungle is still the only place the orchid grows wild, pollinated by native stingless bees that produce Maya honey. The prized Tahitian vanilla, which comes from Mexican stock, must be hand-pollinated.

are most often dried corn husks or fresh corn or banana leaves, but may be fashioned from palm, avocado, or *chaya* (a spinachlike vegetable) leaves.

Yucatecan tamales have a distinctly Maya flavor, filled with pork or chicken marinated in achiote (an earthy, mildly tangy paste made from the annatto seed) and cooked in an underground pit or oven that chars the banana leaf black. Tabasco makes liberal use of freshwater fish and seafood, rice, and an array of exotic produce. Chiapas' eclectic assortment of tamales

The days when you had to carry water purification tablets to return from a trip to Mexico with your intestines intact are long gone. Nearly all restaurants that serve middle-class Mexicans use filtered water, disinfect their vegetables, and buy ice made from purified water. If in doubt, look for ice with a rough cylindrical shape and a hollow center, produced by the same kind of machinery across the country. Street vendors and market stalls are less consistent; look for clean, busy places and stick with cooked foods and unpeeled fruit.

might be filled with *mole, chicharrón* (crispy, fried pork rind), or even flower buds; the best known are *tamales de bola,* with pork rib, a prune, and a small dried chile, all wrapped up in a corn husk tied on top to form a ball (*bola*).

CHILES Hardly a traditional dish in all of Mexico lacks chiles. Appearing in wondrous variety throughout Mexico, they bear different names depending on whether they are fresh or dried. Chiles range from blazing hot with little discernible taste to mild with a rich, complex flavor, and they can be pickled, smoked, stuffed, or stewed. Among the best-known are the pimiento, the large, harmless bell pepper familiar in the U.S.; the fist-sized poblano, ranging from mild to very hot; the short, torpedo-shaped serrano; the skinny and seriously fiery *chile de árbol;* the stubby, hot jalapeño; the chipotle, a dried and smoked jalapeño usually served in adobo (vinegar and garlic paste); and the tiny, five-alarm *pequín.*

If you suffer from misadventure by chile, a drink of milk, a bite of banana or cucumber, a spoonful of yogurt, or—if all else fails—a bottle of beer will help extinguish the fire.

Regional Specialties

The Yucatán evolved in isolation from the rest of the country until recent decades, and its cuisine is an amalgam of native, European, Caribbean, and Middle Eastern flavors and techniques. Some of the most recognizable tastes are achiote, sour oranges, lime juice, pumpkin seeds, and pickled onions. Turkey (*pavo*), still the most common meat in Yucatecan homes, is prominent on most menus, though beef, pork, and chicken have also become staples. Fish and seafood reign along the coast.

Achiote and sour orange came to the Yucatán by way of the Caribbean; Edam cheese through historical trade with the Dutch; and peas likely from the English. A wave of Lebanese immigration around the turn of the 20th century also left its mark; the spit-broiled *tacos al pastor* is basically Mexican gyros, and you might come across *kibbeh* made of beef or potatoes instead of lamb or *dolmas* wrapped in *chaya* instead of grape leaves.

The Yucatán's trademark dishes are *pollo* or *cochinita* (chicken or pork) *pibil,* meat marinated in achiote, bitter orange, and spices, wrapped in banana leaves and barbecued or baked in a pit; *poc chuc,* pork slices marinated in sour orange and garnished with pickled onions; and *sopa de lima* (lime soup), made of shredded, lime-marinated turkey or chicken and topped with sizzling tortilla strips.

Try starting your day with *huevos moluleños*—fried eggs over sliced plantains, beans, and fried tortillas, topped with a dusting of salty cheese, tomato sauce, and peas—but only if you're ravenous. *Cochinita pibil* is also served in the morning. The best place to have the former is in any reputable restaurant; the best place for the latter would be a market such as El Mercado de Santa Ana in Mérida.

Customary dishes for the afternoon meal include *relleno negro,* turkey cooked with a paste of charred chiles and vegetables with bits of hard-boiled eggs; *escabeche blanco,* chicken or turkey cooked in a vinegar-based sauce; or *queso relleno,* mild Edam cheese stuffed with seasoned ground beef. The unique *Tikinxic* (or some variant of this name) is grilled fish that has been lightly marinated in an achiote paste. These also appear on the evening menu in restaurants in Cancún and on the coast. Traditional evening foods are based on turkey and include such finger foods as *salbutes* and *panuchos,* two dishes of tortillas or *masa* cakes layered with shredded turkey or chicken; *panuchos* add a layer of *frijoles.*

Campeche has its own culinary traditions, a marriage of Spanish cuisine, recipes brought by pirates from all over the world, and local fruits and vegetables. The signature dish, *pan de cazón* (baby shark casserole)—layers of tortillas, black beans, and shredded baby shark meat, smothered in tomato sauce—reaches its greatest heights at La Pigua. Lying on the Gulf Coast, Tabasco has more in common with the Caribbean flavors of Veracruz, which developed close ties to Cuba during colonial times. *Veracruzana,* a lightly spiced blend of tomato and onion, bathes fresh fish, meat, and seafood. The specialty is the fish *pejelagarto,* whose mild, nutty taste is enhanced by chile and lemon; La Jangada in Villahermosa is a favorite place to indulge. *Camarón* (shrimp), *ostión* (oyster), and *pulpo* (octopus) are ubiquitous, delicious, and cheap.

A Lebanese restaurant.

A food stall in a Mérida market.

Fresh produce at a local market.

The Maya of Chiapas were great mathematicians and astronomers, like their kin throughout the Yucatán, but they also were particularly accomplished farmers. Though they depended above all on corn, native herbs such as *chipilin,* a fragrant, thin-leaved plant, and *hoja santa,* the large anise-scented leaves that characterize much of southern Mexico's cooking, flavor the many varieties of Chiapas' famous tamales, which are heavier and larger than central Mexican tamales. With the introduction of European cattle, Chiapans also became expert ranchers and, as a corollary, cheese makers. Similar to neighboring Guatemala, Chiapas' cooking uses a lot of beef, either grilled or in a stew.

Be sure to read the food glossary in chapter 10 to learn more about regional dishes.

Drinks

Coca-Cola is nearly as entrenched in Mexico's drinking habits as tequila, having been a fixture since 1926. Pepsi is also sold in every city and town. These and other American *refrescos* outsell Mexican brands such as Manzana, a carbonated apple juice. If you like your soft drinks cold, specify *frío,* or you may get them *clima* (room temperature).

Better yet, treat yourself to **licuados**—refreshing smoothies of fresh fruit (or juice), milk, and ice, sold all over Mexico. **Aguas frescas** ("fresh waters") are lighter drinks made by adding a small amount of fresh fruit juice and sugar to water. Hibiscus, melon, tamarind, and lime are common, but rice, flowers, cactus fruit (*tuna* in Spanish), and other exotic ingredients find their way into these refreshments. In the Yucatán, the most popular of these is **horchata,** a drink made from rice, almonds, cinnamon, and sugar. And inexpensive, fresh-squeezed juices from every fruit you can name—and a few you can't—are one of Mexico's greatest pleasures.

Coffee is one of Mexico's most important exports, and Chiapas grows some of the best. Tarted-up coffee isn't Mexico's style. Your basic choices are *café Americano,* the familiar gringo-style brew; espresso and sometimes cappuccino, served in cafes; and the widely popular *café con leche,* translated as "coffee with milk" but more accurately described as milk with coffee. Potent, delicious *café de olla,* traditionally brewed in a clay pot with raw sugar and cinnamon, is harder to find.

Hot chocolate is a traditional drink, usually made with cinnamon and often some crushed almonds. Another traditional hot drink is *atole,* made from cornmeal, milk, cinnamon, and puréed fresh fruit, often served for breakfast.

Mexican **beer** generally is light and well carbonated, all the better to tame the chile burn. Brands such as Bohemia, Corona, Dos Equis, Pacifica, Tecate, and Modelo are favorites around the world. Mérida's Cerveceria Yucateca, alas, was bought by Modelo in 1979 and closed in 2002, but its León Negra and Montejo beers are still produced in central Mexico.

Tequila's poorer cousins, **pulque** and **mescal,** originated with *octli,* an Aztec agave drink produced strictly for feasts. Mexicans drank *pulque,* made from juice straight from the plant, for more than 5,000 years, but it has recently given way to more refined—and more palatable—spirits. The Spanish learned to create serious firepower by roasting the agave hearts, then extracting, fermenting, and distilling the liquids. Thus were born tequila and *mescal. Mescal,* famous for the traditional worm at the bottom of the bottle, is more potent than *pulque* but easier to swallow. It's also available commercially; *pulque* is found mostly in central Mexico's *pulquerías.*

Tequila, once consigned to a stereotype in bad Westerns, has lately acquired a sophisticated aura. A growing coterie of connoisseurs has spotlighted high-quality varieties and is making inroads on the knock-back-a-shot mentality in favor of sipping and swirling as you would with fine Scotch or French cognac.

Don't overlook southern Mexico's **local spirits.** Kahlúa, the Arabica coffee-flavored liquor ubiquitous in U.S. bars, is the Yucatán's best-known product. Xtabentún, a honey-anisette liqueur based on the Maya's ceremonial drink produced from the morning glory, whose nectar fueled local honey production, is a popular after-dinner cordial. Its best-known maker, D'Aristi of Mérida, also makes Caribe rum and the lesser-known Kalani, a coconut liqueur. Other after-dinner liqueurs are flavored with native flowers such as hibiscus (*jamaica*) or fruit such as bananas (*plátano*) and pomegranate (*granada*).

Tequila 101

Tequila is a variety of *mescal* produced from the *A. tequilana* agave species, or blue agave, in the Tequila area of Jalisco state. Its quality and popularity have soared in the past 15 years. Distillers—all but one still based in Jalisco—have formed an association to establish standards for labeling and denomination. The best tequilas are 100% agave, made with a set minimum of sugar to prime the fermentation process. These tequilas come in three categories based on how they were stored: *Blanco* is white tequila aged very little, usually in steel vats. *Reposado* (reposed) is aged in wooden casks for between 2 months and a year. The coveted *añejo* (aged) tequila is stored in oak barrels for a year or more.

dining service **TIPS**

○ The afternoon meal is the main meal of the day, and many restaurants offer a multicourse daily special called *comida corrida* or *menú del día*. This is the least expensive way to get a full dinner.

○ In Mexico you need to ask for your check; it is considered rude to present the bill to someone who hasn't requested it. If you're in a hurry, ask for the check when your food arrives.

○ Tips are about the same as in the U.S. Restaurants sometimes include a 15% value-added tax, which shows up on the bill as "IVA." This is effectively the tip, which you may augment if you like, but make sure you're not tipping twice.

○ To summon the waiter, wave or raise your hand, but don't motion with your index finger, which is a demeaning gesture. If you need your check, it's OK to summon any waiter and ask, *"La Cuenta, por favor"*—or simply catch someone's eye and pantomime a scribbling motion against the palm of your hand.

WHEN TO GO

High season in the Yucatán begins around December 20 and continues to Easter week. This is the best time for calm, warm weather; snorkeling, diving, and fishing (the calmer weather means clearer and more predictable seas); and for visiting the ruins that dot the interior of the peninsula. Book well in advance if you plan to be in Cancún around the holidays.

Low season begins the day after Easter and continues to mid-December; during low season, prices may drop 20% to 50%. However, in Cancún and along the Riviera Maya, demand by Mexican and European visitors is creating a summer middle season.

Generally speaking, Mexico's **dry season** runs from November to April, with the **rainy season** stretching from May to October. It isn't a problem if you're staying close to the beaches, but for those bent on road-tripping to Chichén Itzá, Uxmal, or other sites, temperatures and humidity in the interior can be downright stifling from May to July. Later in the rainy season, the frequency of **tropical storms** and **hurricanes** increases; such storms, of course, can put a crimp in your vacation. But they can lower temperatures, making climbing ruins more fun, accompanied by cool air and a slight wind. November is especially ideal for Yucatán travels. Cancún, Cozumel, and Isla Mujeres also have a rainy season from November to January, when northern storms hit. This usually means diving visibility is diminished—and conditions may prevent boats from even going out.

Villahermosa is sultry and humid all the time. San Cristóbal de las Casas, at an elevation of approximately 2,100m (7,000 ft.), is much cooler than the lowlands and is downright cold in winter.

Cancún's Average Temperatures

	JAN	FEB	MAR	APR	MAY	JUNE	JULY	AUG	SEPT	OCT	NOV	DEC
AVG. HIGH (°C)	27	28	29	29	31	32	32	32	32	31	29	28
AVG. HIGH (°F)	81	82	84	85	88	89	90	90	89	87	84	82
AVG. LOW (°C)	19	20	22	23	25	26	26	25	24	23	22	21
AVG. LOW (°F)	67	68	71	73	77	78	78	77	76	74	72	69

Calendar of Events

Religious and secular festivals are a part of life in Mexico. Every town, city, and state holds its own specific festivals throughout the year commemorating religious and historic figures. Indeed, in certain parts of the country it sometimes feels like the festivities never die down, and the Yucatán, Tabasco, and Chiapas are no exception.

For an exhaustive list of events beyond those listed here, check **http://events. frommers.com**, where you'll find a searchable, up-to-the-minute roster of what's happening in cities all over the world.

JANUARY

Año Nuevo (New Year's Day), nationwide. This national holiday is perhaps the quietest day in all of Mexico. Most people stay home or attend church. All businesses are closed. In traditional indigenous communities, new tribal leaders are inaugurated with colorful ceremonies rooted in the pre-Hispanic past. January 1.

Día de los Reyes (Three Kings' Day), nationwide. This day commemorates the Three Kings presenting gifts to the Christ Child. On this day, children receive presents, much like they do at Christmas in the United States. Friends and families gather to share the *Rosca de Reyes,* a special cake. Inside the cake is a small doll representing the Christ Child; whoever receives the doll must host a tamales-and-*atole* (a warm drink made of *masa*) party on February 2. January 6.

FEBRUARY

Día de la Candelaria (Candlemas), nationwide. Music, dances, processions, food, and other festivities lead up to a blessing of seed and candles in a ceremony that mixes pre-Hispanic and European traditions marking the end of winter. Those who attended the Three Kings celebration reunite to share *atole*

and tamales at a party hosted by the recipient of the doll found in the *Rosca.* February 2.

Día de la Constitución (Constitution Day), nationwide. This national holiday is in honor of the current Mexican constitution, signed in 1917 as a result of the revolutionary war of 1910. It's celebrated through small parades. February 5.

Carnaval, nationwide. Carnaval takes place the 3 days preceding Ash Wednesday and the beginning of Lent. In Cozumel, the celebration resembles New Orleans's Mardi Gras, with a festive atmosphere and parades. In Chamula, the event harks back to pre-Hispanic times, with ritualistic running on flaming branches. Cancún also celebrates with parade floats and street parties.

Ash Wednesday, nationwide. The start of Lent and time of abstinence, this is a day of reverence nationwide; some towns honor it with folk dancing and fairs.

MARCH

Benito Juárez's Birthday, nationwide. This national holiday celebrating one of Mexico's most beloved leaders is observed through small hometown celebrations, especially in Juárez's birthplace, Guelatao, Oaxaca. March 21.

Spring Equinox, Chichén Itzá. On the first day of spring, the Temple of Kukulkán—Chichén Itzá's main pyramid—aligns with the sun, and the shadow of the plumed serpent moves slowly from the top of the building down. When the shadow reaches the bottom, the body joins the carved stone snake's head at the base of the pyramid. According to ancient legend, at the moment that the serpent is whole, the earth is fertilized. Visitors come from around the world to marvel at this sight, so advance arrangements are advisable. Elsewhere, equinox festivals and celebrations welcome spring, in the custom of the ancient Mexicans, with dances and prayers to the elements and the four cardinal points. It's customary to wear white with a red ribbon. March 21 (the shadow appears Mar 19–23).

APRIL

Semana Santa (Holy Week), nationwide. Mexico celebrates the last week in the life of Christ, from Palm Sunday to Easter Sunday, with somber religious processions, spoofing of Judas, and reenactments of biblical events, plus food and craft fairs. Some businesses close during this traditional week of Mexican national vacations, and almost all close on Maundy Thursday, Good Friday, Saturday, and Easter Sunday.

If you plan to travel to Mexico during Holy Week, make your reservations early. Airline seats into Cancún in particular will be reserved months in advance. Planes and buses to towns across the Yucatán and to almost anywhere else in Mexico will be full, so try arriving on the Wednesday or Thursday before Good Friday. Easter Sunday is quiet, and the week following is a traditional vacation period. Early April.

MAY

Labor Day, nationwide. Workers' parades countrywide; everything closes. May 1.

Cinco de Mayo, nationwide. This holiday celebrates the defeat of the French at the Battle of Puebla, although it (ironically) tends to be a bigger celebration in the United States than in Mexico. May 5.

Feast of San Isidro. The patron saint of farmers is honored with a blessing of seeds and work animals. May 15.

Cancún Jazz Festival. Over Memorial Day weekend, the Parque de las Palapas, as well as the area around the Convention Center, has live performances from jazz musicians from around the world. To confirm dates and schedule information, check www.cancun.travel.

International Gay Festival. This 5-day event in Cancún kicks off with a welcome fiesta of food, drinks, and mariachi music. Additional festivities include a tequila party, tour of Cancún, sunset Caribbean cruise, bar and beach parties, and a final champagne breakfast. For schedule information, check www.cancun.eventguide.com.

JUNE

Navy Day (Día de la Marina). All coastal towns celebrate with naval parades and fireworks. June 1.

Corpus Christi, nationwide. The day honors the Body of Christ (the Eucharist) with religious processions, Masses, and food. Dates vary.

Día de San Pedro (St. Peter and St. Paul's Day), nationwide. Celebrated wherever St. Peter is the patron saint, this holiday honors anyone named Pedro or Peter. June 26.

AUGUST

Assumption of the Virgin Mary, nationwide. This is celebrated throughout the country with special Masses and in some places processions. August 15 to August 17.

SEPTEMBER

Independence Day, nationwide. This day of parades, picnics, and family reunions throughout the country celebrates Mexico's independence from Spain. At 11pm on September 15, the president of Mexico gives the famous independence *grito* (shout) from the National Palace in Mexico City, and local mayors do the same in every town and municipality all over Mexico. On September 16, every city and town conducts a parade in which both government and civilians display their pride in being Mexican. For these celebrations, all important government buildings are draped in the national colors—red, green, and white—and the towns blaze with decorative lights. September 15 and 16; September 16 is a national holiday.

Fall Equinox, Chichén Itzá. The same shadow play that occurs during the spring equinox repeats at the fall equinox. September 21 to September 22.

OCTOBER

"Ethnicity Day" or Columbus Day (Día de la Raza), nationwide. This commemorates the fusion of the Spanish and Mexican peoples. October 12.

NOVEMBER

Day of the Dead (Día de los Muertos), nationwide. What's commonly called the Day of the Dead is actually 2 days: All Saints' Day, honoring saints and deceased children, and All Souls' Day, honoring deceased adults. Relatives gather at cemeteries countrywide, carrying candles and food to create an altar, and sometimes spend the night beside the graves of loved ones. Weeks before, bakers begin producing bread (called *pan de muerto*) formed in the shape of mummies or round loaves decorated with bread "bones." Decorated sugar skulls emblazoned with glittery names are sold everywhere. Many days ahead, homes and churches erect special altars laden with Day of the Dead bread, fruit, flowers, candles, favorite foods, and photographs of saints and of the deceased. On the 2 nights, children dress in costumes and masks, often carrying through the streets mock coffins and pumpkin lanterns, into which they expect money to be dropped. November 1 and 2; November 1 is a national holiday.

Annual Yucatán Bird Festival (Festival de las Aves de Yucatán), Mérida, Yucatán. Bird-watching sessions, workshops, and exhibits are the highlights of this festival, designed to illustrate the special role birds play in our environment and in the Yucatán territory. Check out www.yucatan birds.org.mx for details. Mid-November.

Revolution Day, nationwide. This commemorates the start of the Mexican

WHAT'S biting WHEN?

It's fishing season year-round along the Caribbean coast. Here's a general breakdown of what to look for during your trip. A handy guide for more information can be found at www.deepseafishingcancun.com/season.htm.

- **Blue Marlin:** March through August
- **White Marlin:** March through August
- **Sailfish:** January through August
- **Grouper:** Most of the year, except July and August
- **Wahoo:** November through August
- **Amberjack:** August through March

- **Dolphin Fish:** March through September
- **Blackfin Tuna:** December through August
- **Bonita:** February through October
- **Barracuda:** June through March
- **Kingfish:** October through February
- **Red Snapper:** August through June

Revolution in 1910 with parades, speeches, rodeos, and patriotic events. November 20.

Feast of the Virgin of Guadalupe, nationwide. Throughout the country, religious processions, street fairs, dancing, fireworks, and Masses honor the patroness of Mexico. This is one of Mexico's most moving and beautiful displays of traditional culture. The Virgin of Guadalupe appeared to a young man, Juan Diego, in December 1531, on a hill near Mexico City. He convinced the bishop that he had seen the apparition by revealing his cloak, upon which the Virgin was emblazoned. It's customary for children to dress up as Juan Diego, wearing mustaches and red bandannas. One of the most famous and elaborate celebrations takes place at the Basílica of Guadalupe, north of Mexico City, where the Virgin appeared. Every village celebrates this day, though, often with processions of children carrying banners of the Virgin and with *charreadas* (rodeos), bicycle races, dancing, and fireworks. December 12.

Festival of San Cristóbal de las Casas, San Cristóbal de las Casas, Chiapas. This 10-day festival includes a procession by the Tzotzil and Tzetzal Indians, *marimba* music, and a parade of horses. December 12 to December 21.

Christmas Posadas, nationwide. On each of the 9 nights before Christmas, it's customary to reenact the Holy Family's search for an inn, with door-to-door candlelit processions in cities and villages nationwide. These are also hosted by most businesses and community organizations, taking the place of the northern tradition of a Christmas party. December 15 to December 24.

Christmas. Mexicans extend this celebration and often leave their jobs beginning 2 weeks before Christmas all the way through New Year's Day. Many businesses close, and resorts and hotels fill up. Significant celebrations take place on December 24.

New Year's Eve. As in the rest of the world, New Year's Eve in Mexico is celebrated with parties, fireworks, and plenty of noise. December 31.

LAY OF THE LAND

The Yucatán Peninsula is truly a freak of nature—a flat, nearly 134,400-sq.-km (51,900-sq.-mile) slab of limestone with almost 1,600km (1,000 miles) of shoreline that is virtually devoid of surface water. The peninsula's geology, found nowhere else on Earth, was shaped by the same meteor thought to have extinguished the dinosaurs 65 million years ago. The impact fractured the brittle limestone into an immense network of fissures that drain all rainwater away from the surface. You'll see no bridges, no rivers, lakes, or streams in the northern and central Yucatán, but fresh rainwater courses through a vast underground river system stretching for hundreds of miles.

Breaches in the ceiling of this subterranean basin have created an estimated 3,000 cenotes—sinkholes that reveal the underground

The Endemic Birds of the Yucatán

The following 14 bird species are endemic to the Yucatán. See them while you're here, because you won't find them anywhere else on the planet: the black catbird, Cozumel emerald, Cozumel vireo, Cozumel thrasher, ocellated turkey, orange oriole, red-vented woodpecker, rose-throated tanager, yellow-lored (Yucatán) parrot, Yucatán poorwill, Yucatán nightjar, Yucatán flycatcher, Yucatán jay, and the Yucatán wren.

Cenote Xkekén in Valladolid.

to the world above. The Maya called them *dzonots,* or sacred wells, and regarded them as gateways to the underworld. Precious stones, ceramics, and bones unearthed in cenotes suggest that they were ancient ceremonial sites.

Quiet, dark, and cool, cenotes offer respite from the bright, often steamy glare above. Some are underground, with only a small breach in a roof perforated by thirsty tree roots. Others open to the surface like a lake. Most tourists get their introduction to this subterranean world at Chichén Itzá, with its Grand Cenote, and Hidden Worlds Cenotes Park, with underground caverns and waterways north of Tulum. But thousands more lie at the ends of narrow dirt roads throughout the peninsula, the greatest concentration being inland from the Playa del Carmen–Tulum corridor. The largest is Cenote Azul, at the end of Laguna de Bacalar in southern Quintana Roo.

The thin layer of soil coating the Yucatán's limestone shelf supports a nearly uniform terrain of dense, scrubby jungle full of wild ginger and orchids, jaguars, monkeys, and tropical birds. The only elevation is in the Puuc Hills. Rising south of Chichén Itzá and extending into northwestern Campeche, they peak at less than 300m (984 ft.).

The geography changes abruptly at the peninsula's isthmus. Hot, marshy Tabasco is a low-lying state bordering the Gulf of Mexico. With about 30% of Mexico's surface freshwater, Tabasco is said to be more water than land. Parts of the state are cloaked in thick rainforest, which extends through Chiapas. The capital, Villahermosa, lies in a shallow basin about an hour from the coast at the confluence of two rivers. Small lakes break up the landscape, especially in the modern parts of the city.

Chiapas, a much larger state of wildly varying elevations, extends from Tabasco all the way to the Pacific on one side and Guatemala on the other. It is washed by abundant lagoons, waterfalls, and rivers, including the Usumancinta, which forms the border with Guatemala. The high central plateau of a dramatic, pine-covered mountain range is the uncommonly chilly domain of San Cristóbal

Cozumel's Coral Reef

Cozumel has been one of the world's top dive sites since Jacques Cousteau unveiled its wonders in a 1961 documentary film. The island is fringed by a coral reef system that grows into towering walls, peaks, valleys, arches, and tunnels inhabited by more than 4,000 species of fish and thousands of other plants and animals. Its colors and textures rival New England's fall foliage displays. This underwater mountain range, running for 32km (20 miles) along Cozumel's southwest coast, is part of the massive Great Mesoamerican Reef (also called the Great Mayan Reef) stretching from the Gulf of Mexico to Honduras—second in size only to Australia's Great Barrier Reef.

de las Casas, a small and ancient colonial city surrounded by Maya villages. Nearby Sumidero Canyon is a winding river gorge with some walls reaching 1,000m (3,281 ft.) into the sky. Palenque, one of Mexico's most exquisite ruins, sits where the northern highlands slide down to the Gulf coastal plain.

Southern Mexico is blessed with an astounding diversity of wildlife. North America's only two flamingo breeding grounds flank the northern Yucatán's Gulf Coast, and whale sharks convene off the peninsula's northeastern tip. Jaguars, howler monkeys, crocodiles, sea turtles, and hundreds of bird species populate the Sian Ka'an Biosphere Reserve south of the Riviera Maya.

Odd critters such as the paca (kind of a spotted guinea pig on steroids), the coati, and the kinkajou (tree-dwelling raccoon kin), might pop up as you roam ancient Maya cities or hike through mangrove thickets. Though less often seen, jaguars, ocelots, margays, and other smaller cats roam the region's tropical forests.

Marshland in Tabasco.

Most of Mexico's 1,000 species of colorful tropical birds inhabit southern Mexico. The resplendent quetzal, which inspired the "plumed serpent" god of Maya legend, is among the world's most spectacular feathered creatures, with its shimmering, 2-foot-long tail. Its numbers have dwindled, but it can still be found in Chiapas' highlands.

Tabasco's wetlands are a paradise for bird-watchers. Crocodiles are also common, and you might spot howler monkeys, big cats, and manatees. Coastal waters throughout the region teem with dolphins, rays, and sea turtles.

A coati.

And those are just the animals you might have heard of. Others in this region include the Mexican caecilian, a primitive amphibian resembling a half-meter-long (1⅓-ft.) earthworm; the striped basilisk, called the "Jesus Christ lizard" for its ability to skip across the water's surface; the roseate spoonbill, a flamingo burdened with an elongated duck's bill; and other strange and marvelous creatures.

RESPONSIBLE TRAVEL

Mexico's ecological diversity is among the broadest of any country in the world, with an abundance of ecosystems ranging from the northern deserts to the central conifer forests and the southern tropical rainforests. Mexico also supports 111 million people and welcomes more than 20 million visitors each year. Tourism is one of the country's biggest and most lucrative industries, and while tourism has brought jobs and growth to much of Mexico, it has also created and even accelerated many of Mexico's ecological problems. **Cancún** might be the highest-profile example: Rapidly developed from a rural outpost to an international resort destination, Cancún imported turf from Florida for its golf courses, inadvertently introducing a disease that wiped out the local coconut palms. The region's mangroves, a key habitat for native species and vital to protecting the land from hurricanes and erosion, have also suffered.

However, tourism has also encouraged development of ecological conservation. Mexico is home to seven of the world's eight species of sea turtle, and the entire turtle population was decimated on both coasts as a result of tourism growth and local overfishing. A recent success story comes from the **Riviera Maya,** where marine biologists are working with hotels to guard nesting turtles and their eggs.

Mexico's people are proud of their land and culture, and through your travels, especially in rural areas, you will likely encounter *ejidos* and *cooperativos,* or local cooperatives, which offer small-scale tourism services—this may be as simple as taking visitors on a boat ride through a lake or as visible as controlling access to archaeological ruins. *Ejidos* will also run tours to popular ecotourism

Biodegradable Sunscreen

Recent scientific studies have shown that chemicals in commercial sunscreen can do long-term damage to coral reefs, collect in freshwater, and even build up in your body. The Riviera Maya receives more than 2.5 million visitors every year, many of them drawn to its rare marine environment—a unique combination of freshwater cenotes and the world's second-largest coral reef. A few ounces of sunscreen multiplied by 2.5 million are equal to a substantial amount of harmful chemicals suspended in the ocean and freshwater. That's why tours to the **Sian Ka'an Biosphere Reserve** and water parks **Xcaret** and **Xel-Ha** ask that you use only biodegradable sunscreen or wear none at all when swimming in their ocean or cenotes.

The label of a biodegradable sunscreen should state that it is 100% biodegradable (and only 100% will do). You can buy it at the parks, but you'll get a better price at local markets. If you're curious, you can obtain a list of banned chemicals by contacting the parks directly. Buy a supply of biodegradable formula before you go from **www.mexitan.com** or **www. caribbean-sol.com**.

destinations similar to those offered by large travel agencies. When you deal with *ejidos,* everyone you encounter will be from the community, and you know that your money goes directly back to them. States with a strong network of cooperatives include Chiapas, Quintana Roo, and Yucatán. Playa del Carmen's **Alltournative** (www.alltournative.com) is one example of a private company that has created tour options that include local input and grow by sustainable development.

The Mexican Caribbean supports the Great Mesoamerican Barrier Reef, the second-largest reef in the world, which extends down to Honduras. This reef and other marine ecosystems face increasing pressure from sedimentation, pollution, overfishing, and exploitative recreational activities, all newly associated with growing regional tourism. The **Coral Reef Alliance** (CORAL; www.coral. org) is an example of an organization that, by teaming up with the **World Wildlife Fund** (WWF; www.wwf.org) and **United Nations Environmental Program** (UNEP; www.unep.org), has been working to address threats to the Mesoamerican Barrier Reef and improve environmental sustainability throughout the region. CORAL partners with Mexican Amigos de Sian Ka'an, Conservation International, and the Cozumel Reefs National Park in an effort to build sustainability into mass tourism (such as cruise ships and hotels). CORAL assists marine tourism operators in implementing a voluntary code of conduct for best environmental practices. CORAL is soon to spread its influence to the Yum Balam region of the Yucatán Peninsula, where guidelines for whale shark interactions are greatly needed.

One of the best contributions a diver can make to support a healthy reef is to avoid physical contact with the reef during a dive. Talk to your scuba outfitter about proper buoyancy control and body position to avoid damaging these fragile ecosystems.

Tabasco suffered devastating flooding in 2007 that brought widespread suffering to the population, which is among Mexico's poorest. The floods also affected Chiapas, though to a lesser extent. Even more severe flooding came in 2010. Tabasco's sinking land, and the extraction of oil and gas, land erosion, and deforestation all contributed to the state's vulnerability.

Ecotourism and sustainable tourism opportunities abound in **Chiapas,** where a growing number of small, local tourism cooperatives have organized to take tourists on guided hikes, treks, and even kayak expeditions into the state's isolated jungles and nature reserves. The **Chiapas Tourism Secretariat** has information in Spanish about ecotourism at locations across the state (www.turismochiapas.gob.mx). Two private companies that run ecotours throughout Chiapas are **Ecochiapas** (Primero de Marzo 30, San Cristóbal de las Casas; www.ecochiapas.com; ✆ **01-800/397-5072** toll-free in Mexico or 967/674-7498 in San Cristóbal) and **Latitud 16** (Calle Real de Guadalupe 23, San Cristóbal de las Casas; ✆ **967/678-3909**).

The **Mesoamerican Ecotourism Alliance** (www.travelwithmea.org; ✆ **800/682-0584** in the U.S.) offers award-winning ecotours recognized by *National Geographic* to the Yucatán and Chiapas.

Animal-Rights Issues

The Yucatán presents many opportunities to **swim with dolphins.** The capture of wild dolphins was outlawed in Mexico in 2002. The only dolphins added to the country's dolphin swim programs since then were born in captivity. This law may have eased concerns about the death and implications of capturing wild dolphins, but the controversy is not over. Local organizations have been known to staple notes to Dolphin Discovery ads in magazines distributed in Cancún hotels. Marine biologists who run the dolphin swim programs say the mammals are thriving and that the programs provide a forum for research, conservation, education, and rescue operations. Animal-rights advocates maintain that keeping these intelligent mammals in captivity is nothing more than exploitation. Their argument is that these private dolphin programs don't qualify as "public display" under the Marine Mammal Protection Act because the entry fees bar most of the public from participating.

Visit the website of the **Whale and Dolphin Conservation Society** at www.wdcs.org or the **American Cetacean Society,** www.acsonline.org, for further discussion on the topic.

Bullfighting is considered an important part of Latin culture, but you should know, before you attend a *correo,* that the bulls (at least four) will ultimately be killed in a gory spectacle. This is not the case in some countries, such as France and Portugal, but the Mexicans follow the Spanish model. That said, a bullfight is a portal into understanding Mexico's Spanish colonial past, although nowadays bullfights are more of a tourist attraction, especially in tourist-laden Cancún. To read more about the implications of attending a bullfight, visit the website of **People for the Ethical Treatment of Animals (PETA)** at www.peta.org.

TOURS
Academic Trips & Language Classes

For Spanish-language instruction, **IMAC** (www.spanish-school.com.mx; ✆ **866/306-5040**) offers programs in Guadalajara, Puerto Vallarta, and Playa del Carmen. The **Spanish Institute** is affiliated with intensive Spanish language schools in Puebla (http://sipuebla.com; ✆ **800/554-2951**) and Mérida (http://simerida.com; ✆ **800/539-9710**).

To explore your inner Frida or Diego while in Mexico, look into **Mexico Art Tours,** 9323 E. Lupine Ave, Scottsdale, AZ 85260 (www.mexicanarttours.com; ✆ **888/783-1331** or 480/730-1764). Typically led by Jean Grimm, a specialist in the arts and cultures of Mexico, these unique tours feature compelling speakers who are themselves respected scholars and artists. Itineraries include visits to Chiapas, Guadalajara, Guanajuato, Puebla, Puerto Vallarta, Mexico City, San Miguel de Allende, Veracruz, other cities. Special tours involve archaeology, architecture, interior design, and culture, such as a Day of the Dead tour.

ATC Tours and Travel, Av. 16 de Septiembre 16, 29200 San Cristóbal de las Casas, Chis. (www.atctours.com; ✆ **967/678-2550,** -2557; fax 967/678-3145), a Mexico-based tour operator with an excellent reputation, offers specialist-led trips, primarily in southern Mexico. In addition to trips to the ruins of Palenque and Yaxchilán (extending into Belize and Guatemala by river, plane, and bus if desired), ATC runs horseback tours to Chamula or Zinacantán, and day trips to the ruins of Toniná around San Cristóbal de las Casas; birding in the rainforests of Chiapas and Guatemala (including in the El Triunfo Reserve of Chiapas); hikes to the shops and homes of textile artists of the Chiapas highlands; and walks from the Lagos de Montebello in the Montes Azules Biosphere Reserve, with camping and canoeing. The company can also prepare custom itineraries.

Adventure Trips

Mexico Sagaz (Asociación Mexicana de Turismo de Aventura y Ecoturismo; www.amtave.org; ✆ **800/654-4452** toll-free in Mexico or 55/5544-7567) is an active association of ecotourism and adventure tour operators. It publishes an annual catalog of participating firms and their offerings, all of which must meet certain criteria for security, quality, and training of the guides, as well as for sustainability of natural and cultural environments.

The California Native, 6701 W. 87th Place, Los Angeles, CA 90045 (www.calnative.com; ✆ **800/926-1140** or 310/642-1140), offers small-group deluxe 7-, 8-, 11-, and 14-day escorted tours through the Riviera Maya, the Yucatán, and Chiapas.

Trek America, 16/17 Grange Mills, Weir Road, London, SW12 0NE, UK (www.trekamerica.com; ✆ **800/873-5872** in the U.S.; 0844/576-1400 in the UK), organizes lengthy, active trips that combine trekking, hiking, van transportation, and camping along the Maya Route and across the Yucatán.

Food & Wine Trips

If you're looking to eat your way through Mexico, sign up with **Culinary Adventures,** 6023 Reid Dr. NW, Gig Harbor, WA 98335 (www.marilyntausend.com; ✆ **253/851-7676;** fax 253/851-9532). It runs a short but select list of cooking tours in Mexico. Culinary Adventures features well-known cooks, with travel to regions known for excellent cuisine. Destinations vary each year, though often include the Yucatán. The owner, Marilyn Tausend, is the author of *Cocinas de la Familia* (Family Kitchens), *Savoring Mexico,* and *Mexican,* and co-author of *Mexico the Beautiful Cookbook.*

3

SUGGESTED YUCATÁN ITINERARIES

by Shane Christensen

The following itineraries assume you're flying in and out of Cancún, by far the most common, and least expensive, port of entry for the Yucatán. The airport is south of town in the direction of the Riviera Maya, so if you rent a car to drive down the coast, you won't have to deal with city traffic. Those preferring to skip the coast and stick to the peninsula's interior could fly directly to Mérida, capital of the state of Yucatán, and adjust their itineraries accordingly.

For traveling around the Yucatán, rental cars work well. The roads are generally easy to figure out, and there's not much traffic when you move inland. Finding your way around Mérida is a little tricky, but Cancún and the other cities of the peninsula are easy. You can take inexpensive, comfortable buses for long distances during your entire trip, but keep in mind that buses in the Riviera Maya do not run along the small roads that connect the highway to the beach. Your bus may drop you on the side of the highway right at the junction with the road to your paradise, and you'll have to flag a taxi to take you the rest of the way. This is a fine method, but can be time-consuming.

These itineraries are merely suggestions; you should tweak them to your specific tastes and interests. The 14-day itinerary is very busy and will keep you moving quickly; it's an attempt to be comprehensive in hitting the top sites, but you may well want to skip a few of these and spend more time at others. Though I've included an itinerary that takes you south into Tabasco and Chiapas, interested travelers should consider taking a fully dedicated trip to these states on their own. I recommend against being too ambitious with your vacation time. The heat and humidity of summer bring about a lethargy that can only be enjoyable if you're not preoccupied with a timetable. Keep in mind as well that it gets dark early here, and it's not a good idea to do much night driving.

THE REGIONS IN BRIEF

Travelers to the peninsula have an opportunity to see pre-Hispanic ruins—such as **Chichén Itzá, Uxmal,** and **Tulum**—and the living descendants of the cultures that built them, as well as the ultimate in resort Mexico: **Cancún** and **Playa del Carmen.** The Yucatán peninsula borders the aquamarine Gulf of Mexico on the west and north, and the clear blue Caribbean Sea on the east. It covers almost 134,400 sq. km (51,892 sq. miles), with nearly 1,600km (1,000 miles) of shoreline. Underground rivers and natural wells, called cenotes, are a peculiar feature of this region.

Of course, the primary allure of the Yucatán peninsula for tourists is its long Caribbean coast, stretching the entire coast of the state of **Quintana Roo.** The swath of coast from Cancún south to **Tulum** has been dubbed the **Riviera Maya;** the region from the Sian Ka'an Biosphere Reserve's southern boundary to

PREVIOUS PAGE: **Snorkelers at Xel-Ha.**

The beaches at Xel-Ha.

the Belize border is the **Costa Maya.** This coastline has an enormous array of wildlife, including hundreds of species of birds. The Gulf Coast beaches, while good enough, don't compare to those on the Caribbean. National parks near **Celestún** and **Río Lagartos** on the Gulf Coast are home to amazing flocks of flamingos.

Things change when you move inland, into the states of **Yucatán,** the central portion of the peninsula, and **Campeche,** the western portion. The landscape is dotted by crumbling haciendas and the stark ruins of ancient cities. This is the world of the present-day Maya, where life moves slowly in simple villages bordered by rock walls and small cornfields. In the cities and towns, such as **Mérida** and **Izamal** in Yucatán state, and **Campeche** in Campeche state, you'll find the traditional Yucatán, with its highly pronounced regional flavor, and a way of life informed by centuries-old traditions.

To present the Maya world in its entirety, this book also covers the states of **Tabasco** and **Chiapas.** The Gulf Coast state of Tabasco was once home to the Olmec, the mother culture of Mesoamerica. At Villahermosa's Parque–Museo La Venta, you can see the impressive 40-ton carved rock heads that the Olmec left behind.

San Cristóbal de las Casas, in Chiapas, inhabits cooler, greener mountains and is more in the mold of a provincial colonial town. Approaching San Cristóbal from any direction, you see small plots of corn tended by colorfully clad Maya. The surrounding villages are home to many craftspeople, from woodcarvers to potters to weavers. In the eastern lowland jungles of Chiapas lie the classic Maya ruins of **Palenque.** Deeper into the interior, for those willing to make the trek, are the ruins of **Yaxchilán** and **Bonampak.**

The Yucatán state's nature preserves include the 47,200-hectare (116,600-acre) **Ría Lagartos Biosphere Reserve** north of Valladolid—where you'll find North America's largest flock of nesting flamingos—and the 5,600-plus-hectare (13,800-acre) **Celestún Wildlife Refuge,** which harbors most of the flamingos during non-nesting season. The state also has incorporated nature trails into the archaeological site of **Dzibilchaltún,** north of Mérida.

In 1989, the Campeche state set aside 71,480 hectares (176,630 acres) in the **Calakmul Biosphere Reserve** that it shares with Guatemala. The area includes the ruins of Calakmul, as well as acres of thick jungle.

Quintana Roo's protected areas are some of the region's most wild and beautiful lands. In 1986, the state set aside the 520,000-hectare (1.3-million-acre) **Sian Ka'an Biosphere Reserve,** conserving a significant part of the coast in the face of development south of Tulum. **Isla Contoy,** also in Quintana Roo, off the coast of Isla Mujeres and Cancún, is a beautiful island refuge for hundreds of birds, turtles, plants, and other wildlife. Cozumel's **Chankanaab National Park** gives visitors an idea of the biological importance of Yucatán's lengthy shoreline: Four of Mexico's eight marine turtle species—loggerhead, green, hawksbill, and

TOP: **Flamingoes at Ría Lagartos.** BOTTOM: **A kayaker traversing the Sian Ka'an Biosphere Reserve.**

IF YOU HAVE EVEN less TIME . . .

Given Cancún and the Riviera Maya's proximity to the United States, the vast majority of visitors to this region are long weekenders and snowbirds from the East Coast looking for a quick beach fix. Of course, that's what Cancún was made for, and even if you have a mere 3 days, you can still experience a taste of what this fascinating region has to offer.

Here are a few suggestions if you're prepared to leave the beach cabaña of your resort and explore a bit of the area. Ease yourself into a state of relaxation by spending a day and perhaps a night in sleepy **Isla Mujeres** (p. 116), just 15 minutes by ferry from Cancún.

A more ambitious beach vacation would have you head a couple hours south to stylish **Playa del Carmen** (p. 165) and then to either **Tulum** (p. 187) to visit the Maya ruins or **Cozumel** (p. 132) to snorkel or scuba dive next to one of the world's largest reefs. For a bit of culture off the beach, you can easily do a half-day trip to the unforgettable Maya ruins of **Chichén Itzá** (p. 285), stopping for lunch and a stroll in colonial **Valladolid** (p. 294). Since Cancún's **nightlife** is legendary (p. 101), you may want to spend at least one evening in this world-famous resort partying the night away.

leatherback—nest on Quintana Roo's shores, and more than 600 species of birds, reptiles, and mammals have been counted.

Tabasco, though a small state, has set aside a vast preserve of wetlands called **Pantanos de Centla,** just northeast of Villahermosa. Three reserves in Chiapas encompass jungles and lakes, and some of Mexico's most biodiverse lands. The largest by far is the nature preserve called **Montes Azules,** the old homeland of the Lacandón Indians in the extreme eastern lowlands bordering Guatemala. Not far from San Cristóbal de las Casas is also a small preserve of high cloud-forest habitat called **Huitepec.** A good distance west of Tuxtla Gutiérrez, the state capital, is an extensive nature preserve containing upland forests called **Selva del Ocote.**

HIGHLIGHTS OF CANCÚN & THE NORTHERN YUCATÁN

If you want to hit the highlights of Cancún and the Northern Yucatán, you'll first need to decide how much time you want to spend on the coast versus the interior. These highlights offer a sampling of both. You'll need a car to explore these destinations, and you could spend more or less time in any of them depending on your preferences.

DAYS 1 & 2: Cancún

If you arrive in Cancún, then it makes perfect sense to start here, preferably with an afternoon swim at your resort before heading to happy hour. Take a taxi to dinner at a waterfront seafood restaurant in the Hotel Zone, followed

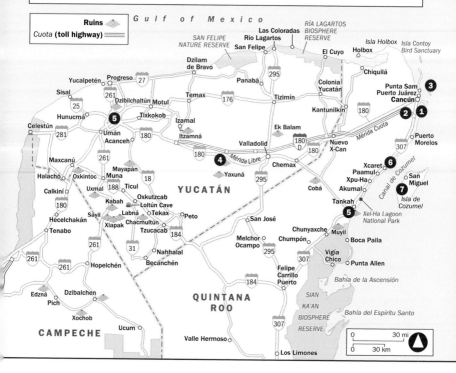

Highlights of Cancún and the Northern Yucatán

Ruins
Cuota (toll highway)

by a wild night out along "party row." Recover on the beach the next morning before an exhilarating afternoon jungle cruise through mangroves of the Nichupté Lagoon. Enjoy duty-free shopping in the evening at La Isla shopping village followed by another vibrant night out.

DAY 3: Isla Mujeres

Although few visitors to Cancún make it to **Isla Mujeres,** this is one of my favorite hideaways. Just a 15-minute ferry ride away, it's a quick trip to a far away time when life moved at the slow pace of sandy flip-flops. Head to Playa Norte for one of the most beautiful swimming beaches anywhere, and then explore the little town's *malecón* (boardwalk) for shopping bargains and a delicious fresh fish meal.

DAY 4: Chichén Itzá ★★★

Even if your plans are for a beach vacation, take time to visit the remarkable Maya ruins of **Chichén Itzá** (p. 285), an easy day trip from Cancún. You can combine this with an excursion to **Ek Balam** (p. 300), another pre-Columbian archaeological site that lies north of the colonial city of **Valladolid** (p. 294).

DAY 5: Mérida ★★ or Tulum ★★★

From **Chichén Itzá,** you have a choice of continuing inland or heading back to the coast. Travel west to **Mérida** (p. 224) to explore the Yucatán's colonial capital, or drive back to the sea by way of **Tulum** (p. 187), which is the gateway to the Mayan Riviera. Exquisite if haunting ruins await you there.

DAY 6: Playa del Carmen ★

The preferred beach destination for visiting Europeans, "Playa" has a vibrant beach chic feel. Put on your tiniest swimsuit for people-watching on the white sand beaches. The shopping, dining, and nightlife action happens along Quinta Avenida, best visited at night. **Xcaret** (p. 176) and **Xel-Ha** (p. 184) are two outstanding eco-parks that lie within an hour's drive and are fun family activities. See p. 165.

DAY 7: Cozumel

Hop on the jet ferry from Playa del Carmen to **Cozumel** for incredible scuba diving and snorkeling adventures. The island's reef system extending along its southern leeward coast is part of the Great Maya Barrier Reef, the second largest reef system in the world. Whether your hotel is in the single town of San Miguel or at a more secluded resort, prepare to be relaxed. Stay here until island fever takes you away.

Tulum's ruins.

A crowded beach in Playa del Carmen.

THE NORTHERN YUCATÁN IN 1 WEEK

You could extend this itinerary to 10 days, even 2 weeks—it all depends on how much time you want to spend on the beach. Once you've spent a little time in that clear blue water, it's hard to pull yourself away to move inland.

DAYS 1 & 2: Playa del Carmen ★ & Tulum ★★★

I recommend starting your trip in fashionable **Playa del Carmen** (p. 165), which offers gorgeous beaches and an artsy main strip called Quinta Avenida with bustling shops, cafes, and restaurants. "Playa," as it is known locally, is the gateway to **Cozumel** (p. 132), which makes for an easy day trip by ferry. **Xcaret** and **Xel-Ha** (p. 176 and 184, respectively), two outstanding eco-parks, also lie within easy driving distance. Spend your second day in any of these tempting spots or in the ancient Maya city of **Tulum** (p. 187) visiting its beaches, ruins, and the Sian Ka'an Biosphere Reserve (p. 199).

DAY 3: Ek Balam ★★★ & Chichén Itzá ★★★

Head for the ruins of **Ek Balam** (p. 300), which lie north of the colonial city of **Valladolid** (p. 294). From Tulum, take the highway to **Cobá** (p. 195) and consider stopping first at the ruins here. When you get to Valladolid, continue north on Hwy. 295 to the turnoff for Ek Balam. After climbing the main pyramid and inspecting the beautifully worked sacred doorway, head back to Valladolid for a late lunch. You can then drive to Chichén Itzá via the old highway. If there's time, stop at **Cenote Dzitnup** (p. 297), just outside Valladolid. Continue on to the ancient Maya city of **Chichén Itzá** (p. 285) and check into a hotel in the area. In the evening, see the sound-and-light show, and then visit the ruins the next morning.

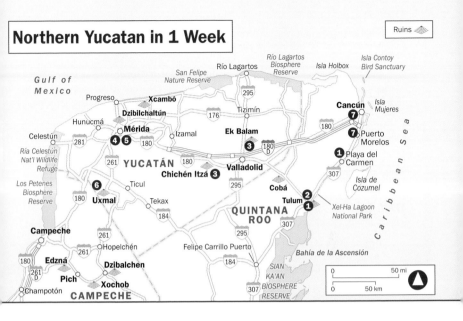

Northern Yucatan in 1 Week

Ruins

Gulf of Mexico

Río Lagartos Biosphere Reserve

San Felipe Nature Reserve

Río Lagartos

Isla Holbox

Isla Contoy Bird Sanctuary

295

Progreso

Xcambó

Tizimín

Cancún **7**

Isla Mujeres

Dzibilchaltún

176

Hunucmá

Mérida **4 5**

Izamal

Ek Balam

180

7 Puerto Morelos

Celestún

281

180

3

180

1 Playa del Carmen

Ría Celestún Nat'l Wildlife Refuge

261

YUCATÁN

180

Chichén Itzá **3**

Valladolid

307

Los Petenes Biosphere Reserve

Ticul

295

Cobá

Isla de Cozumel

180

Uxmal **6**

Tekax

Tulum **2 1**

Xel-Ha Lagoon National Park

QUINTANA ROO

307

Caribbean Sea

Campeche

261

184

Hopelchén

Felipe Carrillo Puerto

295

Bahía de la Ascensión

180

Edzná

261

Dzibalchen

184

SIAN KA'AN BIOSPHERE RESERVE

307

0   50 mi

0   50 km

Pich

Xochob

Champotón

CAMPECHE

DAYS 4 & 5: Mérida ★★

After you've taken in Chichén Itzá, head west to **Mérida** (p. 224) and enjoy an evening in this bustling capital city. The next day, you can further explore the tropical town, or may wish to take a day trip and return to enjoy Mérida in the evening. Choices include the **Celestún National Wildlife Refuge** (p. 255), where you can take a boat ride and see some pink flamingos, or the ruins of **Dzibilchaltún** (p. 237). You might also consider visiting **Progreso** and **Xcambó** (p. 256) for another good chance of seeing flamingos.

DAY 6: Uxmal ★★★

No matter whether you take the short way or the long way, try to get to **Uxmal** by late afternoon so that you can rest and cool off before seeing the sound-and-light show at night. Uxmal's **Pyramid of the Magician** is one of the most dramatic structures in the Maya world, and it becomes even more intriguing when lit at night. The next morning, you can explore the ruins in more detail. See p. 265.

The ruins of Uxmal.

DAY 7: Cancún or Puerto Morelos

This last day will include a good bit of driving. Take the short route back via Umán, then use the loop or *periférico* to avoid entering Mérida. After about 45 minutes, you'll see signs for the highway to Cancún. If you prefer to stay in a quiet beach location near Cancún, try **Puerto Morelos** (p. 154).

THE YUCATÁN IN 2 WEEKS

The Yucatán's quality roads and fairly contained shape allow for a complete circuit of the peninsula within a 2-week time frame. By moving counterclockwise, you'll save the best beach time for the end of your trip. This is a packed itinerary and can be done at a more relaxed pace if you leave out Palenque and San Cristóbal de las Casas in Chiapas. Plan on arriving in and departing from Cancún.

DAY 1: Ría Lagartos Biosphere Reserve ★, Ek Balam ★★★ & Valladolid ★

Begin with a trip from Cancún to **Ría Lagartos** (p. 301), at the peninsula's northern tip, where you can take a boat tour of the wildlife sanctuary, explore the mangrove and saltwater estuaries, as well as lakes filled with pink flamingos, pelicans, eagles, and other bird species. After taking a swim, head south on Hwy. 295 toward the ruins of **Ek Balam** (p. 300), known for a beautifully sculpted sacred doorway on the tallest pyramid in northern Yucatán. Spend the night in **Valladolid** (p. 294).

DAY 2: Cenote Dzitnup ★ & Chichén Itzá ★★★

Shortly after leaving Valladolid on the old highway, stop at cenotes **Dzitnup & Sammulá** (p. 297). Continue to the fascinating ruins of **Chichén Itzá** (p. 295). If you plan to stay near Chichén Itzá, you can watch a surreal sound-and-light show in the evening.

DAY 3: Izamal & Mérida ★★

Go west to the (literally) yellow city of **Izamal** (p. 253) to visit the few remaining Maya buildings, main square, and massive Franciscan convent before continuing to **Mérida** (p. 224), the region's cultural center. Get an overview on a bus/trolley tour and stroll the main plaza surrounded by 500-year-old buildings, built from the stone of Maya pyramids destroyed by the Spanish Conquistadors. Each evening, free cultural events take place in the historic district. Sunday's festivities last all day.

DAY 4: Celestún & Uxmal ★★★

From Mérida, **Celestún** (p. 255) is an easy day trip that allows you to combine a half-day on the beach with a boat trip through flocks of flamingos in the ecological reserve. From there, head south to the Maya ruins of **Uxmal** (p. 265). If you're driving, choose from two different routes (p. 258) that take you past tiny Maya villages, crumbling Spanish haciendas, and more archaeological finds. Check into a hotel near Uxmal in time to catch the evening light show; save touring the ruins for the cool early hours of the next morning.

DAY 5: Campeche ★

Campeche (p. 272) is the best-preserved walled city in the Americas. The United Nations declared it a World Heritage Site in 2000, which secures

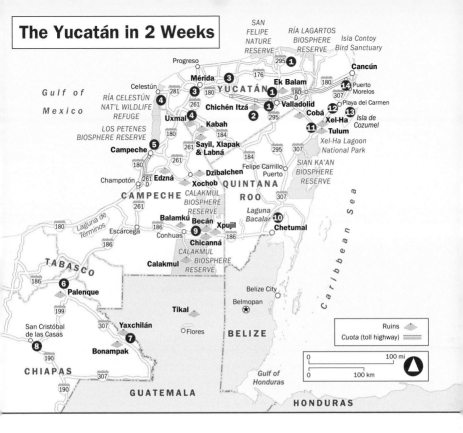

The Yucatán in 2 Weeks

protection for its narrow cobblestone streets and colonial-era buildings, painted in pastel colors. Check in and rest up: The next 3 days involve lots of road time.

DAYS 6, 7 & 8: Palenque & San Cristóbal de las Casas

Head south on Hwys. 180, 186, and finally 199 to **Palenque** (p. 312). You can explore the magnificent pyramids here and, if you like, also see the ruins of **Bonampak** and **Yaxchilán** (p. 320) the next day. Spend the first night in Palenque and the second night in **San Cristóbal de las Casas** (p. 322), the most interesting city in Chiapas. From San Cristóbal, go with one of the local guides to see the fascinating Maya communities of **San Juan Chamula** and **Zinacantán** (p. 330).

DAY 9: Calakmul, Xpujil & the Río Bec Ruins

Leave San Cristóbal early to head back up Hwy. 186 to the Calakmul Biosphere Reserve. It's a long drive through Escárcega to **Xpujil** (p. 216) and the ruins of the **Río Bec** area (p. 212). Easy-to-access local ruins are Xpujil, Chicanná, and Becán. The ruins of **Calakmul** (p. 217) are perhaps the Yucatán's most mysterious and difficult to reach—a 90-minute drive off the highway. The best way to see these ruins is to overnight near Xpujil and set out at dawn. If you decide to go to Calakmul, devote an extra day.

DAY 10: Lago Bacalar ★

Xpujil marks the geographic halfway point; from here you're on your way back to Cancún. Head west toward **Laguna Bacalar** (p. 207), stopping on the way to see the stone masks in the **Kohunlich** ruins (p. 215). Detour into **Chetumal** to see the fantastic Museum of Maya Culture (p. 210). Spend the night 37km (23 miles) north of the capital at one of the eco-lodges or simple inns on the edge of Laguna Bacalar.

Lago Bacalar at sunset.

DAY 11: Tulum ★★

After an hour-and-a-half drive north to **Tulum** (p. 187), you'll reach one of Mexico's most alluring Caribbean towns. Plan to spend a night at a beach hotel, allowing time to visit the **Tulum ruins** (p. 189) and check out the incredible beach in front of them. Also consider a nature tour of the **Sian Ka'an Biosphere** (p. 199), just south of town, with one of the local guide collectives.

DAYS 12 & 13: Playa del Carmen ★ & Cozumel

Take the drive up to **Playa del Carmen** (p. 165), which can serve as a base to explore cenotes or even the ruins of **Cobá** (p. 195). Playa is a chic

Dock jumping in Puerto Morelos.

town with a European flavor; be sure to allow time to take in the cobblestone Quinta Avenida. The next morning, you can take the ferry to **Cozumel** (p. 132) for a day of diving, snorkeling, swimming with dolphins, or simply enjoying the beach. Stay for an early dinner and return to Playa for the night.

DAY 14: Puerto Morelos

Spend your last day in **Puerto Morelos** (p. 154), a slow-paced beach town with stellar snorkeling just 31km (19 miles) south of Cancún.

AN ECO-ADVENTURE FOR THE WHOLE FAMILY

If you've got your own gear, bring it along for this trip; you can always get rentals, but you're better off with gear that fits well.

DAY 1: The Lower Riviera Maya

For this itinerary, I recommend staying in the lower Riviera Maya in or near **Playa del Carmen** (p. 165) or **Tulum** (p. 187). This puts you close to most of the places you'll be visiting. The drive from the airport to this part of the coast is at most 2 hours.

DAY 2: Xel-Ha & the Ruins of Tulum ★★★

Spend a day snorkeling, swimming, and frolicking in **Xel-Ha**'s natural lagoons and open-sea aquarium (p. 184). You can stay here the entire day or combine this with a trip to see the mystical ruins in **Tulum** (best in the morning, when the air is cooler). See p. 189.

Xel-Ha Lagoon.

An Eco-Adventure for the Whole Family

DAY 3: Hidden Worlds ★★★ & Aktun Chen ★

Between Akumal and Tulum are two attractions, each interesting in its own way. At **Hidden Worlds** (p. 185), you can snorkel in cenotes and subterranean rivers. Wet suits and snorkel gear are provided if you don't bring your own. **Aktun Chen** (p. 184) is a cavern that you can hike through and see lots of rock formations. The small zoo houses local species such as spider monkeys and tropical birds.

DAY 4: Alltournative

Consider spending today with **Alltournative,** an adventure tour agency based in Playa del Carmen. Its day trips combine adventure with nature and interactions with contemporary Maya in their own villages. The company will pick you up at almost any hotel in the Riviera Maya. See p. 175.

DAY 5: Sian Ka'an Biosphere Reserve ★

Explore the largest wildlife preserve in the Yucatán; snorkel down canals built by the Maya, visit the large, pristine lagoon at the center of the park, and observe various forms of wildlife as you get an up-close-and-personal view of the peninsula's natural habitat. See p. 199.

DAY 6: Chichén Itzá ★★★

Go for a morning snorkel trip with one of the local dive shops, and then drive to **Chichén Itzá** in the afternoon. Check into a hotel, and in the evening you can enjoy the sound-and-light show at the ruins. Return the next morning to get a closer look in daylight. See p. 285.

DAY 7: Cenote Dzitnup ★, Ek Balam ★★★ & Ría Lagartos Nature Reserve ★

After seeing the ruins, head east on the old federal highway until you get to **Cenote Dzitnup** (p. 297), shortly before the town of Valladolid. You'll find a dark cenote with a beautiful pool of water illuminated by a column of sunlight that penetrates the roof. Nearby is the smaller and less-visited but equally beautiful Cenote Sammulá. After a quick dip, continue into **Valladolid** (p. 294) for lunch. After you're nourished, head north on Hwy. 295 to the remarkable ruins of **Ek Balam** (p. 300). Then continue north, past the town of Tizimín, to the coastal village of **Río Lagartos.** Check in to one of the economical hotels fronting the water and arrange for an early morning boat tour of the flamingo sanctuary. See p. 301.

DAY 8: Cancún

After your visit with pink flamingos, it's time to get back to Cancún and civilization. See chapter 4.

LA RUTA MAYA

This route, which connects the major Maya sites in Mexico, could be done moving quickly over 2 weeks, more slowly in a month, or perhaps broken up into two trips. I've condensed the trip by leaving out Mérida, but visiting the beautiful Yucatán capital makes a fine urban break and gives you a glimpse of contemporary Maya culture. You can overdose by seeing too many ruins in too short a time, so pick and choose at your own pace. The best mode of travel is by rental car: The highways have little traffic and are, for the most part, in good shape.

DAY 1: Cancún

After you arrive, enjoy the rest of the day with a swim in the Caribbean or an afternoon by the pool. See chapter 4.

DAY 2: Ek Balam ★★★ & Chichén Itzá ★★★

Take the modern toll highway toward Mérida and exit at Valladolid. Head north, away from town, to visit the ruins of **Ek Balam** (p. 300). Then head

Chichén Itzá ruins.

The San Cristóbal de las Casas cathedral.

back to **Valladolid** (p. 294) for lunch before driving the short distance to **Chichén Itzá** (p. 285). Either visit the lovely Cenote Zací in town or stop to see the cenotes of **Dzitnup** and **Sammulá** (p. 297), just outside of Valladolid. Farther on is the **Balankanché Cave** (p. 293). When you get to Chichén Itzá, check into your hotel, and then go to the **ruins** later in the evening for the sound-and-light show. See p. 285.

DAY 3: Uxmal ★★★

Spend more time at the ruins of **Chichén Itzá** in the morning, then continue west on the toll highway toward Mérida. Turn off at Ticopó and head south toward the town of **Acanceh** (p. 260) and Hwy. 18. Stop to see the small but interesting ruins in the middle of town, and then proceed down Hwy. 18 to the ruins of **Mayapán** (p. 260). Afterward, continue through Ticul to Santa Elena and **Uxmal** (p. 265) for the sound-and-light show.

DAY 4: Edzná

Visit **Uxmal** (p. 265) in the morning, then drive back toward Santa Elena and take Hwy. 261 south to Hopelchén and on to the elegant ruins of **Edzná** (p. 279). Consider having lunch at the haunting hacienda-turned-hotel nearby, called **Uayamón** (p. 249). In **Campeche's** historic center (p. 272), you can stay at its sister property, **Hacienda Puerta Campeche,** or choose from several more modest digs.

DAYS 5 & 6: Palenque ★★, Bonampak & Yaxchilán

Stay on Hwy. 261 to Escárcega, then head west on Hwy. 186 toward Villahermosa, and south on Hwy. 199 to the town of **Palenque** (p. 312) with

La Ruta Maya

its magnificent pyramids. The next day, go to the ruins of **Bonampak** and **Yaxchilán** (p. 320).

DAYS 7 & 8: San Cristóbal de las Casas ★★

Keep south on Hwy. 199 toward **San Cristóbal de las Casas** (p. 322). On the way, take a swim at **Agua Azul** or **Misol Ha** (p. 320), and visit the ruins of **Toniná** (p. 321) outside of Ocosingo. From San Cristóbal, go with one of the local guides to see the Maya communities of **San Juan Chamula** and **Zinacantán** (p. 330).

DAY 9: Calakmul ★★★

Retrace your steps to Escárcega and continue east on Hwy. 186. If you have time, visit the fascinating sculptures of **Balamkú** (p. 220). Spend the night at one of the hotels in the vicinity of the turnoff for less-visited **Calakmul,** one of the prime city-states of the Classic age of the Maya.

DAY 10: Calakmul & Becán ★★★

Get to **Calakmul** (p. 217) early. Keep your eyes open for wildlife as you ride along the narrow jungle road. A vast area surrounding the city is a wildlife preserve. Afterward, continue east on Hwy. 186 to see the ruins of **Becán** (p. 216), a large ceremonial center with tall temples. Also in the vicinity are **Xpujil** (p. 216) and **Chicanná** (p. 217). Spend the night on the shores of **Laguna Bacalar** (p. 207), where you can cool off in its blue waters.

Tulum overlooks sandy beaches.

DAYS 11, 12 & 13: Tulum

Drive north on Hwy. 307 to **Tulum,** and settle into one of the small beach hotels there. In the morning, walk through the ruins and enjoy the view of the coast. Depending on your schedule, enjoy some more beach time on your last day, or head to the airport (25 min. south of Cancún) and depart.

CANCÚN

by Shane Christensen

4

Powdery white sand and a Caribbean sea the color of blue Curaçao—believe the brochures about Cancún. No matter how high-rise this city gets with all-inclusive megaresorts and supermalls, it's the beach that puts it on the map—and no hurricane or swine flu has been able to sweep it away. Get up from your poolside lounge and discover why millions flock to this sun-drenched destination—turtle-spotting off Isla Mujeres, discovering Chichén Itzá's iconic Maya pyramid, and swaying to reggaetón in the Hotel Zone's tequila-slamming bars.

Things to Do While it's tempting just to laze on **Playa Langosta**'s bleached sand, life beyond Cancún's beaches beckons with adventure in easy reach of a day trip. Scuba dive or snorkel off the islands of **Isla Mujeres** and **Cozumel,** both with quieter waters than Cancún. The enigmatic culture of the Maya comes alive at nearby **Tulum**'s seafront ruins. Or take a day trip to the pyramid temples of **Chichén Itzá** and jungly **Uxmal.** Kids in tow? Let them swim with dolphins in **Xel-Ha** eco–theme park's gigantic natural aquarium.

Shopping Cancún's glossy malls, such as **Plaza Las Americas** and **Plaza Kukulcán,** have an American flavor with their brand-name stores, cinemas, and food courts. **La Isla Shopping Village,** though, has Venetian-style canals and a spectacular aquarium. For a more Mexican experience, root around downtown **El Centro** for crafts, fresh produce, and authentic street chow. Pick up unique gifts from handmade *sombreros* and hammocks to *huaraches* (sandals) and artisan silver jewelry.

Eating & Drinking Tuck into sizzling **fajitas** in party-mad Tex-Mex joints or **fresh shrimp and lobster** while being serenaded by mariachis in the seafront restaurants in the **Zona Hotelera.** Food is cheaper and the atmosphere more authentically Mexican in **El Centro,** where locals eat incendiary **tacos, enchiladas** with chocolate-chile *mole* sauce, and succulent **tamales** (corn dough studded with meat or beans, wrapped in a banana leaf or corn husk). For an inexpensive snack, graze the food stalls in **Parque Las Palapas.**

Entertainment & Nightlife Nightlife here is loud, sexy, and relentless. Hop (or crawl) from a pool party to a pumping open-air club. Forget about quiet cantinas—Cancún is about pulsating discos with theme shows and party favors. Many of the monster clubs, from the **The City** to **CoCo Bongo,** lie within the same block, routinely turning the area into a sidewalk party. In El Centro's clubs playing bouncy *cumbia* music, sip tequila in a refreshing margarita or slam it with lime and salt.

PREVIOUS PAGE: **An infinity pool overlooking the Caribbean Sea.**

A BRIEF HISTORY OF cancún

Due to Cancún's ideal mix of elements—its transparent turquoise sea, powdery white sand, and immense potential for growth—a group of Mexican government computer analysts targeted the town for tourism development in 1974, transforming it from a deserted beach area to a five-star resort. Since then, Cancún has sustained the devastations of hurricanes and other powerful tropical storms, only to emerge stronger and more irresistible. In the wake of Hurricane Wilma, which tore through the Yucatán peninsula in 2005, wreckage rapidly gave way to exacting renovations, luxurious upgrades, and brand-new destinations. However, the double whammy of the worldwide economic crisis and worries caused by swine flu has not made for an easy time in Cancún in the past couple years. Hotels, restaurants, and tourist services across the board have suffered here, just as they have elsewhere in the region. With a struggling economy and more budget-minded travelers, Cancún's resorts have been moving increasingly to all-inclusive options, which typically include lodging, meals, domestic drinks, and a variety of discounts on activities.

Cancún embodies Caribbean splendor and the exotic joys of Mexico, but even a Western traveler feeling apprehensive about visiting foreign soil will feel completely at ease here. English is spoken and dollars accepted; roads are well paved and lawns manicured. Some travelers are surprised to find that Cancún is more like a U.S. beach resort than a part of Mexico. Indeed, signs of Americanism are rampant. U.S. college students continue to descend in droves during spring break—which, depending on your perspective, may be reason to rush headlong into the party or stay far, far away during this season. One astonishing statistic suggests that more Americans travel to Cancún than to any other foreign destination in the world. Indeed, almost three million people visit annually—most of them on their first trip to Mexico.

THE BEST CANCÚN EXPERIENCES

- **Carving out a piece of paradise:** Cancún is synonymous with the Mexican Caribbean, and daytime activity in this hedonistic paradise revolves around the sea. The beaches are among the best anywhere, the swimming and snorkeling are spectacular, and divers enjoy world-class scuba sites nearby. Endless water sports make both the Caribbean and Nichupté Lagoon natural playgrounds.

- **Duty-free shopping:** For a respite from the sun and sea, luxury malls dot the Hotel Zone with international designer fashions and duty-free shopping. More traditional and typically cheaper local handicrafts, jewelry, and clothes fill the local shops and markets of Cancún City. The best flea markets are located downtown, where bargaining is common.

- **Taking the kids to see tropical fish, dolphins, and even Jaws:** The interactive aquarium at La Isla shopping plaza is a blast for kids, and includes a chance to swim with dolphins and even feed sharks. The outdoor-plaza facing the lagoon also has canal rides resembling Venetian gondolas.

Cancún's famous white-sand beach runs south along the Caribbean Sea for 22km (14 miles).

- **Did someone say lobster?** Outside the all-inclusive resorts, Cancún's independent restaurants are among the most varied and highest quality in Latin America. Longstanding seafood establishments situated along the lagoon serve Caribbean lobster, grilled local fish, and succulent shrimp. Inexpensive Mexican eateries cluster in Cancún City, so head downtown for cheap spicy tacos.

- **Going wild in Cancún:** A Cancún vacation implies raucous nightlife, and this town is a year-round, sun-drenched Caribbean party that rocks hardest at spring break. By sundown, beachgoers have folded up their towels, packed up their snorkels, and put away their shopping bags, rolling en masse to any of the countless margarita-charged happy hours to kick off the night. The Hotel Zone is where the ladies and gents go wild, jamming indoor and outdoor bars that pump out party beats as if competing to be heard by a distant island. Downtown Cancún houses authentic cantinas serving somewhat quieter shots of tequila and bottles of Mexican beer.

ESSENTIALS
Arriving

BY PLANE   If this is not your first trip to Cancún, you'll notice that the **airport's** (www.cancun-airport.com) facilities and services continue to expand. Most international flights, including those to and from the U.S. (except for Jet-Blue and AirTran, which use Terminal 2), now go through the new Terminal 3, which has money-exchange services, duty-free shops, restaurants, medical services, an express spa, and even a welcome bar serving beer and margaritas just outside the terminal. **Aeroméxico** operates connecting service to Cancún through Mexico City. In addition to these carriers, many **charter** companies—such as Apple Vacations (www.applevacations.com) and Funjet (www.funjet.com)—travel to Cancún; these package tours make up as many as half of arrivals by U.S. visitors.

InterJet (www.interjet.com.mx; ☏ **866/285-9525** in the U.S. or 01-800/011-2345 in Mexico) and **Volaris** (www.volaris.com.mx; ☏ **866/988-3527** in the U.S. or 01-800/122-8000 in Mexico) are two regional carriers that fly to Cancún from Mexico City. Domestic flights generally use Terminal 1, and flights to and from other destinations in Latin America use Terminal 2. **Mayair** (www.mayair.com.mx; ☏ **998/881-9413** in Mexico) flies between Cancún and Cozumel.

The following major international carriers serve Cancún: **AirTran** (www.airtran.com; ☏ 800/868-8833 in the U.S.), **American** (www.aa.com; ☏ 800/433-7300 in the U.S.), **Continental** (www.continental.com; ☏ 800/231-0856 in the U.S.), **Delta** (www.delta.com; ☏ 800/221-1212 in the U.S.), **Frontier** (www.frontierairlines.com; ☏ 800/432-1359 in the U.S.), **JetBlue** (www.jetblue.com; ☏ 800/538-2583 in the U.S.), **Spirit** (www.spirit.com; ☏ 800/772-7117 in the U.S.), **United** (www.united.com; ☏ 800/241-6522 in the U.S.), and **US Airways** (www.usairways.com; ☏ 800/428-4322 in the U.S.).

Most major car-rental firms have outlets at the airport, so if you're renting a car, consider picking it up and dropping it off at the airport to save on airport-transportation costs. Another way to save money is to arrange for the rental before you leave home. If you wait until you arrive, the daily cost will be around $50 to $75 for a compact vehicle. Major agencies include **Alamo, Avis, Budget, Dollar, Hertz, National,** and **Thrifty.** The Zona Hotelera (Hotel Zone) lies 10km (6¼ miles)—a 20-minute drive—from the airport along wide, well-paved roads. Online quotes often do not include taxes and insurance.

The rate for a **private taxi** from the airport is $60 to Ciudad Cancún (downtown) or the Hotel Zone. The return trip with an airport taxi is discounted by 50%. The **Green Line** and **Taxi by Hertz** both run shuttles

An aerial view of the Cancún Hotel Zone.

THE BEST CANCÚN websites

o **All About Cancún: www.cancun mx.com** This site is a good place to start planning. It includes Cancún-specific information, bookings for regional tours, and a visitors' blog.

o **Cancún Convention & Visitors Bureau: www.cancun.travel** The official site of the Cancún Convention & Visitors Bureau lists excellent information on events and attractions. Its hotel guide is one of the most complete available and includes events and news related to Cancún.

o **Cancún Online: www.cancun. com** This comprehensive guide has lots of information about things to do and see in and around Cancún, though most details come from paying advertisers. The site lets you reserve package trips, accommodations, activities, and tours.

o **Cancún Travel Guide: www. go2cancun.com** These online information specialists are also a good resource for Cancún travel deals offered by paying advertisers.

(called *colectivos*) from the airport into town approximately every 20 minutes. Buy tickets, which cost about $15, from the booth to the far right as you exit the airport. These services accept U.S. dollars, though you'll get a more favorable rate if you pay in pesos. **Local bus** transportation on ADO ($4) goes from the airport to Ciudad Cancún. From there, you can take another bus for less than a dollar to Puerto Juárez, where passenger ferries leave to Isla Mujeres regularly. There is no shuttle service returning to the airport from Ciudad Cancún or the Hotel Zone, so you'll have to take a taxi, but the rate will be much less than for the trip from the airport. (Only federally chartered taxis may take fares *from* the airport, but any taxi may bring passengers *to* the airport.) Ask at your hotel what the fare should be, but expect to pay about half what you paid from the airport to your hotel.

BY CAR From Mérida or Campeche, take **Hwy. 180** east to Cancún. This is mostly a winding, two-lane road that branches off into the express **toll road 180D** between Izamal and Nuevo Xcan. Nuevo Xcan is approximately 40km (25 miles) from Cancún. Mérida is about 320km (200 miles) away.

BY BUS Cancún's **ADO bus terminal** (www.ado.com.mx; ✆ **01-800/702-8000**) sits in downtown Ciudad Cancún at the intersection of avenidas Tulum and Uxmal. All out-of-town buses arrive here. Buses run to Playa del Carmen, Tulum, Chichén Itzá, other nearby beach and archaeological zones, and other points within Mexico. ADO buses also operate between the airport and downtown, as well as from the airport directly to Playa del Carmen (from where ferries depart for Cozumel).

Visitor Information

The **Cancún Municipal Tourism Office** is downtown at Avenida Nader at the corner of Avenida Cobá (http://cancun.travel; ✆ **998/887-3379**). It's open Monday through Friday from 9am to 4pm. The office lists hotels and their rates, as well as ferry schedules. For information prior to your arrival in Cancún, visit the Convention Bureau's website, **www.cancun.travel**. The state tourism website is in Spanish, at www.qroo.gob.mx.

Pick up copies of the free booklet *Cancún Tips* (www.cancuntips.com.mx), which can also be downloaded from the site.

City Layout

There are really two Cancúns: **Ciudad Cancún (Cancún City)** and **Isla Cancún (Cancún Island).** Ciudad Cancún, on the mainland, is the original downtown area, where most of the local population lives. It's home to traditional restaurants, shops, and less expensive hotels, as well as pharmacies, dentists, automotive shops, banks, travel and airline agencies, and car-rental firms—all within an area of about 9 square blocks. The city's main thoroughfare is **Avenida Tulum.** Heading south, Avenida Tulum becomes the highway to the airport and to Tulum and Chetumal; heading north, it intersects the highway to Mérida and the road to Puerto Juárez and the Isla Mujeres ferries.

Not technically an island, Isla Cancún is a thin strip 22km (14 miles) long wrapped like a "7" around the Nichupté Lagoon. It's home to the famed **Zona Hotelera,** or Hotel Zone (also called the Zona Turística, or Tourist Zone), connected to the mainland by the Playa Linda Bridge at the north end and the Punta Nizuc Bridge at the southern end. Between the two areas lies Laguna Nichupté. Avenida Cobá leading from Cancún City becomes Bulevar Kukulcán in the Hotel Zone, the tourist zone's main traffic artery. Cancún's international airport is just inland from the south end of the strip.

FINDING AN ADDRESS Cancún City's street-numbering system is a holdover from its early days. Addresses are still given by the number of the building lot and by the *manzana* (block) or *supermanzana* (group of blocks). The city is relatively compact, and the downtown commercial section is easy to cover on foot.

On the island, addresses are given by kilometer number on Bulevar Kukulcán or by reference to some well-known location. In Cancún, streets are named after famous Maya cities. Boulevards are named for nearby archaeological sites Chichén Itzá, Tulum, and Uxmal.

Getting Around

BY TAXI Taxi prices in Cancún are clearly set by zone, although keeping track of what's in which zone can take some practice. The minimum fare within the Hotel Zone is 90 pesos per ride, making it one of the most expensive taxi areas in Mexico. In addition, taxis operating in the Hotel Zone feel perfectly justified in having a discriminatory pricing structure: Local residents pay about half of what tourists pay, and prices for guests at higher-priced hotels are about double those for budget hotel guests—these are all established by the taxi union. Rates should be posted outside your hotel; if you have a question, all drivers are required to have an official rate card in their taxis, though it's generally in Spanish. Taxi drivers will accept dollars, though at a less favorable rate than pesos.

Within the downtown area, the cost is about 25 pesos per cab ride (not per person); within any other zone, it's 70 to 110 pesos. It'll cost about 200 pesos to travel between the Hotel Zone and downtown. Settle on a price in advance, or check at your hotel. Trips to the airport from most zones cost about 350 pesos (up to four people). Taxis can also be rented for 350 pesos per hour (2-hr. minimum) for travel around the city and Hotel Zone. If you want to hire a taxi for an all-day tour, for example to Chichén Itzá or along the Riviera Maya, expect to pay about 3,500 pesos total (up to four people)—many taxi drivers feel that they are also providing guide services.

A Ruta 2 bus heading to the Hotel Zone.

BY BUS Bus travel is a cheap, safe way for getting up and down the Hotel Zone. In downtown Cancún, almost everything lies within walking distance. **Ruta 1, Ruta 2,** and **Ruta 15** city buses travel frequently from downtown Cancún to the Hotel Zone. **Ruta 1** buses continue to Puerto Juárez for ferries to Isla Mujeres. All these city buses run between 6am and 10pm daily. Buses also go up and down the main strip of the Hotel Zone day and night. Public buses have the fare painted on the front; at press time, the fare was about 10 pesos.

BY SCOOTER Scooters are a convenient but dangerous way to cruise through the very congested traffic. Rentals start at about $50 for a day, not including insurance, and a credit card voucher is required as security. You should receive a crash helmet (it's the law) and instructions on how to lock the wheels when you park. Make sure the vehicle is in adequate condition and has been serviced. Also read the fine print on the back of the rental agreement regarding liability for repairs or replacement in case of accident, theft, or vandalism, and make sure you have adequate insurance coverage in case of an accident.

[Fast FACTS] CANCÚN

Area Code The telephone area code is **998.**

ATMs & Banks Most banks sit downtown along Avenida Tulum and are usually open Monday through Friday from 9am to 3pm, although some are open later and even half the day on **Saturday.** Many have ATMs for after-hours cash withdrawals. In the Hotel Zone, you'll find an HSBC bank in Kukulcán Plaza that's open Monday through Saturday from 9am to 7pm.

Consulates The **U.S. Consular Agent** is in the Torre La Europea, Bulevar Kukulcán Km 13 (http://merida.usconsulate.gov; ✆ **998/883-0272**); open Monday through Friday from 8am to 1pm. The **Canadian Consulate** is in the Centro Empresarial, Bulevar Kukulcán Km 12 (www.mexico.gc.ca; ✆ **998/883-3360**); open Monday through Friday from 9am to 1pm. The **United Kingdom** has a consular office at the Royal Sands Hotel, Bulevar Kukulcán Km 12 (http://ukinmexico.fco.gov.uk/en;

998/881-0100); open Monday through Friday from 9am to 3pm. Irish, Australian, and New Zealand citizens should contact their embassies in Mexico City.

Crime Car break-ins are a frequent crime here, especially around the shopping centers in the Hotel Zone. Rapes and sexual assault are serious concerns. Most have taken place at night or in the early morning. Some bars and nightclubs can be havens for drug dealers and petty criminals. Be sure to travel in pairs or small groups; women should not walk alone at night.

Currency Exchange Payment in dollars is no longer accepted in Mexico per federal law. Cancún has many *casas de cambio* (exchange houses) with varying exchange rates. Hotels will change money for guests. Avoid changing money at the airport as you arrive, especially at the first exchange booth you see— its rates are less favorable than those of any in town or others farther inside the airport. The easiest way to draw money is at an ATM machine, which will dispense money in pesos and charge a small transaction fee (usually around 25 pesos).

Drugstores Across the street from Señor Frog's in the Hotel Zone, at Bulevar Kukulcán Km 9.5, **Farmacías del Ahorro** (ℂ **998/892-7291** for call center offering deliveries) is open 24 hours. Plenty of drugstores sit in the major shopping malls in the Hotel Zone and are open until 10pm. In downtown Cancún, **Farmacías del Ahorro** is located in front of the Rey del Caribe hotel at the corner of Av. Uxmal and Nadar. It's open daily from 7am to 11pm. You can stock up on over-the-counter and many prescription drugs without a prescription.

Emergencies The local **Red Cross** (ℂ **998/884-1616**) is open 24 hours on Avenida Yaxchilán between avenidas Xcaret and Labná, next to the Telmex building.

Hospital **Galenia Hospital** is one of the city's most modern, offering full emergency and other services with excellent care, at Av. Tulum, SM 12, at Nizuc (www.hospitalgalenia.com; ℂ **998/891-5200**). **U.S. Air Ambulance** (Global Ambulance) service is available by calling ℂ **800/948-1214** (www.usairambulance.net).

Internet Access All of **Kukulcán Plaza,** Bulevar Kukulcán Km 13, offers free Wi-Fi. You'll need to pick up a password at Customer Services, near the main entrance. Most hotels now have Internet access, and five-star hotels have business centers.

Luggage Storage & Lockers Hotels will generally tag and store luggage while you travel elsewhere.

Newspapers & Magazines Most hotel gift shops and newsstands carry English-language magazines and English-language, Mexican-edition newspapers, such as *USA Today*. *Cancún Tips* (www.cancuntips.com.mx) is an entertainment magazine that offers descriptions of local activities, maps, and tourist information.

Police Dial ℂ **066** for the police in an emergency. Cancún also has a fleet of tourist police to help travelers. Dial ℂ **998/885-2277.**

Post Office The main *correo* lies at the intersection of avenidas Sunyaxchen and Xel-Ha (ℂ **998/884-1418**). It's open Monday through Friday from 9am to 4pm, and Saturday from 9am to noon for the purchase of stamps only.

Seasons High season runs from December 15 to April; low season extends from May to December 15, when prices drop 10% to 30%. Some hotels are starting to charge high-season rates during June and July, when Mexican, European, and school-holiday visitors often travel, although rates may still be lower than in winter months.

Weather The days are warm and, in summer, sultry. The rainy season runs May through October. August to November is hurricane season, which brings erratic weather. November through February can be partly cloudy, windy, and occasionally rainy. Evenings can get cool.

EXPLORING
Beaches, Watersports & Boat Tours

BEACHES   Cancún's beaches are among the most beautiful in the world. Resort hotels dominate most of them. All of Mexico's beaches are public property, so you can use the beach of any hotel by walking through the lobby or directly onto the sand. Be especially careful on the east-facing beaches fronting the open Caribbean, where the undertow can be quite strong. In the Caribbean, storms can arrive and conditions can change from safe to unsafe in a matter of minutes, so be alert: If you see dark clouds heading your way, make for the shore and wait until the storm passes. Get to know Cancún's water-safety pennant system, and make sure to check the flag at any beach or hotel before entering the water. Here's how it goes:

White	Excellent
Green	Normal conditions (safe)
Yellow	Changeable, uncertain (use caution)
Black or **red**	Unsafe—use the swimming pool instead!

By contrast, the northern beaches facing Isla Mujeres just above the Hotel Zone are protected by a bay, leaving them calm and ideal for swimming. Playa Tortuga (Turtle Beach), Playa Langosta (Lobster Beach), Playa Linda (Pretty Beach), and Playa Las Perlas (Beach of the Pearls) are some of the public beaches. At most of them, you can rent a sailboard and take lessons, ride a parasail, or partake in a variety of watersports. There's a small but beautiful portion of public beach on Playa Caracol, popular with families because of its shallow sandy bottom.

WATERSPORTS   Many beachside hotels offer watersports concessions that rent kayaks and snorkeling equipment. On the calm Nichupté lagoon are outlets for renting small **sailboats, jet skis, windsurfing gear,** and **water skis.** Prices vary and are often negotiable, so check around.

DEEP-SEA FISHING   You can arrange a shared or private deep-sea fishing charter at one of the numerous piers or travel agencies. Prices fluctuate widely depending on the length of the excursion (there's usually a 4-hr. minimum), number of people, and quality of the boat. Marinas will sometimes assist in putting together a group. Charters include a captain, a first mate, bait, gear, and beverages. Rates are lower if you depart from Isla Mujeres or from Cozumel—and, frankly, the fishing is better closer to those departure points.

SCUBA & SNORKELING   Known for its shallow reefs, dazzling color, and diversity of life, Cancún is one of the best places in the world for beginning scuba diving. Punta Nizuc is the northern tip of the **Gran Arrecife Maya (Great Mesoamerican Reef),** the largest reef in the Western Hemisphere and one of the largest in the world. In addition to the sea life along this reef system, several sunken boats add a variety of dive options. Inland, a series of caverns and cenotes (wellsprings) are fascinating venues for the more experienced diver. Drift diving is the norm here, with popular dives going to the reefs at **El Garrafón** and the **Caves of the Sleeping Sharks**—although be aware that the famed "sleeping sharks" have departed, driven off by too many people watching them snooze.

A variety of hotels offer resort courses that teach the basics of diving—enough to make shallow dives and slowly ease your way into this underwater world of unimaginable beauty. One preferred dive operator is **Scuba Cancún,** Bulevar Kukulcán Km 5 (www.scubacancun.com.mx; ✆ 998/849-7508), on the lagoon side. Full open-water PADI certification takes 3 days and costs $410. A half-day "discover scuba diving"

Sailing off of the Cancún coast.

course for beginners with theory, pool practice, and a one-tank dive at a reef costs $88. Scuba Cancún is open daily from 7am to 8pm. For certified divers, Scuba Cancún also offers PADI specialty courses and diving trips in good weather to 18 nearby reefs, as well as to cenotes (9m/30 ft.) and Cozumel. The average dive is around 11m (36 ft.), while advanced divers descend farther (up to 18m/59 ft.). Two-tank dives to reefs around Cancún cost $68, and one-tank dives cost $54; those to farther destinations cost $140. Discounts apply if you bring your own gear. Dives usually start around 9:30am and return by 1:30pm. Snorkeling trips cost $29 and leave daily at 1:30 and 4pm for shallow reefs about a 20-minute boat ride away.

The largest dive operator is **Aquaworld,** across from the Meliá Cancún at Bulevar Kukulcán Km 15.2 (www.aquaworld.com.mx; ✆ 998/848-8300). It offers resort courses and diving to reefs, wrecks, or caverns—as

Learn to scuba dive in Cancún's clear, vibrant waters.

Snorkelers look for sea life off of the Cancún coast.

A frigate bird at Isla Contoy.

well as snorkeling, parasailing, jet-ski "jungle tours," fishing, day trips to Isla Mujeres and Cozumel, and other watersports activities. Aquaworld has the **SubSee Explorer,** a boat with picture windows beneath the surface. The vessel doesn't submerge—it's an updated version of a glass-bottom boat— but it does provide nondivers with a worthwhile peek at life beneath the sea. The 30-minute voyage costs $45 for adults, $25 for children under 12. Aquaworld also offers a snorkeling tour to the impressive new **La Musa (Underwater Museum of Art)** off Isla Mujeres, where more than 400 sunken sculptures form an artificial reef. This attraction costs $45 per person.

Besides snorkeling at **El Garrafón Natural Park** (see "Boating Excursions," below), travel agencies offer an all-day excursion to the natural wildlife habitat of **Isla Contoy,** which usually includes time for snorkeling. The island, 90 minutes past Isla Mujeres, is a major nesting area for birds and a treat for nature lovers. You can call any travel agent or see any hotel tour desk to get a selection of boat tours to Isla Contoy. Prices range from $65 to $95, depending on the length of the trip, and generally include drinks and snorkeling equipment.

The Great Mesoamerican Reef also offers exceptional snorkeling opportunities. In **Puerto Morelos,** 37km (23 miles; p. 154) south of Cancún, the reef hugs the coastline for 15km (9⅓ miles). The reef is so close to the shore (about 460m/1,509 ft.) that it forms a natural barrier for the village and keeps the waters calm on the inside of the reef. The water here is shallow, from 1.5 to 9m (5–30 ft.), resulting in ideal conditions for snorkeling. Stringent environmental regulations implemented by the local community have kept the reef here unspoiled. Only a select few companies are allowed to offer snorkel trips, and they must adhere to guidelines that will ensure the reef's preservation. **Cancún Mermaid** (www.cancunmermaid.com; ✆ **998/273-4257**), in Puerto Morelos, is considered the best—it's a family-run ecotour company that has operated in the area since the 1970s. It's known for highly personalized service. The 8-hour tour typically takes snorkelers to two sections of the reef, spending about an hour in each area. When conditions allow, the boat drops off snorkelers and then follows them along with the current—an activity known as "drift snorkeling," which enables snorkelers to see as much of the reef as possible. The "Snorkeling in Puerto Morelos" trip costs $68, which includes boat, snorkeling gear, life jackets, a light lunch, bottled water, sodas and beer, entrance to the park, and round-trip transportation to and from Puerto Morelos from Cancún hotels. Departures are Monday through Saturday at 9am. Reservations are required at least 1 day in advance; MasterCard and Visa are accepted.

JET-SKI/FAST BOAT TOURS   Several companies offer the thrilling **Jungle Cruise,** in which you drive your own small speedboat (called a *lancha*) or WaveRunner rapidly through Cancún's lagoon and mangrove estuaries out into the Caribbean Sea and a shallow reef. The excursion lasts about 2½ hours and costs $60 to $80, including snorkeling equipment. Many people prefer the companies offering two-person boats rather than WaveRunners, since they can sit side by side rather than one behind the other.

Jungle Cruise operators and names offering excursions change often. To find out what's available, check with a local travel agent or hotel tour desk. The popular **Aquaworld,** Bulevar Kukulcán Km 15.2 (www.aquaworld.com. mx; ✆ **998/848-8327**), calls its trip the Jungle Tour and charges $67 for the 2-hour excursion, which includes 30 minutes of snorkeling time. It even gives you a free snorkel and has the WaveRunner-style one-behind-the-other seating configuration. Multiple departures happen daily from 9am to 3pm. If you'd prefer a side-by-side boat so that you and your partner can talk or at least look at each other, try **Blue Ray,** Bulevar Kukulcán Km 13.5, next to Mambo Café (www.blueray.com.mx; ✆ **998/885-1108**), which charges $67, with departures every hour between 9am and 3pm. Expect to get wet, and wear plenty of sunscreen. Bring $5 for entrance to the national park, and tips are expected. If you just want to rent a WaveRunner, Aquaworld offers them for $50 per half-hour or $91 per hour.

Boating Excursions

ISLA MUJERES   The island of **Isla Mujeres,** just 13km (8 miles) offshore, is one of the most pleasant day trips from Cancún. At one end is **El Garrafón Natural Park,** which is good for snorkeling. At the other end is a captivating village with small shops, restaurants, and hotels, and **Playa Norte,** the island's best beach. If you're looking for relaxation and can spare the time, it's worth several days. For complete information about the island, see chapter 5.

The easiest way to get to Isla Mujeres is by **public ferry** from Puerto Juárez, which takes between 15 and 20 minutes, or with one of the less frequent ferries from any of the Hotel Zone departure points, which include El Embarcadero (at Playa Linda), Playa Tortuga, or Playa Caracol. There are also **water taxis** (more expensive, but faster), that run to the island from these departure points, and daylong **pleasure-boat cruises,** most of which leave from El Embarcadero.

The inexpensive Puerto Juárez **public ferries** lie just a few kilometers north of downtown Cancún. From Cancún City, take the Ruta 1 bus on Avenida Tulum to Puerto Juárez. The air-conditioned **Ultramar** (www. granpuerto.com.mx; ✆ **998/881-5890**) boats cost 70 pesos per person each way and take 15 to 20 minutes. Departures are every half-hour from 5am to 8:30pm and then at 9:30, 10:30, and 11:30pm. Ultramar also runs ferries between Isla Mujeres and El Embarcadero at Playa Linda, in the Hotel Zone. The cost is $11 one-way, $17 round-trip. Upon arrival, the ferry docks in downtown Isla Mujeres near all the shops, restaurants, hotels, and Playa Norte. You'll need a taxi to get to El Garrafón park at the other end of the island. You can stay as long as you like on the island and return by ferry, but be sure to confirm the time of the last returning ferry.

Pleasure-boat cruises to Isla Mujeres are a favorite pastime. Modern motorboats, yachts, sailboats (including the "Sea Passion" catamaran; www.seapassion.net), and even old-time sloops—more than 25 boats a day—take swimmers, sun lovers, snorkelers, and shoppers out on the translucent waters. Some tours include a snorkeling stop at El Garrafón, lunch on the beach, and a little time for shopping in downtown Isla Mujeres. Most leave at 9:30 or 10am, last about 5 or 6 hours, and include continental breakfast, lunch, and rental of snorkel gear. Others, particularly sunset and night cruises, go to beaches away from town for pseudo-pirate shows and include a lobster dinner (p. 93). If you want to actually see Isla Mujeres, go on a morning cruise, or travel on your own using the public ferry from Puerto Juárez. Prices for the day cruises vary depending on length and services included. Reservations aren't necessary.

An all-inclusive entrance fee of $74 ($54 for children) to **Garrafón Natural Reef Park ★★** (www.garrafon.com; ☎ **998/849-4748**) includes transportation from Playa Langosta in Cancún; meals; open bar with domestic drinks; access to the reef; and use of snorkel gear, kayaks, inner tubes, life vests, the pool, hammocks, and public facilities and showers (but not towels, so bring your own). There are also nature trails and several on-site restaurants.

Outdoor Activities & Attractions

DOLPHIN SWIMS On Isla Mujeres, you have the opportunity to swim with dolphins at **Dolphin Discovery ★★** (www.dolphindiscovery.com; ☎ **998/193-3360** or 193-3350). Groups of eight people swim with two dolphins and one trainer. Swimmers view an educational video and spend time in the water with the trainer and the dolphins before enjoying 15 minutes of free swimming time with them. Reservations are recommended (you can book online), and you must arrive an hour before your assigned swimming time, at 10:30am, 12:15pm, 1:50pm, or 3:30pm. The cost is $129 per person for the Dolphin Royal Swim. There are less expensive programs that allow you to learn about, touch, and hold the dolphins (but not swim with them) starting at $69. Ferry transfers from Playa Langosta in Cancún are available.

La Isla Shopping Village, Bulevar Kukulcán Km 12.5, has an impressive **Interactive Aquarium** (www.aquariumcancun.com.mx; ☎ **998/883-0411**), with dolphin swims and shows and the chance to feed a shark while immersed in the water in an acrylic cage. Guides inside the main tank use underwater microphones to point out the sea life, and even answer your questions. Open exhibition tanks enable visitors to touch a variety of marine life, including sea stars and manta rays. The dolphin educational program costs $85; the advanced program (which includes swimming with dolphins) costs $135; and the shark-feeding experience runs $70. The Aquarium now offers

The Hilton Cancún Golf club.

"dolphin-assisted therapy" designed to enhance personal well-being, as well. The entrance fee to the aquarium is $10, and it's open daily from 9am to 6pm.

GOLF & TENNIS   The 18-hole **Cancún Golf Club at Pok-Ta-Pok** (www. cancungolfclub.com; ℭ **998/883-0871**), located at Bulevar Kukulcán Km 7.5, is a Robert Trent Jones II design on the northern leg of the island. Greens fees run $175 for 18 holes in high season, $145 in low season, including shared golf cart (discounted fees after 2pm), with clubs renting for $45. A caddy costs $20 plus tip. The club is open daily from dawn to dusk.

Formerly part of the Hilton, the **Iberostar Playa Paraiso Golf Club** (www.iberostar.com; ℭ **984/877-2828**) has a championship 18-hole, par-72 course. Greens fees during high season for the public are typically $199 for 18 holes and $135 for twilight, which includes a shared golf cart, snacks, and soft drinks. Golf clubs and shoes are available for rent. The club is open daily from 6am to 6pm and accepts American Express, MasterCard, and Visa. The **Gran Meliá Cancún** (www.granmeliacancun.com; ℭ **998/881-1100**) has a 9-hole executive course; the greens fee is $35. The club is open daily from 7am to 3pm (last tee time is 2pm).

The Moon Palace Spa & Golf Club (www.palaceresorts.com; ℭ **998/ 881-6000**) is home to a Jack Nicklaus Signature Golf Course, the first along the Riviera Maya. The $260 greens fee ($160 for twilight) includes cart, snacks, and drinks.

WHERE TO EAT

A wide range of dining options spanning Mexican, American, European, and Asian cuisines dot Cancún's Hotel Zone and downtown, with some of Mexico's top restaurants located right here. Restaurants divide into roughly three categories: expensive and international in resort hotels; independent establishments along the lagoon (with great sunset views); and inexpensive Mexican eateries in El Centro (Cancún City). The establishments listed below are typically locally owned, one-of-a-kind restaurants or exceptional selections at area hotels. Many schedule live music. Unless otherwise indicated, parking is free.

One unique way to combine dinner with sightseeing is aboard the **Columbus Lobster Dinner Cruise** (www.thelobsterdinner.com; ℭ **998/193-3360**).

Cruising around the tranquil, turquoise waters of the lagoon, passengers feast on steak and lobster dinners accompanied by wine and live saxophone music. Cost is $89 per person for the lobster, surf-and-turf, or the "veggie lovers" menu. The two daily departures are from the Marina Aquatours Pier (Bulevar Kukulcán 6.25). A sunset cruise leaves at 5pm during the winter and 5:30pm during the summer; a moonlight cruise leaves at 8pm winter, 8:30pm summer. Another—albeit livelier—lobster dinner option is the **Captain Hook Lobster Dinner Cruise** (www.pirateshipcancun.com; ⓒ **998/849-4451**), which is similar, but with the added attraction of a pirate show involving two 28m (92-ft.) replicas of 18th-century Spanish galleons, making this a fun choice for families. The steak option costs $82 per person, and the lobster (or steak and lobster) option is $92 per person, including open bar. It departs at 7pm from El Embarcadero at Playa Linda, and returns at 10:30pm.

Isla Cancún

VERY EXPENSIVE

Aioli ★ MEDITERRANEAN   Le Méridien's signature restaurant offers Mediterranean gourmet specialties in an exquisite French setting. Wrought-iron chandeliers, hand-painted Talavera vases, original artwork, and candlelit tables define the elegant dining room. Examples of excellent appetizers include foie gras medallions and caramelized figs with a cherry brandy sauce, as well as Caesar salad tossed with jumbo shrimp. Favorite mains include the red snapper with a Spanish sausage risotto, and tender rack of lamb with couscous. The in-house pastry chef (whose dessert preparation you can watch in action) creates decadent sweets—I recommend the rich "Fifth Element" with chocolate and a berry sauce. Live flamenco music accompanies the highly attentive dinner service.

In Le Méridien Cancún Resort & Spa (p. 108), Retorno del Rey Km 14. ⓒ **998/881-2200.** Reservations recommended. No sandals or tennis shoes; men must wear long pants. Main courses 250–420 pesos. AE, MC, V. Daily 6:30–11am and 6–11pm.

The Club Grill ★★★ INTERNATIONAL   The Ritz-Carlton's Club Grill is one of Mexico's top-ranked restaurants. In a resort town that's increasingly going with the all-inclusive concept, this jazz and supper club stands out as an outstanding hotel restaurant open to the wider public. The gracious service starts in the anteroom, with its elegant seating and superb selection of cocktails and wines. It continues in the candlelit dining room, with shimmering silver and crystal. Gourmet appetizers include caramelized scallops, escargot, and sautéed foie gras. Among the excellent mains, you'll find roasted duck with chipotle; herbed rack of lamb; crispy organic chicken breast; and braised veal cheeks with vegetables, a fine potato puree, and a vanilla sauce. Finish with a pistachio crème brûlée or any of three impeccable soufflé selections (I suggest the caramel coconut). Guests seeking an even more gastronomically rich experience can sign up for the chef's table or take a gourmet cooking class at the hotel's renowned Culinary Center. The five-course chef's tasting menu changes seasonally and can be paired with wine.

In the Ritz-Carlton Cancún (p. 109), Retorno del Rey 36, Bulevar Kukulcán Km 13.5. ⓒ **998/881-0808.** Reservations required. No sandals or tennis shoes; men must wear long pants and collared shirts. Main courses 410–670 pesos. AE, DC, MC, V. Tues–Sun 7–11pm.

Lorenzillo's ★★ ☺ SEAFOOD   Almost always crowded, this Cancún favorite serves the best seafood in town. Lobster remains the star, and part of the appeal is plucking your dinner right out of the giant lobster tank set in the lagoon. Twinkle lights line the dock between Lorenzillo's and Limoncelle, the waterfront Italian restaurant next door, creating a magical reflection off the water. When Lorenzillo's main dining room is packed, a wharf-side bar handles the overflow. To start, I recommend *El Botin,* which consists of two soft-shell crabs breaded and fried to perfection. In addition to lobster (prepared in any of 20 different ways), you can also choose from shrimp stuffed with cheese and wrapped in bacon, *El Mastelero* (Caribbean grouper, sea bass, or hog fish, prepared to taste), and steak and seafood combinations. Climb into the large built-in wine cellar for a tasting of one of the 280 labels, from 16 countries, with some very high-end bottles available by the glass. For dessert, the chocolate volcano cake dripping with fudge blows the mind and expands the stomach. Lorenzillo's remains as popular with families as with couples looking for lagoon-side romance.

Bulevar Kukulcán Km 10.5. http://lorenzillos.com.mx. ✆ **998/883-1254.** Reservations recommended. Main courses 280–580 pesos. AE, MC, V. Daily 1pm–midnight.

EXPENSIVE

Casa Rolandi ★★ SWISS/ITALIAN   Casa Rolandi moved to a lagoon-front setting in 2011, an ideal spot for sunset dinners. Famous personalities, from international actors to Mexican presidents, have dined at this Cancún institution over the years. The core dishes are Swiss-Italian, although monthly thematic festivals—featuring, for example, seafood, venison, or asparagus—infuse the menu with creative selections using seasonal ingredients. The best starters include carpaccios and fresh salads. Among my favorite main courses are veal cheeks in wine served over polenta, jumbo shrimps baked in banana leaves with a Mayan *achiote* sauce, fresh seafood *tagliolini* draped in black ink, and grilled tuna served on a bed of arugula. Finish with the sublime tiramisu soaked in espresso and a rich chocolate and rum cream.

Bulevar Kukulcán Km 13.5. www.casarolandirestaurants.com. ✆ **998/883-1817.** Reservations recommended. Main courses 178–500 pesos. AE, MC, V. Daily 1pm–1am.

Elefanta ★ INDIAN   A partner restaurant to Thai (p. 97), Elefanta is one of the trendiest spots on Cancún's dining scene. The exotic waterfront space has two open kitchens overseen by an Indian chef—one for cooking in the clay tandoor oven, and the other for curries. Two extremely flavorful dishes are cinnamon-spiced tandoori shrimp and creamy lamb curry with cashews. The kitchens focus on fish, shrimp, and chicken dishes; this is also one of the few places in Cancún serving a substantial selection of quality vegetarian plates. Elefanta's chill-out music is coordinated with Thai, next door, and a DJ here spins hot mixes Thursday through Saturday nights. If you're in the mood for a cocktail, try one of the 30 exotic martinis.

La Isla Shopping Village, Bulevar Kukulcán 12.5. ✆ **998/176-8070.** Reservations recommended during high season. Main courses 170–505 pesos. AE, MC, V. Daily 5–11:30pm.

Gustino ★★★ ITALIAN   JW Marriott's signature restaurant Gustino offers romantic Italian dining unsurpassed in Cancún. The exquisite dining room boasts a gorgeous centerpiece candle display, well-spaced white linen tables, and floor-to-ceiling windows looking out to a lazy man-made lagoon and the beach beyond. The meal begins with a heaping basket of fresh-made Italian breads, including a flavorful basil and tomato focaccia. For an antipasto, the unusual pear carpaccio with red beet and fig puree tastes sublime, as does the *foie gras* with a pomegranate reduction and hint of pistachio. I also love the warm tossed spinach salad, topped with bacon, mushrooms, and walnut vinaigrette. Examples of expertly prepared main dishes are garlic and saffron sautéed seafood over pasta as well as a braised veal chop with prosciutto and wild mushrooms. The menu, which changes seasonally, features other homemade pastas and succulent steak and seafood selections. Gustino houses a wine cellar with an excellent variety of international grapes. Service is outstanding.

In the JW Marriott (p. 108), Bulevar Kukulcán Km 14.5. www.gustinorestaurant.jwmarriottcancun restaurants.com. ✆ **998/848-6849.** Reservations required. Dress code requires no beachwear. Main courses 210–585 pesos. AE, DC, MC, V. Daily 6–11pm.

Harry's ★★ STEAK   Situated adjacent to the Nichupté Lagoon, this is the Hotel Zone's top steakhouse. The dining room and waterfront terrace combine local stone and wood with burnt orange marble and large expanses of glass to create a sense of Californian chic. The attentive waitstaff brings to your table an impressive selection of beef cuts, as well as a presentation of ice-cold shellfish from the raw bar. The New York strips, rib-eyes, and other cuts of beef are broiled in a 927°C (1,700°F) oven, while the fish and seafood are grilled on a *parilla*. A variety of butters and sauces, such as chipotle lime and pepper corn, are available to choose from. A la carte selections blend Mexican and Asian influences, with fascinating results such as lobster *pozole*, black cod with miso and bok choy, and tuna steak with a spicy mayo and eel sauce served with jasmine rice and wasabi. Don't expect a kids' menu here: Even the Kobe beef burger is so big (and expensive) it could feed a family. A selection of more than 500 international and Mexican boutique wines accompanies the menu. This is also one of the few restaurants in Cancún serving kosher options.

Bulevar Kukulcán Km 14.2. www.harrys.com.mx. ✆ **998/840-6550.** Reservations recommended. Main courses 240–1,100 pesos. AE, MC, V. Daily 1pm–1am.

Puerto Madero ★★ ARGENTINE/SEAFOOD/STEAK   A tribute to the famed Puerto Madero of Buenos Aires, this trendy restaurant has earned a reputation for its steak and fish as well as its unique urban atmosphere. Overlooking the Nichupté Lagoon, the decor re-creates a 20th-century dock warehouse similar to what you'd find in the real Puerto Madero, with dark woods, exposed brick, visible pipes, and a marble-lit bar. A wall of glass separates the bustling dining room from the patio, where smoking is allowed. Puerto Madero offers an extensive selection of prime-quality beef cuts (not authentically Argentine, but tasty nevertheless), local and imported fish, seafood, and pasta. For a more traditional Argentine starter, the crispy tuna-filled empanada comes with a delectable *chimichurri* dipping sauce. Excellent mains include sea bass with shiitake mushrooms in soy sauce, black cod laced with hazelnut butter, and creative pastas such as crab tortellini smothered in white Parmesan sauce. Steak lovers will appreciate the selection of Kobe beef alongside more traditional cuts. Service is gracious and warm, and the wine and champagne list extensive.

Marina Barracuda, Bulevar Kukulcán Km 14.1. www.puertomaderorestaurantes.com. ✆ **998/885-2829,** -2831. Reservations recommended. Main courses 170–740 pesos. AE, MC, V. Daily 1pm–1am.

Mikado ☺ JAPANESE   Even if it's not the most authentic Japanese food, Mikado makes for a delightful evening for families and celebrating friends. Expect a loud, spirited atmosphere rather than a quiet, romantic experience. Dinners are prepared *teppanyaki*-style, with each communal table featuring a chef performing culinary tricks such as steaming onion volcanoes, spinning eggs, flying shrimp, and flaming zucchini. Complete dinners include miso soup, steamed rice, and a rich assortment of greens (so tasty they'll make converts of veggie-averse children) with a choice of chicken, steak, fresh fish, or seafood—all cooked to order. Cheerful Mexican cooks compete with each other for theatrical talent and are spurred on by the applauding diners. Among the a la carte selections are sushi, tempura, and udon noodles. Sasi Thai is an excellent open-air Thai restaurant just next door.

At the Marriott CasaMagna (p. 111), Bulevar Kukulcán Km 14.5. www.mikado.marriottcancun restaurants.com. ✆ **998/881-2030.** Reservations recommended. Main courses 175–450 pesos. AE, MC, V. Daily 5:30–11pm.

Sedona Grill ★ SOUTHWEST Sedona Grill successfully adapts French culinary techniques to Southwestern American cuisine. The result is exceptional, with fresh Mexican Caribbean ingredients infusing the original menu. Start with a light shrimp ceviche served with mango, Key lime, and Navajo fry bread, or the roasted corn bisque filled with country flavor. Excellent mains include *chimichurri* red snapper served with chile-lemon risotto, thick seared filet mignon so tender it almost cuts through like butter, and vegetarian chiles rellenos with sweet bell pepper rice and Oaxaca cheese. The high-ceiling wood beam dining room, created with subtle Southwestern decor, looks out to the JW Marriott pools and Caribbean Sea. An expansive breakfast buffet is offered here daily.

In the JW Marriott (p. 108), Bulevar Kukulcán Km 14.5. www.sedona.jwmarriottcancun.com. ✆ **998/848-9648.** Reservations required. Main courses 160–450 pesos. Breakfast buffet 320 pesos. AE, DC, MC, V. Daily 6:30am–11pm.

Thai ★★★ 📷 THAI Stepping into this exotic waterfront restaurant and lounge feels worlds removed from the adjacent Mexican shopping plaza. The tropical outdoor setting includes thick foliage and bamboo, where the best dining tables are a handful of intimate *palapas* (open-air huts, each with its own table, sofa, and flickering candles) constructed like tiny islands over the expansive lagoon. Unobtrusive service, soft red and blue lighting, and Asian chill-out music contribute to the ultra-chic ambience. Specialties prepared by Thai chefs include Pad Thai, chicken and shrimp curries, stir-fried beef, and an exquisite crunchy fried fish infused with a ginger, garlic, and electrifying habanero sauce. A DJ works the mesmerizing venue on weekends. Thai opens at sunset.

La Isla Shopping Village, Bulevar Kukulcán Km 12.5. www.thai.com.mx. ✆ **998/176-8070.** Reservations recommended during high season. Main courses 230–519 pesos. AE, MC, V. Daily 6pm–midnight (lounge open until 1am).

MODERATE
La Destilería ☺ MEXICAN For quality Mexican food and a sampling of Mexico's potent export, this lagoon-front restaurant is your place (keep an eye out for Pancho, the lagoon crocodile who often comes to visit). La Destilería is more than a tequila-inspired restaurant; it's a mini-museum honoring the "spirit" of Mexico with more than 150 brands of tequila, including some treasures that never find their way across the border. A tequila tour takes place at various times between 1 and 5pm daily, and patrons can always order tequila "samplers" at their tables. No surprise, the margaritas are among the island's best. You'll also find a creative Mexican menu, with everything from quesadillas with zucchini flower, cheese, and green peppers to *arrachera* steak fajitas served in a hot *molcajete* pot with chorizo,

black beans, and avocado. Live mariachi music plays nightly from 8 to 9pm, and there's a kids' playroom and menu with tacos, chicken, and fish.

Bulevar Kukulcán Km 12.65, across from Kukulcán Plaza. www.ladestileria.com.mx. ℂ **998/885-1086,** -1087. Main courses 140–305 pesos. Tequila tour 85 pesos. AE, MC, V. Daily 1pm–midnight.

La Madonna SWISS/ITALIAN   This architecturally dazzling restaurant and bar emerges unexpectedly from La Isla Shopping Village like an Italian Renaissance showroom along the canal. Inside, the dining room resembles one of the mystical international Buddha Bars, with an enormous replica of the Mona Lisa looking over the dazzled clientele. La Madonna offers Italian and Swiss cuisine, including assorted seafood, antipasti, pasta and risotto, grilled fish, steak, and fondues. Main dishes include chicken in limoncello sauce, homemade meatballs topped with mozzarella, and a veal chop in prosciutto sauce. For dessert, request the tableside flambéed strawberries. Many people come just for dessert and drinks (p. 103).

La Isla Shopping Village, Bulevar Kukulcán 12.5. www.lamadonna.com.mx. ℂ **998/883-2222.** Reservations recommended. Main courses 160–475 pesos. AE, MC, V. Daily noon–1am.

INEXPENSIVE

El Fish Fritanga Pescadillas MEXICAN/SEAFOOD   Simple beach chairs and tables sit in the sand among beached fishing boats and a small dock. Just below La Destilería (above), Pescadillas—as it's known to locals—offers friendly service, refreshing (and promptly served) beverages, and tasty snacks. Munch on any number of appetizers, such as tostadas packed with sizzling fish, shrimp, or octopus, or snappy, lemon-drenched ceviches of all kinds. Chicken and pasta are available for more conventional palates, but I'd recommend diving into the "aphrodisiac lobster," grilled to perfection with fragrant cloves of garlic and butter. Alongside the seafood specialties are sizzling platters of fajitas served with rice and beans, and the best salsa I've had on the island. This is a fun, casual place for lingering over simple food and drinks, and perfect for sunsets over the lagoon.

Bulevar Kukulcán Km 12.6. ℂ **998/840-6216.** Main courses 80–300 pesos. AE, MC, V. Daily 11am–10pm.

Ciudad Cancún

MODERATE

Labná YUCATECAN   Coming for a meal at Labná is like a very special trip to a Yucatecan home, a place that serves delicious Mayan food and treats you like a friend. Even before you order, you'll have a chance to sample a squash-based Mayan sauce and grilled red onions with tortilla chips. Specialties include a sublime lime soup, *poc chuc* (marinated, barbecue-style pork), chicken or pork *pibil* (sweet and spicy barbecue sauce served over shredded meat wrapped in banana leaves), and unusual appetizers such as *papadzules* (tortillas stuffed with boiled eggs in a pumpkin-seed sauce). The Labná Special is a sampler of four typically Yucatecan main courses, including *poc chuc* (grilled marinated pork), while another specialty of the house is baked suckling pig, served with guacamole. The refreshing Yucatecan beverage, *agua de chaya*—a blend of sweetened water and the leaf of the *chaya* plant, to which sweet Xtabentun liquor (a type of anise) can be added for an extra kick—is also served here. The vaulted-ceiling dining room is decorated with a mural of a pre-Hispanic Yucatecan scene, as well as with black-and-white photographs of Mérida, the capital of the Yucatán, dating from the 1900s. A local trio plays weekends at lunch.

Margaritas 29, next to Cristo Rey church and La Habichuela restaurant. www.labna.com. ✆ **998/884-3158.** Reservations recommended. Main courses 84–233 pesos. AE, MC, V. Daily noon–10pm.

La Habichuela ★★★ 📷 SEAFOOD   Boasting a musically accented sculpture garden with flowering white-lit hibiscus trees and replicas of Mayan artifacts, this award-winning restaurant remains downtown's most elegant table. For an unforgettable culinary adventure, order crème of *habichuela* (string bean) soup; giant shrimp in any number of sauces, including Jamaican tamarind, tequila, or ginger and mushroom; and exotic Mayan coffee prepared tableside with Xtabentun (a strong, sweet, anise-based liqueur). The menu of family recipes includes luscious ceviches, Caribbean lobsters, an inventive seafood "parade," and shish kabob flambé with shrimp and lobster or beef. For something divine, try *cocobichuela*, lobster and shrimp in sweet curry served in a coconut shell with rice and topped with fruit. Finish your meal with a boozy butterscotch crepe. La Habichuela, in operation since 1977, now has a second branch in the Hotel Zone called **La Habichuela Sunset,** which features giant windows overlooking the lagoon and is close to La Isla Shopping Village. It's open daily from noon to midnight and features a pre-Hispanic Mayan show Monday, Wednesday, and Friday at 8pm.

Margaritas 25 (in downtown). www.lahabichuela.com. ✆ **998/884-3158.** La Habichuela Sunset at Bulevar Kukulcán Km 12.6 (in Hotel Zone). ✆ **998/840-6280.** Reservations recommended in high season. Main courses 170–450 pesos. AE, MC, V. Daily noon–midnight.

La Parilla ★ MEXICAN   A downtown institution, La Parilla is a celebration of Mexican tradition featuring a colorful open-air dining room, nightly mariachi music, and a rich menu delivering excellent food. You'll find authentic dishes from the garden and the Caribbean, as well as Mexican specialties such as *mole* enchiladas or grilled Aztec steak wrapped in cactus leaves and stuffed with onions. There are also tacos of every variety (*pastor* is the specialty), sumptuous grilled steaks and seafood, mixed grill plates for two served sizzling hot, and Maya treats such as *poc-chuc* pork tenderloin. This is a place to eat, drink, and be merry, and tequila samplers are available for those willing to risk a hangover the next morning. One drawback: There are fans but no air-conditioning, so take a cold shower before you come here on a hot night.

Av. Yaxchilán 51. ✆ **998/287-8118.** Main courses 103–510 pesos. AE, MC, V. Daily 11:30am–1:30am.

Pericos MEXICAN   A rowdy spectacle of Mexican folklore, this restaurant-cantina resembling a Latin carnival is a touristy place to come with friends looking to fiesta. Live entertainment is the key attraction, with a marimba orchestra, would-be comedians, and theatrical waiters on the lookout for closet performers among the clientele. Expect costume-clad hosts peddling tequila shots, photos, and party favors. The menu features meat and seafood brochettes, sizzling fajitas, juicy steaks, and Caribbean seafood, as well as an inexpensive selection of tacos and a full bar. The experience here is less about the food than the atmosphere, though.

Av. Yaxchilán 61. ✆ **998/884-3152.** Main courses 120–520 pesos. AE, MC, V. Daily noon–1am.

INEXPENSIVE

100% Natural BREAKFAST/HEALTH FOOD   If you want a healthy reprieve from an overindulgent night—or just like your meals as fresh and natural as possible—this favorite national chain is your oasis. No matter what your dining preference, you owe it to yourself to try a Mexican tradition, the fresh-fruit *licuados* (tropical juices served in creative combinations—the "traditional" blends orange, grapefruit, and carrot). Milk smoothies, yogurt shakes, aloe vera drinks, and other healthy beverages round out the menu. You'll find more than just quality drinks, though—there's a bountiful selection of healthy Mexican plates and terrific sandwiches served on whole-grain bread, with multiple options for vegetarians. Breakfast is delightful, and the attached bakery features all-natural baked goods such as chocolate croissants and banana muffins.

Av. Sunyaxchen 63. www.100natural.com.mx. ✆ **998/884-0102.** Breakfast 50–75 pesos; main courses 68–190 pesos. AE, MC, V. Daily 7am–10:30pm.

Rolandi's Pizzeria ☺ ITALIAN   At this patio restaurant-bar and pizzeria known for dependable Italian delights, you can choose from an enticing selection of antipasti and salads, calzones, and baked dishes, such as roast beef, garlic shrimp, and tender chicken. There are also almost two dozen delicious, if greasy, wood-oven pizzas (individual size) ranging from simple to exotic. Why not try the deliciously spicy "Fiesta Mexicana" pizza with tomato, cheese, Mexican sausage, and jalapeños, or the veggie-lover's "Jardinera" with tomato, cheese, asparagus, mushrooms, green peppers, carrots, and olives? A Cancún institution since 1979, Rolandi's has additional branches in Cozumel and Isla Mujeres (see chapter 5). It's as popular with locals as with tourists.

Av. Cobá 12 (at Av. Tulum). www.rolandi.com. ✆ **998/884-4047.** Pasta 112–140 pesos; pizza and main courses 99–180 pesos. AE, MC, V. Daily 12:30pm–12:30am.

SHOPPING

Aside from the surrounding natural splendor, Cancún is known throughout Mexico for its diverse shops and festive malls catering to international tourists. Visitors from the United States may find apparel more expensive in Cancún, but the selection is much broader than at other Mexican resorts. Numerous duty-free shops offer excellent value on European goods. **Ultrafemme,** Av. Tulum Sur 260 in Plaza las Americas (www.ultrafemme.com; ✆ **998/272-5476**), specializes in imported cosmetics, perfumes, and fine jewelry and watches. This downtown Cancún location offers slightly lower prices than Hotel Zone branches in Plaza Caracol, La Isla, and Luxury Avenue in Kukulcán Plaza. It's open Monday to Saturday from 10am to 7pm.

Handicrafts are more limited and more expensive in Cancún than in other regions of Mexico because they are not produced here. They are available, though; the best open-air crafts market is **Mercado 28** in Cancún City. A less enticing open-air market in the Hotel Zone is **Coral Negro,** Bulevar Kukulcán Km 9.5, next to Plaza Dady'O, open daily from 7am to 11pm. **Plaza La Fiesta,** next to the Cancún Center (✆ **998/883-4519**), is a large Mexican outlet store selling handicrafts, jewelry, tequila, leather, and accessories. It's typically open daily from 9am to 10pm or later.

Cancún's main venues are the **malls**—not quite as grand as their U.S. counterparts, but close. All are air-conditioned, sleek, and sophisticated. Most lie on Bulevar Kukulcán between Km 7 and Km 12. Kukulcán Plaza and La Isla offer the most extensive parking garages.

The **Kukulcán Plaza** (www.kukulcanplaza.com; ✆ **998/885-2200**) houses hundreds of shops, restaurants, and entertainment. It has a bank, a bowling alley, several crafts stores, a Play City with gambling machines, a liquor and tobacco store, several bathing-suit specialty stores, music stores, a drugstore, a leather-goods shop (including shoes and sandals), and a store specializing in silver from

La Isla Shopping Village by night.

Taxco. U.S. eateries include Häagen-Dazs and Ruth's Chris Steak House, and there's an extensive food court. The adjacent Luxury Avenue complex features designer labels such as Cartier, Coach, Fendi, Louis Vuitton, Salvatore Ferragamo, and Ultrafemme. The mall is open daily from 8am to 10pm, until 11pm during high season. Assistance for those with disabilities is available upon request, and wheelchairs, strollers, and lockers are available at the information desk.

Most people come to entertainment-oriented **Forum by the Sea,** Bulevar Kukulcán Km 9 (www.forumbythesea.com.mx; © **998/883-4425**), for the food and fun, choosing from Hard Rock Cafe, Carlos 'n' Charlie's, Chili's, and CoCo Bongo, plus an extensive food court. The few shops and restaurants include Harley-Davidson, Nike, Señor Frog's, Sunglass Island, and Zingara Beachwear and Swimwear. The mall is open daily from 10am to midnight (bars remain open later).

One of Mexico's most appealing malls is **La Isla Shopping Village,** Bulevar Kukulcán Km 12.5 (www.laislacancun.com.mx; © **998/883-5025**), a wonderful open-air complex that borders the lagoon. Walkways lined with quality shops and restaurants cross little canals (boat rides are even offered), and an attractive boardwalk lines the lagoon itself, as well as an interactive aquarium and dolphin swim facility (p. 92). Shops include Brooks Brothers, Guess, Hugo Boss, Nautica, Massimo Dutti, Nine West, Puma, Tommy Hilfiger, and Zara, as well as Mexican handicrafts stores Casa Mexicana and Plaza La Fiesta. Among the dining choices are Johnny Rockets, Chili's, Italianni's, Planet Hollywood, the romantic Thai restaurant (p. 97), and Elefanta (p. 95). You will also find a movie theater and several lounges, including those at La Madonna (p. 98) and Thai. La Isla is open daily from 9am to 11pm.

ENTERTAINMENT & NIGHTLIFE

Cancún's party reputation is not confined to spring break—the action here continues year-round. While the revelry often begins by day at the beach, the sun-drenched crowd heads to happy hour at the rocking bars located along the Hotel Zone, which often serve two-for-one drinks at sunset. Hotels play in the happy hour scene, with drink specials to entice visitors and guests from other resorts. Come night, the hottest centers of action are also along Kukulcán, and include **Plaza Dady'O, Forum**

by the Sea, and **La Isla Shopping Village.** These entertainment plazas transform into true spring break madness for most of March and April.

The Club & Music Scene

Clubbing in Cancún is a favorite part of the vacation experience and can go on each night until the sun rises over that incredibly blue sea. Several big hotels have nightclubs or schedule live music in their lobby bars. At the clubs, expect to stand in lines on weekends and pay a cover charge equivalent to about $40 with open bar ($15–$25 without open bar, and then about $10 per drink). Some of the higher-priced clubs include live entertainment. The places listed in this section are air-conditioned and accept American Express, MasterCard, and Visa.

Numerous restaurants, such as **Carlos 'n' Charlie's, Hard Rock Cafe,** and **Señor Frog's,** double as nighttime party spots, offering wildish fun at a fraction of the price of more costly clubs.

Grupo Dady offers a package deal enticing clubbers to party in all of its neighboring bars, including Dady'O, Terresta, UltraClub, Sweet Club, and Dos Equis Bar. It costs $45 to $55 per person depending on the night and includes open bar; buy tickets at any of the Grupo Dady bars.

If you have been drinking when you're ready to go back to your accommodations, take public transportation or have someone with you rather than drive or get in a taxi alone.

The City ★★ One of the largest nightclubs in the world, The City features nine bars over three floors with progressive electronic music spun by visiting DJs from New York, L.A., and Mexico City (the DJ booth looks like an airport control tower). This is where celebrities often come to party when they're in town. You actually need never leave, as The City is a day-and-night club. The Cabana Beach opens at 10am and features beach cabanas, a pool, and food and bar service

with frequent activities, pool parties, and bikini contests. The City Discotheque accommodates up to 6,000 unrelenting club-goers. Open from 10:30pm to 4am, the 743-sq.-m (8,000-sq.-ft.) nightclub features a one-million-watt sound system, stunning light shows, and several VIP areas. Bulevar Kukulcán Km 9.5. www.thecitycancun.com. ✆ **998/848-8380.** Cover $25; $45 with open bar.

CoCo Bongo ★★★ Continuing its reputation as the hottest night spot in town, CoCo Bongo combines an enormous dance club with extravagant theme shows: Think flying acrobats, bar-top conga lines, soap bubbles, and confetti streamers. It has no set dance floor—you dance anywhere, and that includes on the tables, on the bar, and even on the stage with the occasional live band. This place regularly packs in as many as 1,800 people—you have to experience it to believe it. Despite its capacity, lines are long on weekends and in high season. The music alternates between

Clubgoers wait to get in to CoCo Bongo.

Caribbean, salsa, house, hip-hop, techno, and classics from the '70s, '80s, and '90s. Open from 10:30pm to 3:30am, CoCo Bongo draws a hip young crowd. Plaza Forum by the Sea, Bulevar Kukulcán Km 9.5. www.cocobongo.com.mx. ℭ **998/883-5061.** Weekend cover $65 with open bar; $55 weekdays with open bar.

Dady'O This is a popular rave among the young and brave, with frequent long lines. Grupo Dady offers a package deal that includes open bar and entrance to all five of its neighboring bars (see above), and this is the granddaddy of them. It opens nightly at 10pm and has a giant dance floor and awesome light system. Bulevar Kukulcán Km 9.5. www.dadyo.com. ℭ **998/883-3333.** Cover $20–$25.

Mandala Next to The City, Mandala is a hot addition to Cancún's vibrant nightlife. The imposing facade of this Asian-inspired club is open to the street, also known here as Party Row, so anyone passing by can get a clear sense of Mandala's vibe. The sexy crowd parties on all three of the red-lit floors, dancing into the wee hours. Mandala opens nightly at 9:30pm. Bulevar Kukulcán Km 9. www.mandalanightclub.com. ℭ **998/848-8380.** Cover $20–$25.

The Lobby Lounge at The Ritz-Carlton ★ CoCo Bongo it's not, but for socialites who want a more refined experience than what they'll find along Cancún's party row, the Ritz-Carlton's lobby bar offers a good place to start. Live music is offered nightly (the singer takes requests), while patrons choose from flavored margaritas, creative martinis, and single-malt whiskeys. It's open daily from 5pm to midnight. The Ritz-Carlton Cancún (p. 109), Retorno del Rey 36, off Bulevar Kukulcán Km 13.5. ℭ **998/881-0808.**

La Madonna With more than 150 creative martini selections accompanied by ambient music, this trendy restaurant-bar in La Isla shopping center also offers authentic Swiss-Italian cuisine, as well as delicious desserts (p. 98). Enjoy your red mandarin, lychee, or green apple martini, or glass of wine elbow to elbow with Cancún's beautiful people on the outdoor patio. Cognac and cigars are served upstairs, and there's an international wine selection. Bossa nova and lounge music are the norm. It's open daily from noon to 1am. La Isla Shopping Village, Bulevar Kukulcán Km 12.5. www.lamadonna.com.mx. ℭ **998/883-2222.**

Light ★ On the lagoon front joined to the trendy Katsu-Ya Japanese restaurant, Light Nightclub caters to a sushi-loving and slightly older crowd than what you'll find along the Hotel Zone's party row. Martini specials, ladies' nights, karaoke, guest DJs, and other themed events happen regularly, and live music kicks off at midnight. The sexy clientele from Katsu-Ya tends to spill over to Light's dance floor following dinner and cocktails at the bar. It's open Monday to Saturday from 6pm until 2am. Bulevar Kukulcán Km 13.5. www.katsuya.com.mx. ℭ **998/840-6014.** Cover including open bar 250–350 pesos.

The Performing Arts

Several hotels host **Mexican fiesta nights,** including a buffet dinner and a folk-loric dance show; admission with dinner and open bar costs about 550 pesos unless you're at an all-inclusive resort that includes this as part of the package. Check out the show at **Hacienda Sisal** (www.haciendasisal.com; ℭ **998/848-8220**), located at Bulevar Kukulcán Km 13.5, which is offered Tuesday and Thursday nights starting at 8pm. **La Habichuela Sunset** (www.lahabichuela.com; ℭ **998/840-6240**), at Bulevar Kukulcán Km 12.6 in front of Kukulcán Plaza, offers a pre-Hispanic show with Mayan influences Monday, Wednesday, and Friday nights at 8pm.

WHERE TO STAY

Island hotels—almost all of them offering modern facilities and English-speaking staffs—line the beach like concrete dominoes. The water on the upper end of the island facing Bahía de Mujeres is placid, while beaches lining the long side of the island facing the Caribbean are subject to choppier water and even waves on windy days. (For more information on swimming safety, see "Beaches, Watersports & Boat Tours," earlier in this chapter.) Be aware that the farther south you go on the island, the longer it takes (20–30 min. in traffic) to get back to the "action spots," which are primarily between the Plaza Flamingo and Punta Cancún on the island and along Avenida Tulum on the mainland.

In the wake of the international economic crisis, hotels and resorts here have increasingly turned to all-inclusive concepts, either in full or as an option. This puts an emphasis on quantity of consumption at lower prices, but with quality sometimes compromised. It also means an occasional dip in service, activities, and amenities, particularly at hotels that have dramatically reduced prices. Some of the more expensive hotels have struggled to survive in this environment, and more changes to Cancún's hotel landscape are likely. Among the resorts that are not all-inclusive are the Fiesta Americana Grand Coral Beach, Le Méridien, the Marriott hotels, and The Ritz-Carlton. These resorts are, in my opinion, the best on Isla Cancún (Cancún Island, also known as the "Hotel Zone").

Many major hotel chains have real estate in the Hotel Zone. The reality is that Cancún is so popular as a **package destination** from the U.S. that prices and special deals are often the deciding factor for consumers rather than loyalty to any one hotel brand. Ciudad Cancún offers independently owned, smaller, less expensive lodging (which is typically not all-inclusive). For condo, home, and villa rentals, check with **Cancún Hideaways** (www.cancun-hideaways.com; ☎ **817/522-4466**), an American company specializing in vacation rentals in downtown and the Hotel Zone—many at prices much lower than comparable hotel stays. Owner Maggie Rodriguez, a former resident of Cancún, has made this niche market her specialty.

The "concrete dominoes" of Cancún's Hotel Zone.

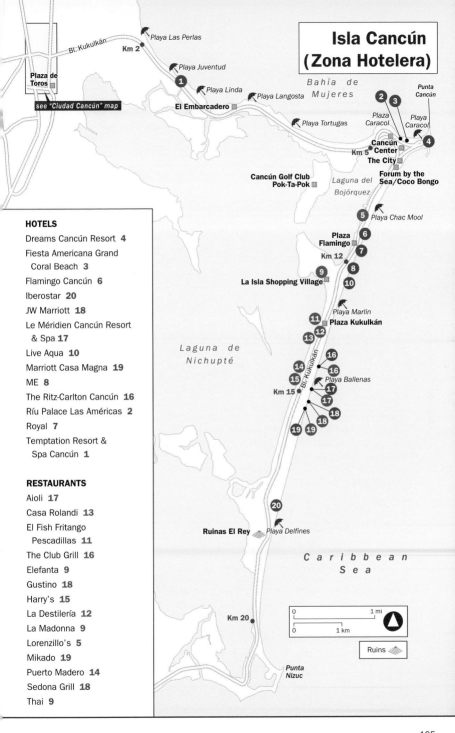

Isla Cancún (Zona Hotelera)

Bl. Kukulkán
Km 2

Playa Las Perlas

Plaza de Toros

see "Ciudad Cancún" map

Playa Juventud
1
Playa Linda
Playa Langosta
El Embarcadero

Bahía de Mujeres

Punta Cancún

2 **3**

Plaza Caracol

Playa Caracol

Playa Tortugas

Cancún Center
Km 5
The City

4

Cancún Golf Club Pok-Ta-Pok

Laguna del Bojórquez

Forum by the Sea/Coco Bongo

5 Playa Chac Mool

Plaza Flamingo
6
7
Km 12
8

9
La Isla Shopping Village
10

Playa Marlin
11 **Plaza Kukulkán**
13 **12**

Laguna de Nichupté

16
14 **16**
15 Playa Ballenas
Km 15 **17**
17
18
19 **19** **18**

20
Ruinas El Rey Playa Delfines

Caribbean Sea

Km 20

Punta Nizuc

0 — 1 mi
0 — 1 km

Ruins

HOTELS

Dreams Cancún Resort **4**
Fiesta Americana Grand Coral Beach **3**
Flamingo Cancún **6**
Iberostar **20**
JW Marriott **18**
Le Méridien Cancún Resort & Spa **17**
Live Aqua **10**
Marriott Casa Magna **19**
ME **8**
The Ritz-Carlton Cancún **16**
Ríu Palace Las Américas **2**
Royal **7**
Temptation Resort & Spa Cancún **1**

RESTAURANTS

Aioli **17**
Casa Rolandi **13**
El Fish Fritango Pescadillas **11**
The Club Grill **16**
Elefanta **9**
Gustino **18**
Harry's **15**
La Destilería **12**
La Madonna **9**
Lorenzillo's **5**
Mikado **19**
Puerto Madero **14**
Sedona Grill **18**
Thai **9**

Ruins near a modern Cancún hotel.

The hotel listings in this chapter begin on Cancún Island and finish in Cancún City (the real downtown). Stay in the Hotel Zone to be next to the stunning Caribbean beaches by day and the vibrant entertainment by night. If you prefer a more authentic Mexico and are interested in bargain accommodations, downtown Cancún is preferable. Unless otherwise indicated, parking is free at Cancún's hotels.

Isla Cancún

VERY EXPENSIVE

Fiesta Americana Grand Coral Beach Resort & Spa ★★★ ☺ This grand coral-colored resort sits on Punta Cancún, offering relative seclusion despite its easy walking distance to the Hotel Zone's key entertainment. It's one of the top-rated resorts in Mexico and attracts an international clientele for good reason. In front, the whitest sand beach glides into emerald waters, where the surf is calm and perfect for swimming. Yet you may feel tempted not to leave the beautiful multi-tiered pools with waterfalls, fountains, swim-up bars, and lush surroundings. The all-suites hotel includes junior suites with sunken sitting areas, whitewashed furniture, marble bathrooms, and soothing California colors. The marvelous 40,000-square-foot spa—the best in Cancún—includes a hydrotherapy program and innovative "gemstone" treatments. The Fiesta Kids club challenges the little ones to sand castle building, shell hunting, and other beach-front contests, and there are daylong sports and social activities planned for adults as well. Service throughout this luxury property is gracious and attentive. La Jolla is the hotel's excellent Mexican restaurant.

Bulevar Kukulcán Km 9.5, 77500 Cancún, Q. Roo. www.fiestamericanagrand.com. ☏ **877/927-7666** in the U.S., or 998/881-3200. Fax 998/881-3288. 602 units. High season $300 and up double, $400 and up club-floor double; low season $200 and up double, $300 and up club-floor double. AE, MC, V. **Amenities:** 5 restaurants; 4 bars; babysitting; children's programs; concierge w/multilingual staff; concierge-level rooms; fitness center; outdoor pool w/swim-up bars; sauna; world-class spa; watersports. *In room:* A/C, flatscreen TV, hair dryer, minibar, MP3 docking station, Wi-Fi (for a fee).

Iberostar ☺ This Spanish resort chain took over the Hilton Cancún in late 2011, renovating the public areas and pools, but keeping the cool minimalist decor of the guest rooms. It sits on 100 hectares (247 acres) of prime beachside property, which means every room has a sea view (some have both sea and lagoon views). And there's an 18-hole par-72 golf course across the street, which is among the city's best. The sprawling multi-section swimming pool stretches out to the gorgeous beach, and there's a full-length soccer field on the other side as well as a mini waterpark for kids. The four restaurants include a Mexican,

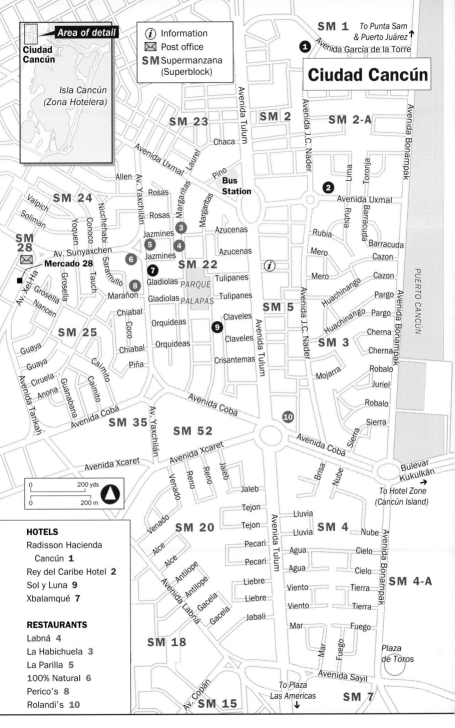

Ciudad Cancún

Japanese, steakhouse, and gourmet option. Despite the hotel's vibrant energy and wide range of activities, don't expect highly personalized service. This is a giant all-inclusive resort attached to a convention center.

Bulevar Kukulcán Km 17, Retorno Lacandones, 77500 Cancún, Q. Roo. www.iberostar.com. © **998/ 881-8000.** Fax 998/881-8080. 426 units. $348 and up double all-inclusive. 3-night minimum. AE, DC, MC, V. **Amenities:** 4 restaurants; 2 bars; amphitheater; children's programs; golf club; 7 inter-connected outdoor pools w/swim-up bar; 2 whirlpools; full service spa; soccer field; 2 lighted tennis courts. *In room:* A/C, flatscreen TV, CD/MP3 player, hair dryer, minibar, Wi-Fi (for a fee).

JW Marriott Cancún Resort & Spa ★★★   This remains my favorite resort in Cancún, a refined oasis that offers exceptional service without pretense. Despite its many touches of elegance, the JW is friendly and even family-friendly—although more families stay at the neighboring and less expensive Marriott CasaMagna (p. 111). From the beautifully decorated marble and flower-filled lobby to the luxurious oceanview rooms, the resort combines classic and Caribbean styling with warm Mexican service. Guest rooms and suites feature exquisite marble bathrooms with separate tub and shower, private balconies, flatscreen TVs, bathrobes and slippers, and twice-daily maid service. The breathtaking infinity pools meander through the property and overlook the sea. A spectacular 3,252-sq.-m (35,000-sq.-ft.) spa includes an indoor pool and whirlpool, high-tech fitness center, and full range of massages, body scrubs and polishes, facials, and healing water treatments. **Gustino** (p. 95) is the hotel's outstanding Italian restaurant, while **Sedona Grill** (p. 97) combines Southwestern U.S. and Caribbean flavors.

Bulevar Kukulcán Km 14.5, 77500 Cancún, Q. Roo. www.jwmarriottcancun.com. © **800/223- 6388** in the U.S., or 998/848-9600. Fax 998/848-9601. 448 units. High season $350 and up double; low season $200 and up double. AE, DC, MC, V. **Amenities:** 2 restaurants; deli; lobby bar and pool bar; club floor w/special amenities and complimentary cocktails; concierge; access to children's programs at Marriott CasaMagna; indoor pool; dive pool w/waterfalls; expansive outdoor pool; sauna; full-service spa w/fitness center and aerobics studio; steam room; 3 whirlpools. *In room:* A/C, flatscreen TV, hair dryer, minibar, Wi-Fi (for a fee).

Le Méridien Cancún Resort & Spa ★★   Frequented by Europeans familiar with this French-inspired hotel line, Le Méridien is among Cancún's most inviting luxury options. The elegant lobby, featuring original artwork, fresh flowers, and subtle lighting, creates a sense of intimacy that extends throughout the hotel. Guest rooms are generous in size, with small balconies overlooking the three-tiered infinity pool; due to the hotel's design, the rooms do not have full ocean views. Each has a large marble bathroom with a separate tub and glassed-in shower. The resort's **Spa del Mar** is one of Mexico's top European spas. Among the creative treatments using local ingredients such as coffee, chocolate, and honey is the "chocolate fondue wrap." **Aioli** (p. 94) is the splendid fine-dining restaurant connected to the lobby. The hotel staff offers calm, personalized service. An all-inclusive option is now offered as well.

Retorno del Rey Km 14, Zona Hotelera, 77500 Cancún, Q. Roo. www.starwoodhotels.com/le meridien. © **800/543-4300** in the U.S., or 998/881-2200. Fax 998/881-2201. 213 units. $230 and up double. Ask about all-inclusive and special spa packages. AE, DC, MC, V. Small dogs accepted with prior reservation. **Amenities:** 2 restaurants; bar; babysitting; supervised children's program w/clubhouse, play equipment, and wading pool; concierge; florist; 3 cascading outdoor pools; European spa w/salon, whirlpool, steam room, treatment rooms, fitness center, and yoga classes; 2 lighted championship tennis courts. *In room:* A/C, flatscreen TV, CD player, hair dryer, minibar, Wi-Fi (for a fee).

Deciphering Hotel Prices

In all price categories, Cancún's hotels generally set their rates in dollars, so they are immune to variations in the peso. Travel agents and wholesalers always have air/hotel packages available. Cancún also has numerous all-inclusive properties, which allow you to take a fixed-cost vacation. Note that the price quoted when you call a hotel's reservation number may not include Cancún's 14% tax. Prices can vary considerably throughout the year and have dropped considerably during the global financial crisis, so it pays to consult a travel agent or shop around.

Live Aqua ★   The all-inclusive Live Aqua is one of the most stylish resorts in the Hotel Zone—New Age music emanates from each corner, behind every palm tree, and around the eight tempting pools. The spa is outstanding, with indoor and outdoor treatments that incorporate the best techniques from around the globe. All of the soothing guest rooms have balconies facing the ocean, iHome sound systems, luxury bath amenities, and artisan soaps. I don't remember the last time I slept in such a comfortable bed; Egyptian cotton sheets share company with a plush collection of form-fitting pillows. The only things calling you out of bed are likely to be the clear blue skies, deep turquoise waters, and brilliant white sand outside your window—as well as the fact that everything is included, except for some spa services.

Bulevar Kukulcán Km 12.5, 77500 Cancún, Q. Roo. www.feel-aqua.com. ℂ **800/343-7821** in the U.S., or 998/881-7600. Fax 998/881-7635. 371 units. High season $490 and up double; low season $290 and up double. All-inclusive. AE, MC, V. **Amenities:** 3 gourmet restaurants; 3 bars; beach club; 8 outdoor pools; room service; sauna; boutique spa and gym; 2 tennis courts; yoga and other fitness activities. *In room:* A/C, flatscreen TV w/DVD, hair dryer, minibar, MP3 docking station, Wi-Fi.

The Ritz-Carlton, Cancún ★★★ ☺   Elegant public areas and guest rooms overlook the magnificent pools and beach, offering refinement that's a hallmark of the Ritz chain—think exquisite artwork, carpets, chandeliers, and fresh flowers in the public areas, and spacious guest rooms with marble baths and fluffy featherbeds. The resort's restaurants are among the best in all of Mexico, including **The Club Grill** (p. 94); **Fantino,** which offers the most elegant dining in Cancún; and **Casitas,** for a romantic beachside meal in a candlelit cabaña. A world-class Culinary Center offers gourmet cooking classes in a lavish Caribbean-front kitchen along with an option to dine with the chef. In addition to the daytime Kids Camp, the Ritz offers a "Kids' Night Out" program that allows parents to steal away for the evening. The beachfront Kayantá Spa bases many of its treatments on traditional Mayan rituals and therapies. Guests can enjoy a drink in the **Lobby Lounge** (p. 103), a refined space for a nightcap.

Retorno del Rey 36, off Bulevar Kukulcán Km 13.5, 77500 Cancún, Q. Roo. www.ritzcarlton.com. ℂ **800/241-3333** in the U.S. and Canada, or 998/881-0808. Fax 998/881-0815. 365 units. May 1–Dec 21 $280 and up double, $430 and up club floor and suites; Dec 22–Jan 3 $700 and up double, $1,000 and up club floor and suites; Jan 4–Apr 30 $400 double, $640 and up club floor and suites. AE, MC, V. **Amenities:** 6 restaurants; lounge w/sushi bar; babysitting; children's programs; concierge; club floors; culinary center; fitness center; 2 outdoor pools; spa; Cliff Drysdale tennis center w/3 lighted tennis courts; tequila tastings. *In room:* A/C, flatscreen TV, CD player, hair dryer, minibar, Wi-Fi (for a fee).

4

CANCÚN | Where to Stay

Riu Palace Las Américas ★ ☺ One of Cancún's original all-inclusives, the Riu Palace is part of a family of Riu resorts known for their grand, opulent style. This is the smallest of them and the most over-the-top, steeped in pearl-white Greco architecture. It looks more like it belongs on the Las Vegas strip than next to the Caribbean Sea, but then again, no one ever said Cancún had a consistent style. The location is prime—near the central shopping, dining, and nightlife centers, and just a 5-minute walk to the Convention Center. All rooms are spacious junior suites with an ocean or lagoon view, separate seating area with sofa or sofa bed, and a balcony or terrace. Eight have whirlpools. The beautiful central pools overlook the ocean and a small stretch of beach. Riu Palace offers guests virtually 24 hours of all-inclusive snacks, meals, and beverages. Activities include watersports, daytime entertainment for adults and kids, live music and shows at night, and access to other Riu hotels in Cancún. The hotel's European opulence stands in contrast to the mostly informal North American guests.

Bulevar Kukulcán Km 8.5, Lote 4, 77500 Cancún, Q. Roo. http://cancun.riu.com. ℂ **888/666-8816** in the U.S., or 998/891-4300. Fax 998/891-4301. 372 units. High season $380 and up double; low season $300 and up double. Rates are all-inclusive, and a 2-night stay may be required. AE, MC, V. **Amenities:** 5 restaurants; 5 bars; beach games for kids and adults; live shows; 2 outdoor pools; spa w/fitness center, sauna, and whirlpool; access to golf and tennis; nonmotorized watersports, including introductory scuba lessons; Wi-Fi (in lobby). *In room:* A/C, satellite TV, hair dryer, minibar.

Royal ★★ This adults-only all-suites hotel is one of my favorite Cancún all-inclusive establishments, offering a level of services and amenities unmatched almost anywhere. From the stunning infinity pools and gorgeous beach to the gourmet restaurants and sophisticated spa, the owners have spared no expense. The elegant marble lobby looks out one side to the Caribbean and the other to the lagoon, with sit-down check-in and a champagne welcome. All of the innovative suites feature flatscreen TVs with CD/DVD players, marble bathrooms with rain showers, two-person whirlpools, and oceanview balconies with hammocks. Swim-up master suites have semiprivate plunge pools facing the resort's pool and beach; guests in the top-category suites enjoy "Royal Service," which includes upgraded amenities, Bose stereo systems, pillow menus, the ability to preselect your suite online, and 1-hour use of a Mini Cooper. The Maya-inspired oceanview spa includes "ecoholistic" massages, whirlpool, sauna, traditional *temazcal* steam bath, massage waterfall, and state-of-the-art fitness center. Actually, the range of services is almost hard to believe, except that you will be paying top dollar for it. The all-inclusive package includes gourmet meals, premium drinks, and evening entertainment.

Bulevar Kukulcán Km 11.5, 77500 Cancún, Q. Roo. www.realresorts.com. ℂ **800/760-0944** in the U.S., or 998/881-7340. Fax 998/881-7399. 288 units. $500 and up double. Rates are all-inclusive. AE, DC, MC, V. No children 15 and younger. **Amenities:** 6 restaurants; 8 bars; concierge; expansive outdoor pool; ocean view spa w/steam room, sauna, whirlpool, and well-equipped fitness center. *In room:* A/C, flatscreen TV, CD/DVD player, hair dryer, minibar, Wi-Fi.

EXPENSIVE

Dreams Cancún Resort & Spa ☺ The all-inclusive Dreams Resort enjoys one of the island's most idyllic locations at the tip of Punta Cancún. The setting is casual and family-friendly. Bright colors and strategic angles define the design, which now looks somewhat dated relative to Cancún's newer establishments. Choose from two sets of rooms: those in the 17-story club tower with ocean views and extra services and amenities, and those in the pyramid overlooking the dolphin-filled lagoon. The all-inclusive concept here includes meals, 24-hour room service, and premium-brand drinks, as well as the use of all resort amenities, nonmotorized watersports, theme-night entertainment, and tips. Unfortunately, service at the resort is inconsistent.

Bulevar Kukulcán, 77500 Punta Cancún (Apdo. Postal 14), Cancún, Q. Roo. www.dreamsresorts. com. ✆ **866/237-3267** in the U.S., or 998/848-7000. Fax 998/848-7001. 376 units. $350 and up double. Rates are all-inclusive. AE, DC, MC, V. **Amenities:** 5 restaurants; 5 bars; babysitting; bikes; children's programs; private saltwater lagoon w/dolphins and tropical fish; 2 outdoor pools; spa w/fitness center, steam bath, and whirlpool; Spanish and cooking classes; lighted tennis court; ocean trampoline; watersports including kayaks, catamarans, paddleboats, snorkeling equipment, and scuba lessons; beach volleyball; yoga. *In room:* A/C, TV w/DVD/CD player, hair dryer, minibar.

Marriott CasaMagna ★★★ ☺ This picture-perfect Marriott resort is one of the most enticing family destinations in Cancún. Entering through a half-circle of Roman columns, you'll pass through a domed foyer to a wide, lavishly marbled lobby filled with plants and shallow pools. It looks out to the sparkling pool and enormous whirlpool at the edge of the beach. Guest rooms are decorated with Mexican-Caribbean furnishings and have balconies facing the sea or lagoon. The Marriott caters to family travelers (up to two children stay free with parent), and the supervised children's program is one of the best of any resort here. That said, the resort never feels overrun by kids, and young couples will also have a wonderful time. Among the many places to dine, the most fun is the *teppanyaki*-style (cook-at-your-table) Mikado Japanese restaurant (p. 96). Service throughout the resort is excellent. Guests can also pay to use the more luxurious JW Marriott spa next door.

Bulevar Kukulcán Km 14.5, 77500 Cancún, Q. Roo. www.marriott.com. ✆ **800/228-9290** in the U.S., or 998/881-2000. Fax 998/881-2085. 450 units. $180 and up double; $300 and up suite. Ask about family packages and all-inclusive options. AE, MC, V. **Amenities:** 4 restaurants; lobby bar w/ live music; babysitting; children's programs; concierge; fitness center and massage service; outdoor pool and whirlpool; 2 lighted tennis courts. *In room:* A/C, flatscreen TV, hair dryer, minibar.

ME ★ The now all-inclusive ME hotel by Meliá brings to Cancún a level of minimalist chic with an atmosphere befitting a trendy nightclub more than a beach resort. Bathed in hues of beige and mauve, with polished marble, onyx lamps, and modern artwork, the hotel creates its own fashion statement—and the hip clientele reflects it. The modern lobby feels a bit like an urban cocktail lounge, with designer bars and chill-out music filling the space. Guest rooms have distinctive contemporary furnishings, flatscreen TVs, iPod docking stations, and marble bathrooms with rain showers and Aveda bath products; half look to the Caribbean Sea and the other half to the lagoon. The super-stylish Yhi Spa overlooks the ocean and offers a hydrotherapy center, aromatherapy massages, body masks, and wraps. The Beach House restaurant appears sunken into the main pool and joins the beach in front, and the daytime Beach Club (open on weekends) recreates a South Beach party scene with live music and DJs.

Bulevar Kukulcán Km 12, 77500 Cancún, Q. Roo. www.me-cancun.com. ✆ **877/954-8363** in the U.S., or 998/881-2500. Fax 998/881-2501. 448 units. $370 and up double. Rates are all-inclusive. AE, MC, V. **Amenities:** 3 restaurants; 2 bars; beach club; concierge; concierge-level rooms; Internet cafe; 3 outdoor pools; full-service luxury spa w/fitness center; whirlpool. *In room:* A/C, flatscreen TV, hair dryer, minibar, MP3 player, Wi-Fi.

MODERATE

Flamingo Cancún ☺   The Flamingo seems to have been inspired by the dramatic, slope-sided architecture of Dreams Cancún and is similarly aging, but it's considerably smaller and less expensive (guests can opt out of the all-inclusive package, which includes three meals and domestic drinks). With two pools and a casual vibe, it's also a friendly, accommodating choice for families. The bright guest rooms—all with balconies—border a courtyard facing the interior swimming pool and *palapa* pool bar. Some, but not all, of the rooms have been remodeled in recent years. The Flamingo lies in the heart of the island hotel district, opposite the Flamingo Shopping Center and close to other hotels, shopping centers, and restaurants.

Bulevar Kukulcán Km 11, 77500 Cancún, Q. Roo. www.flamingocancun.com. ✆ **877/319-8464** in the U.S., or 998/848-8870. Fax 998/883-1029. 260 units. $85–$145 double. All-inclusive option available. AE, MC, V. **Amenities:** 2 restaurants; 2 bars; babysitting; fitness center; kids' area; 2 outdoor pools; Wi-Fi (in lobby). *In room:* A/C, TV, hair dryer, minibar.

Temptation Resort & Spa Cancún   This adults-only (21 and over) getaway is a "tempting" all-inclusive resort favored by those looking for significant social interaction. Although it's not advertised as such, the hotel is widely known for its popularity with "swingers." By day, pool time is all about flirting, seducing, and getting a little wacky with adult games such as teasing time and a dirty jokes contest. The main pools are top-optional. Note that tops are also optional on the beach in front, which has calm waters for swimming. Come night, theme dinners, shows, a DJ, and other live entertainment keep the party going. The small, somewhat dated rooms are housed in two sections, with quiet rooms in one and "sexy" rooms, complete with red lighting, in another. Surrounded by acres of tropical gardens, this moderate hotel lies at the northern end of the Hotel Zone, close to the major shopping plazas, restaurants, and nightlife. It reminds me of a Carnival Cruise, but on land.

Bulevar Kukulcán Km 3.5, 77500 Cancún, Q. Roo. www.temptationresort.com. ✆ **877/485-8367** in the U.S., or 998/848-7900. Fax 998/848-7994. 384 units. High season $189 per person per night double occupancy; low season $149 per person per night double occupancy. Rates include food, beverages, and activities. AE, MC, V. Guests must be at least 21 years old. **Amenities:** 6 restaurants; 5 bars; exercise room w/daily classes; 3 outdoor pools; pool and beach games; limited room service; spa; 7 whirlpools; nonmotorized watersports including snorkeling and scuba lessons. *In room:* A/C, TV, hair dryer, Wi-Fi (for a fee).

Ciudad Cancún

You won't find much in the way of authentic Mexican charm in the Hotel Zone, but you can get a glimpse of it in Ciudad Cancún, where most of the local population lives. You'll find inexpensive hotels, a number of outstanding traditional restaurants, and some good value shopping here.

MODERATE

Radisson Hacienda Cancún ★ ☺   This is the top business hotel in downtown Cancún, and one of the best values in the area. The Radisson offers all the expected comforts of the chain, yet resembles a hacienda with the distinct manner of Mexican hospitality. Guest rooms surround a warm, rotunda-style lobby with a cool onyx bar, as well as lush gardens and an inviting pool area. All have brightly colored fabric accents; views of the garden, the pool, or the street; and a small sitting area and balcony. The hotel lies within walking distance of downtown Cancún. Kids 12 and under stay for free.

Av. Nader 1, SM2, Centro, 77500 Cancún, Q. Roo. www.radissoncancun.com. ☎ **800/395-7046** in the U.S., or 998/881-6500. Fax 998/884-7954. 247 units. $80 and up double; $100 and up junior suite. AE, MC, V. **Amenities:** Restaurant; lobby bar and snack bar; babysitting; small gym; outdoor pool w/adjoining bar and separate wading area for children; limited room service; sauna; lighted tennis courts; Wi-Fi (in lobby). *In room:* A/C, TV, iron, hair dryer.

Rey del Caribe Hotel ★★ 🎁   This acclaimed ecofriendly hotel is a unique oasis where every detail works toward establishing harmony with the environment. You might easily forget you're in the midst of downtown Cancún in the tropical garden setting, with local palms, blooming orchids, and other flowering plants. The lovely grounds include statues of Maya deities, hammocks, and a tiled swimming pool. Yoga, as well as special classes on astrology, ancestral traditions, and other subjects are periodically offered. Good value massages are available in two cabins near the pool. Individually decorated guest rooms are large and sunny, with a kitchenette and your choice of one king-size or two full-size beds; some have a terrace. The extent of ecological sensitivity is a model for sustainable tourism—ranging from the use of collected rainwater to waste composting. Recycling is encouraged, and solar power is used wherever possible.

Av. Uxmal SM 24 (corner of Nader), 77500 Cancún, Q. Roo. www.elreydelcaribe.com. ☎ **998/884-2028.** Fax 988/884-9857. 31 units. High season $85 double; low season $65 double. Street parking. Rates include breakfast. MC, V. **Amenities:** Airport transfer 280 pesos; outdoor pool; whirlpool; massage service. *In room:* A/C, TV, kitchenette, Wi-Fi (free).

INEXPENSIVE

Sol y Luna 🍃   This simple but cheerful hotel next to the Parque Las Palapas has 11 individually decorated rooms on three floors with small balconies and mosaic-trimmed baths with showers only. A tiny bridge crosses the small pool at the entrance. Come here if you want to explore the downtown and experience Cancún's more local flavor on the cheap, but don't expect much in the way of service or amenities.

Calle Alcatraces 33, at Parque Las Palapas, 77500 Cancún, Q. Roo. www.hotelsolylunacancun.com. ☎ **998/887-5579.** 11 units. 650 pesos double. Cash only. Street parking. **Amenities:** Small outdoor pool. *In room:* A/C, TV, fridge, Wi-Fi (free).

Xbalamqué ★★   Designed to resemble a Maya temple, this imaginative downtown hotel features inviting outdoor spaces, including a waterfall pool adjacent to an authentic Mexican cantina. Live music plays evenings in the library-cafe adjacent to the lobby. Guest rooms and 10 junior suites offer rustic furnishings with regional touches, colorful tilework, and simple bathrooms with showers. Ask for a room overlooking the ivy-filled courtyard and pool. A tour desk is available to help you plan your vacation activities, and the small spa offers some of the best rates of any hotel in Cancún. The small theater offers programs on weekends for children and adults alike.

Av. Yaxchilán 31, Sm. 22, Mza. 18, 77500 Cancún, Q. Roo. www.xbalamque.com. ☎ **998/884-9690.** Fax 998/884-9690. 99 units. 950 pesos double; 1,050 pesos suite. AE, MC, V. American breakfast included. **Amenities:** Restaurant; cafe; cantina; bar; outdoor pool; spa; weekend theater; tour desk. *In room:* A/C, TV, Wi-Fi (free).

ISLA MUJERES & COZUMEL

by Shane Christensen

These two Caribbean islands are among the most peaceful beach destinations in Mexico, both easy jaunts from Cancún and the Riviera Maya. Although day-trippers and cruise-ship visitors come ashore during high season, the islands never feel overrun. Come evening, the uncrowded streets and relaxed energy of the residents exemplify the enduring tranquillity of the islands. Neither Isla Mujeres nor Cozumel is particularly large, and they each still have that small island feel—pristine beaches, bumpy roads that don't go far, a welcoming remoteness, and a seemingly timeless setting.

Fish-shaped **Isla Mujeres** lies 13km (8 miles) northeast of Cancún, a quick boat ride away but what feels like a world removed from its glittery neighbor. Despite this proximity, I consider Isla Mujeres a little-known gem filled with historic and rustic charm. During pre-Hispanic times, Maya women would cross over to the island to make offerings to the goddess of fertility, Ixchel. More than 40 sites containing shrines remain around the island, and archaeologists still uncover the small dolls that were customarily part of those offerings. Hotels range from rustic to boutique, and the value of accommodation and dining are among the best one can find in this part of Mexico. Passenger ferries travel to Isla Mujeres from Cancún's Puerto Juárez and the Hotel Zone's Embarcadero at Playa Linda; car ferries leave from Punta Sam.

Larger than Isla Mujeres and farther from the mainland (19km/12 miles off the coast from Playa del Carmen), **Cozumel** has its own mini-international airport. Life here revolves around two major activities: scuba diving and cruise ships making a port of call. Yet a strong sense of family and community continues to prevail here. There are less than 100,000 people on the island, a couple thousand of whom are Americans and the rest of whom are mostly Maya, Yucatecan, and Mexican from elsewhere in the country. There's just one town, San Miguel de Cozumel; to the north and south lie resorts. The rest of the shore is deserted and predominantly rocky, with a scattering of small sandy coves that you can have all to yourself. Because Cozumel remains a frequent stop on the cruise ship circuit, the town's waterfront is lined with jewelry stores and duty-free and souvenir shops. This and the area around the town's main square are about as far as most cruise-ship passengers venture, and they're usually just here for a few hours in the middle of the day.

Unfortunately, there's no way to travel directly between Cozumel and Isla Mujeres, but you can get from one to the other by traveling via Cancún and Playa del Carmen.

THE BEST TRAVEL EXPERIENCES

o **Swimming with Tropical Fish:** These two islands are home to some of the most colorful snorkeling and scuba diving in the world. On Isla, bring your snorkels and flippers to Garrafón Natural Reef Park or to the new MUSA

PREVIOUS PAGE: **An isolated beach on Cozumel.**

Underwater Sculpture Garden, while in Cozumel enjoy drift-diving among one of the world's largest and best visibility reefs, including at Chankanaab National Park, where you can also swim with dolphins.

o **Experiencing Caribbean Wonders from a Comfortable Chair:** Those less comfortable with getting wet can explore the sea while remaining fully clothed on board the Atlantis Submarine in Cozumel. A number of the snorkeling trips here and in Isla Mujeres use glass-bottom boats for those who prefer to stay dry.

o **Exploring Ancient Ruins:** Visit the temple dedicated to the Maya goddess Ixchel, located at the southern tip of Isla Mujeres. While here, you can also walk through a sculpture garden and along the breathtaking Cliff of the Dawn. To see Maya ruins on Cozumel, take an island excursion to San Gervasio.

o **Shopping and Eating, the Traditional Way:** At the end of the day, shop for good value authentic handicrafts in either of the two islands' main towns and then sit down for a simple Mexican Caribbean meal at any of the local seafood restaurants.

o **Taking a Day Trip off the Islands:** If island fever strikes, the 45-minute ferry from Cozumel to Playa del Carmen lets you explore this chic beach town and then do a day trip along the Mayan Riviera. Discover the incredible seaside ruins of Tulum, swim in the crystal-clear waters of Xel-Ha natural water park, or visit Mexico's top eco-archaeological park at Xcaret.

ISLA MUJERES ★★★

13km (8 miles) N of Cancún

Only a quick boat ride from the swarming beaches of Cancún, Isla Mujeres feels like a different world. Bathed in the warm waters of the Caribbean Sea, the sleepy island attracts visitors who prefer a laid-back lifestyle focused around the beach and watersports such as diving and snorkeling. The name translates as "the island of women," but few islanders agree on the origin. While Isla Mujeres has a healthy nightlife, relaxed *isleños* frown upon spring break antics; if you're looking for parties, stick to Cancún.

Beaches **Playa Norte,** which runs along the northernmost edge of town, is a picture-perfect Caribbean dream, ideal for relaxing with a cool beverage or wading in the waist-deep water. For stunning views across the turquoise waters to Cancún, head to **Playa Lancheros,** on the southern side of the island. Enjoy the spectacular sunset from the **Casa Rolandi** restaurant, on the waterfront of the Villa Rolandi resort.

Things to Do Fans of ancient cultures can tour the crumbling Maya temple at the southernmost tip of the island, thought to be dedicated to Ixchel, goddess of fertility. Wander through the multicolored sculpture garden, or venture just beyond to the **Cliff of the Dawn** for extraordinary views. Get up close to sea turtles at the **Tortugranja,** a sea turtle sanctuary that protects the marine reptiles. Bypass the Isla's downtown T-shirt stores in favor of boutiques where you can shop for Mexican artworks ranging from Day of the Dead skeletons to seaglass jewelry.

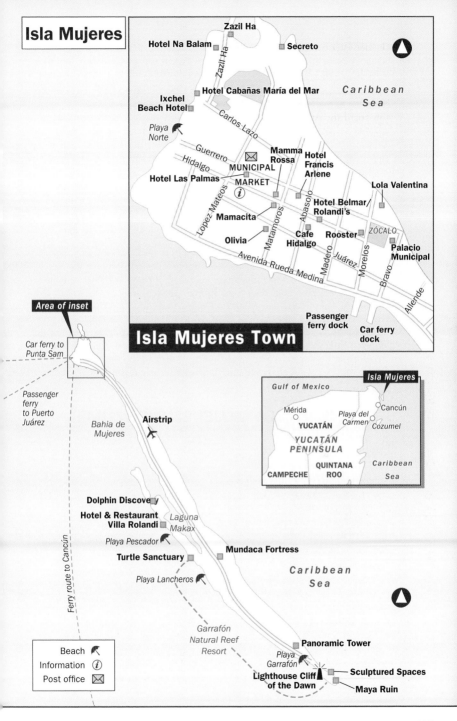

Isla Mujeres

Isla Mujeres Town

Zazil Ha

Hotel Na Balam

Secreto

Caribbean Sea

Zazil Ha

Hotel Cabañas María del Mar

Ixchel
Beach Hotel

Carlos Lazo

Playa
Norte

Guerrero

Mamma
Rossa

Hotel
Francis
Arlene

Hidalgo

MUNICIPAL
MARKET

Hotel Las Palmas

Lola Valentina

Lopez Mateos

Hotel Belmar/
Rolandi's

Mamacita

Abasolo

ZÓCALO

Olivia

Matamoros

Cafe
Hidalgo

Rooster

Palacio
Municipal

Madero

Morelos

Avenida Rueda Medina

Juárez

Bravo

Allende

Passenger
ferry dock

Car ferry
dock

Area of inset

Car ferry to
Punta Sam

Passenger
ferry
to Puerto
Juárez

Bahia de
Mujeres

Airstrip

Isla Mujeres

Gulf of Mexico

Mérida

Cancún

YUCATÁN

Playa del
Carmen

Cozumel

YUCATÁN
PENINSULA

QUINTANA
ROO

Caribbean Sea

CAMPECHE

Ferry route to Cancún

Dolphin Discovery

Hotel & Restaurant
Villa Rolandi

Laguna
Makax

Playa Pescador

Turtle Sanctuary

Mundaca Fortress

Playa Lancheros

Caribbean Sea

Garrafón
Natural Reef
Resort

Panoramic Tower

Playa
Garrafón

Lighthouse Cliff
of the Dawn

Sculptured Spaces

Maya Ruin

Beach
Information
Post office

117

Eating & Drinking   The island's culinary specialty is **seafood,** best enjoyed at any of the simple beachside restaurants where you can sink your feet into the sand by day or dine by tiki torch at night. A local favorite dish of Maya origin is *Tikinxic*—whole fish marinated in achiote and sour oranges, then wrapped in a banana leaf and cooked in an earthen oven. While tequila isn't made on the island, it's the most popular spirit here, especially when included in freshly made margaritas.

Nature   Divers and snorkelers have a wealth of sites to discover off of Isla Mujeres. The diving spot is the **Caves of the Sleeping Sharks,** once famous as a meeting point for slow-moving sharks. Snorkelers prefer the calm, shallow water of the island's western side, with Lighthouse and Manchones being the best spots to see the coral reef. On a day trip to **Isla Contoy,** a national park with mangrove lagoons, you'll spot more than 150 species of birds.

Essentials

GETTING THERE   You can travel to Isla Mujeres from the "Gran Puerto" dock at Puerto Juárez, just north of Cancún, or from the Embarcadero in the Hotel Zone. **Ultramar** (www.granpuerto.com.mx; ✆ **998/881-5890**) runs fast boats leaving every half-hour from **Puerto Juárez,** making the trip in 15 minutes. There is storage space for luggage and the fare is 70 pesos each way. These boats operate daily, starting at 5:30am and usually ending at midnight (check beforehand for latest schedules). They might leave early if they're full, so arrive ahead of schedule. From the Hotel Zone's **Embarcadero** at Playa Linda, located at Bulevar Kukulcán Km 4 on the northern tip of the Hotel Zone/Isla Cancún, Ultramar ferries to Isla Mujeres depart

THE BEST ISLA MUJERES & COZUMEL
websites

o **Isla Mujeres Tourist Information: www.isla-mujeres.net**   The official site of the Isla Mujeres Tourism Board provides complete informa- tion on Isla, including places to eat, where to stay, and things to do.

o **My Isla Mujeres: www.myisla mujeres.com**   Get a local's view of the island; check out the section called "My Isla Guide Book."

o **Cozumel.net: www.cozumel. net**   This site is a cut above the typical dining/lodging/activities sites. Click on "About Cozumel" to find weather, articles of interest, and links to services and events. There's

also a comprehensive listing of B&Bs and vacation-home rentals.

o **Cozumel Travel Planner: www. go2cozumel.com**   This is a well-done guide to area businesses and attractions by an online Mexico specialist.

o **Cozumel Hotel Association: www. islacozumel.com.mx**   Operated by the tourism-promotion arm of the hotel association, this site gives more than just listings of the member hotels. There's info on the island's history, culture, and ecology, plus useful descriptions of things to do and how to do them.

The Isla Mujeres Ferry Terminal.

less frequently and cost $11 one-way or $17 round-trip. There are up to eight scheduled departures per day. Depending on the season, Ultramar also operates ferries to Isla Mujeres from the Hotel Zone's Playa Tortugas, at Bulevar Kukulcán Km 6.5, and from Playa Caracol at Bulevar Kukulcán Km 9.5.

Isla Mujeres is so small that a vehicle isn't necessary, but if you're taking one to the island, you'll use the **Punta Sam** port a little beyond Puerto Juárez. The 40-minute car ferry (© **998/877-0065**) runs five or six times daily between 8am and 8pm year-round except in bad weather. Always check with the tourist office in Cancún to verify this schedule. Cars should arrive an hour before the ferry departure to register for a place in line and pay the posted fee, which is 185 pesos per car. A gas pump is at Avenida Rueda Medina and Calle Abasolo, northwest of the ferry docks.

To get to Puerto Juárez from **Cancún,** take the Ruta 1 city bus. From the Cancún airport, take the shuttle bus to the pier (160 pesos).

GETTING AROUND   A popular form of transportation on Isla Mujeres is the electric **golf cart,** available for rent at many hotels or rental shops for 180 pesos per hour, 500 pesos from 9am to 5pm, or 600 pesos for 24 hours. Prices are the same at all rental locations. **El Sol Golf Cart Rental,** Av. Benito Juárez Mza. 3 no. 20 (corner of Matamoros; © **998/877-0791**), is one good option in the town center. The golf carts don't go more than 30kmph (19 mph), but they're fun. Anyway, you aren't on Isla Mujeres to hurry. Many people enjoy touring the island by *moto* (motorized bike or scooter). **Gomar** (© **998/877-0604**), at the corner of Madero and Hidalgo, rents reliable scooters. Fully automatic versions are available for 100 pesos per hour, 250 pesos for 8 hours, or 350 pesos for 24 hours. They come with

Avenida Rueda Medina, or the *malecón*.

helmets and seats for two people. There's only one main road with a couple of offshoots, so you won't get lost. Be aware that the rental price does not include insurance, and any injury to yourself or the vehicle will come out of your pocket. **Bicycles** are also available for rent at some hotels for about 35 pesos an hour or 200 pesos for 24 hours, usually including a basket and a lock.

Tricycle taxis are the least expensive and easiest way to get to your hotel if it's in town. From the ferry pier to any of the downtown hotels will cost about 30 to 40 pesos. If you ask the driver for the price, they might just say "Oh, whatever you care to give."

If you prefer to use a taxi, rates are about 40 pesos for trips within the downtown area, or 78 pesos for a trip to the southern end of Isla. You can also hire them for about 210 pesos per hour. Regular taxis are always lined up in a parking lot to the right of the pier, with their rates posted. The number to call for taxis is ✆ **998/877-1838.**

ISLAND LAYOUT Isla Mujeres is about 8km (5 miles) long and 4km (2½ miles) wide, with the town at the northern tip. "Downtown" is a compact 4 blocks by 6 blocks, so it's very easy to get around. The **passenger ferry docks** are at the center of town, within walking distance of most hotels, restaurants, and shops. The street running along the waterfront and in front of the ferry docks is **Avenida Rueda Medina,** commonly called the *malecón* (boardwalk). The **Mercado Municipal** (town market) is by the post office on **Calle Guerrero,** an inland street at the north edge of town, which, like most streets in the town, is unmarked.

VISITOR INFORMATION The **City Tourist Office** (www.isla-mujeres.net/tourism/home.htm; ✆ **998/877-0307**) is at Av. Rueda Medina 130, just across the street from the pier. It's open Monday through Friday from 9am to 4pm, closed on Saturday and Sunday.

[FastFACTS] ISLA MUJERES

Area Code The telephone area code is **998.**

ATMs & Banks Isla has only one bank, **HSBC Bank** (☎ **998/877-0005**), across from the ferry docks. It's open Monday through Friday from 8:30am to 6pm, and Saturday from 9am to 2pm. It has ATM machines.

Currency Exchange Isla Mujeres has numerous *casas de cambio,* or currency exchanges, along the main streets. Most of the hotels listed here change money for their guests, although often at less favorable rates than the commercial enterprises.

Drugstore **YZA Farmacia** (☎ **998/877-1836**), located at the corner of Juárez and Morelos, stays open 24 hours.

Hospital The **Hospital Integral** is on Avenida Guerrero, a block before the beginning of the *malecón* (☎ **998/877-0117**).

Internet Access **Europa Computer Internet,** at Abasolo between Hidalgo and Juárez, offers Wi-Fi and computers for 20 pesos per hour. It's open Monday to Saturday from 9am to 10pm.

Post Office The *correo* is at Calle Guerrero 12 (☎ **998/877-0085**), at the corner of López Mateos, near the market. It's open Monday through Friday from 9am to 5:30pm, Saturday 9am to 1pm.

Seasons Isla Mujeres's tourist season (when hotel rates are higher) is a bit different from that of other places in Mexico. High season runs December through May, a month longer than in Cancún. Some hotels raise their rates in August, and some raise their rates beginning in mid-November. Low season runs from June to mid-November.

Exploring
BEACHES & OUTDOOR ACTIVITIES

BEACHES & SWIMMING **Playa Norte ★★★,** which extends around the northern tip of the island, is perhaps the world's best municipal beach—a gorgeous swath of fine white sand and calm, translucent turquoise-blue water that stays shallow far off the shore. It's just a short walk to the beach from the ferry and downtown hotels. Watersports equipment, beach umbrellas, and lounge chairs are widely available for rent. This is a terrific place for swimming and snorkeling. Areas in front of restaurants usually cost nothing if you use the restaurant as your headquarters for drinks and food, and the best of them have hammocks and swings from which to sip your piña coladas.

Garrafón Natural Reef Park ★★ (p. 124) offers beautiful snorkeling areas, but there's also a nice stretch of beach on either side of the park for those who want to avoid the expensive entrance fee. The **Beach Club Garrafón de Castilla,** located right next to the park, has a wonderful swimming area, snorkeling equipment for rent, and a beachside snack shop. The entrance fee is about 50 pesos. **Playa Lancheros** sits on the Caribbean side of Laguna Makax and is another lovely swimming beach. Local buses travel to Lancheros from downtown.

Isla Mujeres has no lifeguards on duty and does not use the system of water-safety flags employed in Cancún and Cozumel. The bay between Cancún and Isla Mujeres is calm, with warm, transparent waters ideal for swimming, snorkeling, and diving. The east side of the island facing the open Caribbean Sea is typically rougher, with much stronger currents.

Playa Norte Beach in Isla Mujeres.

FISHING   To arrange a day of fishing, ask at the **Cooperativa Isla Mujeres** (the boatmen's cooperative), a small shop on the right side of the pier off Avenida Rueda Medina, next to Las Brisas restaurant. Four hours of fishing costs $220 for up to eight people. Year-round you'll find bonito, mackerel, kingfish, and amberjack. Sailfish and sharks (hammerhead, bull, nurse, lemon, and tiger) are in good supply in April and May. In winter, larger grouper and jewfish are prevalent. The cooperative is open daily from 8am to 6:30pm.

SCUBA DIVING   Most of the dive shops on the island offer the same trips for similar prices, including reef, drift, deep, and night dives: One-tank dives cost about $55 to $75; two-tank dives about $70 to $90. **Squaloadventures,** Madero 10 between Hidalgo and Guerrero (www.squaloadventures. com.mx; ✆ **998/877-0607**), is a full-service shop that offers resort courses, dive packages, and certifications. Another respected dive shop is **Carey Dive Center,** at Matamoros 13A and Rueda Medina (www.careydivecenter. com; ✆ **998/877-0763**). Both offer 2-hour snorkeling trips for about $25.

    Cuevas de los Tiburones (Caves of the Sleeping Sharks) is Isla's most renowned dive site—but the name is slightly misleading, as shark sightings are uncommon these days. Two sites where you could traditionally see the sleeping sharks are the Cuevas de los Tiburones and **La Punta.** The sharks have mostly been driven off, and a storm collapsed the arch featured in a Jacques Cousteau film showing them. However, the caves survive. Although sleeping shark sightings are rare, giant whale sharks by the hundreds migrate through these waters about 12 to 15 miles offshore between mid-June and mid-August.

    A recent addition to the Isla Mujeres diving scene is **La MUSA Underwater Museum of Art** (www.musacancun.com), where more than 400 sunken life-size sculptures form an impressive artificial reef. Scuba and snorkeling trips are offered here. Other dive sites include a **wreck** 15km (9⅓ miles) offshore; **Banderas** reef, between Isla Mujeres and Cancún, where there's always a strong current; **Tabos** reef on the eastern shore; and **Manchones** reef, 1km (⅔ mile) off the southeastern tip of the island, where the water is 4.5 to 11m (15–36 ft.) deep. **The Cross of the Bay** is close to Manchones reef. A bronze cross, weighing 1 ton and standing 12m

(39 ft.) high, was placed in the water between Manchones and Isla in 1994, as a memorial to those who have lost their lives at sea.

SNORKELING   One of the most popular places to snorkel is **Garrafón Natural Reef Park ★★** (p. 124). **Manchones** reef, off the southeastern coast, is also good. It's just offshore and accessible by boat. You can snorkel around *el faro* (the lighthouse) in the **Bahía de Mujeres** at the southern tip of the island. The water is about 2m (6½ ft.) deep. Boatmen will take you for around 300 pesos per person if you have your own snorkeling equipment or 350 pesos if you use theirs.

YOGA   Increasingly, Isla is becoming popular among yoga enthusiasts. The trend began at **Hotel Na Balam ★★** (p. 130; www.nabalam.com; ✆ **998/881-4770**), which offers ashtanga, vinyasa, and hatha flow yoga classes weekday mornings and evenings under its large poolside *palapa,* complete with yoga mats and props. The hotel also offers yoga vacations featuring respected teachers and a more extensive practice schedule; call for more information. Individual yoga classes cost $12, with discounts available for multiple classes. Another reputable yoga center offering weekday morning classes is **Elements of the Island** (www.elementsoftheisland.com; ✆ **998/274-0098**). The breakfast and lunch cafe and studio apartments for rent are located at Juárez 64, between López Mateos and Matamoros.

ATTRACTIONS

Dolphin Discovery ★★ WATER PARK   You can swim with dolphins (www. dolphindiscovery.com; ✆ **998/849-4748** or -4757) at the "Dolphinario," located midway along the island near Villa Rolandi (on the side of Isla Mujeres facing Cancún). Groups of up to eight people swim with two dolphins and a trainer. Swimmers view an educational video and spend time in the water with the trainer and the dolphins before enjoying swimming time with the dolphins. Reservations are necessary, and you must arrive an hour before your assigned swimming time, at 10:30am, 12:15, 1:50, or 3:30pm. The cost is $129 per person for

Snorkeling off of Isla Mujeres.

Cliff of the Dawn.

the Dolphin Royal Swim. There are less expensive programs that allow you to learn about, touch, and hold the dolphins (but not swim with them), starting at $79 ($69 for kids). The park is open from 9am to 5pm, and the fee includes ferry transport from Aquatours in Cancún.

Turtle Farm ★★ FARM   Years ago, fishermen converged on the island nightly from May to September to capture turtles when they would come ashore to lay eggs. Then a concerned fisherman, Gonzalo Chale Maldonado, began convincing others to spare the eggs, which he protected. It was a start. Following his lead, the fishing ministry founded the **Centro de Investigaciones Pesqueras** to find ways to protect the species and increase the turtle populations. Although the local government provides some assistance, most of the funding comes from private-sector donations. Since the center opened, tens of thousands of young turtles have been released, and local schoolchildren have participated, helping to educate a new generation of islanders for the cause. Releases are scheduled from May to November, and visitors are invited to take part. Inquire at the center.

Three species of sea turtles nest on Isla Mujeres. An adult green turtle, the most abundant species, is 1 to 1.5m (3⅓–5 ft.) long and can weigh 204kg (450 lb.). At the Tortugranja, as the Turtle Farm is called in Spanish, visitors walk through the indoor and outdoor turtle pool areas, where the creatures paddle around. Turtles are separated by age, from newly hatched up to 1 year. People who come here usually end up staying about an hour, especially if they opt for the guided tour, which I recommend. They also have a small gift shop. The sanctuary is on a spit of land jutting out from the island's west coast. The address is Carretera Sac Bajo no. 5; you'll need a taxi to get there. Admission is 30 pesos; the shelter is open daily from 9am to 5pm. For more information, call ✆ **998/877-0595.**

Garrafón Natural Reef Resort ★★ NATURE RESERVE   Garrafón (www.garrafon.com; ✆ **998/849-4748**) sits at the southern end of the island near Punta Sur. Once a public national underwater park, Garrafón is now operated by Dolphin Discovery and has myriad water activities that include snorkeling, kayaks, a dive platform, and swimming. Although the tropical fish are dazzling to see, most of the reef has sadly died. The pricey ecopark also offers a swimming pool, zip line, bicycle tour, restaurant and bar, beach chairs, shaded hammocks, changing rooms with showers and lockers, and gift shop. Admission costs $74 ($54 for children under 12); the all-inclusive package includes round-trip transportation between Cancún and Isla Mujeres, buffet lunch, domestic open bar, and use of snorkeling equipment and kayaks. Swim with dolphin packages are also available. The park stays open daily in high season from 10am to 5pm. In low season, it may close a couple days per week.

Just south of Garrafón, the small **Caribbean Village** has colorful clapboard buildings that house cafes and shops displaying folk art. You can have lunch or a snack here and stroll around before heading on to Sculptured Spaces and the Maya ruins.

Walking toward the southern tip of the island, you'll find **Sculptured Spaces,** a sculpture garden with pieces donated to Isla Mujeres by internationally renowned sculptors. Among Mexican sculptors represented are José Luis Cuevas and Vladimir Cora. A small **Maya ruin** dedicated to the fertility goddess Ixchel rests here, as well (below). There's a 30-peso entrance fee for the garden and Maya ruin; a lighthouse is also located here. It's open daily from 9am to 5pm.

The **Cliff of the Dawn ★★★** lies just beyond the sculpture garden, at the southeasternmost point of Mexico. The cliff has extraordinary views, and pathways leading nearly to the water's edge. The cafe and restrooms on-site are generally open from 9am to 5pm, but you can enter at any time; if you make it there to see the sunrise, you can claim you were the first person in Mexico that day to be touched by the sun.

Isla Contoy ★ NATURE RESERVE   Try to visit this pristine uninhabited island, 30km (19 miles) by boat from Isla Mujeres. It became a national wildlife reserve in 1981. The 6km-long (3¾-mile) island is covered in lush vegetation and harbors 70 species of birds, as well as a host of marine and animal life. Bird species that nest on the island include pelicans, brown boobies, frigates, egrets, terns, and cormorants. Flocks of flamingos arrive in April. Most excursions troll for fish (which will be your lunch), anchor en route for a snorkeling expedition, skirt the island at a leisurely pace for close viewing of the birds without disturbing the habitat, and then pull ashore. While the captain prepares lunch, visitors can swim, sun, follow the nature trails, and visit the fine nature museum, which has bathroom facilities. The trip from Isla Mujeres takes about 45 minutes each way and can be longer if the waves are choppy. Because of the tight-knit boatmen's cooperative, prices for this excursion are the same everywhere: $65. You can buy a ticket at the **Cooperativa Isla Mujeres** (no phone), on Avenida Rueda Medina, next to Mexico Divers and Las Brisas restaurant. Trips leave at 9am and return around 4pm. Boat captains should respect the cooperative's regulations regarding ecological sensitivity and boat safety, including the availability of life jackets for everyone on board. If you're not given a life jacket, ask for one. Sodas, beer, and snorkeling equipment are usually included in the price, but double-check before heading out.

A Maya Ruin ★★ RUINS   Just beyond the lighthouse, at the southern end of the island, lie the remains of a small Maya temple. Archaeologists believe it was dedicated to the moon and fertility goddess Ixchel. The location, on a lofty bluff overlooking the sea, is worth seeing and makes a great place for photos. It is believed that Maya women traveled here on annual pilgrimages to seek Ixchel's blessings of fertility.

The Maya ruins of Isla Mujeres.

Hacienda Mundaca, an old pirate's fortress.

A Pirate's Fortress HISTORIC SITE   Almost in the middle of the island is a large building purported to have been a pirate fortress. A slave trader who arrived here in the early 19th century claimed to have been the pirate Mundaca Marecheaga. He set up a business selling slaves to Cuba and Belize, and prospered here. According to island lore, a charming local girl captivated him, only to spurn him in favor of a local.

Where to Eat

At the **Municipal Market,** next to the post office on Avenida Guerrero, obliging, hardworking women operate several little food stands as well as lunch spots. If you want to experience authentic Mexican food, come here.

EXPENSIVE

Casa Rolandi ★★★ ITALIAN/SEAFOOD   The hotel Villa Rolandi's restaurant is the best on the island, a stunning open-air setting gazing across the sea to Cancún and serving exquisitely prepared fresh seafood, meats, and homemade pasta. The Northern Italian menu here is even more sophisticated than Rolandi's downtown, taking advantage of an open kitchen and brick oven to transform Caribbean lobster, fish filets, shrimp brochettes, rack of lamb, suckling pig, and other creatively prepared dishes into delectable meals. Dinners include hot baked bread that leaves the oven looking like a puffer fish; with black olives and a dash of olive oil, it's an irresistible temptation, but don't fill up! This is a great place to enjoy the sunset, and there's a selection of fine international wines and premium tequilas. Breakfast selections, which come with complimentary fresh fruit and French toast, include spicy omelets and creative egg dishes, and Mexican specialties such as *chilaquiles rojos.*

On the pier of Villa Rolandi (p. 130), located in the center of the island, Lagunamar SM 7. ✆ **998/877-0700.** Reservations necessary. Main courses 200–450 pesos. Breakfast 76–120 pesos. AE, MC, V. Daily 7am–10:30pm.

MODERATE

Lola Valentina MEXICAN FUSION   Opened in late 2011, this hot addition to the Isla Mujeres dining scene adds Caribbean and American touches to

Mexican fusion cuisine. The open-air restaurant resembles a modern tequila hacienda with a centerpiece bar and warm lighting. The menu changes regularly, but samples of imaginative dishes include grilled shrimp on a plantain mash with a sweet mole; seafood enchiladas stuffed with fish, crab, and shrimp topped with a creamy pumpkin seed sauce; and a Black Angus filet mignon on a bed of blue cheese with a raspberry-chipotle sauce. Wash it down with a zesty jalapeño-watermelon margarita. When she's not interacting with diners, American owner Lola Valentina can sometimes be seen salsa dancing to the beats of the nightly band. American breakfasts with Mexican flavors are also served, along with vegetarian and gluten-free options.

Av. Hidalgo 16. ℂ **998/274-0314.** Breakfasts 60–120 pesos; main courses 165–320 pesos. No credit cards. Daily 8am–11pm.

Mamacita MEXICAN   Despite being owned by Italians, there's no pasta in sight at this otherwise authentic Mexican restaurant. Juicy ceviches, tasty tacos, big burritos, and sizzling fajitas decorate the menu, along with traditional meat dishes and fishy selections *del mar* (fresh from the Caribbean sea). Dishes use local ingredients, fresh vegetables, and homemade corn tortillas. The tender *arrachera* beef steak and the *chile relleno* stuffed with meat and cheese are especially delicious. Waiters tend to move a little slowly in this colorful open-air restaurant at the end of Hidalgo, so expect to stay for a while.

Av. Hidalgo (under the youth hostel). ℂ **998/877-1811.** Main courses 95–225 pesos. MC, V. Daily 4pm–midnight.

Mamma Rosa ITALIAN   Mamma Rosa serves mouthwatering pizzas and homemade pasta to happy patrons seated at candlelit sidewalk tables. The most extravagant pizza is the Diamante smothered with lobster, mozzarella, and tomatoes. For pasta, I recommend the simple meat lasagna or tortellini with ricotta cheese and spinach. The filet of grouper with fresh tomato and garlic makes for a perfect main course, unless you're in the mood for an Angus steak with green pepper. Lots of olive oil is used in the light, Mediterranean-inspired cooking. Accompany your meal with an Italian wine and finish with the rich tiramisu. Waiters here speak Italian and little Spanish or English.

Av. Hidalgo 10 (at Matamoros). ℂ **998/200-1969.** Pizzas and pasta 85–220 pesos; main courses 105–220 pesos. MC, V. Daily 4–11pm.

Olivia ★★ MEDITERRANEAN   This intimate dinner spot attracting a well-heeled clientele combines Greek, Turkish, and Moroccan influences in one tempting menu by the Balkan family owners. To start, the family-style Greek tapas features eggplant salad, *tzatziki,* and marinated green olives served with fresh Parmesan bread. Delicious mains prepared in the open kitchen include moussaka with ground beef and eggplant as well as pastilla with layers of phyllo dough and chicken; I also like the Moroccan-style fish filet slowly cooked in a red sauce with lime, garlic, coriander, and chickpeas served over couscous. The candlelit dining room leads out to an equally enchanted courtyard with tiki torches and luminarias. Soothing lounge music plays in the background.

Av. Matamoros (corner of Juárez). www.olivia-isla-mujeres.com. ℂ **998/877-1765.** Main courses 80–270 pesos. No credit cards. Tues–Sat 5–9:30pm (also open Mon in high season).

Rolandi's ITALIAN/SEAFOOD   This casual Italian eatery is an Isla institution, and usually the most crowded place in town. The thin-crust pizzas and calzones feature wide-ranging ingredients—from traditional tomato, cheese, ham, and oregano to more exotic seafood selections. A wood-burning oven imparts the signature flavor of the pizzas, as well as fish kabobs, baked chicken, and roast beef. The extensive menu offers a wealth of salads and appetizers, plus an ample array of homemade pasta dishes, steaks, fish, and desserts. Rolandi's also serves tasty breakfast items such as sweet and savory crepes, spicy omelets, flour and corn tortilla quesadillas, richly filled croissants, and fresh fruit plates. The restaurant sits adjacent to the Hotel Belmar (p. 131), with sidewalk tables brushing up against the action on Avenida Hidalgo.

Av. Hidalgo 110 (3½ blocks inland from the pier, btw. Madero and Abasolo). © **998/877-0430.** Reservations recommended. Breakfast 35–60 pesos; pizzas and pastas 110–175; main courses 110–200 pesos. AE, MC, V. Daily 7:30am–11:30pm.

Rooster CAFE Mexican chef Sergio Carrillo's casual eatery offers great breakfasts and lunches and a creative if small dinner menu. Wake up to a delicious omelet, *huevos rancheros, chilaquiles,* steak and eggs, or the "Veggie Benedictine" with poached eggs, spinach, feta cheese, and tomatoes. Customers rave about the lobster Benedict, as well (ask for it even if you don't see it on the menu). Creative salads and sandwiches mark the lunch menu, along with duck tacos and burritos flavored with ham, chipotle cream cheese, sliced avocado, and salsa. The "Roosters at Night" dinner menu changes seasonally and may feature specialties such as roasted duck, *osso buco,* and surf and turf. Most tables are outdoors, and service is friendly and relaxed.

Calle Hidalgo 1, at Plaza Isla Mujeres. © **998/274-0152.** Reservations recommended for dinner. Breakfast 55–120 pesos; sandwiches 85–90 pesos; dinner 130–250 pesos. No credit cards. Daily 7am–3pm and 6–9pm (dinner only Wed–Sat).

Zazil Ha 🍴 SEAFOOD Beachfront tables look out to one of the island's most alluring Caribbean scenes with the whitest sand and most turquoise of waters. Come night, candlelit tables sparkle underneath the open-air *palapa.* Specialties include *ceviche* with pineapple, cucumber, and mango, fresh fish filet *al pastor* served with a Parmesan risotto, shrimp enchiladas accompanied by rice and beans, and a seafood platter with scallops, shrimp, fish, octopus, and mussels. A juicy tenderloin steak is also on the menu. Between the set meal times, you can order all sorts of enticing snacks, such as tacos and sandwiches, as well as natural fruit juices and classic cocktails. Service is inconsistent.

At the Hotel Na Balam (at the end of Playa Norte, almost at the end of Calle Zazil Ha; p. 130). www.nabalam.com. © **998/881-4770.** Reservations recommended. Tacos and sandwiches 80–130 pesos; main courses 130–200 pesos. AE, MC, V. Daily noon–9:30pm.

INEXPENSIVE

Café Hidalgo ★ CAFE This adorable cafe serves delicious breakfasts, marvelous sweet and savory crepes, panini, croissant sandwiches, and rich Mexican coffee. For breakfast, I recommend scrambled eggs served with sautéed potatoes, grilled zucchini, and sliced tomato, along with a fresh fruit crepe packed with strawberries, bananas, mango, kiwi, cantaloupe, and pineapple. Come evening, enjoy a dessert crepe and cocktail on one of the sidewalk tables as you watch the people go by. The owner oversees each one of the carefully presented dishes herself, making the crepes right at the cafe entrance.

Calle Hidalgo 14. No phone. Crepes 30–50 pesos; breakfast 40–60 pesos; salads and sandwiches 30–70 pesos. No credit cards. Tues–Sun 8am–11pm.

Shopping

Shopping is a casual activity here. Several shops, especially concentrated on Avenida Hidalgo, sell Saltillo rugs, onyx, silver, Guatemalan clothing, blown glassware, masks, folk art, crafts, beach paraphernalia, and T-shirts in abundance. Prices are lower than in Cancún or Cozumel, and bargaining is expected.

Entertainment & Nightlife

Those in a party mood by day's end may want to start out at the beach bar and lounge of the **Na Balam** hotel on Playa Norte, which serves tapas and creative cocktails to a cool crowd. **Jax Bar & Grill,** on Avenida Rueda Medina, close to Hotel Posada del Mar, is a Texas-style sports bar offering live music nightly. **Las Palapas Chimbo's** restaurant on the beach becomes a jammin' dance joint with a live band from 9pm until whenever. Farther along the same stretch of beach, **Buho's,** the beach bar of the Cabañas María del Mar, has its moments as a popular, low-key hangout, complete with swinging seats under a giant beachfront *palapa.* It's open from midday until 11pm. A rock-'n'-roll–loving yacht set fueled by close to 100 tequila brands keeps the party going at **Fayne's,** located at Av. Hidalgo 12 and open nightly from 7pm to midnight or later. It offers excellent live music and dancing that usually gets going after 10pm. Also in the town center at the corner of Av. Hidalgo and Abasolo, the super-casual **La Terraza** hosts excellent Latin American bands. It's open from 7pm to midnight or later except for Sundays, when it's closed. A DJ spins tunes at **Poc-Na** (essentially a beach party thrown by the youth hostel) on the waterfront off the end of Av. Hidalgo, where a 20- and 30-something crowd dances on the sand until 4am.

Where to Stay

You'll find plenty of hotels in all price ranges on Isla Mujeres. The rates listed below do not include the 14% room tax. They also do not necessarily apply to the

Open-air restaurants line the streets of Isla Mujeres.

brief Christmas/New Year's season, when many hotels charge extra. High season runs from December through May and sometimes includes August. Low season is the rest of the year.

Those interested in private home rentals or longer-term stays can contact **Mundaca Travel and Real Estate** on Isla Mujeres (www.mundaca.com.mx; ✆ **866/646-0536** in the U.S., or 998/877-0025), or book online with **Isla Beckons** vacation rental service (www.islabeckons.com). More upscale vacation rentals are available through **Isla Home Services** (www.islahomeservices.com; ✆ **998/888-0948**). If you're looking for a quality all-inclusive resort near the town center, consider **Privilege Aluxes** (www.privilegehotels.com; ✆ **866/947-6002** in the U.S. or 998/848-8470), located at Av. Adolfo Lopez Mateos.

VERY EXPENSIVE

Hotel Villa Rolandi Gourmet & Beach Club ★★★ 📷

Villa Rolandi is a romantic escape on a little sheltered cove with a pristine white-sand beach. Each of the luxurious junior and master suites has a terrace or balcony with private whirlpool overlooking the sea. The large marble bathrooms feature enticing showers with multiple showerheads that convert into steam baths. Breakfast is served in the oceanfront restaurant or in bed, delivered to the room through a small portal. Three small but dazzling infinity pools look over the idyllic private beach. The spa offers an outdoor Thalasso therapy whirlpool and beachside massages. You can eat exceedingly well at **Casa Rolandi** (p. 126) without having to go off property, which is reached directly by yacht from Cancún's Embarcadero (provided complimentary by the resort) or via a 20-minute drive from town.

Fracc. Lagunamar, SM 7, Mza. 75, Locs. 15 and 16, 77400 Isla Mujeres, Q. Roo. www.villarolandi. com. ✆ **800/525-4800** in the U.S., or 998/999-2000. Fax 998/877-0100. 35 units. $337 and up junior suite, $428 and up master suite. Rates include full American breakfast. No children 12 and under. AE, MC, V. **Amenities:** Restaurant (see "Where to Eat," above); airport transfer via van (for a fee) and yacht (included); small fitness room; saltwater Jacuzzi; kayaks; 2 infinity pools; room service; spa. *In room:* Flatscreen TV, hair dryer, minibar, Wi-Fi.

EXPENSIVE

Hotel Na Balam ★★★ 🏨

This ecologically friendly hotel on Playa Norte promises a piece of Maya heaven on the beach, which is one of the most beautiful anywhere. Bleached white rooms lie in three sections separated only by sand, palms, and flowers; some face the beach and others lie in a garden setting with a swimming pool. They're individually decorated with a king-size or two double beds, folk art, and terrace or balcony with hammocks. Master suites feature additional amenities, including small pools with hydromassage. The older section is well kept and surrounds a lush inner courtyard and Playa Norte. Yoga practitioners take advantage of the numerous classes offered throughout the week; check with the reception for schedules. The beautiful turquoise cove in front of the hotel makes for perfect swimming and snorkeling. Na Balam's restaurant, **Zazil Ha** (p. 128), remains one of the island's most popular, and the beachside bar and lounge is a beautiful spot for sunsets. Na Balam is also popular for weddings.

Zazil Ha 118, 77400 Isla Mujeres, Q. Roo. www.nabalam.com. ✆ **998/881-4770.** Fax 998/877-0446. 32 units. High season $200–$275 double, $310 master suite; low season $120–$185 double, $200 master suite. Children 11 and under stay free. AE, MC, V. **Amenities:** Restaurant; bar; diving and snorkeling trips available; massages; yoga classes; Wi-Fi (free). *In room:* A/C, hair dryer, minibar, no phone.

Secreto ★   One of the Caribbean's top-rated resorts in the last decade, this hidden boutique hotel oozes a chic Mediterranean feel. Twelve suites overlook an infinity pool, Jacuzzi, and the open sea. Located on the northern end of the island, Secreto lies within walking distance of town, yet feels removed enough to make for an idyllic retreat. Tropical gardens surround the exquisite pool, and an outdoor living area offers large couches. The ultra-modern guest rooms feature simple and bold design lines along with featherbeds, large plasma TVs with DVD players and Bose docking stations, advanced dimming lighting, and deep balconies with sunbeds. Nine suites include king-size beds, while the remaining three have two double beds. There's no restaurant on-site, but several deliver to the hotel. A spa is expected to open in 2012.

Sección Rocas, Lote 1, 77400 Isla Mujeres, Q. Roo. www.hotelsecreto.com. ✆ **998/877-1039.** Fax 998/877-1048. 12 units. High season $250–$300 double; low season $200–$230. Extra person $25. AE, MC, V. **Amenities:** Bar; outdoor pool; fitness center. *In room:* A/C, flatscreen TV/DVD, fridge, hair dryer, minibar, MP3 docking station.

MODERATE

Hotel Cabañas María del Mar ★   A good choice for simple beach accommodations, the Cabañas María del Mar sits on the beautiful Playa Norte. Rooms in the older "tower" section behind the reception area offer partial ocean views and lie just a few steps from the beach. Single-story cabañas closer to the pool and garden are decorated in a rustic Mexican style with private terraces. The recently remodeled "castle" section sits in the same building as the restaurant. Upgraded rooms here offer air-conditioning, king-size beds, and balconies with partial ocean views. Beachfront Buho's offers casual all-day dining and drinks with swings and hammocks surrounding the three popular *palapa* bars. The central courtyard contains a small pool, as well.

Av. Arq. Carlos Lazo 1 (on Playa Norte, a half-block from the Hotel Na Balam), 77400 Isla Mujeres, Q. Roo. www.cabanasdelmar.com. ✆ **998/877-0179.** Fax 998/877-0213. 73 units. High season $120–$135 double; low season $75–$90 double. MC, V. Rates include Continental breakfast. **Amenities:** Restaurant; bar; outdoor pool. *In room:* A/C, TV, fridge.

Ixchel Beach Hotel ☺   This moderately priced "condohotel" enjoys a privileged location on Playa Norte. Most of the comfortable if indistinctive rooms in the two whitewashed towers offer large balconies with ocean and pool views; the one-bedroom suites also have kitchenettes and sitting areas with a futon. Especially popular with families, Ixchel sits right on an idyllic stretch of beach with lounge chairs and umbrellas and nearby access to watersports. The small swimming pool and bar sit adjacent to the beach, and the hotel lies less than a 10-minute walk from the ferry dock and town center.

Calle Guerrero at Playa Norte, 77400 Isla Mujeres, Q. Roo. www.ixchelbeachhotel.com. ✆ **998/999-2010.** Fax 998/877-2011. 117 units. High season $139 standard double, $230–$430 suite; low season $119 standard double, $150–$265 suite. AE, MC, V. **Amenities:** Restaurant; bar; direct beach access; 2 outdoor pools; small gym. *In room:* A/C, TV w/DVD, kitchenette (in all but standard rooms), Wi-Fi (free).

INEXPENSIVE

Hotel Belmar ★   Right in the center of Isla's entertainment district, this charming three-story hotel (no elevator) sits above the usually packed Rolandi's restaurant. The simple, attractive rooms come with tile floors, whitewashed furniture, and either a king bed or two twins or two doubles. The rooms are well maintained and have quiet air-conditioning. One large suite features a sitting area, large patio, and whirlpool. Though I had little trouble with noise from the restaurant in my third-floor room, light sleepers might want to look elsewhere. Although there's no beach here, it's easy to walk to one. A full breakfast is included.

Av. Hidalgo 110 (btw. Madero and Abasolo, 3½ blocks from the passenger-ferry pier), 77400 Isla Mujeres, Q. Roo. www.rolandi.com. © **998/877-0430.** Fax 998/877-0429. 11 units. High season $70 double, $100 suite; low season $42 double, $100 suite. Full breakfast included. AE, MC, V. **Amenities:** Restaurant/bar (see "Where to Eat," above); room service; Wi-Fi. *In room:* A/C, fan, TV.

Hotel las Palmas
This colorful family-run hotel features individually decorated rooms surrounding a palm-filled courtyard. Most rooms have murals designed by the owner and one king or two double beds with excellent mattresses. Guests, most of whom hail from North America and Europe, enjoy interacting in the hotel's friendly common areas, including on the rooftop deck where there's a communal kitchen and small dipping pool. Mother and daughter team Kate and Safari go out of their way to make guests feel at home. Las Palmas sits across the street from the municipal market and is a 5-minute walk from the beach.

Av. Guerrero 20, 77400 Isla Mujeres, Q. Roo. www.laspalmasonisla.com. © **998/236-5803.** 17 units. High season $80 double; low season $60 double. No credit cards. **Amenities:** Communal kitchen and library, dipping pool, rooftop deck, Wi-Fi (free). *In room:* A/C, fan, fridge, no phone.

Hotel Francis Arlene
This small family-run inn sits on a quiet street near the center of town. It's bright, cheerful, and well managed, and features attractive common spaces. For these reasons, it gets a lot of return guests and remains especially popular with families and seniors. Some rooms have ocean views, and many are remodeled or updated each year. They are comfortable, with tile floors, tiled bathrooms, balconies or patios, and face a central courtyard. Standard rooms include a coffeemaker and refrigerator; top-floor rooms come with kitchenettes and offer an ocean view. Ten rooms have only a ceiling fan and are the lowest-priced doubles; don't expect high-quality mattresses.

Guerrero 7 (5½ blocks inland from the ferry pier, btw. Abasolo and Matamoros), 77400 Isla Mujeres, Q. Roo. www.francisarlene.com. ©/fax **998/877-0310,** -0861. 24 units. High season $60–$75 double, $90 top-floor double; low season $50–$65 double, $80 top-floor double. MC, V. *In room:* A/C (in some), fridge, kitchenette (in some), no phone.

COZUMEL ★★★

70km (43 miles) S of Cancún; 19km (12 miles) SE of Playa del Carmen

Although otherwise a sleepy little Caribbean island, Cozumel's clear waters and exquisite coral reefs make it a world-famous destination for snorkeling and scuba diving. Far quieter than neighboring Cancún, without highways, high-rises, or construction projects, the only town on the island is San Miguel. Avenida Rafael Melgar lazily runs through it, the main waterfront road that includes a boardwalk with casual restaurants and a chilled-out bit of nightlife. Staying in town is fun and convenient. Alternatively, several peaceful dive resorts are along the island's western coast.

The Coast Cozumel is 45km (28 miles) long and 18km (11 miles) wide, and lies just 19km (12 miles) from the mainland. Most of the terrain is flat and clothed in a low tropical forest. Tall reefs line the **southwest coast,** creating towering walls

that offer divers a fairytale seascape to explore. The water on the protected side, the **western shore,** stays as calm as an aquarium, unless a front is blowing through. The rougher, wild **eastern shore** remains more lightly traveled for those preferring to wander off the beaten path. **Chankanaab National Park,** along the south-western shore of the island, offers beautiful sightseeing and sunning spots.

Things to Do   Come to Cozumel to sink your toes into the same dreamy white sand and turquoise waters that Cancún offers, but without its commercialism or party atmosphere. Put on a snorkel mask to peek underwater near the **light-house,** even if you don't dive here. Explore the crocodile-filled **Faro Celerain** ecological reserve and drive through the inland jungle on the way to the Maya ruins at **San Gervasio.**

Eating & Drinking   Dining in Cozumel is not particularly sophisticated, with Italian and Mexican predominating. Caribbean-caught **seafood** fills restaurant menus (with **lobster** in abundance), while traditional Yucatán influences bring zest to chicken and pork by infusing them with *mole*, achiote, and garlic. For a more refined dining experience, the island's few resorts offer the best options.

Underwater   **Scuba diving** in Cozumel is the finest in the Western Hemisphere, with a tremendous diversity of reefs, caves, and canyons teeming with tropical fish and coral. The colors of the underwater life here shimmer with resplendence and breathtaking biodiversity. Whether you are a novice toying with the idea of a beginner dive, or an expert seeking new underwater frontiers, don't leave Cozumel without submersing yourself below the surface.

Essentials
GETTING THERE

BY PLANE   During high season, several more international commercial flights fly in and out of Cozumel's airport (CZM) than in low season, including a few flights from northern U.S. cities. Airlines include **Interjet** (a Mexican domestic carrier), **Maya Air** (which flies between Cozumel and Cancún), **American, Continental, Delta, Frontier, United,** and **US Airways.** You might also inquire about buying a ticket on one of the charter flights in high season. Several of the island's independent hotels work with packagers.

BY FERRY   Passenger ferries run to and from Playa del Carmen. **México Waterjets** (www.mexicowaterjets.com; ✆ **987/872-1508**) and **Ultramar** (www.granpuerto.com.mx; ✆ **998/881-5890**) offer departures almost every hour in the morning and about every 2 hours in the afternoon. The schedules change according to seasons but generally start at 7am and continue until 9 or 10pm. The trip takes 30 to 45 minutes, depending on conditions, and costs about 160 pesos each way. The boats are air-conditioned. In Playa del Carmen, the ferry dock is 1½ blocks from the main square. In Cozumel, the ferries use Muelle Fiscal, the town pier, a block from the main square. Luggage storage at the Cozumel dock costs 20 pesos per day.

The car ferry that used to operate from Puerto Morelos now uses the Calica pier just south of Playa del Carmen. The fare for a standard car is 683 pesos. **Trans-Caribe** (www.transcaribe. net; ✆ **987/872-7688**) has four departures daily; check the website for exact scheduling. The ferry docks in Cozumel at the **Muelle Internacional** (the **International Pier,** which is south of town near La Ceiba Hotel).

BY BUS   If you plan to travel on the mainland by bus, purchase tickets in advance from the ticket office for **ADO buses** called **Ticket**

The ferry runs between Cozumel and Playa del Carmen.

AN all-inclusive **VACATION IN COZUMEL**

Booking a room at an all-inclusive resort should be done through a vacation packager. Booking lodging directly through the hotel usually doesn't make sense, even with frequent-flier mileage to burn, because the discounts offered by most packagers are so deep. I include websites for you to find out more info about the properties, but don't expect to find clear info on rates. The game of setting rates with these hotels is complicated and always in flux.

Two all-inclusives are north of town: **El Cozumeleño** (www.elcozumeleno.com) and the **Meliá Cozumel** (www.solmelia.com). Both occupy multistory modern buildings and have attractive rooms. El Cozumeleño is the larger of the two resorts and has the nicest hotel pool on the island. It's best suited for active types. The Meliá is quieter and offers golf discounts for the nearby golf course. The Cozumeleño's small beach has to be replenished with sand periodically. The Meliá's beach is long, narrow, and pretty, but occasionally seaweed washes up, which doesn't happen on the rest of the island's coast. The advantages of staying in these two are the proximity to town, with its restaurants, clubs, movie theaters, and so on, and the fact that most rooms at these hotels come with views of the ocean.

The **Cozumel Palace** (www.palaceresorts.com) lies right on the water on the southern fringes of town. Despite the location, it doesn't have a beach. But that's not so bad. The water is usually so calm on Cozumel's west shore that swimming here is like swimming in a pool, and you can snorkel right out of the hotel.

Of the all-inclusives to the south, my favorites are the **Occidental** resort (**Grand Cozumel** and **Allegro Cozumel;** www.occidentalhotels.com) and the **Iberostar Cozumel** (www.iberostar.com). These are "village" style resorts with two- and three-story buildings, often with thatched roofs, spread over a large area at the center of which is the pool and activities area. Rooms at the Grand Cozumel are larger and more attractive than the all-inclusives in the south. Like the Occidental chain, Iberostar has several properties in the Mexican Caribbean. This one is the smallest. I like its food and service and the beauty of the grounds. The rooms are attractive and well maintained. The advantage to staying in these places is that you're close to a lot of dive sites; the disadvantage is that you're somewhat isolated from town, and you don't have many rooms with ocean views.

The **Fiesta Americana Cozumel All-Inclusive** (www.fiestamericana.com), on a pristine stretch of beach off the road toward Chankanaab, features an excellent dive center next to the oldest and largest coral reef in the hemisphere. The friendly **Hotel Cozumel & Resort** (www.hotelcozumel.com.mx) lies within short walking distance of the town and also offers diving packages.

Bus on the municipal pier (open while the ferries are running). Another is on Calle 2 Norte and Avenida 10 (📞 **987/872-1706**). Hours are from 8:30am to 9:30pm daily. ADO buses make the 1-hour trip from Cancún airport to Playa del Carmen (and back) throughout the day for 116 pesos; you can easily catch the ferry to Cozumel from Playa.

ORIENTATION

ARRIVING Cozumel's **airport** is just a 5-minute drive from downtown. **Transportes Terrestre** (𝄐 **987/872-1323**) provides hotel transportation in multi-passenger vans. Buy your ticket as you exit the terminal. To hotels downtown, the fare is 57 pesos per person; to hotels along the north and south shore, 96 pesos. A private taxi to downtown costs 134 pesos. Passenger ferries arrive at the Muelle Fiscal, the municipal pier, by the town's main square. Cruise ships dock at the **Punta Langosta** pier, several blocks south of the Muelle Fiscal, and at the **International Pier,** which is at Km 4 of the southern coastal road. A third cruise-ship pier, the **Puerta Maya** near the International Pier, is also operational.

 Be Streetwise

North–south streets—the *avenidas*—have the right of way, and traffic doesn't slow down or stop.

CITY LAYOUT San Miguel's main waterfront street is **Avenida Rafael Melgar.** Running parallel to Rafael Melgar are *avenidas* numbered in multiples of five—5, 10, 15. **Avenida Juárez** runs perpendicular to these, heading inland from the ferry dock. Avenida Juárez divides the town into northern and southern halves. The *calles* (streets) that parallel Juárez to the north have even numbers. The ones to the south have odd numbers, except for Calle Rosado Salas, which runs between calles 1 and 3. Vehicles on the *avenidas* have the right of way.

ISLAND LAYOUT One road runs along the western coast of the island, which faces the Yucatán mainland. It has different names. North of town, it's **Santa Pilar** or **San Juan;** in the city, it is **Avenida Rafael Melgar;** south of town, it's **Costera Sur.** Hotels stretch along this road north and south of town. The road runs to the southern tip of the island (Punta Sur), passing **Chankanaab National Park.** **Avenida Juárez** (and its extension, the **Carretera Transversal**) runs east from the town across the island. It passes the airport and the turnoff to the ruins of San Gervasio before reaching the undeveloped ocean side of the island. It then turns south and follows the coast to the southern tip, where it meets the Costera Sur.

GETTING AROUND You can walk to most destinations in town, and it's very safe. Getting to outlying hotels and beaches requires a rental car, moped, or taxi.

Car rentals are about $60 for a VW bug and $95 for a Jeep Wrangler. **Avis** (𝄐 **987/872-0099**) and **Hertz** (𝄐 **987/871-6783**) have counters in the airport. Other major rental companies have offices in town, including **Thrifty** (𝄐 **987/869-2957**) at Juárez 181, between avenidas 5 and 10 Norte. Rentals are easy to arrange through your hotel or at any of the many local rental offices.

Scooters are readily available and cost about $35 for a full day including a helmet but not insurance, which runs about $15 extra. **HTL Rentals** (𝄐 **987/869-3097**) at Av. 5 between calles 2 and 4 Norte, is a reliable agency. If you rent a scooter, be careful: Scooter accidents easily rank as the greatest cause of injury in Cozumel. Before renting one, inspect it carefully to see that all the gizmos—horn, light, starter, seat, mirror—are in good shape. I've been offered scooters with unbalanced wheels, which made

Carnaval

Carnaval (similar to Mardi Gras) is Cozumel's most colorful fiesta. It begins the Thursday before Ash Wednesday, with daytime street dancing and nighttime parades on Thursday, Saturday, and Monday (the best).

them unsteady at higher speeds, but the renter quickly exchanged them upon my request. You are required to stay on paved roads. It's illegal to ride a moped without a helmet outside of town (subject to a 500-peso fine).

Cozumel has lots of **taxis** and a strong drivers' union. Fares are standardized—there's no bargaining. Here are a few sample fares for two people (there is an additional charge for extra passengers to most destinations): island tour, 800 pesos; town to southern Hotel Zone, 100 to 200 pesos; town to northern hotels, 50 to 70 pesos; town to Chankanaab, 120 pesos for up to four people; in and around town, 50 pesos.

VISITOR INFORMATION The **Municipal Tourism Office** (www.cozumel.gob. mx; ✆ **987/869-0212**), located at Plaza del Sol, also has information booths at the International Pier and Punta Langosta Pier. It's open 8am to 3pm Monday to Friday.

[Fast FACTS] COZUMEL

Area Code The telephone area code is **987.**

ATMs, Banks & Currency Exchange The island has several banks and *casas de cambio*, as well as ATMs. Most places accept dollars, but you usually get a better deal paying in pesos. **HSBC** has an ATM machine on the corner of the main plaza at Av. 5 Sur and Calle 1 Sur; the fee for withdrawing cash here is less than at other ATM machines along Avenida Melgar.

Climate From October to December, there can be strong winds all over the Yucatán, as well as some rain. June through October is the rainy season.

Consulates The **U.S. Consular Agent** is in the Villa Mar Mall in the Plaza, Parque Juárez between

Avenida Juárez and 5th Av. Norte (✆ **987/872-4574**); open Monday through Friday from noon to 2pm.

Hospital Médica San Miguel (✆ **987/872-0103**) works for most things and includes intensive-care facilities. It's on Calle 6 Norte between avenidas 5 and 10. **Centro Médico Cozumel** (✆ **987/872-9400**) is an alternative. It's at the intersection of Calle 1 Sur and Avenida 50.

Internet Access Several cybercafes are in and around the main square. If you go just a bit off Avenida Rafael Melgar and the main square, prices drop. Rates at **Mexatel,** between Av. Juárez 15 and Calle 2 Norte, are 10 pesos per hour. It's open daily from 9am to 10pm.

Post Office The *correo* is on Avenida Rafael Melgar at Calle 7 Sur (✆ **987/872-0106**), at the southern edge of town. It's open Monday through Friday from 9am to 3pm, Saturday from 9am to noon.

Recompression Chamber Cozumel has three *cámaras de recompresión.* The best are the **Hyperbaric Chamber and Clinic** (www.sssnetwork.com; ✆ **987/872-2387**, -1430), staffed 24 hours, at Calle 5 Sur 21-B, between Avenida Rafael Melgar and Avenida 5 Sur; and the **Hyperbaric Center of Cozumel** (✆ **987/872-3070**), at Calle 6 Norte, between avenidas 5 and 10.

Seasons High season is from Christmas to Easter and August.

5

ISLA MUJERES & COZUMEL

Fast Facts: Cozumel

Exploring

For **diving** and **snorkeling,** you have plenty of dive shops to choose from. For **island tours, ruins tours** on and off the island, **evening cruises,** and other activities, go to a travel agency, such as **Proviajes,** Calle 2 Norte 365, between avenidas 15 and 20 (www.proviajescozumel.com; ℭ **987/869-0516**). Office hours are Monday through Saturday from 9am to 5pm, Saturday from 10am to 3pm.

Carnaval festivities.

WATERSPORTS

SCUBA DIVING   Cozumel is the number-one dive destination in the Western Hemisphere. Don't forget your dive card and dive log, unless you're coming for just an introductory dive or beginner certification course. Dive shops will rent you scuba gear but won't take you out on a boat until you show some documentation. If you have a medical condition, bring a letter signed by a doctor stating that you've been cleared to dive. A two-tank dive trip costs about $70 to $90; some shops offer an additional one-tank dive for a modest additional fee. A lot of divers save some money by buying a dive package with a hotel. These usually include two dives a day.

Diving in Cozumel is drift diving, which can be a little disconcerting for novices. The current that sweeps along Cozumel's reefs, pulling nutrients into them and making them as large as they are, also dictates how you dive here. The problem is that it pulls at different speeds at different depths and in different places. When it's pulling strong, it can quickly scatter a dive group. The role of the dive master becomes more important, especially with choosing the dive location. Cozumel has a lot of dive locations. To mention but a few: the famous **Palancar Reef,** with its caves and canyons, plentiful fish, and sea coral; the monstrous **Santa Rosa Wall,** famous for its depth, sea life, coral, and sponges; the **San Francisco Reef,** with a shallower drop-off wall and fascinating sea life; and the **Yucab Reef,** with its beautiful coral.

For Experienced Divers

Bring proof of your diver's certification and your log. Underwater currents can be strong, and many of the reef drops are quite steep, so dive operators want to make sure divers are experienced.

Finding a dive shop in town is even easier than finding a jewelry store. Cozumel has more than 50 dive operators, including: **Aqua Safari,** which has a location on Av. Rafael Melgar 429 at Calle 5 (www.aquasafari.com; ℭ **987/872-0101**). **Dive Paradise** (www.diveparadise.com; ℭ **987/872-1007**), which has four locations in Cozumel including the central facility between the Hotel Barracuda and Naval Base, has been in business more than 25 years and offers dive training at all levels. **Liquid Blue Divers** (www.liquidbluedivers.com; ℭ **987/869-7794**) arranges tours by

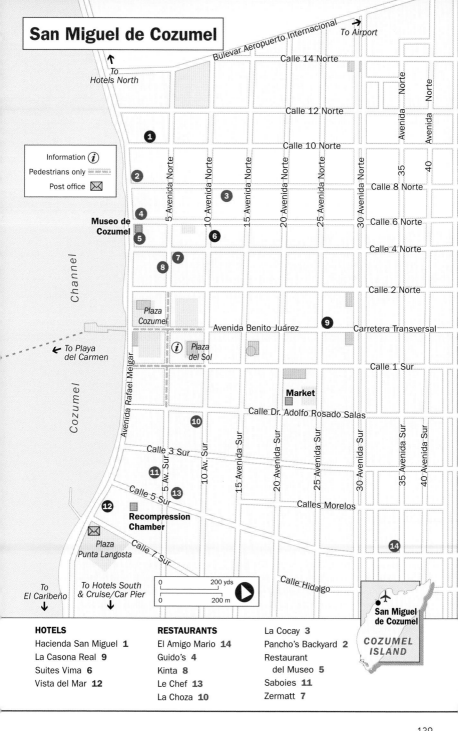

San Miguel de Cozumel

To Airport

Bulevar Aeropuerto Internacional

Calle 14 Norte

To Hotels North

Calle 12 Norte

Calle 10 Norte

Information (i)
Pedestrians only
Post office ✉

Calle 8 Norte

Museo de Cozumel

Calle 6 Norte

Calle 4 Norte

Calle 2 Norte

Plaza Cozumel

Avenida Benito Juárez

Carretera Transversal

To Playa del Carmen

(i) Plaza del Sol

Calle 1 Sur

Market

Calle Dr. Adolfo Rosado Salas

Calle 3 Sur

Calle 5 Sur

Calles Morelos

Recompression Chamber

Plaza Punta Langosta

Calle 7 Sur

To El Caribeño

To Hotels South & Cruise/Car Pier

Calle Hidalgo

0   200 yds
0   200 m

San Miguel de Cozumel

COZUMEL ISLAND

HOTELS	RESTAURANTS		
Hacienda San Miguel **1**	El Amigo Mario **14**	La Cocay **3**	
La Casona Real **9**	Guido's **4**	Pancho's Backyard **2**	
Suites Vima **6**	Kinta **8**	Restaurant del Museo **5**	
Vista del Mar **12**	Le Chef **13**	Saboies **11**	
	La Choza **10**	Zermatt **7**	

appointment and provides high-quality service to small groups. **Scuba Du** (www.scubadu.com; ☏ **987/872-9505**), based at the Presidente Inter-Continental resort (p. 151), offers excellent diving excursions, discovery dives and refresher courses, and all levels of diving certification.

Cozumel has several colorful and vibrant dive sites.

SNORKELING   Most resorts offer snorkeling equipment, and many dive shops do, as well. Even though you won't see a lot of the more delicate structures, such as fan coral, you will still see plenty of sea creatures and enjoy the clear, calm water of Cozumel's protected west side. When contracting for a snorkel tour, stay away from the companies that cater to the cruise ships. Those tours are crowded and not very fun.

BOAT TRIPS   Travel agencies and hotels can arrange boat trips, a popular pastime on Cozumel. Choose from evening cruises, cocktail cruises, glass-bottom boat cruises, and other options. A real submarine tour is offered by **Atlantis Submarines** (www.atlantisadventures.com; ☏ **987/872-5671**). The tour includes 40 minutes at up to 30m (100 ft.) beneath the surface of the Chankanaab protected marine park (total excursion time is 1½ hr.). It costs $89 per adult, $59 for kids ages 4 to 12. This is a far superior experience to the **Sub See Explorer** offered by **AquaWorld** (www.aquaworld.com.mx), which is really just a glorified glass-bottom boat. You can make reservations online and get a bit of a discount.

FISHING   The best months for fishing are March through June, when the catch includes blue and white marlin, sailfish, tarpon, and swordfish. The least expensive option would be to contact a boat owner directly and negotiate a price. A reliable operator offering flats bonefishing and deep-sea fishing in Cozumel is **Aquarius Fishing** (www.aquariusflatsfishing.com;

 Cenote Diving on the Mainland

A popular activity in the Yucatán is cave diving. The peninsula's underground **cenotes** (seh-*noh*-tehs)—sinkholes or wellsprings—lead to a vast system of underground caverns. The gently flowing water is so clear that divers seem to float on air through caves complete with stalactites and stalagmites. If you want to try this but didn't plan a trip to the mainland, contact **Germán Yañez** (www. germanyanez.com; ☏ **987/872-5659**), based at 60 Avenida 117, between Calles 2 and 4 North. He offers all-day cenote tours as well as cave dive training. The cenotes lie 30 to 45 minutes from Playa del Carmen, and a dive in each cenote lasts around 45 minutes. Dives happen within the daylight zone, about 40m (131 ft.) into the caverns, and no more than 18m (59 ft.) deep. Open water certification and at least five logged dives are required. For those without diving certifications, a cenote snorkeling tour is also offered.

ANATOMY OF THE CORAL reef

Corals are polyps, tiny animals with hollow, cylindrical bodies that attach by the thousands to hard surfaces of the sea floor. The polyps extract calcium carbonate from the seawater to create hard, cup-shaped skeletons that assume an endless variety of shapes and sizes. These massive limestone structures shelter nearly one-fourth of all marine life. The soft, delicate polyps retreat into their skeletons during the day, but their protruding tentacles can be seen when they feed at night.

Cozumel boasts the world's second largest reef (after Australia's Great Barrier Reef) with 26 classes of coral. Two distinct types of coral formations dominate its waters. Bases of the less developed platform reefs, such as Colombia Shallows, Paradise, and Yucab, are rarely more than 9 to 15m (30–49 ft.) in depth.

Edge reefs are more complex structures built up over many millennia, and their layered structures peak high above the edge of the drop-off, extending as much as 55m (180 ft.) below the surface. These are found mostly in the south; examples include Palancar, Colombia Deep, Punta Sur, and Maracaibo.

© 987/872-1092), located at Avenida 20 Sur between Calle 3 Sur and Calle Rosado Salas. The cost for an 8-hour excursion is $385 for up to two anglers, and $100 more for each additional angler.

CHANKANAAB NATIONAL PARK & FARO CELERAIN ECOLOGICAL RESERVE (PUNTA SUR)

Chankanaab National Park ★ (www.cozumelparks.com), off the Carretera Costera Sur at Km 9, is the pride of many islanders. In Mayan, Chankanaab means "little sea," which refers to a beautiful land-locked pool connected to the sea through an underwater tunnel. Admission to the park includes a dolphin presentation and sea lion show, manatee exhibition, beach with facilities, and excellent snorkeling. Arrive before 9am to stake out a chair and *palapa* before the cruise-ship crowd arrives. The snorkeling is also best before noon. The park has bathrooms, lockers, a gift shop, several snack huts, a restaurant, and a *palapa* for renting snorkeling gear. The entrance is $21 for adults, $14 for children under 12.

You can also swim with dolphins here. **Dolphin Discovery** (www.dolphindiscovery.com; © **800/293-9698**) has several programs for experiencing these sea creatures. These are popular, so plan ahead—you should make reservations well in advance. The surest way is through the website—make sure to pick the Cozumel location, as there are a couple of others on this coast. There are three different programs for swimming with dolphins. The Dolphin Royal Swim costs $129 and features close interaction with the beautiful swimmers. There are also swim-and-snorkel programs for under $100 that get you in the water with these creatures. The park is open daily from 8am to 5pm and lies south of town, just past the Fiesta Americana Hotel. Taxis run constantly between the park, the hotels, and town (about 120 pesos from town for up to four people).

Faro Celerain Ecological Reserve (admission $10), also called Punta Sur, is a gorgeous ecological reserve at the southern tip of the island that includes the Columbia Lagoon. A number of crocodiles make the lagoon their home, so swimming is not only a bad idea, it's not allowed. The only practical way of going out to the lighthouse, which lies 8km (5 miles) from the entrance, is to rent a car

Chankanaab National Park.

or scooter; there's no taxi stand, and usually few people. At the entrance to Punta Sur, you'll find a reggae beach bar and a sea turtle nesting area. The lovely beaches just in front are kept as natural as possible, but be cautious about swimming or snorkeling here depending on the winds and currents. Regular hours are daily 9am to 6pm. If you have a rental car, getting here is no problem, and this is usually a great place to get away from the crowds and have a lot of beach to yourself. Occasionally, boat tours of the lagoon are offered. Ask at the information office.

BEACHES

Along both the west and east sides of the island you'll see signs advertising beach clubs. A "beach club" in Cozumel can mean just a *palapa* hut that's open to the public and serves soft drinks, beer, and fried fish. It can also mean a recreational beach with the full gamut of offerings, from banana boats to parasailing. They also usually have locker rooms, a pool, and food. The biggest of these is **Mr. Sancho's** (www.mrsanchos.com; ✆ **987/112-1933**), south of downtown San Miguel at Km 15 on the main road between the Reef Club and Allegro Resort. It offers a restaurant, bar, massage service, and motorized and nonmotorized watersports. Quieter versions of beach clubs are **Playa San Francisco** (no phone) and **Paradise Beach** (www.paradise-beach-cozumel.com), next to Playa San Francisco. All of these beaches are south of Chankanaab Park and easily visible from the road. Several have swimming pools with beach furniture, a restaurant, and snorkel rental. They cost about $12 to enter.

Once you get to the end of the island, the beach clubs become simple places where you can eat, drink, and lie out on the beach. **Paradise Cafe** is on the southern tip of the island across from Punta Sur Nature Park, and as you go up the eastern side of the island you pass **Playa Bonita, Chen Río,** and **Punta Morena.** Except on Sunday, when the locals head for the beaches, these places are practically deserted. Most of the east coast is unsafe for swimming because of the surf. The beaches tend to be small and occupy gaps in the rocky coast.

ISLAND TOURS

Travel agencies can arrange a variety of tours, including horseback, Jeep, and ATV tours. Taxi drivers charge about 800 pesos for a 3-hour tour of the island, which most people would consider only mildly amusing, depending on the driver's personality.

Crocodiles in the Faro Celerain Ecological Reserve.

OTHER ATTRACTIONS

MAYA RUINS A popular island excursion is to **San Gervasio** (100 B.C.–A.D. 1600). Follow the paved transversal road to Km 7.5, and you'll see the well-marked turnoff about halfway between town and the eastern coast. For what you see, it's a bit overpriced. Entrance is $8; camera permits are $5 extra. A small tourist center at the entrance sells handicrafts, cold drinks, and snacks. The ruins are open daily from 7am to 4pm.

When it comes to Cozumel's Mayan ruins, getting there is most of the fun—do it for the mystique and for the trip, not for the size, scale, or condition of the ruins. The buildings, though preserved, are crudely made and would not be much of a tourist attraction if they were not the island's principal ruins. More significant than beautiful, this site was once an important ceremonial center where the Maya gathered, coming even from the mainland. The important deity was Ixchel, the goddess of weaving, women, childbirth, pilgrims, the moon, and medicine. Although you won't see any representations of Ixchel at San Gervasio today, Bruce Hunter, in his *Guide to Ancient Maya Ruins,* writes that priests hid behind a large pottery statue of her and became the voice of the goddess, speaking to pilgrims and answering their petitions. Ixchel was the wife of Itzamná, the sun god.

Guides charge about $35 for a tour for one to six people. Seeing it takes 30 to 60 minutes. Taxi drivers offer transportation for about $50, which includes the driver waiting for you outside the ruins.

A HISTORY MUSEUM The **Museo de la Isla de Cozumel (Cozumel Island Museum) ★**, Avenida Rafael Melgar between calles 4 and 6 Norte (✆ 987/872-1475), is more than just a nice place to spend a rainy hour. On the first floor, an exhibit illustrates endangered species, the origin of the island, and its present-day topography and plant and animal life, including an explanation of coral formation. The second-floor galleries feature the history of the town, artifacts from the island's pre-Hispanic sites, and Colonial-era cannons, swords, and ship paraphernalia. It's open daily from 9am to 5pm (but closes at 4pm on Sun). Admission is $4. There's also a gift shop and a picturesque rooftop cafe that serves breakfast and lunch (p. 147; you don't need to pay admission to eat here unless you plan to visit the museum, too).

GOLF Cozumel has an 18-hole course designed by Jack Nicklaus. It's at the **Cozumel Country Club** (www.cozumelcountryclub.com.mx; ✆ 987/872-9570), north of San Miguel. Greens fees are $169 for a morning tee time, including cart rental and tax. Afternoon tee times cost $105. Tee times

San Gervasio Maya ruins.

can be reserved 3 days in advance. A few hotels have special memberships with discounts for guests and advance tee times; guests at Playa Azul Golf and Beach Club pay no greens fees, but the cart costs $25.

Where to Eat

The island offers a number of tasty restaurants. Taxi drivers will often steer you toward restaurants that pay them commissions; don't heed their advice.

Zermatt (☏ 987/872-1384), a nice little bakery selling homemade breads and desserts, is on Avenida 5 at Calle 4 Norte. It's open Monday to Saturday from 7am to 8:30pm. Morning tacos of *cochinita pibil* (traditionally a breakfast item) are served at **El Amigo Mario** (☏ 987/872-0742), on Calle 5 Sur, between Francisco Mújica and Avenida 35. The doors close at 12:30pm. For traditional Yucatecan food, **Sabores** (no phone), at 316 Avenida 5 between Calle 3 Sur and Calle 5 Sur, offers homemade lunches right in the owner's charming yellow house. Stop by anytime Monday through Saturday between noon and 4pm.

EXPENSIVE

Cabaña del Pescador (Lobster House) ★★ LOBSTER   The story's a little strange, but brothers Fernando and Enrique, who no longer speak with each other due to a business dispute, run adjacent restaurants both called the Lobster House. They have slight differences in decor, but both restaurants are excellent. Fresh lobster is weighed, then grilled or boiled with a hint of spices, and served with melted butter or garlic, accompanied by sides of rice, vegetables, and bread. Does lobster require anything more? Lobster is the only thing on the menu at Fernando's restaurant, but Enrique will also cook up steaks, shrimp, or fish. The setting is pure tropical—a pair of thatched bungalows bordering a pond with lily pads and reeds, traversed by a small footbridge. The open-air rooms flicker with the glow of candles and are furnished with rustic tables and chairs. The restaurants ramble around quite a bit, so explore until you find the spot most to your taste. Finish with the signature Key lime pie.

Carretera Santa Pilar Km 4 (across from Playa Azul Hotel). ☏ **987/872-0795.** Reservations not accepted. Lobster (by weight) 250–450 pesos. No credit cards. Daily 6–10:30pm.

El Caribeño ★ MEXICAN/SEAFOOD   The oversized beachside *palapa* enjoys an uninterrupted view of the Caribbean, making this one of the most scenic open-air restaurants on the island. Gracious Mexican waiters serve Caribbean and Mayan specialties. Start with an order of fresh ceviche, lime soup, or rich guacamole, followed by local fish prepared in a banana leaf with tomato, onion, and achiote sauce. Other tasty delights include coconut shrimp, black shrimp tacos, and Caribbean lobster tail. Finish with a scoop of coconut ice cream. The 10-minute drive from town to the Intercon is worth it just to see this idyllic setting, and the atmosphere of El Caribeño is as casual and relaxed as the island itself.

Costera Sur Km 6.5, next to beach of the Presidente Intercontinental. www.intercontinental cozumel.com. ⓒ **987/872-9500.** Main courses 120–375 pesos. AE, MC, V. Daily 7am–11pm.

Guido's ★★ SWISS/ITALIAN   The inviting terrace, with director's chairs and rustic wood tables, makes this a restful place in daytime and a romantic spot at night. The kitchen blends Mediterranean, Italian, and Swiss influences. The specialties are wood-fired pizzas and homemade pastas, including lasagna with a Bolognese and béchamel sauce and seafood linguine. For something a little more substantive, try prosciutto-wrapped scallops or fresh fish with browned butter, black olives, capers, and lime. Another item people love here is the *pan de ajo*—fresh bread prepared with olive oil, garlic, and rosemary. The impressive wine list includes featured bottles and wines by the glass.

Av. Rafael Melgar (btw. calles 6 and 8 Norte). ⓒ **987/872-0946.** Reservations recommended. Main courses 190–295 pesos; pizzas 155–195 pesos. AE, MC, V. Mon–Sat 11am–11pm; Sun 3–9:30pm.

La Cocay ★★★ MEDITERRANEAN/SEAFOOD   La Cocay, which means "firefly" in Mayan, serves the most original cooking on the island. An open kitchen separates the dining room from the garden patio, glittering with white lights to create an alluring atmosphere. For an appetizer, the empanadas with goat cheese and caramelized apples make for excellent tapas, as does the sesame sashimi tuna with noodles and a peanut sauce. For a main course, try the 8-oz. filet mignon with garlic mashed potatoes or the succulent roasted duck with sweet

A laid-back outdoor restaurant in Cozumel.

potatoes. Give special consideration to the daily specials and the wonderful chocolate torte. It takes a little extra time to prepare, so order it early. The wine list offers excellent selections from South America.

Calle 8 Norte 208 (btw. avs. 10 and 15). www. lacocay.com. ⓒ **987/872-5533.** Reservations recommended. Main courses 116–290 pesos. AE, MC, V. Mon–Sat 5:30–11pm.

MODERATE

Coconuts ★★ 🎁 SEAFOOD This fun-filled beach restaurant and bar sits on the highest point in Cozumel, which really isn't saying much but nevertheless offers a magnificent view of the Caribbean. Coconuts is open only during the day and has no electricity—running only a daytime generator using solar power. Grab a plastic table in the sand or a seat under the open-air *palapa,* and check out the proverbs around you. One says, "beer, so much more than just a breakfast drink," while another advises, "what happens at Coconuts stays at Coconuts." If you do nothing else here, please order the mixed seafood ceviche. It's just too delicious. There are also sumptuous shrimp quesadillas, the freshest guacamole, and all kinds of tacos and fajitas.

Carratera Oriente Km 43.5. No phone. Main courses 100–200 pesos. No credit cards. Daily 10am–dusk.

Kinta ★★ CARIBBEAN   An excellent example of Mexican creativity, this chic restaurant blends tropical decor with a cool urban style. Chill-out music fills the air of the lush garden terrace decorated with palms, tiny white lights, and a pond. Chef Kris Wallenta, who previously worked at Guido's and trained at New York's French Culinary Institute, has created a menu celebrating contemporary Mexican cuisine. I recommend the "Mexikanissimo" to start—crispy warm *panela* cheese over a green tomato sauce with herbs. Then order a chile relleno—a poblano pepper with vegetable ratatouille and cheese, baked and cooked over red sauce with a chipotle cream. The filet mignon with *huitlacoche* (corn mushroom), mashed potatoes, and poblano pepper sauce is terrific, too. A well-balanced and reasonably priced wine list accompanies the menu.

Av. 5 148B (btw. calles 2 and 4 Norte). ✆ **987/869-0544.** Main courses 145–225 pesos. MC, V. Tues–Sun 5:30–11pm; closed Mon.

La Choza ★ MEXICAN/YUCATECAN   A favorite among locals, La Choza is an open-air restaurant with well-spaced tables under a brick dome roof. Flavorful platters of chiles rellenos, fajitas, kebabs, and grilled fish and meat selections are simple and delicious. Be sure to add some of the zesty table sauces and guacamole to your meal. Breakfasts are tasty.

Rosado Salas 198 (at Av. 10 Sur). ✆ **987/872-0958.** Reservations accepted for groups of 6 or more. Breakfast 45–60 pesos; main courses 96–192 pesos. AE, MC, V. Daily 7:30am–10pm.

Le Chef ★ 🏛 MEDITERRANEAN   This artsy European-style bistro is more Mediterranean than Mexican, where the only local dish is tortilla soup. Otherwise, the cooks focus on salads packed with fresh vegetables, creative pastas, and first-rate pizzas. For fish fans, the catch of the day is sourced locally and served with fresh salsa, while land-lovers may prefer a thick Black Angus steak. Grab a table in the small eclectic dining room or on the sidewalk in front. This is an especially popular spot for lunch and a bit quieter at dinner.

398 Av. 5 (corner of Calle 5 Sur). ✆ **987/878-4391.** Pizza and lunch items 85–145 pesos; main courses 105–285 pesos. MC, V. Mon–Sat noon–11pm.

Pancho's Backyard ★★★ MEXICAN   Owned by father and son duo Pancho and Panchito, this imaginative open-air restaurant surrounded by palms, banana trees, and trickling fountains occupies one of the town's original buildings. Cuisine here focuses on traditional Mexican fare—corn, beans, vegetables, and rice—with a healthy selection of chicken and fish plates. My favorite is the mahimahi filet topped with an almond, mango, orange, and pineapple *pico de gallo.* Homemade tortilla chips come with fresh tomato and onion salsa, as well as a bowl of extraordinarily spicy habanero sauce. Wash it all down with one of the island's best margaritas. Waiters wearing white *guayaberas* offer friendly, efficient service. There's also an outstanding artisan store, Los Cinco Soles, here (p. 147).

Av. Melgar 27 at Calle 8 Norte. www.panchosbackyard.com. ℂ **987/872-2141.** Lunch $7–$17; dinner $12–$19. AE, MC, V. Mon–Sat 10am–11pm; Sun 5–11pm.

INEXPENSIVE

El Moro 🍴 REGIONAL   El Moro is an out-of-the-way place that has been around for a long time. It's popular with the locals, who come for the food, service, and prices, but not the decor, which is orange, orange, orange, and Formica. Get here by taxi, which will cost a couple of bucks. Portions are generous. Any of the shrimp dishes use the real jumbo variety when available. For something different, try the *pollo Ticuleño,* a specialty from the town of Ticul layering tomato sauce, mashed potatoes, crispy baked corn tortillas, and fried chicken breast, topped with shredded cheese and green peas. Chicken is prepared half a dozen additional ways, too. Other specialties include enchiladas and fresh seafood, plus grilled steaks and sandwiches.

75 Bis Norte 124 (btw. calles 2 and 4 Norte). ℂ **987/872-3029.** Main courses 60–200 pesos. MC, V. Fri–Wed 1–11pm.

INEXPENSIVE

Restaurant del Museo BREAKFAST/MEXICAN   The museum's rooftop restaurant and cafe remains my favorite place in San Miguel for breakfast or lunch (weather permitting). It offers a serene ocean view, removed from the traffic noise below and sheltered from the sun above. Breakfasts include *huevos rancheros* with corn tortillas, fried eggs, and salsa; Mexican and American omelets; fresh fruit platters; and pancakes. The Spanish menu offers even more choices than the English menu. Simple lunch dishes include sandwiches and enchiladas, while the Mexican platter for two, with chicken and beef tacos, enchiladas, nachos, quesadillas, and guacamole, ensures you won't go home hungry.

Av. Rafael Melgar (corner of Calle 6 Norte). ℂ **987/872-0838.** Breakfast 55–75 pesos; lunch main courses 64–110 pesos. No credit cards. Daily 7am–2pm.

Shopping

If you're looking for silver jewelry or other souvenirs, go no farther than the town's coastal avenue, Rafael Melgar. Along this road, you'll find one store after another selling jewelry, Mexican handicrafts, and other souvenirs and duty-free merchandise. The most impressive of these is **Los Cinco Soles** (www.loscincosoles.com; ℂ 987/872-9004), on the waterfront at 8 Norte, adjacent to Pancho's Backyard restaurant (p. 146). It's open Monday to Saturday from 9am to 8pm and Sunday from 11am to 5pm. There are also some import/export stores in the Punta Langosta Shopping Center in the southern part of town in front of the cruise-ship pier. Prices for serapes, T-shirts, and the like are lower on the side streets off Avenida Melgar.

Souvenir stores line Avenida Rafael Melgar.

Entertainment & Nightlife

Most of the music and dance venues are along Avenida Rafael Melgar. **Carlos 'n' Charlie's** (☎ **987/869-1648**), which is in the Punta Langosta shopping center, is practically next to **Señor Frog's** (☎ **987/869-1650**). Punta Langosta lies just south of Calle 7 Sur. The **Hard Rock Cafe** (☎ **987/872-5271**), which may be the smallest Hard Rock in the world, is also on Avenida Rafael Melgar, at no. 2, just north of the municipal pier, and remains open until 2am or later with live music on weekends.

In town, there are a few Latin music clubs. These open and close with every high season, prospering when people have cash in their pockets, but closing down when the flow of tourism stops bringing in money. Calle 1 Sur between avenidas 5 Sur and 10 Sur is a pedestrian street housing a number of local bars, some with live music. **Wet Wendy's,** at 53 Av. 5 Norte between Calle 2 and Juarez (☎ **987/872-4970**), is a spirited open-air bar with a fun crowd toasting margaritas and other tequila cocktails.

For sports events, the most popular watering hole for locals and expats remains the **French Quarter,** open Wednesday to Monday from 5pm to midnight. On Sunday evenings, the place to be is the main square, which usually has a free concert and lots of people strolling about and visiting with friends. Various cafes and bars surround the square.

San Miguel's **movie theater** is Cinépolis, the modern multicinema in the Chedraui Plaza Shopping Center at the south end of town. It mainly shows Hollywood movies. Most of these are in English with Spanish subtitles (*película subtitulada*); before buying your tickets, make sure the movie hasn't been dubbed (*doblada*).

Where to Stay

I've grouped Cozumel's hotels by location—**north** of town, **in town,** and **south** of town. The prices quoted are public rates and typically do not include the 14% tax. High season is from December to Easter. Expect rates from Christmas to New Year's to be higher than the regular high-season rates quoted here. Low season is the rest of the year, though a few hotels raise their rates in August, when Mexican families go on vacation.

All of the beach hotels in Cozumel, even the small ones, have deals with vacation packagers. Some packagers will offer last-minute deals to Cozumel with hefty discounts; if you're the flexible sort, keep an eye open for these.

Most hotels have an arrangement with a dive shop and offer dive packages. These can be good deals, but if you don't buy a dive package, it's quite okay to stay at one hotel and dive with a third-party operator—any dive boat can pull up to any hotel pier to pick up customers. Most dive shops won't pick up from the hotels north of town.

In addition to the hotels listed below, another reliable option is the **Fiesta Americana All-Inclusive Dive Center** (www.fiestamericana.com; ☎ **987/872-9600**), located on Carretera Chankanaab Km 7.5, which is popular with families and has its own dive center. As an alternative to a hotel, you can try **Cozumel Vacation Villas and Condos,** Av. Rafael Melgar 685 (btw. calles 3 and 5 Sur; www.cozumel-villas.com; ☎ **800/224-5551** in the U.S.), which rents villas and condos by the week.

NORTH OF TOWN

Carretera Santa Pilar, or San Juan, is the name of Avenida Rafael Melgar's northern extension. All the hotels lie close to each other on the beach side of the road a short distance from town and the airport.

Very Expensive
Playa Azul Golf-Scuba-Spa ★
This quiet hotel is among the most relaxing of the island's properties. It's smaller than the others and an excellent choice for golfers; guests pay no greens fees, only cart rental ($30). The hotel's small beautiful beach with shade *palapas* has a quiet little beach bar. All three categories of

Downtown San Miguel de Cozumel.

guest rooms have ocean views. The units in the original section are suites—very large, with oversize bathrooms with showers. The newer wing has mostly standard rooms that are comfortable and large. The corner rooms are master suites with large balconies and Jacuzzis overlooking the sea. If you prefer lots of space over having a Jacuzzi, opt for a suite in the original building. Rooms contain a king-size or two double beds; some suites offer two convertible single sofas in the separate living room. The hotel also offers deep-sea- and fly-fishing trips.

Carretera San Juan Km 4, 77600 Cozumel, Q. Roo. www.playa-azul.com. ✆ **987/869-5160.** Fax 987/869-5173. 51 units. High season $170 double, $215 suite; low season $130 double, $175 suite. Rates include unlimited golf and full breakfast. All-inclusive option available. AE, MC, V. Free guarded parking. **Amenities:** 2 restaurants; 2 bars; dive shop; unlimited golf privileges at Cozumel Country Club; medium-size pool; room service; snorkeling equipment; spa. *In room:* A/C, TV, fridge, hair dryer, Wi-Fi.

Expensive
Condumel Condobeach Apartments ✦ If you want some distance from the crowds, consider lodging here. It's not a full-service hotel, but in some ways, it's more convenient. The 10 one-bedroom waterfront apartments are designed and furnished in practical fashion—airy, with sliding glass doors that face the sea and allow for good cross-ventilation (especially in the upper units). They also have ceiling fans, air-conditioning, and two twin beds or one king-size. Each apartment has a separate living room and a full kitchen with a partially stocked fridge, so you don't have to run to the store on the first day. There's a small, well-tended beach area (with shade *palapas* and a grill for guests' use) that leads to a low, rocky fall-off into the sea.

Carretera Hotelera Norte s/n, 77600 Cozumel, Q. Roo. www.condumel.com. ✆ **987/872-0892.** Fax 987/872-0661. 10 units. High season $142 double; low season $120 double. Dive packages available. No credit cards. *In room:* A/C, kitchen, no phone, Wi-Fi.

IN TOWN

Staying in town is not like staying in the town on Isla Mujeres, where you can walk to the beach. The oceanfront in town is too busy for swimming, and there's no beach, only the *malecón*. Prices are considerably lower, but you'll have to drive or take a cab to the beach; it's pretty easy. English is spoken in almost all of the hotels.

Moderate

Hacienda San Miguel ★ ❦   This is a peaceful hotel built in Mexican colonial style around a large garden courtyard. The property is well maintained and the service is good. It's located a half-block from the shoreline on the town's north side. The large guest rooms offer rustic Mexican furnishings and fully equipped kitchens. Most of the studios have one or two queen-size beds, while the junior suites have more living area and a queen-size as well as a twin bed. The two-bedroom suite comes with four double beds. For this hotel, high season runs from January to August; low season is from September to December, excluding the holiday season.

Calle 10 Norte 500 (btw. Rafael Melgar and Av. 5), 77600 Cozumel, Q. Roo. www.haciendasan miguel.com. ✆ **866/712-6387** in the U.S., or 987/872-1986. Fax 987/872-7043. 11 units. High season $94 studio, $106 junior suite, $154 2-bedroom suite; low season $72 studio, $84 junior suite, $114 2-bedroom suite. Rates include continental breakfast and free entrance to Mr. Sancho's beach club. MC, V. Guarded parking on street. *In room:* A/C, TV, hair dryer, kitchen, no phone, Wi-Fi (free).

Vista del Mar   This budget hotel is connected to a small shopping plaza. Guest rooms are bright and cheerfully decorated with bamboo furnishings. The rooms in front offer ocean views with wrought-iron balconies. Those in back go for slightly less and overlook a small pool. This hotel is operated by the same people who run Hacienda San Miguel, and it has the same high season/low season split, with higher rates for Carnaval and Christmas time.

Av. Rafael Melgar 45 (btw. calles 5 and 7 Sur), 77600 Cozumel, Q. Roo. www.hotelvistadelmar. com. ✆ **888/309-9988** in the U.S., or 987/872-0545. Fax 987/872-7043. 20 units. High season $110 double; low season $78–$90. Rates include Continental breakfast. AE, MC, V. Limited street parking. **Amenities:** Outdoor pool. *In room:* A/C, TV, fridge, hair dryer, free local calls, Wi-Fi (free).

Inexpensive

La Casona Real ❦   Five blocks from the waterfront, this cheerful two-story hotel is a bargain for those wanting a hotel with a pool. The simple rooms are small to medium in size, with a king or two double beds, good air-conditioning, and colorful Mexican decor. A courtyard with an oval pool is on the west side of the building, and some rooms have views of the pool while others look toward the town (and are a bit noisier). Families can make good use out of the one-bedroom suite, which has a futon in the living room, full kitchen, and cable TV.

Av. Juárez 501, 77600 Cozumel, Q. Roo. www.hotel-la-casona-real-cozumel.com. ✆ **987/872-5471.** 16 units. $50–$55 double; $80 suite. MC, V. Limited street parking. **Amenities:** Outdoor pool. *In room:* A/C, TV, no phone, Wi-Fi (free).

Suites Vima ❦   This three-story hotel sits 4 blocks from the main square. It's comfortable, clean, and economical, and each of the spacious rooms comes with its own fridge, which for island visitors can be a handy feature. The rooms are fairly quiet. Choose between two doubles or one king-size bed. There is no restaurant, but there is a pool and lounge area. As is the case with other small hotels on the island, the staff at the front desk doesn't speak English. This is one of the few hotels in town that doesn't use high season/low season rates.

Av. 10 Norte btw. calles 4 and 6, 77600 Cozumel, Q. Roo. ✆ **987/872-5118.** 12 units. 550 pesos double. No credit cards. Limited street parking. **Amenities:** Tiny outdoor pool, free Wi-Fi in lobby. *In room:* A/C, fridge.

SOUTH OF TOWN

The hotels in this area tend to be more spread out and farther from town than hotels to the north. Some are on the inland side of the road; some are on the beach side, which means a difference in price. Those farthest from town are all-inclusive properties. The beaches tend to be slightly better than those to the north, but all the hotels have swimming pools and piers from which you can snorkel, and all of them accommodate divers. Head south on Avenida Rafael Melgar, which becomes the coastal road **Costera Sur** (also called Carretera a Chankanaab).

Expensive

Presidente InterContinental Cozumel ★★★   The best resort in Cozumel, the Presidente spreads out across a magnificent stretch of coast with only distant hotels for neighbors. Rooms come in seven categories offering pool, ocean, or beachfront views, and are separated by quiet corridors displaying vivid original art. Guests enjoy Egyptian cotton sheets, marble bathrooms, Mexican artwork and onyx lamps, Maya-inspired turndown service, and complimentary tea or coffee in the morning. Beachfront "reef" rooms and suites occupy the resort's most exclusive section and include 24-hour butler service and hammocks. There's a full-service spa here, and a pyramid of iguanas out by the pool that is thrilling for children to see. The excellent poolside dive shop (**Scuba Du;** p. 140) offers introductory and one- and two-tank dives as well as certification programs in the clear turquoise sea just in front. A long stretch of sandy beach, dotted with *palapas* and palm trees, fronts the entire hotel, and the sunsets are amazing. Alfredo di Roma serves excellent Italian food, and the open-air **Caribeño** (p. 144) restaurant offers breathtaking views of the sea.

Costera Sur Km 6.5, 77600 Cozumel, Q. Roo. www.intercontinentalcozumel.com. ℗ **800/327-0200** in the U.S., or 987/872-9500. Fax 987/872-9501. 220 units. High season $330 pool view, $398 ocean view, $582 and up beach fronts and suites; low season $257–$291 pool view, $302–$358 ocean view, $370–$504 beach fronts and suites. Internet specials sometimes available. AE, MC, V. Free valet parking. **Amenities:** 3 restaurants; 2 bars; babysitting; 24-hr. butler service in reef section; children's programs; concierge; dive shop; deep-sea fishing trips; access to golf club; putting green; 2 outdoor pools, including adults-only pool; room service; full-service spa with salon and fully equipped fitness center; 2 lighted tennis courts; tennis lessons; watersports; yoga. In room: A/C, flatscreen TV w/pay movies, hair dryer, minibar, MP3 docking station, Wi-Fi (free).

Side Trips

CHICHÉN ITZÁ, TULUM & COBÁ   Travel agencies can arrange day trips to the ruins of **Chichén Itzá.** The ruins of **Tulum,** overlooking the Caribbean, and **Cobá,** in a dense jungle setting, are closer and cost less to visit. A trip to both Cobá and Tulum begins at 8am and returns around 6pm. A shorter, more relaxing excursion goes to Tulum and the nearby nature park of **Xel-Ha.**

PLAYA DEL CARMEN & XCARET   Going on your own to the nearby seaside town of **Playa del Carmen** and the **Xcaret** nature park is as easy as a quick ferry ride from Cozumel (for ferry information, see "Getting There," earlier in this chapter). While at Xcaret, visit their newest park, **Xplor** (℗ **998/849-5275;** www.xplor.travel), next door. For information on Playa, Xcaret, and Xplor, see chapter 6. Cozumel travel agencies offer an Xcaret tour that includes the ferry ride, transportation to the park, and the admission fee.

6

THE RIVIERA MAYA & THE SOUTHERN CARIBBEAN COAST

by Christine Delsol & Maribeth Mellin

The Yucatán's Caribbean coast reaches 380km (236 miles) from Cancún to Chetumal, at the Belize border. The northern coast, from Cancún to Tulum and down the Punta Allen peninsula, has been dubbed the Riviera Maya; the southern half, the Costa Maya. In between is the vast Sian Ka'an Biosphere Reserve. But what you really need to know (and have probably heard before), is that this region is known for its "endless stretch of pristine beach" and "soft white sand caressed by turquoise waves."

The region's greatest geological asset is the **Great Mesoamerican Reef,** which extends south to Honduras and protects most of the Caribbean coast from harsh currents and waves. **Playa del Carmen**'s beaches, such as **Playa El Faro,** are among the area's most beautiful, with soft sand and minimal surf. Lined with small hotels, **Tulum**'s uninterrupted beaches are ideal for getting away from the crowds and strolling on the sand. Head to **Paamul**'s wide, curving beach for a relaxing swim in the warm turquoise water.

The Caribbean coast is culturally rich, too. Here you'll find **Tulum,** one of few Maya archaeological sites on the sea, and nearby **Cobá,** still buried in jungle with resident green parrots and spider monkeys, serves as an important trade link between the numerous Maya cities around the Yucatán Peninsula. Off the beaten path, **Muyil** serves as a gateway to the vast canal system in Sian Ka'an, the coast's largest swath of protected lagoons and beach.

A single highway connects the coast's towns and sights. **Playa del Carmen,** the coast's largest city, is filled with excellent restaurants, small hotels, clubs, and shops. Puerto Morelos has a more laid-back feel, while the town of Tulum is a magnet for international entrepreneurs running beach camps and gourmet restaurants. Though most well-marked side roads now lead from the highway to large resort compounds, you can still find small sandy tracks to more secluded beaches including **Paamul, Xpu-ha,** and **Tankah.** Inland roads take you to the amazing cave system at **Aktun Chen,** the underground river at **Río Secreto,** and a series of freshwater swimming holes called cenotes. Birds and animals from throughout Yucatán are protected at **Xcaret,** a pricey but worthwhile park offering an all-in-one view of Mexico's marvels.

THE BEST TRAVEL EXPERIENCES IN THE RIVIERA MAYA

- **Swimming with Sea Turtles:** Loggerhead and green sea turtles return to Mexico's Caribbean coast to nest every summer; you can spot them swimming around Akumal, Paamul, Sian Ka'an, and Xcalak. Don't touch or bother them in the water or on the sand.

- **Mingling with the Maya:** During tours to Cobá, Alltournative (p. 198) and other tour companies include visits to Maya communities where you can

PREVIOUS PAGE: **Sunbathers at Akumal Bay beach in Akumal.**

sample local cuisine and check out traditional Maya houses complete with wood fire and hammocks.

o **Floating Through Sian Ka'an:** According to its Mayan name, Sian Ka'an Biosphere is the place where the sky is born. It's easy to see why as you float in a boat, kayak, or lifejacket along hidden canals carved through seemingly endless turquoise lagoons.

o **Sampling Tikinxic:** Fish fresh from the sea is rubbed with red achiote and bitter-orange marinade, wrapped in banana leaves, and baked over a wood fire. This centuries-old recipe results in the coast's moist, slightly spicy traditional fish dish served with fresh tortillas and lime.

o **Strolling Along Fifth Avenue:** Locals and visitors mingle on Playa del Carmen's Quinta Avenida, the coast's social hub. Reggae, rock, and mariachi music fills the air, and boutiques display all matter of memorabilia.

PUERTO MORELOS & VICINITY
Between Cancún & Playa del Carmen

The coast directly south of the Cancún airport has several roadside attractions, small cabaña and boutique hotels, and astonishingly luxurious all-inclusive resorts. The agreeable town of **Puerto Morelos** lies midway along this 51km (32-mile) stretch of coast between the airport and Playa del Carmen.

ROADSIDE ATTRACTIONS

CrocoCun ★ ☺ ZOO   This interactive zoo, 1.6km (a mile) north of Puerto Morelos, is especially captivating to children, but the up-close and sometimes hands-on encounters with iguanas, spider monkeys, a boa constrictor, immense

Children will love seeing the reptiles at CrocoCun.

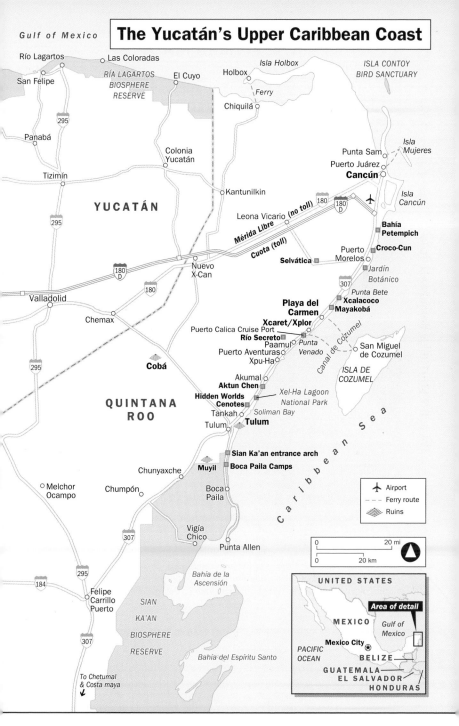

The Yucatán's Upper Caribbean Coast

Gulf of Mexico

Río Lagartos
Las Coloradas
San Felipe
El Cuyo
Holbox
Isla Holbox
ISLA CONTOY
BIRD SANCTUARY
RÍA LAGARTOS
BIOSPHERE
RESERVE
Ferry
Chiquilá
295
Panabá
Colonia
Yucatán
Punta Sam
Puerto Juárez
Cancún
Isla
Mujeres
Tizimín
Kantunilkin
Isla
Cancún
YUCATÁN
Leona Vicario *(no toll)*
Mérida Libre
180
180
D
**Bahía
Petempich**
295
Cuota (toll)
Puerto
Morelos
Croco-Cun
Valladolid
180
D
180
Nuevo
X-Can
Selvática
*Jardín
Botánico*
307
Punta Bete
Xcalacoco
Mayakobá
Chemax
**Playa del
Carmen**
Xcaret/Xplor
Puerto Calica Cruise Port
Río Secreto
Paamul
Puerto Aventuras
Xpu-Ha
*Punta
Venado*
San Miguel
de Cozumel
295
Cobá
Akumal
Aktun Chen
*ISLA DE
COZUMEL*
**Hidden Worlds
Cenotes**
Tankah
*Xel-Ha Lagoon
National Park*
**QUINTANA
ROO**
Tulum
Soliman Bay
Tulum
Sian Ka'an entrance arch
Chunyaxche
Muyil
Boca Paila Camps
Melchor
Ocampo
Chumpón
Boca
Paila
Canal de Cozumel
Caribbean Sea
307
Vigía
Chico
Punta Allen
*Bahía de la
Ascención*

	Airport
	Ferry route
	Ruins

0   20 mi
0   20 km

184
295
Felipe
Carrillo
Puerto
307
*SIAN
KA'AN
BIOSPHERE
RESERVE*
Bahía del Espíritu Santo

*To Chetumal
& Costa maya*

UNITED STATES
Area of detail
MEXICO
*Gulf of
Mexico*
PACIFIC
OCEAN
Mexico City
BELIZE
GUATEMALA
EL SALVADOR
HONDURAS

driving **THE RIVIERA MAYA**

Driving along this coast isn't difficult, but it takes eagle-eyed attention, especially for first-timers. With only one highway, you can't get too lost unless you miss the signs for your hotel. Hwy. 307 traces the coastline for 380km (236 miles) from Cancún to Chetumal, a 4½-hour trip by car. The section between Cancún's airport and Tulum is now a four-lane divided highway with speed limits up to 110kmph (68 mph). It takes about 2 hours to drive the 130km (81 miles) from Cancún airport to Tulum.

Turnoffs can be from either the right or left lane; if you miss the one you want, go a bit farther and circle back. You're not allowed to stop on the highway to make a left turn, but there are several short left-turn lanes at many points across the road from major resorts. It is impossible to overemphasize just how dangerous this highway can be, especially during high season when you've got locals speeding to work, tour buses clogging the lanes, truck and bus drivers barreling along, and confused or distracted tourists changing lanes on whim. Speed limits are clearly posted and seem to change every few kilometers. Keep an eye out for speed signs, especially around towns and resorts. The police have become ever more sophisticated at ticketing speeders and are especially vigilant around stoplights and one-way streets. Several overpasses now carry you over the busiest intersections at Puerto Morelos, Puerto Aventuras, and Playa del Carmen, which greatly

reduce the danger and traffic congestion.

All that said, it's hard to imagine traveling around the Riviera Maya without a rental car. So many wonderful places to explore are right beside the highway and along side roads leading to the beach and jungle. First-class gas station plazas with minimarts and fast-food spots are becoming a common sight. Attendants pump the gas (be sure they don't overfill the tank) and will check your oil. Make sure you receive the right change, and tip attendants if they provide extra services. As long as you study your maps in advance and keep your wits about you, driving allows freedom for serendipitous discoveries.

Always carry plenty of drinking water when driving along the coast. Most hotels offer a couple of small bottles in your room upon arrival, and then charge close to $2 for each new bottle. Have at least one half-gallon bottle in the car and a reusable water bottle with you at all times.

---

tarantulas, and crocs of all ages and sizes disarm adults as well. Once a crocodile farm, CrocoCun now runs a captive breeding program that has helped replenish the toothy reptiles' local population and extends its protection to all animals native to the Yucatán. A guided tour with one of the knowledgeable and enthusiastic veterinary students who volunteer here lasts 1½ hours. Entrance fees are high, but the memories will last. Take bug repellant.

Highway 307, Km 31. www.crococunzoo.com. ⓒ **998/850-3719.** 285 pesos adults, 171 pesos children 6 to 12, free for children 5 and younger. Daily 9am–5pm.

Jardín Botánico Dr. Alfredo Barrera Marín PARK/GARDEN   This fecund 161-acre botanical garden, just south of the Puerto Morelos turnoff, is the largest swath of undeveloped land along the coast, save for the Sian Ka'an Biosphere Reserve (p. 199). Ceiba trees, sacred to the Maya, stand tall amid palms, bromeliads, ferns, and orchids; just when you think you've had enough jungle, a small archaeological site, a reconstructed Maya home, or a *chiclero* camp pop up. Biology students working here eagerly share details (it helps to speak Spanish). Spider monkeys, nearly extinct elsewhere on the coast, frolic here along with tropical birds. This is more a jungle trek than a walk in the park; wear sturdy walking shoes and insect repellent.

Carretera Cancún-Tulum, Km 320. www.ecosur.mx/jb/YaaxChe. © **998/206-9223.** Admission 100 pesos. Mon–Sat 9am–5pm.

Puerto Morelos ★★

36km (22 miles) S of Cancún; 26km (16 miles) S of airport; 32km (20 miles) N of Playa del Carmen

Even though it's the closest town to Cancún, Puerto Morelos resembles the Playa del Carmen that first lured tourists away from the clamor of Cancún. It's the northern Caribbean coast's last real fishing village, perfect for lying on the white-sand beach and reading, with the occasional foray into snorkeling, diving, windsurfing, or kayaking. This was the coast's boomtown 100 years ago, when its port shipped hardwood and *chicle* to the U.S. and Europe. Today, the biggest attraction is its quiet, small-town atmosphere and easy pace.

The townspeople succeeded in protecting Puerto Morelos' section of the Great Maya Reef with a national park designation in 1998. The underwater coral mountain, which buffers the coast from storm surges, rises to within a few feet of the surface and is easy to snorkel. The government-maintained beaches are clean and rarely crowded; the water is shallow, calm, and clear, with sea grass growing on the bottom.

Puerto Morelos brims with foreign tourists during the high season, but low season is so low that many businesses close temporarily, earning it the affectionate nickname Muerto Morelos (*muerto* means "dead").

ESSENTIALS

GETTING THERE

BY CAR   Puerto Morelos is at Km 31, about a half-hour from either Cancún or Playa del Carmen. You'll need to exit the highway onto the frontage road, then turn left under the overpass.

BY BUS   Buses from Cancún to Tulum and Playa del Carmen usually stop at the highway here, but be sure to ask before buying a ticket. A taxi for the 2km (1¼ mile) ride from the highway to the center of town costs 20 pesos.

GETTING AROUND

Puerto Morelos consists of the beach area and the inland pueblo next to the highway. The beach town is so compact that your own two feet are the best transportation for most of what you'll want to do. Taxis are only 20 to 40 pesos around town and up to 60 pesos to the edges of town or the pueblo on the other side of the highway.

EXPLORING IN & AROUND PUERTO MORELOS

The biggest draw is the **coral reef ★★★** rising directly in front of the village about a ½ kilometer offshore. Because it tops out so close to the surface, divers have nothing over snorkelers here; everyone gets a close-up of the convoluted passages and large caverns burgeoning with fish and sea flora. Restrictions on fishing and boating make this the coast's most pristine patch of coral. Several dive

shops in town offer snorkeling tours and gear rentals, but my choice is the local **fishing cooperative ★** (© 998/ 121-1524) of more than 20 families at the foot of the pier. Its members are national park-certified guides who rotate tour gigs to supplement their fishing income. The fixed fee is 300 pesos for a 2-hour trip that visits two snorkeling sites. Tours leave approximately every half-hour Monday through Saturday from 9am to 3pm.

Snorkelers enter the water at Puerto Morelos.

The excellent dive shops around town charge $45 to $60 for one-tank dives; PADI certification costs $350 to $430. One of the best is also among the least expensive. Enrique Juárez of the long-established **Almost Heaven Adventures,** on Javier Rojo Gómez a block north of the plaza (www.almostheavenadventures. com; ©/fax **998/871-0230**), limits groups to five divers and is known for thorough briefings and attentive boat crews. Also recommended: **Aquanuts** (www.aqua-nautsdiveadventures.com; © **998/206-9365**), **Dive In Puerto Morelos** (www. diveinpuertomorelos.com; © **998/206-9084**), and **Wet Set Diving Adventure** (www.wetset.com; © **998/871-0198**).

A pleasant sea walk along the small, modern **central plaza** leads to the main pier with its old landmark **lighthouse,** whose tilt, courtesy of Hurricane Beulah's 1967 rampage, makes the Leaning Tower of Pisa look downright upright—especially against the profile of the larger beacon that replaced it. The plaza itself, while rather simple, is the fulcrum of local life and brims with a fine variety of restaurants. On the south side, **Alma Libre** (www.almalibrebooks.com; © **998/252-2207**) sells more English-language books than any other bookstore in the Yucatán. The owners, Canadians Joanne and Rob Birce, stock everything from beach reads

Puerto Morelos's waterfront.

and English classics to cookbooks and volumes on Maya culture, plus regional maps. The store also serves as a book exchange, tourist information center, and vacation rental agency; they recently added a line of locally made specialty foods. It's open daily November through April 11:30am to 2:30pm and 3:30 to 8pm (hours seem to change each season; check the website for latest info).

About a block south of the plaza on Javier Rojo Gómez, the local artisans' cooperative runs **Hunab Kú market,** a collection of *palapa* stands selling hammocks, hand-embroidered clothes, jewelry, blankets, ceramics, and other handicrafts made in the area. The wares are high quality, and there are some bargains. Vendors don't hustle you, so it's worth a stroll just for the parklike setting. The market is open daily from 9am to 8pm.

The **Little Mexican Cooking School ★★★**, Av. Rojo Gomez 768 (www. thelittlemexicancookingschool.com; ✆ **998/251-8060**), which started out in founder Catriona Brown's home, has moved to expansive new hacienda-style quarters in the former Club Marviya hotel, 3 blocks north of the plaza. Classes, offered Tuesdays through Fridays and some Saturdays, begin with continental breakfast and an introduction to traditional ingredients and modern Mexican cuisine. Chef Pablo Espinosa is as entertaining as he is knowledgeable, combining demonstrations with hands-on preparation. For *comida fuerte,* or full Mexican late lunch, you'll prepare and sample about eight dishes, which give traditional recipes a contemporary spin. Sessions last about 5½ hours and cost $110, including tax.

Authentic Maya massage, in several variations—including a special hangover treatment—is the specialty at the **Jungle Spa ★★** (www.mayaecho.com; ✆ **998/208-9148**), just outside the pueblo, west of Hwy. 307. You can also try an aloe vera/banana leaf or chocolate body wrap, all for a fraction of what you'd pay at resort spas. The women in this cooperative have been trained to incorporate contemporary spa techniques into the traditional Maya healing massages they grew up with. Full-body massages cost $40 for 1 hour or $60 for 1½ hours, and the money directly supports local Maya families. Appointments are available Tuesday through Saturday and sometimes Sunday. The women also perform a traditional Maya dance and sell unique handicrafts at their Sunday Jungle Market, held from mid-December to Easter Sunday.

RUTA DE CENOTES

The road heading inland from Hwy. 307, across from the Jardín Botanico (p. 156), is lined by cenotes along the 17km (10½-mile) stretch between Puerto Morelos and the village of Central Vallarta. It's hard to miss the enormous arch over the turnoff, and the cenotes are also well-marked along a paved section of the road. Some have been turned into "adventure parks," with ATV tours, zip lines, aerial walkways, and parachute jumps that draw streams of tour groups from Cancún. **Selvática,** at Km. 19 (www.selvatica.com.mx; ✆ **866/552-8825** toll-free in the U.S., or 998/847-4581), is the most popular and expensive (starting at $99 adults/ $49 children); **Boca del Puma,** at Km. 16 (www.bocadelpuma.com; ✆ **998/241-2855**), is a better choice. Not only are its prices lower ($76 adults/$45 kids), but it places greater emphasis on the environment and local culture. One option is a horseback tour, and facilities include a *chicle* camp and history museum.

Independent travelers can venture farther off the main road to some truly beautiful, remote cenotes. **Cenote Las Mojarras** (http://cenotelasmojarras.com; ✆ **998/848-2831**), at Km. 12.5, looks like a large pond and has a double zipline and double tower to jump from, as well as restrooms, hammocks, a picnic area, and campground. Among the less-developed cenotes is **Siete Bocas** at Km. 16, consisting of seven "mouths" to an underground river. Three are large enough for stairways straight down into the cool, clear water, and the others funnel light into the underground chamber—the effects are especially dramatic around midday. Camping is permitted (for a fee) here and at **Lucerno Verde,** down the road at Km. 17. This might be the most beautiful swimming hole of all. Jagged rock walls scored by massive tree roots enclose a crater holding clear, seemingly bottomless turquoise water. There's a zip line and a safety rope across its 100-foot diameter, and a rock ledge where you can plunge about 20 feet into the water, but there are no services or even easy places to sit.

WHERE TO EAT

There's been a bit of a shakeup in Puerto Morelos' restaurant scene, with the departure of some longtime favorites and arrival of new ones. One thing that hasn't changed: The number and variety of good restaurants is far greater than you'd expect in a town of this size. Most are on or around the main square, including **Doña Triny's** for Mexican and Yucatecan standards; **Los Pelícanos** for seafood; **David Lau's** and **Asi Aki** (formerly Hola Asia) for Asian food; and **Le Café d'Amancia** for coffee, pastries, and seriously addictive smoothies.

John Gray's Kitchen ★★★ INTERNATIONAL   This is a splurge—and totally worth it. After chef John Gray elevated the Club Grill at The Ritz-Carlton Cancún to iconic status, he cooked his way around the world before settling in Puerto Morelos in 2002. The menu changes with market offerings and Gray's mood; don't be surprised if he bursts out of the kitchen to scribble fresh sword-fish and clams on the menu just as you've made up your mind. For a bargain meal for two, pick out three appetizers or sides, such as crab and shrimp sliders with potato bread or a grilled vegetable brochette in sweet soy and red chile, and split them. If you decide to order an entree, the chef does strange and wonderful things with lobster, mac and cheese, and a pork loin in a Roquefort crust.

Av. Niños Heroes (north of Av. José Morelos). www.johngraysrestaurants.com. ✆ **998/802-1762.** Reservations recommended (available online). Main courses 100–595 pesos. MC, V. Daily 8am–10pm.

Merkadito del Mar ★★ SEAFOOD   This newcomer took over the space vacated by La Suegra and won legions of fans in a short time. Its tostadas, tacos, ceviches, grilled fish, and pastas make liberal use of shrimp, tuna, mussels, salmon, octopus, and whatever else local fishermen are pulling out of the water. The tostadas are always a hit, while the Jack Daniels salmon and cactus stuffed with shrimp are especially artful. Service is attentive and friendly, and doesn't hurt that they mix a mean margarita—in a tin cup, to help keep it cold—on a terrace overlooking the ocean.

Rafael Melgar Lote 8-B. ✆ **998/871-0774.** Main courses 10–200 pesos. AE, DISC, MC, V. Daily 11am–9pm.

Posada Amor ★ BREAKFAST/YUCATECAN   Puerto Morelos's oldest restaurant, now run by the founder's son, has patrons who have been eating here for nearly 30 years. The *palapa*-roofed dining room, a half-block south of the plaza, is a great place for a complete breakfast or the bargain-priced Sunday breakfast buffet. A few sidewalk tables are perfect for nighttime. The dinner menu focuses on fresh seafood and Yucatecan-influenced dishes. The grilled fish is stellar, and the soups—a varied lineup including fish, corn, and other vegetables—were tasty and, with tortillas, hearty enough to be a meal.

Avs. Javier Rojo Gómez and Tulum. ℂ **998/871-0033.** Main courses 48–200 pesos; breakfast 45–70 pesos. AE, MC, V. Daily 7am–10pm.

Rustika MEDITERRANEAN   This new "Jazz Gourmet & Art Gallery," as it's billed, is a little more upscale than is typical for Puerto Morelos, and a little more eclectic, aiming to be a live music venue and art gallery as well as a fine restaurant. The menu is full of fresh ingredients and Mediterranean flair along with other influences. The Tuna Asiatico (Asian tuna ceviche) and clam and mussel pasta (hand-made) are outstanding, and the outdoor seating area is delightful.

Avs. Javier Rojo Gómez and Cozumel. ℂ **998/253-1281.** Main courses 110–180 pesos. MC, V. Daily 4pm–1am.

WHERE TO STAY

For vacation rentals, see the website of Alma Libre books (above), or contact Mayan Rivera Properties (www.mayanrivieraproperties.com; ℂ **248/275-5556** in the U.S. or 998/871-0716).

Carmen Hacienda   The former Hacienda Morelos is a good beachfront alternative to cosseting yourself away in one of the all-inclusives outside of town—just don't expect resort-level service. Rooms, all facing the ocean, are small and basic but refurbished, and bathrooms have plenty of hot water and good pressure. The hotel's main virtues are the ocean views and expansive beachfront patio. Aquanuts, the on-site dive shop, earns consistently high marks. The restaurant is expensive and slow—all the more reason to sample the multitude of restaurants around the square, just a block away.

Av. Rafael E. Melgar no. 5, 77580 Puerto Morelos, Q. Roo. www.carmeninn.com/en/puerto-morelos. ℂ **998/871-0448.** 30 units. High season $159 double; low season $116. AE, MC, PayPal, V. Free off-street parking. **Amenities:** Restaurant; dive shop; outdoor pool. *In room:* A/C, TV, fridge (in some), patio (with ground-floor rooms).

Casa Caribe ★★★   When the Little Mexican Cooking School (p. 159) took over the former Hotelito Marviya—one of Puerto Morelos' oldest buildings—owner Catriona Brown renovated five of the rooms to create this beguiling yet affordable B&B. With primarily white decor enlivened by found furniture, splashes of color, and whimsical use of bathroom tile, rooms project a sense of simple luxury. Heavenly breezes efficiently cool the four upstairs rooms, while the family-size downstairs room is air-conditioned. Though the beach is a block away, the terrific ocean view is unobstructed. Major bonus: Cooking school chef Pablo Espinosa oversees the breakfast menu, based on local ingredients in an artful, and ample, blend of traditional and contemporary favorites.

Av. Javier Rojo Gómez (at Ejército), 77580 Puerto Morelos, Q. Roo. www.casacaribepuertomorelos. com. ℂ **998/159-8890** or 512/410-8146 (U.S.). 5 units. High season $100 double, low season $85. Rates include breakfast. 4-night minimum. MC, PayPal. **Amenities:** Garden terrace lounge; cooking school and kitchen shop; beach 1 block away (beach chairs and umbrellas provided); laundry service; Wi-Fi. *In room:* Ceiling fans (A/C in one), coffeemaker, fridge, private balcony with hammock.

Hotel Ojo de Agua ☺ ✋   This family-run waterfront hotel, 2 long blocks from the main square, was once a great deal. Lately, though, prices have climbed while maintenance lags and the reception seems indifferent. Still, it commands the town's best stretch of beach and has a good dive shop, watersports, and a popular beach restaurant. Utilitarian rooms are brightened by rattan furniture and bold paint. Studios with kitchenettes and small yards come with one king-size bed or a double and two twins—no air-conditioning in these—and are well-suited for families. The beach's excellent snorkeling includes the undersea cenote for which the hotel is named.

Av. Javier Rojo Gómez 16, SM2, M 2, 77580 Puerto Morelos, Q. Roo. www.ojo-de-agua.com. ✆ **998/871-0027.** 36 units. High season 910–1,300 pesos; low season 770–950 pesos. AE, MC, V. **Amenities:** Restaurant; dive shop; outdoor pool. *In room:* Ceiling fans, A/C (in some), kitchen (in some).

Posada El Moro ★★ ☺ ✔ One of the town's most appealing hotels, a half-block off the town square, also happens to be a great deal. Renting a room is akin to ordering dim sum: Add $10 a night for air-conditioning, $5 more for TV, and another $5 for a kitchenette. French-paned sliding doors and windows flood the rooms with natural light, and the tile bathrooms are sparkling clean. Simple, cheery furnishings include queen-size beds with nearly perfect mattresses, plus a futon. Junior suites also have a single bed; full suites have two double beds, a futon, and a kitchenette. The pretty, compact garden has a small pool perfect for kids, and a rooftop *palapa* in the process of becoming a restaurant has sweeping ocean views. Miguel, the attentive manager, speaks perfect English; his family is less conversant but equally eager to please.

Av. Javier Rojo Gómez, SM2, M 5, Lote 17 (north of José Morelos), 77580 Puerto Morelos, Q. Roo. www.posadaelmoro.com. ✆/fax **998/871-0159.** 31 units. High season $60–$75 double, $80–$90 suite; low season $50–$65 double, $70–$80 suite. Rates include continental breakfast. AE, MC, V. **Amenities:** Small outdoor pool; breakfast room/part-time restaurant. *In room:* A/C (in some), TV (in some), Wi-Fi.

South of Puerto Morelos

The beaches, bays, mangrove lagoons, and jungles between Puerto Morelos and Tulum are constantly undergoing transformation. Punta Maroma, home to the coast's first exclusive hideaway, now has several resort and residential compounds. Massive all-inclusives loom above beaches where campgrounds once thrived. Mayakobá, a master-planned resort just north of Playa del Carmen, is a fine example of an ecologically responsible development, though some other resorts use the land without much thought to conservation.

EXPENSIVE

Grand Velas ★★★ From afar, this irresistible resort looks massive and imposing. But the small, Mexican-owned Velas hotel chain has merged all-inclusive with all the luxuries of the area's finest hotels. Suites are clustered in three categories—the adults-only Grand Class, family-friendly Ambassador Suites, and Master Suites located amid jungle vegetation. The first two all have ocean views; jungle suites are located beside the spa and convention center and have the most amenities for business travelers, including large desks facing canals and jungle. Cream-colored walls with sleek, dark furnishings give all suites an open-air feeling. The restaurants are top-notch: The Cocina de Autor has won numerous accolades thanks to its creative Spanish chefs, as has the French restaurant Piaf. You could spend hours in the spa's hydrotherapy area (free with spa treatment), with its bubbling jets, gushing water spouts, "experience showers," saunas, and cushy lounge chairs. The service is impeccable, even keeping kids' clubs open until 11pm to give parents a chance to enjoy romantic evenings.

Carretera 307 Km 62, Playa del Carmen, 77710 Q. Roo. www.rivieramaya.grandvelas.com. ⓒ **866/ 335-4640** in the U.S. and Canada, or 984/877-4414. 481 units. $668 and up double. Rates include meals, drinks, and gratuities. AE, MC, V. Free valet parking. **Amenities:** 8 restaurants; 3 bars; butler service; children's programs; concierge; fitness center; 3 outdoor pools; room service; spa; watersports. *In room:* A/C, fan, TV/CD/DVD, hair dryer, MP3 docking station, Wi-Fi.

Hacienda Tres Rios ★★★ An ecofriendly all-inclusive may seem a contradiction in terms, but this property proves a resort can pamper guests and still care for nature. Its 132-hectare (326-acre) nature park incorporates lush jungle, mangrove forests, and coastal dunes, plus plant nurseries, 10 cenotes, and the three rivers for which the hotel is named. Eco-consciousness is emphasized everywhere. Buffet food is arranged in small individual portions rather than huge bowls and platters; recycling bins are located in all departments; and air-conditioning, heating, and lighting all encompass custom-designed operating systems to reduce water and power consumption. The hotel was built on raised pilings to maintain the surface water's natural flow, and pathways wind through vegetation past meandering rivers and a large pool area. Rooms are elegant and comfortable, the restaurants are very good, and the tours offered throughout the park are great fun. Tres Rios' numerous accolades include Green Globe certification as a World Heritage Alliance for Sustainable Tourism site.

Carretera 307 Km 54, 77760 Q. Roo. www.haciendatresrios.com. ⓒ **866/921-6984** in the U.S. and Canada, or 984/877-2400. 273 units. $500 and up double. Rates include meals, drinks, and gratuities. AE, MC, V. Free valet parking. **Amenities:** 5 restaurants; 4 bars; children's programs; fitness center; 2 outdoor pools; room service; spa; watersports. *In room:* A/C, fan, TV/CD/DVD, hair dryer, Wi-Fi.

Viceroy Riviera Maya ★★ The smallest resort in this area once held sway over a private white beach. New hotels and neighborhoods have risen all around it, but the Viceroy (formerly Tides) has 2.5 hectares (6¼ acres) of waterfront property and is all about seclusion and tranquillity. The resort's original 30 villas are buried in gardens and jungle with resident spider monkeys. Eleven additional villas opened in 2011 and are on the beach or have ocean views. All villas blend with the setting, using louvered shutters, crocheted hammocks, and minimal decorations in a modern, spare style and have plunge pools and outdoor showers. Guests are greeted by a shaman, and Maya healing techniques and traditions, including a *temazcal*, are used in the eco-spa. Thoughtful touches include special scents and a selection of hand-cut soaps. The restaurant takes in sea views from its loft dining room; drinks and snacks are served in the Library Lounge and grilled fish and meats at the beachside grill. Children 17 and older are welcome.

Playa Xcalacoco, Carretera Cancún–Tulum, 77710 Q. Roo. www.viceroyrivieramaya.com. ⓒ **866/332-1672** in the U.S. and Canada, or 984/877-3000. Fax 713/528-3697. 33 units. High season $720 and up double; low season $605 and up double. Rates include full breakfast. AE, MC, V. Free secure parking. No children 16 and under except during some holidays. **Amenities:** Restaurant; 2 bars; concierge; 2 Jacuzzis; large outdoor pool; room service; spa; steam bath; watersports. *In room:* A/C, TV/DVD, hair dryer, minibar, MP3 docking station, Wi-Fi.

MODERATE

Azul Fives ★ ☺ When checking in at this family-friendly all-inclusive, kids are greeted with milkshakes while parents get sparkling wine. Toys are everywhere, from the lobby to the suites, which are also equipped with cribs, changing tables, strollers, bottle warmers, and baby-sized robes. The amazing Kid's Club and play programs were designed with Fisher-Price, and include all sorts of colorful toys and games. There's even a children's gym. Older kids hang out in the video game room, complete with beanbag chairs, while adults rejuvenate in the luxurious spa (kids' treatments available). Both European and all-inclusive plans are available. The Gourmet Inclusive concept includes specialty restaurants, premium liquors, all sorts of activities, and nightly entertainment. The stylish suites work well for honeymooners, who get an instant crash-course in family dynamics. Children under 3 stay free; those 3 to 12 get a 50% discount when sharing a room with parents. Though it's just 10 minutes to Playa del Carmen, taxis cost $15 each way.

Predio El Limonar Fracc. 2, 77710 Xcalacoco, Municipio de Solidaridad, Q. Roo. www.karisma hotels.com. ✆ **888/280-8810** in the U.S. and Canada, or 984/877-2750. 360 units. $351 and up double European Plan; $470 double all-inclusive. AE, MC, V. Free parking. **Amenities:** 4 restaurants; 5 bars; children's programs; gym; 3 outdoor pools; spa; watersports. *In room:* A/C, TV/CD/DVD, hair dryer, Wi-Fi.

Petit Lafitte Hotel ★   One kilometer (⅔ mile) south of the original, venerable Posada Lafitte, this property has the same easygoing attitude that characterized the old one. In relative isolation, you still get all the amenities of a relaxing vacation. Rooms in the three-story building are surrounded by gardens, and bungalows are set amid coconut groves and gardens. Some bungalows and rooms have ocean views. Rooms are spacious and attractive, but have a beach-hotel simplicity. The staff came from the old property, so service is still personal and attentive.

Carretera Cancún–Tulum Km 63 (Punta Bete), 77710 Playa del Carmen, Q. Roo. www.petitlafitte. com. ✆ **800/538-6802** in the U.S. and Canada, or 984/877-4000. 47 units. High season $235–$385 double; low season $170–$285 double. Rates include breakfast and dinner. MC, V. Free guarded parking. **Amenities:** Restaurant; bar; outdoor pool. *In room:* A/C, TV, hair dryer, minibar, Wi-Fi.

Mayakobá Residential Golf & Spa Resort

One of the most impressive ecologically sensitive developments I've seen, **Mayakobá** (www.mayakoba.com) incorporates three upscale hotels (one reviewed below) and a championship golf course into more than 607 hectares (1,500 acres) of healthy mangroves, lagoons, cenotes, and beaches. In 2011, the resort's developers were awarded a Sustainable Standard-Setter Award from the Rainforest Alliance and the Ulysses Award for responsible, sustainable tourism projects from United Nations World Tourism Organization. The compound's concept is unusual—it's a beach resort with precious few oceanview rooms. Instead, the hotels line a series of freshwater canals.

Guests travel about in electric boats and golf carts, and may use the restaurants, spas, and other facilities in all three hotels. Some have trouble with the jungle setting—bug repellent is a must, especially at dusk, and swimming is forbidden in the canals. I've spotted small crocodiles in the canals and have been assured they're removed to more suitable homes on Mayakobá's wild side. The **El Camaleón** golf course, designed by Greg Norman, is an Audubon-certified bird reserve—and a challenge for the pros competing in Mexico's only PGA tournament, usually scheduled for late February/early March. You must have a reservation to get past the gates of this extremely private development. Consider booking a meal or spa treatment at one of the hotels to take a look around.

Fairmont Mayakobá ★★ ☺   Families, groups, and recluses are all happy with Mayakobá's first resort. Active types head for the beach, pool island, 24-hour gym, or golf course. Sybarites spend hours at the Willow Stream Spa. Dining

The Mayakobá development is surrounded by healthy mangroves and lagoons.

choices range from a gourmet deli to two excellent formal restaurants. Rooms come in 13 categories, including a suite on its own island. All open out to gardens, lagoons, or the sea. Wooden shutter doors close off sleeping areas or can be open to nature. Befitting the eco setting, rooms have cans for recyclable materials and the spa uses soaps and lotions made at a local co-op.

Carretera Cancún–Tulum Km 298, 77710 Playa del Carmen, Q. Roo. www.fairmont.com/maya koba. ✆ **800/435-2600** in the U.S. and Canada, or 984/206-3000. 401 units. High season $332 and up double; low season $186 and up. AE, MC, V. Free guarded parking. **Amenities:** 3 restaurants; 3 bars; fitness center; 5 outdoor pools; spa; watersports. *In room:* A/C, fan, TV/CD, hair dryer, Internet, minibar.

PLAYA DEL CARMEN ★★★

32km (20 miles) S of Puerto Morelos; 70km (43 miles) S of Cancún; 10km (6¼ miles) N of Xcaret; 13km (8 miles) N of Puerto Calica

Young adventuresome travelers have long been attracted to the eclectic Playa del Carmen beach scene. It's no longer an idyllic village with seaside campgrounds and budget eateries. In fact, Playa del Carmen is one of Mexico's fastest growing cities, with sprawling neighborhoods on both sides of the highway and nearly every big-box store you can imagine. Fortunately, Playa still retains a laid-back beach vibe, which combines with a cosmopolitan, counterculture ethos to create a distinctly European feel. Many of the earliest hotel and restaurants owners moved to Playa from Italy, so there's no shortage of great pasta and vino. These days, restaurants serve everything from sushi to foie gras, and shops carry Balinese figurines and Brazilian bikinis.

Playa is a logical base for travelers without cars or those who want easy access to public transportation and abundant diversions. It serves as a great base for exploring the Riviera Maya's central coast by tour, taxi, or bus. Delve into Maya culture with a trip south to the limestone ruins of the ancient cities of Tulum and Cobá. A short ferry ride to the nearby island of Cozumel puts you alongside some of the finest scuba diving in the world. Take a day trip to Xcaret or Xel-Ha, dive or snorkel through the cenotes (underwater caves) at Hidden World Cenotes, and spend an afternoon fishing or boating at the Puerto Aventuras marina.

But, save your evenings for in-town exploring. Playa's La Quinta (Fifth Avenue) is the coast's social magnet, with browse-worthy shops and plenty of bars and restaurants studding the pedestrian promenade. Sample the best of Mexico's national spirit—tequila, naturally—or take in the wild acts at CocoBongo. Slip on your dancing shoes for wild nights at all style of dance clubs, from sophisticated lounges to rock-until-dawn discos.

Essentials

GETTING THERE & DEPARTING

BY PLANE Fly into Cancún and take a bus directly from the airport (see "By Bus," below), or fly into Cozumel and take the passenger ferry.

BY CAR **Hwy. 307** is the only highway that passes through Playa. A soaring overpass bypasses the busy city traffic—stay off it unless you're traveling south of Playa. Stick to the main highway and the two main arteries into town. Avenida Constituyentes works well for destinations in northern Playa, while Avenida Juárez leads to the town's main square and ferry pier. Keep to the inside lanes that permit turning left at any of the traffic lights. Don't panic if you miss your turn; just keep going south until you get to the highway's turnaround, then double-back, staying to your right.

BY FERRY Air-conditioned passenger ferries to Cozumel leave from the pier, 1 block from the main square. There is also a car ferry to Cozumel from the Calica pier just south of Playacar. The schedule changes with demand. You can usually count on hourly departures in the morning and late afternoon—just like rush hour on land. Ferries typically depart every 2 hours around midday. For more information about both ferries, see "Getting There" in the Cozumel section of chapter 5.

BY TAXI Taxi fares from the Cancún airport are about $75 one-way.

BY BUS **Autobuses Riviera** offers service from the Cancún airport about 10 times a day between 10:50am and 7pm. Cost is about $10 one-way. Ticket counters are located outside customs at Terminals 2 and 3. At either terminal, you can also pay the driver, in either pesos or U.S. dollars. From the downtown Cancún bus station, buses depart almost every 30 minutes and cost 40 pesos.

VISITOR INFORMATION The Riviera Maya Tourism Board's website, www.rivieramaya.com, is an excellent source of overall info and practical details.

GETTING AROUND

Playa has two bus stations. Buses from Cancún and places along the coast, such as Tulum, arrive at the Riviera bus station at the corner of Juárez and Quinta Avenida, by the town square. Buses from interior destinations arrive at the ADO station on Avenida 20 between calles 12 and 14. Taxi fares around central Playa run between $3 to $10, depending on the destination

Playa del Carmen's ferry terminal.

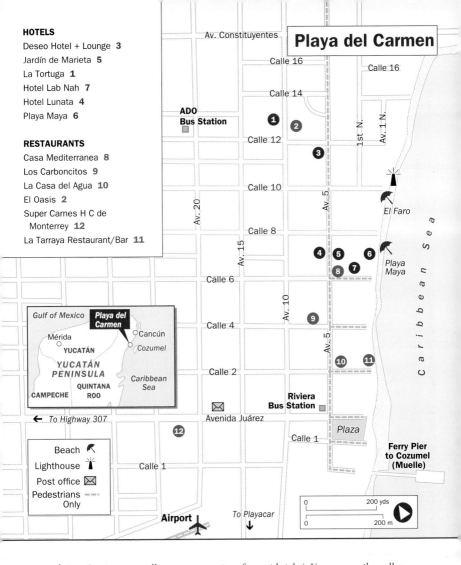

HOTELS

Deseo Hotel + Lounge **3**
Jardín de Marieta **5**
La Tortuga **1**
Hotel Lab Nah **7**
Hotel Lunata **4**
Playa Maya **6**

RESTAURANTS

Casa Mediterranea **8**
Los Carboncitos **9**
La Casa del Agua **10**
El Oasis **2**
Super Carnes H C de
  Monterrey **12**
La Tarraya Restaurant/Bar **11**

Playa del Carmen

Beach
Lighthouse
Post office
Pedestrians
  Only

and time (taxis are usually more expensive after midnight). You can easily walk to the beaches, shops, and restaurants form central hotels.

CITY LAYOUT The main street, Avenida Juárez, leads to the town square from Hwy. 307. On the way, it crosses several numbered avenues running parallel to the beach, all of which are multiples of five. The east-west streets parallel to Juárez are in multiples of two. A wonderful bike path along Avenida 10 provides fairly safe passage for *triciclos* (bike taxis) and cyclists.

Quinta Avenida (Fifth Avenue) runs 1 to 2 blocks inland from the beach and is the most popular street in the Riviera Maya. It's closed to traffic from Avenida Juárez to Calle 12 (and some blocks beyond, in the evening). However, taxis and drivers are allowed to access hotels on side streets. Hotels, restaurants, shops, and clubs line La Quinta and its side streets.

Avenida Constituyentes delineates the newest part of rapidly growing Playa. Several excellent international restaurants and pricey condo developments are located from this main intersection north to Calle 38.

Playacar, a golf-course development with private residences and several resort hotels, is located just south of Avenida Juárez.

[FastFACTS] PLAYA DEL CARMEN

Area Code 984.

ATMs, Banks, and Currency Exchange All available along Quinta Avenida.

Doctor For serious medical attention, go to Hospiten (© **984/803-1002**) on Hwy. 307 at the second Playacar exit.

Drugstore The Farmacía del Carmen, Avenida Juárez between avenidas 5 and 10 (© **984/873-2330**), is open 24 hours.

Internet Access Most hotels have Wi-Fi, at least in public areas, and Internet cafes are available on nearly every block around Quinta Avenida.

Parking Estacionamiento México, at avenidas Juárez and 10, is open daily 24 hours. Ask your hotel about parking. Few have on-site parking, but some can get you reduced rates at nearby lots.

Post Office Avenida Juárez at Calle 15.

Seasons The main high season is from mid-December to Easter. Mini high seasons are in August and around Thanksgiving. Low season is all other months, though many hotels further divide these into several micro seasons.

Special Events The Riviera Maya Jazz Festival, held in November, attracts international headliners for 3 days of music on the beach.

Exploring Playa del Carmen

BEACHES

Playa's most active pursuits revolve around simply enjoying the good life. The hippest sandy beaches for swimming, sunning, and people-watching are north of Avenida Constituyentes; central Playa's beach is more popular with local families and fishermen, and is home to a few inexpensive hotels and restaurants. The best stretch of sand in this area, offering a breather from encroaching hotels, is Playa El Faro, between calles 8 and 10. The most beautiful beach, though—and unfortunately the most crowded—extends from Constituyentes north for 5 blocks to Las Mamitas and Kool beach clubs, between calles 28 and 30. Its gradually deepening waters and breaking waves farther out provide ample fodder for water play. The sublime sands farther north are increasingly being squeezed by condo developments.

DIVING & SNORKELING

Playa's offshore reef offers decent diving, though it doesn't compare to Cozumel (p. 132) or Puerto Morelos (p. 154). Its primary virtue, which has earned it scores of dive shops, is access to Cozumel and a chain of inland cenotes. Reef dives generally cost $45 to $50 for one tank and $70 to $75 for two; two-tank cenote trips are around $110 to $120. Prices for Cozumel trips vary more and are noted below.

Countless watersports outfitters line the beach.

(Cozumel dives almost always require you to take the ferry on your own and board the dive boat on the island.) Playa's dive shops also offer full-day trips (May–Oct) to snorkel with whale sharks off Isla Mujeres and Isla Holbox north of Cancún. Dedicated divers should look for the discounted multi-dive deals and dive/hotel packages offered by many shops. Cyan Ha Dive Center (www.cyanha.com; ℭ 984/803-2517), one of the first shops in Playa and still one of the most respected, has a second site at the Petit Lafitte Hotel (p. 164). Tank-Ha Dive Center (www.tankha.com; ℭ 984/873-0302) takes divers to Cozumel directly on their own boat to Cozumel's reefs. The two-tank trip costs $140. Yucatek Divers (www.yucatek-divers.com; ℭ 984/803-2836) specializes in cenote diving and in dives for people with disabilities. Abyss Dive Center (www.abyssdiveshop. com; ℭ 984/873-2164) has a second shop in Tulum. Snorkeling isn't good in Playa since you can't reach the reefs by swimming from the beach. If you really want to snorkel, you're better off in the waters around Akumal and Xel-Ha.

WATERSPORTS

Countless outfitters line the beach and have stands on La Quinta, offering excursions inland to cenotes, ruins, and adventure parks. Banana boating, tubing, and jet-skiing are just a few of the (pricey) watersports you can enjoy in Playa's calm waters.

Where to Eat

Tiny cafes and fancy restaurants line Fifth Avenue and surrounding streets, and everybody's got an opinion on what's best. You can sample Argentinean beef, sushi, fancy pastas, and basic tacos *al pastor,* but be prepared—dining in Playa isn't cheap. For a taste of old Playa, try Yucatecan *Tikinxic* or impeccably fresh ceviche at a simple stand on the beach.

For a delicious Veracruz-style lunch in pleasant, breezy surroundings, try the upstairs **Marisquería** at the Hotel Básico, at Quinta Avenida and Calle 10 Norte. For fish tacos and inexpensive seafood, try **El Oasis,** on Calle 12, between avenidas 5 and 10 (no phone). For *arrachera* (fajita) tacos, the place to go is **Super Carnes H C de Monterrey,** Calle 1 Sur between avenidas 20 and 25 (℃ **984/803-0488**).

EXPENSIVE

La Casa del Agua ★★ EUROPEAN/MEXICAN   Excellent food in inviting surroundings. Instead of obtrusive background music, you hear the sound of falling water. The German owners do a good job with seafood; try the grilled seafood for two. For a home-style dish try the Chicken Zurich, chicken strips with fresh mushroom sauce served with spaetzle; for something heartier, there's a steak with Roquefort sauce and mashed potatoes. Pastas include a fine crab ravioli. On the Mexican side, the *cochinita pibli* ravioli and *pozole verde* are both excellent. The downstairs bistro is more informal than the second-story dining room, which sits under a large and airy *palapa* roof.

Av. 5 (at Calle 2). ℃ **984/803-0232.** Reservations recommended in high season. Main courses 149–380 pesos. MC, V. Daily noon–midnight.

Yaxché ★★★ YUCATECAN   The menu at this Playa standout, unlike the usual offerings at Yucatecan restaurants, employs native foods and spices in elaborate regional dishes. The sleek decor enhances the artsy section of La Quinta, while the food retains its ancient origins. Excellent examples are a cream of *chaya* (a native leafy vegetable similar to spinach) and an *xcatic* chile stuffed with *cochinita pibil*. The classic Mexican-style fruit salad with lime juice and dried powdered chile is another favorite. Seafood dishes are fresh and well prepared.

Av. 5 (at Calle 22). ℃ **984/873-3011.** Reservations recommended in high season. Main courses 160–280 pesos. AE, MC, V. Daily noon–midnight.

MODERATE

Casa Mediterránea ★ ITALIAN   Tucked away on a quiet little patio off Quinta Avenida, this small, homey restaurant serves excellent Italian cuisine. Maurizio Gabrielli and Maria Michelon routinely greet customers and make recommendations. Maurizio came to Mexico to enjoy the simple life, and it shows in the restaurant's welcoming, unhurried atmosphere. The menu is mostly northern Italian, with several dishes from other parts of Italy. The lobster is prepared beautifully. There are daily specials, too. Pastas (except penne and spaghetti) are made in-house and fresh. Try fish and shrimp ravioli or *penne alla Veneta.* There are several wines, mostly Italian, to choose from.

Av. 5 (btw. calles 6 and 8; look for the Hotel Marieta sign). ℃ **984/876-4679.** Reservations recommended in high season. Main courses 120–220 pesos. No credit cards. Wed–Mon 2–11pm.

La Cueva del Chango ★★ HEALTH FOOD/MEXICAN   Good food in original surroundings with a relaxed attitude makes this quirky place enduringly popular (expect a wait on weekend mornings). True to its name (The Monkey's Cave), the place is cavelike and has wicker and fabric monkeys hanging about. You'll enjoy great juices, blended fruit drinks, salads, soups, Mexican specialties with a natural twist, and handmade tortillas. The fresh fish is delicious, and the warm *panela* cheese with tortillas is divine. Mosquitoes can sometimes be a problem at night, but the management has bug spray on hand.

Calle 38 (btw. Av. 5 and the beach). ℃ **984/147-0271.** Main courses 80–220 pesos. No credit cards. Mon–Sat 8am–11pm; Sun 8am–2pm.

INEXPENSIVE

La Tarraya Restaurant/Bar 🐟 SEAFOOD/YUCATECAN THE RESTAU-
RANT THAT WAS BORN WITH THE TOWN, proclaims the sign. The wood hut doesn't
look like much, but there are tables right on the beach, and the owners are fishermen. The catch of the day is so fresh it's practically wiggling. If you haven't tried
the Yucatecan specialty *Tikinxic*—fish with achiote and bitter-orange sauce,
cooked in a banana leaf—this is a good place to start, and the mixed seafood grill
is a delicious steal.

Calle 2 Norte. (*C*) **984/873-2040.** Main courses 60–100 pesos; whole fish 100 pesos per kilo (2.2
lb.). No credit cards. Daily noon–9pm.

Los Carboncitos ★ MEXICAN Among the top choices at this simple sidewalk hangout are the tacos with *arrachera* (beef) or *al pastor* (pork), served with a
great salsa selection. I also recommend the chicken soup (*caldo xochitl*) and the
traditional *pozole*. For seafood, try the shrimp al chipotle or the shrimp kabobs.
Sides include crispy fried cheese (*chicharrón de queso*) and guacamole, and the
beer is always icy cold.

Calle 4 (btw. avs. 5 and 10). (*C*) **984/873-1382.** Main courses 80–138 pesos; order of tacos 74–89
pesos. No credit cards. Daily 9am–1am.

Shopping

Playa is the Caribbean coast's retail heart, and wandering along Quinta Avenida
and its side streets to ferret out the latest boutiques and shops makes a fine late-
afternoon diversion. Once you get past the ferry terminal area, low-key, locally
owned shops vie for your vacation dollar with high-end clothing, Cuban cigars,
specialty tequila, handicrafts, jewelry, and beach wear. Sadly, chain jewelry and
sportswear shops are claiming prime strolling areas. Abundant folk art and boutiques are concentrated between calles 4 and 10; Calle Corazón, a leafy pedestrian area between calles 12 and 14, has art galleries, restaurants, and still more boutiques. North of Calle Consti-tuyentes, artists and artisans display their creations on the sidewalks on Saturday evenings. Credit cards are widely accepted in shops, most with fixed prices.

Some favorite shops along La Quinta, south to north: **De Beatriz Boutique,** Calle 2, west of Quinta Avenida (*C* **984/879-3272**), an unsung little side-street shop selling locally designed *manta* (Mexican cotton) clothing; **Caracol,** between calles 6 and 8 (*C* **984/803-1504**), with tasteful and unique textiles, crafts, and clothing from throughout Mexico; **La Calaca,** between calles

Stock up on souvenirs at any number of stores
on Quinta Avenida.

Quinta Avenida is bustling at night.

12 and 14 (✆ 984/873-0174), for its wondrous variety of wooden masks, quirky carvings of angels, devils, and skeletons, and *alebrijes* (the famous Oaxacan carved, whimsically painted animals); **Rosalia,** between calles 12 and 14 (✆ 984/803-4904), for fabulous textiles from Chiapas, including embroidered *huipiles* and inexpensive shawls, scarves, and bags; **Casa Tequila,** at Calle 16 (✆ 984/873-0195), for its impressive selection of fine silver jewelry as well as 100 types of specialty tequila (you sample before you buy); and **Ah Cacao,** at Constituyentes (www.ahcacao.com; ✆ 984/803-5748), for its intense and rare *criollo* chocolate, the Maya's "food of the gods," in bars, cocoa, or roasted beans—the cafe's fudgy mochas, frappes, and chocolate shots will ruin you for Starbucks.

North of Constituyentes, artists display their works along Quinta Avenida, wine bars abound, and shops offer high-quality clothing, folk art, and shoes. This section is often used for art shows and festivals. **La Sirena,** at Calle 26 (✆ 984/803-3422), offers trendy folk art with *calaca* (skull), *lucha libre,* and Frida Kahlo themes.

Entertainment & Nightlife

It seems as if everyone in town is out strolling La Quinta until midnight; there's pleasant browsing, dining, and drinking available at any number of establishments. Wild and crazy **CoCo Bongo** (✆ 984/803-5939) presents a must-see show with flying acrobats, strutting rock star impersonators, and an unpredictable array of dancers, followed by long nights of impassioned dancing among the guests. It's at Avenida 10 and Calle 12. On the beach, the **Blue Parrot** (✆ 984/873-0083) at Calle 12 attracts a mixed crowd with its live rock show and nightly fire show on the beach. Just to the south is **Om** (no phone), which gets a younger crowd with louder musical acts. **Fusion** (✆ 984/873-0374), on the beach at Calle 6, hosts live bands Monday through Saturday nights, alternating between jazz, reggae, and rock. **La Santanera,** on Calle 12 between avenidas 5 and 10, has long been the best late-night club.

Though they technically close around sunset, several beach clubs north of Avenida Constituyentes occasionally book live acts. Look for action at the foot of calles 30 to 36.

CHOOSING AN all-inclusive IN THE RIVIERA MAYA

All-inclusive resorts far outnumber regular hotels in the Riviera Maya, and the trend continues to dominate new construction. Most folks are familiar with the AI (short for all-inclusive) concept—large hotels that work with economies of scale to offer lodging, food, and drink all for a single rate. Some AIs offer convenience and low rates good for families with many mouths to feed. Because they are enclosed areas, they make it easy for parents to watch their children. The system works well for multiple-generation family reunions and group meetings, and seasonal deals offer amazingly cheap getaways.

This type of all-inclusive is best booked through a vacation packager or travel agent. Their air and AI packages usually beat anything you can get by booking your own flight and room, even if you have frequent-flier miles to burn. In a recent comparison of package prices with the cost of separate direct air and hotel bookings, for example, a couple could save an average of more than $100 a night through BookIt.com, which offers a particularly good range of all-inclusive resorts among its deals.

I came to understand and appreciate this type of vacation while staying at the **Iberostar** (www.iberostar.com) complex on Paraíso Beach north of Playa del Carmen. The enormous compound includes five hotels in all price ranges, a golf course, shopping center, nightclubs, spacious beach, and terrific spa. A tram travels between the resorts. (Guests at the higher-end hotels can use the amenities at all hotels.) Despite the size, I never felt overwhelmed and enjoyed watching families play together and apart.

With several resorts of varying quality and style, **Karisma Hotels + Resorts** (www.karismahotels.com)

merits attention. Their Azul resorts have a partnership with Fisher-Price, and their kids' clubs are amazing. Their adults-only Dorado resorts pamper grownups with spas and gourmet restaurants. Some of the hotels have Gourmet Inclusive plans offering all the amenities you expect in upscale resorts, all included in the rate.

Another all-inclusive concept offers beyond-luxurious resorts with fabulous suites, spas, pools, and beaches along with exceptional gourmet dining. Daily rates can soar beyond $1,000 per person per day. But more and more resort companies are moving in this direction, and big spenders have outstanding options. The **Grand Velas Riviera Maya** (p. 162) excels in this category. The pricey **Royal Hideaway Playacar** (www.royalhideaway.com) is acclaimed as an idyllic wedding and honeymoon setting. The exclusive resorts sometimes have some odd rules, though. For example, my husband and I weren't able to enjoy the specialty restaurants at one resort because men were required to wear closed-toe dress shoes—even dressy leather sandals were verboten. Be sure you know such things before you go.

Where to Stay

Playa's many small hotels give you a better feel for the town than staying in one of the resorts in Playacar. Don't hesitate to book a place that's not on the beach. Town life here is much of the fun, and staying on the beach has its disadvantages—in particular, the noise from a couple of beach bars. Beaches are public property in Mexico, and you can lay out your towel anywhere you like. At some beach clubs in north Playa, you have use of lounge chairs and towels for a small sum or the price of a meal.

When tourism is slow you can score some great walk-in offers. Promotional rates and packages pop up online as well. Reservations are essential around holidays, however. Rates listed below include the 12% hotel tax, but not the Christmas-to–New Year's rates, which soar well beyond the standard high-season rates.

EXPENSIVE

Deseo Hotel + Lounge ★★   The lounge here serves as a lobby, restaurant, bar, and pool area all at once. Filled with a hip Mexico City clientele during national holidays, this hotel is popular with the 20 to 50 set. Guest rooms are comfortable, original, and striking, but they don't tempt one to stay indoors—no TV, no cushy armchair. Their simplicity gives them an almost Asian feel, heightened by nice touches such as sliding wood-and-frosted-glass doors. The bottom of each bed has a little drawer that slides out with a night kit containing incense, earplugs, and condoms.

The owners also operate the cleverly styled **Hotel Básico** (www.hotel basico.com; ✆ **984/879-4448**). It's a fun mix of industrial and '50s styles, built with concrete, plywood, and plastics. As with Deseo, the common areas are not wasted space.

Av. 5 (at Calle 12), 77710 Playa del Carmen, Q. Roo. www.hoteldeseo.com. ✆ **984/879-3620.** 15 units. $205–$345. Rates include continental breakfast. AE, MC, V. No parking. No children 17 and under. **Amenities:** Bar; Jacuzzi; small rooftop pool; room service. *In room:* A/C, hair dryer (on request), minibar.

MODERATE

Hotel Lunata ★★ ✦   In the middle of Playa, there isn't a more comfortable or more attractive place to stay than this small hotel on Quinta Avenida. Rooms offer character and polished good looks. The few standard rooms are midsize and come with a queen-size or a double bed. Large deluxe rooms come with a king-size bed and small fridge; junior suites come with two doubles. The well-designed bathrooms have good showers. Rooms facing the street have double-glazed glass doors opening to a balcony. When they're shut, the street noise is not bothersome, but light sleepers should ask for a room facing the garden.

Av. 5 (btw. calles 6 and 8), 77710 Playa del Carmen, Q. Roo. www.lunata.com. ✆ **984/873-0884.** Fax 984/873-1240. 10 units. High season $120–$155 double; low season $110–$145 double. Rates include continental breakfast. AE, MC, V. No children 10 and under. **Amenities:** Bikes; watersports. *In room:* A/C, fan, TV, fridge (in some), hair dryer (on request), Wi-Fi (in some).

La Tortuga ★★★   You'll have a hard time staying anywhere else when you can get amiable service, a variety of rooms, and all the amenities you need at these digs. The word's out and travelers fill the rooms—though there's usually a good choice for returning guests. Some rooms edge the sinuous pool; others have balconies overlooking gardens and the pool. Suites have whirlpool tubs, balconies, and extras such as irons and robes. All rooms have coffee machines and alarm clocks. The cozy living-room space by the pool has a bar, a book exchange, and comfy couches, and the El Bistro restaurant is very good, as is the on-site spa.

Av. 10 (at Calle 14), 77710 Playa del Carmen, Q. Roo. www.hotellatortuga.com. ✆ **866/550-6878,** U.S. and Canada 984/873-1484. 51 units. $189 and up double high season; $143 and up low season. Rates include breakfast, and beach passes. MC, V. **Amenities:** Restaurant; bar; spa; outdoor pool; Wi-Fi. *In room:* A/C, fan, TV, Jacuzzi (in suite), minibar, MP3 docking station (in suite).

Playa Maya ★ 🏄 Good location, good price, comfortable rooms, and friendly, helpful management are but a few reasons to choose this over other beach hotels in downtown Playa. But what really sets it apart is that you enter the hotel from the beach. This seemingly inconsequential detail sets the mood and creates a little separation from the busy street. What's more, the design blocks out noise from nearby bars and neighboring hotels. Rooms are large, with midsize bathrooms. A couple units have private garden terraces with Jacuzzis; others have balconies facing the beach. High-season rates here extend from Christmas through August, and minimum stays are required.

Zona FMT (btw. calles 6 and 8 Norte), 77710 Playa del Carmen, Q. Roo. www.playa-maya.com. ✆ **984/803-2022.** 20 units. High season $150 and up double; low season $100 and up double. Rates include continental breakfast. MC, V. Limited street parking. **Amenities:** Restaurant; bar; Jacuzzi; outdoor pool; room service. *In room:* A/C, TV, fridge, hair dryer, Wi-Fi.

INEXPENSIVE

Hotel Lab Nah 🏄 Good rooms in a central location for a good price are the main attraction at this economy hotel in the heart of Playa. Windows in the cheapest rooms face Quinta Avenida, allowing in some noise (mostly of late-night bar hoppers). It's not a big problem, but it's worth the money to get a partial-ocean-view with balcony on the third floor, which is quieter and larger. Garden-view rooms directly below the ocean-views are just as large and quiet, but not quite as fixed up, and there's little difference in price. The largest unit, a rooftop *palapa*, is good for three or four people.

Calle 6 (and Av. 5), 77710 Playa del Carmen, Q. Roo. www.labnah.com. ✆ **984/873-2099.** 33 units. High season $56 and up double, low season $49 and up double. Rates include continental breakfast. MC, V. Limited street parking. **Amenities:** Small outdoor pool. *In room:* A/C, hair dryers (in some), no phone.

Jardín de Marieta 🏨 Besides the reasonable rates, this pleasant, quirky place is appealing for its central yet half-hidden location. Rooms vary, but most are large, bright, and cheerful. Four rooms have kitchenettes adequate for simple meals. Most rooms encircle a tree-shaded patio with a few shops and a restaurant.

Av. 5 Norte 173 (btw. calles 6 and 8), 77710 Playa del Carmen, Q. Roo. www.jardindemarieta. com. ✆ **984/873-0224.** 10 units. High season $60 and up double; low season $40 and up double. No credit cards. Limited street parking. **Amenities:** Restaurant. *In room:* A/C, TV, fridge, kitchenette (in some), no phone, Wi-Fi.

Side Trips

Playa makes a great base for excursions up and down the Riviera Maya. It's easy to shoot out to Cozumel on the ferry, drive south to the nature parks and the ruins at Tulum and Cobá, or drive north to Cancún. Directly south of town is the Playacar development, which has a golf course, several large all-inclusive resorts, and a residential development. My favorite outfitter for unusual trips is **Alltournative,** Hwy. 307 Km 287 (www.alltournative.com; ✆ **877/437-4990** in the U.S., or 984/803-9999; p. 198), in front of the entrance to Playacar just south of Playa del Carmen.

SOUTH OF PLAYA DEL CARMEN

A succession of small communities, resorts, and nature parks flank a 56km (35-mile) stretch of highway leading south from Playa del Carmen. This section covers them from north to south.

Renting a car is the best way to move around here. While buses might get you close to your destination, it can be a hot walk from the highway to the coast. Another option is to hire a car and driver.

Beyond Paamul, you'll see signs for this or that cenote or cave. The Yucatán has thousands of cenotes, and each is slightly different (p. 178). These turnoffs are less visited than the major attractions and can make for a pleasant visit.

Punta Venado: Horseback Riding

A few places along the highway offer horseback rides. The best of these, **Rancho Punta Venado** (www.puntavenado.com; ✆ 984/803-5224), is just south of Playa, past the Calica Pier. This ranch is the least touristy—though it does cater to groups—and the owners take good care of the horses. It has a nice stretch of coast with a sheltered bay and offers horseback riding ($90 for 75 min.), ATV expeditions to caves and cenotes, and other activities. Transportation from Cancún, Playa del Carmen, and Tulum is available for an extra fee. Use of the beach club is included in tour prices. Make arrangements in advance so that they can schedule you on a day when they have fewer customers. The turnoff for the ranch is 2km (1¼ miles) south of the Calica overpass near Km. 279.

Río Secreto: Wondrous Cavern

Río Secreto NATURE RESERVE   More spiritual than commercial, this community-based ecopark teaches visitors about Maya beliefs regarding the "underworld" as they explore a 600m-long (less than a ½ mile) cavern hidden for centuries. As the story goes, a local *campesino* was chasing a meaty lizard into the brush and under a rock pile. The *campesino* followed, digging through rocks, until he heard a splash. The lizard, it seemed, had discovered a hiding place. The man found the entrance to a cave filled with stalactites and stalagmites. Local naturalists discovered a dazzling series of chambers with rock formations dating back 2.5 million years. The area was declared a nature reserve and opened to the public in April 2008.

Visitors must be accompanied by guides and wear short wetsuits and helmets as they walk and swim through the cavern. At times, it is so dark you feel like you're totally blind. Other times, sunshine streams through holes in the roof, illuminating the blue and pink striations caused by mineral-rich water dripping over earth-toned stone. An occasional swim through an emerald green pool adds to the fun, as does the guide's banter and knowledge. From donning your wetsuit to downing a filling lunch after the 90-minute underground tour, it will take about 3½ hours. Hot showers and lockers are available.

Off Hwy. 307, 5 minutes south of Playa del Carmen (btw. Xcaret and the Calica Port). www.rio secreto.com. ✆ **877/357-4242** in the U.S. or 984/877-2377 Basic tour without transportation $69 adults, $35 children 4–11.

Xcaret: Tribute to the Yucatán

A billboard in distant Guadalajara's airport reads in Spanish, AND WHEN VISITING XCARET, DON'T FORGET TO ENJOY THE PLEASURES OF THE RIVIERA MAYA, TOO. An

Marvel at the stalactites and stalagmites of Río Secreto.

exaggeration, yes, but a point well taken: Xcaret ("eesh-ca-*ret*") is the biggest attraction in these parts and even has its own resort. Thousands visit every week; stay away if you like solitude. Xcaret samples everything the Yucatán—and the rest of Mexico—has to offer, and action junkies take full advantage of the pricey admission fee.

The myriad activities include scuba and snorkeling; cavern diving; hiking through tropical forest; horseback riding; an underwater river ride; swinging in a hammock under palms; and meeting native Maya people. Exhibits include a bat cave; a butterfly pavilion; mushroom and orchid nurseries; and a petting aquarium. Native jaguars, manatees, sea turtles, monkeys, macaws, and flamingos are also on display. The best folk art museum in Mexico is housed in the Hacienda Henequenera, a traditional Yucatecan hacienda with rooms decorated as if a family lived there. The wonderful folk art collection from throughout Mexico decorates the rooms, and the displays are always changing. The Cava, an amazing underground wine cellar, displays bottles from Mexico's many excellent wineries and offers wine tastings with advance reservations; the dining rooms looks like somewhere major global negotiations would take place. The Hacienda and Cava both offer guided tours; book them when purchasing your entrance tickets. The evening show celebrates Mexico in music and dance, and the costumes and choreography are unequaled anywhere in Mexico. This show is a genuinely mesmerizing spectacle, presenting so many aspects of the Mexican nation that you feel like you've toured the whole country by the time the performers take their last bow.

A costumed dancer performs at Xcaret.

Paamul: Seaside Getaway ★

About 15km (9⅓ miles) beyond Xcaret and 25km (16 miles) from Playa del Carmen is Paamul (also written Pamul). The exit is clearly marked. You can enjoy the Caribbean in relative quiet here. The water at the out-of-the-way beach is wonderful, but the shoreline is rocky.

UNDERGROUND adventures

The Yucatán Peninsula's land surface is a thin limestone shelf jutting out like a footprint between the Gulf of Mexico and the Caribbean Sea. Rainwater seeps through the surface into cenotes, freshwater sinkholes that dot the underground world. Some cenotes are like small wells. Others are like giant green ponds with high rock walls—tempting sights to would-be Tarzans. Cenotes often provide access to magical caves where sunlight from holes in the land's surface glimmers on icicle-like stalactites and stalagmites. The Riviera Maya is filled with these formations, and it seems every farmer and landowner has posted a sign offering access to their pools and caverns for a few pesos. Some are actually blasting the ground in search of cenotes, unfortunately. More elaborate parks include underground rivers and cenotes among their many attractions. Several, including Xcaret, Hidden Worlds, Río Secreto, and Aktun Chen, are described in this chapter. Dozens of smaller cenotes and caves deserve your attention as well, and entry costs much less than at the big parks. Adventuresome types should seek out newly opened sites marked with rustic wooden signs. Below are a few cenotes accessible from Hwy. 307. Most have bathrooms, are open daily from about 8 or 9am until 5 or 6pm, and charge about 30 to 50 pesos.

Cenote Azul (approximately 2km/1¼ miles south of Puerto Aventuras, just south of Ecopark Kantun Chi): Situated close to the highway with several large pools, Cenote Azul has a fun jump-off point on a section of overhanging rock, and a wooden lounging deck jutting over the water. Walkways along the edge make it easier to get in and swim with the abundant catfish.

Gran Cenote (about 3 km/1¾ miles west of Tulum on the road to Cobá): Divers are especially fond of this aptly named bottomless, crystal-clear cenote leading to caverns that seem to have no end. Snorkelers can follow the dive lights into caves close to the surface and see fantastic rock formations. Since it's off the main highway, this fabulous cenote is less popular with groups and feels like it's buried in jungle.

Jardín del Edén (1.6km/1 mile north of Xpu-Há, just south of Cenote Azul): "El Edén" is one of my favorite cenotes because it's run by an accommodating family and has lots of rocky outcroppings where you can lounge in the warm sun after the freezing water leaves you covered in goose bumps. There's plenty of room along the edges of the cenote, which looks like a huge swimming pool. Shrieks fill the air as daredevils attempt swan dives from a high jump-off point. Snorkelers and divers find plenty of tropical fish and eels.

Manatí (Tankhah, east of the highway 10km/6¼ miles north of Tulum): The large, open lagoon near Casa Cenote restaurant is part of a long underwater cave system that ends at the sea. Freshwater bubbling up into ocean waters creates significant but not dangerous currents that attract a great variety of saltwater and freshwater

Scuba-Mex (www.scubamex.com; ✆ **888/871-6255** in the U.S., or 984/875-1066) is a fully equipped PADI- and SSI-certified dive shop next to the cabañas. Using two boats, the staff takes guests on dives 8km (5 miles) in either direction. If it's too choppy, the reefs in front of the hotel are also good. The cost

fish. The cenote was named for the manatees that used to show up occasionally; the shy creatures have disappeared as the region has gained popularity.

Xunaan ha (outside of Chemuyil, 12km/7½ miles south of Akumal): Gaining popularity because of its sense of authenticity, this one is reached by winding through a Maya village and growing town that is home to locals who work in and around Akumal. Signs point to the small cenote nearly hidden in the jungle, where you can swim, float, or snorkel with schools of fish and the occasional freshwater turtle. *Note:* There are no bathrooms here.

Several dive shops along the Riviera Maya offer cenote and reef diving and snorkeling. Recommended outfitters that specialize in cenotes include **Yukatek Divers** (www.yucatek-divers.com; ☎ **984/803-2836**) and **Go Cenotes** (☎ **984/803-3924**), both in Playa del Carmen, and **Cenote Dive Center** (www.cenotedive.com; ☎ **984/871-2232**) and **Xibalba Dive Center** (www.xibalbadivecenter.com; ☎ **984/871-2953**) in Tulum. Rates start at $55 for a snorkel tour and $120 for two-tank cavern dives, which take place in open cenotes where you are always within reach of air and natural light; cave diving requires advanced technical training and specialized gear, and is more expensive.

Xcaret is 10km (6¼ miles) south of Playa del Carmen; you'll know when you get to the turnoff. It's open daily from 8:30am to 9pm. Basic admission prices are $71 for adults, $35 for

children 5 to 12. Xcaret at Night, with admission after 3pm, is $53 for adults and $27 for children. All-inclusive tickets start at around $100 for adults and $50 for children. Open daily from 8:30am to 9:30pm.

The people who created Xcaret have another park called **Xplor** (www.xplor.travel; ☎ **998/849-5275**) next door. The adventure park has a zip line, four-wheel-drive track, and an underground river ride. Admission is $99 for adults, $49 for children (8 or older); you get a 10% discount for booking online 3 days in advance.

Four kilometers (2½ miles) south of the entrance to Xcaret is the turnoff for **Puerto Calica,** the cruise-ship pier. Passengers disembark here for tours of Playa, Xcaret, the ruins, and other attractions on the coast.

for a one-tank dive with rental gear is $39. They also have multi-dive packages and certification instruction, and offer accommodations in four bedrooms in a beach house for $80 per night.

Avoiding the Cruise-Ship Crowds

Fewer ships arrive on weekends than on weekdays, which makes the weekend a good time for visiting the coast's major attractions.

Cabañas Paamul ★ Paamul works mostly with the trailer crowd, but there are also 13 modern "junior suites" near the water's edge. They are spacious and comfortable, and come with a kitchenette and two queen beds. Trailer guests have access to 12 showers and separate bathrooms for men and women. Laundry service is available nearby. The large *palapa* restaurant is open to the public, and customers are welcome to use the beach, which is rocky along this stretch of the coast. Prices vary according to season.

Carretera Cancún–Tulum Km 85. www.paamul.com. © **984/875-1053** or 612/353-6825. 13 units; 200 trailer spaces (all with full hookups). $100–$150 junior suite. RV space with hookups $30 per day, $600 per month. Ask about discounts for stays longer than 1 week. No credit cards. Free parking. **Amenities:** Restaurant; bar; dive shop; outdoor pool. *In room:* A/C, TV, kitchenette.

Puerto Aventuras: Dolphins & Shipwrecks

Five kilometers (3 miles) south of Paamul and 104km (65 miles) from Cancún, Puerto Aventuras is a condo/marina development with a 9-hole golf course on Chakalal Bay. At its center is a collection of restaurants bordering a dolphin pool that offer Mexican and Italian food, steaks, and pub grub. The major attraction is swimming with the dolphins in a highly interactive program; make reservations well in advance with **Dolphin Discovery** (www.dolphindiscovery.com; © **998/849-4757**). The surest way is through the website.

Puerto Aventuras is also popular for boating and deep-sea fishing. **Capt. Rick's Sportfishing Center** (www.fishyucatan.com; © **888/449-3562** in the U.S., or 984/873-5195) will combine a fishing trip with some snorkeling, which makes for a leisurely day. The best fishing on this coast is from March to August. Puerto Aventuras has a few hotels, but most residential development is condos and homes. The most prominent hotel, the **Omni Puerto Aventuras** (© **888/444-6665** in the U.S., or 984/875-1958), is nice but pricey, starting around $200 per night.

Museo Sub-Acuatico CEDAM ★ MUSEUM This is the region's only maritime museum, a compelling display of coins, weapons, gold dentures, clay dishes, and other items from colonial-era shipwrecks. All were recovered by members of the "Explorations and Water Sports Club of Mexico" (CEDAM), a group of former World War II frogmen. Most of the artifacts came from a Cuban ship that foundered near Akumal in 1741. Other displays include Maya offerings dredged from the peninsula's cenotes, finds from local archaeological sites, vintage diving equipment, and early photos of cenote explorations. The museum is on the second floor of a pink building near the entrance.

Puerto Aventuras. www.puertoaventuras.com/services.html. © **984/873-5000.** Donation requested. Open Mon–Sat 9am–1pm and 2:30–5:30pm. Donations requested.

Xpu-Ha: Sublime Beach

Three kilometers (1¾ miles) beyond Puerto Aventuras is **Xpu-Ha** (eesh-poo-hah) ★★★, a wide bay lined by a broad, beautiful sandy beach. Much of the shore is filled with private houses and condos, along with a few all-inclusive

La Cruz de Caravaca, de significado muy especial para los marineros, quienes creían que los ayudaba a predecir los vientos

The Cross of Caravaca, of special significance to sailors, who believed it helped them to predict winds

A display at the Museo Sub-Acuatico CEDAM.

resorts. The beach is one of the best on the coast and is long enough to accommodate hotel guests, residents, and day-trippers without feeling crowded.

Al Cielo ★   This is a good choice if you want a small hotel on the beach where your rustic digs—local hardwood floors; clapboard walls; no phones, TVs, or clocks; and set on a private, secluded beach—come with air-conditioning, modern bathrooms, and shaded private *palapas* for beach lounging. The four rooms (two upstairs, two down) occupy a large thatched building right on the beach. The restaurant is popular, but the rooms are simple. If you're looking for more amenities, this won't be for you.

Carretera Cancún–Tulum Km 118, 77710 Xpu-Ha, Q. Roo. www.alcielohotel.com. ℂ **984/840-9012.** 4 units. $212–$258 double. Rates include full breakfast. MC, V. Free secure parking. No children. **Amenities:** Restaurant; bar; Hobie cat; room service. *In room:* A/C, fan, hair dryer, no phone, Wi-Fi.

Esencia ★★★   No other property on this coast epitomizes leisure and escape more than Esencia. The hotel includes a few rooms in a villa and guesthouse built as a private getaway for an Italian duchess. I'd be thrilled to spend a few romantic nights in the villa's beach-view rooms—one of those lottery dreams. Families spread out in the two-story cottages surrounded by lush plants and gardens. Every room throughout the property has lots of space, lots of beauty, lots of privacy, and an air of serenity (decorations are tastefully minimalist, such as three oranges on a driftwood tray). Of course, the magnificent beach includes private day beds under A-framed thatch shades. Service is personal and understated (a service fee is added to the room rate) and the food is outstanding. If the spa were any more relaxing, it would be an out-of-body experience.

> ### In Case of Emergency
>
> The Riviera Maya, south of Puerto Aventuras, is susceptible to power failures that can last for hours. Gas pumps and cash machines shut down when this happens, and once the power returns, they attract long lines. It's a good idea to keep a reserve of gas and cash.

Predio Rústico Xpu-Ha, Fracc. 16 y 18, L. 18, 19 (exit Xpu-Ha-2), 77710 Xpu-Ha, Q. Roo. www.hotelesencia.com. ℂ **877/528-3490** in the U.S. or Canada, or 984/873-4830. 29 units. High season $625 and up double or suite; low season $525 and up double or suite. Rates include full breakfast. Internet specials sometimes available. AE, MC, V. Free valet parking. **Amenities:** Restaurant; 2 bars; babysitting; concierge; Jacuzzi; 2 outdoor pools; room service; spa. *In room:* A/C, TV/DVD, hair dryer, Internet, minibar.

Akumal: Beautiful Bays & Cavern Diving

Continuing south on Hwy. 307 for 2km (1¼ miles), the turnoff for Akumal ("Place of the Turtles") is marked by a traffic light. The ecologically oriented tourism community is spread among four bays, with two entrances off the frontage road parallel to the highway. The main entrance, labeled Akumal, leads to hotels, rental condos, and vacation homes. Take the Akumal Aventuras entrance to the Grand Oasis all-inclusive hotel and more condos and homes. No waterside road connects the two, so you'll need to know which exit to take. A white arch delineates the main entrance to the tourism community (years ago, the original residents were moved across the highway to a fast-growing town where many workers and business owners reside). Just before the arch are a couple of grocery stores and a laundry service. Just inside the arch, to the right, is the **Hotel Akumal Caribe.** If you follow the road to the left and keep to the left, you'll reach Half Moon Bay, lined with two- and three-story condos, and eventually Yal-ku Lagoon, a snorkeling park. To rent a local condo, contact **Akumal Vacations** (www.akumalvacations. com; ✆ **800/448-7137** in the U.S.) or **Loco Gringo** (www.locogringo.com).

Both bays have sandy beaches with rocky or silt bottoms. This is a popular diving area and home to Mexico's original diving club. Three dive shops are in town, and at least 30 dive sites are offshore. The **Akumal Dive Shop** (✆ **984/ 875-9032;** www.akumal.com), one of the oldest and best dive shops on the coast, offers cavern-diving trips and courses in technical diving. The friendly owner and dive masters know all the secret spots in the area and can offer all sorts of insider tips. It and **Akumal Dive Adventures** (✆ **888/425-8625** in the U.S., or 984/875-9157), at the Vista del Mar hotel on Half Moon Bay, offer resort courses as well as full open-water certification.

LEFT: **Scuba diving in Akumal.** RIGHT: **Akumal attracts nesting sea turtles from May through September.**

Modern sculptures punctuate gardens beside the clear **Yal-ku Lagoon,** which is about 700m (2,297 ft.) long and 200m (656 ft.) at its widest. You can paddle around comfortably in sheltered water and see fish and turtles. It's a perfect place to learn how to snorkel and let kids swim about safely. Of course, there are many spots along the bays where you can snorkel for free, but this little park is an easy, relaxing outing. It's open daily from 8am to 5:30pm. Admission is 100 pesos for adults, 50 pesos for children 3 to 14.

Centro Ecológico Akumal ★★★ MUSEUM The gentle crescent of **Akumal Bay,** washing a wide, soft beach shaded by coconut palms, is one of the few places where you'll often be surprised by a sea turtle swimming along with you. During nesting season (May–July), visit the center in the morning to sign up for that evening's 9pm turtle walk (Mon–Fri). You'll help staff search for new nests, protect exhausted mothers making their way back to sea, and remove eggs to hatcheries where they can incubate safely.

East side of road at town entrance. www.ceakumal.org. ✆ 984/875-9005.

WHERE TO EAT

Akumal has about 10 places to eat and a convenient grocery store, **Super Cho-mak** (with an ATM), by the arch. A collection of businesses just inside the arch include a bakery and coffeehouse. At the Hotel Akumal Caribe, **Lol-Ha** serves good breakfasts and dinners and has free Wi-Fi, and the **Palapa Snack** bar dishes out everything from ice cream cones to burgers with poblano chiles and avocado. Tell the guards at the hotel's entrance that you're there for a meal, and they'll direct you to special parking areas—and they don't notice if you take some time to wander along the hotel's beautiful beach.

La Buena Vida SEAFOOD/REGIONAL This beach restaurant is just plain fun. Where else can you scale a *mirador* (crow's nest) to dine while under the influence of the best view of Half Moon Bay? The menu is varied and the fare excellent, especially the Maya chicken, *Tikinxic,* and other regional specialties. Afterward, belly up to the sand-floored bar, which blends its own unique cocktails in addition to serving a barrage of special tequilas.

Half Moon Bay beach (btw. Akumal and Yal-ku Lagoon). www.akumalinfo.com/restaurant.htm. ✆ **984/875-9061.** Main courses 80–285 pesos. MC, V. Daily 11am–1am.

Turtle Bay Cafe & Bakery ★ AMERICAN Yummy pancakes with pecan maple syrup, fried eggs with hash browns, and eggs Benedict with Canadian bacon satisfy the expats dining beneath the palms. More adventuresome eaters go for *huevos rancheros* or a breakfast burrito with eggs, corn, and mushrooms. Lunches are equally tempting—you can even get a lentil burger—and cool smoothies and pastries are served throughout the day. Dinner might start with coconut shrimp and move on to crab cakes over mashed potatoes or a bodacious steak sandwich with caramelized onions. There's free Wi-Fi and plenty of friendly folks conversing with travelers in the *palapa*-shaded garden.

Plaza Ukana. ✆ **984/875-9138.** Main courses 125–240 pesos. MC, V. Daily 7am–9pm.

WHERE TO STAY

Rates below are for two people and include taxes. During the holidays, most hotels and condo rentals charge higher rates than those listed.

Hotel Akumal Caribe ★★ ☺ The first accommodations on Akumal Bay were simple thatch-roofed cabañas beside a gorgeous beach. Since then, the property has morphed into a casual resort with tile-roofed bungalows spread about dense gardens. Simply and comfortably furnished, with kitchenettes, spacious showers, and jugs of purified water, the bungalows are great for a night or a week. The rooms in the beachside hotel have kitchenettes and fancier furnishings. The hotel also books condos and villas with multiple bedrooms and a shared pool on Half Moon Bay. The property's best asset is its placement at the edge of beautiful Akumal Bay. Visiting its restaurants and shops will get you past the guards who turn nonguests away.

Carretera Cancún–Tulum (Hwy. 307) Km 104. www.hotelakumalcaribe.com. ℂ **800/351-1622** in the U.S., 800/343-1440 in Canada, or 915/584-3552. 70 units. High season $120 bungalow, $155 double; low season $99 bungalow, $110 double. Low-season packages and reduced Web rates available. Rates include breakfast. AE, MC, V. Free parking. **Amenities:** 2 restaurants; bar; babysitting; seasonal children's activities; dive shop; large outdoor pool. *In room:* A/C, Internet (in some), kitchenette (in some), no phone (in some).

Vista del Mar Hotel and Condos ★ 🏊 This beachside property rents hotel rooms at good prices and large, fully equipped condos that you can rent by the day or week. The lovely, well-tended beach in front of the hotel has chairs and umbrellas. The on-site dive shop eliminates the hassle of organizing dive trips. Hotel rooms are small and contain either a queen-size or a double and a twin bed. The condos consist of a well-equipped kitchen, a living area, two or three bedrooms, and up to three bathrooms. All have balconies or terraces facing the sea and are furnished with hammocks. Several rooms come with whirlpool tubs.

Half Moon Bay, 77760 Akumal, Q. Roo. www.akumalinfo.com. ℂ **888/425-8625** and 505/992-3333 in the U.S. 27 units. High season $110 double, $185–$290 condo; low season $95 double, $110–$175 condo MC, V. Limited free parking. **Amenities:** Restaurant; bar; dive shop; small outdoor pool; watersports. *In room:* A/C, TV, CD player, fridge, kitchenette (in condos), no phone (in some).

Snorkel in Xel-Ha lagoon.

Xel-Ha: Snorkeling & Swimming ★★

Aktun Chen NATURE RESERVE This is one of Yucatán's best caverns, with lots of geological features, good lighting, several underground pools, and large chambers, all carefully preserved. It has thrived under management by the local community rather than outside tour companies. The cavern tour takes about 90 minutes and requires a lot of walking, but the footing is good. Other choices are snorkeling in a cenote or soaring above the jungle on zip lines. There is also a zoo with spider monkeys and other local fauna; some critters are allowed to run about freely. The turnoff is to the right,

Rent Snuba gear in Xel-Ha.

and the cave is about 4km (2½ miles) from the road.

3km/2 miles S of Akumal. www.aktunchen. com. ✆ **984/109-2061.** Cave tour $26 adults, $14 children. Daily 9am–4pm (closed Christmas and New Year's Day).

Xel-Ha ★★ NATURE RESERVE

The centerpiece of this park is a large, beautiful lagoon where freshwater and saltwater meet. You can swim, float, and snorkel in beautifully clear water surrounded by jungle. A small train takes you to a drop-off point upriver, and you float back down on water moving calmly toward the sea. With no waves or currents to pull you around, snorkeling here is more comfortable than in the open sea, and the water has several species of fish, including rays.

The park rents snorkeling equipment and underwater cameras. Platforms allow nonsnorkelers to view the fish. Even better, use the park's Snuba gear, a contraption that allows you to breathe through 6m (20-ft.) tubes connected to scuba tanks floating on the surface. Like Snuba but more involved is sea-trek, an elaborate plastic helmet with air hoses that allows you to walk around on the bottom, breathing normally, and perhaps help to feed the stingrays.

Other attractions include a plant nursery and an apiary for the local stingerless bees. Admission includes use of inner tubes, life vest, shuttle train to the river, and changing rooms and showers.

13km/8 miles S of Akumal. www.xelha.com.mx. ✆ **984/875-6000.** $40 adults, $30 children 5–11. All-inclusive option including all rentals, food and beverages: $79 adults, $39 children. Daily 8:30am–6pm.

Hidden Worlds Cenotes ★★★ NATURE RESERVE Hidden Worlds Cenotes offers an excellent opportunity to snorkel or dive in a couple of nearby caverns. The caverns are part of a vast network that makes up a single underground river system. The water is crystalline (and cold), and the rock formations impressive. These caverns were filmed for the IMAX production Journey into Amazing Caves. The main form of transportation is "jungle mobile," with a guide tossing out information and lore about the jungle plant life you see. You'll be walking some, so take shoes or sandals. If you've toured caverns before, floating through gives you an entirely different perspective. The owners have also installed a 180m (590-ft.) zip line on the property, a zip-line roller-coaster-style ride called Avatar, and a Skycycle that has you riding a recumbent bike over the tree tops. They now offer full-day packages that include several activities. Transportation from Tulum, Akumal, and Puerto Aventuras is included in admission fees.

About 2km (1¼ miles) south of Xel-Ha. www.hiddenworlds.com. ✆ **888/339-8001** U.S. and Canada, or 984/877-8535. Admission including all land activities and snorkeling $80 adults, $40 children. Cenote diving $130. Daily 9am–5pm.

A cenote in Hidden Worlds.

Soliman Bay: Secluded Beauty

Jashita ★★ The setting on the secluded Bahía de Soliman near Tulum couldn't be better. A reef protects the bay from winds, creating a shallow pool filled with sea creatures. The snorkeling and kayaking are fabulous on both sides of the reef, and gear for both sports is at hand for free. Elegantly minimalist, the rooms and suites, including a two-bedroom master suite with two plunge pools, have platform beds dressed in crisp linens and puffy lightweight covers for chilly winter nights, and plasma TVs with SKY service (great music channels). All except the two double rooms have terraces with plunge pools. Top-floor suites claim awe-inspiring views of the sea, lagoons, and seemingly endless vegetation, but the sun shines brightly through high windows beneath the peaked thatch roof. One private five-bedroom villa is also available for rent. Indonesian statues and furnishings decorate the serene Sahara restaurant, where the entire Marchiorello family competes to create divine seafood soup, pastas, and fish.

Bahía Punta Soliman, Tulum, Q. Roo. www.jashitahotel.com. ℭ **984/139-5131.** 14 suites, 1 villa. High season $190–$580 double; low season $140–$450 double. AE, MC, V. Free parking. **Amenities:** Restaurant; bar; outdoor pool; Wi-Fi. *In room:* A/C, TV/DVD, CD player, hair dryer, minibar.

Tankah Bay: Bubbling Cenote

Tankah Bay (about 3km/1¾ miles from Hidden World Cenotes) has a handful of rental houses and condos. The most interesting hotel is **Casa Cenote** (www. casacenote.com; ℭ **998/874-5170**). Its underground river surfaces at a cenote in the back of the property, then goes underground and bubbles up into the sea just a few feet offshore. Casa Cenote has seven beach bungalows. The double rate runs from $125 to $175, depending on the season (excluding holidays) and includes breakfast. A few simple rustic cabins with shared bath and kitchen go for $125 in high season and $75 low season. The American owner provides kayaks and snorkeling gear and can arrange dives, fishing trips, and sailing charters.

TULUM ★★★

Tulum (130km/80 miles from Cancún) is best known for its archaeological site, a walled Maya city of the post-Classic age perched dramatically on a rocky cliff overlooking the Caribbean. The coastline south of the site is packed with *palapa* hotels and upscale retreats for a well-heeled crowd seeking a "rustic" hideaway. This stretch of incredible white beaches has become the unofficial center of the Tulum Hotel Zone—a collection of more than 30 small hotels stretching from the Tulum ruins south to the entrance of the Sian Ka'an Biosphere Reserve. The official town of Tulum is bisected by Hwy. 307, where it intersects the road to Cobá. The commercial center sprawls along both sides of Hwy. 307 for about 20 blocks jam-packed with gas stations, auto repair shops, *farmacias,* banks, markets, tour offices, and eateries. Two *glorietas* (traffic circles) slow the traffic through town; frontage roads allow access to parking spaces and driveways. Restaurants and hotels pop up alongside streets around the plaza. Anyone who thinks of Tulum as a charming pueblo hasn't been here for a few years. The growth is astounding and shows no sign of slowing.

Essentials
GETTING THERE
BY CAR   Highway 307 runs straight from Cancún through the town of Tulum.

BY BUS   Several buses a day leave Playa del Carmen for Tulum.

VISITOR INFORMATION   A particularly handy resource is the travel agency/communications/package center called **Savana** (✆ **984/871-2081**), on the east side of Avenida Tulum between calles Orion and Beta. Most of the staff speaks English and can answer questions about tours and calling home. The website www.todotulum.com is packed with local tips and info.

The Tulum ruins overlook a white-sand beach and the Caribbean Sea.

A Tulum beach.

GETTING AROUND

A rental car makes everything easier in Tulum, especially if you're staying in town and want to spend considerable time at the beach. Bicycles are readily available at hotels, and an excellent bike path runs from the intersection at Hwy. 307 and the road to the coast to several beach hotels. Taxis are abundant.

CITY LAYOUT   From the north, Hwy. 307 passes the entrance to the ruins before you enter town. When you come to an intersection with a traffic light, the highway to the right leads to the ruins of Cobá (p. 195). Turn left to reach Tulum's beach Hotel Zone, beginning about 2km (1¼ miles) away; the road sign reads BOCA PAILA. When you come to a T junction, there will be hotels in both directions. If you turn left (north), you'll be heading toward the back entrance of the ruins. If you take a right, you'll pass a long line of small hotels until you reach the entrance to Sian Ka'an. In the town of Tulum, Hwy. 307 widens and is called Avenida Tulum.

Exploring In & Around Tulum

The main attractions in this area are Tulum's archaeological site and the biosphere reserve at Sian Ka'an, but there are enough other diversions to keep you busy for a week or more.

ECO-TOURS

Mexico Kan Tours (www.mexicokantours.com; ☎ 984/140-7870), at Avenida Tulum and Calle 3, uses local guides for tours to the Maya community of Punta Laguna near Cobá, inland cenotes, and the archaeological site of Muyil. They also run boat tours through Sian Ka'an's Maya canals.

DIVING & SNORKELING

Halocline Diving (www.halocline-diving.com; ☎ 984/120-6402) on Avenida Tulum, between Orion Norte and Centauro Norte, offers two-tank ocean dives

Getting to the Beach

If you're staying elsewhere but want some beach time in Tulum, the easiest way is to drive to El Paraíso (www.el paraisohoteltulum.com; ✆ **984/113-7089**), about 1km (⅔ mile) south of the ruins (take a left at the T junction). This is a great place with a long, broad beach that is pure sand, and access is free. The owners have a restaurant on the sand and make money by selling food and drink, so they ask you not to bring your own. They also have an 11-room hotel with A/C and plasma TVs; rates range from $30 to $155 depending on season and demand. A few tents are available for camping. For true isolation, check out the small hotels in Sian Ka'an and Punta Allen.

for $90 and ocean snorkeling tours for $35. Two-tank cenote dives cost $120, including transportation. Certified cave divers can explore dark cavern systems for $180 for two tanks.

KITEBOARDING

Kiteboarding (also called kite-surfing) is hugely popular in Tulum, and the sea is dotted with bright kites when winds are blowing. **Extreme Control** (www.extremecontrol.net; ✆ **984/745-4555**), one of the first operators in Tulum, has a full-scale facility at El Paraiso Beach Club near the back entrance to the ruins, another facility at Cabañas Tulum, and a shop at the intersection of Avenida Tulum and the road to Cobá in downtown Tulum. Their introductory kiteboarding lesson costs $53. They also rent paddleboards, kayaks, wave kayaks, and surfboards.

Exploring the Tulum Ruins

Thirteen kilometers (8 miles) south of Xel-Ha are the ruins of Tulum, a Maya fortress-city on a cliff above the sea. By A.D. 900, the end of the Classic period, Maya civilization had begun its decline, and the large cities to the south were abandoned. Tulum is one of the small city-states that rose to fill the void. It came to prominence in the 13th century as a seaport, controlling maritime commerce along this section of the coast, and remained inhabited well after the arrival of the Spanish. The primary god here was the diving god, depicted on several buildings as an upside-down figure above doorways. Seen at the Palace at Sayil and Cobá, this curious, almost comical figure is also known as the bee god.

The most imposing building in Tulum is a large stone structure above the cliff called the **Castillo** (castle). A temple as well as a fortress, it was once covered with stucco and paint. In front of the Castillo are several unrestored palace-like buildings partially covered with stucco. Tourists swim and sunbathe on the **beach** below, where the Maya once came ashore.

The **Temple of the Frescoes,** directly in front of the Castillo, contains interesting 13th-century wall paintings, though entrance is no longer permitted. Distinctly Maya, they represent Chaac, the rain god, and Ixchel, goddess of weaving, women, the moon, and medicine. The cornice of this temple has a relief of Chaac's head; from a slight distance, you can make out the eyes, nose, mouth, and chin. Notice the remains of the red-painted stucco—at one time all of Tulum's buildings were painted bright red.

Much of what we know of Tulum at the time of the Spanish Conquest comes from the writings of Diego de Landa, third bishop of the Yucatán. He wrote that Tulum was a small city inhabited by about 600 people who lived in platform dwellings along a street and supervised the trade traffic from Honduras to the Yucatán. Though it was a walled city, most inhabitants probably lived outside the walls, leaving the interior for the ceremonial structures and residences of governors and priests. Tulum survived for about 70 years after the conquest before finally being abandoned.

Because of the great number of visitors this site receives, it is no longer possible to climb all of the ruins (and you should aim to beat the crowds, which arrive around 9:30am). In some cases, visitors are asked to remain behind roped-off areas. Licensed guides at the stand next to the path to the ruins charge 200 pesos for a 45-minute tour in English, French, or Spanish for up to four people. In some ways, they are performers who will tailor their presentation to the responses they get from you.

At the entrance, you'll find artisans' stands, a bookstore, a museum, a restaurant, several large bathrooms, and a ticket booth. It's about a 5-minute walk from the entrance to the archaeological site.

Admission 51 pesos; shuttle 15 pesos; parking 30 pesos, video camera permit 41 pesos. Winter daily 8am–5pm, summer 8am–6pm.

Where to Eat

Tulum's dining scene is surprisingly sophisticated, given its laid-back beach vibe. The variety is best in town, where classy restaurants, rowdy bars, and bare-bones taco stands crowd together along Avenida Tulum and side streets. Many beach hotels have great food as well, though the prices are sometimes appallingly high. Several markets and grocery stores provide do-it-yourself supplies.

Cetli ★★ 🍴 MEXICAN   You'd think chef Claudia Pérez Rívas would be a culinary star in Mexico City or New York, but she's applying her considerable talents to create *alta cocina mexicana* (gourmet Mexican cuisine) in a gorgeous old home in downtown Tulum. She grinds spices and herbs in stone *metates* for authentic *moles* (sauces with multitudinous ingredients), places grilled shrimp atop a bed of *huitlacoche* (a savory corn mushroom), and stuffs chicken breasts with *chaya* (similar to spinach). Linen-covered tables are spaced far enough apart for quiet conversation, though diners tend to share opinions and recommend favorites. Dining here is both a pleasure and a culinary adventure.

Calle Polar Poniente at Calle Orion Norte, downtown Tulum. ✆ **984/108-0681.** Main courses 170–210 pesos. No credit cards. Thurs–Tues 5–10pm.

Don Cafeto's ★ MEXICAN   The first place to go for homestyle *huevos rancheros* or *camarones mojo de ajo* (grilled shrimp with oil and garlic) is this sometimes noisy, always interesting cafe. The coffee's strong, the margaritas are perfectly mixed, and the salsas range from mild to *muy picante*. Background music varies from marimbas to mariachis to romantic guitars, and the waiters are always friendly and patient with non-Spanish speakers. It's like a dependable diner, but with far more interesting cuisine.

Av. Tulum btw. calles Centauro and Orion, downtown Tulum. ✆ **984/871-2207.** Main courses $8–$15. MC, V. Daily 7am–11pm.

El Asadero ★★ 🍴 STEAKHOUSE   In a part of the world where fresh seafood is revered, carnivores will find refuge in perfectly prepared rib-eye, T-bone,

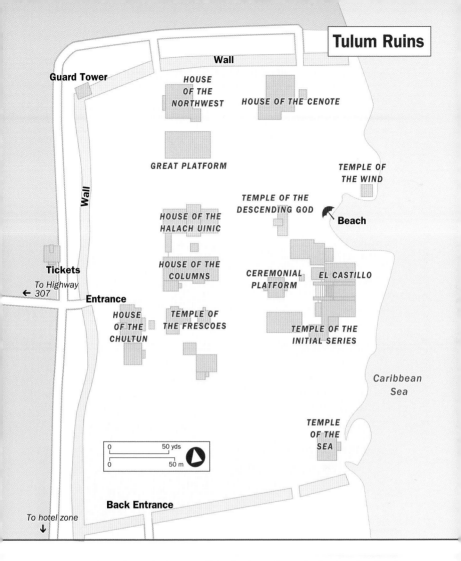

Tulum Ruins

and New York steaks cooked on a grill by the front door. The husband-and-wife team who run this unassuming place out of their home also fire up *arrachera* flank steak, sausage, and chicken. Prices are in line with the setting—bare plastic tables arranged in what looks like it might have once been a garage—but the food would do linen tablecloths proud. For lighter appetites, they also prepare wonderful stuffed potatoes and tacos, and vegetarians will find joy in several *nopal* (roast cactus) concoctions and sautéed vegetables. There's no liquor license, but you can bring your own.

Av. Satelite Norte btw. Sagitario and 2 Poniente, downtown Tulum. ☎ **984/128-6258.** Main courses 80–170 pesos. No credit cards. Daily except Wed 6:30–10pm.

El Camello ★★ 🎁 SEAFOOD   Fishermen deliver their daily catch to a sidewalk *pescadería,* where it's quickly cleaned and passed on to the kitchen next door. There, cooks prepare seafood cocktails, whole fried fish, and other simple dishes for amazingly low prices. Waiters rush about the crowded dining room and along the sidewalk as lines of eager diners wait to claim a simple plastic table. Freshly fried chips arrive almost immediately, followed by chilled beers, *limonada,* and bowls of yummy beans. I ordered a medium-sized *ceviche mixto* on my first visit and could barely eat a third of the portion. I returned the next day for *pulpo* (octopus) with *guajillo* chiles and was sad to leave Tulum without trying the shrimp with garlic. It's on the south side of town as Avenida Tulum becomes Zamná. They may close early if all the fish is gone.

Av. Zamná. btw. Kukulcán and Palenque, downtown Tulum. No phone. Main courses 80–120 pesos. No credit cards. Daily 11am–7pm.

¡Que Fresco! ★★ AMERICAN/MEXICAN   Start the day with fragrant coffee from Chiapas, homemade bread and marmalade, and yogurt with papaya, all served at a bright yellow table on the sand beside a gorgeous beach. Snack on crisp chips and salsas with midday margaritas, and dine on grilled shrimp or filet mignon after dark. Well-deserved rave reviews cover the walls at the Zamas hotel's barefoot cafe, and I've yet to see an unhappy diner even when the place is packed.

Carretera Punta Allen Km 5 on the beach. ✆ **415/387-9806** in the U.S. Main courses $7–$15. No credit cards. Daily 7am–10pm.

Where to Stay

At least 30 small hotels claim any available space on Tulum's soft white-sand beaches, and a confounding collection of signs lines the narrow road along the coast. The drive can be confusing for first-timers trying to dodge bicyclists, pedestrians, and delivery trucks. The beach's popularity has driven prices into the stratosphere, and you'll have a hard time finding a room for less than $100 per

Dozing in a hammock on a peaceful Tulum beach.

Relaxing at a beach in Tulum.

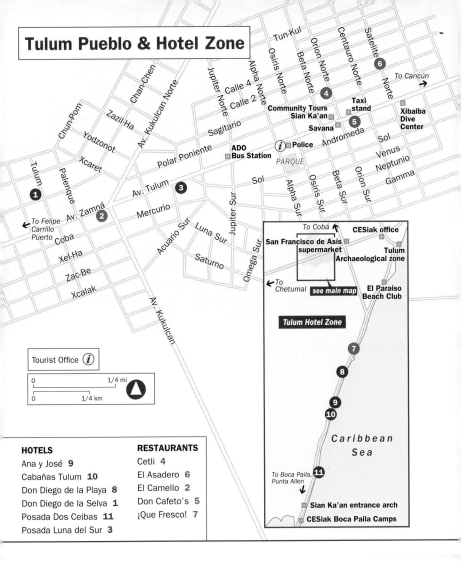

Tulum Pueblo & Hotel Zone

HOTELS
Ana y José **9**
Cabañas Tulum **10**
Don Diego de la Playa **8**
Don Diego de la Selva **1**
Posada Dos Ceibas **11**
Posada Luna del Sur **3**

RESTAURANTS
Cetli **4**
El Asadero **6**
El Camello **2**
Don Cafeto's **5**
¡Que Fresco! **7**

night in high season. Several hotels now have A/C, 24-hour electricity, Wi-Fi, and freshwater pools, and cell service is usually good. Some beach hotels don't accept credit cards (though there's now an ATM on the beach road).

ON THE BEACH

Very Expensive

Ana y José ★★   This *palapa* hotel gets fancier each year. A reception area on the inland side of the road will eventually include a bridge over the road to the seaside rooms and suites, which are decked out with marble countertops, marble tile floors, and furnished wooden terraces. Rooms range from garden- and pool-view doubles with soaring *palapa* ceilings to pricey oceanfront suites with private pools. All have hammocks swinging near the door. Accoutrements include a spa and wedding planners (ceremonies on the excellent white-sand beach are very popular). Ana y José is 6.5km (4 miles) south of the Tulum ruins.

Carretera Punta Allen Km 7 (Apdo. Postal 15), 77780 Tulum, Q. Roo. www.anayjose.com. ✆ **998/880-5629.** Fax 998/880-6021. 23 units. $303–$447 double. AE, MC, V. Free parking. **Amenities:** Restaurant; outdoor pool; spa. *In room:* A/C, fan.

Cabañas Tulum ★★   This old favorite underwent a complete makeover in 2010. Rooms right on the sand offering a sea view from the bed are the priciest, but you'll be happy with a room on the second story when the winds blow sand around. Perfectly functional and simple, the rooms have 24-hour electricity and A/C at night; ceiling fans and open windows are fine in winter. The rates are much higher than they used to be, but are heavily discounted with early booking or 4-night stays. The owners are building a fancier 16-room hotel with a pool next door, and have added a great restaurant, El Bistro, to the beach's restaurant scene. Ziggy's Beach Club, a longtime favorite, has been spruced up with beach beds, tables in the sand, a full bar, and a branch of Extreme Control kiteboarding center.

Carretera Punta Allen Km 7, 77780 Tulum, Q. Roo. ✆ **866/550-6878** in the U.S. and Canada, or 984/151-8754. 16 units. High season $155–$175 double; low season $129–$149 double. Rates include breakfast. MC, V. Free parking. **Amenities:** Restaurant; bar; kiteboarding; yoga. *In room:* A/C, fan, Wi-Fi.

Moderate
Posada Dos Ceibas ★   Of all the places along this coast, this is closest to the way hotels in Tulum used to be: simple, quiet, and ecological without being pretentious. This is a good choice for a no-fuss beach vacation. Bright yellow, blue, and pink cottages are spread throughout dense vegetation. Simply furnished rooms come with ceiling fans and most have private patios or porches with hammocks. Prices are high for what you get. The grounds are well tended. The solar-generated electricity kicks in at 6pm. The hotel is near the entrance to Sian Ka'an and is more private than those bunched together to the north.

Carretera Tulum–Boca Paila Km 10, 77780 Tulum, Q. Roo. www.dosceibas.com. ✆ **984/877-6024.** 8 units. High season $75–$170 double; low season $60–$110 double. MC, V. **Amenities:** Restaurant; Wi-Fi (in restaurant); yoga. *In room:* No phone.

Inexpensive
Don Diego de la Playa ★   An offshoot of the hugely popular Don Diego de la Selva in town, this simple little eco-hotel is buried in palms beside a quiet swath of sand. The least expensive accommodations are in Bedouin tents with wooden floors. Their small net windows catch some breeze, but not enough to keep you cool on sweltering summer nights. Two cement cabañas with thatch roofs are more comfortable. All rooms share common bathrooms with hot-water showers.

Carretera Punta Allen Km 4.5, 77780 Tulum, Q. Roo. www.dtulum.com. ✆ **984/114-9744** in town. 6 units High season $75–$95 tent, $95–$125 cabaña; low season $60–$75 tent, $76–$95 cabaña. No credit cards. Limited parking. **Amenities:** Restaurant. *In room:* Fan, no phone.

IN TOWN
Don Diego de la Selva ★★   The combination of a wild garden setting and easy town and beach accessibility keeps guests coming back to this stylish hotel and restaurant. It feels like you're in the jungle with all the benefits of

civilization—24/7 electricity; immaculate rooms; a large, clear swimming pool; and a huge *palapa* restaurant that attracts diners from town and the beach. The gregarious French owners serve drinks and mingle with guests each night, and the concierge dotes on you like a loving nanny. Spacious, air-conditioned rooms open to garden patios with chairs and hammocks, and include orthopedic mattresses, hot showers with skylights, thick towels, and simple, elegant furnishings. Two large bungalows come with queen-size beds and are cooled by ceiling fans. Breakfast features a different freshly baked cake each day.

Av. Tulum, Mza. 24 Lote 3 (1km/⅔ mile south of ADO bus station), 77780 Tulum, Q. Roo. www. dtulum.com. ✆ **984/114-9744.** 10 units. $95 double with A/C; $75 double with fan. Rates include continental breakfast. MC, V. Parking lot. **Amenities:** Restaurant; bar; shared fridge; outdoor pool. *In room:* A/C (in some), fan, Wi-Fi.

Posada Luna del Sur ★★ 💧 Guests have been known to linger well past their planned departure date at this convenient, comfortable inn. Jugs of purified water, coffeemakers, utensils, and refrigerators make each room feel like home. Ground-floor rooms open to palms, bougainvillea bushes, and banana trees; those on the second story have balconies. The bright decor combines modern sinks and furnishings with Mexican tiles and folk art. Dozens of produce stands, grocery stores, and restaurants are within walking distance, and the beach is a 10-minute drive away.

Calle Luna Sur 5, 77780 Tulum, Q. Roo. www.posadalunadelsur.com. ✆ **984/871-2984.** 12 units. High season $85 double; low season (2-night minimum) $70–$75 double. High-season rates include hot breakfast. No credit cards. Limited covered parking. No children 15 and under. **Amenities:** Rooftop dining area; Wi-Fi. *In room:* A/C, fan, TV, fridge.

COBÁ RUINS ★★★

168km (104 miles) SW of Cancún

Older than most of Chichén Itzá and much larger than Tulum, Cobá was the eastern Yucatán's dominant city before A.D. 1000. The site is widely spread out, with thick forest growing between the temple groups. Rising high above the forest canopy are tall, steep pyramids of the Classic Maya style. Of the major sites, this one is the least reconstructed, with mounds that are likely structures still covered in vines and roots. Left in the condition in which they were found, most of the stone sculptures are worn down and impossible to make out, but the structures themselves, the surrounding jungle, and the twin lakes are impressive and enjoyable. The forest canopy is higher than in the northern part of the peninsula, and the town of Cobá is much like those in Yucatán's interior.

A biker rides along tree-shaded trails in Cobá.

Cobá is my favorite easy escape from the action on the coast. Spending a night here gives you a chance to roam through the archaeological site in early morning when birds chatter, butterflies hover over flowers, and trees shade solitary trails. In the evening, you can easily spot turtles and crocodiles in the lake and graceful white egrets fishing for their dinners. Locals walk along the lakeside and gather outside their simple homes, chatting and watching children run about. I often wish I could spend several nights in this peaceful enclave.

Essentials
GETTING THERE & DEPARTING
BY CAR   The road to Cobá begins in Tulum and continues for 65km (40 miles). Watch out for *topes* (speed bumps) and potholes. The road has been widened and repaved and should be in good condition. Close to the village of Cobá, you will come to a triangle; be sure to follow the road to Cobá and not Nuevo Xcan or Valladolid. The entrance to the ruins is a short distance down the road past some small restaurants and the large lake.

BY BUS   Several buses a day leave Tulum and Playa del Carmen for Cobá. Several companies offer bus tours.

Exploring the Cobá Ruins

The Maya built many intriguing cities in the Yucatán, but few as grand as Cobá ("water stirred by wind"). Much of the 67-sq.-km (26-sq.-mile) site remains unexcavated. Scholars believe Cobá was an important trade link between the Caribbean coast and inland cities. A 100km (62-mile) *sacbé* (raised road) through the jungle linked it to Yaxuná, once an important Maya center 50km (31 miles) south of Chichén Itzá. This is the Maya's longest-known *sacbé*, and at least 50 shorter ones lead from here. An important city-state, Cobá flourished from A.D. 632 (the oldest carved date found here) until after the rise of Chichén Itzá, around 800. Then Cobá faded in importance and population until it was finally abandoned.

Once at the site, keep your bearings—you can get turned around in the maze of dirt roads in the jungle. Branching off from every labeled path, you'll see unofficial narrow paths into the jungle, used as shortcuts by locals. These are good for birding, but be careful to remember the way back.

The **Grupo Cobá** holds an impressive pyramid, **La Iglesia (the Church).** Take the path bearing right after the entrance. Resist the urge to climb the temple; the view is better from El Castillo in the Nohoch Mul group farther back.

Return to the main path and turn right, passing a sign pointing to the restored *juego de pelota* (ball court). Continuing for 5 to 10 minutes, you'll come to a fork in the road, where you'll notice jungle-covered, unexcavated pyramids to the left and right. At one point, a raised portion of the *sacbé* to Yaxuná is visible as it crosses the pathway. Throughout the area, carved stelae stand by pathways or lie forlornly in the underbrush. Although protected by crude thatched roofs, most are weatherworn enough to be indiscernible.

The left fork leads to the **Nohoch Mul Group,** which contains **El Castillo.** Except for Structure 2 in Calakmul, this is the tallest pyramid in the Yucatán, outreaching El Castillo at Chichén Itzá and the Pyramid of the Magician at Uxmal. From the top, you can see unexcavated, jungle-cloaked pyramids poking through the forest canopy all around.

The right fork (more or less straight on) goes to the **Conjunto Las Pinturas,** whose main attraction is the **Pyramid of the Painted Lintel,** a small structure with traces of its original bright colors above the door. You can climb up for a close look. Visit Cobá in the morning or after the heat of the day has passed. Mosquito repellent, drinking water, and comfortable shoes are imperative. Bicycles are available for rent for $3 per hour at a stand just past the entrance. You can also hire a *triciclo* with driver to carry you around the site; rates start at $10. Clever *triciclo* drivers also park at Nohuch Mul to carry hot, tired passengers back to the entrance.

Admission is 51 pesos, free for children younger than 12. Parking is 50 pesos. Open daily 8am to 5pm.

Where to Stay & Eat

Cobá offers a few hotels, restaurants, and markets, and food choices abound at stands near the entrance when the archaeological site is open. Prices are refreshingly realistic. A few truly rustic hostelries offer hard mattresses and cold-water showers for budget travelers, and a couple of hotels are on the road to Tulum. Making reservations is difficult, as phone and Internet service is spotty, but it's a good idea to give it a shot during high season.

Visitors climb the Cobá ruins.

○ A Day in the Life of a Maya Village

In the tropical forest near Cobá, a village of 27 families exists much as their long-ago ancestors did, living in round thatch huts with no electricity, indoor plumbing, or paved roads, gathering plants in the jungle for medicinal and other uses on their way to dip into a hidden cenote, appealing to the gods for successful crops. And every day, the people of Pac Chen open their homes to as many as 80 tourists who want to know what Maya village life is in the 21st century.

The only way to visit Pac Chen is on trips with **Alltournative** (www.alltour native.com; ☎ 877/437-4990 in the U.S., or 984/803-9999), an ecotour company that works with villagers to help them become self-sustaining. Farming continues, but tourism income allows them to survive without burning their land to squeeze out the last remaining nutrients.

The arrangement is a boon to tourists, too. On your own, it would be pretty well impossible to walk into a Maya village and be ushered through the jungle and lowered into a cenote or to glide through the forest canopy on a zip line, kayak a lagoon full of birds, eat lunch cooked by village women and receive a copal-incense blessing from a village elder for a safe trip home. The Maya Encounter tour costs $129 for adults and $89 for children.

Villas Arqueológicas Cobá ★★ 🎁 Lovingly maintained for several decades, this peaceful compound facing the lake is removed from town on a private road. Its cool blue pool, good restaurant, attentive service from faithful local workers, and a superb library make it the best choice close to the ruins. The rooms have a double and a single bed in semiprivate niches, a small bathroom with hot-water shower, a sink outside the bathroom door, and dreadful lighting. Bougainvillea, palms, and ferns flourish in the central courtyard, shading the pool and dining terraces. The restaurant's Mexican/Continental food is very good, if a bit overpriced (meal plan available for $20). An excellent library contains tomes on the Maya, archaeology, and Mexican art—and a pool table for guests bored by the lack of evening activities.

West of the ruins beside the lake. www.villasmex.com. ☎ **984/206-7001.** 43 units. $69–$125 double. MC, V. Parking lot. **Amenities:** Restaurant; bar; outdoor pool; room service; tennis court; Wi-Fi (in public areas). *In room:* A/C, hair dryer.

SIAN KA'AN & THE PUNTA ALLEN PENINSULA ★★★

Just past Tulum's last cabaña hotel is the entrance arch to the vast (526,000-hectare/1.3-million-acre) **Sian Ka'an Biosphere Reserve.** This inexpressibly beautiful tract of wild land is the domain of howler monkeys, ocelots, crocodiles, jaguars, tapirs, sea turtles, and thousands of species of plants. The Mexican government created this reserve in 1986; the following year, the United Nations declared it a World Heritage Site. Sian Ka'an protects 10% of Quintana Roo's land mass, including almost one-third of the Caribbean coastline, from development. Another 319,000 hectares (788,300 acres) of land was added to the reserve in 2010.

The entrance to the Punta Allen Peninsula, a small portion of the reserve, is one of two main entrances to the reserve; the other is from the community of Muyil off Hwy. 307 south of Tulum, where you take a boat down canals built by the Maya to the Boca Paila lagoon.

Legends still swirl about the 4 hours it takes to drive the 50km (31 miles) over potholes, ruts, and rivulets to the town of Punta Allen at road's end. In fact, the road has been much improved, though it is still dirt, still pockmarked to varying degrees, and subject to weather-related conditions. Guards at the entrance gate are fond of declaring it's now a 1-hour trip, and no doubt that's true for the locals who sailed past me in my rented compact sedan. Driving cautiously after a stretch of rainy weather, it took me a little less than 2 hours. Those driving four-wheelers or other robust vehicles should plan to spend about 1½ hours on the road.

If you don't fancy yourself a road warrior, you can drive through the entrance arch in Tulum (entry 25 pesos per person) and continue south about 4km (2½ miles) to where a beach comes into view, pull over, and spread out your beach towel.

The Punta Allen Peninsula

As you drive the skinny peninsula, which separates the Boca Paila Lagoon from the sea, you'll find no trails leading into the jungle and much of the coastal side of the road is fenced off. But you can swim or snorkel off the beaches that come into view. Guided tours are the only way to see most of the reserve. Otherwise, there is no practical way to visit Sian Ka'an except by car.

THE SIAN KA'AN BIOSPHERE RESERVE ★★★

Maya life in ancient times remains essentially a mystery, but there's no wondering why they named this land Sian Ka'an (see-*an* caan), Mayan for "where the sky is born." Sunrise here truly is like witnessing the birth of a day.

The reserve encompasses most of the ecosystems that exist on the entire Yucatán Peninsula: medium- and low-growth jungles, beaches, savannas, marshes, freshwater and brackish lagoons, cenotes, underground rivers, and

Visitors float down a canal in Sian Ka'an.

untouched coral reef. Numerous archaeological sites have also been found within its borders.

More than 2,000 people, most of them Maya, live in Sian Ka'an. All are original residents of the area, or their descendants. Tours to the reserve are often led by locals, who grew up nearby in homes occupied for countless generations. They'll almost never consult a field guide; their knowledge about the birds, the plants, the water, and the ruins are simply a part of their lives.

To access the reserve beyond the road, arrange for a tour in Tulum. Two organizations in particular keep their groups small and work only through the local people.

The **Centro Ecológico Sian Ka'an,** or CESiaK, with an office on Hwy. 307 just south of Tulum ruins turnoff (www.cesiak.org; ✆ **984/871-2499**), is a non-profit group supporting the reserve with education and community development programs. Its popular all-day canal tour ($78 per person, including lunch and tax) includes a guided walk through coastal dunes and jungle and a boat trip across two brackish lagoons where freshwater cenotes well up from under the ground. Boats follow a narrow channel through mangroves to a small temple where Maya traders stopped to make offerings and ask for successful negotiations. You'll don life jackets and float part of the way in the currents of a freshwater lagoon and snorkel in a cenote before the day is over. Other tours include a sunset bird-watching trip and single- and multiday fly-fishing packages. Tours depart from the CESiaK center at the Boca Paila Camps, 4km (2½ miles) south of the reserve entrance.

Community Tours Sian Ka'an, Avenida Tulum between calles Centauro and Orión (www.siankaantours.org; ✆ **984/871-2202**), is a local cooperative that runs snorkeling, birding, and adventure tours into the biosphere. The guides run their tours out of the downtown office and an eco-oriented visitor center near Muyil. Their "Forest and Float" canal tour ($99 per adult, $70 child) begins with an in-depth tour of the Muyil archaeological site, followed by a jungle walk to the edge of a lagoon where snacks are served while guests visit rustic restrooms. Guests then board small boats for an amazing ride through a crystalline lagoon toward canals carved from the landscape by the Maya. After visiting the small ruin, guests don life jackets and float with the current along the canals to a plat-form where they reboard the boats and head back. The tour ends with lunch at

---

Anatomy of a Biosphere Reserve

Unlike its national parks, which focus on historical and aesthetic features, Mexico's biosphere reserves were created purely to protect its last natural ecosystems. Recognition by UNESCO (United Nations Educational, Scientific and Cultural Organization) requires that the biosphere contain at least 10,000 hectares (about 39 sq. miles), at least one pristine area of biological diversity, and threatened or endangered endemic species.

Mexico pioneered the zoning system that allows some carefully managed tourism. The core area—the heart of the reserve—is limited to scientific research and is surrounded by a buffer zone that allows only conservation-related activity. On the periphery, a transition zone permits sustainable use of natural resources to benefit local communities, as CESiaK's tours (above) do. Biosphere reserves allow original residents to remain; local people, in fact, are recruited to research, monitor, and manage the ecosystem while developing sustainable activities such as ecotourism.

SLEEPING WHERE THE sky IS BORN

To see the sun rise in Sian Ka'an as the Maya did, you can stay in CESiaK's **Boca Paila Camps ★ ★**, 4km (2½ miles) past the entrance arch. The eco-lodge's tent cabins are tucked into the edge of the jungle on a clean, white beach, raised on platforms to avoid interfering with the sand's natural processes. The fine linens and solid wood furniture make it feel less like camping, but when night falls and you're stumbling around by candlelight, it feels plenty rustic. Guests share scrupulously clean bathrooms with composting toilets, housed in buildings whose rooftop lookouts grant views of the sea and lagoon that give "panoramic" new meaning—you'll actually see the curvature of the earth. Deluxe tent cabins

with one queen and ocean or lagoon views are $80 to $100. Meals are extra. The camp has no electricity—guests get battery-powered lamps—but wind and solar power provide hot water. Things do not always run perfectly smoothly: The restaurant, which is reasonably priced and turns out better meals than it has any right to in this remote location, sometimes runs out of ingredients for a popular menu item, and one time I was assigned to a tent that was already occupied (and quickly reassigned). But this place makes Tulum's vaunted sands look like Panama City Beach in springtime—and its staff knows the reserve's plants, animals, and local culture backward and forward.

the visitor center, where members of the community are available to chat about their way of life and traditions. Transportation is available from Riviera Maya hotels for an extra charge.

THE ROAD TO PUNTA ALLEN

About 11km (6¾ miles) past the arch, you'll come to the **Boca Paila Fishing Lodge** (www.bocapaila.com). Not for the general traveler, it specializes in week-long, all-inclusive packages for fly-fishers. The peninsula is so narrow here that you see the Boca Paila lagoon on one side and the sea on the other. In another 3km (1¾ miles), you will be flooded by false hope when you reach a smooth, concrete roadway—this is the foot of the Boca Paila Bridge, which spans the inlet between the ocean and the lagoon, and the pavement disappears as quickly as it appeared. You'll often see people fishing off the sides. This is a good place to stop and stretch your legs while taking in ethereal water views from either side.

After the bridge, it's mostly deserted coastline until you get to Punta Allen. About 8km (5 miles) before you do, you'll come to **Rancho Sol Caribe** (www. solcaribe-mexico.com), with four comfortable cabañas and the stunning beach it has all to itself.

Punta Allen

Punta Allen, the peninsula's only town, is a lobster fishing village on a palm-studded beach perched between Ascension Bay and the Caribbean Sea. About 100 families survive by lobster fishing and, increasingly, tourism; many of the young men now are expert fly-fishing guides.

Isolated and rustic, this is very much the end of the road. The town has a lobster cooperative, a few sand streets with modest homes, and a lighthouse. The

Fishing boats in Punta Allen.

generator, when it's working, comes on for a few hours in the morning and a few more at night. Your cellphone won't work here, and no one takes credit cards. Without the help of a friendly local, it's a challenge to figure out when any of the businesses are open.

For now, unless you're a fishing enthusiast, there's not a lot to do in Punta Allen except kick back, snorkel a little, and eat your fill of fresh seafood.

Cuzan Guesthouse One of the town's original fishing lodges, this collection of basic, *palapa*-roofed wood cabañas on a sandy beach also has one of the town's best restaurants and a full bar. Despite the increasing competition, it has a loyal following. Cuzan's bread and butter is its all-inclusive fishing packages, but it will rent a cabaña to anyone interested in passing some time in Punta Allen. The guesthouse also offers a variety of birding, snorkeling, and other boat tours.

Apdo. Postal 24, Felipe Carrillo Puerto, 77200 Q. Roo. www.flyfishmx.com. ✆ **983/834-0358.** 12 units. $50–$110 cabañas. No credit cards. *In room:* No phone.

Serenidad Shardon This retreat on the coastal road just south of town—we're talking about the equivalent of 3 or 4 blocks—can put you in a three-bedroom beach house with two bedrooms, a bath, and kitchen, and an upstairs dorm-style room that sleeps six and has bathroom facilities next door to the house. You can also rent just the downstairs or a sweet, private cabaña with bathroom and kitchen. All have contemporary decoration and views of the Caribbean from decks or windows. The amiable owner can also set you up with tours and think of a dozen other ways to make sure you are happy.

Beach road south of town square. www.shardon.com. ✆ **616/827-0204** in the U.S., or 984/107-4155. 3 units. $200 cabaña; $350 beach house ($250 lower floor only). No credit cards. *In room:* No phone.

En Route to the Lower Caribbean Coast

About 25km (16 miles) south of Tulum on Hwy. 307, a sign points to the small but interesting ruins of **Muyil** (take bug spray), on the western edge of Sian Ka'an. The principal ruins are a small group of buildings and a plaza dominated by the Castillo. It's one of the Caribbean coast's taller structures but is more interesting for the unique, solid round masonry turret at the top. A Maya canal enters Sian Ka'an and empties into a lake; more canals then continue to the saltwater estuary of Boca Paila. This is an alternative entrance for tours of the biosphere (p. 199).

Felipe Carrillo Puerto (pop. 60,000) is the first large town on the road to Chetumal. This was a rebel stronghold during the War of the Castes and home to the millenarian cult of the "Talking Cross." A sizable community of believers

The ruins of Muyil.

still practices its own brand of religion and commands the town's respect. Of primary interest to travelers are Carrillo Puerto's four gas stations, two grocery stores, bus terminal, and a bank next to the gas station in the center of town. The gas stations and grocery stores also have ATMs. Several clean, simple, and inexpensive hotels around the plaza and bus station will serve if you need a break from the highway; the best is **Hotel Esquivel** at Calle 65 No.746, between calles 66 and 68.

Roadwork in the past couple of years has vastly improved Hwy. 307's route through town, eliminating the downtown tangle. Hwy. 184 out of Carrillo Puerto goes into the peninsula's interior and eventually to Mérida, making it a turning point on the "short circuit" of the Yucatán Peninsula.

MAHAHUAL, XCALAK & THE CHINCHORRO REEF

Tourism has been late to arrive on the quiet southern half of the Caribbean coast. The recently dubbed Costa Maya is tucked under the Sian Ka'an Biosphere Reserve on a wide peninsula jutting out from the mainland. It remained largely unnoticed—except by fly-fishers—while resorts gobbled up the beaches of Cancún and the Riviera Maya over the past few decades.

Lying 354km (220 miles) from Cancún's airport and more than 48km (30 miles) from the highway, the Costa Maya's beaches might never see Riviera Maya–scale development, but changes have already come since Carnival Cruise Line and government tourism officials brought a huge cruise port to the tiny fishing village of Mahahual (sometimes spelled Majahual) in 2001. New roads have cut the trip to the even smaller and more remote village of Xcalak (eesh-kah-*lahk*)—the Mexican Caribbean's southernmost settlement—from 4 hours to less than 1. Luxury developments are rumored to be on the drawing boards, but tourism officials vow to abandon the Cancún/Riviera Maya model by integrating the local population into restrained development of small, ecofriendly hotels and nature tours.

Information, please

Good, up-to-date information about the Costa Maya is still scarce, but it's improving. The official tourist site, www.grandcosta maya.com, can be helpful if you read Spanish or are willing to run it through a translator. You can get decent overviews of the coastal areas at www.mahahual.com and www.xcalak.info; for the latest goings-on, sign up for the detailed and gossipy newsletter from Mayan Beach Garden in Mahahual (p. 206). For information about Bacalar and Chetumal, www.bacalarmosaico.com is a good bet.

DIVING THE chinchorro REEF

The **Chinchorro Reef Underwater National Park,** about 30km (19 miles) off this coastline, is by most accounts the largest coral atoll in the Northern Hemisphere, at 38km (24 miles) long and 13km (8 miles) wide. Its coral formations, massive sponges, and abundant sea life are certainly among the most spectacular. The oval reef is as shallow as 1m (3⅓ ft.) at its interior and as deep as 900m (2,953 ft.) at its exterior. It's invisible from the ocean side and has doomed scores of ships. Contrary to popular misconception, diving the 30 or so **shipwrecks** that decorate the underwater landscape is prohibited—they are protected by the Banco Chinchorro Biosphere. However, the reef offers at least a dozen stellar dive sites. And most wrecks, including the famous **40 Cannons** on the northwest side, are shallow enough to be explored by snorkeling. The west side of the reef is a wonderland of walls and coral gardens.

It can be a challenge to get to the reef, partly because of fickle sea conditions and partly because of the strict limit on permits. **XTC Dive Center** (www.xtc divecenter.com; ✆ **983/839-8865**) in Xcalak specializes in trips to Chinchorro—the company's name stands for "Xcalak to Chinchorro." XTC also offers a lineup of dives to local reefs and cenotes. This is an excellent place to see manatees. Whether you're diving, snorkeling, or boating, one of the shy creatures sometimes show itself when you least expect it.

ORIENTATION   About 45 minutes south of Felipe Carrillo Puerto, a few kilometers past the town of Limones at a place called El Cafetal, you reach the clearly marked turnoff for Mahahual and Xcalak. It's 56km (35 miles) on a good paved road to the coast at Mahahual. The turnoff for Xcalak comes 2km (1¼ miles) before you reach Mahahual. Xcalak is 55km (34 miles) to the south, less than an hour's drive.

Mahahual

The cruise ship pier (north of the road entering town) gives Mahahual a split personality. The port has grown into a tourist zone with a beach club, shopping mall, and tour companies offering dozens of excursions, and a minicity with its own suburb of homes and apartments has sprouted nearby. Señor Frog's opened in late 2010, not far from the Hard Rock Cafe—what more is there to say? On port days, the town's packed-sand main street brims with tipsy, sunburned passengers who elect beach time over bus tours, only to empty at night and return to somnolence.

Though Mahahual isn't the most appealing town even when devoid of cruise passengers, it has acquired some good hotels and fine restaurants, and the new *malecón* (seafront promenade) makes for a pleasant walk along a fine white beach. When a ship is in port, the walk is lined with watersports and tour vendors. Most of the town's hotels and services line the sand road running through town and south along the coast.

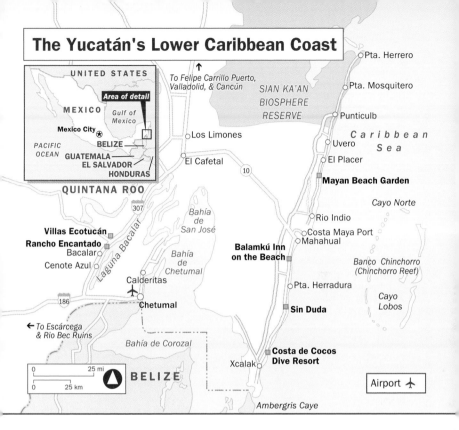

The Yucatán's Lower Caribbean Coast

UNITED STATES

Area of detail

MEXICO
Gulf of
Mexico

Mexico City

PACIFIC
OCEAN

BELIZE

GUATEMALA
EL SALVADOR
HONDURAS

QUINTANA ROO

307

Villas Ecotucán
Rancho Encantado
Bacalar
Cenote Azul

Laguna Bacalar

Calderitas

186

Chetumal

← To Escárcega
& Rio Bec Ruins

0   25 mi
0   25 km

BELIZE

To Felipe Carrillo Puerto,
Valladolid, & Cancún

SIAN KA'AN
BIOSPHERE
RESERVE

Los Limones

El Cafetal

10

Bahía
de
San José

Bahía
de
Chetumal

Bahía de Corozal

Xcalak

Ambergris Caye

Pta. Herrero

Pta. Mosquitero

Punticulb

Caribbean
Sea

Uvero

El Placer

Mayan Beach Garden

Cayo Norte

Rio Indio
Costa Maya Port
Mahahual

Balamkú Inn
on the Beach

Banco Chinchorro
(Chinchorro Reef)

Cayo
Lobos

Pta. Herradura

Sin Duda

Costa de Cocos
Dive Resort

Airport

A couple of newer hotels have elevated the in-town options: **Matan Ka'an** (www.matankaan.it; *℃* **983/834-5679**) and **El Caballo Blanco** (www.hotel elcaballoblanco.com; *℃* **983/126-0319**) offer bright, air-conditioned rooms starting at $60 and $80, respectively; both have restaurants. Beach areas north and south of town, on the other hand, are the stuff of dreams.

Balamkú Inn on the Beach ★★★   This comfortable, friendly place on the coast road south of town rents thatched bungalows on a dazzling white beach fronting a stretch of pristine reef. The large, breezy rooms have comfortable mattresses, large attractive bathrooms, and louvered windows that let you control the breeze. Each has a terrace facing the beach. The environmentally minded Canadian owners derive enough energy from wind to provide 24-hour power without using a generator, and rely on a large rainwater collection system and route shower and sink wastewater to nourish the wetlands. Most impressive of all, they not only allow but urge guests to flush paper down the toilet—it's part of a composting waste system that doesn't pollute as septic tanks do.

Carretera Costera Km 5.7, Mahahual, Q. Roo. www.balamku.com. *℃* **045-983/732-1004** (from U.S. replace 045 with 521). 10 units. High season $90 double; midseason $85 double; low season $80 double. Rates include full breakfast. AE, MC, V for deposits; no credit cards at hotel. Free guarded parking. **Amenities:** Restaurant (breakfast and lunch; Sunday dinner); bar (afternoons); airport transfer; kayaks and snorkeling gear. *In room:* No phone; Wi-Fi.

Mayan Beach Garden Inn ★★   Large, simple but well-furnished, white-washed rooms at this longtime favorite have huge, cushy beds—two have splendid mosaic headboards—situated to take in sea views. A lovely stretch of soft beach near a shallow section of the unspoiled reef; friendly, helpful staff; owners who will show you every prime snorkeling spot and undiscovered Maya site in the area; and fantastic food all add up to an extraordinary stay. Four oceanview rooms and three beachfront cabañas (one suite sleeps four) have large covered decks with hammocks and lounge chairs. Solar power provides 24-hour electricity, but some appliances will run only when the backup generator is running; make sure you get the schedule. Ask Marcia, one of the owners, about driving up into the little-known southern entrance to the Sian Ka'an Biosphere reserve. It's a whole different experience than using the Riviera Maya access points.

Camino Costera Km 20.5, Mahahual, Q. Roo. www.mayanbeachgarden.com. ✆ **983/132-2603.** 7 units. High season $96–$121 double, $125 suite; low season $76–$92 double, $97 suite. 3-night minimum in high season. Rates include full breakfast; all-inclusive packages available. **Amenities:** Restaurant/bar; kayaks (with cabañas). *In room:* Ceiling fans, AC (in some, at night), kitchenettes (in some), Wi-Fi.

Xcalak

Quintana Roo's last stand before the channel marking Mexico's border with Belize, **Xcalak** (eesh-kah-*lahk*) is a former military outpost that had a population as large as 1,200 before a hurricane washed most of the town away in 1958; now it has about 600 permanent residents. Fly-fishers started coming in the 1980s and are still pulling prizes out of the water. The town oozes shabby charm, but the real lure is the inns just beyond town that offer a little patch of paradise, safe from anything resembling a crowd.

You'll likely eat most of your meals wherever you stay, but don't miss the **Leaky Palapa** ★★★ (www.leakypalaparestaurant.com; no phone; Nov–May Sat–Tues 5–10pm) in town. The two women who run the place do wonderful things with the best local ingredients available from day to day. The short but varied menu applies traditional preparation to all manner of contemporary dishes, from 100 to 300 pesos. Reservations recommended.

Costa de Cocos Dive & Fly-Fishing Resort ★   Freestanding cabañas sit around a large, attractive sandy beach graced with coconut palms. Comfortable wooden cabañas have one king- or queen-size bed or two doubles; one is a two-bedroom unit with two bathrooms. They have plenty of cross-ventilation, ceiling fans, hot water, and good mattresses. Wind and solar power provides 24-hour electricity. Activities include kayaking, snorkeling, scuba diving, and fly-fishing. The resort has experienced English-speaking fishing guides and a dive instructor. The casual restaurant/bar, which offers good home-style cooking—pizza is a popular recent addition—is open late. **Note:** At press time, the longtime owners were planning to retire and had the resort up for sale.

Carretera Mahahual–Xcalak Km 52, Q. Roo. www.costadecocos.com. ✆ **983/839-8537.** 16 units. High season $90 double; low season $84 double. Dive and fly-fishing packages available by e-mail request. Rates include breakfast buffet. AE, MC, PayPal, V. Free parking. **Amenities:** Restaurant; bar; dive shop; watersports. *In room:* No phone, Wi-Fi.

Sin Duda Villas ★   There's a reason half of this B&B's guests are repeat customers. It's a bit of a haul on the bouncy road, but the beautiful beach, homey accommodations, and sociable owners are worth the drive. Accommodations open onto the beach and are fan-cooled and comfortably furnished. A roof deck offers dazzling 360-degree views of jungle, lagoon, and sea. The owners are voracious readers, and a bright, well-stocked guest kitchen doubles as a library. Self-serve snorkel gear, kayaks, and bicycles are provided—just be sure to pack it in before cocktail hour with the owners, which will likely turn into the evening's entertainment.

Beach road 8km/5 miles north of town. www.sindudavillas.com. ✆ **415/868-9925** in U.S. (messages only). 6 units. High season $90–$130; low season $75–$114. Rates include light breakfast. AE, DISC, MC, PayPal, V. Free parking. **Amenities:** Bikes; kayaks; communal kitchen/library; snorkel gear; Wi-Fi in living room by request. *In room:* Patio or balcony; no phone.

LAGUNA BACALAR ★★★

104km (65 miles) SW of Felipe Carrillo Puerto; 37km (23 miles) NW of Chetumal

On a sunny day, you will see why Laguna Bacalar is nicknamed *Lago de los Siete Colores* (Lake of the Seven Colors): The white sandy bottom turns the crystalline water pale turquoise in shallow areas, morphing to vivid turquoise and through a spectrum to deep indigo in the deeper center. Colors shift with the passing of the day, making a mesmerizing backdrop.

Considered Mexico's second-largest lake, Bacalar is actually a lagoon, with a series of waterways leading eventually to the ocean. Fed not by surface runoff but by underground cenotes, it is almost 50km (31 miles) long. You'll glimpse the jewel-toned water long before you reach the town of Bacalar, about two-thirds of the way down. This is where you go for swimming or kayaking.

The town of Bacalar is quiet and traditional, though it seems every year brings a new cadre of expats looking for a new start. There's not a lot of action in town, but you shouldn't miss the **Fuerte San Felipe Bacalar,** built in 1733 to protect the Spanish from the pirates and Maya rebels who regularly raided the

Laguna Bacalar.

area. Admission is 57 pesos. Overlooking the lake on the eastern edge of the central plaza, the fort houses an excellent museum devoted to regional history, with a focus on the pirates who repeatedly descended upon these shores.

As if to prove the water gods smile upon Bacalar, it also has Mexico's biggest and deepest cenote, less than 2km (about a mile) south of town at Km 15. Measuring 185m (607 ft.) across, **Cenote Azul** is surrounded by lush flowers and trees, and filled with water so clear that you can see 60m (200 ft.) down into its nearly 91m (300-ft.) depth.

Some lovely inns dot the lagoon's western shore, which makes Bacalar an appealing alternative base to Chetumal for exploring the Maya ruins of the nearby Río Bec area.

ORIENTATION   Driving south on Hwy. 307, the town of Bacalar is 1½ hours beyond Felipe Carrillo Puerto, clearly marked by signs. If you're driving north from Chetumal, it takes about a half-hour. Buses going south from Cancún and Playa del Carmen stop here, and there are frequent buses from Chetumal.

Where to Eat

I've had good, simple meals at **Laguna de Bacalar** on the town square, and great dinners at the more upscale **Los Aluxes** (✆ 983/152-5608) on Avenida Costera, south of Amigos B&B. **Gaia** (www.gaia-maya.com; ✆ 983/834-2963), on Av. 3 a half-block south of the square, is not only a popular, comfortable restaurant serving creative vegetarian dishes as well as chicken and fish—it's also a spa and an art venue. **Restaurante Cenote Azul** (www.cenoteazul.com; ✆ 983/834-2460), with its vantage point overlooking the cenote, wouldn't even have to serve decent food to attract a following, but it does, and with great variety. While you're there, you can swim in the cenote (as long as you aren't wearing lotions or deodorant) or simply watch others take the plunge.

Where to Stay

It doesn't cost much to can stay quite comfortably in Bacalar. My favorite inn is **Amigos B&B Laguna Bacalar** ★ (www.bacalar.net; ✆ 987/872-3868), with five rooms of various sizes and configurations overlooking the water on Avenida

Cenote Azul in Bacalar.

Fuerte San Felipe Bacalar.

Costera, about 1.6km (a mile) south of the plaza. Doubles are 700 pesos with breakfast. A little closer to the center of town on the same road, endearingly quirky **Casita Carolina** (www.casitacarolina.com; ✆ **983/834-2334**) offers three units in a converted family home that share a common living room and kitchen, and three separate casitas scattered through a large, grassy garden sloping to the lake's shore. The owner, who lives on-site, hosts an artist's retreat every February. It's a great value at 300 to 600 pesos a night. You can find newer and brighter rooms from 400 pesos a night at **Hotelito La Ceiba** (www.hotelitola ceiba.com; ✆ **983/834-2565**), but it's a block inland from the lakeshore properties, on Av. 3 between calles 8 and 10—still close enough for a large upstairs terrace to take advantage of lofty lake views.

For a wilder setting, stay on the lakeshore just outside of town. **Villas Ecotucán** ★ (www.villasecotucan.info; ✆ **983/120-5743**) commands about 40 hectares (99 acres) of largely undeveloped land and focuses on the outdoors. Five spacious *palapa*-roofed cabañas (made out of native materials from the property) and two suites have separate sitting rooms and rent for 650 to 850 pesos. They also offer more jungle walks, swimming, and kayaking tours than you could go through in a week. Enter at Hwy. 307, Km 27.3, about 5km (3 miles) north of town and 1km (⅔ mile) off the highway; look for the tall, rainbow-colored tree, flags, and welcome sign. And the well-known **Rancho Encantado** ★ (www. encantado.com; ✆ **877/229-2046** in the U.S., or 998/884-2071) near Hwy. 307 north of town, rents 12 large white stucco cottages scattered over a shady lawn beside the lake, surrounded by native trees, orchids, and bromeliads. It charges $110 to $130 in high season, $65 to $85 in low season.

CHETUMAL

251km (156 miles) S of Tulum; 37km (23 miles) S of Lago Bacalar

Quintana Roo's capital and second-largest city (after Cancún), Chetumal (pop. 210,000) is of interest to tourists primarily as the gateway to Belize, Tikal (Guatemala), and the Río Bec ruins (p. 212). But it also boasts the best museum of Maya culture outside of Mexico City. The federal government is rebuilding the rundown zoo on Avenida Insurgentes at Andrés Quintana Roo into the modern, highly interactive **Biouniverzoo,** devoted to native species. The first phase opened in December 2010 with such exhibits as a cenote populated by bats. As you descend into the cenote, glass viewing walls allow an up-close look at the blind catfish that live deep within the underground water. Signs are in Mayan, Spanish, and English. Reactions from locals attending the opening were generally favorable, but there is much more work to be done on the project, which aims to create Mexico's best zoo. Biouniverzoo is open Wednesday to Sunday 9am to 5pm; admission is 150 pesos adults, 80 pesos ages 3 to 12; younger kids are free.

Essentials
GETTING THERE & DEPARTING

BY PLANE **Mexicana**'s suspension of operations leaves Chetumal (airport code CTM) with no service from the U.S. The Mexican airline **Interjet** (www. interjet.com.mx; ✆ **866/285-9525** in the U.S.), which serves Miami and San Antonio, flies to Chetumal through its Mexico City hub from a dozen airports all over Mexico. The airport is west of town, just north of the entrance from the highway.

BY CAR Chetumal is about 4½ hours from Cancún. If you're continuing to Belize, be aware that rental companies don't allow you to take their cars across the border. To get to the ruins of Tikal in Guatemala, you must go through Belize to the border crossing at Ciudad Melchor de Mencos.

BY BUS The main bus station (© 983/832-5110) is 20 blocks from the town center on Insurgentes at Avenida Héroes. Buses go to Cancún, Tulum, Playa del Carmen, Puerto Morelos, Mérida, Campeche, Villahermosa, and Tikal, Guatemala.

To Belize: Buses run by Belizean companies depart from the Mercado Nuevo (also called Mercado Lázaro Cárdenas) at Calzada Veracruz and Av. Confederación Nacional Campesina. The first-class buses go to the main bus terminal and depart for Belize from there, while the clunky older buses head directly for the border. One of the better bus lines is Premier Line, with approximately three buses daily from the main terminal. Fare is about 140 pesos.

VISITOR INFORMATION

The **State Tourism Office** (© 983/835-0860) is at Calzada del Centenario 622, between Comonfort and Ciricote. It's open Monday to Friday from 9am to 6pm.

ORIENTATION

The telephone **area code** is **983.**

Traffic enters the city from the west on Hwy. 186 and feeds onto Avenida Obregón into town. Stay on Obregón and don't take the exit veering left for Avenida Insurgentes (unless you're looking for the zoo or the huge Plaza Las Americas mall). Turn left on Avenida Héroes, the main north-south street through downtown, to reach the museum, market, and hotels.

A display in the Museo de la Cultura Maya.

A Museum Not to Miss

Museo de la Cultura Maya ★★★

This sophisticated museum unlocks the complex world of the Maya through interactive exhibits and genuine artifacts. Watch a slide show explaining medicinal and domestic uses of plants with their Mayan and scientific names, or learn how to write your birth date in Maya glyphs. One of the most fascinating exhibits describes the Maya's ideal of personal beauty, which prompted them to deform craniums, scar the face and body, and induce *estrabismo*, or cross-eyed vision.

An enormous screen flashes aerial images of more than a dozen Maya sites from Mexico to Honduras. Another large television shows the architectural variety of Maya pyramids and how they were probably built. Then a walk on a glass floor takes you over representative ruins in the Maya world. The museum is built around a stylized three-story ceiba tree, which the Maya believed connected Xibalba (the underworld), Earth, and the heavens, and each floor corresponds to those levels of the Maya cosmos. Try to see the museum before you tour the Río Bec ruins; signs are in Spanish and English.

Av. Héroes s/n (btw. Colón and Gandhi, 8 blocks from Av. Obregón, just past the Holiday Inn). www.educal.gob.mx/directoriolibrerias/interior/87-chetumal-museo-de-la-cultura-maya. ℂ 983/129-2832. Admission 55 pesos. Tues–Sat 9am–7pm; Sun 9am–2pm.

Where to Eat

For local atmosphere on a budget, try **Restaurante Pantoja,** on the corner of calles Ghandi and 16 de Septiembre (ℂ **983/832-3957**), 2 blocks east of the Museum of Maya Culture. It offers a cheap daily special, good green enchiladas, and Yucatecan specialties. It's open Monday to Saturday from 7am to 7pm. To sample excellent *antojitos,* the local supper food, try **El Buen Gusto,** on Calzada Veracruz across from the market (no phone). A Chetumal institution, it serves excellent *salbutes* and *panuchos,* tacos, and sandwiches. It's open from the morning until 2pm and again from about 7pm to midnight. Many locals prefer **La Ideal** next door, which has delicious *tacos de pierna* (soft tacos with thinly sliced pork shoulder) and *agua de horchata* (water flavored with rice, vanilla, and toasted pumpkin seed).

Where to Stay

Chetumal is not nearly as appealing a base for exploring as Bacalar, about 30 minutes away, but it does have some serviceable hotels near the museum.

Hotel Holiday Inn Chetumal Puerta Maya   This modern hotel is a reliable if not inspiring option. It has the best air-conditioning in town and is only a block from the museum. Most rooms are midsize and come with one king-size or two double beds. Bathrooms are roomy and well lit.

Av. Héroes 171 (btw. Aguilar & Mahatma Ghandi), 77000 Chetumal, Q. Roo. www.holidayinn. com. ℂ **800/465-4329** in the U.S., or 983/835-0400. 85 units. $70–$95 double. AE, MC, V. Free secure parking. From Av. Obregón, turn left on Av. Héroes, go 6 blocks, and look for the hotel on the right. **Amenities:** Restaurant; bar; fitness room; midsize outdoor pool; room service. *In room:* A/C, TV, Wi-Fi.

Hotel Los Cocos   Renovated rooms are sleek, bathrooms are scrupulously clean, and the lush garden includes a small but inviting pool. Courtyard-facing rooms are the most pleasant. The terrace restaurant does a good job with Mexican favorites, and is popular with visitors to the museum, two blocks to the north. Unfortunately, recent renovations have reduced the size of the garden and enclosed most of the formerly open-air restaurant.

Av. Héroes 134 (corner of Chapultepec), 77000 Chetumal, Q. Roo. www.hotelloscocos.com.mx. ℂ **983/835-0430.** 176 units. 912–1,026 pesos double. AE, MC, V. Off-street parking. **Amenities:** Restaurant; bar; Internet terminal; 2 outdoor pools; room service. *In room:* A/C, TV, fridge.

Onward from Chetumal

The Maya ruins of Lamanai, in Belize, are an easy day trip if you have transportation (not a rental car). To explore the Río Bec route (see below), take Hwy. 186 to the west.

SIDE TRIPS TO MAYA RUINS FROM CHETUMAL

A few miles west of Bacalar and Chetumal begins an area of Maya settlement known to archaeologists as the Río Bec region. Numerous ruins stretching well into the state of Campeche are intriguing for their heavily stylized, lavishly decorated architecture. Excavation has brought restoration, but these cities have not been rebuilt to the degree found at Uxmal and Chichén Itzá. Buildings here often were in such great shape that reconstruction was unnecessary.

Unlike like the marquee ruins mentioned above, trees and vines grow in profusion here, creating the feel of lost cities. In visiting them, you can imagine what John Lloyd Stephens and Frederick Catherwood must have felt when they traipsed through the Yucatán in the 19th century. The entire route is rich in wildlife; you might see a toucan, a grand curassow, or a macaw hanging about, while orioles, egrets, and several birds of prey are common. Gray fox, wild turkey, *tesquintle* (a bushy-tailed, plant-eating rodent), the coatimundi (raccoon kin with long tapered snout and tail), and armadillos inhabit the area in abundance. Several bands of spider and howler monkeys circulate Calakmul and the surrounding jungle.

THE ROUTE Halfway between Bacalar and Chetumal, about 20km (12 miles) from either, is the well-marked turnoff for Hwy. 186 to Escárcega. This same road leads to Campeche, Palenque, and Villahermosa. A couple of gas stations are en route, including one in the town of Xpujil. Carry plenty of cash, as credit cards are rarely accepted in the area.

The Río Bec sites lie varying distances off this highway. You pass through a checkpoint at the Campeche state border; guards might ask for your travel papers or simply inquire where you've been and where you are going before waving you on. Rarely, they will want to inspect your trunk or even your luggage. You can divide your sightseeing into several day trips from Bacalar or Chetumal, or you can spend the night in this area and see more the next day. With an early start, you can easily visit a few of the sites mentioned here in a day.

Evidence, especially from Becán, shows that these ruins were part of the **trade route** linking the Caribbean coast at Cobá to Edzná and the Gulf Coast, and to Lamanai in Belize and beyond. A great number of cities once thrived here, and much of the land was dedicated to cultivating maize. All of this has been swallowed by the dense jungle blanketing the land from horizon to horizon.

The following sites are listed in east-to-west order, the way you would see them driving from the Caribbean coast—ideally after visiting the Museo de la Cultura Maya (p. 210) in Chetumal to gain some context. If you want a guide to show you the area, **Dan Griffin** (merida07forever@yahoo.com) is based in Mérida but is an archaeologist who works on projects with Harvard and other institutions all over the Yucatán Peninsula. You might meet him guiding for Río Bec Dreams (below), but he also leads independent tours focusing on lesser-known archaeological sites,

---

Opening Hours

The archaeological sites along the Río Bec (except for Calakmul, which has its own opening days and hours) are open daily 8am to 5pm.

Recommended Reading

For a bit of background reading to help you make the most of your visit, try *A Forest of Kings: The Untold Story of the Ancient Maya*, by Linda Schele and David Freidel; *The Blood of Kings: Dynasty and Ritual in Maya Art*, by Linda Schele and Mary Ellen Miller; and *The Maya Cosmos*, by David Freidel and Linda Schele. The best companion book to have is Joyce Kelly's *An Archaeological Guide to Mexico's Yucatán Peninsula*, even though it lacks historical and cultural information, and many sites have expanded since it was written.

abandoned haciendas, and bird-watching. Entry to each site is 35 to 55 pesos. Informational signs are in Mayan, Spanish, and English. Few if any refreshments are available, so bring your own water and food. All the principal sites have toilets.

FOOD & LODGING The only town in the Río Bec region offering basic tourist services is Xpujil, which doesn't have much else going for it. Of the basic affordable hotels in town, the best food and lodging is at **Restaurant y Hotel Calakmul** (✆ 983/871-6029), which rents air-conditioned doubles with TV for 600 pesos. They have tile floors, private bathrooms with hot water, and good beds. The restaurant is reliable and open daily from 6am to midnight. Main courses cost 45 to 120 pesos.

A rental car opens up some better options. Just beyond Xpujil, across from the ruins of the same name, is **Chicanná Eco Village** at Carretera Escárcega–Chetumal Km 144 (www.chicannaecovillageresort.com; ✆ 981/811-9192). Its 42 comfortable, nicely furnished rooms are distributed among several two-story thatched bungalows. They offer doubles or a king-size bed, ceiling fans, a large bathroom, and screened windows. Paths through manicured lawns and flower beds link the bungalows to one another and to the restaurant and swimming pool. Doubles go for 1,200 pesos.

Río Bec Dreams ★★, Carretera 186, Escárcega–Chetumal Km 142 (11km/6¾ miles west of Xpujil; www.riobecdreams.com; ✆ 983/126-3526) rents "jungalows"—small, wooden cabins on stilts—scattered through a tropical forest. They have good screens and such niceties as curtains, tile counters, hand-painted sinks, porches, and very comfortable beds with mosquito netting, for 550 pesos a night. Cabins have wash basins, but guests share spotless bathrooms (one unit with a private bathroom costs 700 pesos; one with a bathroom and a shower is 800 pesos). Rates are for a 2-night minimum stay; for 1 night, add 50 pesos. Three large cabañas with screened-in porches and private bathrooms rent for 1,000 pesos (1 bedroom) to 1,150 pesos (2 bedrooms). The Canadian owners are devoted students of Río Bec architecture who guide tours of the ruins, from short excursions to smaller ruins for 250 pesos to all-day treks through Calakmul for 1,500 pesos. They are a wonderful resource and good companions around the open-air bar. The restaurant is easily the best in the area.

Dzibanché & Kinichná

Dzibanché (or Tzibanché) means "place where they write on wood"—obviously not the original name, which remains unknown. This ancient city dates from the Classic period (A.D. 300–900) and was occupied for around 700 years. Scattered over 42 sq. km (16 sq. miles) are several groupings of buildings and plazas; only

Overgrown trees dominate the ruins of Kinichná.

a small portion is excavated. The turnoff, 37km (23 miles) from the highway intersection, is well marked; another 23km (14 miles) brings you to the ruins. Ask about the condition of the road before setting out. These unpaved roads can go from good to bad pretty quickly, but this is an important enough site that road repair is generally kept up.

TEMPLES & PLAZAS Two large adjoining plazas have been cleared. The most important structure yet excavated is the **Temple of the Owl** in the main plaza, Plaza Xibalba. Archaeologists found a stairway descending from the top of the structure deep into the pyramid to a burial chamber (not open to visitors), where they uncovered some beautiful polychromatic lidded vessels, one of which has an owl painted on the top handle with its wings spreading onto the lid. White owls were messengers of the underworld gods of the Maya religion. Also found here were the remains of a sacrificial victim and what appear to be the remains of a Maya queen, which is unique in Maya archaeology.

Opposite the Temple of the Owl is the **Temple of the Cormorant,** named after the bird depicted on a polychromed drinking vessel found here. Archaeologists also found evidence here of an interior tomb similar to the one in the Temple of the Owl, but excavations have not yet begun. Other magnificently preserved pottery pieces found during excavations include an incense burner with an almost three-dimensional figure of the diving god attached to the outside, and another incense burner with an elaborately dressed representation of the god Itzamná attached.

Situated all by itself is **Structure VI,** a miniature rendition of Teotihuacán's style of *tablero* and *talud* architecture. Each step of the pyramid is made of a *talud* (sloping surface) crowned by a *tablero* (vertical stone facing). Teotihuacán was near present-day Mexico City, but its influence stretched as far as Guatemala. At the top of the pyramid, a doorway with a wooden lintel is still intact after centuries of weathering. This detail gave the site its name. Date glyphs for the year A.D. 733 are carved into the wood.

Another nearby city, **Kinichná** (Kee-neech-*nah*), is about 2.5km (1½ miles) north. The road leading there becomes questionable during the rainy season, but an Olmec-style jade figure was found there. It has a large acropolis with five buildings on three levels, which have been restored and are in good condition. Fragments of the original stucco are visible.

Kohunlich ★

Kohunlich (Koh-*hoon*-leech), 42km (26 miles) from the turnoff for Hwy. 186, dates from around A.D. 100 to 900. Turn left off the road, and the entrance is 9km (5⅔ miles) farther. Enter the grand, parklike site, cross a large, shady ceremonial area flanked by four large pyramids, and continue walking straight ahead.

Just beyond this grouping you'll come to Kohunlich's famous **Pyramid of the Masks** under a thatched covering. Six stucco heads, more than 2.4m (8 ft.) tall, flank the giant staircase. Dating from around A.D. 500, each is slightly different but all are elongated and wear a headdress with a mask on its crest and a mask on the chin piece—essentially masks within masks. The carving on the pupils suggests a solar connection, possibly with the night sun that illuminated the underworld. It's speculated that masks covered much of the facade of this building, which was built in the Río Bec style with rounded corners, a false stairway, and a false temple on the top. At least one theory holds that the masks are a composite of several rulers at Kohunlich.

In the buildings immediately to the left after you enter the site, recent excavations uncovered two intact pre-Hispanic skeletons and five decapitated heads that were probably used in a ceremonial ritual. To the right, follow the shady path through the jungle to another recently excavated plaza. The fine architecture and the high quality of pottery found there suggests this complex housed priests or rulers. Scholars believe overpopulation led to Kohunlich's decline.

An enormous face from Kohunlich's famous Pyramid of the Masks.

Xpujil

Xpujil (Eesh-poo-*heel*; also spelled Xpuhil), meaning either "cattail" or "forest of kapok trees," flourished between A.D. 400 and 900. This small, well-preserved site is easy to get to; look for a highway sign pointing right (north). The entrance is just off the highway; the main structure is a 180m (590-ft.) walk farther. Along the path are some *chechén* trees, recognizable by their blotchy bark. Don't touch; they are poisonous and can cause blisters. On the right, a platform supports a restored two-story building with a central staircase on its eastern side. Remnants of a decorative molding and two galleries are connected by a doorway. About 90m (295 ft.) farther you come to **Structure I,** the site's main structure. This rectangular ceremonial platform, 2m (6½ ft.) high and 50m (164 ft.) long, supports the palace and is decorated with three tall towers shaped like miniature versions of the pyramids in Tikal, Guatemala. These towers are purely decorative, with false stairways and temples that are too small to serve as such. The effect is beautiful. The building holds 12 rooms, which are now in ruins.

Becán ★★★

Becán (Beh-*kahn*) is about 7km (4⅓ miles) beyond Xpujil, visible on the right side of the highway. Becán means "moat filled by water," and it was in fact protected by a moat spanned by seven bridges; the city is a stellar (and rare) example of Maya fortification; dirt from digging the moat was piled up to create a fortified wall around the city. The extensive site dates from the early Classic to the late post-Classic (600 B.C.–A.D. 1200) period. Although it was abandoned by A.D. 850, ceramic remains indicate that there may have been a population resurgence between 900 and 1000, and it was still used as a ceremonial site as late as 1200. Becán was an administrative and ceremonial center with political sway over at least seven other cities in the area, including Chicanná, Hormiguero, and Payán.

The ruins of Xpujil.

The ruins of Becán.

The first plaza group you see after you enter was the center for grand ceremonies. From the highway, you can see the back of **Structure I,** a pyramid with two temples on top. Beyond and in between the two temples you can see the temple atop **Structure IV,** opposite Structure I. When the high priest exited the mouth of the earth monster in the center of this temple (which he reached by way of a hidden side stairway that's now partially exposed), he would have been visible from well beyond the immediate plaza, where it's thought that commoners had to stand. The back of Structure IV is believed to have been a civic plaza where rulers sat on stone benches. The second plaza group dates from around A.D. 850 and has perfect twin towers on top. Under the platform supporting the towers are 10 rooms that are thought to be related to Xibalba (Shee-*bahl*-bah), the underworld. Earth-monster faces probably covered this building (and appeared on other buildings as well). Remains of at least one ball court have been unearthed. Next to the ball court is a well-preserved figure in an elaborate headdress behind glass, excavated not far from where he is now displayed. The markings are well defined, displaying a host of details.

Chicanná

Slightly more than 1.5km (1 mile) beyond Becán, on the left side of the highway, is Chicanná, which means "house of the mouth of snakes." The central square is surrounded by five buildings. **Structure II,** the site's outstanding building, features a monster-mouth doorway and an ornate stone facade with more superimposed masks. As you enter the mouth of the earth monster, you are on a platform configured as the monster's open jaw, with stone teeth on both sides. Again you find a lovely example of an elongated building with ornamental miniature pyramids on each end, typical of Río Bec architecture.

Calakmul ★★★

This area is both a massive Maya archaeological zone, with at least 60 sites, and a 70,000-hectare (172,900-acre) rainforest, designated in 1989 as the Calakmul

Note the monster-mouth doorway of Structure II from the ruins of Chicanná.

Biosphere Reserve with territory in both Mexico and Guatemala. The best way to see Calakmul is to spend the night at Xpujil or Chicanná and leave early in the morning for the reserve. If you're the first to drive down the narrow access road to the ruins (1½ hr. from the highway), you'll probably see plenty of wildlife. On my last trip, I saw two groups of spider monkeys swinging through the trees on the outskirts of the city and a group of howler monkeys sleeping in the trees in front of Structure II.

The site is open Tuesday to Sunday from 7am to 5pm. The rainy season, when the place is soaked, is from June to October.

THE ARCHAEOLOGICAL ZONE   Since 1982, archaeologists have been excavating the ruins of Calakmul, which date from 100 B.C. to A.D. 900. It's the largest of the 60 known Río Bec sites. Nearly 7,000 buildings have been discovered and mapped. At its zenith, at least 60,000 people may have lived around the site, but by the time of the Spanish Conquest in 1519, less than 1,000 lived there. Arriving at a large plaza filled with trees, you immediately see several stelae; Calakmul contains more than 100—more than any other site—but they are much more weathered and indistinguishable than the stelae of Palenque or Copán in Honduras. Looters have cut the faces off of some. By Structure XIII is a stela of a woman thought to have been a ruler that dates from A.D. 652.

Some structures here are built in the Petén style characteristic of Guatemala, with extraordinarily high crested structures, steep staircases, and false facades. Others are typical Río Bec style. **Structure III** must have been the residence of a noble family. Its design is unique and quite lovely; it retains its original form, never having been remodeled. Offerings of shells, beads, and polychromed tripod pottery were found inside. **Structure II** is the tallest pyramid in the Yucatán, at 54m (177 ft.). From the top, you can see the outline of the ruins of El Mirador, 50km (31 miles) across the forest in Guatemala. Two stairways ascend along the sides of the pyramid's principal face in the upper levels, with masks further breaking up the space.

Temple IV charts the line of the sun from June 21, when it falls on the left (north) corner; to September 21 and March 21, when it lines up in the east behind the middle temple on the top of the building; to December 21, when it falls on the right (south) corner. Numerous jade pieces, including spectacular masks, were uncovered here and are on display in the Museum of Mayan Culture in Campeche (p. 278). **Structure VII** is largely unexcavated except for the top, where, in 1984, the most outstanding jade mask yet to be found at Calakmul was uncovered. In their book *A Forest of Kings,* Linda Schele and David Freidel tell of wars among the Calakmul, Tikal, and Naranjo (the latter two in Guatemala), and how Ah-Cacaw, king of Tikal (120km/75 miles south of Calakmul), captured King Jaguar-Paw in A.D. 695 and later Lord Ox-Ha-Te Ixil Ahau, both of Calakmul.

CALAKMUL BIOSPHERE RESERVE   Set aside in 1989, this is the peninsula's only high forest, a rainforest that annually records as much as 5m (16 ft.) of rain. The tree canopy is higher here than in the forest of Quintana Roo. It lies very close to the border with Guatemala, but, of course, there is no way to get there. Among the plants are cactus, epiphytes, and orchids. Endangered animals include the white-lipped peccary, jaguar, and puma. So far, more than 250 species of birds have been recorded. At present, no overnight stay or camping is permitted. If you want a tour of a small part of the forest and you speak Spanish, you can inquire for a guide at one of the two nearby *ejidos* (cooperatives). Some old local *chicleros* (the men who tap sapodilla trees for their gum) have expert knowledge of flora and fauna and can take you on a couple of trails.

A yellow orchid from the Calakmul Biosphere Reserve.

The turnoff on the left for Calakmul is located 53km (33 miles) from Xpujil, just before the village of Conhuas. There's a guard station there where you pay 40 pesos per car. From the turnoff, it's an hour's drive on a paved one-lane-road. Admission to the site is 41 pesos.

It's advisable to take with you some food and drink and, of course, bug spray.

Balamkú ★★

Balamkú (Bah-lahm-*koo*), just off Hwy. 186 about 5km (3 miles) west of Conhuas, is easy to reach and worth the visit. A couple of buildings in the complex were so well preserved that they required almost no reconstruction. Inside the **Temple of the Four Kings,** covered by a later pyramid built over it, is one of the largest stucco friezes in the Maya world. The three major figures—looters made off with a fourth before the frieze was discovered in 1990 and protected— are a rabbit, an alligator, and a crocodile, flanked by many carvings of animals, mythological beings, and kings. The concept behind this temple is life and death, and figures of men sit in the gaping maws of crocodiles and toads as they descend into the underworld. On each stucco figure's head are the eyes, nose, and mouth of a jaguar, followed by the full face of the human figure, then a neck formed by the eyes and nose of another jaguar, and an Olmec-like face on the stomach, with its neck ringed by a necklace. Now the frieze is under lock and key, and visitors must ask the caretaker to let them view the unique art. Much of the original painting remains, so flash photography is not allowed.

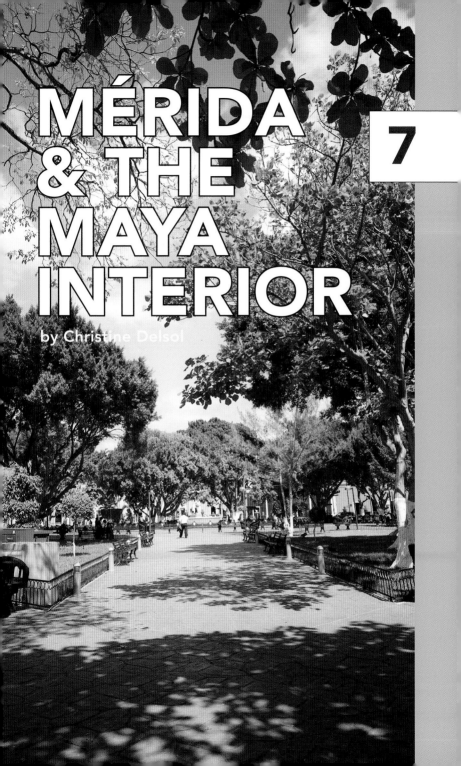

MÉRIDA & THE MAYA INTERIOR

by Christine Delsol

7

ong before Cancún was a glimmer in some computer programmer's eye, all roads led to **Mérida.** The great "White City"—still the region's cultural heart and soul—presided over a peninsula rich with legacies of colliding civilizations. The trove of ancient cities left behind by that cataclysm has enticed visitors ever since New York writer John Lloyd Stephens and illustrator Frederick Catherwood ventured south to investigate rumors of lost cities in the jungle.

The splendors of the ancient Maya world are still the Yucatán's biggest draw beyond the Caribbean coast. **Chichén Itzá,** every bit as wondrous as its coronation as a "new" Wonder of the World suggests, has many worthy companions. **Uxmal, Edzná, Cobá, Calakmul,** and several smaller ancient cities are still infused with a quiet, ancient spirit that seems to be losing ground daily in the glare of Chichén Itzá's celebrity status.

The thoughtful visitor, though, will soon learn the Maya heartland is far more than a living museum revealing an extraordinary culture—it is the evolution of that civilization. Whether you stay in a restored hacienda and indulge in a massage from the granddaughter of a Maya shaman, attend Mérida's weekly *Vaquería* with traditional Yucatecan cowboy music and dancing, or visit a village whose people live in thatch-roof huts and still speak the Yucatec Mayan language, you'll find past and present converging as they do nowhere else.

THE BEST MÉRIDA & MAYA INTERIOR EXPERIENCES

o **Dancing the night away:** Have dinner at Flor de Santiago restaurant, which could be a stand-in for an Argentine coffee house, to get in the mood for 1940s style big-band music in Parque Santiago—and maybe to work up your courage to join the fancy-footed locals on the dance floor. (p. 231)

o **Putting on your explorer's cap:** Thousands of ancient cities and abandoned haciendas slumber under their leafy shrouds all over the peninsula, awaiting the wave of the magic wand. Get someone to lead you to some of these sites, and you'll see the Yucatán as Stephens and Catherwood did. (p. 238)

o **Succumbing to chocolate fever:** Learn what real criollo chocolate tastes like at Ki'Xocolatl in Mérida (p. 244), then visit the Ecomuseo de Cacao (p. 271) to find out how chocolate grows, why the Maya deemed it the "food of the gods," and how it's processed—making your own final touches to the final product.

o **Being master of the hacienda:** Hacienda Yaxcopoil (p. 259) is not restored but simply maintained in a state of arrested decay. After the tourists go home, you can bed down in the guesthouse for a night and have the hacienda to yourself.

PREVIOUS PAGE: **The main square in Valladolid.**

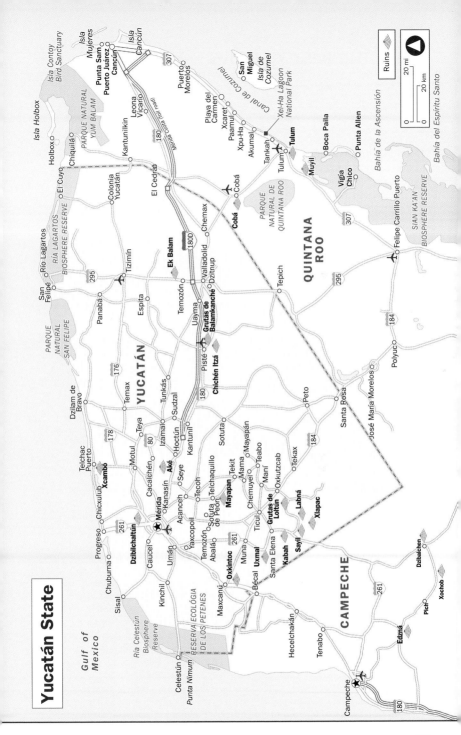

Yucatán State

223

- **Yucatán Today: www.yucatan today.com** One of the least commercial privately run sites, with cultural notes; detailed maps; transportation advice; history; and lists of hotels, restaurants, and events in Yucatán state and beyond, by the editors of an enormously helpful monthly tourist magazine.

- **TravelYucatan.com** Loaded with practical tips and detailed articles by travelers and residents, news roundups, and useful graphics such as photos of authorized taxi cabs and dive-site maps. You might not notice that it's also a booking site until you go to the "accommodations" link.

- **Yucatán Living: www.yucatan living.com** Destination and cultural articles, and in-depth reviews of restaurants and attractions give visitors an inside view on life in Mérida.

- **Yucatán Travel Guide: www. yucatan.travel** Yucatán's Ministry of Tourism site, which has good general information on the state's destinations, activities, and services

- **Buying art at the source:** In the "Yellow City" of Izamal, the artists who produce the jewelry, embroidery, and other crafts that end up in markets and stores all over the peninsula will welcome you into their workshops, where you can witness the birth of what may become your favorite memento of the Yucatán (p. 174).

MÉRIDA: GATEWAY TO THE MAYA HEARTLAND ★★★

1,440km (895 miles) E of Mexico City; 320km (199 miles) W of Cancún

Mérida, capital of the state of Yucatán, has been the peninsula's lodestar since the Spanish Conquest, yet many visitors treat it merely as a base camp for forays to the surrounding ruins. "The White City" (named after its limestone buildings)—more than 470 years old and home to about 1 million people—shares the narrow streets, traffic, and noise common to many colonial cities. But its vibrancy, eye-popping architecture, parks and plazas at every turn, and kind, dignified people are what you remember.

The heady brew of ancient and modern is at its most piquant in the bustling, genial historic center. This is the best place to shop for regional specialties such as hammocks, Panama hats, *guayabera* shirts, and embroidered *huipiles,* the colorful native blouses. Vendors in traditional Maya garb mingle with teenagers swiping at iPads in the leafy central plaza. Mérida enjoys a remarkable bounty of B&B's, converted hotel mansions, and beautifully restored colonial homes.

Expatriates have been flocking to the city in recent years—not just retirees but young couples with boundless energy to explore and show off their adopted home. The resurgence in popularity means prices have been creeping up, yet this is still a haven for the budget traveler in the midst of a cultural explosion where you never have to look far to find a festival, concert, theater production, or art

Mérida's busy Plaza Grande.

exhibition. Best of all, the nonstop festivities are not staged for visitors' entertainment; they are the Meridanos' own celebrations of both their heritage and their aspirations. When you're in Mérida, you're a part of Mérida.

Essentials

GETTING THERE & DEPARTING

BY PLANE Mérida's airport is 13km (8 miles) from the city center on the southwestern outskirts of town, near the entrance to Hwy. 180. The airport has desks for rental cars, hotel reservations, and tourist information. Taxi tickets to town (140 pesos; 200 pesos for a van with up to 7 passengers) are sold outside the airport doors, under the covered walkway.

Aeroméxico (www.aeromexico.com; © 800/237-6639 in the U.S., or 01-800/021-4000 in Mexico) flies nonstop to and from Miami and Mexico City, and has expanded its connecting flights from other U.S. cities since Mexicana suspended operations. Continental (www.continental.com; © 800/523-3273 in the U.S.), in the process of merging with United, flies nonstop to and from Houston. American, Delta, and Alaska also serve Mérida through code shares. Mexican budget line VivaAerobus (www.vivaaerobus.com; © 01-81/8215-0150 in Mexico), which flies to Mérida from Guadalajara, Mexico City, and Monterrey, has connecting flights from Chicago, Houston, Las Vegas, Miami, Orlando, and San Antonio. Interjet (www.interjet.com.mx; © 866/285-9525 in the U.S.), which serves Miami and San Antonio, flies to Mérida through its Mexico City hub.

BY CAR Hwy. 180 is the old *carretera federal* (federal highway) between Mérida and Cancún. The trip takes about 6 hours on a good road that passes through many Maya villages. A four-lane divided *cuota*, or *autopista* (toll road), parallels Hwy. 180 and begins at the town of Kantunil, 56km (35 miles) east of Mérida. For a toll of 381 pesos each way, you avoid the tiny villages and their not-so-tiny speed bumps, cutting the trip to about

3½ hours. Coming from the direction of Cancún, Hwy. 180 feeds into Mérida's Calle 65, which passes 1 block south of the main square.

Coming from the south (Campeche, 2½ hr., or Uxmal, 1½ hr.), you enter the city on Avenida Itzáes. To get to the town center, turn right on Calle 59 (the first street after the zoo).

A *periférico* (loop road) circles Mérida, making it possible to skirt the city. Directional signs into the city are generally good, but lapping the city on the loop requires vigilance.

BY BUS Mérida is the Yucatán's transportation hub. Of its five bus stations, two offer first-class buses and the other three provide local service to nearby destinations. The larger first-class station, **CAME,** is on Calle 70, between calles 69 and 71 (see "City Layout," below). The ADO bus line and its affiliates operate the station, which is also used by other long-distance lines. All the windows sell first-class tickets except for the last couple to the right, which sell tickets for ADO's deluxe services. ADO-GL is a small step up from first class, while ADO Platino (formerly UNO) has superwide seats with lots of leg room. Unless it's a long trip, go for the bus with the most convenient departure time. Tickets can be purchased in advance; ask the agent for ticket options and departure times for the route you need. The old website, www.ticketbus.com. mx, has migrated to **Boletotal** (http://boletotal.mx), a more comprehensive travel ticketing site also affiliated with ADO. It looks better, but isn't much easier to use, and there doesn't seem to be any way to use non-Mexican credit cards to book tickets. It's great, though, for checking schedules.

To and from Cancún: You can pick up a bus almost every hour at the Came; some lines also collect passengers at the Fiesta Americana Hotel on Calle 60 at Avenida Colón, across from the Hyatt. Cancún is 4 hours away; a few buses stop in **Valladolid.**

To and from Chichén Itzá: Three buses per day (1½-hr. trip) depart from the CAME. Tour operators in Mérida hotels also offer day trips.

To and from Playa del Carmen, Tulum, and Chetumal: From the CAME, there are at least 10 departures per day for Playa del Carmen (5 hr. away), six for Tulum (6 hr.), and eight for Chetumal (7 hr.).

To and from Campeche: The CAME station has about 40 departures per day. It's a 2½-hour trip.

To and from Palenque and San Cristóbal de las Casas: There are three departures a day from the Came to San Cristóbal and four to Palenque. Minor thefts have been reported on buses to Palenque; don't take second-class buses, check your luggage so that it's stowed in the cargo bay, and put your carry-on in the overhead rack, not on the floor.

The main **second-class terminal, TAME,** is around the corner from the CAME on Calle 69, between calles 68 and 70.

To and from Uxmal: There are four buses per day from the second-class terminal. (You can also pick up a tour through most hotels or any travel agent or tour operator in town.) The ADO line operates a special tour bus (transportation only; no guide) leaving the second-class terminal at 8am on Fridays, Saturdays, and Sundays. It stops for 30 minutes each at Kabah, Xlapak, Sayil, and Labná; for 1 hour at the new Ecomuseo del Cacao (p. 271); and 2 hours at Uxmal before returning to Mérida. Fare is 159 pesos.

To and from Progreso: Transportes AutoProgreso offers service to and from its downtown station at Calle 62 no. 524, between calles 65 and 67. The trip to Progreso takes an hour by second-class bus.

To Dzibilchaltún: Take the bus for Chablecal, departing several times a day from Autocentro on Calle 62, between calles 67 and 69.

To and from Celestún: Buses depart every hour from the Noroeste second-class station on Calle 50 at Calle 67.

To and from Izamal: Buses leave hourly from the Autobuses del Centro station (second class) on Calle 46 between calles 65 and 67.

To and from Río Lagartos: Second-class buses leave from the Noroeste terminal.

To and from Isla Holbox: An Oriente bus makes the trip from the TAME station at 11:30pm, arriving in Chiquilá (ferry terminal) at 5am; Noroeste departs in the morning and arrives late in the afternoon.

ORIENTATION

VISITOR INFORMATION   The city tourism offices and state tourism offices have different resources; if you can't get the information you're looking for at one, go to the other. The city's **visitor information office** (✆ **999/942-0000**, ext. 80119) is on the ground floor of the Ayuntamiento building on Calle 62, facing the main square. Look for a glass door under the arcade. Hours are Monday to Saturday from 8am to 8pm, and Sunday from 8am to 2pm. The staff offers a free walking tour of the area around the main square at 9:30am, Monday through Saturday. For more complicated questions, you might have better luck at one of the state's two downtown tourism offices: one in the **Teatro Peón Contreras** on Calle 60, facing Parque de la Madre (✆ **999/924-9290**), and the other on the main plaza in the **Palacio de Gobierno** (✆ **999/930-3101**, ext. 10001), immediately to the left as you

Mérida's grand boulevard, Paseo de Montejo.

enter. Both are open daily from 8am to 9pm. The airport and the CAME and TAME bus stations also have state tourism information booths.

Keep your eye out for the free monthly magazine *Yucatán Today;* it's packed with information about Mérida and beyond.

CITY LAYOUT   Downtown Mérida's grid layout is typical of the Yucatán: Even-numbered streets run north and south; odd-numbered streets run east and west. The numbering begins on the north and the east sides of town, so if you're walking on an odd-numbered street and the even numbers of the cross-streets are increasing, you are heading west; likewise, if you are on an even-numbered street and the odd-numbered cross-streets are increasing, you are going south. Most downtown streets are one-way.

NEIGHBORHOODS IN BRIEF   Mérida's main square is the busy **Plaza Grande,** bordered by calles 60, 61, 62, and 63. Calle 60, the *centro's* (downtown's) central artery, runs in front of the cathedral and connects the main square with several smaller plazas, some theaters and churches, and the University of Yucatán, just to the north. Handicraft shops, restaurants, and hotels are concentrated here. Around the plaza are the cathedral, the Palacio de Gobierno (state government building), the Ayuntamiento (town hall), and the Palacio Montejo. The plaza always has a crowd, and it overflows on Sundays, when surrounding streets are closed for an enormous street fair (see "Festivals & Events in Mérida"). The teeming market district is just to the southeast. Walking is by far the easiest way to get around the Centro, supplemented by taxis for occasional forays to spots in more distant neighborhoods. If you've rented a car—which I would recommend only if your visit to Mérida is part of a longer road trip—find a parking lot and forget about it until you leave the city.

Mérida's most fashionable district is the wide, tree-lined boulevard **Paseo de Montejo** and its surrounding neighborhood. The Paseo de Montejo parallels Calle 60 and begins 7 blocks north and a little east of the main square. Though it has trendy restaurants, modern hotels, bank and airline offices, and a few clubs, the boulevard is known mostly for its stately mansions built during the henequén boom times. Near Montejo's intersection with Avenida Colón, you'll find the Hyatt and the Fiesta Americana hotels.

Note: If you are driving into Mérida, avoid arriving on a Sunday, when the Paseo de Montejo and many downtown streets are closed for the Sunday-morning Bici-Ruta bicycle ride and the all-day Mérida en Domingo festival. Most tourists will spend virtually all their time in these two areas.

 ### House Hunting

Address numbers bear little relation to a building's physical location, so addresses almost always include cross-streets. In "Calle 60 no. 549 × 71 y 73," for example, the "×" is shorthand for the word *por* (meaning "by"), and *y* means "and." So this address is on Calle 60 between calles 71 and 73. This tidy system disappears outside of downtown, where street numbering gets erratic (to say the least). It's important to know the name of the *colonia* (neighborhood) where you're going. This is the first thing taxi drivers will ask you.

GETTING AROUND By Car   In general, reserve a car in advance from home to get the best weekly rates during high season (Nov–Feb); in low season, renting a car after you reach Mérida often yields better deals from local companies that offer promotions available only when you are there. Always ask if the price quote includes the IVA tax and insurance coverage. Practically everybody offers free mileage. For tips on saving money on car rentals, see the "Getting There" and "Getting Around" sections in chapter 9. If your visit will be primarily in Mérida except for a couple of day trips, you'll do better to rent for just a day or two, which also spares you the high cost of Mérida's parking lots. These *estacionamentos* often charge one price for the night and double that if you leave your car for the following day. Many hotels offer free parking, but make sure that includes daytime hours.

By Taxi   Taxis are easy to come by and much cheaper than in Cancún, usually 30 to 60 pesos around town and 100 to 120 to the outskirts. For day trips outside of Mérida, you can often hire a taxi for a day or a half-day at rates comparable to a group tour.

By Bus   City buses are tricky to figure out but aren't needed often because almost everything of interest is within walking distance of the main plaza. The most useful buses run between downtown and Paseo de Montejo, which is a bit of a hike from the plaza. Catch an "Itzimná" bus on Calle 59 between calles 56 and 58, or a 52 Norte bus between calles 54 and 56, to visit points along the boulevard. You can also take a *colectivo* (minibus) heading north on Calle 60. Most take you within a couple of blocks of Paseo de Montejo. The *colectivos* or *combis* (usually painted white) line up along the side streets next to the plaza and fan out in several directions along simple routes. Another convenient, if more expensive, way to get to Mérida's main sights is the hop-on, hop-off **Turibus** (p. 230), which even locals use to get around for errands.

[Fast FACTS] MÉRIDA

Area Code   The telephone area code is **999.**

Consulates   The **American Consulate** is at Calle 60 no. 338-K between calles 29 and 31 (*©* **999/942-5700**), 1 block north of the Hyatt hotel (Col. Alcalá Martín). Office hours are Monday to Friday from 9am to 1pm.

Hospitals   Mérida is the Yucatán's center for excellent medical care and is blessed with several outstanding hospitals. The **Clinica de Mérida,** Itzáes 242 at Colón (www.

clinicademerida.com.mx; *©* **999/941-2800**), is accustomed to dealing with foreigners. The hospital most favored by expats is **Star Medica,** Calle 26 No. 199 (btw. calles 15 and 7), Col. Altabrisa (www.starmedica. com; *©* **999/930-2880**). You can also call the **Cruz Roja (Red Cross)** at *©* **999/924-9813.**

Internet Access   You hardly have to walk more than a couple of blocks to find Internet access; rates hover around 15 pesos per

hour. Free Wi-Fi is available in most hotels and in more than 50 city parks, including the Plaza Grande, Parque San Juan, Parque de las Américas, and Parque Zoológico del Centenario.

Mail & Postage   The Centro *correo* on Calle 53, between calles 52 and 54, is open Monday to Friday from 8am to 7pm, Saturday from 9am to 1pm. Airmail (recommended for anything other than local mail) costs 10.5 pesos to the U.S. and Canada.

Pharmacies Both **Farmacía Yza** (© 999/926-6666) and **Farmacías Canto** (© 999/948-1818) have stores all over the city, offer home delivery, and are open 24 hours.

Police Mérida has a special body of English-speaking police to assist tourists. They patrol the downtown area and the Paseo de Montejo, wearing blue pants and white shirts with a POLICIA TURISTICA patch on the sleeve. They can be found at green kiosks in the central plaza and Santa Lucia and Hidalgo parks, or call them at © 999/942-0060.

Newspapers & Magazines *Yucatán Today,* available just about everywhere you look, is packed with tourist information, events, and features about Yucatecan life and culture. For general local news, the ***Yucatán Times*** has had an online English edition.

Safety Mérida has long had the lowest crime rate in Mexico—or in most of the world, for that matter—and that has not changed with the well-publicized drug violence that has escalated in distant parts of Mexico. Crime simply is not tolerated here. You can talk to strangers or walk the streets at all hours of the night without fear.

Exploring Mérida

Most of Mérida's attractions are within walking distance from downtown. One easy way to see more of the city is on the popular, open-air **Carnavalito City Tour Bus.** It leaves Santa Lucia Park (calles 60 and 55) at 10am and 1, 4, and 7pm (no 7pm tour on Sun). The guided tour costs 75 pesos per person and lasts 2 hours, taking in downtown, Paseo de Montejo, past an old 15th-century neighborhood church and many old mansions on Avenida Colón, through the San Juan Arch and back to the starting point. You'll get a chance to stretch your legs at Parque de las Américas. A national company, **Turibus** (www.turibus.com.mx), operates modern, bright-red double-decker buses and provides earphones with a recorded narrative in English and five other languages. It covers essentially the same areas as the Carnavalito bus, also in about 2 hours, but you can hop off at

Mérida's fortresslike cathedral.

Many Mexican cities offer weekend concerts in parks and plazas, but Mérida surpasses them all by offering performances every day of the week. Unless otherwise indicated, admission is free.

Sunday From 9am to 9pm, the Centro stages a fair called Mérida en Domingo (Mérida on Sunday). The plaza and a section of Calle 60 extending to Parque Santa Lucía close to traffic. Parents stroll with their children, taking in the food and drink booths, the lively little flea market and used-book fair, children's art classes, and educational booths. At 11am, musicians play everything from jazz to classical and folk music in front of the Palacio del Gobierno, while the police orchestra performs Yucatecan tunes in Santa Lucía park. At 11:30am, you'll find bawdy comedy acts at Parque Hidalgo, on Calle 60 at Calle 59. After a midafternoon lull, the plaza fills up again as people walk around and visit with friends. Around 7pm in front of the Ayuntamiento, a large band starts playing rumbas, rumbas, and cha-chas with great enthusiasm; you may see 1,000 people dancing in the street. Afterward, folk ballet dancers reenact a typical Yucatecan wedding inside.

Monday At 9pm in front of the Palacio Municipal, performers dance and play Vaquería regional (traditional cowboy music) to celebrate the Vaquerías feast, which was associated originally with the branding of cattle on the haciendas. Performers include dancers with trays of bottles or filled glasses balanced on their heads—a sight to see.

Tuesday At 8:30pm, Auditoio Olimpio, on the Calle 62 side of the plaza, hosts guitar trovas (boleros or ballads) and other live music and theater performances. At 9pm in Parque Santiago, Calle 59 at Calle 72, the Municipal Orchestra plays Latin and American big-band music from the 1940s.

Wednesday At 9pm, Auditorio Olimpio hosts free concerts and theater performances.

Thursday At 9pm in Parque Santa Lucía, the Serenata Yucateca presents regional music, dance, and spoken-word performances.

Friday At 9pm, the University of Yucatán, Calle 60 at Calle 57, presents the University Serenade, including the University Ballet Folklórico performing typical Yucatecan dances.

Saturday At 8pm in the park at Paseo de Montejo and Calle 47, Noche Mexicana features traditional Mexican music and dance performances with craft booths and food stands selling great antojitos (finger foods), drinks, and ice cream. At 9pm, Calle 60 closes between Plaza Grande and Calle 53 for En El Corazón de Mérida, a festival featuring several live bands joined by stilt walkers, mariachis, and crafts and food stands.

any stop to explore at will and grab the next bus when you're ready to continue. Pick them up in front of the cathedral, or at any scheduled stop, every half-hour. The tour costs 100 pesos or $10, 50 pesos/$5 for children 4 to 12 years old. Two-day passes are 140 pesos/$14 adults, 70 pesos/$7 children. (The 10-pesos-per-dollar exchange rate is abysmal; pay in pesos and the adult fare is the equivalent of less than $8.) The most romantic and time-honored way to see the sights is in

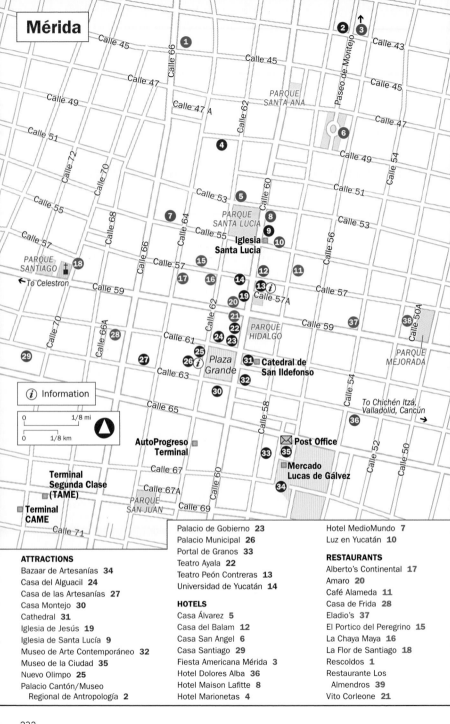

Mérida

a *calesa* (horse-drawn carriage), best at night or on Sunday morning when traffic is light. The traditional 45-minute ride taking in the central plaza, Calle 60 and Paseo de Montejo costs 250 pesos; a double, which lasts longer and adds Avenida Reforma's bullfight ring, García Ginerés and the Parque de las Américas, then leafy Avenida Colón, costs 500 pesos. You can usually find *calesas* beside the cathedral on Calle 61.

PLAZA GRANDE ★★★

Downtown Mérida has a casual, relaxed feel. Buildings lack the severe baroque and neoclassical features that characterize central Mexico; most are finished in stucco and painted light colors. Mérida's many gardens, where plants grow in wild profusion, add to the languid tropical atmosphere. The city's plazas display a similar aesthetic: Unlike the highland plazas with their carefully sculpted trees, Mérida's squares are typically built around large trees that are left to grow as tall as possible.

The plaza (formally the Plaza de la Independencia), a natural starting point for exploring Mérida, is bounded by calles 60, 61, 62, and 63. This is a comfortable and informal place to gather with friends. Even when no orchestrated event is in progress, the park is full of people strolling or sitting on benches and talking. Big as Mérida is, the plaza bestows a personal feel and sense of community. A December 2011 relandscaping project and renovation with new floors, lampposts, and underground wiring make the square an even more fitting centerpiece to Mérida's oldest buildings, beautiful in their scale and composition, which surround the square.

Cathedral de San Ildefonso ★ CATHEDRAL   The fortresslike cathedral—which was in fact designed as a fortress as much as a place of worship—is the oldest on the continent, built between 1561 and 1598. Much of the stone in its walls came from the ruined buildings of the Maya city of T'ho. It was originally finished in stucco, and you can see some remnants still clinging to the bare rock. Inside, decoration is sparse, all smooth white stone, with a conspicuous absence of gold adornments seen in many Mexican cathedrals. The most notable item is a picture of Ah Kukum Tutul Xiú, chief of the Xiú people, visiting the Montejo camp to make peace; it hangs over the side door on the right.

To the left of the main altar is a small shrine with a curious figure of Christ that replicates one recovered from a burned-out church in the town of Ichmul. In the 1500s, a local artist carved the original figure from a miraculous tree that was hit by lightning and burst into flames—but did not char. The statue later became blistered in the church fire at Ichmul, but it survived. In 1645, it was moved to Mérida. The locals attached great powers to the figure, naming it *Cristo de las Ampollas* (Christ of the Blisters). It did not, however, survive the sacking of the cathedral in 1915 by revolutionary forces, so a new figure was modeled after the original. Take a look in the side chapel, which contains a life-size diorama of the Last Supper. The Mexican Jesus is covered with prayer crosses brought by supplicants asking for intercession.

Calles 60 and 61. Daily 8am–noon and 5–8pm.

Museo de Arte Contemporáneo Ateneo de Yucatán (MACAY) ART
MUSEUM   Next door to the cathedral is the old bishop's palace, now converted into the city's contemporary art museum. The palace was confiscated and rebuilt during the Mexican Revolution in 1915. The museum entrance faces the

cathedral from the reconstructed walkway between the two buildings called the Pasaje de la Revolución. The 17 exhibition rooms display work by contemporary artists, mostly from the Yucatán. (The best known are Fernando García Ponce and Fernando Castro Pacheco, whose works also hang in the government palace described below.) Nine rooms hold the museum's permanent collection; the rest are for temporary exhibits.

Pasaje de la Revolución (btw. calles 58 and 60). www.macay.org. ✆ **999/928-3258.** Daily 10am–6pm. Free.

Casa de Montejo ★★ MUSEUM   On the south side of the plaza, the heavy, elaborate decoration around the doorway and windows of the Montejo family home is carved in the Spanish *plateresque* architectural style, but the content is very much a New World creation. Conquering the Yucatán was the Montejo family business, begun by the original Francisco Montejo and continued by his son and nephew, both also named Francisco Montejo. Francisco Montejo El Mozo ("The Younger") began construction of the house in 1542. Bordering the entrance, figures of conquistadors stand on the heads of vanquished Indians—borrowed, perhaps, from the pre-Hispanic custom of portraying victorious Maya kings treading on their defeated foes. The conquistadors' quixotic posture and somewhat cartoonish expressions make them less imposing than the Montejos might have intended. The National Bank of Mexico acquired the house and restored it in 1981. Banamex completed a second restoration between 2007 and 2010 for use as a museum and cultural center. Around a garden courtyard, the living room, office/library, bedroom, and dining room are furnished as they might have been in the late 19th and early 20th centuries, allowing you to imagine what home must have been like for the Montejos and their descendants, who lived here as recently as the 1970s. (Mérida society keeps track of Montejo's descendants, as well as those of the last Maya king, Tutul Xiú.) Three exhibition halls host temporary displays, conferences, and concerts.

Calle 63 (btw. calles 60 and 62). Tues–Sat, 10am–7pm; Sun 10am–2pm. Guided tours Tues–Sat 11am, 1pm, 5pm; Sun 11am. Free.

In stark contrast to the severity of the cathedral and Casa Montejo is the light, unimposing **Ayuntamiento** or **Palacio Municipal** (city hall) on the west side of the plaza on Calle 62. The exterior dates from the mid–19th century, an era when a tropical aesthetic tinged with romanticism began asserting itself across coastal Latin America. On the second floor, you can see the city council's meeting hall and enjoy a view of the plaza from the balcony. Next door to the Ayuntamiento, at the corner of calles 61 and 62, is the **Nuevo Olimpo** (new Olympus). Built in 1999, it follows the lines of the historic building it replaced, but inside it is a large, modern space that hosts art exhibits, films, and lectures. It houses the **Arcadio Poveda Ricalde Planetarium** on the lower level and also holds concert and gallery space, a bookstore, and a lovely courtyard. A comfortable cafe is under the arches.

Cater-corner from the Olimpo is the old **Casa del Alguacil (Magistrate's House).** Under its arcades is something of an institution in Mérida: the **Dulcería y Sorbetería Colón,** an ice cream and sweet shop that will appeal to those who prefer lighter ice creams. A spectacular side doorway on Calle 62 bears viewing, and across the street is the **Teatro Armando Manzanero** (formerly Teatro Mérida), with two movie screens showing art films and one stage for live performances. Returning to the main plaza, down from the ice cream store,

A mural by Fernando Castro Pacheco, located in the Palacio de Gobierno.

is a shopping center of boutiques and convenience food vendors called **Pasaje Picheta.**

Palacio de Gobierno ★★ GOVERNMENT BUILDING   At the end of the arcade is the state government building, dating from 1892. Large murals by Yucatecan artist Fernando Castro Pacheco, completed between 1971 and 1973, decorate the courtyard walls with scenes from Maya myth and Yucatecan history. The painting over the stairway depicts the Maya spirit with ears of sacred corn, the "sunbeams of the gods;" nearby is a painting of mustachioed President Lázaro Cárdenas, who, in 1938, expropriated 17 foreign oil companies and was hailed as a Mexican liberator. The long, wide upstairs gallery holds more of Pacheco's paintings, which have an almost photographic double-exposure effect. It's a heartening experience to visit in the evening, when carefree families mill around, children playing tag and pulling wheeled toys over the tiles, beneath the haunting depictions of Yucatecans subjugated under Spanish rule.

Calle 60 (btw. calles 60 and 62). Mon–Sat 8am–8pm; Sun 9am–5pm. A small tourism office is to the left of the entrance.

Museo de la Ciudad ★★★ MUSEUM   A few blocks from Plaza Grande in the market district (p. 228), the new city museum (1977) now occupies the grand old post office building. An exhibit outlining Mérida's history includes explanatory text in English. Particularly fun is a scale model of the statue for the life-size bronze statue of Felipe Carrillo Puerto, surely Yucatán's most-loved governor. The model for the statue was none other than the museum's director, who happens to be Carrillo Puerto's grandson. The museum also displays old carved stones from the ancient city of T'ho and decorative pieces from churches that were sacked during the Mexican Revolution. Upstairs galleries display the works of local artists.

Calle 56 btw. calles 65 and 65A, Tues–Fri 9am–8pm; Sat–Sun 9am–2pm. Free admission.

CALLE 60

Heading north from Plaza Grande up Calle 60, you'll see many of Mérida's old churches and squares, as well as stores selling jewelry, pottery, clothing, and folk art. A stroll along this street leads to the Parque Santa Ana and continues to the fashionable boulevard Paseo de Montejo.

The **Teatro Daniel Ayala Pérez,** on the left between calles 61 and 59, schedules some interesting performances. On the right side is the small Parque Cepeda Peraza, more often called **Parque Hidalgo,** named for 19th-century Gen. Manuel Cepeda Peraza. It was part of Montejo's original city plan. Small outdoor restaurants front hotels on the park, making it a popular stopping place at any time of day—for locals, tourists, and hammock vendors alike. Across Calle 59 is the **Iglesia de Jesús,** or El Tercer Orden (the Third Order). Built by the Jesuits in 1618, it has the richest interior of any church in Mérida, making it a favorite spot for weddings. If you do nothing else, look carefully at the church's west wall to find stones that still bear Mayan inscriptions from their previous life. The entire block on which the church stands belonged to the Jesuits, who are known for being great educators. The school they left behind after their expulsion became the Universidad de Yucatán.

On the other side of the church is the **Parque de la Madre,** with a copy of Renoir's statue of the *Madonna and Child.* Beyond the park is the **Teatro Peón Contreras ★★,** an opulent theater designed by Italian architect Enrico Deserti a century ago. The theater is noted for its Carrara marble staircase and frescoed dome. This is the home of the Orquesta Sinfónica de Yucatán, and national and international performers appear here often; duck inside and check the schedule for performances taking place during your stay. In the southwest corner of the theater, facing the Parque de la Madre, is a **tourist information office.** Across Calle 60 is the main building of the **Universidad de Yucatán.** The Ballet Folklórico performs in its flagstone courtyard on Friday nights.

A block farther north, across from **Iglesia de Santa Lucía** (1575), is **Parque Santa Lucía.** Bordered by an arcade on the north and west sides, this square was where early visitors first alighted from the stagecoach. The small church facing the park was built in 1575 for Maya residents, who weren't allowed to worship in many Mérida temples. The park holds a used-book market on Sundays and hosts popular entertainment several evenings a week, including a performance of Yucatecan dance, music, and folklore on Thursday nights.

Four blocks farther up Calle 60, at Calle 47, is **Parque Santa Ana,** whose modest *mercado* is a local favorite for breakfast *panuchos.* Two blocks to the right, you'll reach the beginning of Paseo de Montejo.

PASEO DE MONTEJO ★★★

The Paseo de Montejo, a broad, tree-lined boulevard modeled after Paris's Champs Elysées, runs north–south starting at Calle 47, 7 blocks north and 2 blocks east of the main square. In the late 19th century, Mérida's upper crust (mostly plantation owners) decided the city needed something grander than its traditional narrow streets lined by wall-to-wall town houses. They built this monumentally proportioned boulevard and lined it with mansions. It came to a halt when the henequén industry went bust, but numerous mansions survive—some in private hands, others as offices, restaurants, or hotels. Today this is the fashionable part of town, home to restaurants, trendy dance clubs, and upscale hotels.

Museo Regional de Antropología ★★ MUSEUM   Of the surviving mansions, the most notable is the Palacio Cantón, a Beaux Arts confection that houses the Regional Anthropology Museum, Mérida's most impressive museum. Enrico Deserti, the architect of the Teatro Peón Contreras, designed and built this between 1909 and 1911, during the last years of the Porfiriato. It was the home of Gen. Francisco Cantón Rosado, who enjoyed his palace for only 6 years before his death. For a time, the mansion served as the governor's official residence.

A visit to the museum offers the irony of one of Mérida's most extravagant examples of European architecture housing a tribute to the ancient civilization the Europeans did their best to extinguish. The exhibition of pre-Columbian cultures covers the Yucatán's cosmology, history, and culture, with a special focus on the inhabitants' daily life. Displays illustrate such strange Maya customs as tying boards to babies' heads to create the oblong shape that they considered beautiful, and filing or perforating teeth to inset jewels. Drawings and enlarged photos of several archaeological sites illustrate various styles of Maya dwellings. Captions for the permanent displays are mostly in Spanish, but it's a worthwhile stop even if you barely know the language, just for the background it provides for explorations of Maya sites.

Paseo de Montejo (at Calle 43). ℰ **999/923-0557.** Tues–Sun 8am–5pm. 46 pesos.

OUTLYING ATTRACTIONS

Mérida is surrounded by archaeological sites, natural attractions, haciendas, and villages that can be either a day trip or a part of a longer trip to other parts of Yucatán; these are covered in "Side Trips from Mérida" (p. 253). The destinations below are most often visited from a home base in Mérida.

Dzibilchaltún ★ RUINS   This small archaeological site, 14km (8⅔ miles) north of Mérida, was founded about 500 B.C. It flourished around A.D. 750 and began its decline long before the conquistadors arrived. Since their discovery in 1941, more than 8,000 buildings have been mapped, but only about a half-dozen have been excavated. The site covers almost 15 sq. km (5¾ sq. miles); of greatest interest are the buildings surrounding two plazas next to the cenote and a third connected by a *sacbé* (causeway). At least 25 stelae have been found in Dzibilchaltún, which means "place of the stone writing."

The ruins of Dzibilchaltún.

Start with the **Museo del Pueblo Maya** (it was closed in early 2010 for repairs and renovation but should be open by the time you read this), which exhibits artifacts from sites around the Yucatán and provides fairly thorough bilingual explanations. Displays include a beautiful plumed serpent from Chichén Itzá and a finely designed incense vessel from Palenque. The museum moves on to artifacts specifically at Dzibilchaltún, including the curious dolls that gave the site's main attraction its name. Another exhibit covers Maya culture through history, including a collection of *huipiles,* the embroidered dresses worn by Maya women. From here, a door leads out to the site.

You first encounter the *sacbé.* To the left is the **Temple of the Seven Dolls,** whose doorways and the *sacbé* line up with the rising sun at the spring and autumnal equinoxes. To the right are the buildings grouped around the

Cenote Xlacah, the sacred well, and a complex of buildings around **Structure 38,** the **Central Group** of temples. Yucatán's State Department of Ecology has added nature trails and published a booklet (in Spanish) of birds and plants seen along the mapped trail.

Carretera Mérida-Progreso Km. 16. Tues–Sun 8am–4pm. 144 pesos, including museum. Take Calle 60 out of town and follow signs for Progreso and Hwy. 261. Turn right (east) at the sign for Dzibilchaltún, which also reads UNIVERSIDAD DEL MAYAB; the entrance is 4km (2½ miles) east of the highway. If you don't want to drive, take one of the *colectivos* lined up at Parque San Juan.

Hacienda Sotuta de Peón ★★ HISTORIC SITE   It's hard to pass an elegantly decaying hacienda on Yucatán's back roads without wondering what it was really like to live there during the henequén boom days. Naturally, we envision ourselves the owners, not as the Maya laborers who wrangled the stiff, thorny agave plants. At this living museum, 30 minutes south of Mérida on the Convent Route, you'll see hacienda life of a century ago from both sides. The owner didn't just restore the buildings, he put the entire hacienda into working order and is now turning out 10 to 15 tons of henequén per month.

You can arrange a tour from any of Mérida's hotels; if you plan to drive yourself, be sure to get precise directions. You'll start with a tour of the beautiful, tile-festooned main house, visit the henequén fields via mule-drawn "trucks," or carts on rails, see harvesting and processing at the *casa de máquinas*, and learn how to spin the fiber into twine. You'll also learn about the culture surrounding henequén production, visiting one of the workers in his traditional Maya home. Bring your bathing suit for a swim in the **Dzul Ha cenote** on the property. You can also sample fine Yucatecan cooking in the restaurant on the premises. As of this writing, construction of several rental cabanas was under way.

Municipio de Tecoh. www.sotutadepeon.com. ✆ **999/941-8639.** 330 pesos; 165 pesos children 4–12 (under 4 free). Transportation from Merida 200 pesos adults/100 pesos children extra. Tour packages combine entrance fee, transportation, and a meal for 700 pesos. Open daily; tours at 10am and 1pm.

Ecotours & Adventure Trips

The Yucatán Peninsula has many companies that organize nature and adventure tours. Any hotel can arrange a tour, but if you want to go with a known quantity, there are several I can recommend. One well-established outfit with a great track record is **Ecoturismo Yucatán,** Calle 3 no. 235 (btw. calles 32A and 34), Col. Pensiones (www.ecoyuc.com; ✆ **999/920-2772**). Alfonso and Roberta Escobedo create itineraries to meet your special or general interest in the Yucatán or southern Mexico. Alfonso has been creating adventure and nature tours for more than a dozen years. Specialties include archaeology, birding, natural history, and kayaking. The company also offers day trips that explore contemporary Maya culture and life in villages in the Yucatán. Package and customized tours are available.

Mayan Ecotours, Calle 80 no. 561 × 13-1, Col. Pensiones 6a Etapa (www.mayanecotours.com; ✆ **999/987-3710**), also comes highly recommended. The young company specializes in low-impact visits to unspoiled natural areas and pueblos absent from tourist maps. A new Mayan Life tour combines swimming in a cenote, weaving jipijapa (palm leaves that Panama hats are made of) the traditional way—in a cave—and a home cooking lesson in a Maya village. Custom tours are also available.

Mayan Heritage Tours, Calle 79 No. 518 (btw. calles 64 and 64A, Colonia Centro; www.mayanheritage.com.mx; © 999/924-8283), offers a wide range of cultural, nature, adventure, and history tours, ranging from Chichén Itzá, Uxmal, Celestún, and other big attractions to lesser known excursions to Maya towns, the caves in Becal, Campeche, where Panama hats are woven, and the mangrove swamps of Celestún. Circuits of several days and basic transportation services are also available.

William Lawson's Yucatán Excursions (http://lawsonsdriving.blogspot.com; lawson_william@hotmail.com) focuses on getting visitors to places most tourists never hear about—secret cenotes, small towns, ruins still shrouded in jungle vegetation, and unrestored haciendas—delivered with a highly amusing commentary loaded with insight. Run by a Canadian who has spent the past 20 years in the Yucatán, the company has several set itineraries but specializes in personalized excursions.

For a personal guided tour around Mérida or as far away as Calakmul (and points beyond—just ask), call **Dan Griffin** (p. 212), who also has a passion for introducing tourists to the unknown Yucatán. He knows dozens of ruins and nearly as many old haciendas awaiting a fairy godmother, and he'll not only take you to see them but introduce you to the people who live in the nearby villages.

Where to Eat

Downtown Mérida is well endowed with a growing number of good midrange and budget restaurants, including a remarkable number of Middle Eastern restaurants; a large influx of Lebanese immigrants around 1900 exerted such a strong impact on Meridanos' eating habits that kibbe (a concoction of bulgur, minced meat, and spices that can take many forms) is regarded almost the way the U.S. thinks of pizza. The best upscale restaurants are in outlying districts; for something special, treat yourself to a meal at **Hacienda Xcanatún** (p. 252), whose French-trained chef excels at a fusion of French, Caribbean, and Yucatecan dishes. And for the ultimate indulgence in native Yucatecan food, don't miss **Ki'Xocolatl** (p. 244), a cafe in the heart of the centro that has revived Maya chocolate-making traditions.

Cochinita pibil **(pit-baked pork), a Yucatecan specialty.**

Centro
EXPENSIVE
Alberto's Continental LEBANESE/ YUCATECAN There's nothing quite like dining here at night in a softly lit room or on the wonderful old patio framed in Moorish arches. Elegant *mudejar*-patterned tile floors, simple furniture, and a gurgling fountain create a romantic mood, though prices are

on the expensive side. For supper, you can choose a sampler plate of four Lebanese favorites, or traditional Yucatecan specialties, such as *pollo pibil* or fish Celestún (bass stuffed with shrimp), and finish with Turkish coffee.

Calle 64 no. 482 (at Calle 57). ✆ **999/928-5367.** Reservations recommended. Main courses 80–220 pesos. AE, MC, V. Daily 1–11pm.

Casa de Frida ★ MEXICAN   This colorful restaurant serves fresh, healthful classics such as *mole poblano* and an interesting *flan de berenjena*, a kind of eggplant timbale. The classic *chiles en nogada*, a Mexican classic, is hard to find on menus, perhaps because it is a delicate and time-consuming dish. Here, it is the house specialty. This is a comfortable, no-nonsense place with raspberry pink walls and peacock blue trim, a la Frida. The menu's breadth will satisfy any appetite.

Calle 61 no. 526 (at Calle 66). ✆ **999/928-2311.** Reservations recommended. Main courses 100–130 pesos. No credit cards. Mon–Fri 6–10pm; Sat noon–5pm and 6–10pm; Sun noon–5pm.

El Pórtico del Peregrino ♕ INTERNATIONAL   The *berenjenas al horno* here—layers of eggplant, chicken, and cheese baked in tomato sauce—is kind of a hybrid of lasagna and moussaka that seems to personify Mérida's Italian and Lebanese influences, and it is just as delectable as it was when I first had it 10 years ago. And the small, vine-covered patio is one of the sweetest dining areas in Mérida. The higher-priced meat and fish dishes, though—even the Yucatecan specialties—no longer seem to hit the heights they should in order to compete with newer restaurants that now challenge one of Mérida's first upscale restaurants.

Calle 57 no. 501 (btw. calles 60 and 62). ✆ **999/928-6163.** Main courses 70–175 pesos. AE, MC, V. Daily noon–midnight.

Rescoldos Mediterranean Bistro ★★ GREEK/ITALIAN   You won't find a better pizza or calzone than the ones that come out of the traditional wood-fired ovens at this Canadian-run Mediterranean bistro. Even so, it's hard to pass up the specials, which might be sun-dried tomato, basil, and ricotta ravioli, roasted tomato and watermelon soup, or Greek pastitsio made with turkey. I had a falafel piadine that I was still remembering fondly several days later. The outdoor tables are tucked under tall trees augmented by potted palms, with a wall fountain in an alcove whose burbling is so refreshing that you feel like you're ready to take on the entire menu.

Calle 62 No. 366, btw. calles 41 and 43. www.rescoldosbistro.com. ✆ **999/286-1028.** Main courses 60–90 pesos. Paninis, calzones, pizzas 90–100 pesos, entrees 110–120 pesos. Cash only. Tues–Thurs 6–10pm; Fri–Sat 6–11pm.

MODERATE

Amaro VEGETARIAN/YUCATECAN   This peaceful courtyard restaurant, with its walls providing gallery space for local art, lists some interesting vegetarian dishes, such as *crema de calabacitas* (cream of squash soup), apple salad, and avocado pizza. It also offers a few fish and chicken dishes; you might want to try the Yucatecan chicken. The *agua de chaya* (*chaya* is a spinachlike vegetable that has sustained the Maya through the centuries) is refreshing on a hot afternoon. All desserts are made in-house.

Calle 59 no. 507 Interior 6 (btw. calles 60 and 62). ✆ **999/928-2451.** Main courses 50–90 pesos. MC, V. Daily 11am–2am.

La Chaya Maya ★★ YUCATECAN   Ladies in traditional Maya garb slap tortillas onto the grill in an open space in the dining room of this spotless, comfortable restaurant devoted to Yucatecan cooking made with ultrafresh ingredients. I can't imagine skipping the cream of *chaya*. You'll find traditional dishes that rarely grace restaurant menus, such as *mucbil pollo* (chicken tamale casserole), traditionally served for Day of the Dead, and *sikil p'aak,* an earthy paste of ground squash seeds, tomatoes, and chiles served with the complimentary chips. The friendly, professional staff does a better job than most with large groups, too. Be prepared to wait for a table.

Calle 57 no. 481 (at Calle 62). ✆ **999/928-4780.** Main courses 60–90 pesos. Cash only. Daily 7am–11pm.

Restaurante Los Almendros YUCATECAN   As the first place to offer tourists such Yucatecan specialties as *salbutes, panuchos* and *papadzules, cochinita pibil,* and *poc chuc,* this place is an institution. That doesn't mean it produces the best of these dishes, but the food is good and reliable. Photographs on the menu make it a good place to try Yucatecan food for the first time. It's 5 blocks east of Calle 60, facing the Parque de la Mejorada. A newer branch in the Fiesta Americana hotel has better service.

Calle 50A no. 493 at Calle 57. ✆ **999/928-5459.** Reservations recommended Sun. Main courses 60–100 pesos. AE, MC, V. Daily 10am–11pm.

INEXPENSIVE

Café Alameda MIDDLE EASTERN/VEGETARIAN   This simple and informal place (metal tables, plastic chairs) is a good place to catch a light meal. The trick is figuring out the Spanish names for popular Middle Eastern dishes. Kibbe is *quebbe bola* (not *quebbe cruda*), hummus is *garbanza,* and shish kabob is *alambre.* I leave it to you to figure out what a spinach pie is called (and it's excellent). Café Alameda is a treat for vegetarians, and the umbrella-shaded tables on the patio are perfect for morning coffee and *mamules* (walnut-filled pastries).

Calle 58 no. 474 (btw. calles 55 and 57). ✆ **999/928-3635.** Main courses 22–58 pesos. No credit cards. Daily 8am–5pm.

Eladio's ★ YUCATECAN   Locals have come to this open-air restaurant since 1952 to relax, drink very cold beer, and snack on Yucatecan specialties. Five of these restaurants are now scattered about the city; this one is the closest to the historic center. You can order a beer and enjoy *una botana* (a small portion that accompanies a drink—in this case, usually a Yucatecan dish), or order from the menu. *Cochinita, poc chuc,* and *relleno negro* (turkey flavored with burnt chiles) are all good. The restaurant is 3 blocks east of Parque de la Mejorada.

Calle 59 (at Calle 44). ✆ **999/923-1087.** Main courses 40–85 pesos. AE, MC, V. Daily noon–9pm.

La Flor de Santiago YUCATECAN   This is an old-world, atmospheric place with a loyal clientele. The dining area is classic—fans spinning under a high ceiling, dark wood furniture, and a wall lined by bakery cases for fresh treats from a wood-fired stove. The service, though friendly, can be classically slow. It's especially popular for breakfast, but I like to stop in on the way to the weekly big-band dancing in Parque Santiago across the street.

Calle 70 no. 478 (btw. calles 57 and 59). ☏ **999/928-5591.** *Comida corrida* 40 pesos; main courses 40–75 pesos. No credit cards. Daily 7am–11pm.

Paseo de Montejo

EXPENSIVE

Hennessy's Irish Pub ★★★ INTERNATIONAL   Irish food and drink isn't the first thing on your mind in Mexico, but this Irish gastro-pub has consistently packed them in from noon until the wee hours every day since opening New Year's Eve 2010. It's probably appropriate that a traditional dark wood, sparkly bottle Irish pub ensconced in a Spanish colonial building with 20-foot ceilings mixes up fish and chips and shepherd's pie with killer curry, pasta, and chicken breast marinated with Guiness and anise. At least 15 types of Irish whiskey jockey for attention with 200 bottles of other well-known spirits behind the 40-foot bar. You won't be bored here.

Paseo de Montejo btw. calles 41 and 43. www.hennessysirishpub.com. ☏ **999/923-8993.** Main courses 95–220 pesos. MC, V. Daily noon–2am.

INEXPENSIVE

Wayan'e ★★★ MEXICAN   The couple who own Wayan'e seem to be permanent fixtures behind the counter of their little storefront taco stand, chatting with customers and overseeing about 10 staffers who slice and dice and squeeze (fresh *aguas de frutas*). Some 20-odd fillings, from eggs (preferably scrambled with *chaya*) and cactus to tripe and pork loin in smoky chipotle sauce find their way into tacos or tortas (sandwiches on a French roll with cheese). Locals are crowded in by 9am, but gringos unaccustomed to heavy carnivorous breakfasts might want to wait for lunch. Don't wait too long, though: Food is cooked fresh every morning, and doors close when the food runs out, usually around 2pm.

Felipe Carrillo Puerto 11A No. 57C at Calle 4, Col. Itzimná. ☏ **999/938-0676.** 4 tacos for about $5. No credit cards. Mon–Sat 8am–2 or 3pm.

Outlying Districts

EXPENSIVE

Hacienda Teya ★★ YUCATECAN   Widely considered the final word on traditional Yucatecan cooking—right down to being served on stone platters—Hacienda Teya is also one of those gorgeous restored haciendas that makes you wish you were a wealthy Meridano in the 1800s. Once you're sated on *sopa de lima*, *cochinita pibíl*, lomitos de Valladolid, or the unusual specialty, Carne Ahumada Teya (smoked pork), you can walk it off in the surrounding orchards and botanical gardens. If you just can't bear to leave, you can see if one of the six stately suites is available.

Km. 12.5 Carretera Mérida-Cancún. www.haciendateya.com. ☏ **999/988-0800.** Main courses 130–220 pesos. MC, V. Daily noon–6pm.

MODERATE

El Príncipe Tutul Xiú ★★ 🍴 YUCATECAN   Authentic Yucatecan specialties from a limited menu are served here in a Yucatecan village atmosphere by staff in traditional Maya dress. The owner of the original restaurant in the town of Maní opened this location in response to persistent pressure from Meridanos. This is a great place to try the famous *sopa de lima* and one of the six typical main courses, such as *pavo escabeche,* served with great handmade tortillas. Meat is cooked over a charcoal grill. It's a short taxi ride from downtown, and to return you can pick up a local bus that passes by the restaurant. Calle 123 no. 216 (btw. calles 46 and 46b), Colonia Serapio Rendón. © **999/929-7721.** Main courses 58 pesos. MC, V. Daily 11am–7pm.

Shopping

Mérida is known for hammocks, *guayaberas* (lightweight men's shirts worn untucked), and Panama hats. Local baskets and pottery are sold in the central market. Mérida is also the place to pick up prepared adobo, a pastelike mixture of ground achiote seeds (annatto), oregano, garlic, and other spices used as a marinade for such dishes as *cochinita pibil* (pit-baked pork).

A vendor selling balloons in Mérida.

Hordes of people come to Mérida's bustling **market district,** a few blocks southeast of the Plaza Grande, to shop and work. It is by far the most crowded part of town, although new construction and an underground garage have alleviated things a bit. Behind the former post office (at calles 65 and 56, now the city museum), the oldest part of the market is the **Portal de Granos** (Grains Arcade), a row of maroon arches where grain merchants once sold their goods. Just east, between calles 56 and 54, is the market building, **Mercado Lucas de Gálvez.** The city built a new municipal market on the south side of this building, but has had difficulty persuading the market vendors to move. When they do, the city plans to tear down the Lucas de Gálvez and replace it with a plaza. If you can abide the chaos, you can find anything inside from fresh fish and flowers to leather and other locally made goods. A secondary market is on Calle 56, labeled **Bazaar de Artesanías** (crafts market) in big letters. Still another crafts market, **Bazaar García Rejón,** lies a block west of the main market on Calle 65 between calles 58 and 60.

BOOKS

Amate Books ★★ Browse the extensive selection of English titles on Mexican and Latin American art, architecture, anthropology, history, and literature in a serene, library-like atmosphere. Hours are Monday through Saturday 10am to 6pm. Calle 60 453A (btw. calles 51 and 49). © 999/924-2222.

Librería Dante Here, a half-block from the plaza, you'll find a small selection of English-language books on Mexico history and culture. Hours are 8am to 9:30pm Monday through Saturday, 10am to 6pm Sunday. Calle 59 (btw. calles 60 and 62). © 999/928-3674.

Librería-Papelería Burrel This is the place to go for maps; if you'll be driving through the region, stop by to lay in a supply. Hours are Monday through Saturday 8am to 9:30pm, Sunday 10am to 6pm. Calle 59 No. 502 (btw. calles 60 and 62). www.burrel.com.mx. ✆ 999/928-3674.

CHOCOLATE

The Maya's original cacao is Criollo chocolate, now making up only 5% of the chocolate market. Grown almost entirely in Tabasco and Chiapas, this rarest of chocolates is still prized for its delicate, complex taste.

Ki'Xocolatl ★★★ Expat Belgian chocolate makers went back to the roots of their craft, working only with certified organic Criollo chocolate. Disguised as a cafe in the heart of the centro, it's nothing less than a journey into Maya chocolate traditions, beginning with a display of chocolate-making tools. The runaway standout is the fresh dark semi-sweet chocolate bar with red pepper and spices; dark semi-sweet chocolate bars, milk chocolate bars with crisp cocoa nuggets, chocolate-covered coffee beans, and table chocolate (solid tablets the size of a hockey puck, often combined with sugar, vanilla, cinnamon, and other spices) are also available. While you're deciding, indulge in the cafe's hot or cold chocolate, coffee, milkshakes, and all manner of sinful deserts. Hours are Monday through Saturday 9am to 2:30pm and 4:30 to 11pm, Sunday 9am to 6pm. Calle 55 no. 513 (btw. calles 60 and 62). www.ki-xocolatl.com. ✆ **999/920-5869.**

CRAFTS

Pretty much anything made in the Yucatán (and in many other parts of Mexico) go through Mérida, the Peninsula's marketplace. If you'll be here on your trip, save your pesos and do your shopping here. Quality is high, and prices are low.

Alma Mexicana ★★ This extraordinary shop, sharing a house with a two-room B&B, claims to have the most complete folk art collection in the state of Yucatán, and I know of no reason to dispute that. Whether your taste runs to Day of the Dead skeletons or saints and angels, hand-blown glass or Frida Kahlo art, there's sure to be something you can't resist. Visitors with gourmet leanings will find organic Mexican coffee, honey from the native stingless bees, natural vanilla, and copper pot racks, tiles, and sinks. Hours are Monday to Saturday 9:30am to 7pm and Sunday 11am to 3:30pm. Calle 54 no. 476 (btw. calles 55 and 57). www.folkart-mexico.com. ✆ 999/286-7316.

Casa de las Artesanías ★★ This state-run store, occupying the front of a restored monastery, sells a wide selection of crafts, 90% of which come from the Yucatán. The quality of work is higher than elsewhere, as are the prices. The monastery's back courtyard is used as a gallery, with rotating exhibits on folk and fine arts. Make this your first stop to get a benchmark for quality and prices. It's open Monday to Saturday 10am to 8pm, Sunday 10am to 2pm. Calle 63 no. 513 (btw. calles 64 and 66). ✆ **999/928-6676.**

Miniaturas This fun little store is packed to the rafters with miniatures, a traditional Mexican folk art form that has evolved into social and political satire, pop art, and bawdy humor. The owner collects these hand-crafted items from around Mexico and offers plenty of variety, from traditional figures such as doll-house furniture, Day of the Dead figures, and *arboles de vida* (trees of life), to popular cartoon characters and old movie posters. Hours are Monday to Saturday 10am to 8pm. Calle 59 no. 507A-4 (btw. calles 60 and 62). ✆ **999/928-6503.**

GUAYABERAS

Instead of sweltering in business suits in Mérida, businessmen, bankers, and bus drivers alike wear the *guayabera,* a loose-fitting shirt decorated with pin tucks, pockets, and sometimes embroidery, worn over the pants rather than tucked in. Mérida is famous as the best place to buy *guayaberas,* which can go for less than 150 pesos at the market or for more than 650 pesos custom-made; a linen *guayabera* can cost about 800 pesos. Most are cotton, although linen is also popular. Stay away from the less expensive polyester versions; they don't breathe, defeating the purpose of staying cool. The traditional color is white.

Most shops display ready-to-wear shirts in several price ranges. *Guayabera* makers strive to outdo one another with their own updated versions of the shirt. A few things to keep in mind: When Yucatecans say *seda,* they mean polyester; *lino* is linen or a linen/polyester combination. Look closely at the stitching and the way the tucks line up over the pockets; with *guayaberas,* details are everything.

Guayaberas Jack   The craftsmanship is good, the place has a reputation to maintain, and some of the salespeople speak English. Prices are as marked. This will give you a good basis of comparison if you want to hunt for a bargain elsewhere. If the staff does not have the style and color of shirt you want, they will make it for you in within hours. This shop also sells regular shirts and women's blouses. Hours are Monday to Saturday 10am to 8pm, Sunday 10am to 2pm. Calle 59 no. 507A (btw. calles 60 and 62). ✆ **999/928-6002.**

HAMMOCKS

Natives across tropical America used hammocks long before Europeans reached the New World, and they are still used throughout Latin America. None are as comfortable as the traditional Yucatecan hammock, woven with cotton string in a fine mesh. While we might think of a hammock as garden furniture to laze in for an hour or two, they are beds for most Yucatecans, who generally eschew mattresses. Hotels that cater to Yucatecans always provide hammock hooks in the walls because many guests travel with their own.

A good shop will gladly hang a hammock for you to test-drive. Look to see that there are no untied strings. The woven part should be cotton, it should be made with fine string, and the strings should be so numerous that when you get in it and stretch out diagonally (as you're meant to sleep in them), the gaps between the strings remain small. Don't pay attention to descriptions of a hammock's size; they have become practically meaningless. Good hammocks don't cost a lot of money (250–350 pesos), but be prepared to pay as much as 1,000 pesos and up for superior hammocks made with *hilo de crochet,* a fine crochet thread.

You can also see what street vendors are offering, but you have to know what to look for, or they are likely to take advantage of you.

Hamacas El Aguacate   El Aguacate, 6 blocks from the main square, sells hammocks wholesale and retail. It has the greatest variety and is the place to go for a really fancy or extra-large hammock. A good choice is the no. 6 in cotton; it runs around 340 pesos. The store is open Monday to Friday 8:30am to 7:30pm, Saturday 8am to 5pm. Calle 58 no. 604 (at Calle 73). ✆ **999/923-0152.**

Tejidos y Cordeles Nacionales   This place near the municipal market sells only cotton hammocks, priced by weight—a pretty good practice because hammock lengths are fairly standardized. The prices are better than at El Aguacate, but quality control isn't as good. My idea of a good hammock is one that weighs about 1.5kg (3⅓ lb.) and runs about 270 pesos. Calle 56 no. 516-B (btw. calles 63 and 65). © **999/928-5561.**

PANAMA HATS

Another useful and popular item is this soft, pliable hat made from the fibers of the jipijapa palm in several towns south of Mérida along Hwy. 180, especially Becal, in the neighboring state of Campeche. Hat makers in these towns work inside caves so that the moist air keeps the palm fibers pliant.

Jipi hats come in various grades determined by the pliability, softness, and fineness of the fibers and closeness of the weave. A fine weave gives the hat more body and helps it to retain its shape. Panama hats are sold in most craft shops along Calle 60, but you'll find better selections and prices with the specialists in the main market and neighboring streets.

El Sombrero Popular   This friendly little shop opposite the market is piled high with handmade panamas in all kinds of styles and sizes. Calle 65 Depto. 18 (btw. calles 58 and 60).

Entertainment & Nightlife

You could spend a week in Mérida and never run out of free, city-sponsored nighttime entertainment (see "Festivals & Events in Mérida," p. 231). But unregenerate night owls also have a rich array of bars, sidewalk cafes, dance venues, and theaters to choose from. Things don't get hopping until at least 10pm here.

Teatro Peón Contreras, Calle 60 at Calle 57, and **Teatro Daniel Ayala,** Calle 60 at Calle 61, host a wide range of performing artists from Mexico and around the world; check to see what's scheduled during your stay. **El Nuevo Olimpo,** on the main square, schedules frequent concerts, and **Teatro Armando Manzanero,** a half-block north of the Olimpo, has two screens showing classic and art films, and one live stage. On Thursday through Saturday night, the Santiago neighborhood's **LA68 Cultural Center** (Calle 68 btw. 55 and 57) hosts open-air movies and dinner at 9pm.

Mérida's club scene offers everything from ubiquitous rock/dance music to some one-of-a-kind spots. **Ay Caray,** Calle 60 btw. calles 55 and 57, is an upstairs bar popular with a young, noise-loving crowd. In the same building, **El Nuevo Tucho,** a cabaret with live salsa, and **Azul Picante,** a salsa club, are other places where you can dance the night away. But for hard-core salsa, join the locals at **Mambo Café** in the Plaza las Américas shopping center, where touring Dominicana and Cuban bands often perform. Young locals and tourists mix it up at the revolutionary-themed (think waiters in sombreros and bandoliers) **Pancho's** (Calle 59 No. 502, btw. calles 60 and 62), where live salsa and English pop keep the tiny dance floor hopping.

Nightlife along trendy Paseo de Montejo takes on a different tone. The all-white, ever-so-cool **El Cielo Lounge,** Prolongación Montejo and Calle 25, Col. Campestre (www.elcielobar.com), open Thursday through Saturday, might be your style if you're accustomed to enjoying eclectic music with beautiful people. The Rosas y Xocolate hotel's rooftop **Moon Lounge,** Paseo de Montejo at Calle 41, a relative newcomer, has garnered a loyal, upscale following for cocktails enhanced by a sparkly view of both the night sky and the Paseo de Montejo. Three bar-restaurants—**Slavia, Cubaro,** and **Tobago**—on Prolongación Montejo across from the massive Monumento a la Patria, are magnets for martini aficionados.

Where to Stay

Mérida soothes the budget, especially if you've come from the Caribbean resorts. Though winter is the most popular time, the stream of visitors is steadier than on the coast, so high- and low-season rate fluctuations are less pronounced. Reservations are a good idea during the two high seasons: July and August, when Mexicans take their vacations, and between November 15 (or sometimes later) and Easter Sunday, when winter-weary Canadians and Americans flock to the Yucatán.

Most hotels in Mérida offer at least a few air-conditioned rooms, and some also have pools. But many inexpensive places have hard beds or a bottom sheet too small to stay tucked in. Prices quoted here include the 17% tax; most hotels include tax in their rates, but always ask to be sure. The best variety of hotels is in and near the Centro, where most of what you'll want to see is within walking distance. The closer you stay to the central plaza, the more subject you are to street noise, so choose your room with that in mind. Hotels along the Paseo de Montejo tend to be more luxurious (and expensive). Outlying areas have some nice, inexpensive hotels and inns, but I don't find it worth the hassle of dealing with transportation. The exception is hacienda hotels on the edge or just outside of the city. Downtown hotels that don't have their own parking lots usually have arrangements with nearby garages, letting you park for a fee. If you can find parking on the street, cars are generally safe from vandalism. Some hotels offer free parking, but sometimes it's free only at night, with a charge incurred during the day.

CENTRO

Expensive

Casa del Balam ★★ 📷 Mérida's oldest hotel offers colonial grandeur at an easy price. Even with a king-size bed and massive wooden furniture, suites in the original owners' bedrooms of this onetime colonial mansion, converted in 1968, have space enough to do cartwheels. Those overlooking Calle 60 have heavy cedar doors opening onto the street and windows onto the lush courtyard dining room, where piano strains waft up at times. Standard rooms in the newer annex are more pedestrian but comfortable and outfitted with colonial touches such as tile floors and wrought-iron headboards. The plaza is just 2 blocks away, and staff members treat you like their favorite niece or nephew.

Calle 60 no. 488 at Calle 57, 97000 Mérida, Yuc. www.casadelbalam.com. ✆ **800/624-8451** in the U.S. and Canada, or 999/924-8844. 51 units. $86–$117 double; $96–$146 honeymoon; $110–$187 master suite. AE, DISC, MC, V. Free parking. **Amenities:** Restaurant; bar; babysitting; concierge; golf club access; outdoor pool; room service; spa services; Wi-Fi. *In room:* A/C, TV, hair dryer, minibar.

Hotel Marionetas ★ This quiet, attractive B&B, 6 blocks north of the main square, has a comforting feel. Sofi (Macedonian) and Daniel (Argentinean) are engaging, interesting people and attentive innkeepers who have created a lovely space with common areas in front, rooms in back, and a lush garden/pool area in between. Each room is different, but all have handmade tile floors, liberal use of bold but not overbearing color, and large, colonial-style windows and doors.

Calle 49 no. 516 (btw. calles 62 and 64), 97000 Mérida, Yuc. www.hotelmarionetas.com. ✆ **999/928-3377.** 8 units. High season $95 double; $140 junior suite; low season $85 double, $100 junior suite. Rates include continental breakfast. MC, V. Free secure parking for compact cars. No children under 10. **Amenities:** Small outdoor pool. *In room:* A/C, TV, phone, fridge, hair dryer, Wi-Fi.

Moderate

Casa Santiago ★★★   This B&B's four recently remodeled guest rooms open off the wide central corridor of a lovely colonial home that offers an ideal blend of comfort and privacy, traditional detail and modern style. Casa Santiago is part of a compound that includes Casa Feliz, whose two large, newly restored rooms are available individually when the entire house isn't rented, and Casa Navidad, with one more guest room. Each has its own distinct theme, but all have the original *mosaico* tile floors (made in Mérida for centuries with a technology brought over from Spain), handmade furniture, and some of the most comfortable mattresses in Mexico. Its Parque Santiago neighborhood is 5 easy blocks from the main plaza.

Calle 63 no. 562 (btw. calles 70 and 72), 97000 Mérida, Yuc. www.casasantiago.net. ℂ **314/266-1888** in the U.S. and Canada, or 999/997-4058. 7 units. $64–$125 double. Rates include full breakfast. No credit cards (PayPal for deposits). Limited free parking. No children 13 and under. **Amenities:** Common kitchen; phone for local calls; 2 outdoor pools. *In room:* A/C, Wi-Fi.

Hotel Maison Lafitte ★   This three-story hotel has modern, attractive rooms in muted Caribbean colors and tropical touches such as wooden window louvers. Rooms are medium to large, with midsize bathrooms that have great showers and good lighting. Most come with either two doubles or a king-size bed. Rooms are quiet and overlook a pretty little garden with a fountain, though a few don't have windows—check before you book. The location is excellent.

Calle 60 no. 472 (btw. calles 53 and 55), 97000 Mérida, Yuc. www.maisonlafitte.com.mx. ℂ **999/928-1243**. Fax 999/923-9159. 30 units. $80 double. Rates include full breakfast. AE, MC, V. Free limited secure parking for compact cars. **Amenities:** Restaurant; bar; small outdoor pool; room service. *In room:* A/C, TV, hair dryer, minibar, Wi-Fi.

Hotel MedioMundo ★ 📷   Bright colors and lush gardens distinguish this quiet courtyard hotel, 3 blocks north of the main plaza. The simple, beautiful rooms have their original tile floors. The English-speaking owners, Nicole and Nelson, have invested their money in the right places, going for pillow-top mattresses, good lighting, quiet air-conditioning, lots of space, and good bathrooms with strong showers. What they didn't invest in were TVs, which adds to the serenity. The eight rooms with air-conditioning cost $10 more, but all units have windows with good screens and get ample ventilation. A generous breakfast is served in one of the two attractive courtyards.

Calle 55 no. 533 (btw. calles 64 and 66), 97000 Mérida, Yuc. www.hotelmediomundo.com. ℂ/fax **999/924-5472**. 12 units. High season, $75–$90 double; low season, $70–$85. MC, V. Limited street parking. No children 7 and under. **Amenities:** Small outdoor pool; Wi-Fi (in public areas). *In room:* A/C (in some), no phone.

Luz en Yucatán ★★★ ✒   Behind a deceptively plain wall next to Santa Lucia Church, this inn offers a dizzying variety of rooms, suites, studios, and apartments in the main building (rumored to have been Santa Lucia's convent) and tucked into the garden around the pool. Every unit is different, thoughtfully decorated with Mexican arts and crafts, and the place is full of nooks and crannies for visiting or lounging. A large kitchen and dining room that seats 10 at a beautiful wooden table are available for guests in rooms without kitchens. The

haciendas & HOTELS

During the colonial period, **haciendas** in the Yucatán were isolated, self-sufficient fiefdoms. Mostly they produced foodstuffs—enough for the needs of the owners and peasants, plus a little extra that the owners could sell for a small sum in the city. The owners, though sometimes politically powerful, were never rich.

This changed in the 19th century, when the expanding world market created high demand for henequén—more commonly known in the U.S. as sisal—an agave cactus fiber that was used to bale hay. Haciendas shifted to henequén production en masse, and the owners became wealthy as prices and profits climbed through the end of the century and into the 20th. Then came the bust. Throughout the 1920s, prices and demand fell, and no other commodity could replace sisal. The haciendas entered a long decline, but by then, henequén cultivation and processing had become part of local culture.

Visiting a hacienda is a way to see and understand what the golden age was like. **Sotuta de Peón** (p. 238) has been refurbished and operates much as in the old days—a living museum involving an entire community. At another, **Yaxcopoil** (p. 259), you can wander about the shell of a once-bustling estate and take in the faded splendor.

Today another boom of sorts has brought haciendas back, this time as hotels, retreats, and country residences. The hotels convey an air of the past—elegant gateways, thick walls, open arches, and high ceilings—with extravagant suites and personal service.

Six of the region's hacienda hotels are pure luxury. The most opulent is **Hacienda Xcanatún ★★★** (p. 252) on the outskirts of Mérida, off the highway to Progreso.

Four more luxury hotels are owned by Roberto Hernández, one of Mexico's richest men, and are affiliated with Starwood Hotels (www.luxurycollection.com; ☏ **800/325-3589** in the U.S. and Canada). They are restored to their original condition, and are quite beautiful. **Temozón** (p. 252), off the highway to Uxmal, is the most magnificent. **Uayamón ★★★**, located between the colonial city of Campeche and the ruins of Edzná, is perhaps the most romantic, with its exterior preserved in a state of arrested decay. **Hacienda San José Cholul ★** is east of Mérida toward Izamal, and picturesque **Santa Rosa** lies southwest of Mérida, near the town of Maxcanú. Packages are available for staying at more than one of these haciendas. All offer personal service, activities, and spas.

Another luxury hotel, **Hacienda Misné ★★** (p. 251), is within Mérida city limits and is run by the family who once used it as a summer home.

One of the more affordable options on the eastern outskirts of Mérida on the highway to Cancún is **Hacienda San Pedro Nohpat** (p. 252).

Two more haciendas can be leased by small groups for retreats and vacations: **Hacienda Petac** (www.hacienda petac.com; ☏ **800/225-4255** in the U.S., or 999/911-2601) and **Hacienda San Antonio** (www.haciendasanantonio. com.mx; ☏ **999/910-6144**). Both have beautiful rooms, common areas, and grounds.

beds are among the best in Yucatán. The amiable and knowledgeable manager, who lives on-site, delights in taking guests under his wing. The owners recently renovated a 2-bedroom colonial home, less than a block away, that is also available for rent.

Calle 55 no. 499 (btw. calles 60 and 58), 97000 Mérida, Yuc. www.luzenyucatan.com. ©/fax **999/924-0035.** 15 units. $50–$74 double; $64–$69 studio with kitchen; $74–$84 apartment; $84–$94 rooftop terrace room or apartment. Weekly and monthly discounts. No credit cards. Discounted parking in secure lot $5 a day. **Amenities:** Communal kitchen and dining room; outdoor pool; Wi-Fi. *In room:* A/C, TV, fridge.

Inexpensive

Casa Alvarez Guest House ★ ☺ 🎁　Many guests come to this inn, 4 blocks from the plaza, for extended stays with the kind and hospitable Enrique and Miriam Álvarez. Each spacious room in the 19th-century colonial house is different, all featuring light but vivid colors and a variety of wooden, iron, and painted headboards. Larger rooms have air-conditioning and command higher prices. The eat-in kitchen where guests may prepare their own meals is stocked with coffee, tea, spices, and sometimes breakfast food, and invariably becomes a social center. The owners go out of their way to keep children (over 7) happy.

Calle 62 no. 448 at Calle 53, 97000 Mérida, Yuc. www.casaalvarezguesthouse.com. © **999/924-3060.** 8 units. $38–$46. No credit cards. Free parking. **Amenities:** Kitchen for guests' use; pool. *In room:* A/C, ceiling fan, TV, fridge, Wi-Fi.

Hotel Dolores Alba 🍴　Cheerful, comfortable rooms offer respite from a busy and not particularly pleasant street 3½ blocks from the main square. It's a good deal for an inviting swimming pool, good air-conditioning, and free parking. The newer three-story section (with elevator) surrounding the courtyard offers spacious, more stylish rooms with good-size bathrooms. All rooms have windows or balconies looking over the pool. Older rooms are decorated with local crafts and have small bathrooms. Beds tend to be hard. The family that owns the Hotel Dolores Alba outside Chichén Itzá manages this hotel; you can make reservations at one hotel for the other.

Calle 63 no. 464 (btw. calles 52 and 54), 97000 Mérida, Yuc. www.doloresalba.com. © **999/928-5650.** Fax 999/928-3163. 100 units. 600–650 pesos double. MC, V (with 8% surcharge). Free guarded, covered parking. **Amenities:** Restaurant; bar; outdoor pool; room service; Internet service. *In room:* A/C, TV.

PASEO DE MONTEJO

Very Expensive

Rosas y Xocolate ★　Paseo de Montejo claimed a spot of its former grandeur when two long-abandoned mansions emerged after a 3-year transformation into this boutique hotel. Despite the restored antiques, ornate "rugs" created from original and reproduction *mosaico* tiles, and walls restored with a *chukum* resin technique borrowed from ancient Maya architects, the vibe is cool, sleek, and modern, with all the amenities and technology to back it up. A delightful design twist: Double-height ceilings enclosing tubs and showers are open to the sky. The hotel's Chocolate Boutique is overseen by its own Belgian chocolatier, and the spa makes liberal use of the "food of the gods" to invoke its mood-elevating and aphrodisiac properties.

Paseo de Montejo no. 480 at Calle 41, 97000 Mérida, Yuc. www.rosasandxocolate.com. ✆ **999/ 924-2992.** 17 units. $256–$315 double; $417–$774 suite. MC, V. **Amenities:** Restaurant; 2 bars; concierge; library; 2 outdoor pools; room service; spa. *In room:* A/C, TV/DVD, CD player, mini-bar, MP3 docking station, Wi-Fi.

Expensive

Casa San Angel ★ It's hard to guess which draws more people in to this lovely, family-run former converted mansion—the exuberant, largely *trompe l'oeil* jungle that serves as lobby and lounge, or the hotel's own bakery shop, piled high with delectable treats. Colorful guest rooms are roomy and uncluttered but well furnished. The lobby is an appealing place to have dessert and coffee even if you aren't staying here. You can also browse elegant accessories and fine handicrafts from all over Mexico in the hotel's two gift shops. One caveat: The hotel normally is blessedly quiet, but it's right next to the staging ground for *Noche Mexicana* on Saturdays—one of Mérida's free weekly cultural celebrations. The best way around the noise problem is to step outside and join in the fun.

Paseo de Montejo no. 1 at Calle 49, 97000 Mérida, Yuc. www.hotelcasasanangel.com. ✆ **999/ 928-1800.** 15 units. High season $102–$127 double; $161 suite; low season $76–$85 double, $102 suite. Rates include full breakfast. AE, MC, V. Free parking. No children 14 and under. **Amenities:** Restaurant; outdoor pool. *In room:* A/C, filtered water, Wi-Fi.

Fiesta Americana Mérida This six-story hotel on Paseo de Montejo, built in the *fin-de-siècle* style of the old mansions along the boulevard, is the grand dame of Mérida's luxury chain hotels. Guest rooms around the soaring lobby, with its stained-glass ceiling, face outward and have views of one of the avenues. Rooms are comfortable and large, with innocuous modern furnishings and decorations in light, tropical colors. The hotel was built with local materials and at least a nod to Mexican design—infinitely preferable to the cookie-cutter Hyatt across the street, and with more attentive service.

Av. Colón 451, corner of Paseo de Montejo, 92127 Mérida, Yuc. www.fiestaamericana.com.mx. ✆ **877/927-7666** in the U.S. and Canada, or 999/942-1111. Fax 999/942-1112. 350 units. $131 double; $175 executive level; $240 junior suite. AE, MC, PayPal, V. Free secure parking. **Amenities:** 2 restaurants; bar; babysitting; children's programs; concierge; executive-level rooms; health club w/saunas, men's steam room; whirlpool; midsize outdoor pool; room service; tennis court. *In room:* A/C, TV w/pay movies, hair dryer, Internet, minibar.

OUTLYING AREAS

Very Expensive

Hotel Indigo Mérida Hacienda Misné ★★ 🛍 This is a rarity among the region's hacienda hotels: a country estate located just within Mérida's city limits, operated by the family who made it their summer home years before it became a hotel in 2007. It's a beauty, with long red-tiled colonnades stretching along vast gardens peppered with ponds and fountains. The family preserved the hacienda's original character while creating luxurious modern rooms inside. Some even have private sitting pools. It's about a 15-minute drive from downtown, just off Calle 65 (the road to and from Cancún) about a half-kilometer (less than ⅓ mile) from the *periférico*.

Calle 19 no. 172 (at Calle 6B), Fracc. Misné 1, 97173 Mérida, Yuc. www.haciendamisne.com.mx. ✆ **999/940-7150.** Fax 999/940-7160. 50 units. $145–$510 double. See website for promotional rates. AE, DC, DISC, MC, V. Free parking. **Amenities:** Restaurant; bar; concierge; library; 2 outdoor pools; room service; spa. *In room:* A/C, TV, CD player, hair dryer, MP3 player, Wi-Fi.

Hacienda Temozón ★★★ This magnificent 17th-century estancia presides over 37 hectares (91 acres) of subtropical gardens and cenotes, 39km (24 miles) from Mérida. Built in 1655 by Don Diego de Mendoza, Temozón was the region's most productive livestock ranch in the early 18th century, then the top sisal producer in the late 1800s. Meticulously restored in 1997, it's now part of the Starwood luxury collection employing local workers and using organic produce from nearby farms in the restaurant. Spacious Spanish colonial–style rooms have 5.5m (18-ft.) ceilings with exposed rafters, fans, thick whitewashed walls, and Spanish-tile floors and baths. The large, cushy beds are adorned daily with fresh flowers. Suites have tubs, private terraces, and plunge pools. The Casa del Patrón suite has accommodated many global heads of state.

Carretera Mérida–Uxmal, Km 182 Carr. Mérida-Uxmal, 97825 Temozón Sur, Yuc. www.starwood hotels.com/luxury. ✆ **800/325-3589** in the U.S. and Canada, or 999/923-8089. Fax 999/923-7963. 28 units. Doubles from $180; suite from $290. AE, MC, V. **Amenities:** Restaurant; free airport transfers; bikes; concierge; health club; horseback riding; outdoor pool; room service; spa; outdoor tennis court. *In room:* A/C, fan, CD player, Internet, MP3 docking station.

Hacienda Xcanatún ★★★ This magnificent example of the Yucatán's converted haciendas, built in the mid–18th century just outside of present-day Mérida, became one of the region's most important henequén plantations. Restoration with handcrafted local hardwood, wrought iron, marble, and stone has resuscitated its original luster and then some: The capacious bathrooms have double-sized, carved-stone waterfall tubs, and its Casa de Piedra, occupying the old machinery house, is one of Mexico's top-rated restaurants. Fountains and a bridged stream grace the extensive, junglelike gardens, and the spa's ancient Maya healing techniques use local plants and flowers.

Carretera Mérida–Progreso Km 12, Mérida, Yuc. www.xcanatun.com. ✆ **888/883-3633** in the U.S. and Canada, or 999/930-2140. Fax 999/941-0319. 18 units. High season $319 double, $403–$438 suite; low season $302 double, $349–$385 suite. Rates include breakfast. Check website for promotional rates. AE, MC, V. Free parking. No children under 12 without prior arrangement. **Amenities:** Restaurant; 2 bars; concierge; private day-trip program; garden; golf privileges at nearby Jack Nicklaus course; 2 outdoor pools; spa; Wi-Fi on patios, in restaurant, and lobby. *In room:* A/C, hair dryer, minibar, outdoor whirlpool tubs (in suites).

Moderate
Hacienda San Pedro Nohpat ★★ ☺ 🌿 The large, comfortable rooms, vast lawn and gardens, and large pool and hot tub make an ideal retreat in a village just off Hwy. 180, about 1.6km (1 mile) from Mérida's *periférico*. Rooms retain their sometimes grandiose hacienda flourishes but are furnished for contemporary travelers. Four of the rooms opening onto the large, clean swimming pool sleep four to six people and are set up with families in mind, including space for a child's crib. Children love the dogs, cats, burros, and birds that wander the grounds. The outgoing Canadian owner, a font of local knowledge, has become a master at organizing weddings at the picturesque hacienda for half of what hotels and haciendas typically charge.

Chichén Km 8, Mérida, Yuc. www.haciendaholidays.com. ✆ **999/988-0542.** 11 units. $95–$195. Rates include full breakfast. MC, V. **Amenities:** Restaurant; library; outdoor pool. *In room:* A/C, TV/VCR (in some), Jacuzzi (in some).

SIDE TRIPS FROM MÉRIDA

Izamal ★★

80km (50 miles) E of Mérida

Izamal presents one of Mexico's most vivid juxtapositions of three cultures: Ancient pyramids surround one of the largest monasteries the Spanish ever built in Mexico, while contemporary Maya artisans do a brisk trade in their traditional crafts.

The entire city center glows with ochre-yellow paint—the market, all the colonial buildings, and the grandest of all Franciscan buildings in the Yucatán: the massive Franciscan convent of **San Antonio de Padua ★★★**, Izamal's claim to fame. Walking along the colonnades high over the plaza, you know why priests believed they were close to God. The porticoed atrium, reputedly second in size only to the Vatican's, presents a sound-and-light show Monday to Saturday at 8:30pm. Admission is 84 pesos; headphones with English narration cost another 30. Bishop Fray Diego de Landa, who became infamous for his brutal *auto-da-fé* at Maní—burning all the native scripts and later trying to rectify his deed by writing down all he could remember of Maya ways—leveled a pyramid here to build the monastery and church. Inside is a beautifully restored altarpiece and, among many statues, the Nuestra Señora de Izamal, brought from Guatemala in 1652 and still drawing pilgrims every August to climb the staircase on their knees to plead for miracles.

The **Centro Cultural y Artesanal ★★**, in a colonial building across the square from the convent, provides an excellent introduction to Izamal's abundance of handicrafts. A beautiful and highly informative exhibition (20 pesos) displays many examples of crafts produced throughout Mexico. The shop sells top-quality hammocks, clothing, and other work of local artists. The courtyard

Izamal's ochre-colored convent of San Antonio de Padua.

has a spa and a cafe that butt up against another pyramid, the Kabul. Follow up with a self-guided tour of folk art workshops in town. The center no longer provides self-guiding tour maps, but they are available from Macan ché (below). A good way to reach them is by *victoria*, the horse-drawn buggies that serve as taxis here (120 pesos for 45 min.).

Izamal is superimposed over a pre-Hispanic city, and remnants of ancient Maya structures emerge through the layer of contemporary life—forming a retaining wall or the foundation for a church, or as a derelict but recognizable pyramid looming over the town. The largest of the four Maya pyramids enduring in the city center, **Kinich Kakmó,** on Calle 28 at Calle 25 (daily 8am–5pm; free admission), measures 200×80m (656×262 ft.) and is, by many accounts, the Yucatán's largest pre-Hispanic building. Impressing with sheer size rather than fine architecture, it looks like an oddly symmetrical hill, but if you climb the restored stairways on its south face to the temple at the top, you can look down on the lofty convent building and spot leafy mounds on the landscape for miles in every direction—undoubtedly more vestiges of Maya structures. The original city could have tucked the Izamal of today into its pocket.

The easiest way to get to Izamal from Mérida is to take Hwy. 180 toward Cancún. At Hoctún, take the overpass with signs for Izamal via Hwy. 11. Bypass the towns of Kimbila and Citilculm to reach Izamal 24km (15 miles) later.

From Cancún, take Hwy. 180 west toward Mérida. Just before you reach Km 68, turn right at Kantunil and head north, passing through the villages of Xanaba and Sudzal, for 7.7km (4¾ miles) to Izamal.

WHERE TO STAY & EAT

Izamal, which had meager lodging options only a few years ago, seems to be on the upswing. Restaurants are a different story. **Kinich,** Calle 27 (btw. calles 28 and 30), a white-tablecloth restaurant under a *palapa* roof in the middle of town, constantly goes through ups and downs—most recently up, but reliability is not its strong suit. **Los Mestizos,** Calle 33, behind the market, is a better bet, with friendly service and well-executed regional specialties, but it's a bit of a trek—best for starting or ending a day of sightseeing. Fortunately, our hotel picks have excellent restaurants.

Macan ché Bed and Breakfast ★★ ☺ This long-standing favorite in the middle of town offers a varied collection of bungalows, each with its own theme, veiled by junglelike gardens. The property also has two houses suited for families and long-term stays. The four quirky, highly designed rooms—in a new building with its own little garden and fountain at the back of the property—are sublimely comfortable and private. The restaurant's Yucatecan-inspired menu is probably the best in town; every meal is individually prepared, so give the kitchen at least an hour's notice. This is a popular place for retreats and workshops.

Calle 22 no. 305 btw. calles 33 and 35. www.macanche.com. ✆ **988/954-0287.** 17 units. Doubles $45–$65; house $90–$135. Rates include full breakfast. Discounts for long-term stays. MC, V. **Amenities:** Restaurant; bar; pool; yoga workshop space; secure parking; Wi-Fi. Yoga lessons, cooking classes, Spanish and Mayan lessons, massage and tour packages available. *In room:* A/C (in most).

Romantic Hotel Santo Domingo ★★★ ☺ ✦ An Austrian entrepreneur has turned this former ranch into a rural hacienda-style retreat a few steps from the center of town. Attention to detail and some decidedly upscale touches at very reasonable prices make this a top choice. Bright, modern rooms and suites

are set in a tropical garden that will only become lusher as it matures. Options include a small Maya-style cabaña with *palapa* roof and separate shared bathroom for budget travelers (or children staying in their own room), spacious standard rooms, large junior suites, and Casa Maya, a luxurious house with full kitchen that sleeps four. At press time, two more rooms were to be added.

Calle 18 (btw. calles 33 and 35). www.izamalhotel.com. ℂ **988/967-6136.** 9 units. Doubles $39–$95 low season, $50–$110 high, including breakfast. 3-night minimum for Casa Maya. Long-term discounts available. No credit cards. **Amenities:** Restaurant; bar; pool; computer lounge; parking; Wi-Fi (in common areas). Spanish and Mayan classes, massages, excursions available. *In room:* A/C (in all but cabaña); sound system (all but cabaña); TV/DVD player (in some); Wi-Fi (in Casa Maya only).

Celestún National Wildlife Refuge: Flamingos & Other Waterfowl

89km (55 miles) SW of Mérida

On the Gulf Coast west of Mérida, Celestún is the gateway to a wildlife reserve harboring one of North America's only two flamingo breeding colonies (the other is Ría Lagartos, p. 301). The long, shallow estuary, where salty Gulf waters mix with freshwater from about 80 cenotes, is sheltered from the open sea by a skinny strip of land, creating ideal habitat for flamingos and other waterfowl. This *ría* (estuary) is shallow (.3–1m/1–3⅓ ft. deep) and thick with mangroves. You can ride a launch through an open channel just .5km (a third-mile) wide and 50km (31 miles) long to see flamingos dredging the shallows for small crustaceans and favorite insects. You might also see frigate birds, pelicans, spoonbills, egrets, sandpipers, and other waterfowl. At least 15 duck species have been counted. Nonbreeding flamingos remain year-round; breeding birds take off around April to nest in Ría Lagartos, returning to Celestún in October.

Flamingos flock to Celestún National Wildlife Refuge.

Immediately to the left after you cross the bridge into town is a modern visitor center with a small museum, snack bar, clean bathrooms, and a ticket window. Tour prices are fixed at about 720 pesos for a 1-hour tour for up to six people, or 1,320 pesos for a 2-hour tour. You can join others or hire a boat by yourself. In addition to flamingos, you'll see mangroves close up, and you might stop for a swim in a cenote. It's a pleasant ride through calm waters on wide, flat-bottom skiffs with canopies for shade. *Don't ask boatmen to get closer to the flamingos than they are allowed to.* If pestered too much, the birds will abandon the area for another, less-fitting habitat.

Celestún is an easy 90-minute drive from Mérida. (For bus info, see "Getting There & Departing: By Bus," p. 226.) Leave downtown on Calle 57, which ends just past Santiago Church and doglegs onto Calle 59-A. After crossing Avenida Itzáes, it becomes Jacinto Canek; continue until you see signs for Celestún Hwy. 178. After Hunucmá, the road joins Hwy. 281. Continue to the bridge, and you are in Celestún.

WHERE TO STAY

Casa de Celeste Vida ★★ ☺ 🎁 This newish guesthouse, 1.5 km (1 mile) north of town on a quiet, unspoiled beach, hits the perfect balance between comfort and economy, seclusion and convenience. Two studios and a one-bedroom apartment have ocean views, kitchens stocked with utensils and food staples, and use of bikes, kayaks, and outdoor grills. The studios are roomy enough to bring in another bed, and kids stay free. The amiable Canadian owners, who live on-site, gladly arrange tours and sometimes even accompany guests on errands in town. They are highly tuned in to local culture and provide enormous insights into the lives of local fishermen and their families.

Calle 12 49-E, Celestún, Yuc. www.hotelcelestevida.com. ✆ **988/916-2536.** 3 units. $75 studios; $100 apartment. Weekly/monthly rates available. AE, DISC, MC, V. Free parking. **Amenities:** Bikes; kayaks; kitchen; Wi-Fi.

Hotel Eco Paraíso Xixim ✋ This resort draws accolades for its scrupulous ecological practices, such as composting, reusing treated wastewater, and developing barely more than 1% of its 25 hectares (62 acres). The 5km (3 miles) of unsullied beach are sublime. All good, and the *palapa*-roof bungalows are exquisitely private and generally comfortable. The problem? Rates were already higher than seemed justified for the property, and in a year when room rates are generally flat or even lower around the Yucatán, rates here have taken a significant leap. And if you don't relish bouncing over 11km (6¾ miles) of potholes whenever you want to explore, you are captive to the resort's services.

Antigua Carretera a Sisal Km 10, 97367 Celestún, Yuc. www.ecoparaiso.com. ✆ **988/916-2100.** Fax 988/916-2111. 15 units. High season $319–$383 doubles; low season $290–$348. Rates include breakfast. AE, MC, V. Free parking. **Amenities:** Restaurant; bar; outdoor pool. *In room:* Hair dryer.

Progreso, Uaymitun & Xcambó: Gulf Coast City, Flamingo Lookout & More Maya Ruins

Puerto Progreso is Mérida's refuge when the weight of summer heat descends on the city. And though it doesn't occur to most U.S. travelers, it is also a gateway to the trove of undiscovered white sands and mangrove-lined estuaries. Except for the vacation homes within easy reach of Mérida, most of the Yucatán's 378 seafront kilometers (235 miles)—stretching from near Isla Holbox to

A church in the village of Telchac Puerto.

The Catholic church in Xcambó.

Celestún—belongs to some scattered fishing villages, a lot of flamingos, and an increasing number of American and Canadian expats and snowbirds.

Progreso has been the Yucatán's main port of entry since the 1870s, when henequén shipped all over the world. Today, it's a major stop for cruise ships. The cruise business has allowed the city to spruce up the *malecón*, its 16-block seaside promenade that skims past well-groomed, white-sand beaches. You can enjoy a swim anywhere along the way. Though the water is green and murky compared with the Caribbean, it's clean and good for swimming. Fancy restaurants have been added (many sell good seafood), and vendors now ply their wares on the beach, but it's still pretty quiet most of the time. The 7km (4⅓-mile) pier, which seems to disappear in the distance, became the world's longest when a new section was added to accommodate the cruise ships that dock here several times a week. The sea is so shallow here that large ships cannot get any closer to shore.

From Mérida (37km/23 miles south), buses to Progreso leave from the AutoProgreso terminal (p. 227) every 15 minutes or so, taking almost an hour and costing 25 pesos round-trip. If you drive, take Paseo Montejo or Calle 60 north; either funnels you onto Hwy. 261 leading to Progreso.

A drive east on the coastal road toward Telchac Puerto, 69km (43 miles) away, reveals the other side of the Yucatán's coast. The shoreline along Hwy. 27 from Chuburna to the village of Dzilam de Bravo is dubbed La Costa Esmeralda (the Emerald Coast), after the clear, green Gulf waters. First up: the sleepy beach town of **Chicxulub,** about 8km (5 miles) east of Progreso. To winter-phobic northerners, it's a bit of paradise. To scientists, it's the site of a buried impact crater, about 161km (100 miles) in diameter, left by a meteor that smashed into Earth 65 million years ago; it is blamed for extinguishing the dinosaurs and probably created the Yucatán's cenotes. Less than 10km (6¼ miles) farther, in **Uaymitun,** a large wooden tower looming on the right is an observation post for viewing a new colony of flamingos that migrated from Celestún. Binoculars are provided free of charge. You might also spot some of the rosy birds about 20 minutes down near the turnoff for the road to Dzemul.

The road to Dzemul also leads to the small but intriguing Maya site of **Xcambó,** which was (and still is) a salt production center. Archaeologists have reconstructed the small ceremonial center, including several platforms and temples. A rough-hewn Catholic church, complete with altar, flowers, and statues, rises from some of the ruins. Admission is free.

You can continue on the same road through the small town of Dzemul to Baca, where you can pick up Hwy. 176 back to Mérida or Progreso, or you can return to the coast road and continue east until it ends in **Dzilam de Bravo,** final resting place of "gentleman pirate" Jean Lafitte. On the way, you'll pass through **Telchac Puerto,** which holds little interest unless you're hungry for some decent seafood, and the appealing village of **San Crisanto,** where a group of local fishermen will paddle you through shallow canals in the mangroves to an array of newly accessible cenotes (40 pesos).

WHERE TO STAY

Hotel Yakunah ★★ ☺   This beautiful former colonial home is owned by a generous, outgoing Dutch family who have turned it into an expat gathering place as well as an exemplary B&B. The quiet location is a 10-minute walk from the Progreso city center but right across the street from the beach. Spacious rooms have a romantic air, with large beds, pasta tile, and armoires. Gleaming tiled bathrooms have large showers. A two-bedroom garden apartment with fully equipped kitchen and private terrace is also available. Co-owner Gerben Hartskeerl is a talented chef who turns out breakfasts and dinners (extra charge) that will spare you the tribulations of finding a restaurant.

Calle 23 no. 64 (btw. calles 48 and 50), Col. Ismael García, Progreso, Yuc. www.hotelyakunah. com.mx. ⓒ **969/935-5600.** 7 units. 750–850 pesos double; 1,400 pesos 2-bedroom casita. Rates include light breakfast; extra charge for full breakfast. Minimum stay 2 nights. MC, V. **Amenities:** Restaurant; bar; library; outdoor pool; nonsmoking rooms. *In room:* A/C, TV, Wi-Fi.

En Route to Uxmal

Two routes go to Uxmal, about 80km (50 miles) south of Mérida. The most direct is Hwy. 261, via Umán and Muna. Hwy. 18 is a longer, more scenic road sometimes called the Convent Route. You might also make the trip to Uxmal as a loop by going one way and coming back the other, with an overnight stay at Uxmal. Arriving at Uxmal in late afternoon, you could attend the evening sound-and-light show, and see the ruins the next morning while it is cool and uncrowded.

Both of these roads will lead you to the central square in one small village after another, and many lack signs to point you in the right direction. Get used to poking your head out the window and saying, *"Buenos días. ¿Dónde está el camino para . . . ?"* ("Good day. Where is the road to . . . ?") You might have to ask more than one person before you get back on track. Streets in these villages are full of children, bicycles, and animals, so drive carefully, and learn to recognize unmarked *topes* from a distance.

⊙ A Night in the 17th century

Hacienda Yaxcopoil is no secret, but few travelers seem to know you can stay overnight in the **Casa de Visitas ★★★**, a guesthouse behind the manor house that is not open to the public. While the rest of the hacienda property exists in a state of suspended animation, this one room's interior has been restored to the condition it might have been in during the hacienda's 19th-century heyday. It is quite roomy and charming, with sitting and dining room areas, a simple but modern bathroom, patterned tile floor, and colonial-style furniture. You can lounge on the back terrace or step out the front door and have run of the garden. After the tour groups leave at 6pm, it's just you, the entire empty hacienda, and the starry starry night. This is a unique experience that I look forward to repeating, but it's not for travelers who require a front desk ready to snap to attention at any hour of the day or night—or for those who believe in ghosts, based on some of the stories I've heard. The guesthouse rents for $70 a night; and another $25 per person gets you a traditional homemade dinner (*sopa de lima*, three types of tamales, seasonal fruit, and horchata) and a hearty breakfast, cooked, delivered, and served at your convenience by a woman in town.

Churches on these routes don't keep strict hours but are open daily from roughly 10am to 1pm and 4 to 6pm, so you might want to plan for lunch and a visit to a ruin midday. Ruins are open daily from 8am to 5pm.

HWY. 261: YAXCOPOIL & MUNA   From downtown Mérida, take Calle 65 or 69 west and then turn left on Avenida Itzáes, which feeds onto the highway. To save some time by looping around the busy market town of Umán, take the exit for Hwy. 180 to Cancún and Campeche, and follow signs toward Campeche. Keep going south on Hwy. 180 until it intersects with Hwy. 261 and take the Uxmal exit.

You'll soon come to **Hacienda Yaxcopoil ★★** (yash-koh-po-*eel*; www.yaxcopoil.com; ✆ **999/900-1193**) and the town that grew up around it and took its name. Thirty-two kilometers (20 miles) south of Mérida, the ruined hacienda, immediately identifiable by its double Moorish arches, has been preserved but not restored, making for an eerie but particularly vivid trip back in time. Tours take in the *casa principa,* with its large lounges and drawing rooms, the extensive gardens, a small Maya museum, and the henequén factory. It's open Monday to Saturday from 8am to 6pm, and Sunday 9am to 5pm. Admission is 50 pesos.

South of Yaxcopoil, the little market town of **Muna** (65km/40 miles from Mérida) sells excellent **reproductions of Maya ceramics,** created by artisan Rodrigo Martín Morales, who has worked 25 years to replicate the ancient Maya's style and methods. As you enter Muna, watch for two large ceiba trees on the right side of the road, with handicraft and food stalls in a small plaza under the branches. Turn right, and in about 45m (148 ft.) the **Taller de Artesanía Los Ceibos** (✆ **997/971-0036**) will be on your left. The family works in the back, and only Spanish is spoken. The store is open from 9am to 6pm daily. Uxmal is 15km (9⅓ miles) beyond Muna.

HWY. 18: THE CONVENT ROUTE   From downtown Mérida, take Calle 63 east to Circuito Colonias and turn right, then look for a traffic circle with a small fountain and turn left. This feeds onto Hwy. 18 to Kanasín (kah-nah-*seen*)

An artisan crafts a ceramic vase in Muna.

and then Acanceh (ah-kahn-*keh*). In **Kanasín,** the highway divides into two; go to the right, and the road curves to flow into the next parallel street. Pass the market, church, and main square on your left, and then stay to the right when you get to a fork.

Shortly after Kanasín, the road bypasses a lot of villages. Follow the sign pointing left to **Acanceh.** Across the street from and overlooking Acanceh's church is a restored pyramid. On top, under a makeshift roof, are some stucco figures of Maya deities. The caretaker will guide you up to see them and give you a little explanation (in Spanish). A few blocks away, at some other ruins called **El Palace de los Stuccoes,** a stucco mural was found in mint condition in 1908. Exposure deteriorated it somewhat, but it is sheltered now. You can still distinguish the painted figures in their original colors. Admission is 31 pesos. To leave Acanceh, head back to the highway on the street that passes between the church and the plaza.

The next turnoff will be for **Tecoh,** on the right side. Its ornate and crumbling parish church and convent sit on the base of a massive pre-Columbian ceremonial complex that was sacrificed to build the church. The three carved *retablos* (altarpieces) inside are covered in gold leaf and unmistakably Indian in style. About 9km (5⅔ miles) farther on, you come to the ruins of Mayapán, the last of the great city-states.

Mayapán ★

50km (31 miles) SE of Merida

Founded, according to Maya lore, by the man-god Kukulkán (Quetzalcóatl in central Mexico) in about A.D. 1007, Mayapán quickly established itself as northern Yucatán's most important city. For almost 2 centuries, it was the capital of a Maya confederation of city-states that included Chichén Itzá (which it equaled in size) and Uxmal. Sometime before 1200, Mayapán attacked and subjugated the other two cities, leading to a revolt that eventually toppled Mayapán. It was abandoned during the mid-1400s.

The walled city, considered the last great Maya capital, extended out at least 4 sq. km (1½ sq. miles), but the ceremonial center is quite compact. Several buildings bordering the principal plaza have been reconstructed, including one that looks eerily like Chichén Itzá's El Castillo (and also named El Castillo) and another much like the observatory. Excavation has uncovered murals and stucco figures that provide more grist for the mill of conjecture: atlantes (supporting columns in the form of a human figure), skeletal soldiers, macaws, entwined snakes, and a stucco jaguar. With some 4,000 mounds, and only half a dozen in different stages of restoration, Mayapán shows the full spectrum of ruins in their original discovered state, some in mid-transformation and others in stages of advanced restoration. Well worth a stop.

The site is open daily from 8am to 5pm. Admission is 31 pesos. Use of a personal video camera is 45 pesos.

WHERE TO STAY

Hotel Na' Lu'um ★ 🏕 Whether you need a place to stay because you've run out of steam while exploring the Puuc or Convent routes, or you're looking for a tranquil retreat in the heart of the Mundo Maya, this ecohotel will fit the bill. Spacious *palapa*-roofed cabañas fit unobtrusively into the well-tended gardens and surrounding natural landscape. Their rustic Maya design uses clay and wood to keep them cool and windows in every direction to pull in cross-breezes. Inside, they offer every modern comfort and a few unusual touches, such as a pull-out clothesline in the oversized shower. The hotel restaurant, which is becoming a popular roadside stop on the way to the Mayapán ruins, specializes in regional dishes and is very good. On Saturdays, the hotel opens the *temazcal* for Maya-style ritual steam cleansings.

Carretera Mérida–Chetumal Km 22.9 (before Mayapán archaeological zone), Libramiento Tecoh, Yuc. www.naluumtm.com. ✆ **999/195-6294.** 10 units. 1,000–1,100 pesos double. Includes full breakfast. AE, MC, V. Free parking. **Amenities:** Restaurant; jogging track; outdoor pool; *temazcal. In room:* Ceiling fan; no phone.

The ruins of Mayapán.

FROM MAYAPÁN TO TICUL   About 20km (12 miles) after Mayapán, take the highway for **Mama** on your right, and the narrow road quickly enters town. Some parts of this village are quite pretty. The main attraction is the church and former convent, with several fascinating *retablos* sculpted in a native form of baroque. Colonial-age murals and designs were uncovered and restored during the restoration of these buildings. You can peek at them in the sacristy. From Mama, continue on another 20km (12 miles) to Ticul, a large (for this area) market town with a couple of simple hotels.

Ticul

98km (61 miles) S of Mérida via Hwy. 18

Best known for the cottage industry of *huipil* (native blouse) embroidery and the manufacture of women's dress shoes, Ticul is both an exciting stop and a convenient place to wash up and spend the night. It's also a center for large-scale pottery production—most of the widely sold sienna-colored pottery painted with Maya designs is made here. If it's a cloudy, humid day, potters may not be working; part of the process requires sun drying. They still welcome visitors to purchase finished pieces.

Ticul is only 20km (12 miles) northeast of Uxmal, making a good alternative to the expensive hotels at the ruins, especially if you plan to do the Puuc Route one day and the Convent Route the next. On the main square is the **Hotel Plaza,** Calle 23 no. 202, near Calle 26 (www.hotelplazayucatan.com; ✆ **997/ 972-0484**). It's a modest but comfortable 30-room hotel with air-conditioning, TVs, and a decent restaurant. A double room with air-conditioning costs 340 pesos. A 5% charge applies to payments made by credit card (MasterCard and Visa accepted). Get an interior room to avoid noise from Ticul's lively plaza. From Ticul, you can head straight for Uxmal via Santa Elena, or loop around the Puuc Route (p. 268) the long way to Santa Elena.

Ticul is known for its pottery.

FROM TICUL TO UXMAL   Follow the main street (Calle 23) west through town. Turn left on Calle 34 and drive 15km (9⅓ miles) to Santa Elena; it will be another 15km (9⅓ miles) to Uxmal. In Santa Elena, by the side of Hwy. 261, is a clean restaurant with good food, **El Chaac Mool,** and on the opposite side of the road the **Flycatcher Inn B&B** (see listing, below).

THE RUINS OF UXMAL ★★★

80km (50 miles) SW of Mérida; 19km (12 miles) W of Ticul; 19km (12 miles) S of Muna

The ceremonial complex of Uxmal ("oosh-*mahl*") is one of the masterworks of Maya civilization. Expansive and intricate facades of carved stone make it strikingly different from all other Maya cities. Unlike other sites in northern Yucatán, such as Chichén Itzá and Mayapán, Uxmal isn't built on a flat plane, but incorporates the varied elevations of the hilly landscape. And then there is the strange and beautiful oval-shaped Pyramid of the Magician, unique among the Maya. The great building period took place between A.D. 700 and 1000, when the population probably reached 25,000. After 1000, Uxmal fell under the sway of the Xiú princes (who may have come from central Mexico). In the 1440s, the Xiú conquered Mayapán, and not long afterward, the age of the Maya ended with the arrival of the Spanish conquistadors.

Close to Uxmal, four smaller sites—**Sayil, Kabah, Xlapak,** and **Labná**—can be visited in quick succession. With Uxmal, these ruins (p. 268) are collectively known as the **Puuc route.**

Essentials

GETTING THERE & DEPARTING   **By Car**   The two main routes to Uxmal from Mérida are described in "En Route to Uxmal," earlier. *Note:* There's no gasoline at Uxmal.

   By Bus   See "Getting There & Departing" (p. 226) for information about bus service between Mérida and Uxmal. To return, wait for the bus on the highway at the entrance to the ruins. To see the sound-and-light show, sign up with a tour operator from Mérida.

ORIENTATION   Entrance to the ruins is through the visitor center where you buy tickets (two per person; hold on to both). It has a restaurant; toilets; a first-aid station; shops selling soft drinks, ice cream, film, batteries, and books; a state-run Casa de Artesanía (crafts house); and a small museum, which isn't especially informative. The site is open daily from 8am to 5pm. Admission to the archaeological site is 234 pesos; the evening sound-and-light show is an additional 72 pesos. Bringing in a video camera costs 45 pesos, and parking is 10 pesos. If you're staying the night in Uxmal, consider getting to the site late in the day, viewing the sound-and-light show that evening and visiting the ruins the next morning before it gets hot. (Make sure the ticket vendor knows what you intend to do, and keep the ticket.)

   Guides at the entrance of Uxmal give tours in several languages, charging about 550 pesos for a single person or a group. The guides frown on it, but you can ask other English speakers if they'd like to join you in a tour and split the cost. The 45-minute **sound-and-light show** begins each evening at 7pm during standard time and 8pm during daylight saving. It's in Spanish, but you can rent headsets for 25 pesos that narrate the program in several languages. It's part Hollywood, part high school, but the surreal effect of colored lights playing on the buildings is worth it. After the show, the chant *"Cha-a-ac, Cha-a-ac"* will echo in your mind for weeks.

A Tour of the Ruins

THE PYRAMID OF THE MAGICIAN ★★   As you enter the ruins, note a *chultún*, or cistern, where Uxmal stored its water. Unlike most of the major Maya sites, Uxmal stands about 30m (100 ft.) above sea level, so it has no cenotes to supply freshwater from the subterranean rivers. The city's inhabitants depended on rainwater, and consequently venerated the rain god Chaac with unusual devotion.

Rising in front of you is the Pirámide del Adivino, the city's tallest structure at 38m (125 ft.). The name comes from a myth about a magician-dwarf who reached adulthood in a single day after being hatched from an egg and built this pyramid in a night. It is built over five earlier structures. The pyramid has an oval base and rounded sides. You are looking at the east side. Walk around the left, or south, side to see the main face on the west side. The pyramid was designed so that the east side rises less steeply than the west side, which shifts the crowning temples to the west of the central axis of the building, causing them to loom above the plaza below. The temple doorway is heavily ornamented, characteristic of the Chenes style, with 12 stylized masks representing Chaac.

THE NUNNERY QUADRANGLE   To get from the plaza to the large Nunnery Quadrangle, walk out the way you walked into the plaza, turn right, and follow the wall of this long stone building until you get to the building's main door—a corbeled arch that leads into the quadrangle. You'll be in another plaza, bordered on each side by stone buildings with elaborate facades. The 16th-century Spanish historian Fray Diego López de Cogullado gave the quadrangle its name when he decided its layout resembled a Spanish convent.

The quadrangle does have a lot of small rooms, about the size of a nun's cell. They don't warrant much exploration, being long ago abandoned to the

Uxmal's Pyramid of the Magician.

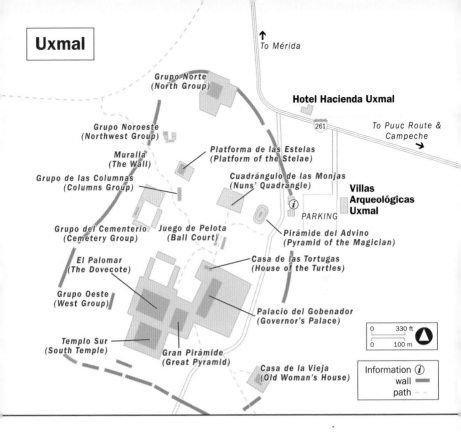

Uxmal

To Mérida ↑

Grupo Norte
(North Group)

Hotel Hacienda Uxmal

Grupo Noroeste
(Northwest Group)

261

To Puuc Route &
Campeche →

Muralla
(The Wall)

Platforma de las Estelas
(Platform of the Stelae)

Grupo de las Columnas
(Columns Group)

Cuadrángulo de las Monjas
(Nuns' Quadrangle)

Villas
Arqueológicas
Uxmal

ⓘ

PARKING

Grupo del Cementerio
(Cemetery Group)

Juego de Pelota
(Ball Court)

Pirámide del Advino
(Pyramid of the Magician)

El Palomar
(The Dovecote)

Casa de las Tortugas
(House of the Turtles)

Grupo Oeste
(West Group)

Palacio del Gobenador
(Governor's Palace)

0	330 ft
0	100 m

Templo Sur
(South Temple)

Gran Pirámide
(Great Pyramid)

Casa de la Vieja
(Old Woman's House)

Information ⓘ
wall ▬▬▬
path - - -

swallows that fly above the city, but poke your head into one to see the shape and size. No interior murals or stucco work have been found here. The richness of Uxmal lies in the stonework on its exterior walls.

The Nunnery is a stunning example. The first building that catches your eye when you enter the plaza is the north building in front of you. It is the tallest, and the view from the top includes all the city's major buildings, making it useful for the sound-and-light show. The central stairway is bordered by doorways supported by rounded columns, a common element in Puuc architecture. Remnants of the facade on the second level show elements used in the other three buildings and elsewhere in the city: a cross-hatch pattern and a pattern of square curlicues, called a step-and-fret design, and the vertical repetitions of the long-nosed god masks—found so often on the corners of Uxmal's buildings that they have been dubbed "Chaac stacks." Though the facades of these buildings share these and other common elements, their composition varies. On the west building, long, feathered serpents are intertwined at head and tail. A human head stares out from a serpent's open mouth. There are many interpretations of this motif, repeated elsewhere in Maya art, and that's the trouble with symbols: They are usually the condensed expression of multiple meanings, so any one interpretation could be true, but only partially true.

THE BALL COURT   Leaving the Nunnery the same way you entered, you will see a ball court straight ahead. This one is a particularly good representative of the hundreds found elsewhere in the Maya world. It even has a replica of one of the stone rings the players aimed at, using their knees, hips, and maybe their arms to strike a solid rubber ball (the Maya knew about natural rubber and extracted latex from a couple of species of rubber trees). Spectators are thought to have observed the game from atop the two structures.

THE GOVERNOR'S PALACE   Continuing south, you come to the large raised plaza supporting the Governor's Palace, which runs north and south. The surface area of the raised plaza measures 140m×170m (459 ft.×558 ft.), and it is raised about 10m (33 ft.) above the ground—quite a bit of earth moving. Most of this surface is used as a ceremonial space facing the front (east side) of the palace. In the center is a double-headed jaguar throne, which is seen elsewhere in the Maya world. From here, you get the best view of the building's remarkable facade. Like the other palaces here, the first level is smooth and the second is ornate. A series of Chaac masks moves diagonally across a crosshatch pattern. Crowning the building is an elegant cornice projecting slightly outward from above a double border, which could be an architectural reference to the original crested thatched roofs of the Maya. Human figures adorned the main doors, though only the headdress of the central figure survives.

THE GREAT PYRAMID   Behind the palace, the platform descends in terraces to another plaza with a large temple, known as the Great (or Grand) Pyramid, on its south side. On top is the Temple of the Macaws, named for the repeated macaw image on the face of the temple, and the ruins of three other temples. The view from the top is extraordinary.

THE DOVECOTE   This building is remarkable, in that roof combs weren't a common feature of temples in the Puuc hills, although Sayil's El Mirador has one of a very different style.

The Governor's Palace (left) and the Great Pyramid (right) in Uxmal.

Where to Stay & Eat

Lodging at or near the ruins' entrance is expensive without any justification beyond their location. You can eat well at the **Lodge at Uxmal** if you stay with the Yucatecan specialties, which are fresh and well prepared. More affordable rooms are available in the village of Santa Elena, 15 minutes southeast of the ruins just off Hwy. 261. In addition to the Pickled Onion (below), **El Chac Mool** in Santa Elena offers decent, inexpensive local food.

AT THE RUINS

Hacienda Uxmal ★★   The Hacienda is the oldest hotel in Uxmal. Located just up the road from the ruins, it was built for the original archaeology staff. Large, airy rooms exude a feel of days gone by, with patterned tile floors, heavy furniture, and louvered windows. Room nos. 202 through 214 and 302 through 305 are the nicest of the superiors. Larger corner rooms are labeled A through F and come with Jacuzzi tubs. A handsome garden courtyard with towering royal palms, a bar, and a pool adds to the air of tranquillity.

Carretera Mérida–Uxmal Km 80, 97844 Uxmal, Yuc. www.mayaland.com. ⓒ **800/235-4079** in the U.S., or 997/976-2012. Fax 987/976-2011. 82 units. High season $69–$104 double, $153 suite; low season $69 double, $87 suite. AE, MC, V. Free guarded parking. **Amenities:** Restaurant; bar; 2 outdoor pools. *In room:* A/C, TV; Jacuzzi (in some), hair dryer (upon request), minibar.

Villas Arqueológicas Uxmal ★ 🗡   Still the best value among the hotels at the ruins' entrance, the Villas consist of a basic two-story quadrangle around a garden patio and pool. Lush vegetation, Maya statues, and a paint job with a semblance of traditional style pretty the place up nicely. Guests have use of a tennis court, a library, and an audiovisual show on the ruins in English, French, and Spanish. The small, modern rooms each have a double and a twin bed fit into alcoves walled on three sides (very tall people should look elsewhere). Ask about rates for half- (breakfast plus lunch or dinner) or full (3 meals) board.

Ruinas Uxmal, Carretera Mérida–Campeche Km 76, 97890 Uxmal, Yuc. www.villasarqueologicas. com.mx. ⓒ **222/273-7900.** 43 units. $59–$97 double. AE, MC, V. Free guarded parking. **Amenities:** Restaurant; bar; outdoor pool; tennis court; spa; TV/game room; Wi-Fi (in public areas). *In room:* A/C, hair dryer, Wi-Fi (in some).

SANTA ELENA

Flycatcher Inn B&B ★★   This pleasant bed-and-breakfast offers quiet, attractive rooms. Beds come with pillow-top orthopedic mattresses and decorative ironwork made by one of the owners, Santiago Domínguez. His wife, Kristine Ellingson, has voluminous information on travel and local culture to share with guests. Most of the inn's 15-acre grounds remain a wildlife sanctuary and include a recently discovered little Maya ruin along the nature trail that runs through the property. The new Owl's Cottage, a secluded house with a small kitchen and large living/dining room, is designed for longer stays.

Carretera Uxmal–Kabah, 97840 Santa Elena, Yuc. www.flycatcherinn.com. ⓒ **997/102-0865.** 8 units. $60–$75 double; $85 suite; $80–$95 cottage. Weekly/monthly rates available. 4-night minimum for Owl's Cottage. Rates include full breakfast. No credit cards except for online advance deposit. Not set up to accommodate young children. **Amenities:** Free secure parking; laundry service. *In room:* A/C.

The Pickled Onion Restaurant and B&B ★★★ 🗡   After 5 years of building up a reputation for her restaurant, the Pickled Onion—offering a mostly

Mexican menu with a few international twists (35–98 pesos)—British (by way of Canada) expat Valerie Pickles has extended her legendary hospitality to overnight guests. She has built four handsome Maya-style rental cabañas out of traditional materials; another was due for completion in July 2012 and a sixth by the end of the year. They are simple but neat and cozy, with exceptionally comfortable beds and modern bathrooms. Cabañas are in a large garden that includes a massage hut and a large pool with a lofty view (also available to restaurant guests free of charge). This is the best value in the area.

Carretera Uxmal-Kabah, 98760 Santa Elena, Yuc. www.thepickledonionyucatan.com. © **997/ 111-7922.** 5 units. $35 doubles; $45–$65 larger units. Rates include continental breakfast. No credit cards (advance deposits through PayPal). **Amenities:** Restaurant; pool; Wi-Fi (in restaurant area); laundry service; massage available; parking. *In room:* Ceiling fan, mini fridge (in one).

THE PUUC MAYA ROUTE

South and east of Uxmal are several other ancient Maya cities, small and largely unexcavated but worth visiting for their unique architecture.

Kabah is 28km (17 miles) southeast of Uxmal via Hwy. 261 through Santa Elena, and only a couple kilometers (1¼ miles) farther to Sayil. Xlapak is almost walking distance (through the jungle) from Sayil, and Labná is just a bit farther east. A short drive beyond Labná brings you to the caves of Loltún. Oxkutzcab is at the road's intersection with Hwy. 184, which you can follow west to Ticul or east all the way to Felipe Carrillo Puerto. If you aren't driving, a daily bus from Mérida (p. 226) goes to all these sites, with the exception of Loltún.

Puuc Maya Sites

KABAH ★   From Uxmal, head southwest on Hwy. 261 to Santa Elena (1km/⅔ mile), then south to Kabah (13km/8 miles). The ancient city lies along both sides of the highway. Turn right into the parking lot.

The Palace of Masks in Kabah.

These sites are undergoing excavation and reconstruction, and some buildings may be roped off when you visit. The sites are open daily from 8am to 5pm. Admission ranges from 37 to 43 pesos for each city (except Xlapak, which is free) and 95 pesos for Loltún. Loltún has tours at 9:30 and 11am, and 12:30, 2, 3, and 4pm. Even if you're the only person there when a tour is scheduled, the guide must give you a tour, and he can't charge you as if you were contracting his services for an individual tour (though sometimes they try). Fee for use of a video camera is 45 pesos; if you visit Uxmal the same day, you pay only once for video permission and present your receipt as proof at each ruin.

The outstanding building at Kabah, to the right as you enter, is the **Palace of Masks,** or Codz Poop ("rolled-up mat"), named for its decorative motif. Its Chenes-style facade is completely covered in a repeated pattern of 250 masks of Chaac, each with curling remnants of the god's elephant trunk–like nose. It is unique in all of Maya architecture. For years, parts of this building lay lined up in the weeds like pieces of a puzzle awaiting assembly. Sculptures from this building are in the anthropology museums of Mérida and Mexico City.

Just behind and to the left of the Codz Poop is the **Palace Group** (also called the East Group), with a fine Puuc-style colonnaded facade. Originally, it had 32 rooms. On the front are seven doors, two divided by columns—a common feature of Puuc architecture. Across the highway is what was once the **Great Temple,** and beyond that is a **great arch.** It was much wider at one time and may have been a monumental gate into the city. A *sacbé* linked this arch to Uxmal. Compare this corbeled arch to the one at Labná (below), which is in much better shape.

SAYIL   About 4km (2½ miles) south of Kabah is the turnoff (left, or east) to Sayil, Xlapak, Labná, Loltún, and Oxkutzcab. The ruins of **Sayil** ("place of the ants") are 4km (2½ miles) along this road.

Sayil is famous for **El Palacio ★★**. With more than 90 rooms, the palace is impressive for its size alone. Climbing is not permitted, but the

The ruins of Sayil.

facade that makes this a masterpiece of Maya architecture is best appreciated from the ground. It stretches across three terraced levels, and its rows of columns give it a Minoan appearance. The upside-down stone figure known to archaeologists as the Diving God, or Descending God, over the doorway on the second level is the same motif used at Tulum a couple of centuries later. The large circular basin on the ground below the palace is an artificial catch basin for a *chultún* (cistern); this region has no natural cenotes (wells) for irrigation.

In the jungle beyond El Palacio is **El Mirador,** a small temple with an oddly slotted roof comb. Beyond El Mirador, a crude stela (tall, carved stone) is carved with a fertility god burdened with a phallus of monstrous proportions. Another building group, the Southern Group, is a short distance down a trail that branches off from the one heading to El Mirador.

XLAPAK Xlapak (*shla*-pahk) is a small site with one building; it's 5.5km (3½ miles) down the road from Sayil. The Palace at Xlapak bears the masks of the rain god Chaac. If you're running out of steam, this is the one to skip.

LABNÁ Labná, dating from between A.D. 600 and 900, is 30km (19 miles) from Uxmal and only 3km (2 miles) past Xlapak. The entrance has a snack stand and toilets. Descriptive placards fronting the main buildings are in Spanish, English, and German.

As soon as you enter you'll see **El Palacio,** a magnificent Puuc-style building on your left that is much like the one at Sayil, but in poorer condition. Over one doorway is a large, well-conserved mask of Chaac with eyes, a huge snout nose, and jagged teeth around a small mouth that seems on the verge of speaking. Jutting out on one corner is a highly stylized serpent's mouth from which pops a human head with an unexpectedly serene expression. From the front, you can gaze out to the enormous grassy interior grounds flanked by vestiges of unrestored buildings and jungle.

Labná's El Palacio.

sweet STOP ON THE PUUC ROUTE

Paris, Bruges, and Prague had chocolate museums first, but the Maya had chocolate first (see "A Debt of Gratitude," p. 45). Now they have a museum as well. The owners of Ki'Xocolatl (p. 244) have created the **Ecomuseo del Cacao ★★★** on their Tikul Plantation, between Labná and Xlapak on the Puuc Route (119km/ 74 miles south of Mérida). The museum focuses as much on cocoa's mystical significance to the Maya as on the confection itself. A stone path leads to traditional thatched-roof huts, each with its own theme: cocoa's sacred role in the Maya's spiritual world; daily Maya life (demonstrated in an outdoor kitchen, a wild orchid garden and a colony of the native stingless bees that are crucial to cocoa's growth); and the laborious chocolate-making process.

Paths between the huts lead through a veritable botanical garden, with signs explaining the importance of such plants as henequén, pomegranate, habanero pepper, tamarind, lime, guava, and of course the cacao tree (which actually isn't grown much in the Yucatán because of its thin, rocky soil). You'll also see bits and pieces of ancient Maya structures. The tour culminates in a demonstration of the grinding and preparation of a chocolate drink, to which you get to add your own embellishments. Don't shy away from the chile—it was traditional in the Maya drink, and once you try it, you'll find Hershey's unbearably dull.

The museum, Km 20, Route Puuc, Yotholin, Ticul, Yuc. (www.ecomuseo delcacao.com; ✆ **999/192-5385**), is open daily 9am to 6pm. Admission is 90 pesos adults, 60 pesos seniors, students, and children; kids 6 and under free. A craft store, playground, and cafeteria are also on-site.

From El Palacio, you can walk on a reconstructed *sacbé* leading to Labná's **corbeled arch.** At one time, there were probably several such arches through the region. This one has been extensively restored, although only remnants of the roof comb are visible. It was once part of a more elaborate structure now lost to history. Chaac's face occupies the corners of one facade, and stylized Maya huts are fashioned in stone above the two small doorways. You can pass through the arch to reach **El Mirador** or El Castillo. Towering above a large pile of rubble, the remains of a pyramid, is a singular room crowned with a roof comb piercing the sky.

LOLTÚN The caverns of Loltún are 31km (19 miles) past Labná on the way to Oxkutzcab, on the left side of the road. One of the Yucatán's largest and most fascinating cave systems, they were home to the ancient Maya and were used as a refuge during the War of the Castes (1847–1901). Inside are statues, wall carvings, and paintings, *chultunes* (cisterns), and other signs of Maya habitation. Guides will explain much of what you see, though their English isn't always easy to understand.

The admission price includes a 90-minute tour. These begin daily at 9:30 and 11am, and 12:30, 2, 3, and 4pm. The bilingual guides do not charge for their services but appreciate tips. The floor of the cavern can be slippery in places; take a flashlight if you have one.

To return to Mérida from Loltún, drive the 7km (4⅓ miles) to Oxkutzcab. From there, you can take the slow route through Maní and

Teabo, which will allow you to see some convents and return by Hwy. 18, known as the "Convent Route" (p. 259). The other option is to head toward Muna to hook up with Hwy. 261 (p. 259).

Oxkutzcab

Oxkutzcab (ohsh-kootz-*kahb*), 11km (6¾ miles) from Loltún, is the center of the Yucatán's fruit-growing region. Oranges abound. The tidy village of 21,000 centers on a beautiful 16th-century church and the market. **Su Cabaña Suiza** (no phone) is a dependable restaurant in town. The last week of October and first week of November is the **Orange Festival,** when the village turns exuberant, with a carnival and orange displays in and around the central plaza.

En Route to Campeche

From Oxkutzcab, head back 43km (27 miles) to Sayil, and then drive south on Hwy. 261 to Campeche (126km/78 miles). After crossing the state line, you'll pass through the towns of Bolonchén and Hopelchén, both of which have gas stations. It's a pleasant drive with little traffic. Watch carefully for directional traffic signs in these towns to stay on the highway. From Hopelchén, Hwy. 261 heads west. After 42km (26 miles), you'll find yourself at Cayal and the well-marked turnoff for the ruins of the city of Edzná (p. 279), 18km (11 miles) farther south. If you're taking this route to Campeche, this could be the time to see this tranquil, underappreciated ancient city.

CAMPECHE ★★

180 km (112 miles) SW of Mérida via Hwy. 180; 251km (156 miles) via Hwy. 261 376km (234 miles) NE of Villahermosa

Campeche, capital of the state of the same name, is a splendidly restored colonial city that has been largely overlooked by English-speaking travelers accustomed to being coddled in Cancún. Within its 17th-century walls, all the historic center's facades have been repaired and painted, electrical and telephone cables moved underground, and the streets paved to resemble cobblestone. Several period films have been shot here, including *Che,* Steven Soderbergh's epic biography of Che Guevara starring Benicio del Toro (2008), and *Original Sin* (2001) with Angelina Jolie and Antonio Banderas. Foreign tourists who did come to Campeche typically were on their way to the ruins at Palenque (chapter 8) or the Río Bec region (chapter 6). Though you'll still find less English translation at museums, ruins, and services, and little nightlife—except on Saturday and Sunday nights when the main square becomes one huge street party—Campeche has made great strides in recent years.

The city has a decent supply of reasonably priced hotels with such niceties as good lighting, washcloths, and toiletries (still not a given in Mexico), as well as several stunning luxury hotels. Information in English is much easier to come by. On my last two trips there, I've found hotel staff, waiters, and store clerks speaking better English than I do Spanish. The state now publishes (in Spanish) a weekly booklet of event listings, and the last one I picked up had 28 pages' worth—signifying the end of the nightlife shortage. Calle 59, the main street crossing the old city from the Puerta de Mar (Sea Gate) to the Puerta de Tierra (Land Gate), was renovated and widened recently, and it has an innovation I've yet to see in the United States—with a row of dots down the middle of the

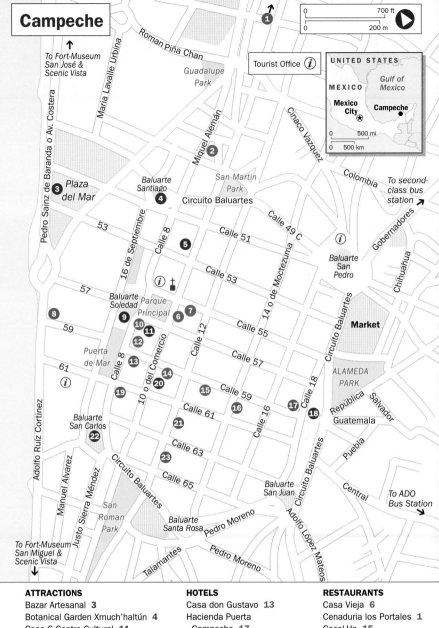

Campeche

↑
To Fort-Museum
San José &
Scenic Vista

Roman Piña Chan

Guadalupe
Park

0 ———— 700 ft
0 ———— 200 m

Tourist Office (i)

UNITED STATES

MEXICO

Gulf of
Mexico

Mexico
City ✪   Campeche ●

0 ———— 500 mi
0 ———— 500 km

María Lavalle Urbina

Pedro Sainz de Baranda o Av. Costera

Cinaco Vázquez

Colombia

To second-
class bus
station ↗

Gobernadores

Chihuahua

Miguel Alemán

Baluarte
Santiago ④

San Martín
Park

Circuito Baluartes

③ Plaza
del Mar

53

16 de Septiembre

Calle 8

Calle 51

Calle 49 C

⑤

Calle 53

(i)
Baluarte
San
Pedro

14 o Moctezuma

57

(i) †

Baluarte
Soledad Parque
Principal

⑥ ⑦

Calle 55

Circuito Baluartes

Market

⑧

59

⑨

⑩ ⑪

Calle 12

⑫

Puerta
de Mar

Calle 8

⑬

61

10 o del Comercio

⑭

⑳

Calle 57

ALAMEDA
PARK

(i)

⑲

⑮

Calle 59

Calle 18

República

Salvador

Calle 61

⑯

Calle 16

⑰

⑱

Guatemala

Adolfo Ruiz Cortinez

Baluarte
San Carlos

㉑

Puebla

㉒

Calle 63

Manuel Álvarez

Justo Sierra Méndez

Circuito Baluartes

㉓

Calle 65

Central

To ADO
Bus Station ↘

San
Roman
Park

Baluarte
Santa Rosa

Baluarte
San Juan

Circuito Baluartes

Adolfo López Mateos

To Fort-Museum
San Miguel &
Scenic Vista ↓

Pedro Moreno

Talamantes

Pedro Moreno

Campeche's Parque Principal by night.

sidewalk so that blind people can negotiate their way, as well as shoulder-height street signs embedded with Braille. All of which make it easier for visitors to discover one of Mexico's most beautiful and well-maintained city centers, populated by some of its warmest and most unassuming people.

Essentials

GETTING THERE & DEPARTING

BY PLANE   **Aeroméxico** (www.aeromexico.com.mx; 𝄽 **800/237-6399** in the U.S., 01-800/021-4000 in Mexico or 981/816-6656) flies daily to and from Mexico City. **VivaAerobus** (www.vivaaerobus.com; 𝄽 **01-818/215-0150** in Mexico), which flies to Campeche from Mexico City, has connecting flights from Chicago, Houston, Las Vegas, Miami, Orlando, and San Antonio. Campeche's **airport** is several kilometers northeast of the town center, and you'll have to take a taxi into town (about 100 pesos).

BY CAR   Hwy. 180 goes south from Mérida, passing near the basket-making village of Halacho and near Becal, known for its Panama-hat weavers. The trip takes 2½ hours. The longer way from Mérida is along Hwy. 261 past Uxmal.

When driving from Campeche to Mérida via Hwy. 180, go north on Avenida Ruiz Cortines, bearing left to follow the water (this becomes Av. Pedro Sainz de Baranda, but there's no sign). Follow the road as it turns inland to Hwy. 180, where you turn left (there's a gas station and an Oxxo at the intersection).

To go from Campeche to Edzná and Uxmal, take the Circuito Baluartes to Avenida Governadores, which begins at Baluarte San Pedro; it will funnel you to drive north on either Ruiz Cortines or Gobernadores and turn right on Madero, which feeds onto Hwy. 281. To go south to Villahermosa, take Ruiz Cortines south.

BY BUS   **ADO** (www.boletotal.com; ☎ **981/811-9910**) offers first-class *de paso* (passing through) buses to Palenque (6 hr.; 266 pesos) four times a day, and two or three times per hour to Mérida (2½ hr.; 152 pesos) around the clock. The ADO **bus station** is on Avenida Patricio Trueba at Avenida Casa de Justicia, almost 2km (1¼ miles) from the Puerta de Tierra. The second-class bus station, with service to nearby cities and to Mérida, is at Avenida Gobernadores and Calle 45 (also called Calle Chile on the east side of Gobernadores).

ORIENTATION

VISITOR INFORMATION   The **State of Campeche Office of Tourism** (www. campeche.travel; ☎ **981/811-9229;** fax 981/816-6767) is in Plaza Moch-Couoh, Avenida Ruiz Cortines (btw. calles 63 and 65). Hours are daily 8am to 4pm and 6 to 9pm, among the state buildings between the historic center and the shore. Tourist information offices are also at Baluarte San Pedro (daily 9am–1pm and 5–9pm) and in Casa 6 (daily 9am–9pm). The city's **Tourism and Culture Office,** Calle 55 between calles 10 and 8 (☎ **981/811-3989**), is open daily 9am to 9pm. It's good for picking up brochures and maps, but it's not as helpful as the state office.

CITY LAYOUT   By far the most interesting feature of the city is the old, restored historic center, most of which once lay within the walls. The Circuito Baluarte traces the original walls' path. Originally, the seaward wall was at the water's edge, but land has been gained from the sea between the old walls

 UP AGAINST THE wall

Campeche's history is laden with drama. The conquistadors arrived in 1517, when Francisco Hernández de Córdoba landed here while exploring the coast and stayed just long enough to celebrate Mass—irascible Maya killed most of his men and fatally injured Córdoba when the interlopers failed to move on quickly enough. Native resistance thwarted attempts to settle here until Montejo the Younger gained a foothold in 1540.

In the 17th and 18th centuries, pirates repeatedly sacked the city. The list of attackers reads like a who's who of piracy. On one occasion, several outfits banded together under the famous Dutch pirate Peg Leg, inspiration for many a fictional one-legged sailor, and captured the city. Campechanos, tired of hosting pirate parties, persuaded Spain to erect walls around the city—one of only three North American walled cities built by Europeans—with *baluartes* (bastions) at critical points. The walls were built from 1686 to 1704; in the late 18th century, two forts, complete with moats and drawbridges, were built on the hills flanking Campeche. Four gates breached the wall, two of which still stand: the reconstructed **Puerta de Mar** (Sea Gate) and the **Puerta de Tierra** (Land Gate). The pirates never cared to return, but in the course of Mexico's turbulent political history, the city did withstand a couple of sieges by different armies. The wall was razed in the early 1900s, but the bastions and main gates remain, along with the two hilltop fortresses. Most of the bastions and both forts now house museums.

and the coastline. This is where you'll find most of the state government buildings, built in glaringly modernist style around **Plaza Moch-Couoh**—buildings such as the **Palacio de Gobierno** (headquarters for the state of Campeche), and the futuristic **Cámara de Diputados** (Chamber of Deputies), which looks like a cubist clam.

Campeche's street-numbering system is typical of the Yucatán, except that numbers of the north–south streets increase as you go east instead of the reverse.

GETTING AROUND   Most recommended sights, restaurants, and hotels are within walking distance of the old city, except for the two fort-museums. Campeche isn't easy to negotiate by bus, so take taxis for sights beyond walking distance—they are inexpensive.

[FastFACTS] CAMPECHE

Area Code   The telephone area code is **981.**

ATMs   More than 10 cash machines are around the downtown area, as well as HSBC, Bancomer, and Manorte banks.

Post Office   The *correo* is in the Edificio Federal, at Avenida 16 de Septiembre and Calle 53 (✆ **981/816-2134**), near the Baluarte de Santiago; open Monday to Saturday from 7:30am to 8pm.

Exploring Campeche

With beautiful surroundings, friendly people, and an easy pace of life, Campeche is made for walking. Its more than 1,000 refurbished facades and renovations, grand mansions, monumental buildings, and ornate churches can be sampled in half a day or savored, along with a few day trips, over a week.

WITHIN THE CITY WALLS

The modest but exceedingly pretty *zócalo*, or **Parque Principal ★**, is bounded by calles 55 and 57 running east and west, and calles 8 and 10 running north and south. On Saturday nights and Sundays, bands tune up in the gazebo and the square fills with people. A recent art installation has placed bronze figures representing Campeche's history in and around the square, so you might find yourself amidst a water delivery truck and driver

A colorful cobblestone street in Campeche.

or a fisherman, to name just two. Construction of the **cathedral** on the north side, whose crown-shaped bell towers dominate the square, began in 1650 and was finally completed 150 years later. A pleasant way to see the city is to take the *tranvía* (trolley) tour leaving the plaza approximately every hour between 9am and 1pm and 5 to 9pm. The cost is 80 pesos for a 45-minute tour.

Baluarte San Juan HISTORIC SITE/MUSEUM The city's smallest bastion holds an exhibition on the history of the baluartes and an old underground dungeon. The only remaining chunk of the old city wall connects San Juan with the Puerta de Tierra. The short walk between the two offers incomparable views of the new and old city.

Calle 18 btw. calles 8 and 10. No phone. Free admission. Tues–Sun 8am–7:30pm.

Botanical Garden PARK/GARDEN The Jardín Botánico Xmuch'haltún is a riot of some 250 species of exotic and common plants, in a tiny courtyard surrounded by the stone walls of the last bastion Campeche built (Baluarte de Santiago).

Av. 16 de Septiembre and Calle 49. No phone. Free admission. Mon–Sat 9am–9pm; Sun 9am–4pm.

Casa 6 Centro Cultural ★★ CULTURAL INSTITUTION Some rooms in this remodeled colonial house are decorated with period furniture and accessories. The traditional stucco and terra-cotta kitchen is arranged just as many Campechanos use them today. The patio of mixtilinear arches supported by simple Doric columns is striking. The front of the house is now a cultural center with a patio restaurant and a bookstore focusing on Campeche's history. One bedroom has been turned over to exhibition space. A play about the use of the house is presented at 9:30pm, Friday through Sunday evenings.

Calle 57 no. 6. ℭ **981/816-1782.** Free admission. Daily 9am–9pm.

Mansion Carvajal ★ HISTORIC HOME Another remarkable colonial mansion, built by one of the Yucatán's wealthiest *hacendados* in the early 19th century, has been put to more prosaic contemporary use for state offices but is open to the public on weekdays. It is most famous for its massive Carrara marble stairway, curving to the open, light-filled second story. Surrounded by pale mint-green walls punctuated by white columns and sinuous Moorish arches, you feel like you're standing on a colossal tiered wedding cake. Art Nouveau curlicues in the iron railings and black-and-white checkerboard floors are, well, the icing on the cake.

Calle 10 btw. calles 51 and 53. No phone. Free admission. Mon–Fri 8am–2:45pm.

Museo de la Arquitectura Maya MUSEUM/HISTORIC SITE The Baluarte de la Soledad, next to the Sea Gate, houses the Maya Stele Museum. Four rooms of Maya artifacts recovered from throughout the state, including columns from Edzná, provide an excellent overview of Maya writing, sculpture, and architecture. Many of the stelae are badly worn, but line drawings beside the stones allow you to appreciate their former design.

Calle 57 and Calle 8, opposite Plaza Principal. No phone. Admission 31 pesos. Daily 9am–5:45pm.

Museo de la Ciudad MUSEUM/HISTORIC SITE The Museo de la Ciudad, or city museum, with the Baluarte de San Carlos, deals primarily with the design and construction of the fortifications. A model of the city shows how it looked in its glory days and provides a good overview for touring within the city walls. There are several excellent ship models as well. All text is in Spanish.

Circuito Baluartes and Av. Justo Sierra. No phone. Admission 31 pesos. Tues–Sat 8am–8pm; Sun 9am–1pm.

Puerta de Tierra ☺ ⓞ ICON   The Land Gate, unlike the reconstructed Sea Gate at the opposite end of Calle 59, is the original, and is connected to the last remaining patch of the old city wall. A small museum displays portraits of pirates and the city founders. The 1732 French 5-ton cannon in the entryway was discovered in 1990. On Thursdays through Sundays at 8pm, it holds a light-and-sound show. A variation on the popular shows at the archaeological sites, this reenacts pirate tales with blazing cannons and flashing lights. A little over the top, but fun, and kids are enthralled.

Calle 59 at Circuito Baluartes/Av. Gobernadores. No phone. Free admission to museum; show 52 pesos adults, 15 pesos children younger than 11. Daily 9am–9pm.

OUTSIDE THE WALLS: SCENIC VISTAS

Fuerte–Museo San José el Alto ☺ MUSEUM/HISTORIC SITE   This fort is higher and has more sweeping city and coastline views than Fuerte San Miguel, and its sloping lawns are a popular picnic spot, especially at sunset. It houses the Museo de Barcos y Armas, a small exhibit of 16th- and 17th-century weapons and scale miniatures of sailing vessels. The rogue's gallery of pirates is irresistible. Take a cab; you will pass a colossal statue of Benito Juárez on the way.

Av. Morazán s/n. No phone. Admission 31 pesos. Tues–Sun 9:30am–5:30pm.

Fuerte–Museo San Miguel ★★ MUSEUM/HISTORIC SITE   For a good view of the city and a great little museum, take a cab up to Fuerte–Museo San Miguel, a small fort with a moat and a drawbridge. Built in 1771, it was the most important of the city's defenses. General Santa Anna captured it when he attacked Campeche in 1842. In the **Museum of Mayan Culture ★,** a room devoted to Maya concepts of the afterlife displays a captivating *in situ* burial

A rampart of the Fuerte–Museo San José el Alto.

The city walls of Campeche.

scene with jade masks and jewelry from Maya tombs at Calakmul. Another room explains Maya cosmology, one depicts war, and another explains the gods. The history of the fort has its own exhibits.

Ruta Escénica s/n. No phone. Admission 34 pesos. Mon 9am–3pm (fort only); Tues–Sun 9am–5:30pm; Sun 8am–noon.

Malecón ★★ Not everything Campeche has to offer is lodged in the past. The flurry of renovation also lined about 3km (1¾ miles) of the waterfront with this broad, palm-lined sea walk, encompassing fountains, cannons, exercise stations, gardens, and monuments. The jogging and bike path bustles with energetic locals in the cool of early morning and late-night hours. Join them as the day's heat breaks for a sunset you won't soon forget.

Outlying Attractions
BEACHES

Campeche is a coastal city, but if it ever had beaches, they were long ago obliterated by pirate-proof walls and landfill. The closest real swimming beach is **Playa Bonita,** about 13km (8 miles) south of Campeche just past the fishing village of Lerma, which serves as Campeche's main port. Shade *palapas* are equipped with hammock hooks and concession stands sell drinks. This is a popular place with locals looking to cool off, so it can get crowded on weekends and holidays.

If you're willing to drive a little farther for a lot more beach, continue south through Champotón, a pleasant enough seaside town. (A crumbling little fort at the mouth of the Champotón River commemorates it as the place where the first Spanish landfall on mainland Mexico took place in 1517, with disastrous effect; see p. 275). Ten or 15 minutes south of town—you'll pass a cluster of luxury resort developments that have been stopping and starting for nearly a decade—pull over at the **Bahía de Tortugas** restaurant, where for the price of a snack you can use the property's pool and beach chairs on a white sandy beach lapped by calm, clean waters. This is the beginning of a beautiful stretch of deserted white beach that seems to go on forever, or at least to Ciudad del Carmen. It's one of the most important breeding grounds for Kemp's Ridley and hawksbill **sea turtles,** which nest here from May to September. Nearly a dozen turtle sanctuaries dot these miles of beach; ask restaurant staff about the one nearby.

EDZNÁ ★★

64km (40 miles) SE of Campeche; 194km (121 miles) SW of Merida

Don't skip **Edzná** just because you've seen Chichén Itzá, Uxmal, or other famous ruins. There are several reasons to see this city. The area was populated as early as 600 B.C., with urban formation by 300 B.C. Edzná grew impressively, displaying

Edzná's Pyramid of Five Stories.

considerable urban-planning skills. It has an ambitious and elaborate canal system that must have taken decades to complete, but would have allowed for a great expansion in agricultural production and therefore, concentration of population.

Another construction boom began around A.D. 500, during the Classic period—the city's most prominent feature, the **Great Acropolis,** was started then—and rose to its height as a grand regional capital between A.D. 600 and 900. This was a crossroads between cities in present-day Chiapas, Yucatán, and Guatemala, and influences from all those areas appear in the city's elegant architecture.

Sitting atop the Great Acropolis are five main pyramids, the largest being the much-photographed **Pyramid of Five Stories.** It combines the features of temple platform and palace. Maya architecture typically consists of palace buildings with many vaulted chambers or solid pyramidal platforms with a couple of interior temples or burial passages. The two types of construction are mutually exclusive—except here. Such a mix is found only in the Puuc and Río Bec areas, and in only a few examples there. None are similar to this, which makes this pyramid a bold architectural statement.

Each of the Acropolis's four lesser pyramids is constructed in a different style, and each is a pure example of that style. It's as if the city's rulers were flaunting their cosmopolitanism, showing that they could build in any style they chose but preferred creating their own, superior architecture.

West of the Acropolis, across a large open plaza, is a long, raised building whose purpose isn't quite clear. But its size, as well as that of the plaza, makes you wonder just how many people this city actually held to necessitate such a large public space. Other major structures to explore include the **Platform of the Knives,** where flint knives were recovered, and the **Temple of the Big Masks,** flanked by twin sun-god faces with protruding crossed eyes (a sign of elite status).

To reach Edzná, take Hwy. 261 east from Campeche to Cayal, then Hwy. 188 south for 18km (11 miles). Buses from Campeche leave from a small station behind Parque Alameda, which is next to the market. Plan to spend an hour or two. The site is open daily from 8am to 5pm. Admission is 46 pesos, including the evening light-and-sound show, plus 45 pesos if you use a video camera.

Tours

Once you get beyond the capital, much of what Campeche has to offer is sparsely documented and hard to find. Taking a tour can save a lot of frustration. Prices vary with the length and type of tour, but figure 1,000 pesos a day as a rough guide. Resist the temptation to take a marathon day trip to Calakmul, however; leaving at 5am and returning around 7pm, you'll spend more time in the van than at the ruins. Either opt for an overnight tour or stay overnight around Xpujil on your own and book a tour through your hotel (p. 213).

Operadora Turística Edzná (www.edzna.com.mx; ✆ **981/816-5452**) is an especially good local tour operator with friendly, knowledgeable, English-speaking guides. Their offerings include comprehensive city tours by day or night, half-day guided tours of Edzná, full-days tour of the Chenes Route to the northeast, and many other excursions that will show you sides of Campeche that you didn't know existed. They also offer car rentals and travel booking services.

Xtampak Tours (xtampac_7@hotmail.com; ✆ **981/811-6473**), one of the historic center's most highly recommended agencies, offers comprehensive city tours, shuttle service to Edzná, as well as guided tours and tours of the Chenes sites and eastern Campeche.

To create your own private tour, I highly recommend **Erik Mendicuti** (emobile2@hotmail.com; ✆ **981/121-0892**), who is a translator and a guide with extensive experience and a passion for Campeche. His base price is 800 pesos a day, depending on time, distance, and transportation arrangements.

Where to Eat

Campeche is a fishing town, known for its fresh seafood, but restaurants also offer classic Yucatecan pork, chicken, turkey, and beef dishes. Campeche also has its own regional cuisine, fusing Spanish dishes, recipes brought by pirates from all over the world, and the region's own exotic fruits and vegetables. Make a point to try the No. 1 specialty, *pan de cazón* (baby shark casserole)—a stack of tortillas layered with baby shark and refried beans, then smothered with tomato sauce. For an inexpensive introduction to Campechano cuisine, sample the home-cooked food served in stalls around the *zócalo* on weekend evenings.

EXPENSIVE

La Pigua ★★★ SEAFOOD   The dining area is an air-conditioned version of a traditional Yucatecan cabin, but with walls of glass looking out on green vegetation. Sure to be on the menu is fish stuffed with shellfish, which I recommend. If you're lucky, you'll also find pompano in a green sauce seasoned with a peppery herb known as *hierba santa*. Other standouts are coconut-battered shrimp with applesauce and chiles rellenos with shark. Service is excellent, and the accommodating owner can have your favorite seafood prepared in any style you want.

Av. Miguel Alemán no. 179A (btw. calles 49A and 49B). ✆ **981/811-3365.** Reservations recommended. Main courses 120–260 pesos. AE, MC, V. Daily 1–9pm. From Plaza Principal, walk north on Calle 8 for 3 blocks; cross Av. Circuito by the botanical garden where Calle 8 becomes Miguel Alemán; the restaurant is 1½ blocks farther, on the right.

MODERATE

Casa Vieja ✋YUCATECAN   Casa Vieja has gotten a little, well, old. While the blend of Yucatecan and Cuban food still holds interest, there's been a drop in effort. But this is still the city's prettiest dining space, in an upstairs arcade overlooking the main square. Stick with simple regional dishes, and if you're lucky, they'll be on the upswing in that mysterious cycle of quality that seems to rule so many restaurants.

Calle 10 no. 319 altos, Portales Revolución. ℂ **981/811-8016.** Main courses 60–160 pesos. No credit cards. Tues–Sat 8:30am–midnight; Sun 4pm–midnight.

Marganzo ★ SEAFOOD   The menu veers toward the expensive side if you indulge in the seafood—its specialty—but if you stick to the Yucatecan dishes such as *poc chuc* and *pollo pibíl*, you'll eat quite well for 75 pesos or so. If you spring for seafood, whitefish filled with seafood is a local favorite. Either way, you'll leave satisfied; the kitchen knows what it's doing. Though it isn't the bargain it used to be, breakfast is still the most popular meal here.

Calle 8 no. 267 (in front of the Sea Gate). www.marganzo.com. ℂ **981/811-3899.** Main courses 82–228 pesos. MC, V. Daily 7am–11pm.

INEXPENSIVE

El Bastion YUCATECAN   This pretty but very casual place offers a variety of Mexican food—the emphasis is on breakfast, which is available all day—including a good number of regional dishes and regional twists on traditional dishes, such as *motuleños* or *tacos de cochinita pibíl* (highly recommended). Salsa campechana, the rich tomato-based sauce with a distinct Caribbean tang that is served with seafood cocktails, might show up just about anywhere here. Drop in any time of day or night, even if you don't quite know what you feel like eating, and you'll find satisfaction here.

Calle 57 no. 2A (btw. calles 8 and 10). ℂ **981/816-2128.** Breakfast 42–99 pesos, main courses 55–90 pesos. Daily 6am–midnight. No credit cards.

Cenaduría los Portales ★ ANTOJITOS   This is a traditional Campechano supper place, a small restaurant under the stone arches facing the Plaza San Francisco in the *barrio* (neighborhood) of San Francisco. This is the oldest part of town, but it lies just outside the walls to the north. Start with the *horchata* (a sweet, milky-white drink made, in this case, with coconut). Try the delicious turkey soup and the *sincronizadas* (tostadas) and *panuchos*.

Calle 10 no. 86, bajo Portales San Francisco. ℂ **981/811-1491.** *Antojitos* 4–15 pesos. No credit cards. Daily 6pm–midnight.

Chocol-Ha ★★★ INTERNATIONAL   Chocolate is the *raison d'être* here—good, robust, not overly sweet chocolate in more than a dozen hot and cold drinks plus crepes, cakes, and even a tamal. But this place will also calm a coffee jones, and if you're a bit peckish in the evening, campechao-style tamales, croissant sandwiches, and veggie-filled crepes are available. If you've had your fill of caffeine, choose from a variety of natural fruit juices. It's a simple menu done to perfection, and the air-conditioned cafe is as comfortable and friendly as it is cute.

Calle 59 no. 30 (btw. calles 12 and 14). ℂ **981/811-7893.** Drinks 18–39 pesos; small plates & desserts 20–55 pesos. No credit cards. Mon–Thurs 5:30–11:30pm; Fri–Sat 5:30pm–12:30am.

La Parroquia MEXICAN   This local hangout offers good, inexpensive fare. It's best for breakfasts and the afternoon *comida corrida,* which might offer pot roast, meatballs, pork, or fish, with rice or squash, beans, tortillas, and fresh fruit–flavored water. Service can be slow.

Calle 55 no. 8 (btw. calles 10 and 12). ⓒ **981/816-2530.** Breakfast 50 pesos; main courses 50–130 pesos; *comida corrida* (noon–3pm) 45–55 pesos. MC, V. Daily 24 hr.

Luz de Luna ★★ 🍴 INTERNATIONAL   Whether you're looking for regional food or are in a more international mood, this hole-in-the-wall restaurant delivers sophisticated meals at unassuming prices. My chicken breast with lime and red pepper was simple perfection, and the lime-marinated cucumber strips dipped in a Tajín chile powder mix was an inspired departure from chips and salsa. Everything in the compact space—I don't think there are more than 8 tables—is a feast for the eyes, from the hand-carved and -painted chairs to the multitude of fans, star-shaped lamps, and lanterns hanging from the ceiling, all from local artists.

Calle 59 no. 6 (btw. calles 10 and 12). ⓒ **981/100-8556.** Breakfast 35–75 pesos; main courses 55–80 pesos. No credit cards. Mon–Sat 8am–9pm; Sun 9am–6pm.

Shopping

Bazar Artesanal ★   Imagine a traditional Mexican market, with all its variety of handmade goods and crafts, but without the crowding, the heat, or the haggling. This state-run indoor, air-conditioned artisan market on the *malecón* offers a wide variety of local crafts with some items, such as bull horns carved into mirror frames and jewelry, rarely found elsewhere. If you won't get to Becal, this is a good place to look for a Panama hat. If you enjoy bargaining as sport, be aware that prices here are fixed. They aren't the cheapest prices you'll find, either, but the merchandise is top quality. Av. Pedro Sainz de Baranda, Centro Comercial Ah Kiim Pech, 201-223. ⓒ **981/127-1036.** Daily 10am–10pm.

Casa de Artesanías Tukulná   This store, run by a government family-assistance agency, occupies a restored mansion and sells top-quality examples of everything that is produced in the state, from textiles to clothing to furniture. An elaborate display of regional arts and crafts in the back includes a hammock in the making and a replica of a mud-walled Maya house. Calle 10 no. 333 (btw. calles 59 and 61). ⓒ **981/816-9088.** Mon–Sat 10am–8pm; Sun 10am–2pm.

Where to Stay

Rates quoted include the 17% tax.

VERY EXPENSIVE

Casa don Gustavo ★★★   The first challenger to Hacienda Puerta Campeche's hold on the luxury crown began life as the 18th-century home of a wealthy merchant. Renovated 2 years ago, it retains many original details—some of the *mosaico* tiles, for example, were reconstituted to create a rug effect—remodeled into light and airy spaces and accommodating modern, European-style bathrooms. Rooms with 13-foot ceilings are filled with 200-year-old furniture, including such remarkable pieces as a bed that the National Institute of Anthropology and History believes belonged to the Empress Carlotta and a clock that might have belonged to Napoleon. Yet somehow, you don't feel like you're sleeping in a museum; you feel like a successful merchant enjoying your elegant home.

Calle 59 no. 4 (btw. Calles 8 and 10) 24000 Campeche, Camp. www.casadongustavo.com. ⓒ **981/ 811-2350.** 10 units. $250–$350 double. (**Note:** These are rack rates; lower rates often available through online booking sites.) Rates include breakfast. AE, MC, V. Limited free parking. **Amenities:** Restaurant; bar; outdoor pool; rooftop terrace; concierge; room service; Wi-Fi (in common areas). *In room:* A/C, TV, iPod docking station; clock radio; hair dryer.

Hacienda Puerta Campeche ★★★ This beautiful and original hotel is not actually a hacienda—it was created from several adjoining colonial homes, just inside the Puerta de Tierra in Campeche's historic center. The houses surround a tropical garden, and a pool runs through the ruined walls of one house. Rooms are colonial with flair—large with old tile floors, distinctive colors, and beamed ceilings. "Hacienda" is part of the name to make it apparent that this hotel is connected to the hacienda properties managed by Starwood hotels (p. 249).

Calle 59 no. 71 (btw. Calles 16 and 18), 24000 Campeche, Camp. www.luxurycollection.com. © **800/325-3589** in the U.S. or Canada, or 981/816-7508. Fax 999/923-7963. 15 units. High season $290–$460 double; low season $189–$380. AE, MC, V. Free guarded parking. **Amenities:** Restaurant; 2 bars; airport transfer; babysitting; concierge; outdoor pool; room service; spa. *In room:* A/C, TV, fridge, hair dryer, Internet, minibar.

EXPENSIVE

Hotel Del Mar ★ It's your typical uninspiring concrete rectangle, but rooms in this modern four-story hotel are large, bright, and comfortably furnished. All have balconies facing the Gulf of Mexico. The beds (two doubles or one king-size) are comfortable. The Del Mar is on the main oceanfront boulevard, between the coast and the city walls. You can make a reservation here to stay in the Río Bec area, or you can buy a package that includes guide and transportation.

Av. Ruiz Cortines 51 (at Calle 59), 24000 Campeche, Camp. www.delmarhotel.com.mx. ©/fax **981/811-9191.** 164 units. $80 double. AE, MC, V. Free parking. **Amenities:** 2 restaurants; bar; babysitting; gym w/sauna; large outdoor pool; room service. *In room:* A/C, TV, hair dryer.

MODERATE

Hotel Castelmar ★★ ☺ This remarkable transformation of a one-time flophouse was restored with pillars, archways, and tall wooden doors reminiscent of Puerta de Campeche. The original floor plans and tiles (different patterns in each room) remain, and rooms are all shapes and sizes. But the bathrooms, swimming pool, and sun deck are new. I like the rooms with double doors opening onto a tiny balcony, though some people find them too noisy. It's a great *centro histórico* (historical district) location, 2 blocks from the *zócalo.*

Calle 61 no. 2 (btw. calles 8 and 10), 24000 Campeche, Camp. www.castelmarhotel.com. © **981/811-1204.** Fax 702/297-6826. 22 units. 750 pesos double; 850 pesos superior; 1,050 pesos junior suite. AE, MC, V. Free parking. **Amenities:** Concierge; outdoor pool; sun deck. *In room:* A/C, TV, hair dryer (on request), Wi-Fi.

Hotel Francis Drake ★ ✦ This three-story hotel in a quiet *centro histórico* location has comfortable, midsize rooms with upscale touches not often seen at the rates they charge. The modern marble bathrooms have large showers. Suites are larger and better furnished than the standard rooms. Service is attentive, if not particularly warm by Campeche standards. The small restaurant serves fine examples of local dishes at very reasonable prices.

Calle 12 no. 207 (btw. calles 63 and 65), 24000 Campeche, Camp. www.hotelfrancisdrake.com. © **981/811-5626,** -5627. 24 units. 795 pesos double; 905 pesos junior suite; 1,030 pesos suite. AE, MC, V. Limited free parking. **Amenities:** Restaurant; concierge; room service. *In room:* A/C, TV, hair dryer, minibar.

INEXPENSIVE

H177 🗝 Bright, modern rooms, pleasant common areas, and some amenities that go beyond the basics—flatscreen TV and in-room phones—put this newcomer a rung above the usual budget hotel. The spare, urban design won't appeal to everyone, but the small rooms are comfortable and manage a certain sense of intimacy. Rates are exceptionally good for the comforts and practical conveniences the hotel offers.

Calle 14 no. 177 (btw. calles 59 and 61), 24000 Campeche, Camp. www.h177hotel.com. ☏ **981/816-4463.** 24 units. 560–640 pesos double. MC, V. **Amenities:** Coffee bar; Jacuzzi; laundry; Wi-Fi. *In room:* A/C, TV, Wi-Fi.

Hotel López 🗝 Unique among the historic center's hotels, the López is all Art Deco verve, with curlicued ironwork swooping around layers of curved walkways above an oval-shaped, open-air courtyard. The 1950 building was rehabilitated several years ago, adding gleaming tile bathrooms, a new waterfall pool, and a small cafe. Guest rooms are small and not nearly as stylish as the public areas, but they are comfortable and clean.

Calle 12 no. 189 (btw. calles 61 and 63), 24000 Campeche, Camp. www.hotellopezcampeche. com.mx. ☏ **981/816-3344.** 48 units. 500 pesos. MC, V. **Amenities:** Outdoor pool. *In room:* A/C, TV, Wi-Fi.

Side Trips from Campeche
CALAKMUL & RÍO BEC

The ruins along the Río Bec route, though in Campeche state, are more often visited from Quintana Roo; see "Side Trips to Maya Ruins from Chetumal," in chapter 6. **Calakmul** ★★★ (p. 217) is one of Mexico's most important sites, with the tallest pyramid on the Yucatán peninsula; Balamkú and other Río Bec sites are well worth seeing while you're in the area. You can get information and book a tour in Campeche, or rent a car. Although tour companies offer Calakmul as a day trip from Campeche, it is too far away to enjoy, let alone appreciate, without staying overnight in the area.

From the Calakmul area, it's easy to cross over the peninsula to Yucatán's southern Caribbean coast. Then you can head up the coast and complete a loop of the peninsula.

THE RUINS OF CHICHÉN ITZÁ ★★★

179km (111 miles) W of Cancún; 120km (75 miles) E of Mérida; 138km (86 miles) NW of Tulum

The fabled ruins of Chichén Itzá (Chee-*chen* Eet-*zah*) are by far the Yucatán's best-known ancient monuments. Sadly, its coronation as a "New World Wonder" has made the great city harder to appreciate. Still, walking among these stone temples, pyramids, and ball courts gives you a feel for this civilization that books cannot approach, and there's no other way to comprehend the city's sheer scale. The ceremonial center's plazas would have been filled with thousands of people during one of the mass rituals that occurred here a millennium ago—and that is the saving grace for hordes of tourists that now flow through every day.

Much of what is said about the Maya (especially by tour guides) is merely educated guessing. We do know the area was settled by farmers as far back as the

The fabled ruins of Chichén Itzá.

4th century A.D. The first signs of an urban society appear in the 7th century in construction of stone temples and palaces in the Puuc Maya style, found in the "Old Chichén" section of the city. In the 10th century (the post-Classic Era), Chichén Itzá came under the rule of the Itzáes, who arrived from central Mexico by way of the Gulf Coast. They may have been a mix of highland Toltec Indians, who built the city of Tula in central Mexico, and lowland Putún Maya, a thriving population of traders. Following centuries brought Chichén Itzá's greatest growth. The style of the grand architecture built during this age clearly reveals Toltec influence.

The new rulers might have been refugees from Tula. A pre-Columbian myth from central Mexico tells of a fight between the gods Quetzalcóatl and Tezcatlipoca that forced Quetzalcóatl to leave his homeland and venture east. In another mythic tale, the losers of a war between Tula's religious factions fled to the Yucatán, where they were welcomed by the local Maya. Over time, the Itzáes adopted more and more the ways of the Maya. Sometime at the end of the 12th century, the city was captured by its rival, Mayapán.

Though it's possible to make a day trip from Cancún or Mérida, staying overnight here or in nearby Valladolid makes for a more relaxing trip. You can see the light show in the evening and return to see the ruins early the next morning when it is cool and before the tour buses start arriving.

Essentials

GETTING THERE & DEPARTING **By Car** Chichén Itzá is on old Hwy. 180 between Mérida and Cancún. The fastest way to get there from either city is to take the *autopista* (or *cuota*). The toll is 78 pesos from Mérida (1½ hr.), 267 pesos from Cancún (2½ hr.). From Tulum, take the highway leading to Cobá and Chemax, which connects to Hwy. 180 a bit east of Valladolid. Exiting the *autopista,* turn onto the road to Pisté. In the village, you'll reach a T junction at Hwy. 180 and turn left to the ruins; the entrance is well marked. On the same highway a few kilometers beyond, you'll come to the Hotel Zone exit at Km 121 (first, you'll pass the eastern entrance to the ruins, which is usually closed).

By Bus First-class buses run from Mérida's CAME station nearly every hour, and some first-class buses to Cancún and Playa also stop here.

Cancún and Valladolid also have first-class service. Day trips to Chichén Itzá are also widely available from Mérida, Cancún, and Playa del Carmen (and almost any destination in the Yucatán).

AREA LAYOUT   The village of **Pisté,** where most of the budget hotels and restaurants are located, is about 2.5km (1½ miles) west of the ruins. Public buses can drop you off here. Another budget hotel, the Dolores Alba (p. 250), is on the old highway 2.5km (1½ miles) east of the ruins. Three luxury hotels are situated right at Chichén Itzá's entrance.

Exploring the Ruins

The site occupies 6.5 sq. km (2½ sq. miles), requiring most of a day to see it all. The ruins are open daily from 8am to 5pm, service areas from 8am to 10pm. Admission for foreigners is 234 pesos, free for children 11 and younger. A video camera permit costs 45 pesos. Parking is extra. *You can use your ticket to reenter on the same day.* The **sound-and-light show** is held at 7pm fall and winter and 8pm spring and summer, and costs 72 pesos. The narrative is in Spanish, but headsets are available for rent in several languages. The real reason for attending is the lights, which show off the beautiful geometry of the city.

The large, modern visitor center at the main entrance consists of a museum, an auditorium, a restaurant, a bookstore, and bathrooms. Licensed guides who speak English or Spanish usually wait at the entrance and charge around 450 pesos for one to six people (there's nothing wrong with approaching a group of people who speak the same language and offering to share a guide). You can also see the site on your own, but the guides can point out architectural details you might miss on your own.

Chichén Itzá has two parts: the central (new) zone, which shows distinct Toltec influence, and the southern (old) zone, with mostly Puuc architecture. The most important structures are in New Chichén, but the older ones are also worth seeing. For more information, go to http://chichenitza.inah.gob.mx.

EL CASTILLO   As you enter from the tourist center, the icon of Yucatán tourism, the magnificent 25m (82-ft.) El Castillo (also called the Pyramid of

The sound-and-light show illuminates the pyramids of Chichén Itzá.

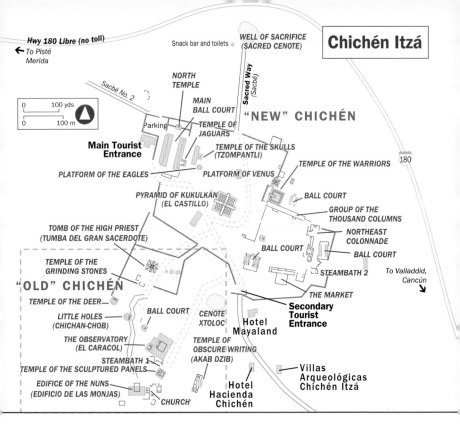

Kukulkán) is straight ahead across a large, open grassy area. It was built with the Maya calendar in mind. The four stairways leading up to the central platform each have 91 steps, which, added to the platform, totals the 365 days of the solar year. The 18 terraces flanking the stairways on each face of the pyramid add up to the number of months in the Maya religious calendar. The terraces contain a total of 52 panels representing the 52-year cycle when the solar and religious calendars reconverge. The pyramid, now closed to climbers, is aligned so that the **spring** or **fall equinox** (Mar 21 or Sept 21) triggers an optical illusion: The setting sun casts the terraces' shadow onto the northern stairway, forming a diamond pattern suggestive of a snake's geometric designs. As it meets the giant serpent's head at the bottom, the shadow appears to slither down the pyramid as the sun sets, a phenomenon that brings hordes of visitors every year. (The effect is more conceptual than visual, and frankly, the ruins are much more enjoyable on other days when they are less crowded.)

Like most Maya pyramids, El Castillo was built over an earlier structure. A narrow stairway at the western edge of the north staircase leads inside to a sacrificial altar-throne—a red jaguar encrusted with jade. The stairway is open from 11am to 3pm and is cramped, usually crowded, humid, and uncomfortable. A visit early in the day is best. Taking photos of the jaguar figure is not allowed.

JUEGO DE PELOTA (MAIN BALL COURT)   Northwest of El Castillo is Chichén's main ball court, the largest and best preserved anywhere, and only one of nine ball courts built in this city. Carved on both walls are scenes showing Maya figures dressed as ball players and decked out in heavy protective padding. A headless player kneels with blood shooting from his neck; another player holding the head looks on.

Players on two teams tried to knock a hard rubber ball through one of the two stone rings placed high on either wall, using only their elbows, knees, and hips. According to legend, losers paid for defeat with their lives. However, some experts say the victors were the only appropriate sacrifices for the gods. Either way, the game, called *pok-ta-pok*, must have been riveting, heightened by the ball court's wonderful acoustics.

THE NORTH TEMPLE   Temples stand at both ends of the ball court. The North Temple has sculptured pillars and more sculptures inside, as well as badly ruined murals. The acoustics of the ball court are so good that from the North Temple, a person speaking can be heard clearly at the opposite end, about 135m (443 ft.) away.

TEMPLE OF JAGUARS   Near the southeastern corner of the main ball court is a small temple with serpent columns and carved panels showing warriors and jaguars. Up the steps and inside the temple, a mural chronicles a battle in a Maya village.

TZOMPANTLI (TEMPLE OF THE SKULLS)   To the right of the ball court, the Temple of the Skulls obviously borrows from the post-Classic cities of central Mexico. Notice the rows of skulls carved into the stone platform; when a sacrificial victim's head was cut off, it was impaled on a pole and displayed with others in a tidy row. Also carved into the stone are pictures of eagles tearing hearts from human victims. The word "Tzompantli" is not Mayan, but comes from central Mexico.

PLATFORM OF THE EAGLES   Next to the Tzompantli, this small platform has reliefs showing eagles and jaguars clutching human hearts in their talons and claws, as well as a human head emerging from the mouth of a serpent.

PLATFORM OF VENUS   East of the Tzompantli and north of El Castillo, near the road to the Sacred Cenote, is the Platform of Venus. In Maya and Toltec lore, a feathered monster or a feathered serpent with a human head in its mouth represented Venus. This is also called the tomb of Chaac-Mool, for the figure that was discovered "buried" within the structure.

SACRED CENOTE   Follow the dirt road (actually an ancient *sacbé,* or causeway) leading north from the

Pelota players tried to knock a hard rubber ball through this stone ring on the Ball Court.

Platform of Venus for 5 minutes to get to the great natural well that may have given Chichén Itzá (the Well of the Itzáes) its name. This well was used for ceremonial purposes, and the bones of both children and adult sacrificial victims were found at the bottom.

Edward Thompson, who was the American consul in Mérida and a Harvard professor, purchased the ruins of Chichén early in the 20th century and explored the cenote with dredges and divers. He uncovered a fortune in gold and jade, most of which ended up in Harvard's Peabody Museum of Archaeology and Ethnology—a matter that disconcerts Mexican classicists to this day. Excavations in the 1960s yielded more treasure, and studies of the recovered objects show that the offerings came from throughout the Yucatán and even farther away.

TEMPLO DE LOS GUERREROS (TEMPLE OF THE WARRIORS) The Toltec influence is especially evident on the eastern edge of the plaza. Due east of El Castillo is one of Chichén Itzá's most impressive structures, the Temple of the Warriors, named for the carvings of warriors marching along its walls. The temple and the rows of almost Greco-Roman columns flanking it are also called the Group of the Thousand Columns, and it recalls the great Toltec site of Tula. A figure of Chaac-Mool sits at the top of the temple (visible only from a distance now that the temple is closed to climbers), surrounded by columns carved in relief to look like enormous feathered serpents. South of the temple was a square building that archaeologists call **El Mercado** (The Market); a colonnade surrounds its central court.

The main Mérida–Cancún highway once ran straight through the ruins of Chichén, and though it has been diverted, you can still see the great swath it cut. South and west of the old highway's path are more impressive ruined buildings.

TUMBA DEL GRAN SACERDOTE (TOMB OF THE HIGH PRIEST) Past the refreshment stand to the right of the path, the Tomb of the High Priest shows both Toltec and Puuc influence. The 9m (30-ft.) pyramid, with stairways on each side depicting feathered serpents, bears a distinct resemblance to El Castillo. Beneath its foundation is an ossuary (a communal graveyard) in a natural limestone cave, where skeletons and offerings have been found.

CASA DE LOS METATES (TEMPLE OF THE GRINDING STONES) This building, the next one on your right, is named after the Maya's concave corn-grinding stones.

TEMPLO DEL VENADO (TEMPLE OF THE DEER) Past Casa de los Metates is this fairly tall, though

Columns leading to the Temple of the Warriors.

ruined, building. The relief of a stag that gave the temple its name is long gone.

CHICHANCHOB (LITTLE HOLES) This temple has a roof comb with little holes, three masks of the rain god Chaac, three rooms, and a good view of surrounding structures. It's one of Chichén's oldest buildings, built in the Puuc style during the late Classic period.

EL CARACOL (THE OBSERVATORY) One of Chichén Itzá's most intriguing structures is in the old part of the city. From a distance, the rounded tower of El Caracol ("The Snail," for its shape), sometimes called The Observatory, looks like any modern observatory. Construction of this complex building with its circular tower was carried out over centuries, acquiring additions and modifications as the Maya's careful celestial observations required increasingly exact measurements. Quite unlike other Maya buildings, the entrances, staircases, and angles are not aligned with one another. The tower's circular chamber has a spiral staircase leading to the upper level. The slits in the roof are aligned with the sun's equinoxes. Astronomers observed the cardinal directions and the approach of the all-important spring and autumn equinoxes, as well as the summer solstice.

On the east side of El Caracol, a path leads north into the bush to the **Cenote Xtoloc,** a natural limestone well that provided the city's daily water supply. If you see lizards sunning there, they may well be *xtoloc,* the species for which this cenote is named.

TEMPLO DE LOS TABLEROS (TEMPLE OF THE PANELS) Just south of El Caracol are the ruins of a *temazcalli* (a steam bath) and the Temple of Panels, named for the carved panels on top. A few traces remain of the much larger structure that once covered the temple.

EDIFICIO DE LAS MONJAS (EDIFICE OF THE NUNS) This enormous nunnery is reminiscent of the palaces at sites along the Puuc route. The new edifice was built in the late Classic period over an older one. To prove this, an early 20th-century archaeologist put dynamite between the two and blew away part of the exterior, revealing the older structures within. Indelicate, perhaps, but effective.

Chichén Itzá's El Caracol is shaped like a snail shell.

On the east side of the Edifice of the Nuns is **Anexo Este** (annex), constructed in highly ornate Chenes style with Chaac masks and serpents.

LA IGLESIA (THE CHURCH)   Next to the annex is another of Chichén's oldest buildings, the Church. Masks of Chaac decorate two upper stories; a close look reveals armadillo, crab, snail, and tortoise symbols among the crowd of Chaacs. These represent the Maya gods, called *bacab,* whose job it was to hold up the sky.

AKAB DZIB (TEMPLE OF OBSCURE WRITING)   Beloved of travel writers, this temple lies east of the Edifice of the Nuns. Above a door in one of the rooms are some Mayan glyphs, which gave the temple its name because the writings are hard to make out. In other rooms, traces of red handprints are still visible. Reconstructed and expanded over the centuries, Akab Dzib might be the oldest building on the site.

CHICHÉN VIEJO (OLD CHICHÉN)   For a look at more of Chichén's oldest buildings, constructed well before the time of Toltec influence, follow signs from the Edifice of the Nuns southwest into the bush to Old Chichén, about 1km (²⁄₃ mile) away. Be prepared for this trek with long trousers, insect repellent, and a local guide. Attractions here include the **Templo de los Inscripciones Iniciales** (Temple of the First Inscriptions), with the oldest inscriptions discovered at Chichén, and the restored **Templo de los Dinteles** (Temple of the Lintels), a fine Puuc building. Some of these buildings are being restored.

Where to Stay & Eat

The expensive hotels in Chichén occupy beautiful grounds, are close to the ruins, serve decent food, and have toll-free reservations numbers. They do a brisk business with tour operators—they can be empty one day and full the next. From these hotels, you can easily walk to the back entrance of the ruins, next to the Hotel Mayaland. **Hotel Chichén Itzá** (www.mayaland.com; ✆ 998/887-2495) is the best of several inexpensive hotels just west of the ruins in the village of Pisté, which has little else to recommend it. Another option is to stay in the colonial town of Valladolid (p. 294), 40 minutes away.

This area has no great food, but it has plenty of adequate food; simple choices are best. The ruins' visitor center serves decent snack food. Hotel restaurants do a fair job but are more expensive than they should be. In the Pisté, try the Hotel Chichén Itzá or one of the restaurants along the highway that cater to bus tours (best during early lunch or regular supper hours, when the buses are gone).

EXPENSIVE

Hacienda Chichén Resort ★★   The smallest and most private of the hotels at the ruins' entrance is also the quietest. A one-time hacienda that served as headquarters for the Carnegie Institute's excavations in 1923, the bungalows built for institute staff residences now house one or two units with a dehumidifier, a ceiling fan, and good air-conditioning. The floors are ceramic tile, ceilings are stucco with wood beams, and walls are adorned with carved stone. Trees and tropical plants fill manicured gardens that you can enjoy from your private porch or from the terrace restaurant, which occupies part of the original main house.

Zona Arqueológica, 97751 Chichén Itzá, Yuc. www.haciendachichen.com. ✆ **985/851-0045.** (Reservations office in Mérida: ✆ 877/631-4005 in the U.S., or 999/920-8407.) 28 units. High season $169–$265 double; $280 suite; low season $120–$169 double; $180 suite. Promotional rates available. AE, MC, V. Free guarded parking. **Amenities:** Restaurant; 2 bars; large outdoor pool; spa. *In room:* A/C, hair dryer, minibar, no phone.

MODERATE

Villas Arqueológicas Chichén Itzá ★ ☺ Similar to its sister property at Uxmal, this hotel is built around a courtyard and pool and is a happy compromise between low-budget lodging and the more lavish hotels nearby. It's by far the best deal if you want to stay near the entrance to the ruins (a 5- to 10-min. walk on a peaceful road). Rooms are modern, clean, and quite comfortable, unless you're 1.9m (6 ft. 2 in.) or taller—each bed is in a niche, with walls at the head and foot. Most rooms have one double bed and a twin bed, and Islander has added a few suites. You can also book a half- or full-board plan.

Zona Arqueológica, Carretera Mérida–Valladolid Km 120, 97751 Chichén Itzá, Yuc. www.villas arqueologicas.com.mx. ✆ **222/273-7900.** Fax 985/856-6008. 45 units. $59–$84 double; $121–$173 suite. Rates include continental breakfast. Half-board (breakfast plus lunch or dinner) $20 per person; full board (3 meals) $35 per person. AE, MC, V. Free parking. **Amenities:** Restaurant; bar; large outdoor pool; tennis court; Wi-Fi (in public areas). *In room:* A/C, hair dryer.

INEXPENSIVE

Hotel Dolores Alba 🏄 This longtime budget favorite is of the motel variety, and it is a bargain for what you get: two pools (one fed by a natural spring); hammocks hanging under *palapas*; and large, comfortable rooms with some colorful hacienda-style accents that come with two double beds. The restaurant serves good meals at moderate prices. The hotel provides free transportation to the ruins and the Cave of Balankanché, though you will have to take a taxi back. It is on the highway 2.5km (1½ miles) east of the ruins (toward Valladolid).

Carretera Mérida–Valladolid Km 122, Yuc. www.doloresalba.com. ✆ **985/858-1555.** 40 units. 650 pesos double. MC, V (8% service charge). Free parking. **Amenities:** Restaurant; bar; 2 outdoor pools; room service. *In room:* A/C, TV, no phone.

Other Area Attractions

Ik-Kil (70 pesos; daily 8am–6pm) is a large, deep cenote on the highway across from the Hotel Dolores Alba, 2.5km (1½ miles) east of the main entrance to the ruins. Getting down to the water's edge requires navigating many steps, but they are easier to manage than those at Dzitnup. The view from both the top and the bottom is dramatic, with lots of tropical vegetation and hanging tree roots stretching to the water's surface. Go swimming before 11:30am, when bus tours begin to arrive. These tours are the main business of Ik-Kil, which also has a restaurant and souvenir shops.

The **Cave of Balankanché** (95 pesos; kids 6 and under not permitted) is 5.5km (3½ miles) from Chichén Itzá on the road to Valladolid and Cancún. Taxis will make the trip and wait. The entire excursion takes about a half-hour, but the walk inside is hot and humid. This is the tamest of the Yucatán's cave tours, with good footing and the least amount of walking and climbing. It includes a cheesy and uninformative recorded tour. The highlight is a round chamber with a central column that resembles a large tree. The cave became a hideout during the War of the Castes, and you can still see traces of carving and incense burning, as well as an underground stream that supplied water to the refugees. Outside, meander through the botanical gardens, where nearly everything is labeled with common and botanical names. Tours in English 11am and 1 and 3pm; in Spanish, 9am, noon, and 2 and 4pm. Double-check hours at Chichén Itzá's main entrance. Use of video camera 45 pesos (free with video permit bought in Chichén the same day).

VALLADOLID

40km (25 miles) E of Chichén Itzá; 160km (99 miles) SW of Cancún; 98km (61 miles) NW of Tulum

Valladolid (pronounced "bah-yah-doh-*leed*") is a small colonial city halfway between Mérida and Cancún. One of the first Spanish strongholds and crucible of the War of the Castes (p. 27), the city still has handsome colonial buildings and 19th-century structures that make it a pleasant place to bask in the real Yucatán. People are friendly and informal, and the only real challenge is the heat. The city's economy is based on commerce and small-scale manufacturing. It's close to a couple of famous cenotes, the intriguing ruins of Ek Balam, Ría Lagartos' nesting flamingos, and the sandy beaches of Isla Holbox (p. 302). It's closer to Chichén Itzá than Mérida is, and it is an inexpensive town, making it a good alternative base for exploring.

Essentials

GETTING THERE & DEPARTING

BY CAR From Mérida or Cancún, you can take either the Hwy. 180 *cuota* (toll road) or Hwy. 180 *libre* (free). The toll is 233 pesos from Cancún and 135 pesos from Mérida. The **cuota** passes 2km (1¼ miles) north of the city; the exit is at the crossing of Hwy. 295 to Tizimín. Hwy. 180 *libre,* passing through a number of villages (with their requisite *topes*) takes significantly longer. Both 180 and 295 lead straight to downtown. Leaving is just as easy: From the main square, Calle 41 turns into 180 E. to Cancún; Calle 39 heads to 180 W. to Chichén Itzá and Mérida. To take the *cuota* to Mérida or Cancún, take Calle 40 (see "City Layout," below).

BY BUS Buses leave throughout the day for Mérida (134 pesos) and Cancún (82 pesos). You can also get several buses a day to Playa del Carmen (96 pesos) and Tulum (64 pesos). To get to Chichén Itzá, take a second-class bus, which leaves at least every hour. The recently remodeled bus station is at the corner of calles 39 and 46.

ORIENTATION

VISITOR INFORMATION The small **tourism office** is in the Palacio Municipal, open Monday to Friday from 8am to 9pm, Saturday and Sunday 9am to 9pm.

CITY LAYOUT Valladolid's layout is the standard for towns in the Yucatán: Streets running north–south are even numbers; those running east–west are odd numbers. The main plaza is bordered by Calle 39 on the north, 41 on the south, 40 on the east, and 42 on the west. The plaza is named Parque Francisco Cantón Rosado, but everyone calls it **El Centro.** Taxis are easy to come by.

Exploring Valladolid

THE MAIN PLAZA

Valladolid's **main plaza** is the town's social center and a thriving market for Yucatecan dresses. The square was renovated in the winter of 2009–2010, and all of the lush old shade trees were preserved. The Old World benches and *confidenciales* (S-shaped chairs inviting friends or lovers to chat or nuzzle face-to-face), were either replaced or repainted. One downside: The Maya women who used to hang their brilliant embroidery on the fence for sale have been moved to stalls in the **Bazar Municipal,** next door to the Mesón del Marqués. Buildings

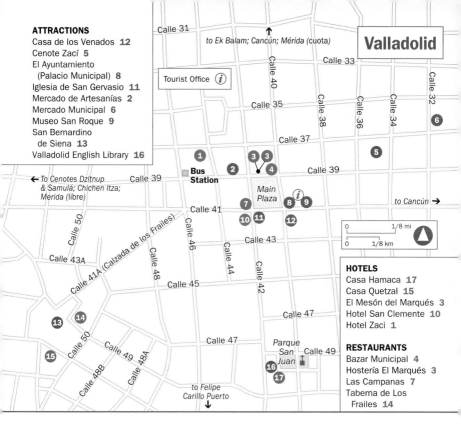

ATTRACTIONS
Casa de los Venados **12**
Cenote Zací **5**
El Ayuntamiento
  (Palacio Municipal) **8**
Iglesia de San Gervasio **11**
Mercado de Artesanías **2**
Mercado Municipal **6**
Museo San Roque **9**
San Bernardino
  de Siena **13**
Valladolid English Library **16**

Valladolid

Calle 31
to Ek Balam; Cancún; Mérida (cuota)
Tourist Office
Calle 33
Calle 40
Calle 35
Calle 38
Calle 36
Calle 34
Calle 32
Calle 37
Calle 39
Bus Station
Main Plaza
to Cancún →
← To Cenotes Dzitnup & Samulá; Chichen Itza; Mérida (libre)
Calle 39
Calle 41
Calle 50
Calle 41A (Calzada de los Frailes)
Calle 46
Calle 48
Calle 44
Calle 42
Calle 43
Calle 43A
Calle 45
Calle 47
Calle 47
Parque San Juan
Calle 49
Calle 50
Calle 49
Calle 48A
Calle 48B
to Felipe Carillo Puerto
0   1/8 mi
0   1/8 km

HOTELS
Casa Hamaca **17**
Casa Quetzal **15**
El Mesón del Marqués **3**
Hotel San Clemente **10**
Hotel Zaci **1**

RESTAURANTS
Bazar Municipal **4**
Hostería El Marqués **3**
Las Campanas **7**
Taberna de Los
  Frailes **14**

flanking the square were repainted, new lighting was added, and walking paths were repaved, yet the square still retains its old colonial feel.

On the plaza's south side is the imposing **Iglesia de San Gervasio** cathedral (sometimes called Parroquia de San Servacio). Its thick stone walls weren't enough to stop the Maya rebels who sacked it in 1847, touching off the War of the Castes. Vallesoletanos, as the locals are known, believe most all cathedrals in Mexico point east, and they cherish a local legend to explain why theirs points north—don't believe a word of it. On the east side, the municipal building, **El Ayuntamiento,** is the repository for dramatic paintings outlining the peninsula's history, including a wonderful depiction of a horrified Maya priest foreseeing the arrival of Spanish galleons. On Sunday nights, beneath the stone arches of the Ayuntamiento, the municipal band plays *jaranas* and other traditional regional music.

When is a museum not a museum? **Casa de los Venados** (www.casadelos venados.com; © **312/944-5215** in the U.S., or **985/856-2289**) is a private collection of Mexican folk art exhibited in the owners' 18,000-square-foot home, less than a half-block from the plaza's southeast corner. The house itself is a work of art, its 9-year renovation designed by the architect who resuscitated Mérida's exquisite Hacienda Xcanatun. But its highest purpose is to display the artwork that owners John and Dorianne Venator have collected over decades of travel. Outstanding examples of every kind of Mexican folk art I've seen in museums reside here—from miniatures and furniture to Day of the Dead skeletons and

Cenote Zací.

trees of life—all awaiting nose-to-nose inspection. It's best to e-mail javenator1@ gmail.com for an appointment; otherwise, stop in at 10am, the default time for tours.

AROUND TOWN

Before it became Valladolid, the city was a Maya settlement called Zací (zah-*kee*), which means "white hawk." The old name lives on in the cenote in a small park at the intersection of calles 39 and 36. The long but easily navigable stepped trail at **Cenote Zací ★** leads past caves, stalactites, and hanging vines that give the place a prehistoric feel, but the cenote's partially open roof lightens the atmosphere. It's a fine place to cool off, whether you jump in for a swim, dangle your feet in the water and let the fish nibble your toes, or just walk down to escape city heat and noise. I find Zací more peaceful and just as pretty as the famous cenotes outside of town (p. 297). The park, which has a large *palapa* restaurant overlooking the cenote, is free; entry to the cenote is 15 pesos.

For an overview of arts and crafts from surrounding Maya villages, find the pink, fortresslike building that houses **Museo San Roque** on Calle 41 between calles 38 and 40. Signs are in Spanish, but the displays mostly speak for themselves. Ancient stone masks, pottery, and bones unearthed at nearby Ek Balam (p. 300) are also on exhibit. The museum is open Monday through Saturday 9am to 9pm. Entry is free.

Ten blocks southwest of the main square is the Franciscan monastery of **San Bernardino de Siena ★★**, dating from 1552. The monastery complex was sacked during the War of the Castes, but a fine baroque altarpiece and some striking 17th-century paintings remain. Most of the compound was built in the early 1600s; a large underground river is believed to pass under the convent and surrounding neighborhood, which is called Barrio Sisal. ("Sisal," in this case, is a corruption of the Mayan phrase *sis-ha,* meaning "cold water.") The *barrio* has been extensively restored and is a delight. For a real treat, walk there just before sunset along the **Calzada de los Frailes (Walkway of the Friars) ★**. From the corner of calles 41 and 46, follow Calle 41A, the cobblestone street running diagonally to the southwest, about 1km (⅔ mile) to the monastery. The road is lined by huge clay planters and passes elegantly painted colonial homes.

Iglesia de San Gervasio.

The **Valladolid English library,** Calle 49 at Calle 40 on Parque San Juan, which opened on Thanksgiving Day in 2011, has quickly built up a collection of English-language books on all sorts of topics, including some rare titles on Maya history and culture. They are available for loan if you've run out of reading material, but the Language Exchange Hour (Tues 5pm) may be of more interest to travelers; you'll be able to help Spanish speakers learn English while they return the favor. At 8:15pm on the third Thursday of each month, the library's lecture series hosts talks by local authors, teachers, environmentalists, and other successful professionals. For information, e-mail denislarsen@yahoo.com.

OUTLYING AREAS

Jalisco state, as we all know, has a lock on the word "tequila" for the seductive liquor made from blue agave. That doesn't mean it isn't made anywhere else—only that it can't be *called* tequila. Valladolid's **Mayapán Distillery** (www.mayapan.mx; ✆ **985/856-1727**) produces some very good Mayapán from blue agave plants imported from Jalisco. You can buy blanco, reposado, or aged versions of Mayapán as well as many other brands at the distillery's Tequila Store, which shares space with what might be the best gift shop in Valladolid. Visitors are also invited to take a tour (30 pesos) to follow the entire process from growth and harvest of the agave to cooking, crushing (by a horse pulling a 1-ton stone around a stone *molienda*), fermentation, and distilling. The capstone is sampling three shots, one each of blanco, reposado, and añejo (aged) Mayapán.

The distillery, located north of town on the beltway at the intersection with the access road to the Hwy. 180 toll road, is open Monday to Friday 7am to 6pm and Saturday 7am to 1pm (Sun by request).

The **Cenote Dzitnup** (also known as Cenote Xkekén) is 4km (2½ miles) west of Valladolid off Hwy. 180 toward Chichén Itzá. It's said to be the most photographed cenote in the Yucatán, and it's easy to see why. The deep, glassy blue water, beneath a thicket of stalactites and ropy tree roots straining for a drink, is a spectacle. The beautiful pictures, however, don't reveal the treacherous stone

San Bernardino de Siena monastery.

steps, the unrelenting humidity even on an otherwise comfortable day (wear contacts instead of glasses, which will be constantly fogged), and the claustrophobic feeling if you're there with a crowd (which is most of the time). It's an awesome sight, and you should see it at least once. Bring a suit and take a swim; it will revive you for the climb back out.

The cenote is open daily from 7am to 7pm; admission is 52 pesos. If it's crowded, you can go for a swim about 90m (295 ft.) down the road on the opposite side in a smaller, less developed but also beautiful cenote, **Sammulá.**

Where to Eat

Valladolid is not a hotbed of haute cuisine, but the regional specialties are reliably good. **Hostería El Marqués ★★**, at the Hotel El Mesón del Marqués, turns out wonderful Yucatecan classics and international dishes in an achingly romantic setting. Also on the main square, friendly, informal **Las Campanas** serves tasty food for reasonable prices. At **Taberna de Los Frailes** (Calle 49 at Calle 41-A), near the San Bernardino Monastery, regional cuisine made from fresh local ingredients approach perfection. Locals like to visit over a meal at the stalls in the **Bazar Municipal,** next door to the Mesón del Marqués; I like them for a quick, cheap breakfast or a fresh-squeezed orange juice when the heat gets to me (you can also take it to go in a plastic bag with a straw).

Shopping

The **Mercado de Artesanías de Valladolid** (crafts market), at the corner of Calle 44 at Calle 39, gives you an overview of the local merchandise. Perhaps the town's primary handicraft is embroidered Maya dresses, which you can buy here or from women in the Bazar Municipal. Being in cattle country, Valladolid is a good place to buy inexpensive, locally made leather goods such as *huaraches* (sandals) and bags. **Yalat,** on Calle 39 at Calle 40, sells unique

 Cenote Etiquette

If you swim in a cenote, be sure you don't have creams or other chemicals on your skin—including deodorant. They damage the habitat of the small fish and other organisms living in the water. No alcohol, food, or smoking is allowed.

folk art from throughout Mexico, specializing in the Yucatán. The **Mercado Municipal,** where you can find just about anything, is on Calle 32 between calles 35 and 37.

Where to Stay

Aside from lodging listed below, Valladolid's best budget hotels are **Hotel San Clemente,** on Calle 42 between calles 41 and 43 (www.hotelsanclemente.com. mx; ✆ 985/856-3161; 448 pesos per night), and **Hotel Zací,** Calle 44 between calles 37 and 39 (✆ 985/856-2167; 468 pesos; no credit cards).

For change of pace, stay in a small ecohotel in the nearby village of Ek Balam, close to the ruins, at **Genesis Retreat Ek Balam** (www.genesisretreat. com; ✆ 985/858-9375; 499–699 pesos). The Canadian owner takes guests on village tours that unveil the contemporary Maya's daily life. She rents simple cabañas (with shared or private bathrooms) surrounding a lovely pool and a restaurant.

Casa Hamaca ★★   A lovely house in a junglelike garden ensconces guests in eight large rooms, each with its own theme. All the comforts you could ask for are here, but the greatest asset is Denis Larsen, the owner. He is a serious student of his adopted culture and a serious gadabout in the community (he's president of the Valladolid English Library, housed on the property), and spending a little time with him will inevitably pull you deeper into local life. At press time, the inn was ready to open a restaurant as soon as the license wended its way through the bureaucracy.

Calle 49 no. 202-A (at Calle 40), 97780 Valladolid, Yuc. www.casahamaca.com. ✆ **985/856-5287.** 8 units. High season $110 doubles, $135–$150 suites; low season $80 doubles, $110–$135 suite. Rates include full breakfast. No credit cards. Free secure parking. **Amenities:** Small outdoor pool; on-site parking; cooking and Spanish classes, massage and bodywork available. *In room:* A/C, no phone, Wi-Fi.

Women embroider fabric in Valladolid.

Casa Quetzal ★ The landlady, Judith Fernández, is a gracious Mexican woman who moved to Valladolid to slow down. She has created airy, attractive lodging in the refurbished Barrio Sisal, within walking distance of the main square. Emphasis is on comfort and service—good linens and mattresses, quiet air-conditioning, and a large and inviting central courtyard. English is spoken, and Sra. Fernández has lined up a good guide to take you to outlying areas.

Calle 51 no. 218, Barrio Sisal, 97780 Valladolid, Yuc. www.casa-quetzal.com. ℂ/fax **985/856-4796.** 8 units. High season $75–$80 doubles; low season $55–$70. Rates include full breakfast. No credit cards. Free secure parking. **Amenities:** Babysitting; small outdoor pool; room service; spa. In room: A/C, TV, no phone, Wi-Fi.

El Mesón del Marqués ★★ Originally an early 17th-century house, the doyen of Valladolid's plaza has grown by adding new construction in back. All the rooms (most with two double beds) are quite comfortable, though the new buildings don't have the wow factor of the original porticoed courtyard, which drips with bougainvillea and hanging plants and is mostly occupied by the restaurant (p. 298). The pretty, fairly large pool is another modern addition. The hotel is on the north side of the plaza, opposite the church.

Calle 39 no. 203 (btw. calles 40 and 42), 97780 Valladolid, Yuc. www.mesondelmarques.com. ℂ **985/856-2073.** Fax 985/856-2280. 90 units. 735–900 pesos double; 1,300 pesos junior suite. AE, MC, V. Free secure parking. **Amenities:** Restaurant; bar; outdoor pool; room service. In room: A/C, TV, Wi-Fi.

Side Trips from Valladolid

EK BALAM: DARK JAGUAR ★★★

About 18km (11 miles) north of Valladolid, off the highway to Río Lagartos, are the spectacular ruins of **Ek Balam,** which, owing to a certain ambiguity in Mayan, may mean "black jaguar," "dark jaguar," or "star jaguar." Though tourists have yet to catch on, these ruins could prove to be a more important discovery than Chichén Itzá. Archaeologists began work only in 1997, and their findings have Maya scholars all aquiver. Built between 100 B.C. and A.D. 1200, the smaller buildings are architecturally unique—especially the large, perfectly restored **Oval Palace** (also sometimes called La Redonda or Caracol).

The imposing central pyramid, known as **El Torre** ★★, or the Acropolis, is about 160m (525 ft.) long and 60m (197 ft.) wide. At more than 30m (98 ft.) high, it easily surpasses El Castillo in Chichén Itzá. To the left of the main stairway, archaeologists have uncovered a large ceremonial doorway of perfectly preserved stucco work. Designed in the Chenes style

The ruins of Ek Balam.

Flamingos in Ría Lagartos.

associated with Campeche, it forms an astonishingly elaborate representation of the gaping mouth of the underworld god. Around it are several beautifully detailed human figures, including what appear to be winged warriors. Known as Mayan Angels, they are unique in Maya architecture. Excavation inside the pyramid revealed a long chamber (so far closed to the public) filled with hieroglyphic writing that suggests the scribes probably came from Guatemala. The script revealed the name of one of the city's principal kings—Ukit Kan Le'k Tok', whose tomb was uncovered about two-thirds of the way up the pyramid. Climb to the top, and you see untouched ruins masquerading as overgrown hills to the north, and the tallest structures of **Cobá,** 50km (31 miles) to the southeast.

Also visible are the Maya's *sacbeob,* or raised causeways, appearing as raised lines in the forest. More than any of the better-known sites, Ek Balam inspires a sense of mystery and awe at the scale of Maya civilization and the utter ruin to which it fell.

A new road runs from the highway to the ruins. Take Calle 40 north out of Valladolid to Hwy. 295 and go 20km (12 miles) to a large marked turnoff. Ek Balam is 13km (8 miles) from the highway; admission is 130 pesos, 45 pesos per video camera. The site is open daily from 8am to 5pm.

RÍA LAGARTOS NATURE RESERVE ★

About 80km (50 miles) north of Valladolid (40km/25 miles north of Tizimín) on Hwy. 295, Ría Lagartos is a 50,000-hectare (123,500-acre) refuge established in 1979 to protect the largest nesting flamingo population in North America. The nesting area is off-limits, but you can see plenty of flamingos, as well as many other species of waterfowl, on an enjoyable boat ride around the estuary.

Whale sharks congregate off Isla Holbox from May to September.

Río Lagartos, at the west end of the estuary, is the place to get boats to the flamingos. Misnamed by Spaniards who mistook the long, narrow *ría* (estuary) for a *río* (river), it's a small fishing village of about 3,000 people who make their living from the sea and from the occasional tourist who shows up to see the flamingos. Colorful houses face the *malecón* (oceanfront street), and brightly painted boats dock here and there.

When you drive into town, keep going straight until you get to the shore. Where Calle 10 intersects with the *malecón,* near a modern church, is a little kiosk where the guides can be found (no phone). You can book a 2-hour tour, which costs about 750 pesos for two to three people. The guides also like to show you the evaporation pools used by the local salt producer at Las Coloradas (a good source of employment for the locals until it was mechanized) and a freshwater spring bubbling out from below the saltwater estuary.

The best time to see flamingos is in the early morning, so you might want to stay overnight in town. Río Lagartos has a few simple hotels, the best of which is **Hotel Villa de Pescadores** (ⓒ **986/862-0020**) on the waterfront. Another is **Hotel San Felipe** (ⓒ **986/862-2067**) in the pleasant fishing village of San Felipe, 9km (5⅔ miles) to the west.

> ### A Matter of Timing
>
> You'll see some flamingos any time of year (and probably ducks, hawks, cranes, cormorants, and osprey as well), but to see great rosy masses of them, go between April and October. After the birds complete their courtship rituals in Celestún, they fly to Ría Lagartos to nest, lay their eggs, and prepare their young for the return journey in October.

ISLA HOLBOX ★

A sandy strip of an island off the northeastern corner of the Yucatán Peninsula, Isla Holbox (pronounced "hohl-*bosh*") is in Quintana Roo, and is actually closer to

Visiting the Whale Sharks of Isla Holbox

In 2002, Mexico's whale sharks were designated an endangered species. The government, along with environmental groups, closely monitors their activity and the tours that visit them off Isla Holbox. Several restrictions apply to how tours are run, and all tour operators must abide by them. See details of the restrictions, and learn more about the whale sharks, at www.domino.conanp.gob.mx/rules.htm.

Whale shark tours are kept small; just two people at a time are allowed to snorkel with the sharks. Tours typically cost around $80 to $100 per person and last 4 to 6 hours. Many hotels or outfitters on the island can arrange a tour

Cancún than Valladolid. But, unless Cancún tourists take a boat tour, they have to drive almost to the Yucatán border to get to the road north. Given the challenges of driving in Cancún, it makes sense to visit Holbox from the Yucatán side.

Holbox was a half-deserted fishing village in a remote corner of the world before tourists started showing up for the beach. Now it's a semiprosperous little community that makes its livelihood from tourist services, employment at the beach hotels, and tours. It's most popular with visitors from May to September, when more than a hundred **whale sharks ★★★** congregate in nearby waters to feed on the plankton and krill churned up by the collision of Gulf and Caribbean waters. Whale sharks are much larger than other sharks, reaching as much as 18m (59 ft.), and they filter their food much as baleen whales do. These peaceable giants swim slowly along the surface of the water and don't seem to mind the boat tours and snorkelers that come for the thrill of swimming alongside them. That said, they can do some mischief if you annoy them.

Besides swimming with whale sharks, most tourists come to Holbox to laze on the broad beach of fine-textured sand. The water, though, is not the amazing blue of the Caribbean but a murkier green. Diving, snorkeling, sportfishing, and nature tours of **Laguna Yalahu,** the shallow lagoon separating Holbox from the mainland, are the primary other diversions.

Posada Mawimbi (www.mawimbi.net; ✆ 984/875-2003), starting at $90 to $105 a night depending on season, hits the best balance between price and comfort among the beach hotels in town. **Casa Sandra** (www.casasandra.com; ✆ 984/875-2171) charges $250 to $410 double in low season and $320 to $470 in high season, but travelers who want only the best will find it here, along with air-conditioning, a rarity in Holbox. Just beyond town, **Villas Delfines,** which has an office in Cancún (www.villasdelfines.com; ✆ 998/884-8606), is an ecohotel with thatched-roof beach bungalows charging $1,368 to $2,280 pesos a night in low season and $1,022 to $1,710 high season.

From Valladolid, take Hwy. 180 east for about 90km (56 miles) toward Cancún; turn north after Nuevo Xcan at the tiny crossroads of El Ideal. Drive nearly 100km (62 miles) north on a state highway to the tiny port of Chiquilá, where you can park your car in a secure parking lot; walk 180m (590 ft.) to the pier, and catch the ferry to the island. It runs 10 times per day and costs 70 pesos per person. When you arrive in the village, you can contract with one of the golf-cart taxis for a ride to your hotel.

TABASCO
& CHIAPAS

by Christine Delsol & Maribeth Mellin

n startling contrast to the flat, dry Yucatán landscape, the states of Tabasco and Chiapas, in southernmost Mexico, are largely covered in jungle, wetlands, and rainforest. Yet in both pre-Classic and Classic times (A.D. 300–900), this, too, was the domain of the Maya, whose descendants still populate the region. In pre-Classic times (before A.D. 300) much of this area was home to Mexico's "mother culture," the Olmec, who in many ways gave form to the cultural development of the civilizations that would come afterward. The ruins that these people left behind, as well as the present-day Maya villages, attract many visitors to this region. Travelers here tend to be pilgrims seeking out the giant stone heads of the Olmec, the ancient ceremonial centers of the Maya, such as Palenque and Toniná, and today's Maya cultures.

The lowland jungle with its high canopy offers a tremendous variety of flora and fauna. Placid lakes dot the land and provide the only open vistas in the densely packed landscape. The mountainous central highlands of Chiapas are also thickly forested and often shrouded in mist. Rivers, including Mexico's two largest, the Grijalva and the Usumacinta, slice down to the lowlands through rugged canyons and tumbling waterfalls. The cool mountain air is refreshing after the heat and humidity of the lowlands.

Tabasco, mostly flat and scored by waterways, is a small, oil-rich state along the Gulf Coast. The capital, **Villahermosa,** is the main port of entry into this region. It has a boomtown feel and an intriguing history. Still, the large and topographically varied state of **Chiapas** holds more attractions. In its eastern lowland jungle is the ancient ceremonial center of **Palenque.** Near the border with Guatemala are the smaller but dramatic sites of **Yaxchilán** and **Bonampak.** Between these lowlands and the central highlands are many waterfalls and rapids, as well as the ruins of **Toniná.** High in the mountains, the colonial city of **San Cristóbal de las Casas,** with its beautiful old town and market center, is surrounded by Indian communities

THE BEST TABASCO & CHIAPAS EXPERIENCES

- o **Raging Waters:** Plunge into clear blue pools, created by waters cascading down from mountain slopes where rivers converge, at **Misol Há** and **Agua Azul.** See p. 320.
- o **Forever Amber:** Chiapas' amber is prized for its clarity and colors. In addition to numerous reputable shops in San Cristóbal de las Casas, the **Museo del Ambar** (p. 328) explains all you need to know about this beautiful fossil and sells exquisite raw and carved pieces.

PREVIOUS PAGE: **The Canyon of El Sumidero.**

- **Sumidero Canyon:** Cruise through the waterway and sheer, 1,000-foot rock cliffs of spectacular **Sumidero Canyon,** spotting crocodiles and fantastically shaped mineral deposits along the way. See p. 343.

- **Ancient Mysteries:** Have a go at figuring out how the Olmec moved those colossal heads on display at **Parque-Museo La Venta** (p. 310), and what the ancient Maya really thought about the year 2012 at the **Carlos Pellicer Museum of Anthropology** (p. 309).

- **Marimba Mojo:** A tribute to the masters of marimba and the music of Chiapas, Tuxtla Gutierrez' beautiful **Parque Jardín de la Marimba** (p. 340) stages live music every night; listen and enjoy, or join the locals on the dance floor to try some of the region's traditional dance moves.

VILLAHERMOSA

142km (88 miles) NW of Palenque; 469km (291 miles) SW of Campeche; 160km (99 miles) N of San Cristóbal de las Casas

Villahermosa (pop. 600,000) is the capital of Tabasco state and its largest city. It lies in a shallow depression about an hour's drive from the Gulf Coast, at the confluence of two rivers, the Grijalva and the Carrizal, which makes the city susceptible to flooding. The land is marshy, with shallow lakes scattered here and there. For most of the year it's hot and humid.

Oil has brought money pouring into this city, which holds more than one-fourth of Tabasco's population, and pushed prices relentlessly up. Villahermosa is one of the most expensive cities in the country, contrasting sharply with inexpensive Chiapas. The lucre has gravitated to the modern western sections surrounding a development called Tabasco 2000. This area, especially the neighborhoods around the **Parque–Museo La Venta,** is the most attractive part of town, dotted by small lakes. The steamy, crowded historic center, where the least expensive hotels are, is not nearly as pleasant. Once the traffic dies down in the evening, though, walking the pedestrianized streets and the bustling *malecón* in the Zona Luz—the historic downtown core, where buildings are gradually being restored—is a pleasure.

Two names that you will likely see and hear are Carlos Pellicer Cámara and Tomás Garrido Canabal; both were interesting people. The first was a mid-20th-century Tabascan poet and intellectual. The best known of Mexico's *modernista* poets, he was a fiercely independent thinker and a tireless promoter of Mexican art and literature. Garrido Canabal, socialist governor of Tabasco in the 1920s and 1930s, was even more fiercely independent. He wanted to turn the conservative, backwater state of Tabasco into a model of socialism and fought for many socialist causes. But his anti-Catholic clericalism campaigning is what he is most remembered for today. He went so far as to name his son

> ### Weather Watching
>
> The winter of 2011–12 was the first time in the past 6 years that some part of Tabasco has not been inundated by floods, causing long delays for travelers trying to get between Veracruz and the Yucatán. In some cases it's taken weeks to clear the highway. Most of the flooding has occurred in Villahermosa and the western part of the state, so check the forecast before heading down to Tabasco.

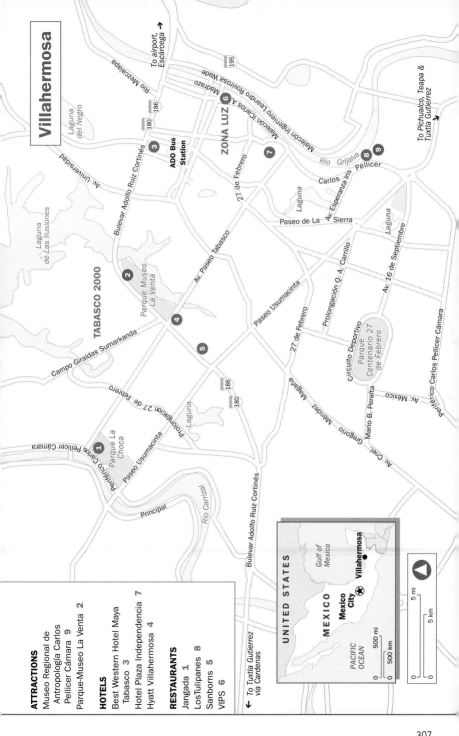

Villahermosa

TABASCO 2000

ZONA LUZ

ADO Bus
Station

To airport,
Escárcega →

To Pichucalco, Teapa &
Tuxtla Gutierrez →

To Tuxtla Gutierrez
via Cardenas →

Laguna
del Negro

Laguna
de Las Ilusiones

Parque Museo
La Venta

Parque La
Choca

Parque
Centenario 27
de Febrero

Río Mezcalapa

Río Carrizal

Río Grijalva

Malecón Icarios Aa

Malecón Ingeniero Leandro Rovirosa Wade

Carlos Pellicer

Av. Esperanza Iris

Paseo de La Sierra

Av. Paseo Tabasco

Paseo Usumacinta

Prolongación Q. A. Carrillo

27 de Febrero

27 de Febrero

Av. 16 de Septiembre

Av. Chnel. Gregorio Méndez Magaña

Mario B. Peralta

Av. Mexico

Periférico Carlos Pellicer Cámara

Circuito Deportivo

Bulevar Adolfo Ruiz Cortinés

Av. Universidad

Campo Giraldas Sumarkanda

Prolongación 27 de Febrero

Paseo Usumacinta

Principal

Bulevar Adolfo Ruiz Cortinés

Periférico Carlos Pellicer Cámara

Madrazo

180 186

180 186

195

Laguna

Laguna

Laguna

ATTRACTIONS
Museo Regional de
Antropología Carlos
Pellicer Cámara **9**
Parque-Museo La Venta **2**

HOTELS
Best Western Hotel Maya
Tabasco **3**
Hotel Plaza Independencia **7**
Hyatt Villahermosa **4**

RESTAURANTS
Jangada **1**
LosTulipanes **8**
Sanborns **5**
VIPS **6**

UNITED STATES

MEXICO

Mexico
City

Villahermosa

Gulf of
Mexico

PACIFIC
OCEAN

0   500 mi
0   500 km

0   5 mi
0   5 km

307

Lenin and his farm animals God, Jesus, and the Virgin of Guadalupe. He also had a son named Luzbel (Lucifer).

Essentials

ARRIVING & DEPARTING

BY PLANE   Villahermosa's airport (airport code: VSA), the main port of entry into this region, is 16km (10 miles) east of town. The trip takes between 20 and 30 minutes. Once you cross the bridge over the Río Grijalva, turn left to reach downtown. Taxis to downtown cost about 200 pesos.

Continental ExpressJet (www.continental.com; ✆ 800/525-0280 in the U.S., or 01-800/900-5000 in Mexico) has direct service to and from Houston. **Aeroméxico** (www.aeromexico.com; ✆ 800/237-6639 in the U.S., or 01-800/021-4000 in Mexico) has direct flights to Mexico City. **VivaAerobus** (www.vivaaerobus.com; ✆ 01-81/8215-0150 in Mexico) has direct flights to Cancún, Guadalajara, Mexico City, and Monterrey. **Interjet** (www.interjet.com.mx; ✆ 866/285-9525 in the U.S. or 01-80/0011-2345 in Mexico) has flights to Mexico City.

BY CAR   Hwy. 180 connects Villahermosa to Campeche (6 hr.). Hwy. 186, which passes by the airport, joins Hwy. 199 to Palenque and San Cristóbal de las Casas. The road to Palenque is a good one, and the drive takes 2 hours. Between Palenque and San Cristóbal, the road enters the mountains and takes close to 5 hours. Conditions on the mountain roads are apt to worsen during the rainy season, from May to October.

BY BUS   The **bus station** is at Mina and Merino (✆ 993/312-8900), 3 blocks off Hwy. 180.

ORIENTATION

VISITOR INFORMATION   The **State Tourism Office** (www.visitetabasco.com; ✆ 993/316-5122, ext. 229) has information booths at the **airport,** staffed daily from 10am to 5pm, and at **Parque–Museo La Venta,** staffed Monday to Friday from 9am to 1pm. They aren't a great help; they have some leaflets, and their hours are mostly theoretical.

GETTING AROUND   Parking downtown can be difficult; it's best to find a parking lot. Use one that's guarded round-the-clock. **Taxis** are your best way to get around town. Villahermosa is rare for being a Mexican city without a capable public transportation system.

CITY LAYOUT   The downtown area, including the pedestrian-only **Zona Luz,** is on the west bank of the Grijalva River. About 1.5km (1 mile) upstream (south) is **CICOM,** an academic organization with the large archaeology museum named for the poet Carlos Pellicer Cámara. The **airport** is on the east side of the river. Hwy. 180 passes the airport and crosses the river just north of downtown, becoming **Bulevar Ruiz Cortines.** To get to the downtown area, turn left onto **Madero** or **Pino Suárez.** Hwy. 180 comes from the north and meets Hwy. 186 about 2km (1.25 miles) east of the river and also merges into Bulevar Ruiz Cortines on its way through town. By staying on Ruiz Cortines you can reach the city's biggest attraction, the Parque–Museo la Venta. It's well marked. Just beyond that is the intersection with **Paseo Tabasco,** the heart of the modern hotel and shopping district.

FAST FACTS   The telephone **area code** is **993.** There aren't a lot of *casas de cambio,* but you can exchange money at the airport, the hotels, and downtown banks on calles Juárez and Madero. ATMs are plentiful.

Exploring Villahermosa

Except for passing a few pleasant hours in the Zona Luz, the main reason to be downtown is for the inexpensive hotels. The modern western part of the city is picturesque in places because the land is broken up by lots of shallow lakes, but you don't need to budget a lot of time for the city. The two major attractions, the **Parque–Museo La Venta** and the **Museo Regional de Antropología Carlos Pellicer Cámara** can be seen in a day.

If you want to explore the city, take a stroll about the pedestrian-only Zona Luz in the old city center, and you'll see signs that investment might be returning to the downtown area. Outside the Zona Luz, things get more unpleasant, with lots of traffic and crowds of pedestrians. You can walk south along the banks of the Grijalva until you come to a pedestrian bridge with an observation tower. And that's really the highlight.

Museo Regional de Antropología Carlos Pellicer Cámara ★★ MUSEUM   This museum on the west bank of the river about 1.5km (1 mile) south of the town center was wrecked in the flood of 2007. It finally opened in a new, larger structure on the same site in December 2011. The most notable piece here is the now-infamous **Tortuguero Monument No. 6 ★★★**, the only existing Maya reference to the end of the 13th bak'tun—a 5,125-year calendar cycle—coinciding with the date Dec. 21, 2012. Freshly mounted in its new home, it is fragmented and incomplete. An account of events in the life of the early 7th-century king Bahlam Ajaw ends with "In two days, nine-score days,

A giant Olmec head in Parque–Museo La Venta.

three years, eight score years, and three times four hundred years, the 13th bak'tun will end, and 4 Ahaw, 3 K'ank'in will happen." The last few glyphs, which might or might not have indicated the significance of this date, are missing. These are the words around which the entire 2012 doomsday mythology has grown.

The museum's permanent collection of pre-Columbian sculpture and pottery is well worth a visit. It focuses on the region's Olmec, Zapotec, and Maya cultures, but also includes pieces from other parts of Mexico. One fantastic addition to the museum is a room-sized mosaic of pale green stone that forms a stylized face, installed in the floor as it was found in the sacred complex of the La Venta archaeological site. This was one of four similar layers of mosaic layered with clay and buried under a platform. Because so much work went into these massive mosaics that no one would ever see, it could only mean it was constructed as an offering to the gods.

CICOM Center, Av. Carlos Pellicer Cámara 511. ℂ **993/312-6344.** Admission 45 pesos. Tues–Sun 9am–5pm.

Parque–Museo La Venta ★★ MUSEUM The Olmec created the first civilization in Mexico and developed several cultural traits that later would be adopted by all subsequent civilizations throughout Mesoamerica. In addition to their monumental works, they carved small, exquisite figurines in jade and serpentine, which can be seen in the Museo Regional de Antropología (above). This *parque-museo* occupies a portion of a larger park named after Tomás Garrido Canabal, which includes a serene lake, a zoo, a natural history museum, and a lot of green space with several walkways frequented by joggers. Once inside the *parque-museo,* a trail leads you from one sculpture to the next. Most of the pieces are massive heads or altars. These can be as tall as 2m (6½ ft.) and weigh as much as 40 tons. The faces seem to be half adult, half infant. Most have highly stylized mouths with thick fleshy lips that turn down (known as the "jaguar mouth," this is one of the identifying characteristics of Olmec art). At least 17 heads have been found: 4 at La Venta, 10 at San Lorenzo, and 3 at Tres Zapotes—all Olmec cities on Mexico's east coast. The pieces in this park were taken from La Venta, a major city during the pre-Classic period (2000 B.C.–A.D. 300). Most were sculpted around 1000 B.C. without the use of metal chisels. The basalt rock used for these heads and altars was transported to La Venta from more than 113km (70 miles) away. It is thought that the rock was transported most of the distance by raft. Most of these pieces were first discovered in 1938. Now all that remains at La Venta are some grass-covered mounds that were once earthen pyramids. An exhibition area at the entrance to the park does a good job of illustrating how La Venta was laid out and what archaeologists think the Olmec were like.

As you stroll along, you will see labels identifying many species of local trees, including a grand ceiba tree of special significance to the Olmec and, later, the Maya. A few varieties of local critters scurry about, seemingly unconcerned with the presence of humans or with escaping from the park. Allow at least 2 hours for wandering through the jungle sanctuary and examining the 3,000-year-old sculpture. *Note:* Don't forget the mosquito repellent.

Bulevar Adolfo Ruiz Cortines s/n. ℂ **993/314-1652.** 40 pesos. Daily 8am–4pm.

Where to Eat

Like other Mexican cities, Villahermosa has seen the arrival of U.S. franchise restaurants, but I prefer the Mexican variety: **Sanborns,** Av. Ruiz Cortines 1310, near Parque–Museo La Venta (✆ **993/316-5710**), and **VIPS,** Av. Fco. I. Madero 402, downtown (✆ **993/314-3971**). Both usually do an okay job with traditional dishes such as enchiladas or *antojitos.*

Jangada ★★ SEAFOOD   This all-you-can-eat seafood buffet is in the fancy western part of town in La Choca neighborhood. Start with a small glass of delicious seafood broth and an appetizing empanada of *pejelagarto,* a freshwater fish for which Tabasco is famous. The salad and cold seafood bar offers a seafood salad of freshwater lobster, different kinds of ceviche, and seafood cocktails made to order. Among the variety of soups, the shrimp-and-*yuca* chowder is especially good. Main dishes include charcoal-grilled *pejelagarto* (mild taste—light and almost nutty) and fish kabobs. Jangada closes early, but Rodizio, a good Brazilian-style steakhouse next door, stays open until 9pm.

Paseo de la Choca 126-A, Fracc. La Choca. (✆ **993/317-6050.** 365 pesos per person, excluding drinks and dessert. AE, DC, MC, V. Daily 12:30–7pm.

Los Tulipanes REGIONAL/SEAFOOD/STEAKS   Los Tulipanes is an old-school Mexican restaurant downtown, next to the Pellicer Museum of Anthropology. If you choose the Mexican over the international dishes, you'll eat well here. Before you order, *tostones de plátano macho*—mashed and fried plantain crisps—are brought to your table as an appetizer. The menu mixes such Mexican specialties as chiles rellenos, tacos, and enchiladas with some out-of-the-ordinary dishes such as *tortilla de maíz nuevo* (oversize tortilla made with fresh corn and stuffed with shrimp or other seafood). For breakfast, the *tamales de chipilín* (an herb) are quite good.

CICOM Center, Periférico Carlos Pellicer Cámara 511. (✆ **993/312-9217.** Main courses 90–210 pesos. MC, V. Mon–Sat 8am–7pm; Sun 12:30–7pm.

Where to Stay

Hotel rooms in Villahermosa are pricier than in other Mexican cities. Rates listed below, which include the 18% tax, can go up during conventions, but there is no high-season/low-season split. Most hotels have live music on weekends. This makes it difficult to sleep in several of the inexpensive downtown hotels.

VERY EXPENSIVE

Hyatt Villahermosa ★★   This property enjoys a better location and offers better service than the Camino Real (the city's other top hotel). It's a short walk away from the Parque–Museo La Venta. Sleek, modern rooms have sharp-looking furnishings, fixtures, and accents. The same is true of the bathrooms, which are large and made to feel larger by the use of sliding doors and minimal clutter. The pool is a good place to relax in the heat of the afternoon.

Av. Juárez 106, 86000 Villahermosa, Tab. www.villahermosa.regency.hyatt.com. (✆ **800/633-7313** in the U.S., or 993/310-1234. Fax 993/315-1963. 206 units. $115 and up double. Weekend rates often discounted. AE, DC, MC, V. Free guarded parking. **Amenities:** Restaurant; 2 bars (1 w/live music, 1 sports bar); concierge; concierge-level rooms; well-equipped exercise room; outdoor pool and wading pool; room service. *In room:* A/C, TV, hair dryer, Internet, minibar.

EXPENSIVE

Best Western Hotel Maya Tabasco   This hotel is centrally located between the downtown area and the modern western section. It's close to the Parque–Museo La Venta, the bus station, and the city's principal restaurant district.

Rooms are larger than the norm. Most have ceramic tile floors and are simply furnished. Midsize bathrooms are attractive and have good counter space. A lush pool area separates the hotel from the hotel's bar, which gets fairly good live talent.

Bulevar Ruiz Cortines 907, 86000 Villahermosa, Tab. www.hotelmaya.com.mx. © **800/528-1234** in the U.S. and Canada, or 993/358-1111, ext. 822. Fax 993/358-1118. 151 units. 850 pesos and up double. MC, V. Free guarded parking. **Amenities:** Restaurant; bar; airport transfer; large outdoor pool; room service. *In room:* A/C, TV, hair dryer, Wi-Fi.

INEXPENSIVE

Hotel Plaza Independencia ✦   The Plaza Independencia is the only hotel in this price range with a pool and enclosed parking. It's also the only one that doesn't have a noise problem with live music on weekends. It's downtown, by the pedestrian bridge, and not far from the Anthropology Museum. Rooms are on the small side but are better lit than the norm. Ask for an end room, whose numbers end in 01, 02, 14, and 15, which have balconies.

Independencia 123, 86000 Villahermosa, Tab. www.hotelesplaza.com.mx. © **993/312-1299,** -7541. Fax 993/314-4724. 90 units. 668 pesos and up double. MC, V. Free secure parking. **Amenities:** Restaurant; bar; small outdoor pool; room service; Wi-Fi (in common areas). *In room:* A/C, TV, hair dryer, minibar.

PALENQUE ★★

142km (88 miles) SE of Villahermosa; 229km (142 miles) NE of San Cristóbal de las Casas

The ruins of Palenque look out over the jungle from a tall ridge that juts out from the base of steep, thickly forested mountains. It is a dramatic sight colored by the mysterious feel of the ruins themselves. The temples here are in the Classic style, with high-pitched roofs crowned with elaborate combs. Inside many are representations in stone and plaster of the rulers and their gods, which give evidence of a cosmology that is—and perhaps will remain—impenetrable to our understanding. This is one of the grand archaeological sites of Mexico.

Eight kilometers (5 miles) from the ruins is the town of Palenque, where you can find lodging and food, and make travel arrangements. Transportation between the town and ruins is cheap and convenient.

Essentials

ARRIVING & DEPARTING

BY CAR   **Hwy. 186** from Villahermosa should take about 2 hours. Drive only during the day. You may encounter military roadblocks that involve a cursory inspection of your travel credentials and perhaps your vehicle. The 230km (143-mile) trip from San Cristóbal to Palenque takes 5 hours and passes through lush jungle and mountain scenery. Take it easy, though, and watch out for potholes and other hindrances.

BY BUS   **ADO/Cristóbal Colón** (© **916/345-1344**) has regular service to and from Villahermosa and Campeche, Tulum, San Cristóbal de Las Casa, and Tuxla Gutierrez. The station is located on Avenida Juárez between the town center and La Cañada.

VISITOR INFORMATION   The downtown tourism office is a block from the main square at the corner of Avenida Juárez and Abasolo. It's open Monday to

Saturday from 9am to 9pm, Sunday from 9am to 1pm. There's no phone at the downtown office. To get info over the phone, call the tourism office's business office (☎ 916/345-0356).

ORIENTATION

VISITOR INFORMATION   The tourist office, in the Plaza de Artesanías on Juárez at Abosolo (☎ 916/345-0356), a block below the main plaza, has a booth on the east side of the plaza with friendly, helpful staff. It's open daily, 9am to 2pm and 6 to 9pm.

CITY LAYOUT   Avenida Juárez is Palenque's main street. At one end is the **plaza,** at the other a traffic circle is adorned with a monument imitating the iconic figure of a Maya head, which was discovered at the ruins. To the right of the statue is the entrance to La Cañada, to the left is the road to the ruins, and straight ahead past the statue is the highway to Villahermosa. The distance between the town's main square and the monument is about 1.5km (1 mile).

La Cañada is a restaurant and Hotel Zone tucked away in the forest. Aside from the main plaza area, this is the best location for travelers without cars, because the town is within a few blocks, and the buses that run to the ruins pass right by.

GETTING AROUND   The cheapest way to get back and forth from the ruins is on the white vans *(colectivos)* that run down Juárez every 15 minutes from 6am to 6pm. The buses pass La Cañada and hotels along the road to the ruins, and can be flagged down at any point, but they may not stop if they're full. The cost is 10 pesos per person.

FAST FACTS   The telephone **area code** is **916.** As for the **climate,** Palenque's high humidity is downright oppressive in the summer, especially after rain showers. During the winter, the damp air can occasionally be chilly in the evening. Rain gear is handy at any time of year. **Internet service** and **ATMs** are easily available.

Exploring Palenque

The ruins are the reason you're here; although you can tour them in a morning, many people savor Palenque (admission 84 pesos; daily 8am–5pm [last entry 4:30pm]; parking free) for days. There are no must-see sights in town.

PARQUE NACIONAL PALENQUE ★★★

A **museum and visitor center** sits not far from the entrance to the ruins. Though it's not large, the museum is worth the time it takes to see; it's open Tuesday to Sunday from 10am to 5pm and is included in the price of admission to the ruins. It contains well-chosen and artistically displayed exhibits, including jade from recently excavated tombs. Text in Spanish and English explains the life and times of this magnificent city. New pieces are sometimes added as they are uncovered in ongoing excavations.

The **main entrance,** about 1km (⅔ mile) beyond the museum, is at the end of the paved highway. There you'll find a large parking lot, a refreshment stand, a ticket booth, and several shops. Among the vendors selling souvenirs are often some Lacandón Indians wearing white tunics and hawking bows and arrows. INAH-trained guides will likely approach you before you reach the entrance; the going rate is about 900 pesos for a full-day tour including the ruins and

Palenque Ruins

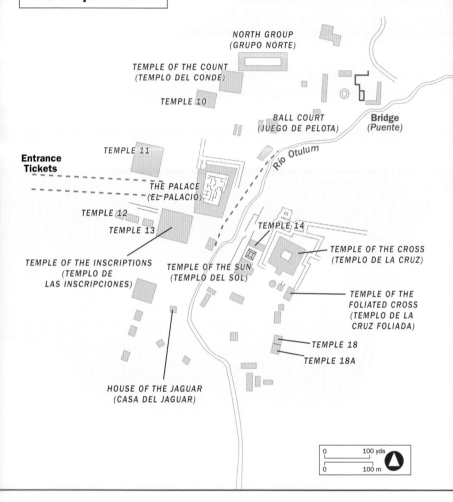

NORTH GROUP
(GRUPO NORTE)

TEMPLE OF THE COUNT
(TEMPLO DEL CONDE)

TEMPLE 10

BALL COURT
(JUEGO DE PELOTA)

Bridge
(Puente)

TEMPLE 11

**Entrance
Tickets**

Río Otulum

THE PALACE
(EL PALACIO)

TEMPLE 12

TEMPLE 13

TEMPLE 14

TEMPLE OF THE CROSS
(TEMPLO DE LA CRUZ)

TEMPLE OF THE INSCRIPTIONS
(TEMPLO DE
LAS INSCRIPCIONES)

TEMPLE OF THE SUN
(TEMPLO DEL SOL)

TEMPLE OF THE
FOLIATED CROSS
(TEMPLO DE LA
CRUZ FOLIADA)

TEMPLE 18

TEMPLE 18A

HOUSE OF THE JAGUAR
(CASA DEL JAGUAR)

0   100 yds
0   100 m

surrounding jungle, but you can scale that down to meet your needs. Ask for **José Luis Zuñiga** (tentzun@gmail.com; ☎ **916/109-2955**), who grew up a few steps from the Temple of the Inscriptions (his family was forced to move to town because the tourists didn't appreciate their chickens running around) and has been guiding since he was in elementary school. Now an independent professional guide who has taken INAH training, he is also available for customized jungle and ruins trips throughout the area. He belongs to a union of guides and can also provide referrals.

TOURING THE RUINS   Pottery shards found during the excavations show that people lived in this area as early as 300 B.C. By the Classic period (A.D. 300–900), Palenque was an important ceremonial center. It peaked around A.D. 600 to 700.

The Temple of the Inscriptions in Palenque.

When John Stephens visited the site in the 1840s, the ruins that you see today were buried under centuries of accumulated earth and a thick canopy of jungle. The dense jungle surrounding the cleared portion still covers unexcavated temples, which are easily discernible in the forest even to the untrained eye. But be careful not to drift too far from the main path—there have been a few incidents where tourists venturing alone into the rainforest were assaulted.

Of all Mexico's ruins, this is the most haunting, because of its majesty; its history, recovered by epigraphers; and its mysterious setting. Scholars have identified the rulers and constructed their family histories, putting visitors on a first-name basis with these ancient people etched in stone. You can read about it in *A Forest of Kings,* by Linda Schele and David Freidel.

As you enter the ruins, the building on your right is the **Temple of the Inscriptions,** named for the great stone hieroglyphic panels found inside. (Most of the panels, which portray the family tree of King Pacal, are in the National Anthropological Museum in Mexico City.) This temple is famous for the crypt of King Pacal deep inside

Ornate stone carvings from the ruins of Palenque.

315

The Palace in the ruins of Palenque.

the pyramid, but the crypt is closed to the public. The archaeologist Alberto Ruz Lhuillier discovered the tomb in the depths of the temple in 1952—an accomplishment many scholars consider one of the great discoveries of the Maya world. In exploratory excavations, Ruz Lhuillier found a stairway leading from the temple floor deep into the base of the pyramid. The original builders had carefully concealed the entrance by filling the stairway with stone. After several months of excavation, Ruz Lhuillier finally reached King Pacal's crypt, which contained several fascinating objects, including a magnificent carved stone sarcophagus. Ruz Lhuillier's own gravesite is opposite the Temple of the Inscriptions, on the left as you enter the park.

Just to your right as you face the Temple of the Inscriptions is **Temple 13.** Archaeologists recently discovered the burial of another richly adorned personage, accompanied in death by an adult female and an adolescent. Some of the artifacts found there are on display in the museum.

Back on the main pathway, the building directly in front of you is the **Palace,** with its unique tower. The explorer John Stephens camped in the Palace when it was completely covered in vegetation, spending sleepless nights fighting off mosquitoes. A pathway between the Palace and the Temple of the Inscriptions leads to the **Temple of the Sun,** the **Temple of the Foliated Cross,** the **Temple of the Cross,** and **Temple 14.** This group of temples, now in various stages of reconstruction, was built by Pacal's son, Chan-Bahlum, who is usually shown on inscriptions with six toes. Chan-Bahlum's plaster mask was found in Temple 14 next to the Temple of the Sun. Archaeologists have begun probing the Temple of the Cross for Chan-Bahlum's tomb. Little remains of this temple's exterior carving. Inside, however, behind a fence, a carving of Chan-Bahlum shows him ascending the throne in A.D. 684. The panels depict Chan-Bahlum's version of his historic link to the throne.

To the left of the Palace is the North Group, also undergoing restoration. Included in this area are the **Ball Court** and the **Temple of the Count.** At least three tombs, complete with offerings for the underworld journey, have been found here, and the lineage of at least 12 kings has been deciphered from inscriptions left at this site.

Just past the North Group is a small building (once a museum) now used for storing the artifacts found during restorations. It is closed to the public. To the right of the building, a stone bridge crosses the river, leading to a pathway down the hillside to the new museum. The rock-lined path descends along a cascading stream, where giant ceiba trees grow. Benches are placed along the way as rest areas, and some small temples have been reconstructed near the base of the trail. In the early morning and evening, you may hear monkeys crashing through the thick foliage by the path; if you keep noise to a minimum, you may spot wild parrots as well. Walking downhill (by far the best way to go), it will take you about 20 minutes to reach the main highway. The path ends at the paved road across from the museum. The *colectivos* (minibuses) going back to the village will stop here if you wave them down.

Where to Eat

Palenque isn't known for its great food, but there are a few good Mexican spots.

MODERATE

La Selva INTERNATIONAL/MEXICAN   At La Selva (the jungle), you dine under a large, attractive thatched roof beside well-tended gardens. The menu includes seafood, freshwater fish, steaks, and Mexican specialties. The most expensive thing on the menu is *pigua*, freshwater lobster caught in the large rivers of southeast Mexico. These can grow quite large—the size of small saltwater lobsters. This and the finer cuts of meat have been frozen, but you wouldn't want otherwise in Palenque. I liked the fish stuffed with shrimp and the *mole* enchiladas. La Selva is on the highway to the ruins, near the statue of the Maya head.

Carretera Palenque Ruinas Km 0.5. ✆ **916/345-0363.** Main courses 177–235 pesos. MC, V. Daily 11:30am–11:30pm.

INEXPENSIVE

Café de Yara MEXICAN   A small, modern cafe and restaurant with a comforting, not overly ambitious menu. The cafe's strong suit is healthful salads (with disinfected greens) and home-style Mexican entrees, such as the beef or chicken *milanesa* or chicken cooked in a *chile pasilla* sauce. It also offers decent tamales. In the evenings it occasionally offers live music.

Av. Hidalgo 66 (at Abasolo). ✆ **916/345-0269.** Main courses 68–105 pesos. MC, V. Daily 7am–11pm.

Restaurante Maya and Maya Cañada ★ MEXICAN   These two are the most consistently good restaurants in Palenque. One faces the main plaza from the corner of Independencia and Hidalgo, the other is in La Cañada (✆ **916/345-0216**). Both do a good job with the basics—good, strong, locally grown coffee and soft, pliant tortillas. The menu offers Mexican standards and regional specialties such as *mole chiapaneco* (dark red, like *mole poblano,* but less sweet) and dishes based on *chaya* or *chipilin* (mild-flavored local greens), such as the soup with *chipilin* and *bolitas de masa* (corn dumplings). For something more comforting, go for the chicken, rice, and vegetable soup, or the *sopa azteca.* The plantains stuffed with cheese and fried, Mexican-style, are wonderful. You can also try *tascalate,* a pre-Hispanic drink made of water, *masa,* chocolate, and achiote, and served room temperature or cold.

Av. Independencia s/n (at Hidalgo). ✆ **916/345-0042.** Breakfast 50–80 pesos; main courses 60–185 pesos. MC, V. Daily 7am–11pm.

Where to Stay

English is spoken in all the more expensive hotels and about half of the inexpensive ones. The quoted rates include the 18% tax. High season in Palenque is limited to Easter week, July to August, and December. Palenque gets most of its visitors through bus tours; if you want to avoid running into large groups, pick a small hotel.

EXPENSIVE

Chan-Kah Resort Village ★   This is a pretty property located between the town and the ruins. It's a grouping of comfortable bungalows, called casitas, surrounded by tropical forest. Staying here offers a measure of privacy and quiet in the tropical surroundings. The grounds are well tended, and an inviting freshwater pool fed by a stream runs through the property. The bungalows are made of stone and plaster. They are spacious, and each comes with its own terrace and two rocking chairs. The master suites are two-bedroom bungalows.

Carretera Las Ruinas Km 3, 29960 Palenque, Chi. www.chan-kah.com.mx. ✆ **916/345-1100.** Fax 916/345-1134. 79 units. 1,720 pesos casita 2,550 pesos master suite. MC, V. Free guarded parking. **Amenities:** Restaurant; bar; 3 outdoor pools (1 large w/natural spring); room service; Wi-Fi (in common areas). *In room:* A/C, TV, hair dryer.

MODERATE

Hotel Ciudad Real   Though not fancy, this hotel does the important things right—the rooms are ample, quiet, well-lit, and comfortably furnished. All rooms have a small balcony, which, in the best case, overlooks tropical vegetation. When making a reservation, specify the hotel in Palenque (there's also a Ciudad Real in San Cristóbal). It's at the edge of town in the direction of the airport. Though it works with bus tours, as other large hotels do, this hotel works well for individual travelers who have their own car.

Carretera a Pakal-Na Km 1.5, 29960 Palenque, Chi. www.ciudadreal.com.mx. ✆ **916/345-1343,** or ✆ 967/678-4400 reservations. 72 units. High season $144 and up double. Internet discounts sometimes available. AE, MC, V. Free secured parking. **Amenities:** Restaurant; bar; outdoor pool and children's pool; room service; Wi-Fi (in lobby and restaurant). *In room:* A/C, TV, hair dryer.

Hotel La Aldea ✍   This hotel on the way to the ruins enjoys the same lush surroundings as the more expensive Chan-Kah Resort Village, but it's smaller and most often quieter. It is a family-owned hotel, designed and managed by an architect. The rooms show that a good deal of thought went into making them attractive and functional. They are in a collection of free-standing bungalows set on rising ground (mostly two rooms per bungalow). A few of the rooms (no. 10 in particular) have great views of the surrounding forest. All rooms are large, with good space for luggage. Each has an outdoor sitting area. In terms of layout and decor, I like them better than those in the neighboring Chan-Kah Village.

Carretera Las Ruinas Km 2.8, 29960 Palenque, Chi. www.hotellaaldea.net. ✆/fax **916/345-1693.** 28 units. $60–$70 double. Low season discounts of 20%–30%. MC, V. Free secured parking. **Amenities:** Restaurant; bar; outdoor pool; Wi-Fi (in common areas). *In room:* A/C, no phone.

Hotel Maya Tulipanes   This is an attractive hotel tucked away in the Cañada. I like it for its location and management. Service and upkeep are both good. Rooms are medium to large and come with a queen-size, a king-size, or two double beds. Tropical vegetation adorns the grounds, along with some reproductions of famous Maya architecture. The Maya Tulipanes has an arrangement with a sister hotel at the ruins of Tikal, in Guatemala. The travel agency operates daily tours to Bonampak and other attractions.

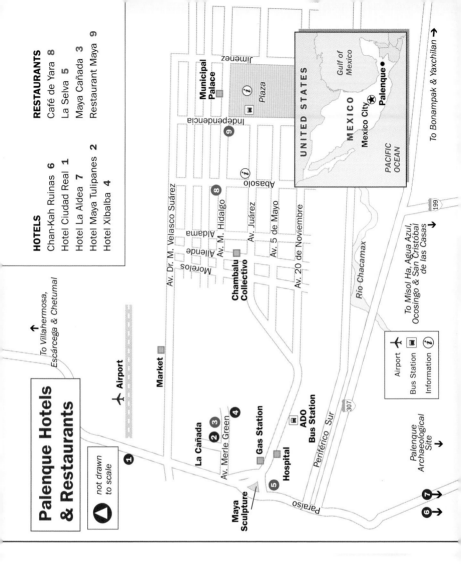

Palenque Hotels & Restaurants

not drawn to scale

HOTELS
Chan-Kah Ruinas **6**
Hotel Ciudad Real **1**
Hotel La Aldea **7**
Hotel Maya Tulipanes **2**
Hotel Xibalba **4**

RESTAURANTS
Café de Yara **8**
La Selva **5**
Maya Cañada **3**
Restaurant Maya **9**

To Villahermosa, Escárcega & Chetumal

Airport

Market

La Cañada

Av. Merle Green

Maya Sculpture

Gas Station

Hospital

ADO Bus Station

Periférico Sur

Paraíso

Av. Dr. M. Velasco Suárez

Morelos

Allende

Aldama

Av. M. Hidalgo

Abasolo

Av. Juárez

Av. 5 de Mayo

Av. 20 de Noviembre

Chambalu Collectivo

Río Chacamax

Independencia

Jiménez

Municipal Palace

Plaza

To Bonampak & Yaxchilan

To Misol Ha, Agua Azul, Ocosingo & San Cristóbal de las Casas

Palenque Archaeological Site

199

307

UNITED STATES

MEXICO

Gulf of Mexico

Mexico City

Palenque

PACIFIC OCEAN

Airport
Bus Station
Information

Calle Cañada 6, 29960 Palenque, Chi. www.mayatulipanes.com.mx. ℂ **916/345-0201,** -0258. Fax 916/345-1004. 74 units. High season 925 pesos and up double. Internet packages available. AE, MC, V. Free secured parking. **Amenities:** Restaurant; bar; ground transportation to/from Villahermosa airport; outdoor pool; room service. *In room:* A/C, TV, hair dryer, Wi-Fi.

INEXPENSIVE

Hotel Xibalba This budget hotel recently expanded to handle larger groups, but the price is still right. You can ask for a room in back if a group is being noisy. The medium-to-small rooms are basic but clean, with functioning air-conditioning, which is not always the case at the budget level. Rooms are small but well-equipped. The upstairs units are a little smaller than the downstairs units. Most of the beds have firm mattresses. Check out the full-size replica of Pacal's sarcophagus lid on the premises.

319

Calle Merle Green 9, Col. La Cañada, 29960 Palenque, Chi. www.hotelxibalba.com. ☏ **916/345-0392.** Fax 916/345-0411. 35 units. 460–650 pesos double. MC, V. Free parking. **Amenities:** Restaurant; bar; Wi-Fi. *In room:* A/C, TV, no phone.

Road Trips from Palenque
BONAMPAK & YAXCHILÁN: MURALS IN THE JUNGLE

Intrepid travelers may want to consider the day trip to the Maya ruins of Bonampak and Yaxchilán. The **ruins of Bonampak ★** (daily 8am–5pm; 46 pesos), southeast of Palenque on the Guatemalan border, were discovered in 1946. The site is important for the vivid and well-preserved **murals** of the Maya on the interior walls of one temple. Particularly striking is an impressive battle scene, perhaps the most important painting of pre-Hispanic Mexico.

Several tour companies offer a day trip. The drive to Bonampak is 3 hours. From there you continue by boat to the **ruins of Yaxchilán ★**, famous for its highly ornamented buildings. Bring rain gear, boots, a flashlight, and bug repellent. All tours include meals and cost about 1,000 pesos per person. No matter what agency you sign up with, the hours of departure and return are the same. You leave at 6am and return at 7pm.

Viajes Na Chan Kan (www.viajesnachankan.com.mx; ☏ **916/345-0263**), at Hidalgo 5 across from the main square, offers all the usual side trips as well as ecological and cultural tours to outlying Indian communities.

WATERFALLS AT MISOL HA & AGUA AZUL

Misol Ha is 20km (12 miles) from Palenque, in the direction of Ocosingo. It takes about 30 minutes to get there, depending on the traffic. The turnoff is clearly marked; you'll turn right and drive another 1.5km (1 mile). The place is

Vivid Maya murals from Bonampak.

A Lacandón Indian near Bonampak.

absolutely beautiful. Water pours from a rocky cliff into a broad pool of green water bordered by thick tropical vegetation. There's a small restaurant and some rustic cabins for rent for around 500 pesos per night, depending on the size of the cabin. The place is run by the *ejido* cooperative that owns the site, and it does a good job of maintaining the place. To inquire about the cabins, call ☎ **916/345-1506.** Admission for the day is 35 pesos.

Approximately 44km (27 miles) beyond Misol Ha are the **Agua Azul** waterfalls—270m (886 ft.) of tumbling falls with water so blue that it looks like it spilled in from the Caribbean (courtesy of the limestone in the rocks). There are cabins for rent here, too, but I would rather stay at Misol Ha. You can swim either above or below the falls, but make sure you don't get pulled by the current. You can see both places in the same day or stop to see them on your way to Ocosingo and San Cristóbal. Agua Azul is prettiest after 3 or 4 consecutive dry days; heavy rains can make the water murky. Check with guides or other travelers about the water quality before you decide to go. The cost to enter is 38 pesos per person. Trips to both of these places can be arranged through just about any hotel.

OCOSINGO & THE RUINS OF TONINÁ

By the time you get to Agua Azul, you're halfway to Ocosingo, which lies halfway between Palenque and San Cristóbal; instead of returning for the night to Palenque, you could go on to Ocosingo. It's higher up and more comfortable than Palenque. It's a nice little town, not touristy, not a lot to do other than see the ruins of Toniná. But it is a pleasant place to spend the night so that you can see the ruins early before moving on to San Cristóbal. Of about a half-dozen small hotels in town, the best are the vine-draped **Hospedaje Esmeralda** (☎ 919/673-0014), on Calle Central Norte a block north of the plaza, and the **Hotel Central** (☎ 919/673-0024), on the north side of the square. The latter has an attractive terrace overlooking the activity on the pretty plaza. Both are small and simple but very welcoming. The restaurant in front of Hotel Central has good cooking.

RUINS OF TONINÁ ★★ The ruins of Toniná (the name translates as "house of rocks") are 14km (8⅔ miles) east of Ocosingo. You can take a cab there and catch a *colectivo* to return. The city dates from the Classic period and covered a large area, but the excavated and restored part is all on one steep hillside that faces a broad valley. This site is not set up to handle lots of tourists (and doesn't really receive many). There is a good bit of climbing involved, and some of it is a little precarious. This is not a good place to take kids. Admission is 47 pesos.

This complex of courtyards, rooms, and stairways is built on multiple levels that are irregular and asymmetrical. The overall effect is that of a ceremonial area with multiple foci instead of a clearly discernible center. It affords beautiful and intriguing perspectives from just about any spot.

As early as A.D. 350, Toniná emerged as a dynastic center. In the 7th and 8th centuries, it was locked in a struggle with rival Palenque and, to a lesser degree, with faraway Calakmul. This has led some scholars to see Toniná as more militaristic than its neighbors—a sort of Sparta of the Classic Maya. Toniná's greatest victory came in 711, when, under the rule of Kan B'alam, it attacked Palenque and captured its king, K'an Joy Chitam, depicted on a stone frieze twisted, his arms bound with rope.

But the single most important artifact yet found at Toniná is up around the fifth level of the acropolis—a large stucco frieze divided into panels by a feathered framework adorned with the heads of sacrificial victims (displayed upside down) and some rather horrid creatures. The largest figure is a skeletal image holding a decapitated head—very vivid and very puzzling. There is actually a stylistic parallel with some murals of the Teotihuacán culture of central Mexico. The other special thing about Toniná is that it holds the distinction of having the last ever date recorded in the long count (A.D. 909), which marks the end of the Classic period.

SAN CRISTÓBAL DE LAS CASAS ★★★

229km (142 miles) SW of Palenque; 80km (50 miles) E of Tuxtla Gutiérrez; 74km (46 miles) NW of Comitán; 166km (103 miles) NW of Cuauhtémoc; 451km (280 miles) E of Oaxaca

San Cristóbal is a colonial town of white stucco walls and red-tile roofs, cobblestone streets and narrow sidewalks, graceful arcades, and open plazas. It lies in a green valley 2,100m (6,890 ft.) high. The city owes part of its name to the 16th-century cleric Fray Bartolomé de las Casas, who was the town's first bishop and spent the rest of his life waging a political campaign to protect the indigenous peoples of the Americas.

Surrounding the city are many villages of Mayan-speaking Indians who display great variety in their language, dress, and customs, making this area one of the most ethnically diverse in Mexico. San Cristóbal is the principal market town for these Indians, and their point of contact with the outside world. Most trek down from the surrounding mountains to sell goods and run errands.

San Cristóbal de las Casas

Several Indian villages lie within reach of San Cristóbal by road: **Chamula,** with its weavers and unorthodox church; **Zinacantán,** whose residents practice their own syncretic religion; **Tenejapa, San Andrés Larrainzar,** and **Santa Magdalena,** known for brocaded textiles; **Amatenango del Valle,** a town of potters; and

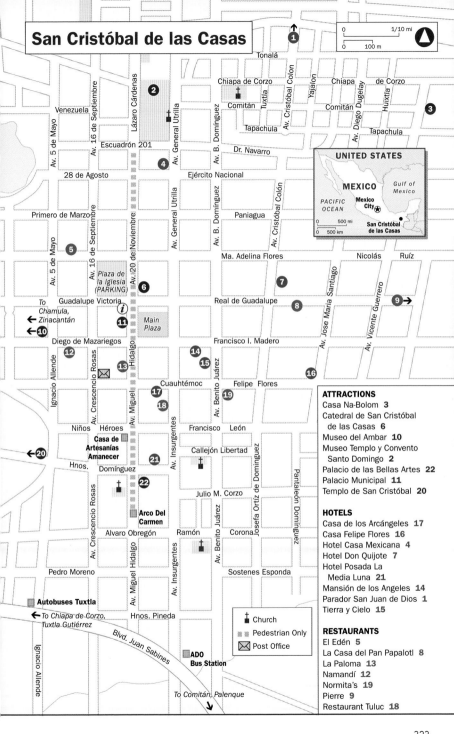

San Cristóbal de las Casas

Tonalá

Chiapa de Corzo · Yajalón · Chiapa · de Corzo

Comitán · Tuxtla · Comitán · Tapachula

Tapachula · Dr. Navarro · Ejército Nacional

Venezuela · Escuadrón 201 · 28 de Agosto

Primero de Marzo · Paniagua · Nicolás · Ruíz

Ma. Adelina Flores

Plaza de la Iglesia (PARKING)

Guadalupe Victoria · Real de Guadalupe

To Chamula, Zinacantán

Main Plaza

Diego de Mazariegos · Francisco I. Madero

Cuauhtémoc · Felipe Flores

Niños Héroes · Francisco León

Casa de Artesanías Amanecer

Hnos. Domínguez · Callejón Libertad

Julio M. Corzo

Arco Del Carmen

Alvaro Obregón · Ramón · Corona

Pedro Moreno · Sostenes Esponda

Autobuses Tuxtla

To Chiapa de Corzo, Tuxtla Gutiérrez · Hnos. Pineda

Blvd. Juan Sabines

ADO Bus Station

To Comitán, Palenque

Street names (columns)
Av. 5 de Mayo · Av. 16 de Septiembre · Lázaro Cárdenas · Av. General Utrilla · Av. B. Domínguez · Av. Cristóbal Colón · Av. Diego Dugelay · Huïxtla · Av. 20 de Noviembre · Av. José María Santiago · Av. Vicente Guerrero · Ignacio Allende · Av. Crescencio Rosas · Av. Miguel Hidalgo · Av. Benito Juárez · Av. Insurgentes · Josefa Ortíz de Dominguez · Pantaleón Domínguez · Ignacio Allende

0 — 1/10 mi
0 — 100 m

Inset map
UNITED STATES
MEXICO
Gulf of Mexico
PACIFIC OCEAN
Mexico City
San Cristóbal de las Casas
0 — 500 mi
0 — 500 km

ATTRACTIONS
Casa Na-Bolom **3**
Catedral de San Cristóbal de las Casas **6**
Museo del Ambar **10**
Museo Templo y Convento Santo Domingo **2**
Palacio de las Bellas Artes **22**
Palacio Municipal **11**
Templo de San Cristóbal **20**

HOTELS
Casa de los Arcángeles **17**
Casa Felipe Flores **16**
Hotel Casa Mexicana **4**
Hotel Don Quijote **7**
Hotel Posada La Media Luna **21**
Mansión de los Angeles **14**
Parador San Juan de Dios **1**
Tierra y Cielo **15**

RESTAURANTS
El Edén **5**
La Casa del Pan Papalotl **8**
La Paloma **13**
Namandí **12**
Normita's **19**
Pierre **9**
Restaurant Tuluc **18**

† Church
▨ Pedestrian Only
✉ Post Office

Personal Safety

Though criminal organizations are active in the state of Chiapas (smuggling drugs overland from Guatemala and preying upon Central American immigrants attempting to get to the U.S.), they mostly work in the state's Pacific coast region, far from San Cristóbal. Life here remains normal. The city doesn't have a gang problem and is by and large a safe place to visit.

Aguacatenango, known for embroidery. Most of these "villages" consist of little more than a church and the municipal government building, with homes scattered for miles around and a general gathering only for church and market days (usually Sun).

Many Indians now live on the outskirts of town because they've been expelled from their villages over religious differences. Known as *los expulsados,* they no longer farm but now make their living in commerce and handicrafts. Most still wear traditional dress, but they've adopted Protestant religious beliefs that prevent them from partaking in many of their community's civic and religious celebrations.

The greatest threat to these unique cultures is not tourism, but the action of large market forces, population pressures, environmental damage, and poverty. The Indians might steal glances or even stare at tourists, but mainly they pay little attention to outsiders, except as potential buyers for handicrafts.

You may see or hear the word *Jovel,* San Cristóbal's Indian name, incorporated into business names. You will hear the word *coleto* referring to someone or something from San Cristóbal. You'll see signs for *tamales coletos, pan coleto,* and *desayuno coleto* (Cristóbal breakfast).

Essentials
ARRIVING & DEPARTING

BY PLANE   The local airport is little used, and the closest airport with regular service is in Tuxtla Gutiérrez (p. 339).

BY CAR   From Palenque (5 hr.), the beautiful road provides jungle scenery, but portions of it may be heavily potholed or obstructed during rainy season. Check with the local state tourism office before driving. From Tuxtla Gutiérrez, the 1½-hour trip winds through beautiful mountain country.

BY TAXI   Taxis from Tuxtla Gutiérrez to San Cristóbal cost around 650 pesos.

BY BUS   The **ADO** station (which also handles the affiliates Altos, Cristóbal Colón, and Maya de Oro) is at the corner of Insurgentes and Bulevar Juan Sabines, 8 blocks south of the main square. This company offers service to and from Tuxtla Palenque, and several other destinations: Mérida (two buses per day), Villahermosa, Oaxaca, and Puerto Escondido. San Cristobal has a total of about a dozen bus terminals, all in this same general area, To buy a bus ticket without going down to the station, go to the **Boletotal** office, Real de Guadalupe 24 (𝄐 **967/678-8503**), open daily from 8am to 9pm.

The best cheap way to get to and from nearby Tuxtla Gutiérrez is by microbus, 16-seat buses that depart every 5 to 15 minutes from the south side of Juan Sabines. The company is called **Omnibus de Chiapas** (no phone). Look for white buses that say *omni* or *expreso* on the front. The fare is 38 pesos, and the trip takes about an hour. There are also vans making the

THE zapatista MOVEMENT & CHIAPAS

In January 1994, Indians from this area rebelled against the Mexican government over healthcare, education, land distribution, and representative government. Their organization, the **Zapatista Liberation Army,** known as EZLN (Ejército Zapatista de Liberación Nacional), and its leader, Subcomandante Marcos, became symbols of the struggle for social justice. Times have changed. The situation has long since quieted, and there is no longer any talk of armed revolt. Subcomandante Marcos has become a social critic and commentator, and the EZLN has become an independent political organization not tied to any particular party. Even the town's graffiti reflects the new mood, with political exhortations disappearing in favor of the more artsy, obscure scribblings resembling graffiti in the U.S.

run every 15 to 30 minutes. They can be found just off Juan Sabines by the bus station. You'll have to ask someone to point them out to you because there isn't a sign. The problem with these is that they pack too many passengers in them for comfort.

ORIENTATION

VISITOR INFORMATION   The **Municipal Tourism Office** (©/fax **967/678-0665**) in the town hall, west of the main square, is open daily from 9am to 9pm. Check the bulletin board for apartments, shared rides, cultural events, and local tours.

San Cristóbal's Avenida 20 de Noviembre.

GETTING AROUND   Most of the sights and shopping in San Cristóbal are within walking distance of the plaza. To get to the town square from the highway, turn on to **Avenida Insurgentes** (at the traffic light). From the bus station, the main plaza is 8 blocks north up Avenida Insurgentes (a 10-min. walk, slightly uphill). Cabs are cheap and plentiful.

Urbano **buses** (minibuses) take passengers between town and the residential neighborhoods. All buses pass by the market and central plaza on their way through town. Utrilla and Avenida 16 de Septiembre are the two main arteries; all buses use the market area as the last stop. Any bus on Utrilla will take you to the market.

Colectivos to outlying villages depart from the public market at Avenida Utrilla. Buses late in the day are usually very crowded. Always check to see when the last or next-to-last bus returns from wherever you're going, and then take the one before that—those last buses sometimes don't materialize, and you might be stranded.

Recommended Books

The People of the Bat: Mayan Tales and Dreams from Zinacantán, by Robert M. Laughlin, is a priceless collection of beliefs from that village (p. 330) near San Cristóbal. Another good book with a completely different view of today's Maya is *The Heart of the Sky,* by Peter Canby, who traveled among the Maya to chronicle their struggles (and wrote his book before the Zapatista uprising).

Rental cars come in handy for trips to the outlying villages and may be worth the expense when shared by a group, but keep in mind that insurance is invalid on unpaved roads. Try **Optima Car Rental,** Av. Mazariegos 39 (ⓒ **967/674-5409**). **Scooters** and **mountain bikes** can be rented from **Croozy Scooters,** at Belisario Domínguez 7-A (http://croozyscooter rental.com; ⓒ **967/114-2862**). **Bikes** are another option for getting around the city; a day's rental is about 140 pesos. **Los Pingüinos,** Calle Ecuador 4B (www.bikemexico.com/pinguinos; ⓒ **967/678-0202**), offers bike rentals and bike tours out of town.

CITY LAYOUT   San Cristóbal is laid out on the traditional grid. The main north-south axis is **Insurgentes/Utrilla;** the east-west axis is **Mazariegos/ Madero.** All streets change names when they cross either of these streets. The *zócalo* (main plaza) lies where they intersect. An important street to know is **Real de Guadalupe,** which runs from the plaza eastward to the church of Guadalupe, and has many hotels and restaurants. The market is 7 blocks north of the *zócalo* along Utrilla.

Cutting through the heart of town is the **Andador,** a pedestrian street to Av. Miguel Hidalgo/Av. 20 de Noviembre from the Templo del Carmen, south of the plaza next to the Arco del Carmen (onetime entrance to the city), to the Templo de Santo Domingo, 4 blocks north of the plaza. It's lined with shops, clubs, and restaurants and is a welcome respite from busy streets.

Note that this town has at least three streets named Domínguez and two streets named Flores. There are Hermanos Domínguez, Belisario Domínguez, and Pantaleón Domínguez, and María Adelina Flores and Dr. Felipe Flores.

[FastFACTS] SAN CRISTÓBAL DE LAS CASAS

Area Code The telephone area code is **967.**

ATMs San Cristóbal has a number of ATMs.

Currency Exchange There are at least five *casas de cambio* on Real de Guadalupe, near the main square, and a couple under the colonnade facing the square. Most are open until 8pm, and some are open Sunday.

Internet Access Internet cafes are everywhere.

Medical Care Chiapas uses a central phone number for all emergency services, ☎ **066.**

Parking Use the underground public lot in front of the cathedral, just off the main square, on 16 de Septiembre. Entry is from Calle 5 de Febrero.

Post Office The *correo* is at Crescencio Rosas and Cuauhtémoc, a block south and west of the main square. It's open Monday to Friday from 8am to 7pm, Saturday from 9am to 1pm.

Spanish Classes The **El Puente Language Classes** at the Centro Cultural El Puente, Real de Guadalupe 55, 29250 San Cristóbal de las Casas, Chi. (www.elpuenteweb.com; ☎/fax 967/678-3723), offers Spanish classes and can arrange home stays.

Weather San Cristóbal can be chilly when the sun isn't out, especially during the winter. Most hotels are not heated, although some have fireplaces. There is always a possibility of rain, but I would avoid visiting during the height of the rainy season, from late August to late October.

Exploring San Cristóbal

San Cristóbal is a lovely town in a lovely region. The scenic beauty is a major draw, but the main appeal is the highland Maya. They can be seen anywhere in San Cristóbal, but most travelers take at least one trip to the outlying villages to get a close-up of Maya life.

Casa Na-Bolom ★ CULTURAL INSTITUTION   This is the old headquarters of anthropologists Frans and Trudy Blom, who made this little corner of the world their home and their passion. It became a gathering place for those studying in the region. Frans Blom (1893–1963) led many early archaeological studies in Mexico, and Trudy (1901–93) was noted for her photographs of the Lacandón

A display from Casa Na-Bolom.

Indians and her efforts to save them and their forest homeland. A room at Na-Bolom contains a selection of her Lacandón photographs, and postcards of the photographs are on sale in the gift shop. The house is now a museum. A tour covers the displays of pre-Hispanic artifacts collected by Frans Blom; the cozy library, with its numerous volumes about the region and the Maya; and the gardens Trudy Blom started for the ongoing reforestation of the Lacandón jungle. The tour ends with a showing of *La Reina de la Selva,* an excellent 50-minute film on the Bloms, the Lacandón, and Na-Bolom.

The 17 guest rooms, named for surrounding villages, are decorated with local objects and textiles. All rooms have fireplaces and private bathrooms. Room rate includes a guided museum tour. Prices are 830 pesos and up double; 1,520 pesos and up suite.

Even if you're not a guest here, you can come for a meal, usually an assortment of vegetarian and other dishes. Just be sure to make a reservation at least 2½ hours in advance, and be on time. The colorful dining room has one large table, and the eclectic mix of travelers sometimes makes for interesting conversation. The restaurant is open from 7:30am to 10pm. Dinner (reservations only) is a set menu and starts at 7pm.

Av. Vicente Guerrero 33, 29200 San Cristóbal de las Casas, Chi. www.nabolom.org. ✆ **967/678-1418.** Fax 967/678-5586. Group tour and film 50 pesos. Open daily 10am–7pm; tours 11:30am (Spanish only) and 4:30pm.

Catedral de San Cristóbal de las Casas CATHEDRAL   San Cristóbal's main cathedral was built in the 1500s. Make note of the interesting beamed ceiling and a carved wooden pulpit.

Calle 20 de Noviembre at Guadalupe Victoria. No phone. Free admission. Daily 7am–6pm.

El Mercado MARKET   Once you've visited Santo Domingo (p. 329), meander through the San Cristóbal town market and the surrounding area. Every time I do, I see something different to elicit my curiosity.

By Santo Domingo church. No phone. Mon–Sat 8am–7pm.

Museo del Ambar MUSEUM   Chiapas is the third-largest producer of amber in the world, and many experts prefer its amber for its colors and clarity. Exhibits at this museum move methodically through all the issues surrounding amber—mining, shaping, and identification, as well as the varieties found elsewhere. It's

LEFT: **San Cristóbal's main cathedral.**
ABOVE: **A display from the Museo del Ambar.**

A gilded altar from Museo Templo y Convento Santo Domingo.

interesting and inexpensive, and you get to see the restored area of the old convent it occupies. A couple of beautiful pieces of worked amber are on permanent loan—make sure you see them. In mid-August, the museum holds a contest for local artisans who work in amber; they do remarkable work.

Exconvento de la Merced, Diego de Mazariegos s/n. www.museumdelambar.com.mx. *C* **967/678-9716.** Admission 20 pesos. Tues–Sun 10am–2pm.

Museo Templo y Convento Santo Domingo CHURCH/CONVENT/MUSEUM Inside the front door of the carved-stone facade are a beautiful gilded wooden altarpiece built in 1560, walls with saints, and gilt-framed paintings. Attached to the church is the former Convent of Santo Domingo, now a small museum about San Cristóbal and Chiapas. It has changing exhibits and often shows cultural films. It's 5 blocks north of the *zócalo*, in the market area.

Av. 20 de Noviembre. *C* **967/678-1609.** Free admission to church; museum 44 pesos. Museum Tues–Sun 9am–6pm; church daily 10am–2pm and 5–8pm.

Palacio de las Bellas Artes CULTURAL INSTITUTION Bellas Artes periodically hosts dance events, art shows, and other performances. The schedule of events is usually posted on the door if they're not open. A public library is next door. Around the corner, the Centro Cultural holds concerts and other performances; check the posters on the door to see what's scheduled.

Av. Hidalgo, 4 blocks south of the plaza. No phone.

Templo de San Cristóbal CHURCH For the best view of San Cristóbal, climb the seemingly endless steps to this church and *mirador* (lookout point). A visit here requires stamina. There are 22 more churches in town, some of which also demand strenuous climbs.

At the very end of Calle Hermanos Domínguez.

HORSEBACK RIDING

Horseback riding, one of the most important forms of recreation in San Cristóbal, is also a popular and inexpensive ($10–$15 per person) mode of touring. Most hotels can book a horseback tour; the Felipe Flores B&B (www.felipeflores.com; *C* **967/678-3996**) specializes in tours. You can also try showing up at the Cafetería del Centro (Real de Guadalupe 7, ½ block east of the plaza), at 9am or 1pm for a 4-hour horseback tour to the village of Chamula with an English-speaking guide.

THE NEARBY MAYA VILLAGES & COUNTRYSIDE

The Indian communities around San Cristóbal are fascinating worlds unto themselves. If you are unfamiliar with these indigenous cultures, you will understand

and appreciate more of what you see by visiting them with a guide, at least for your first foray out into the villages. Guides are acquainted with members of the communities and are viewed with less suspicion than newcomers. These communities have their own laws and customs—and visitors' ignorance is no excuse. Entering these communities is tantamount to leaving Mexico, and if something happens, the state and federal authorities will not intervene except in case of a serious crime.

The best guided trips are the locally grown ones. Two operators go to the neighboring villages in small groups. They charge about the same price (175 pesos per person), use minivans for transportation, and speak English. They do, however, have their own interpretations and focus.

Guides leave from **Casa Na-Bolom** (p. 327) for daily trips to San Juan Chamula, and Zinacantán

Alex Aranda of **Cielo y Tierra Tours** (www.cieloytierratours.com; info@ cieloytierratours.com) specializes in private and group tours to Maya villages around San Cristobal (including some of the more remote villages that receive very little tourism) as well as the Maya ruins of Tonina, Chinkultik, and Tenam Puente.

Raúl and **Caesar,** longtime guides with good connections with the Indians in nearby communities, can be found in front of the cathedral around 9am. They can be reached at alexyraultours@yahoo.com.mx.

Palenque-based **José Luis Zuñiga** (p. 314), a very good independent, INAH-trained guide, will also customize tours in and around San Cristóbal.

For excursions farther afield, see "Road Trips from San Cristóbal" on p. 337.

CHAMULA & ZINACANTÁN   A visit to the village of San Juan Chamula will demonstrate just how different life in the highland villages is from anything within your experience, unless perhaps you've visited an Amish community. Sunday, when the market is in full swing, is the best day to go for shopping; other days, when you'll be less impeded by eager children selling their crafts, are better for seeing the village and church.

The village, 8km (5 miles) northeast of San Cristóbal, has a large church, a plaza, and a municipal building. Each year, a new group of citizens is chosen to live in the municipal center as caretakers of the saints, settlers of disputes, and enforcers of village rules. As in other nearby villages, local leaders wear their leadership costumes on Sunday, donning beautifully woven straw hats loaded with colorful ribbons befitting their high position and sitting solemnly together somewhere around the central square. Chamula is typical of other villages, in that men are often away working in the "hot lands," harvesting coffee or cacao, while women stay home to tend the sheep, the children, the cornfields, and the fires.

Don't leave Chamula without seeing the **church interior.** The receipt for your 20-peso fee warns that **photography inside the church is forbidden.** Take heed; the ban is vigorously enforced—much to transgressors' regret. As you step from bright sunlight into the candlelit interior, you enter the Chamula's sacred space. The air is heavy with the smell of copal, a native incense. Pine needles and burning candles cover the tile floor. Saints line the walls, and people kneel before them, praying aloud while passing around bottles of Pepsi-Cola. Shamans are often on hand, passing eggs over sick people or using live or dead chickens in a curing ritual. The statues of saints are similar to those in any Mexican Catholic church, and they have

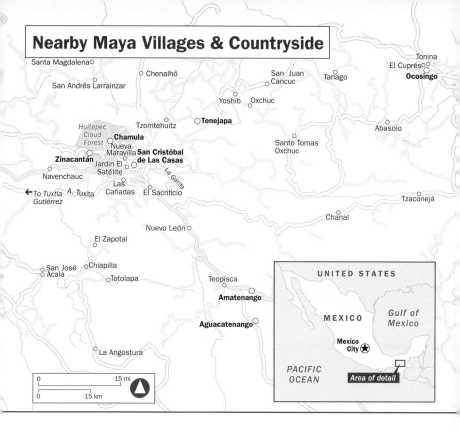

Nearby Maya Villages & Countryside

Santa Magdalena○

○ Chenalhō

San Andrés Larrainzar

San Juan Cancuc ○

Tanago ○

Tonina
El Cuprés○○
Ocosingo

Yoshib ○Oxchuc

Huitepec
Cloud
Forest ○**Chamula**
Nueva
Maravilla **San Cristóbal**
Zinacantán Jardin El ○**de Las Casas**
Satélite
Navenchauc
Las
○ ○
A. Tuxita Cañadas El Sacrificio

Tzomtehuitz ○**Tenejapa**

Santo Tomas
Oxchuc

Abasolo

←To Tuxtla
Gutiérrez

La Garita

Tzaconejá

Chanal ○

Nuevo León ○

El Zapotal
○

○Chiapilla
San José
○ Acala
○Totolapa

Teopisca
○
Amatenango

Aguacatenango○

○ La Angostura

| 0 | 15 mi |
| 0 | 15 km |

UNITED STATES

MEXICO

Gulf of
Mexico

Mexico
City ★

PACIFIC
OCEAN

Area of detail

the same names, but they mean something completely different to the Chamula. Visitors can walk carefully through the church to see the saints or stand quietly in the background.

Just to the south, Zinacantán is a wealthier, tidier, and less insular village than Chamula. Though you are required to sign a form promising not to take any photographs before you see the two side-by-side **sanctuaries,** the village overall feels much friendlier than Chamula. Once permission is granted and you have paid a small fee, an escort will usually show you the church, or you may be allowed to see it on your own. Floors may be covered in pine needles here, too, and the rooms are brightly sunlit. You will likely be approached by children or women who will offer to take you to their homes where their female relatives will be weaving or working at other crafts. Don't hesitate to accept one of these invitations; some of these home workshops are stunning. This is where it helps to have a guide who knows where the best quality and selections are. You aren't obligated to buy anything, but if you are in the market for textiles, clothing, or small animal figures, this is a good place to buy them.

AMATENANGO DEL VALLE   About an hour's ride south of San Cristóbal is Amatenango, a town known mostly for its **women potters.** You'll see their work in San Cristóbal—small animals, jars, and large water jugs—but in the village, you can visit the potters in their homes. Just walk down the dirt streets. Villagers will lean over the walls of family compounds and invite you in to select from their inventory. You may even see them firing the pieces under piles of wood in the open courtyard or painting them with color derived from rusty iron water. The women wear beautiful red-and-yellow *huipiles,* but if you want to take a photograph, you'll have to pay. To get here, take a *colectivo* from the market in San Cristóbal. Before it lets you off, be sure to ask about the return-trip schedule.

A female potter from Amatenango.

AGUACATENANGO   This village, 16km (10 miles) south of Amatenango, is known for its **embroidery.** If you've visited San Cristóbal's shops, you'll recognize the white-on-white and black-on-black floral patterns on dresses and blouses for sale. The locals' own regional blouses, however, are quite different.

TENEJAPA   The **weavers** of Tenejapa, 28km (17 miles) northeast from San Cristóbal, make some of the most beautiful and expensive work you'll see in the region. The best time to visit is on market day (Sun and Thurs, though Sun is better). The Tenejapa weavers taught the weavers of San Andrés and Magdalena—which accounts for the similarity in their designs and colors. To get to Tenejapa, try to find a *colectivo* in the very last row by the market, or hire a taxi. On Tenejapa's main street, several stores sell locally woven regional clothing, and you can bargain for the price.

THE HUITEPEC CLOUD FOREST   **Pronatura,** Calle Pedro Moreno 1 (© 967/ 678-5000), a private, nonprofit, ecological organization, offers environmentally sensitive tours of the cloud forest. The forest is a haven for **migratory birds,** and more than 100 bird species and 600 plant species have been identified here. Guided tours run from 9am to noon Tuesday to Sunday. Guided birding trips and general nature tours cost 70 to 100 pesos per person. Make reservations a day in advance. To reach the reserve on your own, take the Chamula road north; the turnoff is at Km 3.5. The reserve is open Tuesday to Sunday from 8am to 3pm.

Where to Eat

San Cristóbal is not known for its cuisine, but it has a great number and variety of restaurants, so you can eat well. For baked goods, try the **Panadería La Hojaldra,** Insurgentes 33 (© 967/678-4286). It's a traditional Mexican bakery that's open daily from 8am to 9:30pm.

MODERATE

El Edén ★ INTERNATIONAL   This is a small, quiet restaurant inside the Hotel El Paraíso where the food and service are consistently good (better than in most restaurants in San Cristóbal). The steaks are tender, and the margaritas are especially dangerous (one is all it takes). Specialties include Swiss cheese fondue for two, Edén salad, and brochettes.

In the Hotel El Paraíso, Av. 5 de Febrero 19. ✆ **967/678-0085.** Breakfast 35–55 pesos; main courses 60–150 pesos. MC, V. Daily 8am–10:30pm.

La Paloma ★ INTERNATIONAL/MEXICAN   I particularly like this place in the evening because the lighting is so well done. For starters, try the squash blossoms stuffed with *huitlaoche* mousse. Mexican classics include *albóndigas en chipotle* (meatballs in a thick chipotle sauce), Oaxacan black *mole,* abalone with chipotle, and a variety of *chiles rellenos.* Live music nightly at 9pm.

Hidalgo 3. ✆ **967/678-1547.** Main courses 120–165 pesos. MC, V. Daily 9am–midnight.

INEXPENSIVE

La Casa del Pan Papalotl VEGETARIAN   This place is best known for its vegetarian lunch buffet with salad bar. The vegetables and most of the grains are organic. Kippy, the owner, has a home garden and a field near town where she grows vegetables. She buys locally grown, organic red wheat for her breads. These are all sourdough breads, which she likes because she feels they are easily digested and have good texture and taste. The pizzas are a popular item. The restaurant shares space with other facilities in the cultural center El Puente, which has gallery space, a language school, and cinema.

Real de Guadalupe 55 (btw. Diego Dugelay and Cristóbal Colón). ✆ **967/678-7215.** Main courses 50–70 pesos; pizzas 50–140 pesos; lunch buffet 60–75 pesos. No credit cards. Mon–Sat 9am–10pm (lunch buffet 2–5pm).

Namandí INTERNATIONAL/REGIONAL   If you're looking for a light meal, snack, or belly-busting huevos rancheros, this place is the perfect choice. Excellent-quality fair-trade coffee is served with delicious Mexican items such as enchiladas or tostadas. The crepes are excellent, but if you want to sample local fare, try the delicious tamales. The restaurant space is modern, light, and airy.

Mazarriegos 16. ✆ **967/678-8054.** Breakfast 19–97 pesos; lunch and dinner entrees 43–119 pesos. MC, V. Mon–Sat 8am–11pm; Sun 8:30am–10:30pm.

Normita's MEXICAN   Normita's is famous for its *pozole,* a chicken and hominy soup to which you add extra ingredients at the table. It also offers cheap, short-order Mexican mainstays. This is a "people's" restaurant; the open kitchen takes up one corner of the room, the rest of which is filled with simple tables and chairs.

Av. Juárez 6 (at Dr. José Flores). No phone. Breakfast 35–50 pesos; *pozole* 40 pesos; tacos 35 pesos. No credit cards. Daily 7am–11pm.

Restaurant Tuluc ✦ MEXICAN/INTERNATIONAL   The owner hails from Puebla, but learned the restaurant business in Germany and Belgium. He's often seen tending to his customers. The house specialty is *filete Tuluc,* a beef filet wrapped around spinach and cheese served with fried potatoes and green beans—a well-priced (80 pesos), savory dish with meltingly tender beef cooked expertly to order. The *tampiqueña* steak, served with a plethora of sides, is good and filling. The Chiapaneco breakfast is a quartet of juice, toast, two Chiapanecan tamales, and coffee. Lighter favorites include the sandwiches and enchiladas.

Av. Insurgentes 5 (btw. Cuauhtémoc and Francisco León). ✆ **967/678-2090.** Breakfast 35–50 pesos; main courses 40–100 pesos; *comida corrida* (served 2–5pm) 65 pesos. MC, V. Daily 7am–10pm.

COFFEEHOUSES

Because Chiapas-grown coffee is highly regarded, it's not surprising that coffee-houses proliferate here. Most are concealed in the nooks and crannies of San Cristóbal's side streets. Try **Café La Selva,** Crescencio Rosas 9 (✆ **967/678-7244**), for coffee served in all its varieties and brewed from organic beans; it is open daily from 9am to 11pm. A more traditional-style cafe, where locals meet to talk over the day's news, is **Café San Cristóbal,** Cuauhtémoc 1 (✆ **967/678-3861**), between Hidalgo and Insurgentes. It's open daily 7:30am to 10pm, Sunday from 9am to 9pm.

Shopping

Many Indian villages near San Cristóbal are noted for **weaving, embroidery, brocade work, leather,** and **pottery,** making the area one of the best in the country for shopping. You'll see beautiful woolen shawls and skirts, colorful native shirts, and magnificently woven *huipiles,* which often come in vivid geometric patterns. A good place to find textiles as well as other handicrafts, besides what's mentioned below, is in and around Santo Domingo and the market. The stalls and small shops in that neighborhood make for interesting shopping. Working in leather, the craftspeople are artisans of the highest caliber. Tie-dyed *jaspe* from Guatemala comes in bolts and is made into clothing. The town is also known for **amber,** sold in several shops; two of the best are mentioned below.

For the best selection of new and used books and reading material in English, go to **La Pared,** Andador Eclesiásticos 13 (✆ **967/678-6367**). The owners keep a large collection of books on the Maya, and Mexico in general, both fiction and nonfiction. Shops typically open around 9am; some close for a mid-day break.

CRAFTS

La Galería del Corazón Abierto   This art gallery beneath a cafe shows the work of national and international painters. Also for sale are paintings and greeting cards by Kiki Suarez, the owner, a German artist who has found her niche in San Cristóbal. There are some Oaxacan rugs and pottery, plus unusual silver jewelry. Hidalgo 3. ✆ **967/674-7273.**

Lágrimas de la Selva   "Tears of the Jungle" sells amber and amber jewelry, offering the best variety, quality, and artistry in San Cristóbal. It's not a bargain hunter's turf, but if you want to see high-quality amber, visit this place or Piedra Escondida, listed below. Often you can watch the jewelers in action. Hidalgo 1-C (half-block south of the main square). ✆ **967/674-6348.**

The Amber Test

Like any hot commodity, amber has its imitators. You can usually count on what's sold in the shops to be genuine, but some vendors working the streets are selling the cheap imitation. If in doubt, rub the amber briskly over your sleeve or pant leg. Real amber will give off a faint scent like honey. If you don't catch a whiff of honey, the offering is probably acrylic—even if it has an insect trapped inside.

Piedra Escondida   This is another excellent choice for out-of-the-ordinary amber and jewelry. 20 de Noviembre 22. No phone.

Tienda Chiapas   This showroom has examples of every craft practiced in the state. It is run by the government in support of Indian crafts. You should take a look, if only to survey what crafts the region practices. Niños Héroes at Hidalgo. ☏ **967/678-1180.**

TEXTILES

El Telar "The Loom" sells textiles all handmade in San Cristóbal, and most are from the store's workshop, which you can visit in the northwest part of town, next to the hotel Rincón del Arco. It specializes in textiles made on large floor looms. Calle 28 de Agosto 3 (next door to Hotel Casa Mexicana). ☏ **967/678-4422.** www.eltelar. com.mx.

Plaza de Santo Domingo The plazas around this church and the nearby Templo de Caridad fill with women in native garb selling their wares. Here you'll find women from Chamula weaving belts or embroidering, surrounded by piles of loomed woolen textiles from their village. Their inventory includes Guatemalan shawls, belts, and bags. There are also some excellent buys on Chiapanecan-made wool vests, jackets, rugs, and shawls, similar to those at Sna Jolobil (below), if you take the time to look and bargain Av. Utrilla. No phone.

Sna Jolobil Meaning "weaver's house" in Mayan, this place is in the former convent (monastery) of Santo Domingo, next to the church of Santo Domingo. Groups of Tzotzil and Tzeltal craftspeople operate the cooperative store, which has about 3,000 members who contribute products, help run the store, and share in the moderate profits. You'll find some elegant *huipiles* and other weavings; prices are high, as is the quality. Calzada Lázaro Cárdenas 42 (Plaza Santo Domingo, btw. Navarro and Nicaragua). ☏ **967/678-2646.**

Unión Regional de Artesanías de los Altos Also known as J'pas Jolovi-letic, this cooperative of weavers is smaller than Sna Jolobil (above) and not as sophisticated in its approach to potential shoppers. It sells blouses, textiles, pillow covers, vests, sashes, napkins, baskets, and purses. It's near the market and worth looking around. Av. Utrilla 43. ☏ **967/678-2848.**

Entertainment & Nightlife

San Cristóbal is blessed with a variety of nightlife, both resident and migratory. There is a lot of live music, surprisingly good and varied. The bars and restaurants are cheap, and they are easy to get to: You can hit all the places mentioned here without setting foot in a cab. Weekends are best, but on any night you'll find something going on.

Almost all the clubs in San Cristóbal host Latin music of one genre or another. **El Cocodrilo** (☏ **967/678-0871**), a comfortable lounge on the main plaza in the Hotel Santa Clara, has live bands from time to time, and more frequently in summer; a group from Argentina was scheduled to play on my last visit. When a band is on the roster, they play from 9pm to midnight. Relax at a table in what is usually a not-too-crowded environment. After that, your choices vary. One of the two most popular bars is **Café Bar Revolución** (☏ **967/678-6664**), on the pedestrian-only 20 de Noviembre at 1 de Marzo. Its decor backs up the name, and it has two live acts every night—usually blues, reggae, Latin, or rock, and always rock on Saturday nights. Usually it winds down around midnight. For Latin dance music, **Latino's,** on the corner of Madero and Juárez at Calle Madero 33 (☏ **967/678-9972**), has good bands playing a mix of salsa, merengue, and *cumbia.* Weekends get crowded, but it has a good-size dance floor. There's a small cover on weekends. The place is dark and has a bit of an urban edge to it. For a relaxing place to have a drink, try the bar at the **Hotel Posada Real de Chiapas,** across the street from Latino's. It has a piano player on Saturdays and soft recorded music the rest of the week.

Where to Stay

Among the most interesting places to stay in town is the seminary-turned-hotel-and-museum **Casa Na-Bolom** (p. 327).

Hotels in San Cristóbal are inexpensive; you can do well for $50 to $70 per night for a double. Rates listed here include taxes. High season is Easter week, July, August, and December.

EXPENSIVE

Parador San Juan de Dios ★★ This is San Cristóbal's handsomest property. It's in the north end of town in some 17th-century farm buildings. The rooms are large, plush, and distinctive, with something of the air of the old adobe and stone buildings. Most have fireplaces and period pieces mixed with a few modern comforts. Bathrooms are large and beautifully finished. Suites include Jacuzzi tubs. Most rooms have their own stone terraces (in some cases two) with views of the extensive grounds. The hotel is a long walk or short taxi ride from the main square. In 2011, it opened a small spa and a large gallery exhibiting traditional art from the region.

Calzada Roberta 16, Col. 31 de Marzo, 29229 San Cristóbal de las Casas, Chi. www.sanjuandios. com. ℰ/fax **967/678-1167,** -4290. 12 units. High season 1,800 pesos double, 3,400–6,000 pesos suite; low season 1,600 pesos double, 2,400–6,000 pesos suite. AE, MC, V. Free secure parking. **Amenities:** Restaurant; bar; room service; Wi-Fi (in common areas). *In room:* TV, hair dryer, Internet.

MODERATE

Casa de los Arcángeles ✦ The owner of a large courtyard restaurant decided to convert the rooms surrounding the courtyard into hotel rooms. This kind of afterthought is often a recipe for disaster, but it works in this case. The rooms, each with a queen-size bed, are large, comfortable, attractive, and well priced. The restaurant closes early so noise isn't a factor, and the location just south of the main square is excellent.

Cuauhtémoc 4, 29200 San Cristóbal de las Casas, Chi. ℰ **967/678-1531,** -1936. casadelos arcangeles@hotmail.com. 7 units. 1,485 pesos double. Rates include full breakfast. MC, V. Free parking. **Amenities:** Restaurant; bar; spa. *In room:* TV, hair dryer, minibar, Wi-Fi.

Casa Felipe Flores ★ This beautifully restored colonial house is the perfect setting for getting a feel for San Cristóbal. The patios and common rooms are relaxing and comfortable, and their architectural details are so very *coleto*. Guest rooms are nicely furnished and full of character—and heated in winter. The owners, Nancy and David Orr, enjoy sharing their appreciation and knowledge of Chiapas and the Maya.

Calle Dr. Felipe Flores 36, 29230 San Cristóbal de las Casas, Chi. www.felipeflores.com. ℰ/fax **967/678-3996.** 5 units. $95–$125 double. Rates include full breakfast. No credit cards. Limited street parking. **Amenities:** Library. *In room:* No phone.

Hotel Casa Mexicana ★ This colonial hotel with well-manicured courtyards offers attractive, comfortable lodging and attentive management. Standard rooms are carpeted and come with two double beds or one king-size. They have good lighting, electric heaters, and spacious bathrooms. Across the street in another colonial house are several much larger suites that have distinctive clay tile floors and larger bathrooms. The hotel handles many tour groups; it can be quiet and peaceful one day, full and bustling the next.

28 de Agosto 1 (at General Utrilla), 29200 San Cristóbal de las Casas, Chi. www.hotelcasa mexicana.com. ✆ **967/678-0698.** Fax 967/678-2627. 55 units. High season $125 double, $180 junior suite, $200 suite. AE, MC, V. Free secure parking 1½ blocks away. **Amenities:** Restaurant; bar; babysitting; room service; sauna. *In room:* TV, hair dryer, Wi-Fi.

Tierra y Cielo   With its modern architecture incorporating traditional materials and shapes, flatscreen TVs, and reliable Wi-Fi, this small boutique inn has a chic style and comfortable ambience. Rooms are large and easily include a heavy wooden desk. Rooms on the street side do get some traffic noise, but not enough to mar your stay. The restaurant is one of the city's most popular, and the bright, airy courtyard a pleasant spot for relaxing and mingling with other guests.

Av. Benito Juárez No. 1, 29200 San Cristóbal de las Casas, Chi. www.tierraycielo.com.mx. ✆ **967/678-1053.** 12 units. 1,050–1,650 pesos double. AE, DISC, MC, V. Free parking. **Amenities:** Room service. *In room:* TV, Wi-Fi.

INEXPENSIVE

Hotel Don Quijote ✦   Rooms in this three-story hotel (no elevator) are small but quiet, carpeted, and well lit, but a little worn. All have two double beds with reading lamps over them, tiled bathrooms, and plenty of hot water. There's complimentary coffee in the mornings.

Cristóbal Colón 7 (near Real de Guadalupe), 29200 San Cristóbal de las Casas, Chi. www.hotel donquijote.com.mx. ✆ **967/678-0346.** 25 units. 280–370 pesos double. MC, V. Free parking 1 block away. *In room:* TV.

Hotel Posada La Media Luna ✦   A modern two-story hotel in the downtown area with medium-size, attractive rooms for a good price. The bathrooms are larger than the norm, and the staff is helpful and friendly; some speak English. Room rate includes purified water.

Hermanos Domínguez 5, 29200 San Cristóbal de las Casas, Chi. www.hotel-lamedialuna.com. ✆ **967/631-5590.** 11 units. 400–500 pesos double. MC, V. **Amenities:** Restaurant. *In room:* TV, no phone, Wi-Fi.

Mansión de los Angeles   This clean, attractive colonial hotel has an accommodating staff. Guest rooms are medium size and come with either a single and a double bed or two double beds. They are more attractive, warmer, and better lit than most hotels in this town. They are also quiet. Bathrooms are small for the size of the rooms. Windows in most rooms open onto a pretty courtyard with a fountain; rooms in back have their own little mini-courtyard. Ground-floor rooms don't get as much light. The rooftop sun deck is a great siesta spot.

Calle Francisco Madero 17, 29200 San Cristóbal de las Casas, Chi. ✆ **967/678-1173,** -4371. 20 units. 600–740 pesos double. AE, MC, V. Limited secure parking 5 blocks away. *In room:* TV, Wi-Fi.

Road Trips from San Cristóbal

For excursions to nearby villages, see "The Nearby Maya Villages & Countryside," earlier in this chapter; for destinations farther away, there are several local travel agencies. But first, try **Alex and Caesar** (p. 330) or **Jose Luis Zuñiga** (p. 314). You can also try **ATC Travel and Tours,** Calle 5 de Febrero 15, at the corner of 16 de Septiembre (☏ **967/678-2550;** fax 967/678-3145), across from El Fogón restaurant. The agency has bilingual guides and reliable vehicles. ATC regional tours focus on birds and orchids, textiles, hiking, and camping.

The cost of the agency trips includes a driver but not necessarily a bilingual guide or guided information of any kind. You pay extra for those services, so when checking prices, be sure to flesh out the details.

PALENQUE, BONAMPAK & YAXCHILÁN

For information on these destinations, see the section on Palenque, earlier in this chapter.

CHINCULTIC RUINS, COMITÁN & MONTEBELLO NATIONAL PARK

Almost 160km (99 miles) southeast of San Cristóbal, near the border with Guatemala, is the **Chincultic** archaeological site and **Montebello National Park,** with 16 multicolored lakes and exuberant pine-forest vegetation. Seventy-four kilometers (46 miles) from San Cristóbal is **Comitán,** a pretty hillside town of 40,000 inhabitants known for its flower cultivation and a sugar cane–based liquor called *comiteco.* This is the last big town along the Pan-American Highway before the Guatemalan border.

The Chincultic ruins, a late Classic site, have barely been excavated, but the main **acropolis,** high up against a cliff, is magnificent to see from below and is worth the walk up for the view. After passing through the gate, you'll see the trail ahead; it passes ruins on both sides. More unexcavated tree-covered ruins flank steep stairs leading up the mountain to the acropolis. From there, you can gaze upon distant Montebello lakes and miles of cornfields and forest. The paved road to the lakes passes six lakes, all different colors and sizes, ringed by cool pine forests; most have parking lots and lookouts. The paved road ends at a small restaurant. The lakes are best seen on a sunny day, when their famous brilliant colors are optimal.

The Montebello lakes.

Most travel agencies in San Cristóbal offer a daylong trip that includes the lakes, the ruins, lunch in Comitán, and a stop in the pottery-making village of Amatenango del Valle. If you're driving, follow Hwy. 190 south from San Cristóbal through the pretty village of Teopisca and then through Comitán; turn left at La Trinitaria, where there's a sign to the lakes. After the Trinitaria turnoff and before you reach the lakes, there's a sign pointing left down a narrow dirt road to the Chincultic ruins.

TUXTLA GUTIÉRREZ

82km (51 miles) W of San Cristóbal; 277km (172 miles) S of Villahermosa; 242km (150 miles) NW of Ciudad Cuauhtémoc on the Guatemalan border

Tuxtla Gutiérrez (altitude 557m/1,827 ft.) is the commercial center of Chiapas. Coffee is the basis of the region's economy, along with recent oil discoveries. Tuxtla (pop. 567,787) is a business town, and not a particularly attractive one at first glance. Most travelers simply pass through Tuxtla on their way to San Cristóbal, the Sumidero Canyon, or Oaxaca. But if you stay a day or two, it has the virtue of being easy to get around in, having some pleasant parks, and being the jumping-off point for forays into the gorgeous Sumidero Canyon.

Essentials

ARRIVING & DEPARTING

BY PLANE   Tuxtla's airport (airport code: TGZ) is 45 minutes south of the city. There is taxi service at the airport. **Aeroméxico** (www.aeromexico.com; ✆ **800/237-6639** in the U.S., or 01-800/021-4000 in Mexico), **VivaAerobus** (www.vivaaerobus.com; ✆ **01-81/8215-0150** in Mexico), and **Interjet** (www.interjet.com.mx; ✆ **866/285-9525** from the U.S., or 01-80/0011-2345 in Mexico) offer flights to Tuxtla from destinations within Mexico.

BY CAR   From Oaxaca, you'll enter Tuxtla by Hwy. 190. From Villahermosa, or Palenque and San Cristóbal, you'll enter at the opposite end of town on the same highway from the east. In both cases, you'll arrive at the large main square at the center of town, La Plaza Cívica (see "Exploring Tuxtla," below).

From Tuxtla to Villahermosa, take Hwy. 190 east past the town of Chiapa de Corzo; soon you'll see a sign for Hwy. 195 north to Villahermosa. To San Cristóbal and Palenque, take Hwy. 190 east. The road is beautiful but tortuous. It's in good repair to San Cristóbal, but there may be bad spots between San Cristóbal and Palenque. The trip from Tuxtla to Villahermosa takes 4½ hours by car; the scenery is beautiful.

BY BUS   The main **bus station** (✆ **961/612-2624**) is a mile northwest of the city center on Avenida 5 Norte Poniente, at the Plaza del Sol. There are eight buses a day to Villahermosa, three or four buses a day to Oaxaca, and five to Palenque. Purchase tickets in advance for first-class service through http://boletotal.mx. There's usually no need to buy a ticket ahead of time, except during holidays. Small buses (microbuses) to San Cristóbal leave every 5 to 15 minutes from the station at the intersection of Avenida 4 Sur and Calle 15 Oriente.

ORIENTATION

VISITOR INFORMATION   Information desks are on the main square and on Avenida Central across from Parque de la Marimba. Some staff speak English and can provide good maps. The Chiapas state website, www.chiapas.gob.mx/ciudad-de-tuxtla-gutierrez, has good info on attractions and history.

GETTING AROUND   Taxis are the easiest transport in this city. They are plentiful and easy to come by. **Buses** to all parts of the city converge upon the Plaza Cívica along Calle Central.

CITY LAYOUT   Tuxtla is laid out on a grid. The main street, **Avenida Central,** is the east-west axis and is the artery through town for Hwy. 190. It's one of the few cities that you can drive straight through without fear of getting lost. West of the central district, it's called **Bulevar Belisario Domínguez;** in the east, it's **Bulevar Angel Albino Corzo. Calle Central** is the north-south axis. Cross streets are numbered with the directions Norte (North) or Sur (South).

FAST FACTS   The **area code** is 961. If you need medical help, the best **clinic** in town is Sanatorio Rojas, Calle 2 Sur Poniente no. 1847 (www.sanatorio rojas.com.mx; © 961/602-5004 or 612-5024).

Exploring Tuxtla

Tuxtla's downtown is centered on the **Plaza Cívica,** a large plaza framed by government buildings. On one end, the white **Catedral de San Marcos** is significant for its bell tower, where a series of Apostles appear each hour accompanied by ringing bells. **Parque Jardín de la Marimba,** at Av. Central between Calle 8 Poniente Norte and C. 9 Poniente Norte, is a prettier square where marimba bands play every evening. Although boats into **Sumidero Canyon** leave from nearby Chiapa de Corzo, Tuxtla is the gateway to the canyon for drivers, who need only follow Calzada Sumidero (which becomes 3a Av. Sur Poniente) north to reach the series of *miradors* where you can pull over for a bird's-eye view into the canyon.

Miguel Alvarez del Toro Zoo (ZOOMAT) ★★ ☺ ZOO   Located in the forest called El Zapotal Ecological Reserve, ZOOMAT is one of the best zoos in Mexico. The collection of animals and birds indigenous to this area gives the visitor a tangible sense of what the wilds of Chiapas are like. The zoo keeps jaguars, howler monkeys, owls, and many more exotic animals in roomy cages that replicate their home terrain; the whole zoo is so deeply buried in vegetation that you can almost pretend you're in a natural habitat. Unlike at other zoos I've visited, the animals are almost always on view.

Bulevar Samuel León Brinois, southeast of downtown. No phone. General admission adults 20 pesos, children under 13 10 pesos. Tues–Sun 8:30am–5:30pm. The zoo is about 8km (5 miles) southeast of downtown; catch a bus along Av. Central and at the Calzada.

Where to Eat

For a full sit-down meal, you can try local Chiapan food at **Las Pichanchas,** Av. Central Oriente 837 (© 961/612-5351). It's festively decorated and pretty to look at. The emphasis is on meat, with several heavy dishes on the menu. I would recommend the *filete simojovel* (a thin steak in a not-spicy chile sauce) or the *comida grande,* which is beef in a pumpkinseed sauce. Eating here is a cultural experience, but I usually prefer to head over to the **Flamingo,** 1 Poniente Sur 168, just off Avenida Central (© 961/612-0922), which serves standard Mexican dishes: enchiladas, *mole,* roast chicken. The Spanish owner also owns an elegant steakhouse called El Asador Castellano, on the west side of town. Take a taxi.

   If all you want is tacos, several good places are around the **El Parque de la Marimba** (Av. Central Poniente, 8 blocks west of main square). This splendid plaza has statues honoring some of Chiapas' masters of *marimba* and hosts free *marimba* music nightly. Of the local taco restaurants bordering the plaza,

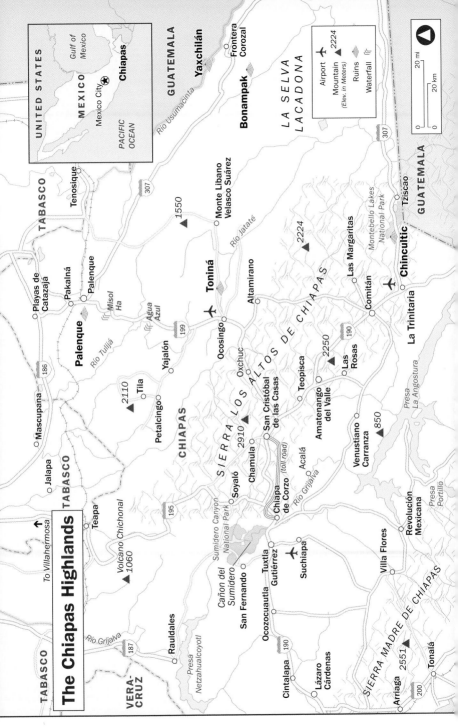

The Chiapas Highlands

TABASCO

To Villahermosa

UNITED STATES

MEXICO

Gulf of Mexico

Chiapas

Mexico City

PACIFIC OCEAN

GUATEMALA

Yaxchilán

Frontera Corozal

Bonampak

LA SELVA LACADONA

Airport

Mountain (Elev. in Meters) ▲2224

Ruins

Waterfall

20 mi

20 km

307

GUATEMALA

Tziscao

Chincultic

Montebello Lakes National Park

La Trinitaria

190

Comitán

Las Margaritas

2224

Presa La Angostura

Altamirano

ALTOS DE CHIAPAS

2250

Las Rosas

Teopisca

Amatenango del Valle

Venustiano Carranza

850

Oxchuc

SIERRA LOS

San Cristóbal de las Casas

2910

Chamula

Soyaló

Acalá

Chiapa de Corzo

(toll road)

Río Grijalva

195

Revolución Mexicana

Presa Portillo

Villa Flores

SIERRA MADRE DE CHIAPAS

2551

Tonalá

200

Arriaga

190

Cintalapa

Lázaro Cárdenas

Ocozocuautla

Tuxtla Gutiérrez

San Fernando

Suchiapa

Cañon del Sumidero

Sumidero Canyon National Park

187

Raudales

Río Grijalva

Presa Netzahualcoyotl

VERA-CRUZ

TABASCO

Teapa

Jalapa

Mascupana

186

Volcano Chichonal 1060

CHIAPAS

Petalcingo

2110

Tila

Yajalón

Palenque

Palenque

Río Tulijá

Misol Ha

Agua Azul

199

Ocosingo

Toniná

Río Jataté

1550

Monte Líbano Velasco Suárez

Pakalná

Palenque

Playas de Catazajá

Tenosique

307

TABASCO

341

Marimba musicians perform nightly in El Parque de la Marimba.

Parrilla Suiza and **El Fogón Norteño** are two good choices. Both have good grilled tacos.

Shopping

The government-operated **Instituto Casa Chiapas,** Plaza Galería, Blvd. Domínguez 2035 (www.casachiapas.gob.mx/plaza-galeria; © **961/602-9800**), supports artisans and promotes crafts from all parts of the state. The store is subsidized, making the prices here quite reasonable. The extensive collection of crafts is grouped by region and type from throughout the state of Chiapas. It's open Tuesday to Sunday from 11am to 8pm.

Where to Stay

The center of the hotel industry is out of town, west to Hwy. 190. You'll notice business-style hotels, such as the **Crowne Plaza, Hotel Flamboyán, Palace Inn,** and **La Hacienda.**

Camino Real Tuxtla Gutiérrez ★★   Bold modern architecture is the hallmark of the Camino Real chain, and this one is no exception, with stark lines, bright colors, and subtle references to the Maya culture and the local region. The center of the hotel is open-air and filled with a spot of jungle, a small cascade, and tropical birds flying freely about. This is a relaxing hotel; walking to and from your room, you hear bird song and splashing water. Guest rooms have two doubles or a king, are carpeted, and are comfortably furnished. Bathrooms are large.

Bulevar Domínguez 1159, 29060 Tuxtla Gutiérrez, Chi. www.caminoreal.com. © **800/7-CAMINO** (722-6466) in the U.S. or Canada, or 961/617-7777. Fax 961/617-7779. 210 units. 1,300 pesos and up. Internet promotions often available. AE, MC, V. Free secured parking. **Amenities:** 2 restaurants; bar; babysitting; concierge; executive-level rooms; health club and spa; outdoor pool; room service. *In room:* A/C, TV, hair dryer, minibar, Wi-Fi.

Holiday Inn Express La Marimba ★   This business-oriented hotel, which just opened in October 2011, is also a good choice for tourists looking for a few extra comforts without paying for a luxury hotel. It's clean and modern, with an eager-to-please staff. Rooms are large and well-lit, and they have strong Wi-Fi connections, a roomy work desk, and plenty of electrical outlets. The "business center" is basically just an Internet-connected computer, but it comes in handy if you need to print something. Best of all, it's just 3 blocks from the delightful Parque Marimba.

Av. Central Poniente no. 1254 at Calle 12 S. Poniente Norte 29000 Tuxtla Gutiérrez, Chi. www. hiexpress.com. ℰ **961/613-1940.** 36 units. 996 pesos double. AE, MC, DISC, V. Rates include buffet breakfast. Limited free guarded parking. **Amenities:** Small fitness room. *In room:* A/C, TV, hair dryer, Wi-Fi.

Hotel María Eugenia   This is a centrally located, well-managed property with plain, medium-size rooms. The white walls and white ceramic tile make them seem even plainer, but clean and uncluttered. Beds have comfortable mattresses and come either as two doubles or one king. There is good space for luggage.

Av. Central Oriente 507, 29000 Tuxtla Gutiérrez, Chi. www.mariaeugenia.com.mx. ℰ **961/613-3767** or 01-800/716-0149 in Mexico. 83 units. 900 pesos double. AE, MC, V. Free guarded parking. **Amenities:** Restaurant; bar; outdoor pool; room service. *In room:* A/C, TV, Wi-Fi.

Chiapa de Corzo & the Sumidero Canyon

The real reason to stay in Tuxtla is to take a boat trip through the **Canyon of El Sumidero** ★★. The canyon is spectacular, and the boat ride is fun. Boats leave from the docks in **Chiapa de Corzo,** a colonial town of about 50,000 inhabitants that bumps up to Tuxtla. To get there, take a taxi or hop on the bus operated by Transportes Chiapa-Tuxtla (Av. 1 Sur btw. calles 5 and 6 Oriente). Buses leave every couple of minutes and cost 9 pesos. The ride takes a half-hour. Ask to get off at the main square *(parada del parque)*. The two main boat cooperatives have ticket booths under the archways bordering the square. But you don't have to look for these; just go straight to the boats at the pier *(embarcadero)* 1½ blocks below the square. (Those who don't make a boat trip, or just want a different perspective on the canyon, can take a driving tour out of Tuxtla Gutiérrez; see p. 340.)

As you pass the church of Santo Domingo, you'll see a large **ceiba** tree shading the churchyard. In better circumstances these trees get even larger than this, but this one has taken up an interesting position in front of the church. The Maya felt that these trees embodied the connection between the heavens, the world of men, and the underworld because they extend into all three realms.

The **two cooperatives** (the reds and the greens identified by the color of their boats) offer the same service. They work together sharing passengers and such. Boats leave as soon as a minimum of 12 people show up. The interval can be up to an hour or as short as 10 minutes, depending on the season. The cost is 200 pesos. The ride takes 2 hours. This river is the Grijalva, which flows to the Gulf of Mexico from Guatemala and is one of Mexico's largest. Besides the canyon vistas, you're likely to see some crocodiles and other things of interest. The boat's pilot will explain a few things in Spanish, but much of what he says adds little to the tour. At the deepest point in the canyon, the walls stretch up vertically 1,000m (3,281 ft.) above the water, which, in turn, is about 100m (328 ft.) deep at that point. Whether that's accurate or not, the view is awe-inspiring. There are some interesting things happening on the walls; water seeps out in places, creating little micro-environments of moss, grass, and mineral deposits. One of these places is called the Christmas Tree, for its form.

The boats operate from 8am to 4pm. They are fast, and the water is smooth. The best times to see the canyon are early or late in the day, when the sun is at an angle and shines on one or the other of the canyon walls. The boats are necessarily open, so take an adjustable cap or a hat with a drawstring and some sunscreen. A pair of earplugs would come in handy, too.

If you'd rather stay in Chiapa de Corzo than Tuxtla, check out the simple but nice hotel off the main square: **Hotel Los Angeles,** at Av. Julián Grajales 2 (www.hotel-chiapas.com; © **961/616-0048**). It offers rooms with or without air-conditioning for 400 to 500 pesos per night.

PLANNING YOUR TRIP TO THE YUCATÁN, TABASCO & CHIAPAS

9

by Shane Christensen

T raveling to the Yucatán, Tabasco, and Chiapas presents a myriad of options, from well-serviced beaches on the Caribbean that offer every modern comfort to more rustic locations in the South and to the West that require planning, patience, and flexibility. Quintana Roo is by far the most advanced tourist state in this region, playing host to about half of all tourism to Mexico. It's easy to travel between Cancún and the beaches of the Riviera Maya, where tourist infrastructure is well developed. You can either plan on resort-hopping along the Caribbean coast in a rental car or taking buses to visit the Maya ruins in the Yucatán peninsula. Getting to and around Chiapas and Tabasco requires a little more ingenuity, although infrastructure (particularly roads) has improved here in recent years.

Travelers to Mexico should be aware of security concerns in a number of parts of the country and take precautions to maximize their safety. For the most part, this region of Mexico is safe for travelers who steer clear of drugs and those who sell them, but visitors should still exercise caution in unfamiliar areas and remain aware of their surroundings at all times. See "Safety," below, for more details; and visit the U.S. State Department's website, www.state.gov, for up-to-date information on travel to Mexico (U.S. citizens living or traveling in Mexico are encouraged to sign up on the same website for the Smart Traveler Enrollment Program to get updated information on local travel and security).

For additional help in planning your trip and for more on-the-ground resources in the Yucatán peninsula, Tabasco, and Chiapas, turn to "Fast Facts," on p. 356.

GETTING THERE
By Plane

Mexico has dozens of international and domestic airports. Among the airports in the Yucatán region are Cancún (CUN), Cozumel (CZM), and Mérida (MID). The major airport in Chiapas is in Tuxtla Gutiérrez (TGZ) and in Tabasco at Villahermosa (VSA). We list which airlines fly to the local airports in the relevant "Getting There: By Air" sections throughout this book. For a list of the major international airlines with service to Mexico, turn to "Airline Websites," p. 369.

ARRIVING AT THE AIRPORT

Immigration and customs clearance at Mexican airports is generally efficient. Expect longer lines during peak seasons, but you can usually clear immigration and customs within a half-hour. For more on what to expect when passing through Mexican customs, see "Customs," below.

PREVIOUS PAGE: **A Carnaval performer in Cozumel.**

Carrying Car Documents

You must carry your temporary car-importation permit, tourist permit (see "Car Documents," below), and, if you purchased it, your proof of Mexican car insurance in the car at all times. The temporary car-importation permit papers are valid for 6 months (apply online at www.banjercito.com.mx). It's a good idea to overestimate the time you'll spend in Mexico so if you have to (or want to) stay longer, you'll avoid the hassle of getting your papers extended. Whatever you do, don't overstay either permit. Doing so invites heavy fines, confiscation of your vehicle (which will not be returned), or both. Also remember that 6 months does not necessarily equal 180 days—be sure that you return before the earlier expiration date.

By Car

Driving is not the cheapest way to get to Mexico, and it is definitely not the easiest way to get to the Yucatán peninsula. While driving is a convenient way to see the country, you may think twice about taking your own car south of the U.S. border, once you've pondered the bureaucracy involved and security concerns, especially along the border. One option is to rent a car once you arrive and tour around a specific region. The Yucatán peninsula is a great place to do this. Rental cars in Mexico are generally clean and well maintained, although they are often smaller than rentals in the U.S. They may have manual rather than automatic transmission, and are comparatively expensive when taxes and insurance are added. Discounts are often available for rentals of a week or longer, especially when you make arrangements in advance online or from the United States. Be careful about estimated online rates, which often fail to include tax and mandatory insurance costs. (See "Car Rentals," below, for more details.)

If, after reading the section that follows, you have additional questions or you want to confirm the current rules, call your nearest Mexican consulate or the Mexican Government Tourist Office. Although travel insurance companies generally are helpful, they may not have the most accurate information. To check on road conditions or to get help with any travel emergency while in Mexico, call ✆ **55/5089-7500** in Mexico City, which is staffed by English-speaking operators.

In addition, check with the **U.S. Department of State** (www.state.gov) for warnings about dangerous driving areas.

CAR DOCUMENTS

To drive your car into Mexico beyond 25km (16 miles), you'll need a **temporary car-importation permit,** which is granted after you provide a required list of documents (see below). The permit can be obtained after you cross the border into Mexico through Banco del Ejército (Banjercito) officials with Mexican Customs (*Aduanas*), or at Mexican consulates in Austin, Denver, San Francisco, Phoenix, Albuquerque, Chicago, Houston, Dallas, Los Angeles, Sacramento, and San Bernardino. For more information, visit www.banjercito.com.mx or call ✆ **877/210-9469** in the U.S.

The following requirements for border crossing were accurate at press time:

- **Passport.**
- **A valid driver's license,** issued outside of Mexico.

PLANNING YOUR TRIP

Getting There

9

- **Current, original car registration and a copy of the original car title.** If the registration or title is in more than one name and not all the named people are traveling with you, a notarized letter from the absent person(s) authorizing use of the vehicle for the trip is required; have it ready. The registration and your credit card (see below) must be in the same name. If the car is leased or rented, be sure to have a copy of the contract.

- **Original immigration documentation.** Likely your tourist card (see "Visas," p. 367).

- **Processing fee and deposit.** You have three options for covering the car-importation fee: Pay $29 at the border, pay $39 in advance at a Mexican Consulate, or pre-pay $49 online at www.banjercito.com.mx. If you apply online, it takes about 2 weeks before you can go into the Banjercito office in order to obtain your permit. You will generally need a credit card to make this payment. Mexican law also requires payment of a deposit at a Banjercito office to guarantee the export of the car from Mexico within a time period determined at the time of the application. For this purpose, American Express, Visa, or MasterCard credit card holders will be asked to provide credit card information; others will need to make a cash deposit of $200 to $400, depending on the make/model/year of the vehicle. In order to recover this bond or avoid credit card charges, travelers must go to any Mexican Customs office immediately before leaving Mexico.

If you receive your documentation at the border, Mexican officials will make two copies of everything and charge you for the copies. For up-to-the-minute information, a great source is the Customs office in Nuevo Laredo, or *Módulo de Importación Temporal de Automóviles, Aduana Nuevo Laredo* (✆ **867/712-2071**).

Important reminder: Someone else may drive, but the person (or relative of the person) whose name appears on the car-importation permit must *always* be in the car. (If stopped by police, a nonregistered family member driving without the registered driver must be prepared to prove familial relationship to the registered driver—no joke.) Violation of this rule subjects the car to impoundment and the driver to imprisonment, a fine, or both. You can drive a car with foreign license plates only if you have a foreign (non-Mexican) driver's license.

MEXICAN AUTO INSURANCE (SEGUROS DE AUTO)

Liability auto insurance is legally required in Mexico. U.S. insurance is invalid; to be insured in Mexico, you must purchase Mexican insurance. Any party involved in an accident who has no insurance may be sent to jail and have his or her car impounded until all claims are settled. U.S. companies that broker Mexican insurance are commonly found at the border crossing, and several quote daily rates.

You can also buy car insurance through **Sanborn's Mexico Insurance** (www.sanbornsinsurance.com; ✆ **800/222-0158**) in daily, semi-annual, or yearly time periods. The company has offices at all U.S. border crossings. Its policies cost the same as the competition's do, but you get legal assistance (attorney and bail bonds if needed), roadside assistance, and, for a premium, vandalism protection. You also get a detailed guide for your proposed route. Most of the Sanborn's border offices are open Monday through Friday; a few are staffed on Saturday and Sunday. **AAA** auto club (www.aaa.com) also sells insurance.

RETURNING TO THE U.S. WITH YOUR CAR

You *must* return the car documents you obtained when you entered Mexico when you cross back with your car, or within 180 days of your return. (You can cross as many times as you wish within the 180 days.) If the documents aren't returned, fines are imposed, your car may be impounded and confiscated, or you may be jailed if you return to Mexico. You can only return the car documents to a Banjercito official on duty at the Mexican *aduana* building *before* you cross back into the United States. Some border cities have Banjercito officials on duty 24 hours a day, but others do not; some do not have Sunday hours. See www.mexbound.com/mexican-vehicle-permits.php for a listing of office hours.

By Ship

Numerous cruise lines serve Mexico. Some (such as Carnival and Royal Caribbean) cruise from Houston or Miami to the Caribbean (which often includes stops in Cancún, Playa del Carmen, and Cozumel). Several cruise-tour specialists sometimes offer last-minute discounts on unsold cabins. One such company is **CruisesOnly** (www.cruisesonly.com; ✆ **800/278-4737**).

By Bus

Greyhound (www.greyhound.com; ✆ **800/231-2222**), or its affiliates, offers service from around the United States to the Mexican border, where passengers disembark, cross the border, and buy a ticket for travel into Mexico. Many border crossings have scheduled buses from the U.S. bus station to the Mexican bus station.

More than likely, if you travel to the Yucatán by bus from the northern border you will pass through Mexico City, the country's capital and main transportation hub. Expect a trip from the border to last several grueling days of all-day (and/or all-night) travel on roads of varying quality.

We've listed bus arrival information in each applicable section of this book.

Point-to-Point Driving Directions Online

You can get point-to-point driving directions in English for anywhere in Mexico from the website of the Secretary of Communication and Transport. The site will also calculate tolls, distance, and travel time. Go to http://aplicaciones4.sct.gob.mx/sibuac_internet, and click on "Rutas punto a punto" in the left-hand column. Then select the English version.

GETTING AROUND
By Plane

Until recently, Mexico had two large private national carriers, but Mexicana closed operations and filed for bankruptcy in 2010. Now, only **Aeroméxico** remains (www.aeromexico.com; ✆ **800/237-6399** in the U.S., or 01-800/021-4000 in Mexico), in addition to several low-cost carriers. Aeroméxico offers extensive connections to the United States as well as within Mexico.

Low-cost carriers include **Interjet** (www.interjet.com.mx) and **Volaris** (www.volaris.com.mx). In each applicable section of this book, we've mentioned regional carriers with all pertinent telephone numbers.

Because major airlines may book some regional carriers, check your ticket to see if your connecting flight is on a smaller carrier—they may use a different airport or a different counter.

Mexico charges an **airport tax** on all departures. It has become a common practice to include this departure tax in your ticket price.

By Car

Many Mexican roads are not up to U.S., Canadian, and European standards of smoothness, hardness, width of curve, grade of hill, or safety markings. Driving at night is dangerous—the roads are rarely lit; carts and bicycles often have no lights; and you can hit potholes, animals, rocks, dead ends, or uncrossable bridges without warning.

The spirited style of Mexican driving sometimes requires keen vision and reflexes. Be prepared for new customs, as when a truck driver flips on his left turn signal when there's not a crossroad for many kilometers. He's probably telling you the road's clear ahead for you to pass.

GASOLINE   There's one government-owned brand of gas and one gasoline station name throughout the country—**Pemex** (Petroleras Mexicanas). There are two types of gas in Mexico: *magna,* 87-octane unleaded gas, and *premio,* 93 octane. In Mexico, fuel and oil are sold by the liter, which is slightly more than a quart (1 gal. equals about 3.8L). Many franchise Pemex stations have bathroom facilities and convenience stores—a great improvement over the old ones. Gas stations accept both credit and debit cards for gas purchases, and a small tip—5 to 10 pesos—is appreciated for the standard full service.

TOLL ROADS   Mexico charges relatively high tolls for its network of new toll roads, so they are less used. Generally, though, using toll roads cuts travel time. Older toll-free roads are generally in good condition, but travel times tend to be longer as these roads pass directly through small towns and villages.

BREAKDOWNS   If your car breaks down on the road, help might already be on the way. Radio-equipped green repair trucks, run by uniformed English-speaking officers, patrol major highways during daylight hours (usually 8am–6pm). These **Angeles Verdes/Green Angels** perform minor repairs and adjustments for free, but you pay for parts and materials. To contact them in Mexico, dial ✆ **078.** For more information, see www.sectur.gob.mx.

Your best guide to repair shops is the Yellow Pages. For repairs, look under *Automóviles y Camiones: Talleres de Reparación y Servicio;* auto-parts stores are under *Refacciones y Accesorios para Automóviles.* To find a mechanic on the road, look for the sign TALLER MECÁNICO. Places called *vulcanizadora* or *llantera* repair flat tires, and it is common to find them open 24 hours a day on the most traveled highways.

MINOR ACCIDENTS   When possible, many Mexicans drive away from minor accidents, or try to make an immediate settlement, to avoid involving the police. If the police arrive while the involved persons are still at the scene, the cars will probably be confiscated and both parties will likely have to appear in court. Both parties may also be taken into custody until liability is determined. Foreigners who don't speak fluent Spanish are at a distinct disadvantage when trying to explain their version of the event. Three steps may help the foreigner who doesn't wish to do as the Mexicans do: If you were in your own car, notify your Mexican insurance company, whose job it is to intervene on your behalf. If you were in a rental car, notify the rental company immediately and ask how to contact the nearest adjuster. (You did buy insurance with the rental, right?) Finally, if all else fails, ask to contact the nearest Green Angel, who may be able to explain to officials that you are covered by insurance. See also "Mexican Auto Insurance," in "Getting There," earlier in this chapter.

CAR RENTALS   You'll get the best price if you reserve a car on the Internet. Cars are easy to rent if you are 25 or older and have a major credit card, valid driver's license, and passport with you. Without a credit card, you must leave a cash deposit, usually a big one. One-way rentals are usually simple to arrange, but they are more costly.

Car-rental costs are high in Mexico because cars are more expensive. The condition of rental cars has improved greatly over the years, and newer cars are increasingly common. You will pay the least for a manual car without air-conditioning or a radio. Prices may be considerably higher if you rent around a major holiday. Also double-check charges for insurance—some companies will increase the insurance rate after several days. Always ask for detailed information about all charges you will be responsible for. Also make sure the vehicle is in good shape and has been properly serviced before driving away.

Car-rental companies often charge on a credit card.

DEDUCTIBLES   Be careful—these vary greatly; some are as high as $2,500, which comes out of your pocket immediately in case of damage.

INSURANCE   Insurance is offered in two parts: **Collision and damage** insurance covers your car and others if the accident is your fault, and **personal accident** insurance covers you and anyone in your car. Note that insurance may be invalid if you have an accident while driving on an unpaved road. Although some international credit cards include as a benefit collision and damage coverage, they almost never include liability.

DAMAGE   Inspect your car carefully and note every damaged or missing item, no matter how minute, on your rental agreement, or you may be charged.

By Taxi

Taxis are the preferred way to get around almost all of Mexico's resort areas. Fares for short trips within towns are generally preset by zone, and are quite reasonable compared with U.S. and European rates. For longer trips or excursions to nearby cities, taxis can generally be hired for around $20 to $25 per hour, or for a negotiated daily rate. A negotiated one-way price is usually much less than the cost of a rental car for a day, and a taxi travels much faster than a bus. For anyone who is uncomfortable driving in Mexico, this is a convenient, comfortable alternative. A bonus is that you have a Spanish-speaking person with you in case you run into trouble. Many taxi drivers speak at least some English. For safety reasons, *sitio* (radio) taxis should be used rather then *libre* taxis off the street. Your hotel can assist you with the arrangements.

By Bus

Mexican buses run frequently, are readily accessible, and can transport you almost anywhere you want to go. Taking the bus is common in Mexico, and the executive and first-class coaches can be as comfortable as business class on an airplane. Buses are often the only way to get from large cities to other nearby cities and small villages. Don't hesitate to ask questions if you're confused about anything, but note that little English is spoken in bus stations.

Dozens of Mexican companies operate large, air-conditioned, Greyhound-type (or better) buses between most cities. Classes are *segunda* (second), *primera* (first), and *ejecutiva* (deluxe, which could also go by other names, such as luxury or "lujo"). Deluxe buses often have fewer seats than regular buses, show movies, are air-conditioned, and make few stops. Many run express from point to point. They are well worth the few dollars more. In rural areas, buses are often of the school-bus variety, with lots of local color.

Whenever possible, it's best to buy your reserved-seat ticket, often using a computerized system, a day in advance on long-distance routes and especially before holidays.

For each relevant destination, we list bus arrival and contact information. The following website provides reservations and bookings for numerous providers throughout Mexico: http://boletotal.mx.

HEALTH

For the latest information on health risks when traveling to Mexico, and what to do if you get sick, consult the U.S. State Department's website at www.travel. state.gov, the CDC website at www.cdc.gov, or the website of the World Health Organization at www.who.int.

General Availability of Health Care

In most of Mexico's resort destinations, you can usually find health care that meets U.S. standards. Care in more remote areas is limited. Standards of medical training, patient care, and business practices vary greatly among medical facilities in beach resorts throughout Mexico. Cancún has first-rate hospitals, for example, but other cities along the Caribbean coast often do not. In recent years, some U.S. citizens have complained that certain health-care facilities in beach resorts have taken advantage of them by overcharging or providing unnecessary medical care. On the other hand, Mexican doctors often spend more time with patients than doctors do north of the border, and may be just as good. Only rudimentary health care is generally available in much of Chiapas, Tabasco, and the Yucatán.

Prescription medicine is broadly available at Mexico pharmacies, and many drugs that in the U.S. require a prescription can be obtained in Mexico simply by asking. However, be aware that you may still need a copy of your prescription or to obtain a prescription from a local doctor.

Common Ailments

SUN/ELEMENTS/EXTREME WEATHER EXPOSURE   Mexico is synonymous with sunshine; much of the country is bathed in intense sunshine for much of the year. Avoid excessive exposure, especially in the tropics where UV rays are more dangerous. The hottest months in Mexico's south are April and May, but the sun is intense most of the year.

DIETARY RED FLAGS   Travelers' diarrhea, often accompanied by fever, nausea, and vomiting, used to attack many travelers to Mexico. (Some in the U.S. call this "Montezuma's revenge," but you won't hear it called that in

Mexico.) Widespread improvements in infrastructure, sanitation, and education have greatly diminished this ailment, especially in well-developed resort areas. Most travelers make a habit of drinking only bottled water, which also helps to protect against unfamiliar bacteria. In resort areas, and generally throughout Mexico, only purified ice is used. If you do come down with this ailment, nothing beats Pepto Bismol, readily available in Mexico. Imodium is also available in Mexico and is used by many travelers for a quick fix. A good high-potency (or "therapeutic") vitamin supplement and even extra vitamin C can help; yogurt is good for healthy digestion.

Since dehydration can quickly become life-threatening, be careful to replace fluids and electrolytes (potassium, sodium, and the like) during a bout of diarrhea. Drink Pedialyte, a rehydration solution available at most Mexican pharmacies, or natural fruit juice, such as guava or apple (stay away from orange juice, which has laxative properties), with a pinch of salt added.

The U.S. Public Health Service recommends the following measures for preventing travelers' diarrhea: **Drink only purified water** (boiled water, canned, or bottled beverages). Choose food carefully. In general, avoid salads (except in first-class restaurants), uncooked vegetables, undercooked protein, and unpasteurized milk or milk products, including cheese. **Choose food that is freshly cooked and still hot.** Avoid eating food prepared by street vendors. In addition, something as simple as clean hands can go a long way toward preventing an upset stomach.

HIGH-ALTITUDE HAZARDS Travelers to certain regions of Mexico occasionally experience **elevation sickness,** which results from the relative lack of oxygen and the decrease in barometric pressure that characterizes high elevations (more than 1,500m/5,000 ft.). Symptoms include shortness of breath, fatigue, headache, insomnia, and even nausea. Mexico City is at 2,240m (7,349 ft.) above sea level, as are a number of other central and southern cities, such as San Cristóbal de las Casas. At high elevations, it takes about 10 days to acquire the extra red blood corpuscles you need to adjust to the scarcity of oxygen. To help your body acclimate, drink plenty of fluids, avoid alcohol, and don't over-exert yourself during the first few days. If you have heart or lung trouble, consult your doctor before flying above 2,400m (7,874 ft.).

BUGS, BITES & OTHER WILDLIFE CONCERNS **Mosquitoes** and **gnats** are prevalent along the coast and in the Yucatán lowlands. *Repelente contra insectos* (insect repellent) is a must, and you can buy it in most pharmacies. If you'll be in these areas and are prone to bites, bring along a repellent that contains the active ingredient DEET. Another good remedy to keep the mosquitoes away is to mix citronella essential oil with basil, clove, and lavender essential oils. If you're sensitive to bites, pick up some antihistamine cream from a drugstore at home.

Most readers won't ever see an *alacrán* (scorpion), but if one stings you, go immediately to a

Over-the-Counter Drugs in Mexico

Antibiotics and other drugs that you'd need a prescription to buy in the States are often available over the counter in Mexican pharmacies. Mexican pharmacies also carry a limited selection of common over-the-counter cold, sinus, and allergy remedies. Contact lenses can be purchased without an exam or prescription, should you run out.

doctor. The one lethal scorpion found in some parts of Mexico is the *Centruroides,* part of the *Buthidae* family, characterized by a thin body, thick tail, and triangular-shaped sternum. Most deaths from these scorpions result within 24 hours of the sting as a result of respiratory or cardiovascular failure, with children and elderly people most at risk. Scorpions are not aggressive (they don't hunt for prey), but they may sting if touched, especially in their hiding places (which can include shoes). In Mexico, you can buy scorpion-toxin antidote at any drugstore, a good idea if you plan to camp in a remote area where medical assistance can be several hours away. **Note:** Not all scorpion bites are lethal, but a doctor's visit is recommended regardless.

TROPICAL ILLNESSES   You shouldn't be overly concerned about tropical diseases if you stay on the normal tourist routes and don't eat street food. However, both dengue fever and cholera have appeared in Mexico in recent years. Talk to your doctor or to a medical specialist in tropical diseases about precautions you should take. You can protect yourself by taking some simple precautions: Watch what you eat and drink; don't swim in stagnant water (ponds, slow-moving rivers, or wells); and avoid mosquito bites by covering up, using repellent, and sleeping under netting. The most dangerous areas seem to be on Mexico's west coast, away from the big resorts.

On occasion, coastal waters from the Gulf of Mexico can become contaminated with rapid growth in algae (phytoplankton), leading to a phenomenon known as harmful algal bloom or a "red tide." The algal release of neurotoxins threatens marine life and can cause rashes and even flulike symptoms in exposed humans. Although red tides happen infrequently, you should not enter the water if you notice a reddish-brown color or are told there is a red tide.

TIPS ON ACCOMMODATIONS
Mexico's Hotel Rating System

The hotel rating system in Mexico is called "Stars and Diamonds." Hotels may qualify to earn one to five stars or diamonds. Many hotels that have excellent standards are not certified, but all rated hotels adhere to strict standards. The guidelines relate to service, facilities, and hygiene more than to prices.

Five-diamond hotels meet the highest requirements for rating: The beds are comfortable, bathrooms are in excellent working order, all facilities are renovated regularly, infrastructure is top-tier, and services and hygiene meet the highest international standards.

Five-star hotels usually offer similar quality, but with lower levels of service and detail in the rooms. For example, a five-star hotel may have less luxurious linens or, perhaps, room service during limited hours rather than 24 hours.

Four-star hotels are less expensive and more basic, but they still guarantee cleanliness and basic services such as hot water and purified drinking water.

Three-, two-, and one-star hotels are at least working to adhere to certain standards: Bathrooms are cleaned and linens are washed daily, and you can expect a minimum standard of service. Two- and one-star hotels generally provide bottled water rather than purified water.

Hotel Chains

In addition to the major international chains, you'll run across a number of less familiar brands as you plan your trip to Mexico. They include:

- **Las Brisas Hotel Collection** (www.brisashotelonline.com). These were the hotels that originally attracted jet-set travelers to Mexico. Spectacular in a retro way, these properties offer the laid-back luxury that makes a Mexican vacation so unique.

- **Fiesta Americana and Fiesta Inn** (www.posadas.com). Part of the Mexican-owned Grupo Posadas company, these hotels set the country's midrange standard for facilities and services. They generally offer comfortable, spacious rooms and traditional Mexican hospitality. Fiesta Americana hotels offer excellent beach-resort packages. Fiesta Inn hotels are usually more business-oriented. Grupo Posadas also owns the more luxurious Caesar Park hotels and the eco-oriented Explorean hotels.

- **Hoteles Camino Real** (www.caminoreal.com). Hoteles Camino Real remains Mexico's premier hotel chain with beach resorts, city hotels, and colonial inns scattered throughout the country. Its beach hotels are traditionally located on the best beaches in the area. This chain also focuses on the business market. The hotels are famous for their vivid and contrasting colors.

- **NH Hoteles** (www.nh-hotels.com). The NH hotels are noted for their family-friendly facilities and quality standards. The beach properties' signature feature is a pool, framed by columns, overlooking the sea.

- **Quinta Real Grand Class Hotels and Resorts** (www.quintareal.com). These hotels are noted for architectural and cultural details that reflect their individual regions. At these luxury properties, attention to detail and excellent service are the rule. Quinta Real is the top-line Mexican hotel brand.

House Rentals & Swaps

House and villa rentals and swaps are becoming more common in Mexico, but no single recognized agency or business provides this service exclusively for Mexico. In the preceding chapters, we have provided information on independent services that we have found to be reputable.

You'll find the most extensive inventory of homes at **Vacation Rentals by Owner** (**VRBO;** www.vrbo.com). They have thousands of homes and

---

 ## Boutique Lodgings

Mexico lends itself beautifully to the concept of small, private hotels in idyllic settings. They vary in style from grandiose estates to palm-thatched bungalows. **Mexico Boutique Hotels** (www.mexicoboutiquehotels.com; © **322/221-2277**) specializes in smaller places to stay with a high level of personal attention and service. Most options have less than 50 rooms, and the accommodations consist of entire villas, casitas, bungalows, or a combination. The Yucatán is especially noted for the luxury haciendas (p. 249) throughout the peninsula.

condominiums worldwide, including a large selection in Mexico. Another good option is **VacationSpot** (www.vacationspot.com), owned by Expedia and a part of its sister company Hotels.com. It has fewer choices, but the company's criteria for adding inventory are much more selective and often include on-site inspections. They also offer toll-free phone support.

[FastFACTS] CANCÚN & THE YUCATÁN

Area Codes   **998** is the area code in Cancún, Cozumel, and Isla Mujeres. **984** is the area code for Playa del Carmen. **981** is the area code for Campeche, and for Mérida, **999.** For Villahermosa, the area code is **993**, and for San Cristóbal de las Casas, **967.** The Tuxtla Gutiérrez area code is **961.**

Business Hours   Most businesses in larger cities are open between 9am and 7pm; in smaller towns they may close between 2 and 4pm. Many close on Sunday. In resort areas, stores commonly open in the mornings on Sunday, and shops stay open late, until 8 or even 10pm. Bank hours are Monday through Friday from 9 or 9:30am to anywhere between 3 and 7pm. Banks open on Saturday for at least a half-day.

Car Rental   See "By Car" under the "Getting Around" section earlier in this chapter.

Cellphones   See "Mobile Phones," later in this section.

Crime   See "Safety," later in this section.

Customs   Mexican Customs inspection has been streamlined. At most points of entry, tourists are requested to press a button in front of what looks like a traffic signal, which alternates on touch between red and green. Green light and you go through without inspection; red light and your luggage or car may be inspected. If you have an unusual amount of luggage or an oversized piece, you may be subject to inspection anyway. Passengers that arrive by air will be required to put their bags through an X-ray machine, and then move to the kiosk and push a button to determine whether their luggage will be selected for any further inspection.

When you enter Mexico, Customs officials will be tolerant if you are not carrying illegal drugs or firearms. Tourists are allowed to bring in their personal effects duty-free. A laptop computer, camera equipment, and sports equipment that could feasibly be used during your stay are also allowed. The underlying guideline is: Don't bring anything that looks as if it's meant to be resold in Mexico. Those entering Mexico by air or sea can bring in gifts worth a value of up to $300 duty-free, except alcohol or tobacco products. The website for Mexican Customs (*Aduanas*) is **www.aduanas.sat.gob.mx**.

Disabled Travelers   Mexico presents a challenging course to travelers in wheelchairs or on crutches. At airports, you may encounter steep stairs before finding a well-hidden elevator or escalator—if one exists. Airlines will often arrange wheelchair assistance to the baggage area. Porters are generally available to help with luggage at airports and large bus stations, once you've cleared baggage claim.

Mexican airports are upgrading their services, but it is still possible to occasionally board from a remote position, meaning you either descend stairs to a bus that ferries you to the plane, which you board by climbing stairs, or you walk across the tarmac to your plane and ascend the stairs. Deplaning presents the same problem in reverse.

Escalators (and there aren't many in the country) are often out of order. Stairs without handrails abound. Few restrooms are equipped for travelers with disabilities; when one is available, access to it may be through a narrow passage that won't accommodate a wheelchair or a person on crutches. Many deluxe hotels (the most expensive) now have rooms with bathrooms designed for people with disabilities. Those traveling on a budget should stick with one-story hotels or hotels with elevators. Even so, there will probably still be obstacles somewhere. Generally speaking, no matter where you are, someone will lend a hand, although you may have to ask for it.

For a bit of underwater sightseeing, **Yucatek Divers** (www.yucatek-divers.com; ✆ **984/ 803-2836**), in Playa del Carmen, specializes in dives for people with disabilities.

Doctors   Any embassy or consulate staff in Mexico from an English-speaking country can provide a list of area doctors who speak English. If you get sick in Mexico, consider asking your hotel concierge to recommend a local doctor—even his or her own. Some hotels even have in-house medical personnel. You can also try the emergency room at a local hospital or urgent care facility. Mexican doctors may not always have access to the latest technologies, and the quality of medical facilities varies, but they usually spend considerable time with patients and charge much less than their North American counterparts. Before choosing a doctor, you can ask for their qualifications and where they were trained.

Also see "Hospitals" later in this section.

Drinking Laws   The legal drinking age in Mexico is 18; however, asking for ID or denying purchase is extremely rare. Grocery stores sell everything from beer and wine to national and imported liquors. You can buy liquor 24 hours a day, but during major elections, dry laws often are enacted by as much as 72 hours in advance of the election—and they apply to tourists as well as local residents. Mexico does not have laws that apply to transporting liquor in cars, but authorities are beginning to target drunk drivers more aggressively. It's a good idea to drive defensively.

It's illegal to drink in the street, but many tourists do. If you are getting drunk, you shouldn't drink in the street, because you are more likely to get stopped by the police.

Driving Rules See "By Car" under the "Getting Around" section earlier in this chapter.

Electricity The electrical system in Mexico is 110 volts AC (60 cycles), as in the United States and Canada. In reality, however, it may cycle more slowly and overheat your appliances. To compensate, select a medium or low speed on hair dryers. Many older hotels still have electrical outlets for flat two-prong plugs; you'll need an adapter for any plug with an enlarged end on one prong or with three prongs. Adapters are available in most Mexican electronics stores. Many better hotels have three-hole outlets (*trifásicos* in Spanish). Those that don't may loan adapters, but to be sure, it's always better to carry your own.

Embassies & Consulates Typical citizen services provided by country missions include passports, notaries, lists of doctors and lawyers, regulations concerning marriages in Mexico, emergency preparedness information, and other valuable assistance. Contrary to popular belief, your embassy cannot get you out of jail, provide postal or banking services, or fly you home when you run out of money. Consular officers can provide advice on most matters and problems, however. Most countries have an embassy in Mexico City, and many have consular offices or representatives in the provinces.

It is a good idea to register with your embassy or consulate when visiting Mexico. The Smart Traveler Enrollment Program (STEP) is a free service provided by the U.S. government to U.S. citizens who are traveling to, or living in, a foreign country. STEP allows them to enter information about their upcoming trip abroad so that the Department of State can better assist them in an emergency, and also allows Americans residing abroad to obtain routine information from the nearest U.S. embassy or consulate. Visit https://travel registration.state.gov.

The Embassy of **Australia** in Mexico City is at Rubén Darío 55, Col. Polanco (www.mexico. embassy.gov.au; ✆ **55/1101-2200**). It's open Monday through Friday from 8:30am to 5pm.

The Embassy of **Canada** in Mexico City is at Schiller 529, in Polanco (✆ **55/5724-7900** or for emergencies 01-800/706-2900); it's open Monday through Friday from 8:45am to 5:15pm. Visit www.dfait-maeci.gc.ca or www.canada.org.mx for addresses of consular agencies in Mexico. Canadian consulates are in Cancún (✆ **998/883-3360**) and Playa del Carmen (✆ **984/803-2411**).

The Embassy of **Ireland** in Mexico City is at Cda. Bl. Manuel Avila Camacho 76, 3rd Floor, Col. Lomas de Chapultepec (✆ **55/5520-5803**). See www.irishembassy.com.mx. It's open Monday through Thursday from 8:30am to 5pm, and Friday from 8:30am to 1:30pm.

The Embassy of **New Zealand** in Mexico City is at Jaime Balmes 8, 4th Floor, Col. Los Morales, Polanco (www.nzembassy.com/mexico; ✆ **55/5283-9460**). It's open Monday through Thursday from 9:30am to 2pm and 3 to 5pm, and Friday from 8:30am to 2pm.

The Embassy of the **United Kingdom** in Mexico City is at Río Lerma 71, Col. Cuauhtémoc (www.ukinmexico.fco.gov.uk/en; ✆ **55/1670-3200**). It's open Monday through Thursday from 8am to 4pm and Friday from 8am to 1:30pm.

The Embassy of the **United States** in Mexico City is at Paseo de la Reforma 305, next to the Hotel María Isabel Sheraton at the corner of Río Danubio (✆ **55/5080-2000**); hours are Monday through Friday from 8:30am to 5pm. Visit http://mexico.usembassy.gov for information related to U.S. Embassy services. A U.S. consulate is at Calle 60 no. 338-K 29 y 31, Col. Acala Martin, Mérida (✆ 999/942-5700). In addition, there are consular agencies at Blvd. Kukulkan Km 13 (in the Torre La Europa, Despacho 301) in Cancún (✆ 998/883-0272), at Plaza Villa Mar in the Plaza Principal of Cozumel (✆ 987/872-4574), and in Playa del Carmen (✆ 984/873-0303) at "The Palapa," Calle 1 Sur between Av. 15 and Av. 20.

Emergencies In case of emergency, dial 📞 **066** from any phone within Mexico. Dial 📞 **065** for the Red Cross or 📞 **068** for the fire department. For police emergency numbers, turn to the "Fast Facts" sections in each of the individual chapters. The 24-hour Tourist Help Line in Mexico City is 📞 **01-800/006-8839** or 55/5089-7500, or you can now simply dial 📞 **078.** The operators don't always speak English, but they are always willing to help.

Family Travel Children are considered the national treasure of Mexico, and Mexicans will warmly welcome and cater to your children. Many parents were reluctant to bring young children into Mexico in the past, primarily due to health concerns, but I can't think of a better place to introduce children to the exciting adventure of exploring a different culture. One of the best destinations for kids is Cancún. Hotels can often arrange for a babysitter.

Before leaving, ask your doctor which medications to take along. Disposable diapers cost about the same in Mexico but are of poorer quality. You can get Huggies Supreme and Pampers identical to the ones sold in the United States, but at a higher price. Many stores sell Gerber's baby foods. Dry cereals, powdered formulas, baby bottles, and purified water are easily available in midsize and large cities or resorts.

Cribs may present a problem; only the largest and most luxurious hotels provide them. However, rollaway beds are often available. Child seats or high chairs at restaurants are common.

Consider bringing your own car seat; they are not readily available for rent in Mexico.

To locate accommodations, restaurants, and attractions that are particularly kid-friendly, refer to the "Kids" icon throughout this guide.

Gasoline Please see "By Car" under the "Getting Around" section earlier in this chapter.

Hospitals Many hospitals also have walk-in clinics for emergency cases that are not life-threatening; you may not get immediate attention, but you won't pay emergency room prices. The quality varies, but is often quite high, especially in resort towns.

We list "Emergencies" and "Embassies" above.

Insurance For travel to Mexico, you may have to pay all medical costs upfront and be reimbursed later. Before leaving home, find out what medical services your health insurance covers. To protect yourself, consider buying medical travel insurance.

For information on traveler's insurance, trip cancelation insurance, and medical insurance while traveling, please visit www.frommers.com/planning.

Internet & Wi-Fi Wi-Fi is increasingly common in Mexico's major cities and resorts. Mexico's largest airports offer Wi-Fi access provided for a fee by Telcel's Prodigy Internet service. Most five-star hotels now offer Wi-Fi in the guest rooms for free or for a fee. Hotel lobbies often have Wi-Fi as well. To find public Wi-Fi hotspots in Mexico, go to **www.jiwire. com**; its Hotspot Finder holds the world's largest directory of public wireless hotspots.

Many large Mexican airports have Internet kiosks, and quality Mexican hotels usually have business centers with Internet access. You can also check out such copy stores as **FedEx Office** or **OfficeMax,** which offer computer stations with fully loaded software (as well as Wi-Fi).

Language Spanish is the official language in Mexico. English is spoken and understood to some degree in most tourist areas. Mexicans are very accommodating with foreigners who try to speak Spanish, even in broken sentences. See chapter 10 for a glossary of simple phrases for expressing basic needs.

9

PLANNING YOUR TRIP | Language

Legal Aid   Embassies and consulates can often provide a list of respected lawyers in the area who speak English.

LGBT Travelers   Mexico is a conservative country, with deeply rooted Catholic religious traditions. Public displays of same-sex affection are rare and still considered surprising for men, especially outside of urban or resort areas. Women in Mexico frequently walk hand in hand, but anything more would cross the boundary of acceptability. However, gay and lesbian travelers are generally treated with respect and should not experience harassment, assuming they give the appropriate regard to local customs.

Things are changing here. On December 21, 2009, Mexico City became the first Latin American jurisdiction to legalize same-sex marriage, and 14th overall after the Netherlands, Belgium, Spain, Canada, South Africa, Norway, Sweden, and six U.S. jurisdictions.

While much of Mexico is socially conservative, Cancún and Playa del Carmen are not. Popular with many gay travelers, both coastal resorts offer gay-friendly accommodations, bars, and activities. For more information, visit MexGay Vacations at www.mexgay.com. Information about gay-friendly accommodations is available at www.gayplaces2stay.com.

Mail   Postage for a postcard or letter varies depending on its destination; it may take from a few weeks to more than a month to arrive. The price for registered letters and packages depends on the weight. The recommended way to send a package or important mail is through FedEx, DHL, UPS, or another reputable international mail service.

Medical Requirements   Also see "Health," p. 352.

Mobile Phones   **Telcel** is Mexico's expensive, primary cellphone provider. It has upgraded its systems to GSM and offers good coverage in much of the country, including the major cities and resorts. Most Mexicans buy their cellphones without a specific coverage plan and then pay as they go or purchase prepaid cards with set amounts of air-time credit. These cellphone cards with scratch-off PIN numbers can be purchased in Telcel stores as well as many newspaper stands and convenience stores.

Many North American and European cellphone companies offer networks with roaming coverage in Mexico. Rates can be very high, so check with your provider before committing to making calls this way. An increasing number of Mexicans, particularly among the younger generation, prefer the less expensive rates of **Nextel** (www.nextel.com.mx), which features a range of service options. **Cellular Abroad** (www.cellularabroad.com) offers cellphone rentals and purchases as well as SIM cards for travel abroad. Whether you rent or purchase the cellphone, you need to purchase a SIM card that is specific for Mexico.

Money & Costs   Frommer's lists exact prices in the local currency (unless rates are given in U.S. dollars). The currency conversions quoted below were correct at press time. However, rates fluctuate, so before departing consult a currency exchange website such as www.oanda.com/convert/classic to check up-to-the-minute rates.

In general, the southern region of Mexico is considerably cheaper not just than most U.S. and European destinations, but also than many other parts of Mexico, although prices vary significantly depending on the specific location. The most expensive destinations are those with the largest number of foreign visitors, such as Cancún and Playa del Carmen. The least expensive are those off the beaten path and in small rural villages, particularly in the poorer states of Tabasco and Chiapas. In the major cities, prices vary greatly depending on the neighborhood. As you might imagine, tourist zones tend to be more expensive.

The currency in Mexico is the peso. Paper currency comes in denominations of 20, 50, 100, 200, and 500 pesos. Coins come in denominations of 1, 2, 5, 10, and 20 pesos, and 20 and

Pesos	US$	Can$	UK£	Euro (€)	Aus$	NZ$
100	US$7.90	C$7.82	£4.98	€5.99	A$7.45	NZ$9.56

50 **centavos** (100 centavos = 1 peso). The current exchange rate for the U.S. dollar is 13 pesos; at that rate, an item that costs 13 pesos would be equivalent to $1.

Many establishments that deal with tourists, especially in coastal resort areas, quote prices in U.S. dollars. To avoid confusion, they use the abbreviations "Dlls." for dollars and "M.N." (*moneda nacional*, or national currency) or "M.X.P." for Mexican Pesos. **Note:** Establishments that quote their prices primarily in U.S. dollars are listed in this guide with U.S. dollars. However, due to new regulations, acceptance of U.S. dollars in cash is now restricted across Mexico. Payments with credit cards and debit cards remain unaffected.

Getting change is a problem. Small-denomination bills and coins are hard to come by, so start collecting them early in your trip. Shopkeepers and taxi drivers everywhere always seem to be out of change and small bills; that's doubly true in markets. There seems to be an expectation that the customer should provide appropriate change, rather than the other way around.

Don't forget to have enough pesos to carry you over a weekend or Mexican holiday, when banks are closed.

Casas de cambio (exchange houses) are generally more convenient than banks for money exchange because they have more locations and longer hours; the rate of exchange may be the same as at a bank or slightly lower. Before leaving a bank or exchange-house window, count your change in front of the teller before the next client steps up. Also, most major hotels will change money for you.

Large airports have currency-exchange counters that often stay open whenever flights are operating. Though convenient, they generally do not offer the most favorable rates.

Currency Symbols

The **universal currency sign ($)** is sometimes used to indicate pesos in Mexico. The use of this symbol in this book, however, denotes U.S. currency.

The bottom line on exchanging money: Ask first, and shop around. Banks generally pay the top rates.

Banks in Mexico have expanded and improved services. Except in the smallest towns, they tend to be open weekdays from 9am until 5pm, and often for at least a half-day on Saturday. In larger resorts and cities, they can generally accommodate the exchange of dollars (which used to stop at noon) anytime during business hours. Some, but not all, banks charge a 1% fee to exchange traveler's checks. But you can pay for most purchases directly with traveler's checks at the establishment's stated exchange rate. Don't even bother with personal checks drawn on a U.S. bank—the bank will wait for your check to clear, which can take weeks, before giving you your money.

Travelers to Mexico can easily withdraw money from ATMs called *cajeras* in most major cities and resort areas. The U.S. Department of State recommends caution when you're using ATMs in Mexico, stating that they should only be used during business hours and in large protected facilities, but this pertains primarily to Mexico City, where crime remains a

Shuttle from airport to Cancún Hotel Zone	US$15.00
Cancún beachfront double room, moderate	US$120.00
Akumal double room, moderate	US$100.00–$150.00
Tulum beachfront double room, moderate	US$150.00–$250.00
Cancún 3-course dinner for one without wine, moderate	400.00–500.00
Tacos in San Cristóbal de las Casas	30.00
Admission to most archaeological sites	30.00–60.00
Night out in Cancún	US$50.00

significant problem. In most resorts in Mexico, the use of ATMs is perfectly safe—just use the same precautions you would at any ATM. However, beware of using ATMs in dubious locations as there have been reports of people having their card numbers "skimmed" (where information is copied and monies stolen or cards fraudulently charged). The ATM exchange rate is generally more favorable than at *casas de cambio*. Most machines offer Spanish/English menus and dispense pesos, but some offer the option of withdrawing dollars.

In Mexico, Visa, MasterCard, and American Express are the most accepted cards. You'll be able to charge most hotel, restaurant, and store purchases, as well as almost all airline tickets, on your credit card. Most Pemex gas stations now accept credit card purchases for gasoline, though this option may not be available everywhere and often not at night—check before you pump. Generally you receive the favorable bank rate when paying by credit card. However, be aware that some establishments in Mexico add a 5% to 7% surcharge when you pay with a credit card. This is especially true when using American Express. Many times, advertised discounts will not apply if you pay with a credit card.

 A Few Words About Prices

Many hotels in Mexico—except places that receive little foreign tourism—quote prices in U.S. dollars or in both dollars and pesos. Thus, currency fluctuations are unlikely to affect the prices most hotels charge.

Beware of hidden credit card fees while traveling. Check with your credit or debit card issuer to see what fees, if any, will be charged for overseas transactions. Legislation in the U.S. has curbed some exploitative lending practices, but many banks have responded by increasing fees in other areas, including fees for customers who use credit and debit cards while out of the country—even if those charges were made in U.S. dollars. Fees can amount to 3% or more of the purchase price. Check with your bank before departing to avoid any surprise charges on your statement.

For help with currency conversions, tip calculations, and more, download Frommer's convenient Travel Tools app for your mobile device. Go to www.frommers.com/go/mobile, and click on the Travel Tools icon.

Newspapers & Magazines   The *News* (www.thenews.com.mx) is an English-language daily with Mexico-specific news, published in Mexico City. Newspaper kiosks in larger cities also carry a selection of English-language magazines.

Packing   In general, Mexico is an easy destination to pack for, as weather is consistent and predictable, and the style is casual and accepting. However, some fine dining restaurants at resorts require pants, collared shirts, and dress shoes for men. Be sure to ask about dress codes when booking. Check forecasts before you go and always bring something for cool nights. For more helpful information on packing for your trip, download our convenient Travel Tools app for your mobile device. Go to www.frommers.com/go/mobile, and click on the Travel Tools icon.

Passports   See www.frommers.com/planning for information on how to obtain a passport.

Citizens from most countries are required to present a valid passport for entry to Mexico. Citizens from some countries will need a Mexican visa. As of March 1, 2010, all U.S. citizens, including children, have been required to present a valid passport or passport card for travel beyond the "border zone" into Mexico, with the "border zone" defined as an area within 20 to 30km (12–19 miles) of the United States.

All U.S. and Canadian citizens traveling by air or sea to Mexico are required to present a valid passport or other valid travel document to enter or reenter the United States except if returning from a closed-loop cruise. In addition, all travelers, including U.S. and Canadian citizens, attempting to enter the United States by land or sea must have a valid passport or other Western Hemisphere Travel Initiative (WHTI) compliant document.

Other valid travel documents (known as WHTI-compliant documents) include the new Passport Card and SENTRI, NEXUS, FAST, and the U.S. Coast Guard Mariner Document. Members of the U.S. Armed Forces on active duty traveling on orders are exempt from the passport requirement. U.S. citizens may apply for the limited-use, wallet-size Passport Card, available for a cost of $55. The card is valid only for land and sea travel between the U.S. and Canada, Mexico, the Caribbean region, and Bermuda. Beginning March 1, 2010, the Mexican Immigration authorities began to accept the passport card for travel into Mexico by air. However, the card is not valid to board international flights in the U.S. or to return to the U.S. from abroad by air. This card is only available to U.S. citizens. For more details on application restrictions, see www.getyouhome.gov. There is also the new "Global Entry" program for frequent travelers, available at www.globalentry.gov.

From our perspective, it's easiest just to travel with a valid passport. Safeguard your passport in an inconspicuous, inaccessible place, like a money belt, and keep a copy of the critical pages with your passport number in a separate place. If you lose your passport, visit the nearest consulate of your native country as soon as possible for a replacement.

Passport Offices:

○ **Australia**   Australian Passport Office (www.passports.gov.au; ✆ 131-232).

○ **Canada**   Passport Office, Department of Foreign Affairs and International Trade, Ottawa, ON K1A 0G3 (www.ppt.gc.ca; ✆ 800/567-6868).

○ **Ireland**   Passport Office, Frederick Buildings, Molesworth Street, Dublin 2 (www.foreign affairs.gov.ie; ✆ 01/671-1633).

○ **New Zealand**   Passports Office, Department of Internal Affairs, 47 Boulcott St., Wellington, 6011 (www.passports.govt.nz; ✆ 0800/225-050 in New Zealand or 04/463-9360).

○ **United Kingdom**   Visit your nearest passport office, major post office, or travel agency or contact the Identity and Passport Service (IPS; www.ips.gov.uk; ✆ 0300/222-0000).

○ **United States**   To find your regional passport office, check the U.S. State Department website (www.travel.state.gov/passport) or call the National Passport Information Center (✆ 877/487-2778) for automated information.

Petrol   Please see "By Car" under the "Getting Around" section earlier in this chapter.

Police   Several cities, including Cancún, have a special corps of English-speaking Tourist Police to assist with directions, guidance, and more. In case of emergency, dial ℂ **066** from any phone within Mexico. For police emergency numbers, turn to "Fast Facts" in the individual chapters.

Safety   Mexico is one of the world's great travel destinations, and millions of visitors travel safely here each year. Yet drug-related violence and widespread media coverage of Mexico's insecurity have severely impacted its tourism industry. Mexican drug-trafficking organizations have been engaged in brutal fights against each other for control of trafficking routes and with the Mexican government, which has deployed military personnel and federal police across the country. The region covered by this guide, Cancún and the Yucatán, has generally not experienced the violence or insecurity affecting many other parts of the country. The Mexican government is working hard to protect visitors to all major tourist destinations, which do not experience anything like the levels of violence and crime reported in the border region and along major drug trafficking routes, mainly in the north.

In most places, it's uncommon for foreign visitors to face anything worse than petty crime. The risk of pickpockets and petty theft rises considerably during the winter high tourist season. Always use common sense and exercise caution when in unfamiliar areas. Leave valuables and irreplaceable items in a safe place, or don't bring them at all. Use hotel safes when available. Avoid driving alone, especially at night. You can generally trust a person whom you approach for help or directions, but be wary of anyone who approaches you offering the same. The more insistent a person is, the more cautious you should be. Stay away from areas where drug dealing and prostitution occur. These tips should help make your trip even more enjoyable.

The U.S. and Mexico share a border more than 3,000km (nearly 2,000 miles) long and Americans comprise the vast majority of tourists to Mexico. Due to this close and historically intertwined relationship, we recommend that all travelers read the **U.S. Department of State travel advisories for Mexico** (www.state.gov; ℂ **888/407-4747** toll-free in the U.S. and Canada). The U.S. State Department encourages its citizens to use main roads during daylight hours, stay in well-known tourist destinations and tourist areas with better security, cooperate fully with Mexican military and other law enforcement checkpoints, and provide an itinerary to a friend or family member not traveling with them. Kidnapping continues to happen at an alarming rate. It can be useful to travel with a working cellphone, as well. This is good advice for all travelers to Mexico.

For emergency numbers, turn to p. 359.

Crime in Resort Towns: There have been a significant number of rapes reported in Cancún and other resort areas, usually at night or in the early morning involving alcohol and the nightclub scene. Visitors, particularly women, should travel in pairs or groups and not alone. Armed street crime is a serious problem in all the major cities. Some bars and nightclubs, especially in resort cities such as Cancún, can be havens for drug dealers and petty criminals.

The U.S. State Department offers specific safety and security information for travelers on spring break in Mexico: http://travel.state.gov/travel/cis_pa_tw/spring_break_mexico/spring_break_mexico_5014.html.

It is also advised that you should not hike alone in backcountry areas or walk alone on less frequented beaches, ruins, or trails.

Highway Safety: Travelers should exercise caution while traveling Mexican highways, avoiding travel at night, and using toll *(cuota)* roads rather than the less secure free *(libre)* roads whenever possible. Fully cooperate with all official checkpoints, the number of which has increased, when traveling on Mexican highways.

Bus travel should take place during daylight hours on first-class conveyances. Although bus hijackings and robberies have occurred on toll roads, buses on toll roads have a markedly lower rate of incidents than second-class and third-class buses that travel the less secure "free" highways.

Bribes & Scams: As is the case around the world, there are the occasional bribes and scams in Mexico, targeted at people believed to be naive, such as telltale tourists. For years, Mexico was known as a place where bribes—called *mordidas* (bites)—were expected; however, the country is rapidly changing. Frequently, offering a bribe today, especially to a police officer, is considered an insult, and it can land you in deeper trouble.

Many tourists have the impression that everything works better in Mexico if you "tip"; however, in reality, this only perpetuates the *mordida* tradition. If you are pleased with a service, feel free to tip. But you shouldn't tip simply to attempt to get away with something illegal or inappropriate—whether it is evading a ticket that's deserved or a car inspection as you're crossing the border.

Whatever you do, **avoid impoliteness;** you won't do yourself any favors if you insult a Mexican official. Extreme politeness, even in the face of adversity, rules Mexico. In Mexico, "gringos" have a reputation for being loud and demanding. By adopting the local custom of excessive courtesy, you'll have greater success in negotiations of any kind. Stand your ground, but do it politely.

As you travel in Mexico, you may encounter several types of **scams,** which are typical throughout the world. One involves some kind of a **distraction** or feigned commotion. While your **attention is diverted,** for example, a pickpocket makes a grab for your wallet. In another common scam, an unaccompanied child pretends to be lost and frightened and takes your hand for safety. Meanwhile the child or an accomplice plunders your pockets. A third involves **confusing currency.** A shoeshine boy, street musician, guide, or other individual might offer you a service for a price that seems reasonable—in pesos. When it comes time to pay, he or she tells you the price is in dollars, not pesos. Be very clear on the price and currency when services are involved. An ATM scam involves **ATMs** in questionable locations where card numbers are "skimmed" and information is copied, money stolen, or cards fraudulently charged.

Senior Travel   Mexico is a popular country for retirees. For decades, North Americans have been living indefinitely in Mexico by returning to the border and recrossing with a new tourist permit every 6 months. Mexican immigration officials have caught on, and now limit the maximum time in the country to 6 months within any year. This is to encourage even partial residents to acquire proper documentation.

Smoking   In early 2008, the Mexican president signed into law a nationwide smoking ban in workplaces and public buildings, and on public transportation. Under this groundbreaking law, private businesses are only permitted to allow public smoking in enclosed ventilated areas. Hotels may maintain up to 25% of guest rooms for smokers. Violators face stiff fines, and smokers refusing to comply could receive up to 36-hour jail sentences. The law places Mexico—where a significant percentage of the population smokes—at the forefront of efforts to curb smoking and improve public health in Latin America.

Student Travel   Because Mexicans consider higher education a luxury rather than a birthright, there is no formal network of student discounts and programs, and student discount cards are not commonly recognized.

The U.S. State Department offers information designated specifically for students traveling abroad: www.studentsabroad.state.gov.

More hostels have entered the student travel scene; **www.hostels.com/mexico** offers a list of hostels in Cancún, Mérida, Playa del Carmen, and San Cristóbal de las Casas.

Taxes   Mexico has a value-added tax of 16% (*Impuesto de Valor Agregado*, or IVA; pronounced "ee-bah") on most everything, including restaurant meals, bus tickets, and souvenirs. (Exceptions are Cancún, Cozumel, and Los Cabos, where the IVA is 11%; as ports of entry, they receive a break on taxes.) Hotels charge the usual 16% IVA, plus a locally administered bed tax of 3% (in most areas), for a total of 19%. In Cancún, Los Cabos, and Cozumel, hotels charge the 11% IVA plus 3% room tax, for a total of 14%. The prices quoted by hotels and restaurants do not necessarily include IVA. You may find that upper-end properties (three or more stars) often quote prices without IVA included, while lower-priced hotels include IVA. Ask to see a printed price sheet and ask if the tax is included.

Telephones   Mexico's telephone system is slowly but surely catching up with modern times. Most telephone numbers have 10 digits. Every city and town that has telephone access has a two-digit (Mexico City, Monterrey, and Guadalajara) or three-digit (everywhere else) area code. In Mexico City, Monterrey, and Guadalajara, local numbers have eight digits; elsewhere, local numbers have seven digits. To place a local call, you do not need to dial the area code. Many fax numbers are also regular phone numbers; ask whoever answers for the fax tone (*"me da tono de fax, por favor"*). The country code for Mexico is 52.

To call Mexico:

1. Dial the international access code: 011 from the U.S. and Canada; 00 from the U.K., Ireland, or New Zealand; or 0011 from Australia.

2. Dial the country code: 52.

3. Dial the two- or three-digit area code, then the eight- or seven-digit number. For example, if you wanted to call the U.S. consulate in Acapulco, the entire number would be 011-52-744-469-0556. If you wanted to dial the U.S. embassy in Mexico City, the entire number would be 011-52-55-5209-9100.

To make international calls: To make international calls from Mexico, dial 00, then the country code (U.S. or Canada 1, U.K. 44, Ireland 353, Australia 61, New Zealand 64). Next, dial the area code and number. For example, to call the British Embassy in Washington, you would dial 00-1-202-588-7800.

To call a Mexican cellular number: From the same area code, dial 044 and then the number. To dial the cellular phone from anywhere else in Mexico, first dial 01, and then the three-digit area code and the seven-digit number. To place an international call to a cellphone (e.g., from the U.S.), you now must add a 1 after the country code: for example, 011-52-1 + 10-digit number.

For directory assistance: Dial ✆ **040** if you're looking for a number inside Mexico. **Note:** Listings usually appear under the owner's name, not the name of the business, and your chances of finding an English-speaking operator are slim.

For operator assistance: If you need operator assistance in making a call, dial 𝄞 **090** to make an international call, and 𝄞 **020** to call a number in Mexico.

Toll-free numbers: Numbers beginning with 800 within Mexico are toll-free, but calling a U.S. toll-free number from Mexico costs the same as an overseas call. To call an 800 number in the U.S., dial 001-880 and the last seven digits of the toll-free number. To call an 888 number in the U.S., dial 001-881 and the last seven digits of the toll-free number. For a number with an 887 prefix, dial 882; for 866, dial 883.

Time   Central Time prevails throughout the Yucatán, Tabasco, and Chiapas. All of Mexico observes **daylight saving time.**

Tipping   Most service employees in Mexico count on tips for the majority of their income, and this is especially true for bellboys and waiters. Bellboys should receive the equivalent of 5 to 15 pesos per bag; waiters generally receive 10% to 15%, depending on the level of service. It is not customary to tip taxi drivers, unless they are hired by the hour or provide touring or other special services.

Toilets   Public toilets are not common in Mexico, but an increasing number are available, especially at fast-food restaurants and Pemex gas stations. These facilities and restaurant and club restrooms commonly have attendants, who expect a small tip (about 5 pesos).

VAT   See "Taxes" earlier in this section.

Visas   For detailed information regarding visas to Mexico, visit the **Mexican Embassy** at http://embamex.sre.gob.mx/usa.

American and Canadian tourists are not required to have a visa or a tourist card for stays of 72 hours or less within the border zone (20–30km/12–19 miles from the U.S. border). For travel to Mexico beyond the border zone, all travelers from Australia, Canada, New Zealand, the U.K., and the U.S., among others, can get their visas upon arrival. Many other countries require a preapproved visa, although as of May 1, 2010, non-U.S. citizens with valid U.S. visas may enter Mexico with the U.S. visa, and do not have to obtain a Mexican visa. For the latest requirements, please check **www.inm.gob.mx**. Once in Mexico, all travelers must be in possession of a tourist card, also called Tourist Migration Form. This document is provided by airlines or by immigration authorities at the country's points of entry. Be careful not to lose this card, as you will be required to surrender it upon departure and you will be fined if you lose it.

Your tourist card is stamped on arrival. If traveling by bus or car, ensure you obtain such a card at the immigration module located at the border and have it stamped by immigration authorities at the border. If you do not receive a stamped tourist card at the border, ensure that, when you arrive at your destination within Mexico, you immediately go to the closest National Institute of Immigration office, present your bus ticket, and request a tourist card. Travelers who fail to have their tourist card stamped may be fined, detained, or expelled from the country.

An immigration official will determine the number of days you can remain in Mexico. Do not assume that you will be granted the full 180 days. An extension of your stay can be requested for a fee at the National Institute of Immigration of the Ministry of the Interior or its local offices.

If you plan to enter Mexico by car, please read the vehicle's importation requirements (p. 348).

Note on travel of minors: Mexican law requires that any non-Mexican citizen under the age of 18 departing Mexico without both parents must carry notarized written permission from the parent or guardian who is not traveling with the child to or from Mexico. This permission must include the name of the parent, the name of the child, the name of anyone traveling with the child, and the notarized signature(s) of the absent parent(s). The U.S. Department of State recommends that permission include travel dates, destinations, airlines, and a summary of the circumstances surrounding the travel. The child must be carrying the original letter (not a facsimile or scanned copy), and proof of the parent/child relationship (usually a birth certificate or court document) and an original custody decree, if applicable. Travelers can also contact the Mexican Embassy or closest Mexican Consulate for more current information.

Visitor Information   The **Mexico Tourism Board** (www.visitmexico.com; ☏ 800/44-MEXICO [44-63942] in the U.S.; or ☏ 078 from within Mexico) is an excellent source for general information; you can request brochures and get answers to the most common questions from the exceptionally well-trained, knowledgeable staff.

The **Mexican Government Tourist Board**'s main office is in Mexico City (☏ 55/5278-4200). Satellite offices are in the U.S., Canada, and the U.K. In Canada: Toronto (☏ 416/925-2753). In the United Kingdom: London (☏ 020/7488-9392). In the United States: Chicago (☏ 312/228-0517), Houston (☏ 713/772-2581), Los Angeles (☏ 213/739-3663), Miami (☏ 786/621-2909), and New York (☏ 212/308-2110).

The **Chiapas Tourism Board** is at Bulevar Belisario Domínguez 950, 29060 Tuxtla Gutiérrez, Chi. (☏ **961/613-9396**). The **Quintana Roo Tourist Board** is at Carr. a. Calderitas 622, 77010 Chetumal, Q. Roo (☏ **983/835-0860**). The **Tabasco Tourism Board** is at Av. Juan Estrada Torre 101, 86190 Villahermosa, Tab. (☏ **993/310-9700**). The **Yucatán Tourism Board** is at Calle 59 no. 514, Centro, 97000 Mérida, Yuc. (☏ **999/924-9389**).

The **Mexican Embassy** in **Canada** is at 2055 Rue Peel, Bureau 1000, Montreal, QUE, H3A 1V4 (☏ **514/288-2502**); 11 King St. W, Ste. 350, Toronto, ON, M5H 4C7, 199 Bay St., Ste. 4440, Toronto, ON, M5L 1E9 (☏ **416/368-2875**); 411-117 W. Hastings St., 4th Floor, Vancouver, BC, V6E2K3 (☏ **604/684-1859**); and 1500-45 O'Connor St., Ottawa, ON, K1P 1A4 (☏ **613/233-8988;** fax 613/235-9123).

The **Mexican Embassy** (Consular Section) in the **United Kingdom** is at 16 Georges St., London, W1S1FD (☏ **020/7907-9442**).

The **Mexican Embassy** in the **United States** is at 1911 Pennsylvania Ave. NW, Washington, DC 20006 (☏ **202/736-1600**).

Water   Tap water in Mexico is generally not potable. It is safest to drink purified bottled water. Some hotels and restaurants purify their water, but you should ask rather than assume this is the case. Ice may also come from tap water and should be used with caution.

Wi-Fi   See "Internet & Wi-Fi," earlier in this section.

Women Travelers   Women do not frequently travel alone in Mexico, including driving alone on the highways. Walking on the street could net you a catcall, and walking alone at night is not advisable except in well-protected tourist areas. I've known people who have had uncomfortable experiences in crowded places such as subways. In general, however, Mexicans are extremely gracious, and will help a woman carry heavy items, open doors, and provide information, among other courtesies.

AIRLINE WEBSITES

MAJOR AIRLINES

Aeroméxico
www.aeromexico.com

Alaska Airlines/Horizon Air
www.alaskaair.com

American Airlines
www.aa.com

British Airways
www.british-airways.com

Delta Air Lines
www.delta.com

Iberia Airlines
www.iberia.com

United Airlines
www.united.com

US Airways
www.usairways.com

Virgin America
www.virginamerica.com

Virgin Atlantic Airways
www.virgin-atlantic.com

BUDGET AIRLINES

Frontier Airlines
www.frontierairlines.com

Interjet
www.interjet.com.mx

JetBlue Airways
www.jetblue.com

Volaris
www.volaris.com.mx

SPANISH & MAYAN TERMS & PHRASES

0 Most Mexicans are very patient with foreigners who try to speak their language; it helps a lot to know a few basic phrases. Included here are simple phrases for expressing basic needs, followed by some common menu items. We have also included a selection of Mayan words and phrases, since many Maya living on the Yucatán Peninsula today still speak their mother tongue.

ENGLISH-SPANISH PHRASES

English	Spanish	Pronunciation
Good day	Buen día	**Bwehn dee-ah**
Good morning	Buenos días	**Bweh-nohs dee-ahs**
How are you?	¿Cómo está?	**Koh-moh eh-stah**
Very well	Muy bien	**Mwee byehn**
Thank you	Gracias	**Grah-syahs**
You're welcome	De nada	**Deh nah-dah**
Goodbye	Adiós	**Ah-dyohs**
Please	Por favor	**Pohr fah-bohr**
Yes	Sí	**See**
No	No	**Noh**

English	Spanish	Pronunciation
Excuse me	Perdóneme	**Pehr-*doh*-neh-meh**
Give me	Déme	***Deh*-meh**
Where is . . . ?	¿Dónde está . . . ?	***Dohn*-deh eh-*stah***
the station	la estación	**lah eh-stah-*syohn***
a hotel	un hotel	**oon oh-*tehl***
a gas station	una gasolinera	**oo-nah gah-soh-lee-neh-rah**
a restaurant	un restaurante	**oon res-tow-*rahn*-teh**
the toilet	el baño	**el *bah*-nyoh**
a good doctor	un buen médico	**oon bwehn meh-dee-coh**
the road to . . .	el camino a/hacia	**el cah-*mee*-noh ah/ah-syah**
To the right	A la derecha	**Ah lah deh-*reh*-chah**
To the left	A la izquierda	**Ah lah ees-*kyehr*-dah**
Straight ahead	Derecho	**Deh-*reh*-choh**
I would like	Quisiera	**Key-*syeh*-rah**
I want . . .	Quiero . . .	***Kyeh*-roh**
to eat	comer	**koh-*mehr***
a room	una habitación	**oo-nah ah-bee-tah-*syohn***
Do you have . . . ?	¿Tiene usted . . . ?	**Tyeh-neh oo-*sted***
a book	un libro	**oon *lee*-broh**
a dictionary	un diccionario	**oon deek-syoh-nah-ryoh**
How much is it?	¿Cuánto cuesta?	***Kwahn*-toh *kweh*-stah**
When?	¿Cuándo?	***Kwahn*-doh**
What?	¿Qué?	**Keh**
There is (Is there . . . ?)	(¿)Hay (. . . ?)	**Eye**
What is there?	¿Qué hay?	**Keh eye**
Yesterday	Ayer	**Ah-*yer***
Today	Hoy	**Oy**
Tomorrow	Mañana	**Mah-*nyah*-nah**
Good	Bueno	***Bweh*-noh**
Bad	Malo	***Mah*-loh**
Better (best)	(Lo) Mejor	**(Loh) Meh-*hohr***
More	Más	**Mahs**
Less	Menos	***Meh*-nohs**

English	Spanish	Pronunciation
No smoking	Se prohibe fumar	**Seh proh-*ee*-beh foo-*mahr***
Postcard	Tarjeta postal	**Tar-*heh*-tah poh-*stahl***
Insect repellent	Repelente contra insectos	**Reh-peh-*lehn*-teh *cohn*-trah een-*sehk*-tohs**
Do you speak English?	¿Habla usted inglés?	**Ah-blah oo-*sted* een-*glehs***
Is there anyone here who speaks English?	¿Hay alguien aquí que hable inglés?	**Eye *ahl*-gyehn ah-*kee* keh *ah*-bleh een-*glehs***
I speak a little Spanish.	Hablo un poco de español.	**Ah-bloh oon *poh*-koh deh eh-spah-*nyohl***
I don't understand Spanish very well.	No (lo) entiendo muy bien el español.	**Noh (loh) ehn-*tyehn*-doh mwee byehn el eh-spah-*nyohl***
The meal is good.	Me gusta la comida.	**Meh *goo*-stah lah koh-*mee*-dah**
What time is it?	¿Qué hora es?	**Keh *oh*-rah ehs**
May I see your menu?	¿Puedo ver el menú (la carta)?	***Pweh*-doh vehr el meh-*noo* (lah *car*-tah)**
The check, please.	La cuenta, por favor.	**Lah *kwehn*-tah pohr fa-*borh***
What do I owe you?	¿Cuánto le debo?	***Kwahn*-toh leh *deh*-boh**
What did you say?	¿Mande? (formal)	***Mahn*-deh**
	¿Cómo? (informal)	***Koh*-moh**
I want (to see) . . .	Quiero (ver) . . .	***Kyeh*-roh (vehr)**
a room	un cuarto or una habitación	**oon *kwar*-toh, *oo*-nah ah-bee-tah-*syohn***
for two persons	para dos personas	***pah*-rah dohs pehr-*soh*-nahs**
with (without) bathroom	con (sin) baño	**kohn (seen) *bah*-nyoh**
We are staying here only . . .	Nos quedamos aquí solamente . . .	**Nohs keh-*dah*-mohs ah-*kee* soh-lah-*mehn*-teh**
one night	una noche	**oo-nah *noh*-cheh**
one week	una semana	**oo-nah seh-*mah*-nah**
We are leaving . . .	Partimos (Salimos) . . .	**Pahr-*tee*-mohs (Sah-*lee*-mohs)**
tomorrow	mañana	**mah-*nyah*-nah**
Do you accept . . . ?	¿Acepta usted . . . ?	**Ah-*sehp*-tah oo-*sted***
traveler's checks	cheques de viajero	***cheh*-kehs deh byah-*heh*-roh**

NUMBERS

English	Spanish	Pronunciation
one	uno	*ooh*-noh
two	dos	dohs
three	tres	trehs
four	cuatro	*kwah*-troh
five	cinco	*seen*-koh
six	seis	sayes
seven	siete	*syeh*-teh
eight	ocho	*oh*-choh
nine	nueve	*nweh*-beh
ten	diez	dyehs
eleven	once	*ohn*-seh
twelve	doce	*doh*-seh
thirteen	trece	*treh*-seh
fourteen	catorce	kah-*tohr*-seh
fifteen	quince	*keen*-seh
sixteen	dieciséis	dyeh-see-*sayes*
seventeen	diecisiete	dyeh-see-*syeh*-teh
eighteen	dieciocho	dyeh-see-*oh*-choh
nineteen	diecinueve	dyeh-see-*nweh*-beh
twenty	veinte	*bayn*-teh
thirty	treinta	*trayn*-tah
forty	cuarenta	kwah-*ren*-tah
fifty	cincuenta	seen-*kwen*-tah
sixty	sesenta	seh-*sehn*-tah
seventy	setenta	seh-*tehn*-tah
eighty	ochenta	oh-*chehn*-tah
ninety	noventa	noh-*behn*-tah
one hundred	cien	syehn
two hundred	doscientos	do-*syehn*-tohs
five hundred	quinientos	kee-*nyehn*-tohs
one thousand	mil	meel

TRANSPORTATION TERMS

English	Spanish	Pronunciation
Airport	Aeropuerto	**Ah-eh-roh-*pwehr*-toh**
Flight	Vuelo	***Bweh*-loh**
Rental car	Renta de autos	**Ren-tah deh *ow*-tohs**
Bus	Autobús	**Ow-toh-*boos***
Bus or truck	Camión	**Ka-*myohn***
Lane	Carril	**Kah-*reel***
Nonstop (bus)	Directo	**Dee-*rehk*-toh**
Baggage (claim area)	Equipajes	**Eh-kee-*pah*-hehss**
Intercity	Foraneo	**Foh-rah-*neh*-oh**
Luggage storage area	Guarda equipaje	***Gwar*-dah eh-kee-*pah*-heh**
Arrival gates	Llegadas	**Yeh-*gah*-dahss**
Originates at this station	Local	**Loh-*kahl***
Originates elsewhere	De paso	**Deh *pah*-soh**
Are seats available?	Hay lugares disponibles?	**Eye loo-*gah*-rehs dis-pohn-*ee*-blehss**
First class	Primera	**Pree-*meh*-rah**
Second class	Segunda	**Seh-*goon*-dah**
Nonstop (flight)	Sin escala	**Seen ess-*kah*-lah**
Baggage claim area	Recibo de equipajes	**Reh-*see*-boh deh eh-kee-*pah*-hehss**
Waiting room	Sala de espera	***Sah*-lah deh ehss-*peh*-rah**
Toilets	Sanitarios	**Sah-nee-*tah*-ryohss**
Ticket window	Taquilla	**Tah-*kee*-yah**

FOOD GLOSSARY
Meals

desayuno   Breakfast.

comida   Main meal of the day, taken in the afternoon.

cena   Supper.

Courses

botana   A small serving of food that accompanies a beer or drink, usually served free of charge.

entrada   Appetizer.

sopa   Soup course. (Not necessarily a soup—it can be a dish of rice or noodles, called *sopa seca* [dry soup].)

10 | Food Glossary | SPANISH & MAYAN TERMS & PHRASES

ensalada   Salad.

plato fuerte or plato principal   Main course.

postre   Dessert.

comida corrida   Inexpensive daily special usually consisting of three courses.

menú del día   Same as *comida corrida*.

Food Temperatures

término un cuarto   Rare, literally means one-fourth.

término medio   Medium rare, one-half.

término tres cuartos   Medium, three-fourths.

bien cocido   Well-done.

Note: Keep in mind, when ordering a steak, that *medio* does not mean "medium."

Miscellaneous Restaurant Terminology

cucharra   Spoon.

cuchillo   Knife.

la cuenta   The bill.

plato   Plate.

plato hondo   Bowl.

propina   Tip.

servilleta   Napkin.

tenedor   Fork.

vaso   Glass.

IVA   Value-added tax.

fonda   Strictly speaking, a food stall in the market or street, but now used in a loose or nostalgic sense to designate an informal restaurant.

Popular Mexican & Yucatecan Dishes

a la tampiqueña   (Usually *bistec a la t.* or *arrachera a la t.*) A steak served with several sides, including but not limited to an enchilada, guacamole, rice, and beans.

achiote   Small red seed of the annatto tree, with mild flavor, used for both taste and color.

adobo   Marinade made with chiles and tomatoes, often seen in adjectival form *adobado/adobada*.

agua fresca   Any sweetened fruit-flavored water, including *limonada* (limeade), *horchata*, *tamarindo*, *sandía* (watermelon), and *melón* (cantaloupe).

alambre   Brochette.

antojito   Literally means "small temptation." It's a general term for tacos, tostadas, quesadillas, and the like, which are usually eaten for supper or as a snack.

arrachera   Skirt steak, fajitas.

arroz   Rice.

bistec   Steak.

calabaza   Zucchini squash.

camarones   Shrimp. For common cooking methods, see *pescado.*

carne   Meat.

carnitas   Slow-cooked pork dish from Michoacán and parts of central Mexico, served with tortillas, guacamole, and salsa or pickled jalapeños.

cebolla   Onion.

cecina   Thinly sliced pork or beef, dried or marinated, depending on the region.

ceviche   Fresh raw seafood marinated in fresh lime juice and garnished with chopped tomatoes, onions, chiles, and sometimes cilantro.

chalupas poblanas   Simple dish from Puebla consisting of handmade tortillas lightly fried but left soft, and topped with different chile sauces.

chayote   A type of spiny squash boiled and served as an accompaniment to meat dishes.

chilaquiles   Fried tortilla quarters softened in either a red or a green sauce and served with Mexican sour cream, onion, and sometimes chicken *(con pollo).*

chile   Any of the many hot peppers used in Mexican cooking, in fresh, dried, or smoked forms.

chile ancho   A dried *chile poblano,* which serves as the base for many varieties of sauces and *moles.*

chile chilpotle (or **chipotle**)   A smoked jalapeño sold dried or canned in an adobo sauce.

chile en nogada   *Chile poblano* stuffed with a complex filling of shredded meat, nuts, and dried, candied, and fresh fruit, topped with walnut cream sauce and a sprinkling of pomegranate seeds.

chile poblano   Fresh pepper that is usually dark green in color, large, and not usually spicy. Often stuffed with a variety of fillings (chile relleno).

chile relleno   Stuffed pepper.

chivo   Kid or goat.

churro   Fried pastry dusted with sugar and served plain or filled. The Spanish equivalent of a doughnut.

cochinita pibil   Yucatecan dish of pork, pit-baked in a *pibil* sauce of achiote, sour orange, and spices.

consomé   Clear broth, usually with rice.

cortes   Another way of saying steaks; in full, it is *cortes finas de carne* (fine cuts of meat).

cuitlacoche   Variant of *huitlacoche.*

elote   Fresh corn.

empanada   For most of Mexico, a turnover with a savory or sweet filling. In Oaxaca and southern Mexico, it is corn *masa* or a tortilla folded around a savory filling and roasted or fried.

empanizado   Breaded.

enchilada   A lightly fried tortilla, dipped in sauce and folded or rolled around a filling. It has many variations, such as *enchiladas suizas* (made with a cream sauce), *enchiladas del portal* or *enchiladas placeras* (made with a predominantly *chile ancho* sauce), and *enchiladas verdes* (in a green sauce of tomatillos, cilantro, and chiles).

enfrijoladas   Like an enchilada, but made with a bean sauce flavored with toasted avocado leaves.

enmoladas   Enchiladas made with a *mole* sauce.

ensalada   Salad.

entomatadas   Enchiladas made with a tomato sauce.

escabeche   Vegetables pickled in a vinegary liquid.

flan   Custard.

flautas   Tortillas that are rolled up around a filling (usually chicken or shredded beef) and deep-fried; often listed on a menu as *taquitos* or *tacos fritos.*

frijoles refritos   Beans mashed and cooked with lard.

gorditas   Thick, fried corn tortillas, slit open and stuffed with meat or cheese filling.

huevos mexicanos   Scrambled eggs with chopped onions, chiles serranos, and tomatoes.

huevos rancheros   Fried eggs, usually placed on tortillas and bathed in a light tomato sauce.

huitlacoche   Salty and mild-tasting corn fungus that is considered a delicacy in Mexico.

jitomate   Tomato.

lechuga   Lettuce.

limón   A small lime. Mexicans squeeze these limes on everything from soups to tacos.

lomo adobado   Pork loin cooked in an **adobo.**

masa   Soft dough made of corn that is the basis for making tortillas and tamales.

menudo   Soup made with beef tripe and hominy.

milanesa   Beef cutlet breaded and fried.

molcajete   A three-legged mortar made of volcanic stone and used for grinding. Often used now as a cooking dish that is brought to the table steaming hot and filled with meat, chiles, onions, and cheese.

mole   Any variety of thick sauce made with dried chiles, nuts, fruits or vegetables, and spices. Variations include *m. poblano* (Puebla style, with chocolate and sesame), *m. negro* (black *mole* from Oaxaca, also with chocolate), and *m. verde* (made with herbs and/or pumpkin seeds, depending on the region).

pan   Bread. A few of the varieties include *p. dulce* (general term for a variety of sweet breads), *p. de muerto* (bread made for the Day of the Dead holidays), and *p. Bimbo* (packaged sliced white bread).

panuchos   A Yucatecan dish of *masa* cakes stuffed with refried black beans and topped with shredded turkey or chicken, lettuce, and onion.

papadzules   A Yucatecan dish of tortillas stuffed with hard-boiled eggs and topped with a sauce made of pumpkin seeds.

papas   Potatoes.

parrillada   A sampler platter of grilled meats or seafood.

pescado   Fish. Common ways of cooking fish include *al mojo de ajo* (pan seared with oil and garlic), *a la veracruzana* (with tomatoes, olives, and capers), and *al ajillo* (seared with garlic and fine strips or rings of *chile guajillo*).

pibil　See ***cochinita pibil.*** When made with chicken, it is called *pollo pibil.*

pipián　A thick sauce made with ground pumpkin seeds, nuts, herbs, and chiles. Can be red or green.

poc chuc　Pork with onion marinated in sour orange and then grilled; a Yucatecan dish.

pollo　Chicken.

pozole　Soup with chicken or pork, hominy, lettuce, and radishes, served with a small plate of other ingredients to be added according to taste (onion, pepper, lime juice, oregano). In Jalisco it's red (*p. rojo*), in Michoacán it's clear (*p. blanco*), and in Guerrero it's green (*p. verde*). In the rest of Mexico, it can be any one of these.

puerco　Pork.

pulque　A drink made of fermented juice of the maguey plant; most common in the states of Hidalgo, Tlaxcala, Puebla, and Mexico.

quesadilla　Corn or flour tortillas stuffed with white cheese and cooked on a hot griddle. In Mexico City, it is made with raw *masa* folded around any of a variety of fillings (often containing no cheese) and deep-fried.

queso　Cheese.

res　Beef.

salbute　A Yucatecan dish much like a *panucho,* but without bean paste in the middle.

sope　Small fried *masa* cake topped with savory meats and greens.

tacos al pastor　Small tacos made with thinly sliced pork marinated in an adobo and served with pineapple, onion, and cilantro.

tamal　(Not "tamale.") *Masa* mixed with lard and beaten until light and folded around a savory or sweet filling, and encased in a cornhusk or a plant leaf (usually corn or banana) and then steamed. "Tamales" is the plural form.

taquitos　See "flautas."

tinga　Shredded meat stewed in a *chile chipotle* sauce.

torta　A sandwich made with a *bolillo.*

ENGLISH-MAYAN PHRASES

Mayan vowels are pronounced as they are in Spanish. Double vowels are pronounced like their single counterparts but are held longer. The "x" is pronounced "sh," as in "ship"; the "j" sounds like "h," as in "home." Consonants that come before an accent (') are glottalized. Though the difference is hard for a newcomer to discern, glottalized consonants have a harder, more emphatic sound. Accents in Mayan words usually fall on the last syllable (unlike Spanish, which emphasizes the penultimate syllable unless an accent mark indicates otherwise). Plurals in Mayan are formed by adding the suffix -ob.

English	Mayan	Pronunciation
Hello	Ola	***Oh*-lah**
How are you?	Biix a beel?	**Beesh a bell**
What is your name?	Bix a k'aaba?	**Beesh ah k-ah-*bah***
My name is . . .	In k'aaba . . .	**Een k-ah-bah**
So long	Tu heel k'iin	**Too heel k-*een***
Goodbye/Take care/Good luck	Xi'ik tech utsil	**Shee-*eek* tech oot-*seel***

English	Mayan	Pronunciation
See you tomorrow	Asta sa'amal	**Ahs-*ta* sah-ah-*mahl***
Okay (fine, well)	Ma'aloob	**Mah-ah-*lohby***
Yes (That's the way it will be)	He'le'	**Hey-*leh***
No	Ma'	**Mah**
I don't understand	Min na'atik	**Meen na-ah-*teek***
Thank you	Dyos bo'otik	**Dee-*yos* boh-oh-*teek***
You're welcome	Mixba'al	**Meesh-bah-*ahl***
Stop	Wa'alen	**Wah-ah-*lehn***
I'm hungry	Wi'hen	**Wee-*hehn***
I'm going home	Kin bin tin nah	**Keen been teen nah**
Bon appetit	Hach ki' a wi'ih	**Hach kee ah wee-*ee***
Let's (go)	Ko'ox (tun)	**Koh-osh (toon)**
Where is the beach?	Tuxan há?	**Too-*shan* hah**

Mayan Glossary

Ah kin   A high priest.

Aktun   Cave.

Atl-atl   Spear-throwing device.

Bacab   A class of important gods.

Balam   Jaguar spirit that keeps evil away.

Cán   Serpent.

Cenote   A natural waterhole created by the collapse of limestone caves; corruption by the Spanish of the Maya word *dzonot*.

Ch'en   Pool.

Chilan   A soothsayer or medium.

Chultun   A bottle-shaped, underground cistern.

Corte   Indian woman's traditional full-length skirt.

Há   Cacao seed.

Huipil   A traditional Maya wraparound, woven cotton dress, worn leaving the shoulders bare.

Ka'a'anab háal ha   Beach.

Kayab   A turtle-shell drum.

Kayem   Ground maize.

Kin   The sun, the day, unity of time.

Ku'um   Pumpkin.

Manta   A square of cloth, used as a cloak or blanket; still worn by the Maya today.

Milpa   A cornfield.

Muxubbak   Tamale.

Nohoch   Important, big.

P'ac   Tomatoes.

Palapa   Traditional thatched-roof Maya structure built without nails.

Pok-a-tok   A Maya ball game.

Pom   Resin of the copal tree, used for rubber, chewing gum, and incense.

Quetzal   A rare Central American bird, now almost extinct, prized by Maya kings for its long, brilliant blue-green tail feathers.

Sacbé   Literally "white road," a raised limestone causeway linking Maya buildings and settlements.

Xibalbá   The Maya underworld.

Index

Photo Credits